WOMEN AND
GODDESS TRADITIONS

STUDIES IN ANTIQUITY AND CHRISTIANITY

The Roots of Egyptian Christianity
Birger A. Pearson and James E. Goehring, editors

Gnosticism, Judaism, and Egyptian Christianity
Birger A. Pearson

Ascetic Behavior in Greco-Roman Antiquity
Vincent L. Wimbush, editor

Elijah in Upper Egypt
David Frankfurter

The Letters of St. Antony
Samuel Rubenson

Women and Goddess Traditions
Karen L. King, editor

THE INSTITUTE FOR ANTIQUITY AND CHRISTIANITY
Claremont Graduate School
Claremont, California

STUDIES IN ANTIQUITY AND CHRISTIANITY

WOMEN AND GODDESS TRADITIONS

IN ANTIQUITY AND TODAY

Edited by Karen L. King
with an
Introduction by Karen Jo Torjesen

FORTRESS PRESS
MINNEAPOLIS

WOMEN AND GODDESS TRADITIONS
In Antiquity and Today

Library of Congress Cataloging-in-Publication Data

Women and goddess traditions : in antiquity and today / edited by
Karen L. King : with an introduction by Karen Jo Torjesen.
p. cm. — (Studies in antiquity and Christianity)
Includes bibliographical references and index.
ISBN 0-8006-2919-1 (alk. paper)
1. Women and religion. 2. Goddesses—Cult. I. King, Karen L.
II. Series
BL458.W563 1997
200'.82—dc21 97-20399
CIP

The paper used in this publication meets the minimum requirements of the American National Standard for Information Sciences—Permanence of Paper for Printed Library Materials, ANSI Z329.48-1984.

Manufactured in the U.S.A. AF 1-2919

01 00 99 98 97 1 2 3 4 5 6 7 8 9

Contents

Part Two: The Ancient Mediterranean

Part Three: Contemporary Goddess Thealogy

Contributors

SUSAN ACKERMAN is Associate Professor of Religion at Dartmouth College. Her research focuses on the relationships between Israelite religion and the cults of Israel's neighbors. She is author of *Under Every Green Tree: Popular Religion in Sixth-Century Judah.* Her latest book, *Warrior, Dancer, Seductress, Queen: Women in Judges and Biblical Israel,* will appear in the Anchor Bible Reference Library series.

ELEANOR FERRIS BEACH is Associate Professor of Religion at Augustana College (Ill.). Her research focuses on integrating biblical studies with ancient Near Eastern art and archaeology and feminist perspectives. Her publications include "The Samaria Ivories, *Marzeaḥ*, and Biblical Text," and a contribution to *Feminist Approaches to Biblical Methodologies, Strategies, and Approaches.*

CLAUDIA V. CAMP is Professor of Religion at Texas Christian University. Her research interests are in the areas of biblical wisdom literature, feminist interpretation, and methodology. Among her publications are a book, *Wisdom and the Feminine in the Book of Proverbs,* and several articles on the female imagery in Proverbs, as well as contributions to *The Women's Bible Commentary* and *Searching the Scriptures: A Feminist Commentary.*

EMILY ERWIN CULPEPPER is Director of Women's Studies and Associate Professor of Women's Studies and Religion at the University of Redlands. She is a longtime activist passionately committed to grass-roots feminist theory. Her published works include "Contemporary Goddess Thealogy: A Sympathetic Critique," "Are Women's Bodies Sacred? Listening to the Yes's and No's," and "The Spiritual, Political Journey of a Feminist Freethinker."

KATHLEEN M. ERNDL is Associate Professor of Religion at the Florida State University, where she teaches Hindu studies, comparative religions, and women and religion. Her current research focuses on the religious lives of Hindu women. She is the author of several works on modern Hinduism and Goddess worship, including the book *Victory to the Mother: The Hindu Goddess of Northwest India in Myth, Ritual, and Symbol.*

RITA M. GROSS teaches in the Department of Philosophy and Religion at the University of Wisconsin—Eau Claire. She has been an important contributor to feminist studies in religion in the United States for over twenty years, and is active in Buddhist-Christian dialogue in North America. Her many publications include *Unspoken Worlds: Women's Religious Lives* (edited with Nancy Auer Falk), *Buddhism after Patriarchy: A Feminist History, Analysis, and Reconstruction of Buddhism,* and *Feminism and Religion: An Introduction.*

LINA GUPTA is Assistant Professor of Philosophy at Glendale College in Glendale, California. Her main scholarly interests are the Goddess tradition in Hinduism and feminism, in particular ecofeminism. Her articles have appeared in various anthologies, including "Secularism and Sikhism" in *Religion and Political Power* (ed. Gustavo Benavides and M. W. Daly), "Kali the Savior" in *After Patriarchy* (ed. Paula Cooey, William R. Eakin, Jay B. McDaniel), and "Ganga: Purity, Pollution and Hinduism" in *Ecofeminism and the Sacred* (ed. Carol J. Adams). Currently she is working on articles on vegetarianism in Hinduism, the unknown Hindu Goddesses, and Tantrism. She has a book in progress on a feminist approach to the Hindu Goddesses.

SUSAN TOWER HOLLIS specializes in ancient Egyptian Goddesses, women, literature, and religion. Author of *The Ancient Egyptian "Tale of Two Brothers,"* coeditor of *Feminist Theory and the Study of Folklore,* and editor of *Hymns, Prayers, and Songs. An Anthology of Ancient Egyptian Lyric Poetry,* she is currently Center Director and Associate Dean for State University of New York, Empire State College's Central New York Center. She is continuing her work on third millennium B.C.E. Egyptian goddesses, working toward a book on the topic.

CYNTHIA ANN HUMES is Associate Professor of Religious Studies at Claremont McKenna College. Her publications concern contemporary use of Sanskrit literature, modern ritual in North Indian Goddess worship, political and economic dimensions in Hinduism, and women's roles and experience in world religions. She coedited and contributed to *Living Banaras: Hindu Religion in Cultural Context,* and her book *Goddess of Blood, Goddess of Love: Divinity and Power in the Devi Mahatmya and Vindhyachal Temple* is forthcoming.

KAREN L. KING is Professor of Religious Studies at Occidental College in Los Angeles. Her research and teaching focuses on Gnosticism, the history of early Christianity, and women's studies. Her recent work includes feminist commentaries on the *Gospel of Mary Magdalene* and the *Book of Norea: Daughter of Eve* in *Searching the Scriptures* (ed. Elisabeth Schüssler Fiorenza), and "Prophetic Power and Women's Authority" in *Women Preachers and Prophets* (ed. Beverly Kienzle and Pamela Walker).

MIRIAM LEVERING is Associate Professor of Religious Studies and Asian Studies at the University of Tennessee. Her primary area of teaching and research is medieval Chinese religion, particularly its social and cultural dimensions. She is the author of articles on twelfth-century Chinese Zen Buddhism, women and gender in Zen, and Buddhist practice in a contemporary Chinese convent. She has also edited *Rethinking Scripture.* She is currently at work on *The Zen of Women,* a book on enlightened women in Chinese Zen.

JUDITH OCHSHORN, who recently passed away, was professor of Women's Studies at the University of South Florida, taught courses on feminist spirituality, women's history, and feminist theory building. Author of *The Female Experience and the Nature of the Divine,* she coedited *Women's Spirituality, Women's Lives.*

AMY RICHLIN is Professor of Classics and Gender Studies at the University of Southern California. She writes and teaches in the areas of women in antiquity, history of sexuality, Roman culture, and feminist theory. Her publications include *The Garden of Priapus: Sexuality and Aggression in Roman Humor.* She edited *Pornography and Representation in Greece and Rome* and coedited *Feminist Theory and the Classics.*

MIRANDA SHAW is Assistant Professor of Religion at the University of Richmond in Virginia. Her current research focuses on Goddesses and the cultural construction of gender in Indian and Himalayan Buddhism. She is the author of *Passionate Enlightenment: Women in Tantric*

Buddhism, and is currently at work on *Her Waves of Bliss: Buddhist Goddesses of India, Tibet, and Nepal.*

Hal Taussig teaches biblical and religious studies at Chestnut Hill College and the Reconstructionist Rabbinical College in the Philadelphia area, and is the pastor of the Chestnut Hill United Methodist Church. He is the coauthor of *Wisdom's Feast: Sophia in Study and Celebration, Sophia: The Future of Feminist Spirituality,* author of "Dealing Under the Table: Ritual Negotiation of Women's Power in Mark 7:24-30" in *Reimagining Christian Origins* (of which he is also coeditor), and coauthor of *Many Tables: The Eucharist in the New Testament.*

Savina J. Teubal is founder of Sarah's Tent: Sheltering Creative Jewish Spirituality, where she now teaches. She has written and lectured extensively on the feminist aspects of the Hebrew Bible and the ancient Near East. She is the author of *Sarah the Priestess: The First Matriarch of Genesis* and *The Lost Tradition of Hagar and Sarah..*

Karen Jo Torjesen is the Margo L. Goldsmith Professor of Religion at the Claremont Graduate School. She teaches and writes in the areas of early Christianity, women in the history of Christianity, and historical theology. Her most recent book is *When Women Were Priests: Women's Leadership in the Early Church and the Scandal of Their Subordination in the Rise of Christianity.*

Donna M. Wulff is Professor of Religious Studies at Brown University. Her publications include a book on the Sanskrit plays of Rupa Gosvami, as well as articles on Sanskrit aesthetic theory, the sacredness of sound and music, and a contemporary Bengali form of religious performance. With John Stratton Hawley she is the editor of two volumes, *The Divine Consort: Radha and the Goddesses of India* and *Devi: Goddesses of India.*

Abbreviations

AJS	Association of Jewish Studies
AV	*Atharva Veda*
B.C.E.	Before the Common Era; equivalent to B.C.
BASOR	*Bulletin of the American Schools of Oriental Research*
Cant	Canticles (=Song of Songs)
Chr	Chronicles
C.E.	Common Era; equivalent to A.D.
CIL	*Corpus Inscriptionum Latinarum* ("Corpus of Latin Inscriptions")
DD	Damascus Document
Dan	Daniel
Deut	Deuteronomy
DM	*Devi-Mahatmya*
Ex	Exodus
Ezek	Ezekiel
Gen	Genesis
Hos	Hosea
HSM	Harvard Semitic Monographs
Isa	Isaiah
JBL	*Journal of Biblical Literature*
JEA	*Journal of Egyptian Archaeology*
Jer	Jeremiah
JNES	*Journal of Near Eastern Studies*
Judg	Judges
Kgs	Kings
KTU	*Die Keilalphabetischen Texte aus Ugarit* (The cuneiform alphabetic texts from Ugarit)
Lam	Lamentations

LXX	Septuagint (Greek version of the Hebrew Bible)
Mal	Malachi
Matt	Gospel of Matthew
Mic	Micah
Neh	Nehemiah
Num	Numbers
Obad	Obadiah
OLP	*Orientalia Lovaniensia Periodica*
Prov	Proverbs
Ps	Psalms
Pss Sol	Psalms of Solomon
RS	Ras Shamra
RV	*Rig Veda*
Sam	Samuel
Sir	Sirach
VT	*Vetus Testamentum*
ZAW	*Zeitschrift für altestamentliche Wissenschaft*
Zech	Zechariah
ZGDJ	*Zengaku Daijiten*

List of Figures

Introduction

Karen Jo Torjesen

The chapters in this volume were originally presented at a conference, "Women and Goddess Traditions," organized through the Women's Studies in Religion Program at the Claremont Graduate School and sponsored by the Blaisdale Institute. The conference gathered scholars working with both contemporary and historical religions to explore the relationship between Goddesses and women's lives.

As the women's movement of the 1960s in the United States began to demand the full social, economic, and political equality of women, feminist scholars began to explore the ways religions are implicated in the definition and maintenance of gendered social roles. Reflecting on the Christianity that shaped the Catholic world in which she grew up, Mary Daly saw an overwhelming connection between a masculine God and male dominance. In her early manifesto *Beyond God the Father*, she coined the aphorism "If God is male, then the male is God." Jewish feminist Naomi Goldenberg, in *The Changing of the Gods*, prophesied that as Jewish and Christian women formed ideas of God out of a feminist consciousness, the face of patriarchal religion would be forever changed.

Responding to these challenges, feminist scholarship in the United States moved in several new directions. Some Jewish and Christian feminists, working toward a remaking of Western religious traditions, began recovering and inventing new religious imagery, constructing theologies, composing new prayers, and creating new rituals, while remaining within their religious traditions. Others, critical of the religions of their own societies, turned to the Goddess religions of Native American, African, and Asian cultures. Criticism of religion's complicity with patriarchy led some women to look to past religious traditions for positive female imagery for the divine. The Goddesses of ancient

Greece, who had long been a feature of the intellectual landscape of European readers, have recently been resurrected as powerful archetypes for contemporary women through a Jungian/psychoanalytic reading of their stories. More recently, the archaeological work of Marija Gimbutas has captured feminist imagination by suggesting a Goddess-centered religion existed in the societies of prehistoric Europe.

In recent decades feminist scholars have been examining the role of Goddess religion in shaping the social status of women in various cultures. Their initial work has begun to uncover some of the complexities in appropriating elements of Goddess religions. In reaction to the negative assessment of male imagery for God, there has been a tendency to assume that the presence of *female* imagery for the divine would be good for women. This may well be the case. But increasingly scholars recognize that such views have to be balanced by an assessment of the place of Goddess worship within patriarchal forms of society, because worship of a Goddess can also be used to confirm women's subordinate social positions. Equally problematic is the appropriation of native American, Asian, and African Goddess traditions by Western feminists within a framework of colonialism. Often when U.S. feminists have appropriated Goddess traditions, there has been a simultaneous tendency to denigrate the women in those cultures. For example, Indian Goddesses might be highly praised, but too often Indian women are portrayed as victims of a patriarchal society, rather than as religious and cultural agents.

In the last five years, interest in Goddesses has made its way into the American Academy of Religion and the Society of Biblical Literature. Sessions on Goddess religions have drawn large audiences and generated intense excitement. At the same time comparative and cross-cultural studies have begun to flourish and bring together scholars working on women in many of the world's religions. The dialogue generated by these sessions has helped to identify common themes, such as the diverse forms of women's religious authority, connections between Goddesses and queens, symbolic associations of women with evil. At the same time, dialogue has called attention to complex methodological issues raised in making connections between Goddess religions and women's status. In this climate, the Claremont conference on women and Goddess traditions was born. A clear set of questions was beginning to emerge.

What is the relationship between Goddesses, as they appear in myth and ritual, and the social roles and practices of women?

Do female Deities affect the status of women in a society?

How does Goddess worship shape women's consciousness?

How are women's bodies and women's sexualities construed in religions in which the divine can be represented in female form?

How does Goddess religion inform the symbolic meanings of female bodies?

To what extent does the female devotee participate by virtue of her femaleness in the powers of the Goddess?

Can a woman represent the divine?

Do women gain religious authority through Goddess worship?

Do Goddesses enhance the political authority of elite women such as queens?

Does Goddess worship enhance women's status in their familial roles?

How does social class affect the relations of Goddess worship and the relations of women of different social classes with each other in a stratified society?

These are questions that the contributors to this volume have taken up in their studies of both ancient and contemporary Goddess religions. Each of these chapters traces a connection between Goddesses honored through ritual and myth and the lives of women. Together they show the complexity of the nexus where religion, gender, and power intersect.

ASIA

The religions of Asia provide rich resources for the study of Goddess worship because the Goddess traditions in these religions are accessible through the practices of contemporary worshipers, as well as through the study of sacred texts, art, and architecture. Kathleen M. Erndl, Cynthia Ann Humes, Donna M. Wulff, and Lina Gupta present studies of the worship of Goddesses within Hinduism. They have done fieldwork, conducted interviews, and directly observed and even participated in the rituals honoring Goddesses. They have studied how women religious leaders understand their authority, and they have lived in the leaders' communities and thus been able to observe these women within their own social worlds.

These studies of women's relationships to Goddesses in Hindu religion are framed by the question of how Goddess figures might empower women in patriarchal societies where the powerful religious roles of priest and renunciant are generally reserved for men. To answer this question, both Erndl and Humes look to the rituals of devotion to the great Goddess to understand the ways in which women do, in fact, achieve religious authority. Erndl focuses on a village religious leader, Tara Devi, and shows how the power of the Goddess is mediated through her when she becomes the Goddess's manifestation. Humes studies the worship of the Goddess at a great temple. Her chapter explores the differences between male and female religious authority, between male "textual power," which is controlled by priests, and female "ritual" power. Both chapters show how women gain religious authority and with it social status by becoming ritual experts, for example, by manifesting the Goddess at a small shrine or through devotional singing that recounts the feats of the Goddess in songs a woman herself composes and performs.

These two scholars approach the question of whether the worship of a female Deity elevates the social and religious status of women by identifying the rights and privileges ascribed to these women on the basis of their religious authority as ritual experts. Corollary questions are equally important but more difficult to answer: How does the worship of a female Deity influence a woman's sense of self? Does it affect her gendered consciousness? Is it natural to assume that a change in the rights and privileges accorded to a woman would also transform her sense of herself as woman? Although it is difficult to find ways of measuring and assessing changes in female consciousness, Kathleen Erndl argues that Tara Devi, as a Goddess-possessed woman, has had her own consciousness profoundly altered and has gained a new social identity within the community.

Donna M. Wulff analyzes the narrative and dialogues of a widespread Bengali Vaisnava form of musical performance called *kirtan,* which dramatizes episodes in the love affair between Radha—a human woman as well as a Goddess—and Krishna. In performances portraying Radha's ire at Krishna's unfaithfulness, Wulff finds a reflection of the strength of Bengali women. She shows that the type-figure of the audacious woman is pervasive in Bengali poetry and performance from the medieval to the contemporary period. From this material, Wulff argues that the drama of the Goddess reproaching her lover may provide Bengali women with models of assertiveness and resistance. The presence of women leaders in the Vaisnava community, and the relatively high status of literate Vaisnava women mendicants in Bengal who assumed the role of religious teachers, corroborate the status accorded to women in *kirtan* performances.

Lina Gupta, a scholar and practitioner, also reflects on these questions as she writes about two women's family rituals in Hindu Bengal. Gupta selected them for study precisely because these rituals are not mediated by a priest, nor are they dependent on male-controlled scripture or practiced for the benefit of the woman's husband or children. These rituals are significant instances of women's autonomy and ritual authority; they ceremonialize women's relationships within a family and are celebrated with other women who are friends or family members. No description of these domestic rituals has been previously published, nor are they included within any written tradition, although they have been practiced by women in Bengal for centuries. Gupta's article makes a unique contribution to this volume, for Western historians of religion rarely have access to familial rituals connected with Goddesses. As a participant observer and scholar, she provides her own theological and ethnographic analysis of these rituals.

Gupta's analysis shows that through familial rituals women participate in the power and potency of the Goddesses. Through the enactment of rituals, the powers of the Goddesses become part of their own inner power. Here Gupta raises the fundamental question: What is the nature of power? By articulating the Hindu woman's understanding of power, she exposes and critiques the unarticulated assumption of U.S. feminists that power is socioeconomic and political. Yet within the stratification of Hindu society, some manifestations of power are internal, such as generative potency and moral power drawn from *Shakti,* the active feminine principle that is personified in the Goddesses. Hindu religion allows women to transform their self-sacrifice and subordination (misperceived by American feminists as a loss of power) into socio-religious forms of power. Women's rituals ceremonialize the network of relationships in the women's community within a Hindu household, a feminine domain that fosters and mediates the meaning of womanhood.

Miranda Shaw and Miriam Levering, both scholars of Buddhism, study Goddess traditions in the sacred texts and traditions of Ch'an and Tantric Buddhism, respectively. From these texts and traditions, they have gleaned stories of Goddesses, female spirit-beings, and female Bodhisattvas and Buddhas. In the dramatic narrative of these stories, they are able to discover forms of women's religious authority distinctive to Buddhism. Because they are working with Buddhism, a nontheistic religion, the challenges of exploring Western feminist issues through comparative religions are more obvious. How are the meanings of sexuality, gender, and gendered representations to be understood in a religion that ostensibly does not conceive of the divine anthropomorphically? Is it even appropriate to speak of Goddesses within a Buddhist context? How should female Buddhas and Bodhisattvas be named—as female Deities, female consorts, or Goddesses?

Yet Shaw and Levering both note that Hindu Goddess worship

provides resources for valuing femaleness in Tantric and Ch'an Buddhisms. In Tantric Buddhism, Hindu rituals of devotion to the Goddess are directed toward the female guru who is seen as an embodiment of the Goddess. In Chinese Buddhism, the characteristics of the Hindu Goddesses are used to invest the Buddhist Bodhisattva with all the graces and powers of femaleness as they are portrayed in the Hindu epics.

Nevertheless, these two traditions are strikingly different in their ideological construction of woman's body. Miranda Shaw explores the meanings of the female body in the teachings of Tantric Buddhism. Ultimate liberation is achieved through a ritually controlled use of sexual pleasure to attain the nondualistic vision of reality that constitutes enlightenment. Because the path to enlightenment is through the sexuality of the female body, the sexual body is honored and even venerated. Devotion to the Goddess provides the pattern for the relationship between the male disciple and the female guru, who functions as a Goddess figure. Male disciples are taught by the Tantric scriptures to worship and reverence women as embodiments of the Goddess. These ritual practices lead Shaw to these questions: Is the traditional patriarchal gender relationship fundamentally reordered through this religious practice? Does this reversal change the social and religious status of women within Tantric circles or within larger Hindu society? Does the female guru come to a different gendered consciousness herself?

Her study also raises the methodological question of how to document a transformed gender consciousness for either men or women. Do Tantric woman-reverencing ritual practices form the female consciousness of Tantric women? To answer this question, Shaw turns to meditational practice. Here the female guru is instructed to practice envisioning herself in the form of the various Goddesses. Shaw observes that the relationship between the female devotee/guru and the Goddess is actually a practice of *mimesis* (imitation), which has as its goal the transformation of female consciousness. Thus, she argues that the symbolic world of the Goddess, her attributes, and her story mediated by these rituals have a profound effect on women's self-perception.

While in Tantric Buddhism a woman is an embodiment of the Goddess and a woman's sexual body is the vehicle for achieving enlightenment for both her and her male devotee, by contrast, in Ch'an Buddhism, a monastic religion based on celibacy, the male body was a symbol of perfection, while the female body was a symbol of imperfection and impurity. A woman seeking spiritual enlightenment, therefore, was told she must first seek rebirth in the male body as a way of renouncing woman's female sexual power.

Levering asks how women seeking Buddhist enlightenment might have understood the stages of their transformation in light of these doctrines on femaleness. How did the denigration of the female body in the Ch'an symbol system affect women's self-understanding? In Ch'an traditions about enlightened women, Levering finds evidence that women did engage these particular teachings on gender and successfully challenged them on the basis of Buddhist teachings on the emptiness of all things. Because there is neither male nor female, both the female body and sexuality belong to the realm of illusion. Hence, women do not need to be reborn as men.

In conclusion, working with such disparate sources as temple rituals to the great Goddess, Goddess worship in home shrines, women's domestic rituals, Tantric ritual practices and female Bodhisattvas, these scholars of Asian religions show the diverse ways in which Hindu and Buddhist women have found affirmations of their femaleness and have gained in social status through Goddess worship.

THE ANCIENT MEDITERRANEAN

The worship of Goddesses in ancient societies reveals different connections between women and Goddesses. The nature of historical sources forces students of the Goddesses of Egypt, Israel, Greece, and Rome to examine a quite different aspect of the relationship between Goddesses and society. With no access to devotees and worshipers or to priests, priestesses, or ritual experts, historians of Goddess traditions are dependent on the material sources preserved from ancient societies. Often all that remains of the Goddess religions of prehistoric ancient societies are the archaeological artifacts, statues, scenes on bas reliefs, and inscriptions. Even for the earliest historical periods, the textual evidence for Goddess worship (myths, hymns, stories, and histories) is quite limited. Because the record-keeping of ancient societies was in the hands of the elite, often only the histories and perspectives of the ruling dynasties are recorded. Thus, the role of Goddess figures is most accessible at the convergence of the cult of the Goddess and royal politics. The connection between Goddesses and queens served to underwrite royal authority. This fact raises a particular set of questions: What was the nature of the queens' political authority? What were the connections between the queens' political authority and the cults of the Goddesses? What roles did queens have in the cults of Goddesses, and did these further establish their political authority? What attributes of Goddesses transferred to queens?

Susan Ackerman's study focuses on the figure of the Israelite queen mother, the *gĕbîrâ*, who was associated with the cult of the Goddess Asherah and who had both cultic and political roles in the Southern Kingdom. She faces the problems peculiar to documenting the worship of Goddesses when the only sources available for analysis are committed to a distinctly masculine monotheism. She must therefore rely on subtle and insightful readings of texts hostile to devotion to Goddesses. According to Ackerman's reconstruction of the *gĕbîrâ's* role, the queen mother was the representative of the Goddess Asherah. Because the king received political authority through his adoption as the son of God, the Goddess Asherah was the adoptive heavenly mother. The queen mother, as a representative of Asherah, was the official counselor in matters of royal succession. Susan Ackerman's work underlines the importance of understanding not only the political ideology of rulership but also the configuration of human and divine kinship relations through connections made between rulers and Goddesses.

Although the surviving literary texts of the Israelites were committed to a monotheism hostile to images, the archaeological repertoire of Israelite religion is replete with female figures. Susan Tower Hollis ponders the scant remaining evidence of the connections between Egyptian queens and Goddesses. Using the evidence of the royal iconography of the *serekh*, Hollis discovers two queens of the first dynasty, Neith-Hetep and Meret-Neith, who are paired with the Egyptian Goddess Neith. The *serekh* shows both their political authority and their participation in the divinity of the Goddess. Hollis notes that the decline of the importance of the Goddess Neith correlates with the decline in the power of queens through the second and third dynasties. Hollis's observation points to further questions: Does the disappearance of Goddesses in royal iconography indicate the waning of the power of queens? What forms of political ideology correlate with Goddess worship?

Eleanor Ferris Beach undertakes the daunting task of tracing Goddess iconography from art to literature. To study representations of Goddesses appearing in both visual and textual forms, Beach proposes three levels of analysis formulated through three questions: When a Goddess motif appears in a visual setting, what are the accompanying iconographic motifs? What can be learned from the physical location of this particular constellation of Goddess motifs? What are the social or cultic contexts in which these motifs are brought into play? The important move Beach makes is to insist that the meaning of a Goddess motif cannot be interpreted independently of the related elements in its setting, nor independently of the social, cultic, and political context of that setting. With this approach Beach draws much tighter and more complex connections between literary female figures and Goddesses. Once she has made all the connections, it becomes clear that the primary function of the Goddess is not to preside over sexuality, as earlier scholars had proposed, but to preside over politics, to legitimate royal succession, and to invest a ruler with the symbols of justice.

Hal Taussig's study of the web of connections between Hellenistic queens and Greek and Egyptian Goddesses draws on the richer epigraphic and literary sources available for the Hellenistic period. With these sources it is possible to catch a glimpse of how queens themselves used their association with Goddesses. The surviving literary histories and archaeological data allow the political intentions, motivations, and strategies of women rulers to be discerned. Taussig shows that several Hellenistic queens actively promoted themselves as divine by using titles such as "savior," "the saving one," and "great mother of the Gods." This political strategy becomes clear in coins minted by Hellenistic queens on which they portrayed themselves as Goddesses. Taussig's interest in Hellenistic queens grows out of his research on the figure of Sophia (Wisdom), a divinized form of the feminine prominent in the literature of Hellenistic Judaism, such as the Wisdom of Ben Sirach. By setting Ben Sirach's praise of the divine feminine alongside the same writer's denigration of women, Taussig presses the question of whether the prominence of a divine female figure within Hellenistic Judaism might have influenced views of women or women's lives.

Ackerman, Hollis, Beach, and Taussig have explored the connections between Goddesses and queens. Taussig's interest in the figure of Sophia introduces another topic, the meanings of female symbolic figures, which the next two chapters take up. Savina Teubal speculates on the symbolic meanings of female figures in prehistoric religions and Claudia V. Camp explores the use of a female figure to symbolize evil.

The roles of Goddess worship in prehistoric societies are of special interest to feminist scholars because of the vast number of representations of the female body found among archaeological remains. The absence of written records to interpret this archaeological evidence, however, renders the reconstruction of Goddess religion in prehistoric cultures somewhat speculative. Savina Teubal considers the enigmatic iconography of the female body portrayed in prehistoric rock art, cave art, and portable art spanning the period from the Upper Paleolithic period (34,000 B.C.E.) through the Iron Age (500 B.C.E.). Using criteria similar to Beach's, Teubal interprets these figures as depicting women's reproductive functions—menstruation, pregnancy, birth, and lactation.

She proposes that the female figures were part of women's rituals that sacralized menstruation, pregnancy, birth, and lactation. These figures of the female body, which were used to honor the sacredness of women's reproductive capacities, functioned as the axis for women's communities. Her chapter focuses on the question of how prehistoric peoples might have viewed women's reproductive power. The presence of such a large number of representations of the female body suggests to Teubal that these societies honored the enigma of life-giving and nurturing, perceiving these special powers to be innate to the female body. Teubal suggests that these prehistoric representations of the female body expressed an awe of the reproductive power of the female body rather than a divinization of the female. She speculates that the appearance of Goddess figures might well have represented a loss of status for women as the innate powers of women's bodies were projected onto a Goddess figure who then became the personification of female reproductive power. Women's status declined further when the creative powers associated with female sexuality were transferred to the male God of Israelite monotheism. For Teubal these prehistoric Goddess religions carry an important message for contemporary spirituality, in that women were able to retain control over the "mysteries of reproduction" through the sacralizing of the female body.

Although limited to textual and archaeological evidence for Goddess worship, these historical studies have illustrated the role of Goddess religion in underwriting political authority and dynastic legitimacy for kings and queens. Savina Teubal's interpretations of prehistoric female figures have made connections between a reverence for the reproductive power of women's bodies and the evolution of Goddess figures. Claudia V. Camp's chapter traces the dangerous trajectory of the feminization of evil.

Goddess figures have interested contemporary feminists as potential symbols of female status and power, but there is also a dark side to mythical female personae. Claudia V. Camp turns to this dark side in her chapter on the feminization and divinization of evil. The question she asks is: How does a female figure become a cultural symbol for evil? In order to map the process of the feminization of evil in ancient Israel, Camp first identifies the range of familial, cultic, and political concerns the deviant woman represented. She shows the progression from "women" used as metaphors for social deviance to the use of "woman" as a hypostasized or divinized symbol of the forces that are poised to destroy the society. Camp points out that cultural symbols are produced by individuals or groups within a given society. Thus, an analysis of the feminization of evil must probe further to determine which groups produced the symbols that feminized evil, what their social locations were, and what their relationship to women was.

Amy Richlin turns to Roman society to ask how Goddess traditions affect women's religious lives. Working with "tattered sources," as she calls them, Richlin assembles an impressive collage of evidence for women's religious authority. Roman women were leading processions, singing in choruses, offering libations, officiating as priestesses, and wielding the sacrificial knife. To answer the question of how these religious offices affected women's status, she turns to dedicatory inscriptions and funerary epitaphs. Holding a priesthood was itself an indication of status for it showed a woman's membership in the municipal elite class. Through high prestige priesthoods, elite women were able to be active in public life, and, for freedwomen, attaining the priesthood was an avenue toward upward mobility. Through an analysis of the calendar of women's festivals, Richlin ponders how rituals of Goddess worship affected women's lives. She observes that because Roman women's religious rituals were primarily concerned with chastity, lactation, and childbearing, Goddess rituals segregated women both by social class (matrons, freedwomen, slaves) and by sexual status (married, virgin, and prostitute).

THEALOGY

Many contemporary feminists look to Goddess religions—both ancient and modern—for resources for a feminist spirituality. The term *thealogy* is used to signify the fundamental rethinking of religious traditions that moves them away from androcentric conceptions of the divine toward more gynocentric ones. The chapters on Asia and the ancient Mediterranean raise the central question: Where should contemporary feminist spirituality be grounded? When contemporary feminist spirituality draws on the resources of prehistoric, historical, or contemporary Goddess religions, what aspects of Goddess traditions should be appropriated? How can female symbols, which are meaningful in their own distinctive cultural contexts, become meaningful in a radically different context? How should the adequacy of such appropriation of Goddess figures be judged?

Judith Ochshorn questions whether reconstructing prehistoric Goddess religions can be an adequate resource for contemporary feminist spirituality. Her concern is that romanticizing the past by imagining a golden age of Goddess worship detracts from the urgent necessity to confront the past as a powerful force in the denigration of women. Further, Ochshorn sees in the appropriation of Goddess spiritualities that are centered in women's reproductive powers a form of biological reductionism that affirms women only in maternal roles. In the place of a prehistoric mother Goddess who sacralized women's reproduction, she offers the historical Goddesses of Sumeria, Babylonia, and Assyria who presided over war, justice, and succession. She argues that ancient Near Eastern belief in powerful and independent Goddesses, who could and did keep nature and the human community running, did not rest on female reproductive potential alone, but was a reflection of the agency and influence of real women. Her critique points to the need for myths or models of female power that correspond more fully to the diverse lives of contemporary women.

Many contemporary feminist spiritualities have turned to Goddess thealogy in order to sacralize the female body and thereby counteract patriarchal culture's denigration of femaleness. Rita M. Gross proposes another alternative by turning to Buddhism as a source for non-theistic and non-anthropomorphic thealogy. She argues that a non-theistic system allows meaningful but non-reified images of the feminine. The absence of an absolute (either male or female) then allows for mythic or symbolic female personifications of enlightenment. The meditative rituals of visualization in Tantric and Mahayana Buddhism, focused on mythic female figures, can lead a seeker toward enlightenment. Thus, within Buddhism, Goddesses function as fluid symbols that mediate the connections to ultimate reality rather than incarnating it.

Emily Erwin Culpepper, in her chapter, assesses the adequacy of the archetype of the triple Goddess (maiden, mother, and crone). Through self-reflection and narratives of conversation, she probes the question of how the symbolism of the crone—associated with insight, wisdom, judgment, rage, vengeance, justice, and knowledge of death and rebirth—can provide a new sense of self for a woman entering menopause. The focus of Culpepper's question brings into view the particularities of American women's experience of the process of aging, the loss of self-esteem, reinforced by hostile and derogatory images of women's aging. The question Culpepper raises is whether the image of the crone is able to affirm the potency of women's life after the child-bearing years, through that full, mature, thriving adulthood. She suggests that a Goddess is missing. Culpepper argues that a mythic and symbolic dimension celebrating women's experience must be discovered or created, and Goddess archetypes can fulfill this function. With a touch of humor she notes that the pantheon of "found Goddesses" includes figures such as Hilaria and Chocolata.

One purpose of the conference on "Women and Goddess Traditions" was to bring together women scholars who work on various aspects of Goddess religion with women involved in creating contemporary Goddess spiritualities. Many women who have contributed to this volume have been involved in both enterprises. The point of including studies on Asia, the ancient Mediterranean, and thealogy is to highlight and balance both the power of Goddess religions to influence women's lives and the complexities of appropriating Goddess traditions.

We would like to thank the Blaisdale Institute for underwriting much of the cost of this conference, and the Institute for Antiquity and Christianity and the Women's Studies in Religion Program of the Claremont Graduate School for their contributions. A special thanks is due to Scripps College for making their beautiful campus available for meetings. Especial thanks to Laura Ammon, who did much of the administrative work associated with the conference and to the students in the Women's Studies in Religion program who helped with many details.

PART ONE

ASIA

1

KATHLEEN M. ERNDL

The Goddess and Women's Power: A Hindu Case Study

In this chapter, I present an example of a Hindu woman whose life has been transformed, who has been empowered through the worship of the Goddess Jvala Mukhi. Here I present a side of Hinduism that has been little discussed by Western scholars until fairly recently. Hinduism, even in recent works, is usually characterized as a male-dominated tradition in which women have only a subordinate and highly restricted role to play. Certainly a perusal of Sanskrit legal texts and an examination of formal religious institutions such as the Brahmin priesthood and the renunciant orders would tend to support this characterization. Similarly, examination of the cultural categories purity and impurity, which legitimate both caste and gender hierarchy, has led many Western scholars to assume that both women and "the feminine" are devalued in Hindu thought and practice. Yet there are also compelling ways in which female power (*shakti*) is not only recognized in the Hindu tradition but is integral to its worldview. Anthropologist Frédérique Marglin, for example, has argued that in Hindu culture female power is the power of life and death, a power that encompasses both auspicious and inauspicious aspects but is exclusively neither one nor the other. She further argues that the auspiciousness/inauspiciousness principle (that is, *shakti*), is profoundly *nonhierarchical*, presenting a different "axis of value" than the hierarchical purity/impurity principle.[1]

The extent to which this female power—widely recognized and valued in Hindu discourse and often personified as a Goddess—translates into opportunities for religious empowerment for women is a question worth exploring. As a researcher of contemporary Hindu Goddess worship in

India, I have been asked, in both scholarly and nonscholarly contexts, variations of the question: Why is it that the Hindu Goddess is so powerful, while Hindu women are powerless? Sometimes the question is phrased the other way around: Why are Hindu women so oppressed in a religion that exalts the Goddess? Either way, this is a loaded question. The first version assumes that Hindu women are powerless; both assume there should be a direct correlation between the worship of a female Deity and the status of women in a society. The first assumption is easily dismissed, because Hindu women *do* exercise power[2] in a variety of contexts, but the second assumption is less easily dealt with. It has been in the back of my mind for years, and I have been grappling with it on different levels, scholarly and personal. As a historian of religions, I have been trained in the phenomenological method of bracketing one's personal biases in order to understand religious and cultural phenomena on their own terms. As a feminist, I am interested not only in women's welfare but in treating women as active subjects rather than as passive objects. In this chapter, I bring these two voices together to explore the relationship between the Goddess and women's power in a specific Hindu context, focusing on the example of Tara Devi, a female religious leader in a village in Kangra.

Kangra or the Kangra Valley, as it is also called, is nestled in the foothills of the Dhauladhar Range of the Himalayas. Once the home of independent Hindu kings, under the British and up until the reorganization of states in the mid-1960s, Kangra was part of the state of Panjab. Now it is part of the mountainous Hindi-speaking state of Himachal Pradesh. Overwhelmingly Hindu in population, the district is dotted with Goddess temples, many of which host a steady stream of pilgrims from the plains below. Most Kangra villagers are farmers, growing rice in landholdings so small that in most families at least one male member works outside Kangra for economic reasons. The influx of pilgrims and the out-migrant labor pattern have kept Kangra in touch with the mainstream of Indian society, though Kangris pride themselves on their distinctive culture, language, food, dress, festivals, and customs. The dominant caste is Rajput, a large princely caste with numerous ranked subdivisions and a patriarchal social structure.[3] A fascinating but little-studied feature of Kangra culture is the degree to which women take on religious leadership roles through Goddess possession, healing, mediumship, and leadership of devotional song groups. It is a truism in Hindu social discourse that for men there are two possible religious lifestyles, that of a householder and that of a celibate renunciant. Under the category of householder fall both religious specialists such as Brahmin priests and ordinary laymen. For women, on the other hand, the conventional wisdom holds that there is only one role, that of a householder (wife and mother) whose sole religious duty is to serve and protect her husband and children.[4] Such ideas are widely espoused by both men and women in Kangra, yet at the same time almost every village has women of extraordinary religious attainments who function as leaders in their communities, even in the absence of institutionalized roles for women as leaders. These women have carved out niches for themselves as religious practitioners, outside the traditional male roles of priest and renunciant as well as outside or in addition to the traditional female role of conducting domestic rituals for the welfare of their families. Such women draw on the power of the Goddess and become powerful themselves.

Of course, how one defines power lies at the crux of the matter. In *Unspoken Worlds,* Nancy Falk and Rita Gross address this issue, writing, "Women's power, in most traditional societies, was not equivalent to legal, economic, political, social, or religious equality."[5] In other words, power and equality are not the same thing. Falk and Gross further write, "When women *have* powerful or provocative myth-models with which they can identify, or when women *are* exemplary sacred sources, they feel powerful and they are powerful."[6] I intend to show in the following pages that in the case of Tara Devi, both processes are operating. Tara Devi, along with women like her, has powerful myth-models, *shakti* (the concept of female dynamic power) and Devi (the Goddess), with whom she identifies. In turn, Tara Devi, along with other women like her, is an exemplary sacred source for other women (and men). By making this argument, I in no way intend to downplay the subordination of women either in Hindu hegemonic discourse[7] or in the economic, social, or educational realms of Indian society.[8] Neither, however, do I wish to trivialize this spiritual power or claim that it "compensates" for the lack of other kinds of power. To do so would be to devalue the spiritual ideals that are for many Hindus—women and men—of the highest value.

THE GODDESS AS MYTHIC MODEL

The revival of female religious symbolism in the West is strongly connected with and heavily informed by the ideology of political feminist movements. By contrast, the worship of female Deities in contemporary Hinduism is by and large not explicitly connected with modern feminist movements *per se.* The prominence of female Deities has long been a feature of every variety of Hinduism, and Shaktism, the worship of the Goddess (Shakti) as the supreme being, is a traditional cultic orientation in Hinduism, along with Vaishnavism and Shaivism, the worship of the male Deities Vishnu and Shiva. While some Indian women's groups, such as the feminist press "Kali for Women," have appropriated Goddess symbolism, they are drawing on traditions that are current in mainstream Hindu culture, not revalorizing forgotten symbols from an ancient past. The statement "God is a woman" simply does not have the shock value for Hindus that it does for Christians, Jews, or Muslims. I suspect that the reason for this is that Hindu conceptions of both the divine and of femaleness are radically different from those in the West. The divine feminine has long been at the center of Hindu religious symbolism. With the possible exception of the popular Marian cults, the ancient Goddesses of the Western world were long ago replaced by male Gods or by a monotheistic God conceived of in masculine terms. In contrast, the Hindu Goddess has become more and more popular throughout the ages, coexisting with male Gods and in many cases making them superfluous. Her cults throughout India continue to grow in numbers and importance. Hindu Goddess worship is a highly developed complex of myth, ritual, and theology, with many regional variants.

The worship of Devi (the Goddess) is one of the most vigorous and visible of religious phenomena in northwest India, an area that includes present-day Panjab, Haryana, Chandigarh, Delhi, and much of Himachal Pradesh, including Kangra. She is worshiped in a variety of forms and manifestations and enshrined in temples such as Vaishno Devi, Jvala Mukhi, and Chintpurni. While each of these "personalities" has her own iconography, stories, and physical dwelling place, each is considered to be a manifestation of *shakti*. When spoken of in general terms, the Goddess is most commonly called Sheranvali ("Lion Rider," a nickname of the demon-slaying Durga) or simply Mata (Mother). Her cult is one in which esoteric Tantric elements mingle with popular devotional (*bhakti*) worship. Although Seranvali has mythological and ritual associations with the great male Deities Vishnu and Shiva, it is in her independent form that she is worshiped. That is, she is not seen as a consort Deity, like Lakshmi or Parvati, whose significance depends on her relationship with a male Deity. She is both transcendent and immanent, her functions ranging from generalized ones such as the creation, preservation, and destruction of the universe to more specific ones, such as curing diseases and helping people in distress. She is the embodiment of *shakti*, the dynamic power of the universe.

Implicit in the theology of this Goddess is a kind of monism in which matter and spirit are not differentiated but rather are a continuity subsumed within *shakti*, the dynamic feminine creative principle. Whereas the Shaiva and Vaishnava theologies associated with the male Deities Shiva and Vishnu both recognize *shakti* to be the active aspect of the divine, the complement to the inactive aspect, Shakta theology understands *shakti* identified with the Great Goddess to be the ultimate reality itself and the totality of all being. Wendell Beane has rightly stated that *shakti* is the "irreducible (*sui generis*) ground for understanding both the non-Sanskritic, popular, exoteric and the Sanskritic, philosophical, esoteric" aspects of the worship of the Divine Feminine.[9]

The general thrust of Shakta theology is to affirm the reality, power, and life force that pervades the material world. Matter itself, while always changing, is sacred and is not different from spirit. The Goddess is the totality of all existence. Thus, as a reflection of how things really are, she takes on both gentle *(saumya)* and fierce *(raudra)* forms. Creation and destruction, life and death, are two sides of reality. The Goddess encompasses both. As a mythic model for women, the Goddess provides not just a transcendent ideal for women to look up to but also an immanent presence in whose divinity they can participate.

There is evidence to suggest that Shakta traditions tend to be more inclusive of women as practitioners and more accepting of women as leaders or gurus than do Vaishnava or Shaiva traditions. Lisa Hallstrom has stated that the prominence of the woman saint Anandamayi Ma must be viewed against the backdrop of her Shakta-influenced Bengali milieu and, more specifically, the Shakta affiliation of her husband's family.[10] Sanjukta Gupta has observed that Shakta women saints have more religious freedom and higher status than Vaishnava women saints.[11] June McDaniel, in her study of Bengali ecstatics, was able to find many Shakta holy women but no Vaishnava holy women.[12] The fact that holy women or women gurus can exist at all in male-dominated Hindu society is due to the divine model of femaleness that the Goddess provides. The holy woman identifies herself with the Goddess and is so identified by others.

In northwest India the Goddess is worshiped in various contexts and in various manifestations—at pilgrimage sites, religious performances, and household shrines in the form of stone *(pindi)*, flame *(jot)*, and icon *(murti)*. The most dramatic way in which devotees experience the Goddess is through her possession of human, usually female, vehicles. This type of possession is not seen as an affliction but rather as a sign of grace, as the Goddess's chosen method of granting a sacred vision *(darshan)* to her devotees. What I have glossed as "possession" is in northwest India called "playing" (Hindi *khelna,* Panjabi *khedna*).[13] It is seen as her sport or play *(lila, kala)* and also as her response to the faith *(shraddha)* and devotion *(bhakti)* of her worshipers. Devotees approach the possessed person, worship her as the Goddess, ask her for help with their problems, listen to her pronouncements, and receive her blessings. Thus, possession is a means for the Goddess to participate in the world of humans and for the medium and her audience to participate in the Goddess's divinity. In Hinduism there is no clear dividing line between divine and human; Gods can become humans and humans can become Gods, and it is often unclear which is which. The worship of Goddess-possessed women as Matas (Mothers), as manifestations of the Goddess, is a case in point. Such women are said to embody the *shakti* of the Goddess, that is, to become human icons.

TARA DEVI AT PLAY WITH THE GODDESS

During the fall of 1991, I spent several months in Kangra villages studying the religious lives of Hindu women, and particularly practices associated with women who become possessed by the Goddess (Mata).[14] I had previously met many such women from Panjab and Haryana in cities such as Chandigarh and Delhi and at the major Goddess pilgrimage places in the region. My aim now was to focus on village women with local followings in the context of their home communities. My primary informant was Tara Devi, a thirty-four-year-old Rajput married woman with four children. She had been experiencing Goddess possession for the past eight years and was a well-known healer and medium with her own temple attached to her home. I had been introduced to her by Swami Ramanand, a respected local religious leader who presides over a nearby Shiva temple. I believe it was in part due to my association with the Swami that Tara Devi was so open to my presence and willing to answer my questions. The brief account I give of her here is based on my observations in her home temple, where she practices, and on interviews with her and her family members, neighbors, and devotees. Tara Devi would want me to say at the outset that she claims no authority for herself, that she is a simple householder with little education, and that everything she knows, she has learned from the Goddess. She says, "At every breath, I have a vision of her riding a lion." She views all the events of her life as imbued with a special meaning in relation to the Goddess, saying that she has not chosen the Goddess, but rather the Goddess has chosen her. Using the English word, she says that all of her actions are in response to the Goddess's "order." However, as we shall see, there is room for some negotiation.

Tara Devi's parents died when she was young, leaving her, her elder sister, and her younger brother to be cared for by relatives. She was able to study only up to the fourth or fifth class and then entered into an arranged marriage at the age of thirteen. Her husband is a health worker currently posted in another village in Kangra District; he comes home on Sundays and holidays. She sums up her life after marriage as follows:

> And then what? All the work fell upon me. Then I had the children. Then the Mother's grace came upon me, and the world became good. Even crazy people, tied up and brought here, became all right. I have only to give one bit of holy ash. I have only to say one *mantra.* Through that they become all right. The world has become good.

In the phrase "the world has become good," Tara Devi expresses her experience of the transformative power of the Goddess. Prior to the Goddess's coming, Tara Devi had suffered for some years with a debilitating but undiagnosed illness. She tells of that period:

> It so happened that I was not keeping well. I was feeling a very heavy pain. The traditional doctors *[vaid]* and [Western-style] doctors denied it, saying it was nothing. There was pain in the chest, in the back. Some said it was pneumonia; others said it was something else. In Dharmsala [the district headquarters] many x-rays had been done. Then we went to faith healers *[celas]*, but there also our questions were unanswered, because the Power *[kudarat]* was over our house. Mata was about to come out. Through this, physical illness was produced. For years I just sat on the cot. And I was constantly worried that the children would be left behind and I would die.

She had no appetite and was unable to sleep.

Tara Devi's symptoms, similar to the "shaman's sickness," so well known in cross-cultural accounts of ecstatic religious experience,[15] are viewed in retrospect by her devotees as a testing and preparation by the Goddess. But at the time, her family feared she would die. Finally, out of desperation, her husband and mother-in-law visited Jvala Mukhi, the famous Kangra temple where the Goddess is manifested in the form of eternal flames. There they made a vow that if Tara Devi would feel hunger and eat, they would return, bringing her there for *darshan,* the sacred vision. From the tank at Jvala Mukhi they brought home a bottle of water and from the sacrificial fire pit some holy ash. As soon as Tara Devi drank the water and applied the ash to her body, she was able to fill her stomach and get some sleep.

So, to fulfill the vow, Tara Devi went with her family to Jvala Mukhi.

As she tells about the event, she focuses on her illness as having been due possibly to her own sinfulness and to some kind of sorcery having been done to her:

> I don't know what goes on with the Gods. I am caught in home and householding. When we went, that day we had eaten meat, and somehow in my heart it didn't seem right. I asked Mother for forgiveness, saying, "We are *bhuts* and *prets* [evil spirits and ghosts], forgive us." She forgave us. Jvala Ma is like that. Everyone eats meat there. It doesn't matter. Then at 9:00, the *arati* [waving of lamps to worship the Deity] started; the drums began to play. Many people were gathered there together. When I meditated on the Mother, she took me up. And I became afraid. She would lift me up sometimes and bring me down sometimes. I had also been fed some dirty things [that is, by a sorcerer in order to cause harm]. My health had been very good at the time of my marriage, but the sorcery gradually took effect. So I kept begging Ma's forgiveness, saying, "Queen Mother [Mata Rani], if I have done anything wrong, please forgive me." I kept on admitting my own wrongdoing. . . . And so much evil had been done over me through the things that had been fed to me, that through the Mother's power, the whole lion-seat [where the Goddess Jvala Mukhi presides] shook. And I was afraid, saying, "O Mother Queen, what are you doing?" Then the Mother appeared before me in a vision, riding on a lion, and she became part of me. When we left Jvalaji, I didn't vomit. Nothing happened. But then in the bus I vomited a lot. When I arrived home, the Mother gave me so much energy that I cut a whole bunch of grass. I worked for two or three hours. Through the Mother's blessing, all my pains went away. [Then she again tells all the places her pain was.] In those places, it dried up and all the pain went away, and she entered into me. She gave me a direct vision; riding on her lion. My whole body became warm. In the Mother's [Jvala Mukhi's] temple also, I had started to "play." My hair opened up, and even the temple priests couldn't catch me. Even they started saying that the Goddess had come to me. It's all the Mother's grace.

When she returned home, her "playing" continued. She begged the Goddess to desist, saying, "O Mother, I'm not cut out for this work. I have four children and a husband, too. And a cow and a calf, too. I also have the farm work." Then the Goddess became angry and returned Tara Devi to her previous anorexic condition. When her husband would speak to her, he would call her Devi (Goddess), saying, "Devi, eat your food." After eight days, Tara Devi went up on the roof, set up a cot and lay down while the rest of the family was in the kitchen preparing food. All the doors in the house were closed. At nine o'clock, the time of *arati* at the Jvala Mukhi temple, as Tara Devi tried unsuccessfully to sleep, the Mother's order came:

> The Mother ordered me to bring the clay from an anthill and make a small shrine for the Goddess in the room across from mine. I didn't heed this, saying, "Mata, please excuse me. I can't do this work." Then she lifted me up from the cot and all the doors that were closed opened by themselves. Everyone was amazed and distressed, wondering how the doors had opened.

After this, she began to "play" regularly, and as the Mother's orders came, she fulfilled them, making a shrine with clay from an anthill and installing an iron pot and a small picture of the Goddess in her Jvala Mukhi form. Gradually, people began to come to her for healing. It was during this time that Tara Devi says she began to speak in Hindi when people would ask questions. Before that, she knew only the Kangra dialect. Other people, coming into contact with Tara Devi, began to "play" also, and everyone was waiting for the Mother to "come out." Unfortunately, I do not have a very detailed account of what happened the day she "came out," but today there are nine images enshrined in Tara Devi's temple that she and her devotees claim emerged spontaneously out of the ground, along with a large quantity of red votive powder *(sindur)*, during the Navaratra festival, the nine nights dedicated to the worship of the Goddess. Tara Devi tells what happened when the first image "came out":

> We were doing *arati* at nine o'clock. There was quite a crowd present. All the people were "playing" the tongs and drums with great gusto. Mother was about to come out, so two or three people began to "play," saying, "Now take Ma out." I said, "When I myself get Ma's order, then only will we take Ma out." Then the Mother gave me a push to the back of the room, so that I would sit down and meditate. There was a woman there, by the name of Champa, in whom Mahavir [the monkey God, bodyguard to the Goddess] began to "play." He ordered us to make five products of cow and add Ganges water, and said that I should sprinkle this mixture around the room with a flower. Well, we kept doing that. People continued to "play." Suddenly, a huge pile of red powder and a big thread came out of the ground. . . . When the Mother started to come out, the flowers started to shake and started to fly. She ordered us to keep on splashing. Then the ferocious form of the Goddess came to me and gave me the order that the Mother is coming out. My eyes also became very red. I thought, "What is going on?" I didn't know what this *sindur* was, I only knew that it was like *sindur.* When the Mother herself came out, there were tiny earrings and clothes on her body. She was not naked. Here she is. It's Jvalaji Ma. [She shows me the image.]

Subsequently, eight other images came out of the ground. Previously a skeptic and reluctant to obey any of the Goddess's orders, Tara Devi's husband says it was this miracle that made a believer of him. Shortly thereafter, he had a small mud brick temple built for his wife in the courtyard. Later, this was replaced by the concrete temple where she sits now. Exhausted by the endless stream of devotees and Tara Devi's weakening health due to constant "playing," Tara Devi and her husband begged the Goddess to restrict the "playing" to certain times. After five years, the Goddess gave the order to set aside three days—Sunday, Tuesday, and Friday—for people to come and ask questions. Of this arrangement and his own gradual acceptance of the Goddess's presence, Tara Devi's husband says:

> At first I didn't believe in this. Day and night people used to come into one of the two rooms of our house, because the temple at that time had not been built. Because of this, our four children did not get time to study, and we did not get time to eat. And we had to arrange some kind of bedding for those who came from outside. Our children would shiver in the cold all night, because we had to provide bedding for other people. But no one wanted to sleep. Whether there were twenty people or three hundred, some were "playing," some were crying, and some were okay. I didn't have any faith at all in all this. I thought that some ghost or spirit [*bhut-pret*] had entered and taken hold of her, and this was its magical illusion [*mahamaya*]. But I started to believe when a crazy boy was brought here tied up and carried by seven men.

He then went on to tell the story of a mentally disturbed boy who was cured by the Goddess's power and remains fine to this day. This event, followed by the miraculous appearance of the Goddess images and the mounds of red powder, fixed his faith. Now he says philosophically, "Who knows what the fruits of a past life will bring? Otherwise, how could Mata come to people like us?" When I asked him what he thought of these cures, in light of his job as a health supervisor, he replied, "Yes, many times it so happens that someone has pain in the stomach and I give them medicine and the patient doesn't become better, and when she gives them ash and holy water they become better. Therefore, I understand that she is a very great doctor."

Tara Devi believes that the reason the Goddess has come to her is to help people with their problems, cure them of diseases, and rid them of afflictions caused by sorcery. She does genuinely seem to enjoy meeting so many people and being of service to them. At the same time, her experience of the Goddess is also deeply personal. It has filled her with spiritual power. She says, "At the time when I do *arati,* they all give me *darshan.* All 330 million Gods come to me. A to Z they all give me very good *darshan*. Even if the pilgrims don't come, still I get enjoyment. I keep muttering with my rosary, and I keep getting their *darshan*.

TARA DEVI AS SACRED SOURCE

As a vehicle for dispensing the Goddess's grace and healing power, Tara Devi has a never-ending stream of pilgrims, most of whom hear about her through word of mouth, showing up at her door. Tara Devi receives pilgrims on Sundays, Tuesdays, and Fridays from about 8:00 A.M. until noon and again from 3:00 until 6:00 or 7:00 P.M. On the days when Tara Devi is receiving pilgrims, she opens the temple, performs a short worship ceremony *(puja)* in front of the images, feeds the ever-burning flame with ghee, and lights incense. Then she recites the Gayatri Mantra and enters into meditation on the Goddess. If no one were to come, she would continue with this meditation, but usually someone does come. It may be a young woman hoping to become pregnant, a high school boy concerned about his exams, a mother with a sick child, a married couple who fight all the time, a family whose buffalo is not giving milk, or a wife who has lost all enthusiasm for household work (there are many of those). In between, Tara Devi often goes in and out of the house to check on rice cooking for lunch or to ask her fourteen-year-old daughter, if she is home, to make tea. Some people, mostly neighbors, may drop by for a few minutes to pay their respects, touching their foreheads to the threshold of Tara Devi's shrine, or to sing a devotional song and imbibe the highly charged atmosphere. Some have taken upon themselves the task of assisting Tara Devi by serving tea to guests, running errands, talking to pilgrims, or leading devotional singing. In particular, an elderly Brahmin widow, whose son was cured through Tara Devi, is usually on hand. Some come out of curiosity, just to watch, but many of those get caught up in the spirit and end up asking questions of their own.

The general procedure for asking a question is for the pilgrim to place some personal item (watch, ring, clothing, or clay from the house) in front of Tara Devi, along with an offering of a few rupees. One may also offer flowers, sweets, cloth, coconuts, fruit, and the like. Tara Devi then places her hand on this item and goes into a trance, leaning backward and forward in a gentle rhythm. I have not seen her "play" wildly with her hair flying about as other women do. She told me that she used to "play" this way, but that as a result of the Goddess's order, she now "plays" in a more subdued fashion. While in trance, the Goddess begins to speak through her with a marked change in voice, signaling her presence with a phrase like this: "Jay Mata di, Jay Jvala Mata di, Jay Kangrevali Mata di" ("Victory to the Mother, victory to Jvala Mother, victory to the Mother of Kangra"). She begins to talk to the pilgrim, asking questions for clarification, giving a diagnosis, and prescribing a remedy. Sometimes the pilgrim asks questions and engages in a conversation with the Goddess. When she is finished with one pilgrim, she moves on to the next item, asking whose it is. From time to time, Tara Devi will come out of trance, and speak with the pilgrims in her own voice, clarifying and elaborating on what the Goddess has said, particularly if the Goddess has given some elaborate ritual instructions. It is interesting to note that when Tara Devi is in trance, the Goddess speaks in standard Hindi, with even a sprinkling of English words, while Tara Devi in her own voice speaks in the Kangra dialect. Tara Devi, unlike many other women who become possessed, remembers what she has said while in trance.

Tara Devi's diagnostic and ritual system is quite elaborate. Based on what I have observed from other healers in the area, I believe that there are broad general features, but much room is left for individual idiosyncrasies. Tara Devi, as usual, attributes her extensive ritual knowledge to the Goddess herself, saying that she knew none of this before the Goddess started coming to her. Usually the diagnosis falls into one or more of the following categories: (1) sorcery, in which some evilwisher has brought harm by means such as feeding the pilgrim something unwholesome or burying it in her house, (2) an inauspicious astrological aspect, (3) some action or omission on the part of the pilgrim such as quarrelsome behavior or failing to perform a prescribed ritual. She will often describe at great length what problems the family is experiencing as a result of this affliction. The remedy she prescribes usually includes ash, holy water, and performance of a *havan* (fire sacrifice) or some other ritual. Sometimes, as I have witnessed on one occasion, she will have the person vomit up the "dirty things" that are causing the problem. She also gives out protective threads and *jantars,* amulets on which she has written prayers to the Goddess. In particularly stubborn cases, she will go to the person's house and dig the "dirty things" out of the wall with her trident. She explained to me that she knows where to dig because the Goddess takes over her body and her lion points the way by striking his paw on the spot.

Pilgrims who have been cured return later to give a thanks offering. Tara Devi offers them further protection by sweeping them with a peacock feather whisk and shaking an iron chain *(sangal)* around them. She explained to me that the whisk takes the sorcery/illness out of the person, at which point it is deposited in the chain, whereupon the Mother takes all those sorrows into herself and disposes of them.

I have heard numerous testimonials from pilgrims about successful cures. The following, from an elderly woman, is typical:

> I had become very ill. My body had become very weak. I was completely unfit to do any kind of work. I didn't even have the heart to work. Nothing. Then I came here and asked her a question, and she told me, "You have something [sorcery]." So, then I came here and ate some ash and drank some holy water. From that I got some benefit. Since then I always come here and to this day I have not even had a fever. Yes, by coming here to Queen Mother's feet, I became well. I have taken many medicines, I had also brought a needle [that is, had injections], but I did not get better. Then Mata gave me a lot of energy. Now I do a lot of work, and I eat with enjoyment.

From the same woman I learned about another fascinating aspect of Tara Devi's cult. Not only does Tara Devi "play" herself, but she encourages and helps other women to "play." The elderly woman told me, "The 'play' comes to me also. When I am absorbed in meditation near her [Tara Devi], she definitely gives me a push." After we had discussed this, Tara Devi closed her eyes, went into meditation, and mumbled something that sounded like she was asking the Goddess to come to this other woman ("sister"). Almost immediately, the woman started to "play." Her hair opened, and she started to talk. Tara Devi engaged her in conversation, interjecting at various points, "Yes, Matarani, yes Mataji." When the older woman came out of the trance, she seemed relaxed and happy. She told me that she feels a heavy pressure against her body when she "plays" and that the Goddess shows her all the pilgrimage places, even though she has never physically been there. Since then, I have seen numerous other women "play" in Tara Devi's temple, including Tara Devi's sister who lives in the same village. Tara Devi's sister, married to a man whom she described to me as old, ugly, and an alcoholic who beats her, told me that "playing" with the Goddess was her only joy in life. I have seen her "play" several times, once when the "ferocious form" *(virat rup)* of the Goddess spoke and threatened to take revenge against all the enemies who were harming her children. Unlike Tara Devi, her sister and the other women claim not to remember what they said while in trance. Much of what they say is incoherent, but I was particularly struck by recurring themes of family dynamics and interpersonal conflicts. Tara Devi's sister may have been giving expression to real problems in her life. Another woman while in trance spoke of a neighbor woman who was performing sorcery against other women in the village. Yet another complained of the heavy burden of housework and farm work, an all-too-common complaint in a region where large numbers of men are absent from home, working elsewhere for most of the year. In these cases, the women are using a religious idiom as an expression of means of resistance to the various conflicts and sorrows in their lives.[16] Obviously, Goddess possession provides some relief and fulfillment in their otherwise stressful lives. On one occasion, when several women had had particularly cathartic trances, they got up afterwards and danced joyfully while the other women drummed and sang devotional songs.

CONCLUSION

In the preceding discussion, I have attempted to show that Tara Devi has tapped into a traditional source of religious empowerment for women. From a Hindu point of view, there is nothing radical in what Tara Devi has done. True, she has transgressed the expected gender norms for a woman of the Rajput caste, who would normally be expected to devote herself solely to her husband and children, keeping a low profile outside the home. But she transgresses in response to a divine call with which no one can argue. Tara Devi does not face the double bind experienced by the rural Pentecostal women ministers interviewed by Elaine Lawless;[17] those evangelical women simply do not have the divine female role model and sanction Tara Devi has.

Julia Leslie, in the introduction to *Roles and Rituals for Hindu Women,* writes that it is not correct "to assume that women have a radically different world view than the one allocated to them by men or by male-authored texts," but that it is "the small deviations from the norm which may be crucial, perhaps the way the apparently negative is transformed into something positive and powerful."[18] In this case, Tara Devi has gained an immense personal power through her transformation from an invalid to a Goddess-possessed woman. But her power does not end with a sense of personal self-worth. It is also acknowledged in the community. She has the reputation of being an effective and compassionate healer, of being a worthy carrier of the Goddess's *shakti*. She is the only one allowed to touch the images in her temple. Even the Brahmin priest who installed the images is not permitted to touch them. Her husband has acknowledged her power and allowed his home life to be forever disrupted. One might object that it is only through male validation that Tara Devi is allowed to continue her activities. But I would argue that the men in question had no choice but to acknowledge Tara Devi's power because it was derived from an even higher power, the Goddess herself. Tara Devi already had a husband at the time her possession experiences started, so his cooperation had to be obtained. Consider an alternative case, that of a Mata with powers similar to Tara Devi's, whose story was told to me by a psychiatrist at the Civil Hospital in Dharmsala who shares clients with the Mata. This woman, now about thirty-five years old, was married at the age of sixteen. After the ceremony, as she was being lifted into the palanquin to be taken to her husband's home, she fell unconscious. Thereupon, the Goddess entered and ordered her to stay where she was and build a temple. She has never lived with her husband and to this day has continued to live with her parents, practicing as a healer in a prosperous temple establishment which she has built. This Mata, Tara Devi, and countless others like them have drawn on a mythic model, a very real female power, to transform their personal identities. But this transformation is not just a private affair. Their personal experiences have had public consequences. They serve as sacred sources, giving strength and empowerment to other women.[19]

Fig. 1

Fig. 2

Fig. 3

Fig. 1 Jvala Mukhi, Goddess temple in Kangra District, Himachal Pradesh
Fig. 2 Road to Tara Devi's house
Fig. 3 Near Tara Devi's house
Fig. 4 Tara Devi's house; her shrine is inside the addition on the right

Fig. 4

Fig. 5

Fig. 6

Fig. 7

Fig. 5 Tara Devi making an offering to a visiting Swami
Fig. 6 Tara Devi at her shrine
Fig. 7 The pindis *which appeared spontaneously from the ground*
Fig. 8 Tara Devi "playing"

Fig. 8

Fig. 9

Fig. 10

Fig. 9 Tara Devi singing devotional songs
Fig. 10 Tara Devi removing obstacles from a client with an iron chain (sangal)
Fig. 11 Tara Devi "playing"

Fig. 11

Fig. 12

Fig. 13

Fig. 12 A neighbor woman "playing"
Fig. 13 A neighbor woman "playing" while Tara Devi speaks with the Goddess
Fig. 14 Tara Devi with the author

Fig. 14

NOTES

1. Marglin, "Female Sexuality," 40. For a fuller discussion of the difference between purity/impurity and auspiciousness/inauspiciousness, including a review of the pertinent scholarly discussion, see Marglin, "Female Sexuality."

2. A word here about power, though I will have more to say below: I use the word "power" in a broad sense, inspired by Michel Foucault, who sees power as exercised rather than possessed, productive rather than primarily repressive, and as coming from the bottom up (and thus having multiple locations and effects) rather than from a centralized source at the top down (see Sawicki, *Disciplining Power,* 20-24). In some ways, the Hindu *shakti* is more similar to Foucault's idea of power than to traditional Western (i.e., Marxist) ideas of power, though to my knowledge, Foucault was not concerned with the kind of religious or spiritual power that *shakti* embodies. For a classic anthropological work on *shakti,* see Wadley, *Shakti.*

3. For a study of Kangra social structure, see Parry, *Caste and Kinship.* For a discussion of how out-migrant labor patterns affect the women remaining at home, see Sharma, *Women, Work, and Property.* For a description of the major features of the Hindu Goddess cult in northwest India, which includes Kangra, see Erndl, *Victory to the Mother.*

4. Most of the scholarly writing on Hindu women has focused on their religious roles within the family. See, for example, Jacobsen, "Golden Handprints"; Wadley, "Hindu Women's Family"; McGee, "Desired Fruits"; and Harlan, *Religion and Rajput Women.* For a historical overview of women in Hinduism, see Young, "Hinduism."

5. Falk and Gross, *Unspoken Worlds,* 233.

6. Falk and Gross, *Unspoken Worlds,* 233.

7. For typical examples in Sanskrit, see Buhler, *The Laws of Manu,* and Leslie, *The Perfect Wife.* Also, the vernacular languages abound in popular manuals with such titles as *Strisubodhini (Instructions for Women),* delineating appropriate behavior for the faithful wife (*pativrata*).

8. Studies on these aspects of Hindu and Indian society are too numerous to mention. An excellent study on one of the more extreme forms of female subordination is Miller, *The Endangered Sex.*

9. Beane, *Myth, Cult and Symbols,* 41.

10. See Hallstrom, "Beyond the Extraordinary."

11. See Gupta, "Women in the Śaiva/Śākta Ethos," 209.

12. See MacDaniel, *The Madness of the Saints,* 231, 315.

13. This is stated in constructions such as "the Goddess plays in X," "the play of the Goddess comes to X," or even "X plays." For further discussion of the language of possession and its relation to Hindu notions of divine play, see Erndl, *Victory to the Mother,* chapter 5.

14. This research was funded by a Fulbright-Hays Faculty Research Abroad fellowship. Previous trips to India for related research were made possible by a Fulbright-Hays Doctoral Dissertation Research Abroad fellowship (1982-1983) and a faculty appointment with the Himalayan Study Program sponsored by the California Institute of Integral Studies (fall 1989). Some of the material presented

in this section of the chapter has appeared in a different form in Erndl, *Victory to the Mother* and "Śeranvali."

15. See Eliade, *Shamanism*, and Lewis, *Ecstatic Religion*.

16. For an interesting perspective on gender resistance and power, see Oakley, *Defiant Moments*. See also Lewis, *Ecstatic Religion*, especially chapter 4.

17. See Lawless, *Handmaidens of the Lord*.

18. Leslie, *Roles and Rituals*, 9.

19. I regret to inform my readers that Tara Devi passed away on August 8, 1996.

WORKS CITED

Beane, Wendell Charles, *Myth, Cult and Symbols in Śākta Hinduism*. Leiden: E. J. Brill, 1977.

Buhler, G., trans. *The Laws of Manu*, Sacred Books of the East, vol. 25. Delhi: Motilal Banarsidass, 1964.

Eliade, Mircea. *Shamanism: Archaic Techniques of Ecstasy*. Translated by Willard R. Trask. Princeton: Princeton University Press, 1964.

Erndl, Kathleen M. *Victory to the Mother: The Hindu Goddess of Northwest India in Myth, Ritual, and Symbol*. New York: Oxford University Press, 1993.

———. "Śeranvali: The Mother Who Possesses." Pp. 173-94 in *Devī: Goddesses of India*, edited by John S. Hawley and Donna M. Wulff. Berkeley, Calif.: University of California Press, 1996.

Falk, Nancy Auer, and Rita M. Gross. *Unspoken Worlds: Women's Religious Lives*. 2d ed. Belmont, Calif.: Wadsworth, 1989.

Gupta, Sanjukta. "Women in the Śaiva/Śākta Ethos." Pp. 193-210 in Leslie, *The Perfect Wife*.

Harlan, Lindsey. *Religion and Rajput Women: The Ethic of Protection in Contemporary Narratives*. Berkeley, Calif.: University of California Press, 1992.

Hallstrom, Lisa. "Beyond the Extraordinary: The Hindu Woman Saint: Anandamayi Ma." Paper presented at the American Academy of Religion, San Francisco, 1992.

Jacobsen, Doranne. "Golden Handprints and Red-Painted Feet: Hindu Childbirth Rituals in Central India." Pp. 59-71 in Falk and Gross, *Unspoken Worlds*.

Lawless, Elaine. *Handmaidens of the Lord: Pentecostal Women Preachers and Traditional Religion*. Philadelphia: University of Pennsylvania Press, 1988.

Leslie, I. Julia. *The Perfect Wife: The Orthodox Hindu Woman According to the Strīdharmapaddhati of Tryambakayajvan*. Delhi: Oxford University Press, 1989.

———, ed. *Roles and Rituals for Hindu Women.* Rutherford, N.J.: Fairleigh Dickenson University Press, 1991.

Lewis, I. M. *Ecstatic Religion: An Anthropological Study of Spirit Possession and Shamanism.* Harmondsworth: Penguin Books, 1971.

McDaniel, June. *The Madness of the Saints: Ecstatic Religion in Bengal.* Chicago: University of Chicago Press, 1989.

McGee, Mary. "Desired Fruits: Motive and Intention in the Votive Rites of Hindu Women." Pp. 71-88 in Leslie, *Roles and Rituals.*

Marglin, Frédérique Apffel. "Female Sexuality in the Hindu World." Pp. 39-59 in *Immaculate and Powerful: The Female in Sacred Image and Social Reality.* Edited by Clarissa W. Atkinson, Constance H. Buchanan, and Margaret R. Miles. Boston: Beacon Press, 1985.

———. *Wives of the God-King: The Rituals of the Devadasis of Puri.* Oxford: Oxford University Press, 1985.

Miller, Barbara D. *The Endangered Sex: Neglect of Female Children in Rural North India.* Ithaca, N.Y.: Cornell University Press, 1981.

Oakley, Judith. "Defiant Moments: Gender, Resistance and Individuals." *Man* (N.S) 26 (1991), 3-22.

Parry, Jonathan P. *Caste and Kinship in Kangra.* London: Routledge and Kegan Paul, 1979.

Sharma, Ursula. *Women, Work, and Property in Northwest India.* London: Tavistock, 1980.

Sawicki, Jana. *Disciplining Foucault: Feminism, Power, and the Body.* New York: Routledge, 1991.

Wadley, Susan Snow. *Shakti: Power in the Conceptual Structure of Karimpur Religion.* Chicago: University of Chicago, Department of Anthropology, 1975.

———. "Hindu Women's Family and Household Rites in a North Indian Village." Pp. 72-81 in Falk and Gross, *Unspoken Worlds.*

Young, Katherine Y. "Hinduism." Pp. 59-104 in *Women in World Religions.* Ed. by Arvind Sharma. Albany, N.Y.: State University of New York Press, 1987.

2

CYNTHIA ANN HUMES

Glorifying the Great Goddess or Great Woman? Hindu Women's Experience in Ritual Recitation of *Devi-Mahatmya*

In the early strands of religious literature preserved in the sacred tongue of Sanskrit that have come to be called Hindu, Deities of fire and sacrifice predominated. Many of these sacrificial Gods were gendered male. Even the earliest Hindu scriptures, however, describe and extol numerous Goddesses with diverse qualities. Some of these Goddesses are still worshiped today. Many popular practices devoted to Goddesses that were either unreflected or barely mentioned in the early Sanskrit texts eventually were included in the later Hindu corpus. By the fifth to sixth centuries of the Common Era, the texts record a growing tradition of devotion to a single "Great Goddess" who was held to incarnate herself as the myriad local and regional Goddesses found throughout India. This theory accounted for the plurality of Goddesses, even as it affirmed philosophical concepts of a unitary, transcendent Goddess.

In the Sanskrit *Devi-Mahatmya* (literally, "Glorification of the Goddess") from about the sixth century C.E., the Hindu Great Goddess is described as the divine creatrix of the entire universe, including the Gods. Although transcendent, she manifests herself periodically in physical form as an omnipotent warrioress in order to vanquish demons who threaten the Gods. She specifically promises to aid all devotees who beseech her. In addition to restoring righteousness and universal harmony, she bestows enlightenment and benevolently grants mundane desires. Fourteen centuries later, millions of Hindus still recite the *Devi-Mahatmya* throughout India for all manner of ends, and the text remains without question the Sanskrit glorification par excellence of the Great Goddess in India.

Recently the *Devi-Mahatmya* (hereafter, *DM*) has engaged the attention of many scholars, including feminists. Some have studied the text to understand how women are viewed in India, while others have hypothesized that the *DM* and its myths of an omnipotent Goddess can serve as a means of female empowerment by providing a universal model for the latent "powerful everywoman." Both ventures are questionable methodologically because Hindu women and the Goddess are not, and have not historically been, considered isomorphic: Hindus of both sexes routinely note the transcendence of the Goddess and the impropriety of ascribing her qualities to human females or women's qualities to the Goddess. That the myths are "really" discussing women is specifically denied by almost all Hindus who use the text. Further, women have not had a strong connection with the *DM*, which for centuries has been seen by the dominant interpreters as a collection of sacred *mantras*, or words of revelation in Sanskrit, whose greatest meaning lies in its ritual power, not in its story. Recently this situation has changed. The majority of women who now use the *DM* do so in the vernacular rather than Sanskrit, and many are educated in modern schools that emphasize the meaning of religious texts rather than their form. As I will show, these factors may signal a profound transformation in the interpretation of the *DM*; a minority of women today see it as a glorification not only of the Goddess but potentially of woman. I will explore these trends here by studying the history of engagement with the *DM*, concluding with glimpses of three women's practices that suggest indigenous models of female empowerment through the *DM*. I thus hope to shed light on how various women themselves view the Goddess described in the text, the nature of the *DM* itself, and its possible relation to their lives as women.

THE HISTORY OF THE *DEVI-MAHATMYA* IN RITUAL

Even though there appear to be fewer than six hundred verses in the *DM*, many of those who are engaged with the work believe it to be composed of seven hundred *mantras*, special sacred utterances that have intrinsic power independent of semantic signification or meaning. Indeed, the dominant preoccupation of fifteenth- to nineteenth-century commentaries on the text was the separation of the *DM* into such *mantras*, not the meaning of its verses.[1] This preoccupation highlights one of the most significant differences in the way that scholars, East and West, have interpreted the *DM*: Hindu commentaries have consistently been most concerned to explain how the *DM* should be *used;* Western commentaries have been most concerned to explain how the myths should be *interpreted.* Six subsidiary "limbs" have come to be attached to the text in its ritual performance. The three preceding the text are often recited daily by worshipers in lieu of verses from the chapters, demonstrating the fact that the myths and their meaning are for many not the most important part of what has come to be known as the *DM.* According to dozens of informants I interviewed who themselves recite the work, Westerners who seek the *DM*'s meaning actually miss the essence of the very text they hope to elucidate. While I am sensitive to this dominant critique, I intend to examine alternate trends in the life of the *DM* that are concerned with its meaning. My reason is that the dominant Hindu approach privileges an elite perspective to the *DM,* while much of my work involves the deconstruction of the *DM* in nonreligious contexts and from nonelite perspectives.

I conducted extensive field research on the use of the *DM* among different groups at Vindhyachal, Uttar Pradesh, a pilgrimage site devoted to the Goddess Vindhyavasini, "She who dwells in the Vindhyas." Vindhyavasini's abode is considered to be a particularly powerful place to recite the *DM,* and many who perform the text there observe that the land is like a charged battery, imbued with power accumulated through millions of *DM* recitations over the years. They often quote *DM* 12.8 as proof: "Whichever abode of mine in which this [*mahatmya*] is constantly recited properly, never will I abandon that place; my presence is established there." The Goddess then promises that performing or sponsoring the recitation of her glorification with devotion (*bhakti*) will yield any worldly or transcendent goal desired. Just as the *DM* itself advocates, the primary activity associated with the text historically has been ritual recitation. Rather than stressing the devotion that should accompany the recitation, however, the *DM*'s interpreters stress that the work is not myth read for its meaning, but rather *mantra* recited for its effect.[2] Recitation of the *DM* is usually done by high-caste males, particularly Brahmins, who might be hired to recite the text for others' benefit, as again is advocated in the text. According to Brahmin specialists, correct performance of the *DM* produces a scientific, predictable, and automatic effect. This view of ritual and *mantra* is particularly significant when one compares it with women's experience with the *DM.*

Ritual participation with the text is gendered. In a lengthy questionnaire survey of 252 pilgrims to the temple site, only 53 of the 100 women interviewed had ever heard of the *DM,* in contrast with 107 of the 152 men (or 70 percent). Only seven pilgrims claimed to recite the *DM* in both Hindi and Sanskrit; all seven were male. Twenty-eight of 252 pilgrims claimed to recite the text in just Sanskrit; only one of these was female. Nearly the same percentages of females and males recite the text in Hindi only: seven females and nine males recited in Hindi, or 7 percent of females and 5.9 percent of males. Thus, only 8 percent of females recite the *DM* at all, in contrast with 28 percent of males, and those females who do so are far less likely than males to recite in the ritual language of Sanskrit.

Participation with the text is also affected by caste. In the same survey, approximately one of every four Brahmins recited the *DM* in Sanskrit, whereas only one in twenty non-Brahmins recited the *DM* in Sanskrit. Only one in twenty Brahmins recited in Hindi, and one in fifteen non-Brahmins recited in Hindi. Brahmins made up 71.4 percent of all who recited in Sanskrit, and non-Brahmins made up 75 percent of those who recited in Hindi alone. Specific studies of reciters at Vindhyachal Temple confirm that Brahmin men tend to recite in Sanskrit, while women and non-Brahmin men tend to recite in Hindi.

Of the few women or low-caste men who do recite the *DM*, almost all do so in vernacular languages, whereas high-caste men recite the text in its original Sanskrit. When low-caste men do recite in Sanskrit, if their wives recite, generally they do so in the vernacular. One may ask: Is this important? The answer is yes and no. Although reciting her mahatmya in the vernacular may—from the perspective of devotionalism or *bhakti*—please the Goddess, the Sanskrit language is considered by almost all to be more powerful because it is a collection of *mantras.* In the vernacular, this *mantra* effect is lost and only the story and the *mahatmya* remain, and many argue that subtle nuances of the story are lost as well. Further, the Goddess is more "pleased" when spoken to in her "own language" of Sanskrit. Thus, reciting the text in vernacular languages does not draw on the Sanskrit's inherent power, more direct appeal to the Goddess, and fullest description. That *DM* recitation in Sanskrit is gendered and affected by caste, then, is an important socio-religious fact that can be obscured by discussion of the text in English translation. It is easy to assume that the wife reading in Hindi is having the same experience as her husband reciting in Sanskrit, but this is not the case according to most Hindus.

I have discussed elsewhere why these gender and caste differences might exist.[3] To summarize briefly, literacy in India is low and access to Sanskrit education even lower. The *DM* is part of a *purana,* the genre of Hindu sacred literature that is theoretically open to all believers. This includes women and low-caste males, who for the most part are excluded from hearing, reciting, or reading texts, such as the *Vedas*, reserved for male twice-borns. Low-caste people especially, and even higher caste women, however, have not routinely been taught Sanskrit, even if they are literate, because Sanskrit has been reserved as the sacred language for males belonging to the three highest social groups of males. Finally, although for centuries the *DM* has been a popular and fairly accessible text among the privileged classes, inexpensive editions of the *DM* have only become widely available to all segments of society relatively recently.

My data reveal what appear to be important new trends in *DM* recitation today. Increasing numbers of people who before now were not engaged with the text or who used to hire Brahmins to recite it told me that they now wish to perform it themselves. This seems to reflect a downward spread of the "great [textual] tradition" and, with the rise of literacy, the dissemination of various modern and perhaps Western, democratic values. Because literacy in Sanskrit was almost exclusively the domain of high-caste males, local vernacular traditions existed alongside Sanskritic culture. Modern secular education has been the major force in opening up Sanskrit and its textual traditions to new groups. Together with the advent of mass printing, the rise of literacy, increased belief in equality, and access to both Sanskrit and vernacular texts have led to a "return" to the *DM* by groups for whom it has never been a tradition, including most women. This has led to the replacement of or addition to local traditions with a Sanskrit tradition among groups that previously had practiced only local, vernacular traditions or hired Brahmins to recite.

These developments have not gone unnoticed by the privileged elite. Some religious authorities hold that women and low-castes should be excluded from reciting the *DM* because of its special nature as *mantra.* Markandeya Brahmachari, a *pandit* from Banaras, warns that reciting the *DM* ritually can be dangerous for those who are not authorized. Low-castes and women should not be encouraged to recite it, although theoretically they are capable of recitation if given the proper training by a competent guru. Untouchables are not qualified to perform the *DM* in any case; the result of recitation is said to be a curse, not a blessing. Cheap, accessible books popularizing the *DM* merely help unqualified people "drive themselves into deeper hells."[4] Brahmachari feels great sympathy for these people; he is convinced that the adoption of Western models of teaching and equality have led many Hindus to abandon proper transmission of sacred knowledge and the maintenance of divinely ordained caste rules, to their own detriment in future lives, if not this one. People of any background have been deluded into believing they can learn privileged religious information from mere books, as Westerners do; they assume incorrectly that a text purchased on the streets is as sufficient and appropriate a guide as the guru.

Western emphases on the primacy of written documents rather than oral tradition as sources of authority, and beliefs in secular education, the equality of all regardless of birth, and quasi-Protestant theories of equal access to divine knowledge through personal engagement with a religious text have all certainly had an impact on *DM* recitation. Although some traditionalists decry these changes as Western corruptions, others welcome them. For instance, a Brahmin male reciter told me that Gita Press, one of the largest publishers of religious texts (including the *DM*) in India, was actually created as a British plot to ruin Hindu religion by publishing corrupted manuscripts and selling sacred works to improper people. Yet another Brahmin male reciter told me, "These are new, revolutionary times." He wants anyone to be able to recite the text "if he is pure and wants to do recitation in a peaceful way." He explains, "I believe I would give even him the authority. He also should do recitation, for he is my brother. Yes, Hindu, Muslim, Sikh, Christian, whatever one may be."[5] (He affirmed female participation with the text as well.)

Western influence on the life of the *DM* is undeniable. I argue, however, that an indigenous model of dissent against the patriarchal and hierarchical values of the dominant elite preserved in *DM* recitation also promoted egalitarianism and equal access to religion, and that now plays a crucial role in the modern life of the *DM* in *bhakti* (devotionalism). As my description unfolds, I will demonstrate the impropriety of attributing all stirrings of dissatisfaction and dissent among Hindus to Westernization.

THE GODDESS AS "FEMININE" AND HER RELATIONSHIP TO WOMEN

At this point I wish to address the issue of the "femininity" of the Great Goddess, and the process of interpreting her mythology in order to shed light on views of human females. In his first book on the *DM*, Thomas Coburn wrote that the thrust of the text is to argue that "ultimate reality is really ultimate," not that ultimate reality is truly feminine; the text's articulation was not a deliberate alternative to understanding ultimate reality as masculine.[6] Many devotees today agree with this statement, particularly those who espouse *Advaitan* or nondual views that depict ultimate reality as the neuter *Brahman*, the ground of being that completely transcends all qualities and thus gender. Others disagree. According to these informants—generally those from a devotional *(bhaktic), Shakta* (devotion to *Shakti*, the Goddess as power), or *Tantric* (pseudoscientific) bent—the deliberateness with which the author(s) of the *DM* altered prior myths in order to attribute all power to an immanent Great Goddess suggests that depicting ultimate reality as feminine was indeed a deliberate alternative to viewing ultimate reality as masculine. Due to its quality of fertility, or better, creative potentiality, the ground of all being is regarded as feminine; for many, she is a creatrix who gives birth to all from herself. Immanent in all things as potentiality, or *shakti*, she also reacts to the needs of her creation and at times assumes specific incarnations, as does the male God Vishnu. Whereas Vishnu appears in the forms of *avatars* descending from the heavens, however, the Goddess appears from within creation because she *is* all of creation. Unlike male Gods who come from above and use external means to create by word, copulation, or manipulation of matter, the Goddess appears and creates all from out of and within her very self. She is *prakriti*, material nature, as well as the abstract qualities, or *gunas*, that provide shape to that substance. Thus, for those who see ultimate reality as creative potency, the ultimate is really ultimate—and really feminine.

Although it is not possible to determine conclusively how the authors of the *DM* understood the Goddess as feminine, especially in relation to women, there are many clues. I do not believe the *DM*'s view of the divine as feminine was meant to idealize the human female. In addition, the understanding of the Goddess for many reciters of the *DM* today seems to differ dramatically from those previously engaged with the text, reflecting the influence of the rise of intense emotional devotionalism, or *bhakti*, and the concomitant revisioning of the Goddess as a kindly mother. Thus, a concern for history is necessary when speaking about what the *DM* means, for it appears to have meant different things at different times to different people. A brief look at her myths is in order first.

The *DM* is considered today to be divided into thirteen chapters and organized according to three episodes depicting the Goddess's battles against demons for the welfare of the Gods. While earlier versions of each of the three episodes exist in Sanskrit literature, the *DM* is the first work to group them together and to depict the Goddess as the primary cause of the demons' defeat. For instance, Vishnu is known in earlier literature to have defeated the two demons Madhu and Kaitabha, earning him the epithet Madhusudana, or "slayer of Madhu," yet in the first *DM* episode, the "great deluding" Goddess Mahamaya, also known as Yoganidra, or "Yogic sleep," has trapped Vishnu in a deep slumber. When the twins appear from Vishnu's earwax and threaten Lord Brahma, he appeals to the Goddess to delude the demons and to depart from Vishnu so that Vishnu can destroy them. Pleased by his prayer, she goes forth from Vishnu's body and appears to Brahma. Through the Great Goddess's beneficent withdrawal, Vishnu becomes "wise and blessed" (1.72), able to act in Brahma's defense. The two demons, on the other hand, become "intoxicated" and "deluded" by the excess of power (*atibala*) generated in battle and foolishly agree to a boon requested by Vishnu that finally tips the balance against them after a five-thousand-year battle. Thus, here she *withdraws* from Vishnu to give him power and wisdom and *imbues* the demons with excess delusory power to make them foolish. Both the withdrawal and the saturation point to the result of immanence by the Goddess as "Tamasi" (1.68), "she who is [predominated by] the *guna tamas*." *Tamas* is the quality (*guna*) of sleep, darkness, or ignorance in the Hindu triadic understanding of *prakriti*, or matter.

The second episode features the defeat of the buffalo demon Mahisha, who, like the Goddess, is able to change his form at will. Whereas earlier myth cycles credit this victory to Shiva or to his son Skanda, the *DM* posits the Great Goddess as the agent instead. The defeated Gods appeal to Shiva and Vishnu for aid, urging them to "set their minds on destroying the demon," and from the anger concentrated within their foreheads, the two Gods, together with Brahma, emit luster (*tejas*). This *tejas* coalesces into a shimmering mass together with the luster of all the other Gods. The *tejas* assumes the form of a refulgent Goddess who shines throughout the three realms of the universe. Thus, here the Goddess, already immanent within the Gods, takes specific incarnate form from the energy *drawn out* of their anger. Immediately an exciting battle with the Goddess ensues; Mahisha and his army are killed and the Gods' rule is restored. After a long paean, she promises to incarnate herself whenever called upon in order to protect the worlds. Most interpretations of this myth explain that Mahishamardini, the "Crusher of Mahisha," is the manifestation of the Great Goddess when predominated by the *guna rajas*, the darkening quality of passion, emotion, and affection. *Rajas* is often associated with *tejas*, and is said to be an active force in air or the sphere of vapor or mist.[7] Coburn interprets this episode as showing that not only is the Goddess operative in the world, but she is supreme ruler of all creatures. Indeed, the *DM* here draws on the classical Indian model of kingship, which portrays the ruler—*raja*—as a collection of the eternal particles of various Gods, who thereby surpasses all created being in *tejas*.[8]

The third episode describes the slaying of the twin demons Shumbha and Nishumbha, and unlike the other two myths, this story appears to have come from a popular regional Goddess tradition rather than Sanskrit sources, although it is again strongly associated with a male Deity (Krishna-Gopala). The Goddess chooses yet another way to appear after being extolled as the "delusory power" of Vishnu. This time, Kaushiki comes forth from the sheath or *kosha* of Parvati, appearing as Ambika, "Little Mother," in a lovely form. Just as Parvati does not recognize Ambika, so the demon brothers mistake her true nature. The demons see her as a "jewel" to be possessed through marriage, but she refuses the proposal extended through their messenger, saying that she had vowed long before that the only one whom she would marry would be he who conquered her in battle. Decrying her as haughty, the messenger says, "All the Gods, led by Indra, were no match in battle for Shumbha and the others. How can you, a mere woman, go into battle with them?" (5.73). All attempts to conquer and control her fail, however. Despite appearing from the sheath of Parvati, understood in contemporaneous literature as Shiva's wife, she is not a married or marriageable Goddess; she is assailed by her suitors as "an evil woman" for refusing their advances, and they angrily resolve to capture her.

This last episode includes the fascinating myth of the demon Raktabija, literally "red-seed" or "blood-drop," who regenerates identical forms of himself when any of his blood "seeds" the earth. To combat the hordes of demons, the Goddess creates other forms from out of herself. Mirroring the *tejas* model of origination in the second episode, from the forehead of the Great Goddess, "black as ink in anger," the terrible Goddess Kali emerges. When the Goddess, her lion vehicle, and Kali are surrounded on all sides, *shaktis*, or separate female "powers," emerge from a group of male Gods; the last *shakti* emerges from the Great Goddess herself. The *shaktis* wound Raktabija, but even more demons arise from his blood. Kali then eats the demons and laps up any blood before it hits the ground to stop further regeneration. The Goddess proves herself—not the demons or the Gods—to be in control of creation. After she slayed Nishumbha, Shumbha accuses the Goddess of conceit for relying on the strength of others yet claiming victory alone. She denies being aided by the seemingly many Goddesses, explaining, "I alone exist here in the world; what second, other than I, is there?" She reabsorbs all of the *shaktis* and standing alone, slays Shumbha. After being praised by the Gods, the Goddess promises to return whenever needed, and she lists many future incarnations she will take to aid her devotees. Coburn explains that this episode is concerned with establishing the Goddess as the one truly ultimate reality. While seemingly taking on many forms, in actuality she is the ground of all that exists, the internal power within all.[9] Indian interpreters hold that this story highlights the quality of the Goddess predominated by the *guna sattva*, the quality of being, purity, or goodness, reflecting her true essence, nature, disposition of mind or character.

Thus, the Great Goddess is the Deity of both wisdom and delusion who acts at times by kindly withdrawal or punitive excessive saturation. She may manifest herself as a brilliant queen from combined powers, the fiery form in which she exists in all creation; she may appear in specific lesser incarnations that themselves may not understand their connection to the transcendent Great Goddess; and she can also appear as a multitude of separate *shaktis*, or manifested powers, not just from male Deities but also from herself.

The variety of ways the Goddess manifests herself and the deliberateness with which she is portrayed as eschewing marriage and dependence on others reveal that unlike human females, this divine feminine force is entirely self-sufficient and creates by her own power. Thus, while one of the commonly quoted *DM* verses affirms that each woman is a "portion" of her, the verse continues that it is by the Goddess alone that this world has been filled up (11.5); women's role in creation is entirely dependent on the Goddess, and she exists as the latent power within *both* the female and the male.

Is the *DM*'s vision of the Goddess as creative femininity an empowering vision for women?[10] I believe that claiming women are embodiments of the Mother Goddess can be a very effective way to obscure a profound misogyny behind portrayals and conceptions of the Great Goddess. Women are not offered an empowered role outside marriage and family; indeed, the feminine nature of the Goddess and her myths in the *DM* do not make sense unless the patriarchal subjugation of the normal human—or even lesser divine—female is assumed. For example, the twin demons misinterpreted the Goddess as an ordinary haughty female with a bad attitude (*dushta*) toward her superior male suitors; they concluded that what she needed was to be subjugated by a man in order to become a good woman, and several times they say she should be dragged by her hair and humiliated by her male combatants. In other words, a "good woman" is a submissive wife and biological mother. Their misunderstanding is seen as a highly amusing episode in the *DM*, and those who recite it find it particularly noteworthy.

Significantly, reciters do not question male dominance but point out the impropriety of a demon securing a liaison with the far superior Goddess, who is not marriageable. Her battle reveals a lustrous "feminismo"; effortlessly drawing upon the inexhaustible powers within herself, which take the external form of other Goddesses, she proves she is not "a mere woman," as her opponents taunt. Shumbha also misunderstands her relation to these female forms, assuming them to be distinct from her, a view proven wrong by her absorption of them all into herself before finally slaying him. Clearly, the feminine qualities ascribed to the Great Goddess and to women in the *DM* are not isomorphic: her nature as mother is different, her relation to men is different, and her strength and abilities are different from women's.

Turning away from the text's views to current devotees' views of the Goddess, it is noteworthy that whereas medieval *DM* commentaries stress ritual or abstruse philosophical views of the Goddess as all-powerful creatrix and ruler, today the maternal relation of the Goddess to her children is primary. Most *DM* reciters now view the Great Goddess of the *DM* as a kind mother and downplay her transcendence and fierce battles. Her maternal affection is constantly identified as the same sentiment found in human females. As is the case with Goddesses in China documented by Steven Sangren, however, "It is not women as a social category that are symbolized in female Deities, but the idea of women as they stand in a particular relationship to worshipers, that is, as mothers to children."[11]

A brief look at the history of the *DM* sheds light on its interpretation today. Early *bhakti* or devotional literature in India was often modeled on the war genre of popular poetry, or eulogies written by court poets singing the praises of local kings. Thus, *bhakti* poems and texts such as the early *DM* drew upon parallels in the cultural construction of kingship for the cultural construction of Godship. Recall how the second episode of the *DM* depicts the Goddess being constructed from the combined *tejas* of the Gods, following the model of kings. In addition, most *bhaktic* praise of the Deities included the decapitation of enemies, long found in war genre poetry, and the style of directly addressing the king (now God or Goddess), both found abundantly in the *DM*. While in the war genre poetry the kings were lauded for defeating human enemies of their peoples, in the *bhaktic* genre of poetry modeled on this style, the Deities defeat demonic enemies of all. As is suggested in the text itself, at least by the medieval period, the *DM* came to be closely associated with ritual and form, so much so that the text came to be understood as *mantra* to be performed in precise, "scientific" rituals, rather than as a paean to be understood, a view still dominant today among ritual specialists. J. N. Tiwari suggests in an intriguing essay, however, that a variant reading of the *DM* found in Bengal and dating from at least the eighteenth century emphasized the maternal, kind aspects of the Great Goddess rather than the "heroic, fighting figure, [and] destroyer of evil and protector of people in distress" described in the *DM*.[12] Tiwari concludes that the "mother aspect" of the Goddess "must have gradually grown in importance" in recent centuries to warrant the variant, for it is an awkward grammatical construction and contextually inappropriate. For unknown motivations, possibly reflecting a general modern bhakticization that calls for more intense devotional moods, they stressed the nurturing aspect of the Goddess, with a concomitant de-emphasis of her martial qualities. Thus, the Great Goddess in the *DM* originally appeared to relate to human females in the context of her being a cosmic creatrix and queen who answered the calls of her devotees or constituents. She differed from women in her capacity as omnipotent warrior-queen who successfully avoided marriage yet was mother nevertheless. With the de-emphasizing of her martial nature, no longer popular in *bhakti* circles, there now appears to be an increasing correspondence between the vision of Mother Goddess and the vision of ideal human mothers, who are always kind and forgiving to their children.

I think Tiwari is astute in recognizing the start of an increasingly dominant devotional context in which the *DM* now finds itself. One of the specific comments made by dozens of reciters on the femininity of the Great Mother Goddess was that, as a mother, she is easier to please than male Deities. Consequently, the recitation of her Sanskrit text was not as threatening to them as if they were to attempt to please a male Deity with recitation of his text. I contend that this may be a partial explanation for the popularity of the *DM*'s recitation in Sanskrit among nonprofessionals who recite the text out of a devotional stance rather than a ritual or Tantric approach. Their confidence is rooted in the conceptualization of the feminine, both human and transcendent, as naturally forgiving, kind, and motherly. Narayan Shekhavat, a Rajasthani compiler of religious texts devoted to the Goddess, explains, "In this world, it is apparent that fathers have become cruel, and they have great rigidity in them; but mothers are filled to the brim with softness, kindness, heartfelt affection, and motherly love." He explains, "It is said that the worship of Durga is the most difficult of all, and that if there is any impurity,... or mispronunciation, or incorrect practice, . . . then great harm may occur. But how can this be? Would a mother, who calls for her own son, punish him if he lisps in response? Would a mother punish a child who soils his pants and body?"[13] This represents a shift in the understanding of both *DM* recitation and the Goddess. Instead of viewing the *DM* as a *ritual text* to be correctly recited to produce a specific effect, a Vedic-Tantric belief found in medieval commentaries and still popular among ritualists today, recitation is often viewed, particularly by nonspecialist lay people, as an instance of calling upon their Mother, quite consciously modeled on ideal human mothers. That the Great Goddess is now seen as a more human, forgiving mother seems to have had a profound impact on understanding how the *DM* works.

I found that nearly all of over one hundred male and female *DM* reciters questioned at Vindhyachal affirmed the Great Goddess as mother and stressed her kindness and forgiving nature. Both males and females were quick to point out the great differences between the Mother Goddess of the *DM* and women as mothers, however. The Great Goddess is mother of her children, but she has no consort, so there is no father. Woman is the source of ignorance for man, but she is not the source of wisdom, whereas the Goddess is proved to be both in the *DM*'s first episode. Nor is the Goddess "polluted," "weak," or "evil," as human women are.[14] And while both have "natural maternal instincts" of loving and easily forgiving children, human mothers are often powerless to protect and provide for their children and must depend on their husbands.

While most Hindus believe women have *shakti*, or creative power, this has not necessarily proven in practice to be liberating. The Goddess's power is controllable both *by her* and to a certain extent *by her devotees* to whom she is committed. Women are believed to be incapable of channeling their power appropriately when independent. This is so because they are considered by men and women alike to be corrupt, weak-willed creatures. Noble exceptions to this rule are extolled as human "Sitas" or "Savitris," but they are still married. Whereas the Great Goddess excels in "masculine" battle and refuses any consort, such activities are generally unacceptable for human females. The only similarities of women to the Great Goddess, then, are *shakti* (which for women must be controlled by males), bearing children, and "natural maternal instincts" to love and easily forgive children.

Another finding suggests extremely important ramifications in the use of Hindu myths. A male pilgrim told me that the difference between the Goddess and women is like the difference between the stone you worship as Goddess and the rock on which you defecate.[15] A reciter reiterated that while there can be no "bad mothers," even "good mothers" who are human are at their core "bad": "Women are the untouchables of this earth in comparison with Durga [the Great Goddess of the *DM*]. Woman's true nature is composed of eight evils. In all women, all eight faults are found; even in Sita and Savitri. Their very pores are permeated with these evils, so what comparison can there be of women with the Goddess?"[16] When asked if men also are permeated with the evils, he laughed and shook his head no, as if shocked by the question. This negative comparison of the lesser Goddesses and women, echoed by other informants, suggests there may be dramatic differences between the way the Great Goddess is perceived and the understanding of female Goddesses who *do* serve as explicit models of women. Despite recognizing the flaws of human women, the majority of reciters interviewed reiterated the truism that they are all embodiments of *shakti*, and that marriage is essential for both sexes: without a female, a male is powerless.[17] What model of *shakti* should women follow, then? Sita and Savitri are both considered perfect wives and mothers, but according to my informants, even they are still permeated with evil and ignorance. It is noteworthy that both Goddesses are subordinate to their husbands, willing to endure any punishment meted out to them in order to obey and save their husbands, and they are sexual, producing children as human females do. Patriarchal culture not only does not encourage women to believe that they can become the pure, independent, and self-empowered Great Goddess of the *DM*, but it actively promotes females modeling themselves upon those lesser Goddesses who support women's social position as submissive, impure wife and mother. Women cannot be viewed as the Great Goddess, subject as they are to "female conditions" from which the Great Goddess is free. These findings suggest dramatic differences between the way humans may approximate the Divine Transcendent. Ironically, men may more closely express divinity than females, even when the Divine is viewed ultimately as the Goddess, for men are not permeated with evils as women are, and they can channel power. Scholars and Westerners seeking to understand Hindu views of women must pay close attention to the fact that research has demonstrated that myths of Hindu Goddesses do not necessarily reflect Hindu culture's vision of womanhood; indeed, they often accentuate what womanhood is *not*.

While most informants said that the Great Goddess and human females are vastly different and that their similarities in gender are confined to creation, embodying power, and being kind to their children, I did note several exceptions, most voiced by women. Pramila Devi, a woman from Rohtas, Bihar, who daily recites in Sanskrit portions of the *DM*'s limbs and reads the myths for meaning in Hindi, was much more positive in her depiction of human females than all the other reciters I interviewed, both male and female. Identifying Vindhyavasini as the unmarried Great Goddess of the *DM*, she said,

> In my opinion, if a woman has *shakti,* to the same degree as she has *shakti,* is full of compassion, with the will to make the weak strong, then all such women, even if poor or weak, are not less than Vindhyavasini herself. If a woman does anything for the welfare of the world, or works shoulder to shoulder with men, if she offers herself for the welfare of her brother, husband, or children, or upon the battlefield of her country, then she is not less than Vindhyavasini. If she helps somebody who is in pain, or feels sorrow, and sacrifices herself in this way, she is not less than Vindhyavasini.[18]

Pramila Devi continued, the Goddess "uses us for unity and integrity on this earth. . . . Everybody has the same *shakti*. Nobody can see it, nobody can taste it. It exists within and manifests by our usage." Lily Bhardwaj, a successful New Delhi career woman who has taught herself to recite parts of the *DM* daily in Sanskrit tells me she consciously thinks of herself as *shakti* when faced with difficult situations. She appeals to the Mother, the Great Goddess, directly to give her infusions of power, to "battle the demons" she encounters in her work. Nirmala Trivedi, who recites in Hindi, says that although women are only humans, "If we do good deeds, we will be absorbed in Her." Clearly, the Great Goddess does act as an empowering role model for at least some Hindu women today, although these three women are not average Hindus, for they all have been educated in modern secular schools and hold privileged positions of power in the culture and economy.

NEW FORMS OF WOMEN'S ENGAGEMENT WITH THE *DM*

Experience of the *DM* in its most common form, ritual, has largely been vicarious for women. Recently, more women have begun to recite the text ritually. Yet women's experience with the nontextualized "glory of the Goddess" has been vast and unencumbered by abstruse language or painstaking ritual. Rather than performing male ritual patterns, some women have adopted the *DM* on their own terms. I turn now to three women's engagement with the *DM*, including a woman seen as a guru who gives oral glosses of the *Mahatmya* but defers to male Brahmins as the experts on the text; a *mata,* or mother, who through her special nature as conduit of the Great Goddess lends authority to a vernacular rendition of the *DM* in folk ritual; and a female commentator who relies on the authority of her own experience to interpret the meaning of the Sanskrit text for not only modern Hindu but other women as well.

Kamala Pandey: Guru

Kamala Pandey is the stunningly beautiful daughter of a *pandit* whose forefathers have traditionally specialized in *DM* recitation and *Shakta* practices. She studied through the intermediate or twelfth grade, and she told me that "in high school, I took Sanskrit. In this way, ever since I have kept studying the *Vedas* and the *shastras*." Thus, although the other women in her family were not taught to read or recite Sanskrit, Kamala is very involved in recitation, reading, *katha* or oral textual exegesis, and also original composition of hymns to the Goddess in vernacular Hindi. Kamala is married to the head of the Mirzapur branch of the Central Investigation Department, and they live in downtown Mirzapur, a city of some 200,000, which is approximately five miles from Vindhyachal. Mr. Pandey is very obliging in his wife's efforts to spread the worship of the Goddess; indeed, he describes her as his guru. She presides over religious sessions open to the public in a room in their home entirely devoted to worship. During these events—every Tuesday, Saturday, and the day of the full moon—she sings over a microphone that transmits her lovely voice through loudspeakers into Mirzapur's main street. She always includes the Sundar Kand section of the *Ramcharitmanas*, as well as a selection of her own devotional songs inspired by portions of texts such as the *DM* and the *Devi Bhagavata Purana*, and the hymns in the *DM* themselves. She offers her own commentary on Sanskrit texts such as the *Shiva Purana* by raising questions and answering them by quoting various Sanskrit texts, including the *DM*. Even so, it is her family priest who recites the *DM* ritually over the loudspeaker during *Navaratras*, the "nine nights" festivals to the Goddess in the fall and spring. Accepting male dominion over ritual and *mantra*, she explains, "the *Shiva Purana* is story [so I can comment on it]; the *DM* is *mantra*, so the *pandit-ji* recites that."

Mrs. Pandey believes all Gods are devotees of the Great Goddess, who precedes them and grants them continuous aid. This Goddess is Vindhyavasini, who is not subject to marriage or any constraints that the Goddesses who are partial manifestations experience. She looks to the *Shiva Purana* for guidance on how women should act; they should model themselves on Parvati's ideal relation to Shiva. If women do so, they can "finally understand the particle of the Great Goddess within them." Thus, she holds to the distinction I have noted: the Great Goddess is beyond emulation, but women can model their actions on Goddesses who correspond to accepted social visions of ideal women and thus partially manifest the Goddess. She sees no contradiction in her roles as wife and guru; it is her duty to teach all interested in the Goddess, even her husband.

Mrs. Pandey has become a popular and authoritative religious teacher, even celebrity, in the local area. During festivals, she sings her songs about Vindhyavasini to large crowds, and her poetry is featured in Vindhyachal Temple magazines. She is commonly seen on pilgrimages to the many shrines in the area and performs her hymns for streams of admirers who follow along with her.

While she says she does not ritually perform the *DM* publicly nor exegete its verses, Mrs. Pandey often performs the most popular portions of the text—the singing of the hymns in chapters 1, 4, 5, and 11—all to new melodies and in renditions she creates herself. In addition, when she speaks on religious topics, she constantly refers to the text. She guesses that she has composed nearly one thousand songs, most of which exalt the Great Goddess and are variations of the myths of the *DM*. Kamala's combination of devotional songs (traditionally women's practice) with variations of the hymns of the *DM* and textual exegesis of its verses (traditionally men's practice), all directed to a large audience, is an interesting fusion. Thanks are due in part to the grace of the Goddess, a secular education, and last but certainly not least, a supportive and admiring husband.

Rama Rani Maharotra: Mata

Rama Rani Maharotra is founder and priestess of a popular Vindhyavasini temple near the Maldahiya area of Banaras. In addition to her famous healing powers, she performs the *DM* according to a popular folk style, the *jagrata. Jagrata,* literally "awake," is the rite of keeping vigilantly awake throughout the night and singing devotional songs to the Goddess. Her worship involves lighting large ghee lamps, symbolizing the Goddess, before which they perform *jagrata,* conducted in Panjabi and Hindi dialects.

Rama Rani believes she has been blessed with a special vision of Vindhyavasini. After worshiping her, she was healed of a sickness no doctor or Ayurvedic healer could cure. Because the Goddess deigned to come to her home, Rama Rani has been able to speak with the Goddess and provide an "energy conduit" to others in ill health or worldly trouble. Mrs. Maharotra does not claim to be possessed by the Goddess; she merely communicates with the Goddess by writing questions posed by devotees on her left palm with a simple metal key. She then relays whatever answer she finds in her palm, which is visible only to her. After receiving *prasad*, or graceful leftovers of food offered to and "spiritually consumed" by the Goddess, the devotees perform whatever deeds or take whatever treatment the Goddess advises.

The fame of her temple has steadily increased since its establishment in 1975. The Hindi magazine *Saptahik Hindustan* featured Mrs. Maharotra and her temple in their October 8-14, 1989, edition on the fall *Navaratra* festival of the Goddess. In addition to detailing her life history and the origin and growing popularity of her temple, the author documented in words and pictures Rama Rani's ability to channel Vindhyavasini's power to heal instantly the bloody wounds of a devotee who had whipped his back with iron claws while in an ecstatic trance. Her notoriety today is especially interesting, because she had previously observed *purdah* in accordance with the social customs of her family and Khatri caste. Her husband encouraged her to go public, saying that after the Goddess granted her this gift, it was not appropriate to restrict it to her family; she must extend this gift to all who come to her. She is referred to as *mata*, or mother, and as *shaktishali*, or "possessing *shakti*." The women and men who come to the temple ask her blessings and touch her feet in respect. Clearly, by the actions of those who come to her, Rama Rani is not considered an ordinary human female; she is actively worshiped.

Services at her temple take place twice daily, and on special days, three or four times. Until 1985, Mr. Maharotra had performed portions of the *DM* in Sanskrit every day for the temple, as Rama Rani recognized that it was the special text of the Goddess, but she knew no Sanskrit. At her suggestion, however, he discontinued ritual recitation, and instead Rama Rani began to sing a vernacular version of the *DM* that is comprehensible to her and her many female clients. This shift from ritual recitation to devotional singing does not cause any decline in effect because, for Rama Rani, the Goddess is ever present and need not be ritually invoked through *mantra* for the words to be effective.

Written by Pandit "Chaman" Lal Bhardwaj, the Panjabi priest of a Goddess temple in Amritsar, the *Shri Durga Stuti* is a vernacular adaptation into Panjabi of the entire Sanskrit *DM*, complete with the ritual limbs except the *Rahasyas*, which are replaced by numerous prayers to various Goddesses. Chaman's version has been popularized by Narendra Chanchal, a famous Panjabi singer who is considered to be a great devotee of the Goddess and a master of the *jagrata* genre of music.

Chanchal specializes in devotional songs to the Goddess, and is hired by devotees to sing at *jagratas,* for which he commands a very high price. In his three-hour performance on cassette tape, accompanied by a chorus of singers and full orchestra, Chanchal sings Chaman's version of the *DM* in a Panjabi accent and comments at times for clarity.

Rama Rani believes Chaman's version is more accessible, and she enjoys Chanchal's rendition. Therefore, she now sings and teaches Chaman's version of the *DM* according to Chanchal's melodies as a ritual. She sings all three preliminary limbs and the *DM* during festivals, but on normal days, she sings just the three limbs that were appended to the myths. Thus, Rama Rani does not actually sing the myths of the *DM* daily, but as mentioned, many engaged with the Sanskrit text also prefer to recite these limbs rather than *DM* chapter verses.

Chaman/Chanchal's version of the *DM* appeals to Rama Rani and her patrons for obvious reasons. A member of the Khatri caste (Panjabi merchants who claim *kshatriya* status) herself, many of Rama Rani's patrons tend also to be Khatri women, who easily understand and can participate in the Panjabi adaptation. This folk form popular in the Panjab has thus encompassed the *DM* and enjoys a wide audience of devotees who seek more accessible translations of the *DM*, both in language and in style, to meet their religious goals. Further, if Rama Rani is able to channel the Goddess's power, it is only appropriate that she not be excluded from participating in the life of the Goddess's most famous text. What is intriguing is that the access follows the pattern of female participation through a vernacular folk style, which becomes mantra-like in ritual because of the presence of the Goddess assured through the *mata,* or mother, Rama Rani.

Vasanti Jayasawal: Commentator

Mrs. Jayasawal is a Nayar woman from Kerala in southwest India. She now lives in Los Angeles and teaches Indian classical and folk dances. Initiated into the Nambudri system of recitation, she told me that elderly people of her community routinely teach the *DM* to youngsters, so that people learn informally to recite the Sanskrit text verbatim. She notes that in Kerala, *DM* editions commonly include verses in the hymns and conclusion not found in Northern publications. She fondly recalls hearing her father reciting the text in their worship room, often adding extra verses in response to his surroundings and mood. She also used to listen to her family priest discuss the text in her home, as well as overhear priests talking about the text in their local temple. She is currently composing a commentary in English on the Sanskrit *DM* based on her own life experiences and the ideas she heard growing up in Kerala.

Originally Vasanti was motivated to create a *DM* commentary due to an "all-consuming attraction" to the text because of its portrayal of the Ultimate Deity as female. After completing work on its first eight chapters, however, she came to feel herself to be in a transition state. She believes now that although the Mahamaya—the all-powerful force of the *DM* understood as feminine—is undeniably positive, manifested Goddesses in texts such as the *Devi Bhagavata* and others are consistently portrayed as abused females who are subsequently given Sati status, a dubious honor that she finds does not justify their harsh treatment by male Gods. She "cannot lie down and take" such passages in the scriptures any more but must come to terms with the fact that there are many scriptural portrayals of the feminine that are "not pleasant" or helpful for women today. She believes it is more important than ever for women to compose commentaries on religious texts themselves because women feel differently than men, have different experiences, and the "female aspect of God has a lot of loopholes" that must be addressed by women based on their own experiences in order for them to become independent and fulfilled.

One of her concerns in creating a commentary is to remain true to the text as a specific revelation. She believes the *DM* encapsulates a specific moment or instance of the Goddess. People inappropriately read into the text later features, such as the theory of the three Great Goddesses rather than the Unified Goddess. The limbs of the text are granted too much prominence, and this results in people missing the text's theology of the Great Goddess as ultimate force, not manifest form. Many interpret the *DM*'s stories in light of similar later myths, but those are concerned with embodied Goddesses who have different histories in other times. For example, the Kali in the *DM*'s first episode is not the Bengali Kali controlled by Shiva; the destroyer of Mahisha is not the temptress described in later myths; and so on. Thus, her interpretations resonate with my fieldwork findings on the substantial differences perceived between the Great Goddess beyond but within all, and lower manifestations, as well as the need for a concern with historicity when interpreting the text.

Mrs. Jayasawal believes that most women from southern Indian states do not accept the passive and powerless divine models for women in the north such as Sati, Sita, and Savitri. In her own matrilineal Nayar community, she has always seen women in positions of power. When she teaches girls and female dance students about the *DM*, she does not instruct them to model themselves specifically on the Great Goddess, but she has found that some consciously do so. Particularly interesting is her observation that while the *DM* is not popular among the younger generation of Kerala women in India, her American students, both Indian and Anglo, are markedly interested in the work, and some have chosen to dance to songs to the Great Goddess because it makes them feel independent and powerful. She explains, "If a woman feels powerful but has no avenue to express that power, women find consolation or hope that if the Goddess can do it, so can we." She is considering enacting the entire *DM* in the *Kathakali* dance form because of student interest; it has been done in *Bharatnatyam*, and she sees no reason why it could not be adapted, even with modern nuances such as portraying the demons as punk rockers and Gods as pop icons like Elvis.

Vasanti is writing her commentary in English because she believes that the *DM*'s truths are universal and not confined to Hindus. The buffalo demon, for instance, symbolizes all adversity and evil. Thus, as the episode in which the Goddess assumes the form from the combined *tejas* of the Gods teaches us, righteous anger and indignation focused against evil, when fused together in the service of good, can defeat any adversity. We all have divine power within that can be evoked and used in battle against evil. She finds Western feminist views of Hindu and other religious texts overly negative; although Hindu women have been abused and religion has played a role in their subjugation, there is also beauty, life, and truth in the revelations. Her commentary is thus intended to redress the omission of Hindu women's experience in approaches to the *DM*, even as it affirms the essential and universal truths in the revelation.

When questioned about her and other women's ritual use of the text, Mrs. Jayasawal replied that she herself recites the text in Sanskrit because of its form as *mantra*. In fact, when she performs the text, she does not think of her commentary at all or, at times, even the meaning of the verses, because the sound patterns instill in her an intense devotional mood toward the Goddess. In point of contrast, she described a huge ritual she observed known as a *Sahasra Chandi*, or ritual recitation of the *DM* one thousand times, done by a group of male *pandits* drawn from all over the Indian state of Karnataka for the purpose of gaining world peace. The temple officiants had constructed fences around the *pandits*, and women were forced to remain standing outside. What she found ironic and sad was that inside the fence, the men recited the text from books with bored expressions on their faces, scratching themselves, and throwing the *samagri* or ritual substances into the *homa* or fire pit "almost offensively," all for a wage. In contrast, watching from the periphery, reciting by and with heart, were the "impure" women; yet there was more meaning on the faces of the women and others outside than in the faces of the Brahmin ritualists. She was overwhelmed by the dichotomy: she "couldn't take it; there was no heart in it," and she immediately wrote a letter to the editor of the local newspaper decrying the marginalization of the women devotees and the lack of true feeling in the ritualists' performance. While others confirmed her views, she sighed, nothing has been changed to bring women into the ritual life of the text in temple functions. She concluded that women need to become not only more engaged with the *DM* and to explain their views, but also to become more vocal in their demands for equal participation. Her commentary and teaching are her own contributions to that goal.

REFLECTIONS

Many historians of religion and feminists have centered on the theology and meaning of the *DM*'s verses, often relating their interpretations to human females. Such an approach directly contradicts dominant *mantra* theory, which postulates the ultimate meaninglessness of the verses, as well as popular opinion, which affirms the myths are not about women but about the Goddess. While feminists plumb the *DM* as a means to enrich women's lives, using the imagery of the Goddess as a model for the latent powerful everywoman, the text has not functioned in such a way in the past or even among most Hindus today. Women and the Great Goddess have not been considered isomorphic, although most Hindus assert that women should model themselves on Goddesses such as Sati, Sita, and Savitri, "partial manifestations," as Mrs. Pandey describes them, who are also "abused Goddesses," as Mrs. Jayasawal observes. These Deities present impossibly perfect and nonliberating models for women.

Some Hindu women, however, today do see the *DM*'s Great Goddess as a possible model for empowering women in the future. These very few women, most either educated in Christian or secular public schools and aware of Western concepts of Deity and human equality, or living in the West, affirm that the text can serve in a different way than has been maintained by those supportive of the patriarchal ideal. I think this development represents the fusion of indigenous *bhakti*, itself an equalizing agent, with worldwide, modern feminist concerns for women's well-being. Each of the women approaches the Goddess primarily through *bhakti* rather than ritual performance, which, like Western forms of Protestant religion, emphasizes belief, meaning, and religious sentiment rather than form or rite. *Bhakti* emphasizes no body and soul dualism and affirms acceptance of individual freedom of expression and choice in religious performance. Although *bhakti's* history as a dissent movement has not been particularly political, at least on an individual, spiritual level it has promoted egalitarianism in class and gender. Western feminist definitions of women's well-being have not been uncritically adopted by the Hindu women with whom I spoke. I heard much criticism of what some perceived to be an artificiality of religion in the West, overemphasis on independence leading to isolation from others, and harsh estrangement from men. As more communication between feminists develops across the globe, perhaps the profound devotionalism to the Goddess I found in the Hindus I interviewed can enliven the despiritualized appropriations and reinterpretations of the *DM* by many Western feminists. Rather than emphasizing the androcentric historical contexts of Hindu texts and uprooting the Hindu Goddess entirely from her salvific history, Western feminists may see fit to join in the promotion of a transcultural feminist devotionalism to the Great Goddess more in keeping with how she has been understood truly to *be* in Hinduism, but a devotionalism that uplifts rather than degrades women's well-being.

The *DM* was almost certainly composed by men, and its use has been dominated by men. One could argue that women's adoption of ritual recitation in Sanskrit is an imitation of male religious behavior, which ironically may lead to the loss or de-emphasis of ancient forms of women's experience of glorifying the Great Goddess. I do not find it surprising at all, however, that women wish to gain access to *mantra,* which had been off-limits before. Most consider the *DM* as an authoritative text that augments, not replaces, their women's traditions. Further, the *DM* has become a means to enrich many women's lives *on their own terms.* Each of the three women discussed in the last section have sought in varying degrees to redress the patriarchal use and interpretation of the text. More women will be motivated to practice Sanskrit recitation themselves—rather than vicariously as daughter, wife, or client—simply because they can. Still others, believing themselves pure enough, knowledgeable enough, and independent enough, through their performance of the *DM* in whatever form and their own commentaries on that text, may come to conclude as a tiny but growing number of women have that extolling the Great Goddess of the *DM* extols the vision of the divine feminine that they may become.

NOTES

1. Coburn, *Encountering the Goddess*, 27.

2. Interviews were conducted in several ways. For instance, one of my most important data sets was a survey of 252 pilgrims, chosen as randomly as possible. The first forty of these pilgrims' interviews were recorded on tape. After determining the usual responses and excising and adding various questions, I composed a questionnaire. I then interviewed respondents on the grounds of Vindhyachal Temple—a crowded public setting—and recorded their responses on the questionnaire form. Each interview took approximately ten to fifteen minutes. I also interviewed hundreds of reciters of the *DM*, professional and lay, that is, nonprofessional. I always used an interview guide that included the same questions as on the pilgrim questionnaire for comparison purposes, but that also included detailed questions on ritual performance and textual exegesis, as well as allowed for open discussion of unprompted material. These interviews lasted a minimum of thirty minutes. Like the pilgrim data set, the first fifty were tape-recorded to ensure the accuracy of their comments and to determine whether any changes were necessary. Again, the interviews usually took place at Vindhyachal Temple but with as much privacy as possible, effected by using a priest's home as an interview base. I also conducted in-depth interviews of selected pilgrims, temple personnel, lay reciters, and ritual specialists (determined by respondents' receptiveness to the initial interviews and whether they were of particular interest). These were sometimes hours in length. My interviews with the three women I highlight in the last section entailed going to the residences of the first two women several times and conducting lengthy taped interviews with them, and holding follow-up two-hour phone interviews with the third woman after meeting her briefly at a religion conference.

3. For further discussion, see Humes, "Power and the Powerful."

4. November 15, 1989, formal taped interview in Banaras, India.

5. Kaushalendra Mani Tripathi, formal taped lay interview in Vindhyachal, India, March 1988.

6. Coburn, *Devī-Māhātmya*, 304.

7. Monier-Williams, *A Sanskrit-English Dictionary*, 863.

8. Coburn, "Consort of None," 159; *Encountering the Goddess*, 26.

9. Coburn, "Consort of None," 159.

10. For an extended discussion, see Humes, "Is the *Devī-Māhātmya* a Feminist Text?"

11. Sangren, "Female Gender," 1, 4, 23.

12. Tiwari, "An Interesting Variant," 243.

13. Shekhavat, *Bhagavati*, 2.

14. An interesting point that never surfaced in my interviews is the case of some Goddesses who are believed to experience menstruation. At Vindhyachal and in the context of the *DM*, informants told me only of the Great Goddess, who is not subject to such bodily defilements as lesser Goddesses may be.

15. Ramakan Caurasiya, taped formal interview with pilgrim, March 1988.

16. Parashuram Dvivedi, taped formal interview with lay reciter, March 1988.

17. Ram Kumar Pandey, formal taped interview with lay reciter, March 1988.

An interesting comment that surfaced twice was the observation that, yes, women all have *shakti* and are a particle or portion of the Goddess, but human women differ from each other because they have portions of different Goddesses. Women who fight with their husbands have portions of Kali; those who are gentle and "behave" have portions of Lakshmi; those who are more independent and intellectual in spirit have portions of Saraswati (from Damodar Prasad Pandey, formal taped interview with lay reciter, March 1988; and Uma Shankar Pathak, taped formal interview with Vindhyachal professional reciter, July 1988).

18. Pramila Devi, formal taped interview with lay reciter, March 1988.

WORKS CITED

Coburn, Thomas B. *Devī-Māhātmya: The Crystallization of the Goddess Tradition*. Delhi and Columbia, Mo.: Motilal Banarsidass and South Asia Books, 1984.

———. "Consort of None, Śakti of All: The Vision of the *Devī-Māhātmya*." Pp. 153–65 in *The Divine Consort*, edited by John S. Hawley and Donna M. Wulff. Delhi: Motilal Banarsidass, 1984.

———. *Encountering the Goddess: A Translation of the Devī-Māhātmya and a Study of Its Interpretation*. Albany: State University of New York Press, 1991.

Humes, Cynthia Ann. "Is the Devī-Māhātmya a Feminist Text?" In *Writing the Goddess: Feminism and Reflexivity in the Study of the Hindu Goddesses*, edited by Kathleen M. Erndl and Alf Hiltebeitel, forthcoming.

———. "Power and the Powerful: Women, Men, and the Goddess." In *Gender, Religion, and Social Definition*, edited by Julia Leslie. New Delhi: Oxford University Press, forthcoming.

Monier-Williams, Sir Monier. *A Sanskrit-English Dictionary*. Reprint, Banaras: Motilal Banarsidass, 1986

Sangren, P. Steven. "Female Gender in Chinese Religious Symbols." *Signs: Journal of Women in Culture and Society* 9 (1983): 1-25.

Shekhavat, Narayan. *Bhagavati! Mateshvari! Pahi Mam!* Varanasi: Vishnu Press, 1984.

Tiwari, J. N. "An Interesting Variant in the Devī-Māhātmya." *Purāna* 25, no. 2 (1983): 235-45.

3

DONNA M. WULFF

Radha's Audacity in *Kirtan* Performances and Women's Status in Greater Bengal

A strong, defiant stance assumed by women toward men, in which the women bitterly reproach their husbands or lovers, often for their neglect and infidelity, constitutes a prominent theme of a number of literary and performance forms in medieval and modern Bengal. Although such defiance is also found in cultural forms prevalent in other areas of the subcontinent, this theme seems to be especially well developed in Greater Bengal, a region composed of parts of present-day Bihar, Orissa, and Assam, as well as West Bengal and Bangladesh. From the first half of the current millennium, we find an unusually large number of verses on the *māninī*, the "woman offended"—usually by her husband's or lover's infidelity—in two prominent anthologies of Sanskrit poetry from Bengal, the *Subhāṣitaratnakósa*, compiled by the Buddhist abbot Vidyākara in the second half of the eleventh century[1] and the *Saduktikarṇāmṛta*, compiled by Śrīdharadāsa in 1205.[2] Medieval Bengali and Brajabuli verses beginning in the fourteenth century continue this tradition, depicting Rādhā as the heroine offended by her lover Krishna's faithlessness. Several Bengali forms of performance draw on these verses to dramatize such scenes of angry rebuff, presenting Rādhā's modes of reproach in minute detail.

Bengal, and eastern India more generally, is a region in which at least some women have had higher status and greater power than women have had in most of the north.[3] This fact invites speculation on whether there is a correlation between the generally higher status of women in the region and the prevalence of literary and performance forms in which women express their anger and unhappiness with their men through modes of rebuke and censure. The attempt to establish such a correlation between cultural forms and women's experience and status is fraught with difficulties. First, our knowledge is far from adequate. For example, although women in colonial Bengal have been the subject of historical studies, there is a dearth of recent ethnographic studies of women in either West Bengal or Bangladesh. Second, it is difficult to know how to interpret the literary and performative evidence. At least four possibilities suggest themselves: first, that these forms reflect actual occurrences or relationships in Bengali society, past or present; second, that they have worked prescriptively or subversively to mitigate the harsh, patriarchal circumstances of women's lives;[4] third, that they have served as compensation for the oppression experienced by women;[5] and finally, that they have functioned as rituals of reversal,[6] paradoxically helping to ensure women's obedience by allowing them to experience vicarious rebellion at suitable intervals.

The purpose of the present article is to explore the possible correlation between cultural forms that show women—human or divine—reproaching or abusing their men, and women's experiences and status. Toward that end I analyze two representative performances of a single episode in the repertoire of a highly influential Bengali devotional musical form, *padāvalī kīrtan*—an episode in which Rādhā and her friends reproach a wayward Krishna. Although she is portrayed in *padāvalī kīrtan* and other forms of religious performance as a human woman, Rādhā has been understood by Bengali Vaiṣṇava devotees—and indeed throughout Greater Bengal—as a Goddess, Krishna's eternal consort. To provide a broader interpretive context for understanding these performances, we shall begin by reviewing two related types of evidence: first, theological and religious conceptions of Rādhā—and of the feminine more generally—prevalent in Bengal; and second, historical evidence for leadership roles assumed by women in medieval Bengal and in the Bengali Vaiṣṇava movement in particular.

Several theological conceptions prominent in Bengal and especially in Bengali Vaiṣṇava teaching have relevance to Rādhā. The first is an understanding of divinity as female as well as male: in Bengal, the Rādhā-Krishna story has been viewed through a lens in which a male-female duality is conceived to be at the heart of the universe. In accordance with this Tantric paradigm,[7] the two lovers are imaged and worshiped as two aspects of a single divine reality. Vaiṣṇava theologians refer to Rādhā as Krishna's *hlādinī shakti*, his blissful energy.[8] Just as Śiva is said to be nothing but a corpse (*śava)*[9] without his energizing consort, also called his *shakti*, so Rādhā is understood to be an integral and indispensable part of the Divine. Although the technical theological term *hlādinī shakti* may not be widely known, the idea of a dual male-female divinity has been widespread throughout Greater Bengal.[10]

A second, somewhat surprising theological assertion about Rādhā's relation to Krishna is that his love for her is not love within the proper bounds of marriage (*svakīyā rati*) but an illicit love for someone who belongs to another (*parakīyā rati*).[11] Several Bengali literary and performance forms depict Rādhā as married to a man called Āyān Ghosh[12]; her relation to Krishna is thus an extramarital one. The usual theological explanation for this startling fact is that whereas love within the confines of marriage is by its very nature deferential and dully conventional, love outside marriage, free from these conventions, can be intensely passionate. It is noteworthy that it is Krishna's love for Rādhā that is termed *parakīyā*, love for someone who is married to another; it is *her* marital status and not Krishna's that is in question. It is she who must overcome the obstacles constructed by her in-laws and indeed by the entire society, which is bound by the normative strictures of *Dharma*,[13] and it is her intense, single-minded love rather than Krishna's more fickle variety that serves as the model for male and female devotees alike.

An illustration and extension of most Bengali Vaiṣṇava theologians' preference for the passion and intensity of extramarital love over the conventional restraint of love within marriage is found in the writings of Rūpa Gosvāmī, a prominent and influential disciple of Caitanya. In his *Ujjvalanīlamaṇi*, as well as in his two long plays,[14] he contrasts Rādhā with Candrāvalī, her chief rival for Krishna's attention. Like Rādhā, Candrāvalī is married, and she too must resort to deception to elude the watchful eyes of her in-laws. Unlike Rādhā, however, whose relation to Krishna is more playful as well as more passionate, Candrāvalī is constrained in her relation to Krishna by her great respect (*ādara*). Except for occasional irony and mild rebuke, she conceals her true feelings under a facade of politeness. In a remarkable line in the first of his two long plays, the *Vidagdhamādhava*, Rūpa has Krishna himself voice to Candrāvalī his preference for "the sweet wine of your angry words" over "this poison of respect."[15] Unlike Rādhā's more profound posture of hurt, anger, and jealous longing (*māna;* Bengali, *mān*),[16] Candrāvalī 's anger is always short-lived. She thus serves largely as a foil for Rūpa's true heroine, Rādhā. Thus not only is the character exemplifying the highest love for Krishna a married woman who must risk everything to meet with her lover, but she is also an assertive, even feisty mistress.

What bearing has the illicit love affair between Rādhā and Krishna been understood by Vaiṣṇavas to have on life in society? The most widely influential Sanskrit theological narrative of the life of Krishna, the *Bhāgavata Purāṇa* (circa eighth century),[17] states explicitly that Krishna's adulterous love is not to serve as a role model for humans. Similarly, orthodox Bengali Vaiṣṇavas have not portrayed Rādhā's actions as sanctioning extramarital affairs. In this important respect they have drawn a clear line between behavior appropriate to God and behavior appropriate to humans. Rādhā's sulking, by contrast, has close parallels in Bengali family life even today. The classical and medieval model of the offended heroine, exemplified by Rādhā as she is portrayed in *padāvalī kīrtan* and other performance forms, is one that is still available to ordinary women in Bengal. In fact the same term, *mān*—or its common variant, *abhimān*[18]—is frequently used even today to designate the sulking behavior of a hurt or jealous woman toward her husband or lover.[19]

In Bengali Vaiṣṇava teaching, Rādhā's love for Krishna represents the highest possibility for human devotion *(bhakti)*. Her love for Krishna, along with the love of the other cowherd women for them both, is held up for the inspiration and emulation of all. A corollary of that view is that women are considered to be natural devotees; men must become women psychologically and spiritually in their devotion to the divine couple.[20] The elevation of women's devotion above men's and the requirement that men adopt a female persona in their religious lives contrasts sharply with certain Christian ascetic traditions in which spiritually advanced women were understood to have left their femaleness behind and "become men."[21] Women may have been considered natural devotees by Bengali Vaiṣṇavas because of perceived qualities—themselves socially prescribed—of devotion and service. However, the exaltation of these female qualities and the use of strong, even socially defiant women in the stories of Krishna to exemplify the highest religious attainment—self-forgetful, passionate love of God—would seem to be powerful valorizations of the religious capacities of women.

In an earlier article, I presented evidence for the existence from roughly the fourteenth to the eighteenth century of a number of prominent women in Greater Bengal. These include rulers, donors, patrons of literature, authors of prose and poetic works, teachers, and singers.[22] The list is impressive; especially germane for our purposes here is the prominence of several women religious leaders and teachers from the sixteenth century onward in the Bengali Vaiṣṇava community. Who were these women, what were their notable achievements, and how were they regarded by other Vaiṣṇava leaders?

A comprehensive study of women in the Bengali Vaiṣṇava movement remains to be written. Although the texts mention several other women, we shall limit our focus to two contrasting sixteenth-century figures whose portraits are rendered in some detail, Sītā Devī, senior wife of the conservative Brahmin leader Advaitācārya, and Jāhnavā Devī,[23] the second wife of the flamboyant and unorthodox leader Nityānanda.

Two hagiographies[24] of Advaitācārya and one of Sītā Devī narrate her story.[25] They tell of her miraculous birth—as a tiny girl on a lotus flower—and they identify her with the Goddess Lakṣmī. They also relate another miracle, in which she and her sister, as small girls, walk across a river. After Sītā Devī and her sister marry the elderly Advaitācārya, the biographers focus, curiously, on Sītā's cooking skills. Īśāna Nāgara, in particular, is at pains to portray her as a perfect Brahmin housewife, but at the same time as an incarnation of Lakṣmī. Although her chief biographer states that she took disciples, he narrates an incident in which she tells two men who come to her for instruction that she can teach only women.[26]

The simultaneous emphasis on Sītā Devī's cooking and on her miracles may seem paradoxical. Both idealizations, however, serve to decrease the likelihood that women who hear of her will seek to imitate her by becoming religious teachers themselves: the first image—Sītā Devī as perfect wife—minimizes her deviation from orthodox Brahmanical expectations for women, whereas the second—Sītā Devī as Goddess—emphasizes the distance between her and ordinary women. The story of the two men who seek to become her disciples also serves to limit and contain her power: its lesson is that women gurus may have only women as disciples.

The picture of Nityānanda's wife Jāhnavā that emerges from the Vaiṣṇava hagiographies is very different. Although the passages about her likewise recount miraculous occurrences, their focus is not on her wifely virtues but on her energetic activity on behalf of the Vaiṣṇava community. From the accounts it is clear that she realized the importance of establishing strong lines of communication between the Vaiṣṇavas of Bengal and the leaders in Vṛndāvana, and the sources agree that she made the arduous trip to Vṛndāvana herself at least twice. They also portray her as having traveled widely in Bengal in an effort to unify the various subsects, and as having been one of the three organizers of the famous festival at Kheturī. Although she had a large number of disciples—men as well as women—she did not found a subsect of her own. The reverence she inspired is perhaps best indicated by a passage from a biographical work, the *Narottama-vilāsa*,[27] that describes her reception by the leaders of the Bengali Vaiṣṇava community in Vṛndāvana: "All the Gosvāmins, at the sight of her, were greatly moved, and could not control their tears. Falling to the earth, they made obeisance to her feet."[28]

The disparity between the accounts of the religious activities of Sītā Devī and Jāhnavā Devī reveals a tension within the Vaiṣṇava community between the more orthodox, conservative branch headed by Advaitācārya and the more liberal branch headed by Nityānanda over the nature and proper place of women. Judging from the accounts of other prominent women leaders in the hagiographical literature,[29] Vaiṣṇava writers outside Advaita's subsect were reasonably comfortable—and assumed that their audiences would also be comfortable—with women who initiated and taught male as well as female disciples and who assumed major leadership roles in the community. Advaita's biographers, by contrast, apparently uncomfortable with Sītā Devī's role as guru, seek to domesticate her. The two sets of biographies converge, however, in their recounting of miracles, presumably to demarcate Jāhnavā and Sītā Devī from ordinary women.

Partly because of the number of important women leaders and teachers in its ranks, the Caitanya movement is often credited with raising the social and religious status of Bengali women.[30] The Vaiṣṇava community's openness to women is especially striking in view of the fact that Caitanya himself, after his renunciation, is represented by his biographers as shunning women and instructing his ascetic followers to avoid all contact with them.[31] Although the historical evidence especially for the period prior to Caitanya is too fragmentary to allow us to establish clear causal links, it seems evident that the general unorthodoxy of Bengali patterns of social and religious thought and practice in the centuries immediately preceding Caitanya, and especially the strength of the Tantric tradition in the region, were major factors contributing to the freedom and high social and religious status of some women. Edward C. Dimock Jr., in contrasting Caitanya's avoidance of women with the enthusiastic welcome received by a woman teacher named Kṛṣṇapriyā from the ascetic *gosvāmins* and other leaders in Vṛndāvana, attributed the change to the influence of Tantric views as well as to "the increasingly exalted position of Rādhā in all forms of Bengali Vaiṣṇava thought."[32] These two factors are not wholly separable: the exaltation of Rādhā was doubtless itself conditioned by Tantric notions of a dual male-female divinity that were prevalent in the region.

In addition to the impressive number of women leaders, the Vaiṣṇava community is distinguished from other religious communities in Bengal by the high rate of literacy of its women mendicants. This distinction is noted as early as the first half of the nineteenth century by two

British officials. Hunter describes a subsect of Vaiṣṇava women mendicants (*vairāginīs*) who held a theory of women's independence and who were trained as teachers of women in order to propagate the sect's teachings. They were apparently so successful in that role that the British government proposed to establish a school for them so that they could be utilized in the general education of women.[33] William Adam, writing reports to the government on vernacular education in Bengal and Bihar in the 1830s, also notes that the only exceptions to the general condition of illiteracy among ordinary women were found among the groups of mendicant Vaiṣṇavas.[34] Unlike the tradition of women gurus, which the Vaiṣṇavas appear to have taken over from the Tantric Buddhists and Shāktas who preceded them, female literacy distinguished the Vaiṣṇavas from *all* other groups in Bengal, including the Shāktas, who worship the Goddess, usually as Kālī or Durgā. However, if Hitesranjan Sanyal is right that the Bengali Vaiṣṇava movement was the religious expression of the rise of a new middle class, the disparity in literacy may be based as much on class as on sect.[35]

RADHA AS "OFFENDED HEROINE" IN *KIRTAN* PERFORMANCES

From the twelfth century or even earlier, the love of Rādhā and Krishna has been celebrated in forms of devotional performance in eastern India. Under the inspiration of Caitanya (1486-1533), one of these, *padāvalī kīrtan*,[36] became a major vehicle of devotion to Rādhā and Krishna throughout Greater Bengal. In a typical *kīrtan* performance, a single episode of their love is elaborated on for some three or four hours by means of song, commentary, dramatic gesture, and dance. In all such performances, the figure of Rādhā is represented as strong, as are her intimate companions, especially vis-à-vis Krishna, who is often portrayed as weak and foolish.

A *kīrtan* troupe typically consists of a lead singer (*kīrtanīyā*), who may be either male or female, several supporting singers, who are usually of the same sex as the lead singer, and two or sometimes three male drummers who play on both ends of elongated, barrel-shaped drums suspended from straps around their necks. In a performance, the lead singer and the troupe present a kind of musical drama—containing elements of dance—that centers on a single devotional theme. For some three or four hours, the lead singer spins out a narrative to the nearly constant rhythmic background of drums and small brass hand cymbals, punctuating the story at intervals with songs based on the lyrical medieval poems called *padāvalī.* The performance area, often in the center of an audience of devotees who sit on the floor in a circular arrangement, is bare of scenery, and the only props used are the lead singer's shawl, sometimes put over the head to resemble a sari, and perhaps the garland of flowers with which a lead singer is often honored.

Operating within these spare means, however, a skilled singer can create a powerful drama through effective timing, the expressive power of such musical means as variation in tempo and dynamic level, the subtle or expansive use of gesture, and the visual and kinesthetic reinforcement of rhythms by dance. It is mainly the lead singer who tells and enacts the story, but the supporting singers also use gesture as they echo the lines of the lead performer. The drummers' highly trained fingers beat out intricate patterns on the two leather heads of their slender drums,[37] and the drummers amplify these at intervals by sharp vocal sounds. These include the elaborate patterns (*bols*) that are used in learning the meters, as well as such exclamations as "*hāiyā*"—sounds apparently drawn from boatmen's songs. In addition to their strong hand and arm movements and the dramatic swings of their heads, the drummers often dance vigorously with the lead singer during the songs, and the supporting singers, most of whom keep time with hand cymbals, sometimes join in the dance as well.

Kīrtan singers portray Rādhā in a web of emotional relationships in which her love for Krishna unfolds. The successive phases of her love for him constitute the themes of some of the most popular episodes enacted in *kīrtan.* These include a range of occasions when the two are united, as well as various situations of separation. It is in the episodes of separation that Rādhā's nature is most fully revealed.[38]

We have seen that *kīrtan* is a powerful medium for conveying and evoking emotions. An expressive singer is able to move an audience of devotees profoundly, gathering them up in the deep love of the other characters toward Rādhā, as well as in Rādhā's own agony and longing. Rādhā's power over Krishna is nowhere so prominent as in the episodes presenting her responses, and those of her close friends, to Krishna's infidelity. These episodes portray Rādhā in the attitude termed *mān,* [39] a posture of rebuff expressive of the jealousy, hurt, anger, and simultaneous yearning for Krishna that the evidence of his unfaithfulness arouses in her. There are two such episodes, *Khaṇḍitā*, "The Woman Offended," and its sequel, *Kalahāntaritā*, "The Lovers' Quarrel." Throughout these episodes, Rādhā and her friends clearly have the upper hand. Rebuking Krishna through various means, they cause him to regret and suffer for his actions of the previous night. In what follows, I shall illustrate these modes of speech and action, drawing on two performances of *Khaṇḍitā*, one by Nanda Kishor Das, a highly celebrated male *kīrtanīyā*, and one by a popular woman performer named Rādhārāṇī.[40]

The plot of "The Woman Offended" (*Khaṇḍitā*) is well known throughout Bengal. As the story opens, Krishna, who had indicated to Rādhā on the previous day that he would meet her that evening in her forest grove, has instead spent the night with her rival, Candrāvalī. As dawn approaches, he remembers Rādhā and sets out to find her. With her friends she has spent the entire night making elaborate preparations and waiting in vain for his arrival. The two performances depict Rādhā at different stages of her development: in Rādhārāṇī's rendition, a young and inexperienced Rādhā is carefully tutored by her friends in the behavior appropriate to the situation, whereas in Nanda Kishor's, she knows from experience how to assume the proper attitude of rebuff. In both, however, she is portrayed as a *māninī*, a proud, hurt, defiant woman who refuses to accept back the man who has wronged her.

In both performances, Rādhā and her friends employ symbolic actions as well as various forms of speech to convey their feelings to Krishna. Pretending not to recognize him when he arrives at Rādhā's grove, they draw the ends of their saris over their heads and make polite inquiries about Rohinī, the mother of Balarām, Krishna's elder brother. When Krishna points out their mistake, Rādhā asks, "Then who are you?" He responds with puzzlement in words that one would never expect him to have to say: "I'm Krishna. Krishna."[41] Rādhā's friend Lalitā has also indicated their displeasure by offering him a place to sit on the outskirts of Rādhā's grove. He remains in this liminal position throughout the remainder of the episode, appearing and acting rather like a courtier who has fallen into disfavor.[42]

The various modes of speech that Rādhā and her friends employ are likewise subtle but eloquent. At the same time as they increase Krishna's feelings of regret, each of their statements serves to maintain the women's position of superiority over Krishna. We shall review examples of six different ways in which Rādhā addresses Krishna in the course of these performances.

The first and perhaps the most common mode of rebuke employed by Rādhā is that of simply indicating one of the signs of Krishna's erotic encounter that fairly cover his body. In both performances, she begins by pointing out the collyrium (Candrāvalī's eye-shadow) and the vermilion (the powder from the part in her hair) that are smeared all over his face. Nanda Kishor indicates the gravity of Rādhā's words and their effect on Krishna by remarking, "There, she's saying, 'smeared with vermilion and collyrium.' She really did say it. My Govinda [Krishna] felt terribly ashamed." Krishna's response is hardly the sort of thing one would expect the Lord of the universe to say: "What have I done? I am ruined! If I had realized that I had collyrium and vermilion marks on my face, I would have wiped them off before I came. . . . Now what shall I do?"[43] Radharani's Rādhā, prompted by the smudges, asks a tongue-in-cheek question: "What woman did you find who can't even light a lamp?"[44]

Second, in both performances Rādhā uses sarcasm and irony, often saying the opposite of what she really means. Both singers have her feign consolation, assuring Krishna that it is all right for him to come to her in his present condition. Nanda Kishor has Rādhā say, "Don't you know you can come to me in any way you please, just as you've done this time? You can also come dressed in some other outfit. There's no harm in that."[45] Radharani's Rādhā employs subtly biting sarcasm, saying, "You can come to me like this every morning. You've come at dawn—you've made my day!"[46] Rādhā also speaks ironically when she calls him virtuous for donning Candrāvalī's blue silk sari, supposedly in order to show it to Rādhā and her friends. Nanda Kishor underlines the irony by breaking in with, "I say, why did she say 'a virtuous lover'? It's not a laughing matter!"[47]

Third, Rādhā conveys her ambivalence by alternating between praise and censure. After pointing out the telltale black and vermilion marks on his face, for example, she asks him to turn around so she can see his face more clearly and then exclaims, "Ah, the beauty of collyrium enhances your beauty! Oh, what a mess: vermilion and collyrium all smeared together! My lover has vermilion and collyrium smeared on his face. The vermilion mark on your forehead would be the envy of ascetics!"[48] There is special irony in her last remark, for Krishna was anything but ascetic during the preceding night.

Closely related to the use of sarcasm or irony and the juxtaposition of contrasting modes to express ambivalence is a fourth device, that of punning. After pointing out the nail marks on Krishna's body, Rādhā says, "This adornment/punishment (*shājā*) is what you deserve, because you are my lover."[49] If we take the first meaning of *shājā,* the sentence says that he deserves such *adornment* because he is Rādhā's lover. The more pertinent meaning, however, is that he deserves such *punishment* because he is *her* lover (and he was unfaithful to her).

A fifth method employed by Rādhā in order to cause Krishna to repent is of a very different sort from the four preceding ones: she reminds him of her tenderness in applying sandalwood paste to his chest, and she exclaims over the softness of his body. These words must cause him to realize how undeserving she is of the torment he has just put her through, as well as what he himself has missed by not keeping his promise to meet her.[50] Yet even this remark contains a hidden irony: her praise of the softness of his body implies a contrast between that external, seductive softness and his hard heart.[51]

The final and most extreme mode used by Rādhā is one of ridicule and humiliation. This is illustrated most dramatically by Rādhā's lengthy commentary on the footprints of red lac adorning Krishna's chest. After a torturously slow process of deducing their source, she inquires as to whether he implored Candrāvalī to place her feet on his chest with such words as, "Please, please put your two feet on my heart, let me cool this burning breast," or whether Candrāvalī did so on her own initiative. As the culmination of this process of humiliating Krishna, Rādhā concludes, "She must have struck you with her feet after conquering you in the battle of love. That's why you have the marks of her feet on your chest."[52]

It is clear from these illustrations that Rādhā's modes of addressing Krishna are not limited to reproach; in commenting on the myriad signs of his unfaithfulness, she expresses as well her own positive feelings. For instance, in her exclamations over the paradoxical beauty of the vermilion and collyrium marks on his face, she indicates the attraction she feels toward him. In reminding him that he is her lover, she expresses her feelings of hurt and jealousy. In recalling her tenderness toward him, she reveals her love and sense of loss. Finally, in commenting ironically on the softness of his body, she indicates her intense longing for him as well as the hurt she feels at his harsh conduct. It seems likely that these revelations would increase Krishna's desire for her and augment his feelings of regret far more effectively than any amount of simple scolding. They also make it possible for women devotees, and men as well, to identify with her experience.

What is Krishna's response to all this abuse? Nanda Kishor tells us that he is ashamed, and he gives us Krishna's thoughts in response to Rādhā's concluding statement about the meaning of the lac footprints on his chest: "Krishna[53] realized, 'I've been severely punished. They said, "Bright lac looks attractive on your chest."' He is quiet. What's the matter? Has he found the words sweet? Well, let him be—he doesn't have to answer." Elsewhere Nanda Kishor has taken Rādhā's part, addressing Krishna on her behalf,[54] but he here shows sympathy for Krishna.

During the action of *Khaṇḍitā,* Krishna seems to have no choice but to stay in his liminal seat and take whatever Rādhā and her friends hand out. His helplessness is indicated by the lameness of his excuses, which range from half-truths to outright lies.[55] His submissiveness invites comparison to the behavior prescribed for the husband in charms found in the *Caṇḍīmangal*, a popular medieval Bengali work in praise of the Goddess Caṇḍī. According to Tapan Raychaudhuri, "The charms were meant to 'domesticate' the husband, who, ideally, should remain silent like a dead cow's head when the wife abused him."[56] The presence of such charms in a literary-religious text and Krishna's corresponding demeanor in "The Woman Offended" raise the fascinating and perplexing issue of what these representations can tell us about the actual social circumstances of Bengali women.

WOMEN'S REPROACH AND WOMEN'S STATUS IN MEDIEVAL AND MODERN BENGAL

Any conclusions we can draw from the evidence we have just reviewed must be cautious ones; yet, the evidence is tantalizing. The pervasiveness of the image of the strong, outspoken woman who boldly rebukes her man in several Bengali cultural forms from at least the twelfth century to the present suggests that it is an integral part of Bengali culture rather than a recent theological or cultural imposition. My own provisional judgment is that is it a reflection of an early societal pattern, not a corrective or a consciously devised blueprint. Although elements of this type are found elsewhere in India, the pattern is especially prevalent in Bengal. Moreover, the image of the defiant woman who gives voice to her hurt and jealous anger toward her mate clearly antedates the Bengali Vaisnava movement inspired by Caitanya.[57]

Although considerable work remains, there are indications from various quarters that the representation of Rādhā's *mān* in *kīrtan* reflects and has helped to perpetuate the relatively high status of women in Bengali society. One indication is the existence of a curiously parallel tradition likewise dating from medieval times, that of the *pati-nindā* (literally, "husband abuse").[58] This is a highly conventional set piece found throughout the medieval poetry known collectively as *mangala-kāvya*, which was kept alive for centuries through recitation as well as in a popular form of performance called *pāñcālī*.[59] The stylized revilement does not center on the husband's infidelity, brutality, or drunkenness, as one might expect, but rather on such extreme physical defects as elephantiasis and the condition of a hunchback, as well as on such relatively ordinary impairments as blindness.[60] Although these deformities are a far cry from the telltale marks on Krishna's body, the strong, adversarial stance adopted by the women in both seems to place them in a common tradition. Regardless of the exaggeration both involve, the existence of at least two such genres originating from medieval Bengal suggests a social climate in which such protest by women is not automatically deemed illegitimate. Indeed, Raychaudhuri, writing of the women's maligning of their husbands in the *pāñcālī* performances, notes, "One comes across a mild admonition for such 'unvirtuous' conduct only very rarely."[61]

In addition to the existence of several Bengali literary and performative traditions in which women reproach men, there is, as we have seen, a common mode of behavior in contemporary Bengal that mirrors or parallels Rādhā's *mān*. No one who has spent significant time in Bengal and who is familiar with the stories enacted in *kīrtan* can fail to note the similarity between the sulking of a wife toward her husband or the pouting of a child toward a parent, and Rādhā's behavior toward Krishna in "The Woman Offended." The continuity is underlined by the fact that the same term—*mān,* or its variant *abhimān*—is still used today to refer to such sulking. The prominence of such attitudes and actions suggests a close cultural identification between the stories dramatized in *kīrtan* and life in Bengali society. Such closeness of cultural conception suggests further that the stories reflect something of the society during the period in which they arose and that they have served in turn to mold that society in subsequent centuries.

Because of the multiplicity of factors that were and are at work, it is not possible to specify with certainty the direction of influence in these matters. One example of such ambiguity is the matter of the disparity in literacy between Shāktas and Vaiṣṇavas. If we count as a key element of high status the freedom to move about independently and to have male as well as female disciples, Vaiṣṇava women gurus were continuing the strong leadership tradition of their Tantric predecessors. By the early nineteenth century, however, they had distinguished themselves sharply from their Tantric counterparts by their achievements in literacy. In an attempt to account for this differential rate of literacy, one may hypothesize that in contrast to Shākta images of powerful but more distant Goddesses the Vaiṣṇava image of Rādhā as a warmly human, emotionally accessible female Deity, together with the elevation of women as ideal devotees, created a climate favorable to women's education. The fact that it was primarily the mendicant women who were literate, however, suggests that there may also have been important institutional factors.

A final complication likewise involves an internal division in the Hindu community. From the sixteenth century or even earlier, the threat to women's freedom in Bengal appears to have come primarily from conservative Brahmans. Among the Vaiṣṇava, this Brahmanical conservatism is evident in the narrow conception of a woman's role put forth by the biographers of Sītā Devī and Advaitācārya. In the poetic and performance tradition of the *mangala-kāvyas,* it can be seen in certain Brahmanical authors' objections to the stock abuses of the men by their wives, and in these authors' concomitant praise for such wifely virtues as revering and serving one's husband.[62] Although I have found nothing so explicit in *padāvalī kīrtan,* there are moments in the performances discussed above in which a *kīrtanīyā* expresses uncertainty about Rādhā's abuse of Krishna. Whether we understand Nanda Kishor's periodic interjections, such as his questioning of Rādhā's biting irony in calling Krishna a virtuous lover, as his own discomfort with the story he inherits or as his anticipation of objections from devotees in the audience,[63] his comments may reflect an uneasy coexistence in the Vaiṣṇava community of conflicting views on the nature and status of women.

NOTES

1. Ingalls, *Anthology,* 216-29. Ingalls says that it is probable though not certain that Vidyākara was the abbot of the Buddhist monastery at Jagaddala (30).

2. Banerji, *Sadukti-Karṇāmṛta.*

3. The situation of women in the south has been different. See, for example, the collection of articles edited by Wadley under the title *The Powers of Tamil Women.*

4. These first two possibilities—based on Clifford Geertz's classic discussion of cultural patterns as models both of and for social and psychological reality—are not mutually exclusive; see *The Interpretation of Cultures,* 93-94.

5. This possibility is a specific application of a more general theory put forth by Hein: he suggests that Krishna *līlā,* with its erotic and antinomian elements, may have been a compensation for a lack of freedom in the political, social, and religious spheres during the period of Muslim rule. See his "A Revolution in Kṛṣṇaism: The Cult of Gopāla."

6. On rituals of status reversal, see Turner, *The Ritual Process,* 167-68, 177-78, 183-88, and Marriott's delightful essay on the festival of Holi in a north Indian village, "The Feast of Love."

7. The term *tantra* designates a complex of ideas and especially practices that existed in greater Bengal from ancient times and that was taken up and developed somewhat differently by the Buddhist and the Hindu communities. Both revere as ultimate reality a male-female duality—*prajñā-upāya* (wisdom and the means of gaining enlightenment) for the Buddhists, Śiva-Shakti for the Hindus. Interestingly, though, whereas for the Buddhists the female principle, *prajñā,* is passive, in Hindu *tantra* the female principle, *shakti,* is the active one. For a discussion of women and the female principle in Bengali *tantra,* see Banerji, *Tantra in Bengal,* 14-17 and 45.

8. On Rādhā as Krishna's *hlādinī shakti,* see De, *Early History,* 279-81.

9. Theologians pun on these two nearly identical terms, Śiva and śava, which are even closer in Bengali or Sanskrit script than they are in their transliterated forms.

10. On this dual conception in the twelfth-century Sanskrit masterpiece of Jayadeva, the *Gītagovinda,* see Miller, "The Divine Duality of Rādhā and Krishna."

11. On *svakīyā* versus *parakīyā rati,* see De, *Early History,* 204-6, 348-51; Dimock, *Hidden Moon,* 200-14; and Wulff, *Drama as a Mode of Religious Realization,* 132.

12. In the Sanskrit plays of Rūpa Gosvāmī, Rādhā's husband is called Abhimanyu. See my *Drama as a Mode of Religious Realization,* esp. 143-44.

13. The richly multivalent term *Dharma* here means the proper norms of conduct established and guarded by the Brahmins. For a translation and interpretation of the most authoritative treatise on *Dharma,* see Doniger and Smith, *The Laws of Manu.* On the conduct deemed proper for a married woman, see Leslie, *The Perfect Wife.*

14. On Rādhā in Rūpa's plays, see my "A Sanskrit Portrait: Rādhā in the Plays of Rūpa Gosvāmī."

15. Wulff, *Drama as a Mode of Religious Realization,* 139; 245 n. 11.

16. On *māna* in Rūpa's works, see my *Drama as a Mode of Religious Realization,* 151-52.

17. The groundbreaking work of Dennis Hudson has pushed the date of the *Bhāgavata Purāṇa* back from previous estimates (ninth to tenth century) to at least the mid-eighth century. See his recent article, "The Śrīmad Bhāgavata Purāṇa in Stone."

18. The prefix *abhi*—which may mean "front," "proximity," or "all sides"—does not change the basic meaning of the term *mān* in this context.

19. The term is also used for the sulking of a child toward one or both parents.

20. For an exposition of this view and a more specific development of it, in which the devotee is instructed to imagine himself or herself as a *mañjarī,* a young female maidservant who because of her innocence is privileged to attend on the divine couple in their lovemaking, see Haberman, *Acting as a Way of Salvation,* 94-114.

21. See *Gospel of Thomas* 114; *Gospel of Mary* 9.18-20; *Martyrdom of Perpetua and Felicitas* 10.7; Castelli, "'I will make Mary Male'"; Meyer, "Making Mary Male." I am grateful to Karen King for supplying me with these references.

22. Wulff, "Images and Roles of Women in Bengali Vaiṣṇava *padāvalī kīrtan,*" 220-24.

23. Her name is sometimes spelled Jāhnavī.

24. Although these Vaiṣṇava accounts of the lives of religious leaders are more properly called hagiographies or religious biographies, they are sometimes simply called biographies. I use the terms here interchangeably. These accounts form a major genre of Bengali Vaiṣṇava writing. See Dimock, "Religious Biography in India."

25. I am drawing here on an unpublished paper by Rebecca Manring, "Sītādevī and the Status of Women in Early Gauḍīya Hagiography." The paper represents the first substantial study of the ways the Bengali Vaiṣṇava biographers portray prominent women.

26. The story also serves as a fascinating illustration of the way some Vaiṣṇavas have understood the process of "becoming women." After telling the two men she can teach only women, Sītā Devī instructs them in Vaiṣṇava meditation, telling them to imagine themselves as female maidservants waiting on Rādhā and Krishna in their love bower. When Sītā Devī reminds them that only women can be disciples, the two leave, only to return a short time later dressed as women of Krishna's cowherd village. They claim that their religious practice has caused a sex change, and they disrobe before Sītā to prove it. They are henceforth known by women's names as Nandinī and Jangalī (Manring, "Sītādevī and the Status of Women," 8-10).

The usual understanding of the requirement that the male devotee "become female" in his/her devotion is that the transformation is one of imaginatively assuming a female role in one's religious practice. (See note 20, above.) As recently as the mid-twentieth century, however, there has been a celebrated and highly controversial case of an ascetic who enacted outwardly his inner religious transformation, taking the name of Rādhā's close friend Lalitā and dressing in saris in order to concretize his/her new religious identity. Decades after his death, this wo/man, Lalitā Sakhī, is still the subject of vigorous debate in the Bengali Vaiṣṇava community.

27. The *Narottama-vilāsa* is a work of Narahari Dāsa that tells the life of Narottama, a poet and prominent Vaiṣṇava leader of Bengal who lived in the latter half of the sixteenth century. With Jāhnavā Devī and Śrīnivāsa Ācārya, he was one of the organizers of the Kheturī festival.

28. Dimock, *Place of the Hidden Moon,* 102 n. 94.

29. These include Hemalatā Devī, a daughter of Śrīnivāsa Ācārya; Gaurāngapriyā, Śrīnivāsa's second wife; and Kṛṣṇapriyā, a daughter of Gangānārāyaṇa, a resident of Vṛndāvana. See Dimock, *Place of the Hidden Moon,* 96-102.

30. See, for example, Chakrabarti, *Vaiṣṇavism in Bengal,* 1486-1900, 174; and Dimock, *Place of the Hidden Moon,* 98-101. For a dissenting view, see O'Connell, "Do Bhakti Movements Change Hindu Social Structures?" 43-44.

31. Dimock, *Place of the Hidden Moon,* 101.

32. Dimock, *Place of the Hidden Moon,* 99.

33. Cited in Mitra, Antiquities of Orissa, 1.110, according to Kennedy, *The Chaitanya Movement,* 86.

34. Adam, *Adam's Reports on Vernacular Education,* 133.

35. Sanyal, "Transformation of the Regional *Bhakti* Movement."

36. For a more extensive discussion of *padāvalī kīrtan* (also called *līlākīrtan*), see my article "The Play of Emotion: *Līlākīrtan* in Bengal."

37. These rhythmic patterns equal in complexity those of the major classical traditions of north and south India.

38. For a discussion of Rādhā in each of the four types of separation enumerated by Rūpa Gosvāmī, and especially the three that serve as common themes of *kīrtan* performances, see my "Rādhā: Consort and Conqueror of Krishna."

39. Sanskrit, *māna.* See n. 16, above.

40. Two well-known *kīrtanīyās* have used the name Radharani. The first is a celebrated singer and actress from Murshidabad whose performances spanned the period from the 1930s to the 1980s, and the second is a much younger singer from Navadvip who is still performing in Calcutta as well as in the towns and

villages of West Bengal. The performance of *Khaṇḍitā* that I analyze is by the younger Radharani.

41. Radharani, *Khaṇḍitā.*

42. Radharani, *Khaṇḍitā.*

43. Nanda Kishor Das, *Khaṇḍitā.*

44. Radharani, *Khaṇḍitā.*

45. Nanda Kishor Das, *Khaṇḍitā.*

46. Radharani, *Khaṇḍitā.*

47. Nanda Kishor Das, *Khaṇḍitā.*

48. Nanda Kishor Das, *Khaṇḍitā.* The first and last sentences of this brief speech, which praise Krishna's beauty through refined poetic conceits, are in a highly Sanskritic Bengali, whereas the two middle sentences, which abuse him, are in a village dialect.

49. Nanda Kishor Das, *Khaṇḍitā.*

50. Nanda Kishor Das, *Khaṇḍitā.*

51. This is a common conceit. For a verse in which Krishna, disguised as a Goddess, pretends to make a parallel claim in a plea directed to Rādhā, see *Vidagdhamādhava* VII. 55, translated in my *Drama as a Mode of Religious Realization,* 94.

52. Nanda Kishor Das, *Khaṇḍitā.*

53. Madan Mohan, literally, "enchanter of the God of love," is a name of Krishna.

54. For example, he tells Krishna not to hide when Krishna attempts to do so out of embarrassment at Rādhā's sarcastic comments about the fact that he has inadvertently put on Candrāvalī's sari (Nanda Kishor Das, *Khaṇḍitā*).

55. Radharani, *Khaṇḍitā.*

56. Raychaudhuri, *Bengal under Akbar and Jahangir,* 11. This looks like a representation of women's desires or fantasies. Yet *men* wrote the *mangala kāvya* works.

57. We have already noted the presence of this theme in two anthologies of Sanskrit poetry that were compiled in Bengal in the early centuries of the present millennium. The *Gītagovinda,* Jayadeva's dramatic lyric poem dating from the same period (late twelfth century) also gives a prominent place to this theme, representing Rādhā's proud anger (*māna*) after Krishna deserts her to make love with the other cowherd women. See Miller, *Love Song of the Dark Lord,* esp. 36-37. The oldest extant Bengali language account of the love of Rādhā and Krishna, the Middle Bengali *Śrīkṛṣṇakīrtan* of Baṛu Caṇḍidāsa, contains an episode of *mān* in which Rādhā rebukes Krishna for making love with the other cowherd women. See Klaiman, *Singing the Glory of Lord Krishna,* 178.

58. See Smith, "The *Pati-Nindā* in Medieval Bengali Literature."

59. Smith, *Pati-Nindā,* 105-7; Raychaudhuri, *Bengal under Akbar and Jahangir,* 11 n. 5.

60. Smith, *Pati-Nindā,* 107.

61. Raychaudhuri, *Bengal under Akbar and Jahangir,* 11 n. 5.

62. Smith, *Pati-Nindā,* 107.

63. His queries may also be a way to point up the ironies and levels of meaning for his listeners.

WORKS CITED

Adam, William. *Adam's Reports on Vernacular Education in Bengal and Bihar, Submitted to Government in 1835, 1836 and 1838. With a Brief View of Its Past and Present Condition, by the Rev. J. Long*. Calcutta: Home Secretariat Press, 1868.

Banerji, Sures Chandra, ed. *Sadukti-Karṇāmṛta*. Calcutta: Firma K. L. Mukhopadhyay, 1965.

———. *Tantra in Bengal*. Calcutta: Naya Prokash, 1978.

Castelli, Elizabeth. "'I will make Mary Male': Pieties of the Body and Gender Transformations of Christian Women in Late Antiquity." Pp. 29–49 in *Body Guards: The Cultural Politics of Gender Ambiguity*, edited by Julia Epstein and Kristina Straub. New York and London: Routledge, 1991.

Chakrabarti, Ramakanta. *Vaiṣṇavism in Bengal, 1486-1900*. Calcutta: Sanskrit Pustak Bhandar, 1985.

De, S. K. *Early History of the Vaiṣṇava Faith and Movement in Bengal*. 2d ed. Calcutta: K. L. Mukhopadhyay, 1961.

Dimock, Edward C., Jr. *The Place of the Hidden Moon*. Chicago: University of Chicago Press, 1966.

———. "Religious Biography in India: The 'Nectar of the Acts' of Caitanya." Pp. 109–17 in *The Biographal Process: Studies in the History and Psychology of Religion*, edited by Frank E. Reynolds and Donald Capps. The Hague: Mouton, 1976.

Doniger, Wendy, and Brian K. Smith, trans. *The Laws of Manu*. London: Penguin Books, 1991.

Geertz, Clifford. *The Interpretation of Cultures*. New York: Basic Books, 1973.

Haberman, David. *Acting as a Way of Salvation*. New York: Oxford University Press, 1988.

Hawley, John Stratton, and Donna Marie Wulff, eds. *Devī: Goddesses of India*. Berkeley, Calif.: University of California Press, 1996.

———. *The Divine Consort: Rādhā and the Goddesses of India*. Berkeley, Calif.: Berkeley Series in Religious Studies, 1982. Reprint, Boston: Beacon Press, 1986.

Hein, Norvin. "A Revolution in Kṛṣṇaism: The Cult of Gopāla." *History of Religions* 25, no. 4 (1986): 296-317.

Hudson, Dennis. "The Śrīmad Bhāgavata Purāṇa in Stone: The Text as an Eighth-Century Temple and Its Implications." *Journal of Vaiṣṇava Studies* 3, no. 3 (1995): 137-82.

Ingalls, Daniel H. H., trans. *An Anthology of Sanskrit Court Poetry*. Cambridge, Mass.: Harvard University Press, 1965.

Kennedy, Melville T. *The Chaitanya Movement.* Calcutta: Association Press, 1925.

Klaiman, M. H., trans. *Singing the Glory of Lord Krishna.* Chico, Calif.: Scholars Press, 1984.

Leslie, I. Julia. *The Perfect Wife: The Orthodox Hindu Woman according to the Strīdharmapaddhati of Tryambakayajvan.* Delhi: Oxford University Press, 1989.

Manring, Rebecca. "Sītādevī and the Status of Women in Early Gauḍīya Hagiography." Unpublished paper presented at the Annual Meeting of the Association for Asian Studies, April 1995.

Marriott, McKim. "The Feast of Love. " Pp. 200–12 in *Krishna: Myths, Rites and Attitudes,* edited by Milton Singer. Honolulu: East-West Center Press, 1966.

Meyer, Marvin W. "Making Mary Male: The Categories of 'Male' and 'Female' in the Gospel of Thomas." *New Testament Studies* 31 (1985): 554-70.

Miller, Barbara Stoler. "The Divine Duality of Rādhā and Krishna." Pp. 13–26 in *The Divine Consort: Rādhā and the Goddesses of India,* edited by John Stratton Hawley and Donna Marie Wulff. Berkeley, Calif.: Berkeley Series in Religious Studies, 1982.

———, trans. *Love Song of the Dark Lord: Jayadeva's Gītagovinda.* New York: Columbia University Press, 1977.

O'Connell, Joseph T. "Do Bhakti Movements Change Hindu Social Structures? The Case of Caitanya's Vaiṣṇavas in Bengal." Pp. 39–63 in *Boeings and Bullock-Carts: Studies of Change and Continuity in Indian Civilization.* Vol. 4, *Religious Movements and Social Identity,* edited by Barwell L. Smith. Delhi: Chanakya Publications, 1990.

Raychaudhuri, Tapan. *Bengal under Akbar and Jahangir.* Delhi: Munshiram Manoharlal, 1966.

Sanyal, Hitesranjan. "Transformation of the Regional *Bhakti* Movement (Sixteenth and Seventeenth Centuries)." Pp. 59–69 in *Bengal Vaiṣṇavism, Orientalism, Society, and the Arts,* edited by Joseph T. O'Connell. East Lansing, Mich.: Michigan State University Occasional Papers, 1985.

Smith, William L. "The *Pati-Nindā* in Medieval Bengali Literature." *Journal of the American Oriental Society* 99, no. 1 (1979): 105-9.

Turner, Victor W. *The Ritual Process.* Chicago: Aldine Publishing Company, 1969.

Wadley, Susan S. *The Powers of Tamil Women.* Syracuse, N.Y.: Maxwell School of Citizenship and Public Affairs, 1980.

Wulff, Donna Marie. *Drama as a Mode of Religious Realization: The*

Vidagdhamādhava of Rūpa Gosvāmī. Chico, Calif.: Scholars Press, 1984.

———. Images and Roles of Women in Bengali Vaiṣṇava *padāvalī kīrtan*." Pp. 217–45 in *Women, Religion and Social Change,* edited by Yvonne Yazbeck Haddad and Ellison Banks Findly. Albany, N.Y.: State University of New York Press, 1985.

———. "The Play of Emotion: *Līlākīrtan* in Bengal." Pp. 99–114 in *The Gods at Play: Līlā in South Asia,* edited by William S. Sax. New York: Oxford University Press, 1995.

———. "Rādhā: Consort and Conqueror of Krishna." Pp. 109–34 in *Devī: Goddesses of India,* edited by John Stratton Hawley and Donna M. Wulff. Berkeley, Calif.: University of California Press, 1996.

———. "A Sanskrit Portrait: Rādhā in the Plays of Rūpa Gosvāmī." Pp. 27–41 in *The Divine Consort: Rādhā and the Goddesses of India,* edited by John Stratton Hawley and Donna Marie Wulff. Berkeley, Calf.: Berkeley Series in Religious Studies, 1982.

4

LINA GUPTA

Hindu Women and Ritual Empowerment

INTRODUCTION

Who and what is a Hindu woman? This question poses a fundamental problem for any woman's self-image, because her identity, at its best and at its worst, is often drawn from a socio-religious context controlled and manipulated by "others" more powerful in the patriarchy. In recent years she has been criticized in scholarly papers and her oppressed status has been sensationalized through media stories. Scholars of many disciplines, regardless of their academic credibility, are far too eager to point out, often on the basis of isolated events, the misfortune and inferior status of women of Hindu and other cultures.

Yet the extent of the oppression and power of Hindu women differs greatly from their Western counterparts. As Naomi Quinn and Martin King Whyte have pointed out, "Women's status cross culturally should be viewed as a composite of many different variables."[1] In other words, given the cross-cultural variations in women's position and the complexity of Hindu tradition, it is becoming increasingly problematic to analyze the multidimensional nature of Hindu women's status from the usual standpoint of public/private, superior/inferior dichotomy.

If there is a clear distinction between a general powerlessness and the powerlessness one experiences in a particular domain, the following question arises: Do Hindu women—within the range of their daughterhood, wifehood, and motherhood—feel essentially powerless or powerless in certain areas? This chapter examines how, contrary to the Western notion of "power" as merely physical or socio-political power, the Hindu concept of power is to be primarily understood as an inner power essential to human evolution on a spiritual level. I will analyze in general how the Hindu concept of *shakti* or power is understood and utilized by Hindu women to their advantage within the context of Hinduism. I will discuss in particular whether she remains within the patriarchal framework of her relegated position as a daughter, a wife, and a mother, or outside the scriptural boundaries where she establishes her identity as she acquires, controls, and shares her power in and through her rituals. By taking a critical and reflective approach to the process and inherent symbolism of two specific rituals, one of which is performed by a woman before her wedding and the other after her wedding, I will emphasize what I take to be women's empowerment within the egalitarian core of Hinduism.

THREE CENTRAL HINDU NOTIONS

Why does a Hindu woman continue to pursue the ideals portrayed in the epics and Purāṇas? How does a Hindu woman remaining within the many scriptural restrictions and the ideal of womanhood acquire and maintain her power? What is her essential goal, beyond the welfare of her family, in enduring various forms of self-denial, self-control, and austerity in her ritual practices all year round? Part of the answer to these questions could be found in the heart of Hinduism as it is expressed in three important concepts: *dharma* (morality or obligation), *tapas* (penance or austerity), and *shakti* (power).

These three concepts combine to form an integral part of Hinduism from the *Rig Vedas* to recent literature. Given the scope of this paper, however, I will limit my discussion to their essential meanings and connections, which allow a Hindu woman to use her limitations as an asset rather than a liability. She uses self-denial and hardship as a means to an ultimate end of power.

Dharma

Rooted in the notion of *Ṛta*, first mentioned in the *Rig Veda*, the concept of *dharma* has undergone various interpretations in each historical era. *Ṛta*, as it is understood in the Vedas "is the 'law or order of the world'"—literally "'the course of things' . . . *Ṛta* serves as the origin of the basic ethical concept of *dharma* in later Indian philosophy."[2] In the early Vedas, right action or "what men ought to do" was primarily "defined in terms of proper actions in the sacrificial ritual."[3] In the successive stages of Hindu philosophy, the notion of *dharma* has extended from mere ritual order to cosmic order and finally to order in society.

All three of these orders are essentially related in that any action that took place in one would be reflected in the entire realm. Right action, therefore, not only proper action in the sacrificial ritual, stood for "all actions by which men express and define their place in the cosmos."[4]

Literally, the word *dharma* stands for moral obligation or duty, that is, the fulfillment of one's duties with regard to one's station in life. Etymologically, the word *dharma* originates from the root *dhṛi*, which is translated as "something that upholds or sustains." To be specific, *dharma* is that which upholds or sustains moral order. Right action, Hinduism emphasizes, depends on different variables such as *deśa* (the place or the culture in which one is born and lives), *kāla* (the historical time in which one is born and lives), *śrama* (the effort that is necessary for a person to function in various stages and situations in life), and *guṇas* (the karmically inherited impressions or character traits that one has). Given these four factors, right actions stand for fulfillment of one's obligations that are consistent with the norm present in one's kinship and caste system.[5]

For Hinduism, familial discord, discontent, or oppression then arise not from the organization of moral structure in the society, but from the failure to maintain individual obligations toward that structure. On a deeper level, however, as Sudhir Kakar reflects, *dharma* is not merely "the principle of individual action and social relation, but also the ground plan of an ideal life cycle, in the sense that it defines the essence of each of the different stages of life and the way in which each stage should be lived."[6]

In order to comprehend the full implications of *dharma*, one needs to consider the following questions. Beyond maintaining order, what is the ultimate purpose of following one's individual obligations? What motivates one to fulfill one's obligations? As far as the ultimate purpose is concerned, it is only in order that one realizes one's true freedom. As one recognizes that order is essential to one's realization of one's freedom, one chooses actions appropriately. However, mere recognition of an order would not necessarily motivate one to the right course of action. One also needs an attitude of concern and respect both for oneself and one's surroundings. Without concern one would be apathetic toward maintaining order and therefore would be controlled from without. Excessive concern, on the other hand, would cause attachment and ultimately bondage.

To clarify, true freedom grows out of one's moral development. Moral development, as it is ordinarily understood, is one's ability, capacity, and concern to conform to moral structure. Because moral structure is reflected in a social structure, by conforming to the social structure one naturally proceeds toward freedom. That is not to say all social rules are conducive to moral developments and ultimately to freedom. How does this concept of *dharma* apply to Hindu women? How does she take her obligation and restrictions to fulfill her ultimate end? By conducting their life according to their *āśramadharma* (obligations pertaining to stages of life) and *manusya-dharma* (human obligations) in general and gender-specific *strī-dharma* (feminine obligations) and *svadharma* (one's own particular life task) in particular, Hindu women transform their lives from a presumably oppressed status in relation to others to a state of freedom in acknowledging who they are within themselves.

Tapas

> Darkness there was, hidden by darkness, in the beginning: an undistinguished ocean was This All. What generative principle was enveloped by emptiness—by the might of its own fervor *[tapas]* That One was Born [*Rig Veda* X. 129.3].
>
> Desire [creative, perhaps sacrificial impulse] arose then in the beginning, which was the first seed of thought [*Rig Veda* X.129.4].
>
> Cosmic order *[ṛta]* and Truth *[satys]* were born out of kindled Heat *[tapas]*. [*Rig Veda* X.190.1].

In reading the *Rig Vedic* hymns as well as the myth of Prajāpati, one realizes the importance of sacrifice and its resultant heat as the force behind creation on all levels. First cited in the *Rig Veda,* the word *tapas* refers to the original fire, the primal force, the ultimate energy that initiates the cosmic movement and brings forth the universe.

The Vedic notion of *tapas* resonates as Śatapatha Brāhmaṇa explains how Prajāpati, the primal being, created this universe through his desire (to multiply) and his *tapas.* This myth describes the disintegration of Prajāpati at the end of his creation, which symbolizes sacrifice and the restoration of his being with the help of Agni, fire. Agni in this ritual myth represents the physical fire as well as *tapas* attained through sacrifices (*Śatapatha* VII.i).

Originally understood as the creative power generated through sacrifice, *tapas* eventually is believed to be an independent power inherent in the structure of reality and therefore available to Gods and humans alike. It is not created by the Gods but is merely used by the Gods to bring forth and maintain all aspects and levels of creation. Various Purāṇic and epic stories confirm the power of *tapas* that the Gods and the seers achieved in realizing their desired goal of authority over heaven and earth, freedom and immortality. From the emptiness of infinite possibilities, desire and *tapas* finally enabled Prajāpati to create the world of multiplicity and diversity. Similarly, humans, as part of this cosmic world, retain the privilege and the right to avail themselves of the creative power of *tapas* to bring forth their desired worlds.[7]

The word *tapas* generally means religious austerity, penance, mortification, the practice of mental or personal self-denial, or the infliction of bodily tortures. The word *tapas* is a combination of the root *tap,* an intransitive verb meaning "mortifying the body," and the suffix *asun,* meaning "to translate into action." Given its etymological profile, the word *tapas* could be taken as a generative power that not only initiates the creative movement and eventual fulfillment of the desire of Prajāpati on a cosmic plane but that is also the inner heat that helps an individual to translate his or her thoughts and desires into action. *Tapas* seems to be the connecting link between the macrocosm and the microcosm, between the possibilities and the actualities of the power that leads to liberation.[8]

The word *tapas* is also literally understood as the "physical heat" created in the body of the sacrificer due to the sacrificial fire, fasting, preparation, the sacrificial process, and so on. Originally, ascetic practices such as fasting, silence, ritual preparation, meditation, and celibate isolation were included in the process of preparing the priests for ritual activity. The priest who labored over the fire and performed the sacrifice with devotional fervor generated the primordial *tapas* or heat. Through performance of the rituals; through penance, austerities, self-denial, and self-control; and through any form of physical or mental exertion, one is enabled to generate *tapas* within oneself. Thus it appears that there is a causal relation between endurance of all kinds, on one hand, and *tapas* on the other hand. That is, in and through one's tolerance and endurance, one is inwardly "heated up." This *tapas* could, therefore, be understood from two perspectives: initially, the physical *tapas* is generated as a result of the priest's toil over the fire, his preparation, and physical austerity; from another perspective, *tapas* is the inner heat created as a result of his ritual actions as he participates in the sacrifice.

In order to appreciate fully the concept of *tapas,* one must consider the related cognate *tapasyā*. *Tapasyā,* an adjective of the masculine noun *tapas,* is a combination of the root *tapas,* meaning "heat," and the suffix *syā,* meaning "to tolerate." Thus the word *tapasyā* literally means "to tolerate heat." Traditionally the word *tapasyā* refers to physical endurance of any ascetic practice, such as meditation, fasting, and so on. It also includes tolerance or endurance in the face of the impact of one's own thoughts, feelings, and experiences; one's passions and desires; one's pain and sorrow; and one's self-denial for the higher purpose of spiritual gain. Together all of these purify the mind and usher in the power of *tapas* or heat. I would caution that not any and every form of self-denial necessarily produces *tapas*. Only the type of self-denial practiced with intention, discipline, and higher purpose yields inner heat and power. It is the intention of one's self-denial and in one's ritual practices that bring one to the source of ultimate power. The concept of intention, however, does not mean the wish, inclination, or vague hope that some state of affairs be brought about, but the earnest striving to accomplish a moral purpose. With *tapas*, women have equal power to become symbolically the Prajāpati in their own being, creating and recreating the universe and the experiences they desire.

Shakti

Wishing to multiply, One Brahmān, the nameless, formless Reality, becomes dual: male and female, *śiva* (consciousness) and *shakti* (energy). As a result of the association of these dual principles, the universe comes into being. At the end of the cosmic cycle, however, the created universe with all its diversity returns to its source and *shakti* comes to repose within *śiva*. The word *shakti* means "power or energy," the female counterpart of the divine male, existing eternally in *Śiva* as his inseparable attribute. To say, however, that *shakti* resides in *Śiva* or in the Brahmān is merely a figure of speech; in truth, they are one and the same. *Shakti*, as pure potentiality devoid of consciousness, initiates and continues the process of creation (only) in the presence of *śiva*. As such, She-with-*śiva* is the cause of manifestations and is responsible for the differentiation of objects.

The word *shakti* is a feminine noun. "The sound *s* in *shakti* stands for welfare and prosperity and *'kti* refers to prowess."[9] Therefore, the word *shakti* literally means "she who is the embodiment of prosperity and prowess, she who grants prosperity and prowess." In general, the word refers to power of any kind: ability, capacity, strength, energy, or prowess encompassing physical to spiritual power. In both Purāṇic and Tāntric literature,

> Ultimate Reality united with its Śakti is understood to be the feminine principle. In spite of the description of Kālī or Śakti as the consort-wife of Śiva understood in Her highest form—that is, understood as the Ultimate One—She is His creator. As Adyashakti, She is the primordial energy itself; She is the Brahman existing before creation. In the later Śakta phase, the Devī (the Goddess) is transformed into the eternally existing, all-powerful female principle who in her concrete form is often personified as Kālī or Dūrgā.[10]

In other words, the Purāṇic and Tāntric literature exalt the feminine as coequal with or superior in power to the symbolically masculine source of the universe. From the traditional point of view, *shakti* is considered to be the power or energy of the divine manifested in women.

Acquiring *Shakti*

> Hindu law was first codified by Manu in the seventh century B.C.E. Under this reform, women lost much of their freedom. Restrictions were placed upon their autonomy, their movements and their associations with men. Women were placed under the supervision first of their fathers, later of their husbands, and then of their sons or in the absence of a son, any other male member of the family. In short, the roles of women were relegated to wife and mother.[11]

She was not permitted to perform certain Vedic rituals and not allowed to be educated in the knowledge of the scriptures. In addition, she was expected to fulfill the virtues of chastity, subordination, submission, tolerance, endurance, self-control, and last but not least, self-sacrifice. "It seems to me that the sources on which the later patriarchal Hindu tradition is based have been interpreted only by Hindu men who had vested interest in, and who were responsible for, defining the sociological and religious status of Hindu women."[12]

Given the restrictions and the expectations placed upon women, how did the Hindu women attain and maintain their power to protect their identity? It is through their rituals, which reflect their boundaries as well as their own chastity that sometimes appear to be their shackles, that the Hindu women acquired and continued to attain and maintain their *shakti*. Recognizing their predicament, Hindu women have used and manipulated the opportunities and avenues open to them. Accepting the obligation of maintaining their dharmic responsibilities, they continued to conform to their socially given roles, while holding on to the myths and legends of ideal womanhood portrayed and amplified in the virtues of Sītā, Sāvitrī, and others. By nurturing their gender obligations with relation to all of their kin and by fulfilling their virtuous roles, they generate inner heat and inner power.

It is the *shakti* of Sāvitrī, acquired through her *tapasyā*, that is said to be responsible for her superior bargaining position with the Gods, which allowed her husband Satyabān to be brought back to life. It is by her *shakti* that Sītā ultimately led Mother Earth to open up and provide a shelter within her. However subordinated and dominated she may appear to be, a Hindu woman can transcend Manu's restrictions. In spite of the societal restrictions, scriptural injunctions, and moral expectations, she is able to transform her relegated position to generate a self-secure and self-assured individual. Her suffering, due to her self-sacrifice and subordination, no longer appears to be the behavior of a weak person but rather was reconceived and perceived as a journey leading to inner heat and ultimately to power.

WORSHIP

All Hindu rituals—Vedic or non-Vedic, *śāstrīya* (that is, scriptural) or *gārhyasta* (that is, domestic), whether guided by priests or performed alone by individuals—follow some significant pattern or structure. I am discussing this structure in terms of what I take to be the four basic components of Hindu worship: (1) the participants, (2) the preparations, (3) the process, and (4) the promise. Considering each of these basic components will help us understand the dynamics of Hindu ritual and the access they provide for both men and women to attain liberation from forms of oppression, patriarchal or otherwise.

1. The Participants. Traditionally, all Hindu rituals take on the quality of a staged performance involving an interaction between the *bhakta* (the devotee) and the *bhagavān* (the divine). Usually the *bhakta* assumes the role of an entertainer who serves and entertains his audience, the *bhagavān.* There are times, however, when the roles are presumed to be reversed. Either way, the relationship of all participants involved reflects a reciprocal as well as a hierarchical structure that in turn ultimately leads to an experience of oneness. Whether the ritual is mediated by a priest and observed by many or performed alone, order and reciprocity remain the same. Most significantly, even the domestic rituals, which exclude priestly intervention, scriptural instruction, or direct reference to any Deity, exemplify the same pattern.

2. The Preparations. The second component of rituals is twofold: *āntarik* (inner) and *vājhyik* (outer) preparation. The preparation begins with the inner and outer purity of the devotee. To be specific, in all rituals cleansing of the mind with an attitude of sincerity, sacrifice, and discipline is as essential as the actual cleansing of the physical body. In addition, fasting is recommended whenever possible to create the sacrificial mood in the ritual. Outer preparations, such as the selection and the decoration of the worship ground and the gathering of the sacramental objects, are precisely carried out according to the detailed instructions of the scriptures to create a sacred environment. It is significant that the worship of various Gods and Goddesses corresponds to the time designated in the Hindu *pañjikā* (almanac), just as do personal rituals or life-cycle ceremonies. Both priestly and domestic rituals require

sacramental objects such as water from the Ganges, sandalwood paste, incense, oil lamps, candles, flowers, leaves, herbs, oils, spices, grains, vegetables, and fruits and sweets, all of which are elements essential for various rites, *śāstrīya* as well as *gārhyasta*.

Of all the sacramental objects, the two most important categories of necessary ritual implements are *pañchya gavya* (five things from the cow) and *pañchāmrita* (five nectars). *Pañchya gavya* includes milk, yoghurt, clarified butter, cow dung, and urine. *Pañchāmrita* includes sugar, honey, yoghurt, clarified butter, and milk. In addition, various types of grains, especially *dhāna* (unhusked rice) and *chāl* (husked rice), are used frequently in most rituals. Durva grass (three-pronged young grass) is included in all ceremonies for blessing purposes. Among the multitude of objects offered in all forms of Hindu rituals, yoghurt, fish, husked rice, unhusked rice, and durva grass are the ones necessary for the two rituals that form the subject of our investigation.

3. The Process. Regardless of how the rite is being performed, the process involved in both the *śāstrīya* and *gārhyasta* rituals includes traditional forms of prayer, chanting, singing, offering, meditating, and various forms of *mudrā* (hand gestures), all of which reflect diverse aspects of Hindu worship. Depending on the particular nature of the rituals, the devotee applies the scripturally suggested mode of worship. It is believed that the efficacy of a ritual is partly contingent upon the appropriate worship activity. It is important to note that in all facets of a person's ritual performance, a *bhakta* endures inner heat that is created by all the necessary activities, whether the ritual involves fasting, praying, or any other form of worship. As a result of the endurance of this inner heat, the *bhakta* experiences inner *shakti* within the process as much as at the completion of the ritual. That is to say, the process involved in the rituals reflects the *tapasyā-shakti* motif.

4. The Promise. All Hindu rituals exemplify fulfillment of a promise made and carried out by the *bhakta*. The assumption is that the promise will be reciprocated by the divine. The entire scenario of preparation and the process of Hindu rituals culminates in an act of the *praṇām-āśirvāda* complex. The word *praṇāma* signifies bowing down to something or somebody who is superior to the individual. The word *āśirvāda* , in Bengali or in Sanskrit, is usually understood as the offering of the blessing by the older to the younger or from the divine to the human. In addition, it also refers to the blessing offered by someone who may not be superior in terms of age but superior in terms of status. There is a correlation between age or status, on the one hand, and the power to bless on the other. This dichotomy of *praṇām-āśirvāda* is believed to come to fruition

in the realization of oneness of the *bhakta* and the *bhagavān*. To clarify, the very act of *praṇām* necessitates, at least temporarily, an elimination of one's ego, thereby facilitating the *bhakta's* experience of oneness with the *bhagavān*.

A deeper meaning behind *āśirvāda*, however, is more experiential than conceptual. *Āśirvāda* is experienced as a fullness of one's own being that flows out to the other with love, concern, and goodwill. The relationship experienced between the one who blesses and the one who is blessed is more of a reverential nature than a mundane one. In reverence one asks for the blessing from the other. In other words, in humility one sacrifices one's ego and releases the power of one's worthiness in claiming the gift. In response the other returns his/her power in giving the gift of blessing. Both are blessed by the process itself. The custom of *āśirvāda* further reflects the *bhakta-bhagavān.* complex in all Hindu rituals.

FAMILY STRUCTURE

In order to understand the following rituals, it is necessary that we recognize the complexity of the Hindu family structure. Most Hindu families exhibit multifaceted and multilevel gender power relationships. Traditionally, most Indians grow up in a joint or extended family that is called *ekānnabhūkta parivār* (in Sanskrit) or *ekānnavarti parivār* (in Bengali). *Ekānnabhūkta parivār* (extended family) is a partrilineal joint family of two or more generations of males, their wives, married sons and their families, unmarried sons, and unmarried daughters living in a patrilocal residence. Often these families include widowed daughters and their children, widowed or childless aunts and uncles, and distant relatives. The entire family lives in one residence, sharing a common living room, kitchen, and worship room, although the individuals' quarters or rooms are located in different parts of the house.

The rationale for the *ekānnabhūkta parivār* is filial loyalty and fraternal solidarity. Parents take responsibility for raising their children; grown-up children are expected to look after their aging parents, grandparents, and other family members in need of help. Besides sharing space, family members share living expenses, maintenance, rituals, and other activities among themselves. Family members old and young, male and female are required to maintain an environment compatible to collective as well as individual well-being. The general attitude is supposed to be one of caring, sharing, serving, and, most importantly, tolerating. The word *ekānnabhūkta* (meaning "sharing one's rice") encapsulates the essence of this attitude quite clearly; that is, one's rice is shared by the entire family through sickness and health, tragedies and triumphs.

The power structure of *ekānnavarti parivār* is based on a complicated ordering according to principles of age and gender. The elder (meaning "someone who is older even by a few days") had more authority and therefore power over the younger person. The head of the family in a patriarchal society is usually the father or the grandfather. In addition to age, gender creates an interesting form of hierarchical order within the family. For example, the wife of the head of the household or the older brother shares equally in her husband's superior status in relation to his younger siblings. To be specific, regardless of her age, a woman's authority, except in the case of an elderly woman, is usually justified on the basis of the position of her husband.

Despite what we find in the myths and the Purāṇic instructions, an elderly woman in Bengali *ekānnabhūkta parivār* exercises power and authority equal to or even greater than the head of the household, not only in her domestic sphere but in the community as well. Her authority is justified on the basis of her age and experience and has little to do with the presence or absence of her husband. To be specific, there is a clear discrepancy between the cultural norm presented in the scriptures and the stories, and the reality of a woman's, especially an elderly woman's, life in an *ekānnabhūkta parivār*. As the renowned Indian psychologist Sudhir Kakar remarks, "The plain truth is that this is (and perhaps always was) a masculine wish-fulfillment rather than an accurate description of the real life of older Indian women."[13]

A daughter is considered to be the representation of the Goddess Lakṣmī, Goddess of prosperity. By her purity, it is believed she upholds the prosperity and welfare of her family. A daughter is to be treated as a guest by her kin, however, because her stay in her natal home is temporary, for she will take her leave at marriage. For all ceremonies and celebrations in her parents' home, she is to be invited and attended to as a special guest. Even after she is married, she simultaneously remains as an insider as well as an outsider in her natal home.

Division of labor is clearly arranged in a joint family to facilitate the needs and purposes of all members. In the past, the women were supposed to be in charge of the household affairs, as men were responsible for matters outside the household. In the last thirty years, however, things have changed in India, so the organization of present-day households hardly resembles this old categorization or order. "In childhood a female must be subject to her father, in youth to her husband; when her lord is dead, to her sons, a woman must be never independent" *(Manu*

IX.3). The fact of the matter is that the family described above exists only in the pages of *Manu Samhitā*; in reality, Hindu women are changing the course of their destinies by their own power. That is not to overlook some cases of oppression in other parts of India.

In the light of the power politics in an *ekānnabhūkta* family based on age and gender, women's lot is demarcated in the arena of household affairs and child rearing. This clearly arranged division of labor within a joint family created a public/private dichotomy in women's lives. In traditional India, both male and female children are born and raised within a well-defined community of people in their families. Early on, a female begins to recognize her status within her family in relation to all its members. A girl also understands her particular position within a community of women, including her grandmother, mother, sister, aunt, and all other female members of her family. Within this feminine domain, a girl finds opportunities to be creative, to experience joys and sorrows with women of all ages, and most importantly to internalize a distinct sense of autonomy. She learns to achieve, affirm, and exercise her power in ways that are not obvious to her Western counterparts.

Moreover, even as her identity is shaped and nurtured by the multitude of familial relationships, her rites and rituals establish and strengthen her self-identity as well as her status in the society. Traditional ceremonies (formal or informal) and rituals (*śāstrīya* or *gārhyasta*) celebrated within an extended family emphasize the value of the family bond over one's concern for self-identity. The individual as well as the collective identity of a family, especially in the relationships among the women, are reinforced as one approaches major life transitions, such as the birth ceremony, initiation, marriage, funerals, and so on.

WOMEN, MOTHERS, AND GODDESSES

The Hindu concept of divine and human motherhood is unparalleled in the history of the world's religions. In the Purāṇic and Tantric traditions, Shakti, Devī, or Kali is considered to be the Brahmān manifested in its mother aspect as the creator and sustainer of the universe. According to Hinduism, divine motherhood is reflected in human motherhood. To be clearer, regardless of her humanness with all her frailties, once a mother, forever a Devī. As a child, one is sustained by one's mother on all levels. Although as an adult one becomes independent of one's mother on a physical level, one continues to be nurtured by her on an essential level.

Hinduism considers a mother to be the gateway to heaven. Such are the scriptural admonitions, that nothing could be accomplished in the mundane or in the spiritual world without her blessing. She is to be revered at all times. I remember very clearly on one occasion of conflict with my mother when I was reminded by my father never to cross her in the future. The sacredness and power of mothers have been portrayed in numerous songs and literature for thousands of years. In the epic *Rāmāyana*, even God-incarnate Rāma had to take his mother's blessing before he left for his fourteen years of banishment in the wilderness.

WOMEN'S RITUALS

All Hindu rituals could be categorized under two headings: *śāstrīya* (scriptural) and *lokācāra* (domestic). Whereas the *śāstrīya* rituals aided by the Brahmins (members of the priestly class) follow the mainstream formalities and intricacies of the Vedic tradition, *lokācāra* are performed according to folklores, legends, and the informal guidelines of ordinary people. *Lokācāra* is a set of traditional rituals and ceremonies rather than a system of dogmatic beliefs and a definite strict code of ethics. Within the area of *lokācāra* there is a subtradition called *strīācāra*. Partly rooted in Vedas and Purāṇas, *strīācāra* is mostly a tradition defined, observed, and guided by women alone. Without priestly supervision or scriptural restrictions and formalities, *strīācāra* is a tradition of rituals, folk stories, and artistic expressions, many of which have not been documented in the scriptures. Yet they clearly have transmitted much of religious culture and family heritage through the generations. Over thousands of years, women developed a tradition, equal in power to the *śāstrīya* rituals, that has a strong authority over the daily lives of Hindus, both men and women. *Strīācāra* is a broad path offering a pattern of attitudes, rites, experiences, and explanations that harmonize Hindu family and social lives with the many faces of its spiritual environment in the context of an ancient culture.

Although most *strīācāra* exemplify a woman's concern for her male kin (such as in the rituals of Śiva Rātri, in which a Hindu woman is concerned about her husband or her prospective husband, or the Ṣaṣṭhipujā, which she does for the welfare of her children), in some additional rituals she seeks and shares power with other women. These rituals are not directly efficacious to the welfare of others, such as her husband and children. On the contrary, they illustrate a single-minded journey toward her own power. She also involves herself in rituals that identify her with the divine power. These *strīācāra* have two purposes: (1) prophylactic or preventive of pain or loss, and (2) positive or conducive to peace, prosperity, potency, or power, and ultimately freedom *(mokṣa)*.

The rituals included in this chapter are practiced and performed by the Hindu women of the State of Bengal in India. One of these two rituals is the Dadhi-Mangal ceremony, which is observed by both the prospective bride and groom on the day before their Vedic wedding ceremony. The other is called the Yātrā-Mangal ceremony, which is performed in part by both the bride and the groom together on the day after the wedding. The remaining part of the Yātrā-Mangal ceremony is observed by the bride alone.

Dadhi-Mangal

The Dadhi-Mangal ceremony is a ritual observed by both the bride and the groom the day before the wedding in their respective homes. Although somewhat similar in nature and purpose, the celebration in the bride's family is wholly woman centered. The ritual is performed by the bride-to-be and the female family members of her generation who celebrate their solidarity and the joyous occasion of her coming marriage. This ceremony takes place at the bride's natal home sometime before sunrise on her wedding day. Although the exact time, the aspects of the ritual, and the types of food offered to the bride vary from region to region and community to community, the ceremony itself remains essentially the same and is one of the most important parts of all Hindu weddings among the Bengalis.

At a designated time, the bride will be gently awakened from her sleep by her sisters or female cousins. Soon an entourage of female family members and neighbors of her generation will join her for a feast on the last day of her unmarried life. She will be given a carpet to sit on and an elderly woman will bring in a huge decorated silver or brass plateful of cooked rice surrounded by various types of fish and a bowl of yoghurt. The bride-to-be must take at least a few morsels or a spoonful from each one of these three dishes. According to the customs, the elderly woman requests that the girl take a piece from the fish dish first, before she eats from the other dishes. After she takes her first bite, she touches the elderly woman's feet. The elderly woman in turn blesses her with *dhāna* (unhusked rice) and *dūrvā* grass and takes her leave from the room. As soon as she leaves the room, the rest of the group joins in and together they all share the entire meal. While the rest of the household is asleep, the group continues to celebrate the bride's last day as a single woman, a carefree daughter in the safe and secure environment of her natal home. With laughter, stories, and humor, they continue what appears to be an adult slumber party, ending the night wherever they can find a spot to put their heads down for an hour or so of sleep.

It is important that one not confuse the Dadhi-Mangal ceremony with a Western form of bridal shower, because Hindus do have a separate ceremony directly for that purpose. If it is not a bridal shower, what is the purpose of such a meal so early in the morning? It is unusual for anyone to have a meal at that hour. From the religious standpoint, it is a violation of the practice of having one's first meal of the day before the morning worship ritual. From the social standpoint, it reflects a total disregard for the custom of feeding the children, the sick, the elderly, and the men before a woman takes her own meal. She is neither sick nor weak. Yet she is supposed to eat as closely as possible to sunrise. The reason is that both the bride and the groom are supposed to fast on their wedding day. Fasting is believed to purify one's body as well as one's mind, and as such it prepares one for a holy occasion such as matrimony. It is therefore understandable why the bride has to eat a huge meal the day before her wedding.

The question remains, what is the point of eating close to sunrise? The answer lies in the following facts. First, the traditional wedding ceremony, with all its Vedic rituals, takes place closer to the evening, which means the bride had to fast the entire day of the wedding. Second, whereas the Western calendar considers midnight to midnight a day, the Hindu calendar regards sunrise to sunrise a day. Therefore, the closer to the day of the wedding the bride eats, the less hungry she will be and therefore the less distracted from the rituals.

The place of the ceremony is in her bedroom or wherever she chose to sleep that particular night, implying a private affair as opposed to the public spectacle of the Vedic ceremony. All facets of this ritual reflect the nurturing of the bride-to-be by the entire female community of this particular household. Given the Hindu marriage system, whether the marriage is arranged by the parents, which is still the custom, or self-chosen, which is fast becoming the norm, neither the bride nor the groom is familiar with the other's residence or family environment prior to their wedding. Because the bride is going to be living in the groom's joint family after her wedding, it is quite understandable that she would feel rather apprehensive about her new life, regardless of how ecstatic she may be about the marriage itself. Obviously, anything that could be done to make her last night's stay in her natal home less stressful will be arranged.

By being with women of her own age, she reaffirms her bond with the women in her family as well as gathers her strength for her new life. As food stands for physical nourishment, it also reflects the resultant power. Serving and eating represent an exchange of power within a community of women, without the interference of patriarchy. Taking the early morning meal prior to one's daily worship establishes the importance of *strīācarā* (women's ritual) over the *śāstrīya* (male) ritual. Most significantly, this ritual of women having their meal before serving the rest of the household, especially the men, demonstrates her power to oppose patriarchy.

In seeking to go beyond the obvious practical and emotional implications of this ritual, we must understand the Dadhi-Mangal ceremony at various levels. To be specific, this ritual needs to be deciphered at the more essential levels of feminine worldview and symbolism. *Dadhi-Mangal is* a combination of two words, *dadhi* (yoghurt) and *mangal* (auspicious). It is an auspicious ceremony, including all the facets of a worship ritual. The bride-to-be holds the center stage; she is to be cared for and venerated by the elderly woman as well as the other women. She is to be catered to and treated as a guest tonight. She has been fed before but not in such a special way in the middle of the night. Traditionally, from the day a daughter is born, she is considered a temporary guest who will ultimately leave for her husband's home. As a guest, the bride-to-be is to be honored, especially the day before her permanent move from her natal home. Significantly, as a guest, she holds the power to bless the family. The *Āpastamba Dharmaśāstra* declares that "the honor done to a guest brings peace and heavenly bliss (to a family)" (S.II.3.6.6).

This particular ritual shows the *bhogam-āśirvāda* (offering-blessing) complex of Hindu worship ritual. The bride-to-be is the center of the women's attention. She is the honored guest in her natal home. It is necessary that she be pleased. She represents Lakṣmī, the Goddess of prosperity in her natal home. Because she is to be married tomorrow and then to take up a separate residence, she is not to take her entire power to her new household. She must leave some power and prosperity behind for the sake of her family's welfare. As a result of her satisfaction with her meal and her joy in her companions, she leaves her blessing behind. Manu says "when women are honored, there the Gods are pleased; but where they are not honored, no sacred rites yield rewards" (*Manu* III.56).

The Dadhi-Mangal ceremony illustrates two of the most important notions in Hinduism: first, the idea of honoring a guest who is considered to be the Divine in disguise, and second, the idea of *āśirvāda*, blessing. As a daughter, she is simultaneously the Devī as well as a guest in her home. Consequently, she occupies a position of authority, which confirms her power to bless. Furthermore, the efficacy of the entire Vedic wedding ceremony will be nullified, as Manu declares, in the absence of her joy. In short, *shakti* is manifest in the ritual itself, in its sacred format and in the attitude of the participants. In their sharing and exchange, transference of *shakti* takes place. By remaining with the group, she sustains and maintains the power individually and collectively. As a beloved daughter, she is nurtured, and the elderly woman fulfills her role of mother. As the representation of the Divine Mother, she is honored as a special guest in the house of her *bhakta.* The usage of the word *mangal* (auspicious) indicates the sacred element present in an otherwise simple, mundane affair.

Further analysis of the ritual reveals the structural as well as conceptual similarities between the traditional worship and the *strīācāra.* The wedding ceremony is lengthy, lasting for more than fifteen days with all its major and minor rituals before and after the actual ceremony. The symbolic meaning of the priestly as well as the domestic preparations of the entire process is quite complicated and detailed. In order to have a coherent view of each one of these rituals, it is therefore necessary that one understand the ceremonies' practicality as well at their symbolic references to Hindu concepts. Among the elements that need to be understood symbolically is the fish offered on this occasion, because fish is a central element of the ceremony. Although most women may not know the full implications of this symbolism, tradition such as Tantrism places heavy emphasis on its importance.

Fish

Numerous interpretations could be suggested for offering fish to the bride-to-be during her Dadhi-Mangal ceremony. That fish can be a worldwide symbol of the Great Mother is evident in various cultures throughout history. From the Indus Valley civilization to the Puranic era, this particular symbol played a significant role in Hindu ritual, art, literature, and music. According to many Indologists, the beginning of Mother worship can be traced to the ruins of Indus Valley civilization. When explaining a ritual scene found among the artifacts on the Indus Valley, Pupil Jayakar explains, "The fish is a recurrent female symbol in the Indian tradition of the aphrodisiacal [sic] and was later identified with *bhagas* as the sexual, the female, divinity. The *bindu,* the dot within the fish, is the *yoni,* the eye of love, the mark of the Goddess, a symbol of the female generative organ, the doorway to the secret place, mystery of creation."[14]

Circumstantial evidence appears to show that the pre-Vedic religion of India consisted of the cult of the Mother Goddess, worship of *linga* (male generative organ) and *yoni* (female generative organ), sexual dualism (that is, the concept of *purusa* and *prakriti* as male and female principles of creation), and the practice of *yoga,* in which the human body was conceived of as the highest mystery of the universe. All these principles stood in reciprocal relation to one another, being components of an undifferentiated religious and ritualistic complex, which subsequently came to be known as the Tantric tradition. The most distinctive aspect of Tantra is its emphasis on the female principle and how the divine feminine is reflected in the human feminine. *Ādyāśakti* or the primal energy is feminine and created the trinity: Brahma (creator God), Vishnu (the preserver God), and Śiva (God of destruction). Offering fish implies either an invocation of energy latent in the bride-to-be or empowering her with the divine power.

According to one of the Purāṇic myths, as the swallower of Śiva's penis, Kali became Mīnākṣī, the fish-eyed one. This particular myth clearly refers to the ancient symbols of *linga* as the act of cultivation and *yoni* as the representation of mother earth. N. N. Bhattacharyya explains, "It should also be remembered that the primitive hoe was designed to resemble the male organ and the word *lāngala* (plough) is philologically associated with the word *linga.* Later on when metaphysical values were attributed to the principles of the cult of *linga* and *yoni,* they eventually came to be interpreted in terms of a dualistic philosophical outlook."[15]

Still another interpretation can be traced from Yoga philosophy, according to which fish symbolizes "suppression of the vital air."[16] Although the very act of the suppression of the vital air on the physical plane could cause danger and death, for the Yogis it is an essential means to enlightenment. Last but not the least, one of the classic interpretations of the symbol of fish is evident in the appearance of the divine (Vishnu) in the form of a fish in his first incarnation (*Bhāga* 24.1116).

Of course, the availability of fish in the Bengal area makes this element an integral part of these rituals, but more importantly these Tantric interpretations reinforce the generative power as well as moral power of the feminine as embodied in the new bride.

Yatra-Mangal

The Yātrā-Mangal ceremony is the farewell ritual that takes place between the newly married couple and the bride's family. An important part of the ritual includes a separate farewell scene between the mother and the daughter. On the day of the daughter's departure from her natal home to travel to her husband's residence, the new bride spends a considerable amount of time with her family members. At a designated time, usually in the late afternoon or in the early evening, prior to their journey, the bride sits down with her new husband in a room surrounded by her friends and family members to begin this special farewell-blessing ceremony. They are gathered with the rest of the family to be blessed and to bless prior to their journey.

At the end of the ceremony, the daughter/bride will be taken aside alone and will be given some rice by an elderly woman. The rice is to be held in her anchal, the end part of her sārī. Finally, she will be ushered into her mother's quarters. In some cases this particular part of the ritual may take place right near the doorway of the house. With the help of another woman, the daughter will pour out the rice from her anchal to her mother's anchal. As she pours out the rice with tears in her eyes, the daughter says to her mother: "I hereby pay back all my debts to you." The daughter ends the ritual by touching her mother's feet and the mother concludes the ceremony by blessing the daughter with *dhāna* (husked rice) and *dūrvā* grass. The mother and the daughter walk away from each other. It is customary on this occasion for each to walk away without turning back even for one last look. This scene has a sad and somber ending. The tears they shed at this point are quite different from an ordinary parting.

It is a ritual that takes place between two women of closest relation: *kanyā* (the daughter) and *mātā* (the mother). The ritual begins and ends without any mediation of a Brahmin priest or the praying of *mantras.* In fact, this farewell ceremony is guided and mediated preferably by a wise elderly woman of experience and is shared with a group of young women. It illustrates various patterns of kin practices within the realm of *strīācāra.* All the participants, guides or mediators, and the witnesses are women. Women are guiding women, and women are participating with women in the farewell-blessing ceremony.

As indicated before, all of the rituals vary in length and in content depending on the location and the community. The ritual as it is narrated above is usually practiced in the State of Bengal. Although it is difficult to find the actual origin and interpretation of this ritual in the *Vedas,* the *Rig Veda* contains a similar rite: "This bride is endowed with awesome auspicious signs; all of you come to see her bless for a good fortune that shall make her lovable to the husband" (*RV* X.85.33). This rite where the bridegroom addresses the assembled guests and other relatives to bless the newly married girl is referred to in the *Rig Veda* as *Prekṣākanumantrana,* meaning "waiting to be blessed." Assembled guests are invited to behold the auspicious signs of the bride as if one were invited or encouraged to view the image of a Deity. Guests are also requested to bless the bride. This an illustration of a devotee-divine complex inherent in all Hindu rituals. In the *Atharva Veda,* there are two *mantras* (*AV* XIV.228-29) similar to that of *Rig Veda.* According to the interpretation found in the *Kauśika Sutra,* these two Vedic *mantras* are to be used for addressing the women who came to see the bride on her journey to her new home. In the light of the above scriptural citations, there seems to be a question as to whether the groom is addressing the spectators in general or only the women who came to see the bride on the eve of her journey. Either way, the present form of the *Yātrā-Mangal* ceremony is primarily a woman-centered ritual.

In addition to the statements found in the *Vedas,* the *Gobhila Gṛhyasutra* states that after the rite of Saptapadī ("Rite of Seven Steps"), the spectators are to be addressed by the bridegroom with the following *mantra:* "This bride is auspicious, come together and behold her. Having blessed her good fortune, please return to your houses" (*Gobhila G. S.* II.2.13, *Mantra brāhmaṇa* I.2.14). Although it is not directly stated whether the invited guests or the spectators are being blessed, the word auspicious indicates an indirect suggestion of blessing. Having "blessed" her, guests fulfill the reciprocity of the divine and the devotee.

The origin of the second part of the *Yātrā-Mangal* ceremony involving the mother and how it came to be associated with the first part are not known. The second part is not documented in any of the major scriptures, yet it is religiously practiced by all Hindus in Bengal. The general assumption is that in the light of the concept of Devī being the strongest in the Tantric tradition, and because the Tantric tradition is rooted in and has flourished in Bengal, Goddess worship became very popular in Bengal. This ceremonial farewell scene between the mother and the daughter is possibly the mythical reenactment of the Goddess Dūrgā returning to her husband's home after her short stay in her natal home.

The most important celebration of the Hindus in the State of Bengal is the celebration of the Dūrgā Pūjā. On the first day of celebration, there is joy everywhere. Mother Dūrgā is coming to her natal home. She is the Mother Goddess, but she is also a daughter. Her visit to her natal home is a joyful occasion for her family. The last day of the ceremony reflects the pain her family feels in letting her go. The *Yātrā-Mangal* ceremony is a form of reenactment of the daughter's departure from her parental home and the pain of separation they all internalize. It is often interpreted that Dūrgā's departure is reflected in the daughter's departure. Her daughterhood correlates with her human motherhood as well as her Divine Motherhood.

The paradigm of Lakṣmī as feminine prosperity and Alaksmi as feminine deprivation comes into play in the *Yātrā-Mangal* ceremony. The daughter is appreciated as the embodiment of the Goddess Lakṣmī, the Goddess of prosperity, and not Alaksmi, lack of prosperity or misfortune. Therefore, she represents abundance in her life as well as in her environment. Depravity is not part of her lot. As was stated above, the daughter as a daughter is accepted as a temporary guest in her natal home. Since Mother Lakṣmī is the source of prosperity for all her devotees, as a daughter, a woman brings prosperity to all her relatives. As she departs, she takes her prosperity with her, in this case to her husband's family. Yet she continues to feel responsible for her birth family. Her encounter with her mother and the subsequent return of the grain possibly indicates that she is returning part of her wealth or sharing her daughterly wealth with her mother as a favor to her natal family.

Is the rite of returning rice optional or obligatory on the part of the daughter? Is she free to part with her inherent wealth, or is her choice determined by the scriptural restrictions? What is the motivation that leads the daughter into this particular rite? Is it absolutely necessary for the daughter to perform the act for her own sake? If so, what does she expect to accomplish? The following quotation addresses the above questions quite clearly. "The universe is a manifestation of Lakṣmī and she is absolutely independent in converting her will into action. Lakṣmī has a five fold function *Karmapañcakam*, namely *sṛṣti* 'creation,' *sṭhite* 'preservation,' *samhṛti* 'destruction,' *anugraha* 'favor,' 'grace' and *tirobhava* 'disfavor'" (*Lakṣmī Tantra* 12.13b 14b). It is apparent that this quotation emphasizes multiple aspects of the Goddess Lakṣmī. She acts as she will. She creates, destroys, and preserves. Although graceful by nature, she is capable of doing favor or disfavor as she sees fit. The rite of returning rice is obligatory on the part of the daughter, but she does it freely to maintain moral order.

The obvious question arises, why is it that this particular ceremony demands that the daughter use the phrase "repaying her debt"? What is there to repay, and why is it to be returned at this particular time? Most importantly, how is one to understand the expression of repayment in the *Yātrā-Mangal* ceremony? In the light of the Hindu concept of motherhood, as amply illustrated in mythological and Purāṇic stories, it would appear to be impossible for a child to repay his or her parent. In order to answer this question, it is necessary to look into the symbolism of rice as well as the notion of debt or indebtedness.

Rice

In addition to all the commonly accepted references and meanings of rice (abundance, earth, fertility), rice also symbolizes Lakṣmī. The

Goddess Lakṣmī, the Goddess of prosperity, is portrayed as holding rice grain or a basketful of rice in one of her hands. Lakṣmī, in the image of a daughter, is returning the rice or leaving the family prosperity in the hands of her most trusted ally, her mother. Lakṣmī is returning the power of her prosperity to Lakṣmī. Second, rice is not only the staple food of the Indians, it is also a usual means of exchange. In the *Yātrā-Mangal* ceremony, change of power is taking place within the family.

According to the Hindu tradition, debts of all kind are to be returned. Leaving a debt behind creates a karmic debt for which one has to be responsible in another life. To be precise, one will be delayed in one's progress towards *mokṣa* (self-realization). Most of the Hindu scriptures speak of repayment of all debts except one's debts to one's mother. One is not powerful enough to pay back one's parents, especially not one's mother, because the debts are too extensive. The power of prosperity concerns the entire family, however, and it is to be returned not in an ordinary fashion but ceremonially. Because it is symbolic, this repayment has none of the arrogance of mundane repayment.

Power is the nature of *shakti*. The daughter, as the representation of Shakti, is born with the power inherent in her femininity. The *shakti* the daughter receives from her mother in her nurturing and blessing is partly the mother's gift and is not to be returned. On the contrary, the *shakti* conferred on the daughter as the bearer of Lakṣmī power is to be repaid for the welfare and prosperity of her family. The expression or the phrase "repaying all she borrowed" is not to be taken in an ordinary sense but rather is to be understood symbolically as the recycling of the power between these two individuals, or more accurately, returning to the flow.

Rice on this occasion represents nourishment, motherhood, mother earth, and fertility. Returning the rice could easily take place by means of a bowl or a plate. Why is it that this particular transaction takes place from one anchal to another anchal? Rice is being returned to the mother's ancal, the end of her sari that folds over her shoulder. I cannot speak for all Indian women, but traditionally all Bengali women, especially mothers, used to keep the house keys and money tied in the safety of their anchals. Moreover, they used their anchals as temporary safety boxes for important things, as well as for personal belongings that were small in size. The anchal seems to have served as a place of temporary safe-keeping. Rather mysterious, tied in knots, the object or the key inside seem to the onlookers to hold a power. The daughter is transferring a special power to her mother and is repaying the power only to protect her natal home. By returning the power, she neither insults her mother nor is deprived of her own power. With her mother's blessing, she receives a new surge of empowerment. Transferring the rice from the daughter's anchal to the mother's anchal also establishes a personal transaction without the mediation of the patriarchy. It also amplifies the devotee and divine complex. The fact that both of them are not to turn back is an act that symbolizes cutting the bond of dependency, assuming a new sense of responsibility, and looking forward to the future of two individuals learning to continue their lives and their relationship on a different level.

The entire ceremony confirms the structure and the strategy of all Hindu worship rituals, which are based on the dichotomy of offering-blessing and devotee-divine. In all forms of Hindu ritual, one participant is supposed to take on the role of the divine and the other devotee; consequently, the devotee presents the offering to the divine and receives in turn the empowering blessing. At the end, the entire structure is resolved into reciprocity as a process of mutual empowerment. The participants on both sides of the process take on a divine light that sanctifies the entire ritual. The ritual becomes sacred, therefore auspicious, even in the absence of the scriptures, the priest, and the preparation.

The divine mother within the human mother blesses a new gift of armor empowered by the divine energy of wisdom and love. The meaning of the armory has two sides—one public, the other private. The public farewell ceremony enacts a symbolic blessing on the couple for their new journey. The private blessing that takes place between mother and daughter implies an exchange of power, a renewal of power, and most importantly a transference of power.

The minimal amount of speech in this scene typifies the Hindu value on nonverbal communication in matters of deep feeling and wisdom. There is a correlation between a lack of words and the presence of power. The woman's tears also exemplify a strong connection between suffering-sacrifice and the power motif. The formality of the ceremony, the reverential attitude on the part of the participants, the timing, and the central role of the mother (the last stop of the daughter's farewell) amplify the importance of this ritual in the Hindu wedding.

REFLECTIONS

The analysis of these two rituals makes it evident that they have structural as well as conceptual similarities. Both parties involved are women relatives. The rituals are not mediated by any priest. These rituals are not practiced for the direct benefit of one's husband or one's child. Though the rituals take place in the context of marriage in a patriarchal society, they do not celebrate women in relation to men (as daughters, wives, mothers), but they celebrate women in relation to other women (mother and daughter, older woman and younger woman, friends and sisters within a household or community). Despite the hierarchical relations, all people involved are also reciprocally related because all are being mutually empowered.

As indicated above, both of the rituals have a number of important features in common that illustrate the nature of the Hindu notion of power and its ultimate significance for the women and men who follow the traditional beliefs. A Western scholar must remember that contrary to the notion of power as rooted in the socio-economic or political realms, Hinduism recognizes this concept to be essentially internal. As with any cultural group, all Hindu men and women are guided and to an extent restricted and therefore oppressed by their religious and social norms. As much as a Hindu woman may be considered to contribute to her own oppression by conforming to the religious guidelines, however, she actually regains and reaffirms her essential power by observing her rites and rituals. The people involved are in a hierarchical relation.

As she remains within the boundaries of the Vedic tradition and conforms to the Purāṇic traditions, a Hindu woman develops a distinct sense of identity as she passes through the successive stages of daughterhood, wifehood, and motherhood. By fulfilling her obligation toward her family, society, and the world she lives in, she goes beyond the sphere of her relatively restrictive status and achieves a sense of completion.

By living her life according to her *dharma,* whether by choice or by chance, she transforms her apparently relegated status to an absolute sense of identity. As one completes one's obligation, whether to one's family or to one's society, one liberates oneself from a form of experience that is relative to a particular time, place, and station to experience an absolute neutrality, the ground of her own "Being."

By conforming, she negates the pressure of patriarchy. By reflecting, she recognizes the necessity of following her moral responsibilities. By fulfilling her obligations, she regains her power. By participating in her rituals, she ultimately redefines her own status. The suffering that accompanies her self-sacrifice and subordination, then, no longer appears to be the behavior of an oppressed individual, but rather the behavior of one on a journey leading to inner heat and finally to enlightenment.

NOTES

1. Stockard and Johnson, *Sex and Gender,* 91.
2. Müller, *Rig-Veda,* 127.
3. Hopkins, *The Hindu Religious Tradition,* 73.
4. Hopkins, *The Hindu Religious Tradition,* 73.
5. Kakar, *The Inner World,* 37.
6. Kakar, *The Inner World,* 42.
7. Chapple, *Karma,* 14.
8. Chapple, *Karma,* 12.
9. Cooey, et al., *Patriarchy,* 26.
10. Cooey, et al., *Patriarchy,* 26.
11. Cooey, et al., *Patriarchy,* 18.
12. Cooey, et al., *Patriarchy,* 18.
13. Kakar, *The Inner World,* 118.
14. Jayakar, *The Earth Mother,* 74.
15. Bhattacharyya, *History,* 128.
16. Bhattacharyya, *History,* 141.

WORKS CONSULTED

Allen, Michael, and S. N. Mukherjee, eds. *Women in India and Nepal.* New Delhi: Sterling Publishers, 1990.

Bhattacharyya, N. N. *History of the Tāntric Religion.* New Delhi: Manohar Publishers, 1992.

Bloomfield, Maurice, trans. *Hymns of the Atharva Veda.* Reprint of Sacred Books of the East XLII. Delhi: Motilal Banarasidass, 1964.

Bühler, G., trans. *The Laws of Manu.* Translated with extracts from seven commentaries and edited by F. Max Müller. Delhi: Motilal Banarasidass, 1982.

Chapple, Christopher. *Karma and Creativity.* Albany, N.Y.: State University of New York Press, 1986.

Chatterjee, Chanchal Kumar. *Studies in the Rites and Rituals of Hindu Marriage in Ancient India.* Calcutta: Sanskrit Pustak Bhandar, 1978.

Cooey, Paula M., Williams R. Eakin, and Jay B. McDaniel, eds. *After Patriarchy: Feminist Transformations of the World Religions.* Maryknoll: Orbis Press, 1991.

Dhal, U. N. *Goddess Lakṣmī: Original Development.* Delhi: Oriental Publishers, 1978.

Dhar, S., and M. K. Dhar. *Evolution of Hindu Family Law (Vedas to Vaśiṣṭha).* Delhi: Dupty Publications, 1986.

Eggeling, Julious, trans. *Śatapatha Brāhmaṇa according to the Text of the Madhyandina School.* Delhi: Motilal Banarasidass, 1972.

Ghadially, Rehana, ed. *Women in Indian Society.* New Delhi: Sage Publications, 1988.

Hopkins, Thomas J. *The Hindu Religious Tradition.* Belmont, Calif.: Wadsworth, 1971.

Jayakar, Pupul. *The Mother Earth.* New Delhi: Penguin Books, 1989.

Kakar, Sudhir. *The Inner World: A Psychoanalytic Study of Childhood and Society in India.* Oxford: Oxford University Press, 1981.

Mani, Vettam. *Pūraṇic Encyclopedia: A Comprehensive Dictionary with Special Reference to the Epic and Puranic Literature.* Delhi: Motilal Banarasidass, 1979.

Müller, F. Max, ed. *Rig-Veda Samhita: The Sacred Hymns of the Brahmans, Together with the Commentary of Sayanakarya.* 2d ed. London: H. Frowde, 1980-92.

Panikkar, Raimundo, ed. and trans. *The Vedic Experience Mantra Mañjarī. An Anthology of the Vedas for Modern Man and Contemporary Celebration.* Berkeley and Los Angeles: University of California Press, 1977.

Potter, Karl H. *Presuppositions of India's Philosophies.* Englewood Cliffs, N.J.: Prentice-Hall, 1963.

Radhakrishnan, Sarvapalli, ed. and trans. *The Principal Upanishads.* London: George Allen & Irwin, 1968.

Radhakrishnan, Sarvapalli, and Charles A. Moor, ed. *A Source Book in Indian Philosophy.* Princeton, N.J.: Princeton University Press, 1957.

Shastri, Yajneshwar S. *Foundations of Hinduism.* Ahmedabad: Yogeshwar Prakashan, 1993.

Stockard, Jean, and Miriam M. Johnson. *Sex and Gender in Society.* Englewood Cliffs, N.J.: Prentice-Hall, 1992.

Swarup, Hem Lata, and Sarojini Bisaria, eds. *Women, Politics and Religion.* Etawah, India: A. C. Brothers, 1991.

Tagre, Ganesh Vasudeo, trans. *The Bhagavata Purana.* Delhi: Motilal Banarasidass, 1976.

Wadley, Susan S., ed. *The Powers of Tamil Women.* New Delhi: Manohar Publication, 1980.

Walker, Barbara J. *The Women's Dictionary of Symbols and Sacred Objects.* San Francisco: Harper and Row, 1988.

5

MIRANDA SHAW

Worship of Women in Tantric Buddhism: Male Is to Female as Devotee Is to Goddess

INTRODUCTION

Tantric Buddhism was the most creative and influential religious movement of Pāla-period India (seventh to twelfth centuries C.E.). This radically new form of Buddhism was vivified by fresh infusions of cultural energy from Hindu Tantra and *Shākta* (Goddess-worshiping) traditions. Female Deities filled the pantheon to the bursting point and took possession of its highest echelon. Among the values that made it distinctive among Buddhist subtraditions was an acceptance of the body and sense experience as sources of knowledge and power. Tantric Buddhists eulogized the body as an abode of bliss and boldly affirmed that desire, pleasure, and sexuality can be embraced on the path to enlightenment. In keeping with this life-affirming orientation, the Tantric pioneers envisioned the possibility of liberating relationships between men and women. The male and female founders of the movement developed disciplines that men and women can perform together in order to transform the ardor of their intimacy and passion into blissful, enlightened states of awareness.[1]

The ritual and yogic methods of Tantric Buddhism include the worship of women (*strīpūjā*) by their male partners, a practice meant to refine the man's emotions and provide the woman with experiences useful to her pursuit of liberation. This worship requires that a man adopt the role of devotee and supplicant in relation to his female partner or companion, who is seen as the living embodiment of a Goddess. In the role of worshiper, the man makes a series of offerings and symbolic and concrete expressions of subordinate status. The culmination of the worship is an offering of sexual pleasure that assists the woman in her yogic practices, spiritual cultivation, and transformation of eros into divine ecstasy.

This practice of worshiping women provides evidence of how the identification of women with Goddesses affected religious practices and gender relations in Tantric Buddhist circles. This evidence in turn is relevant for cross-cultural inquiry into how women fare in Goddess traditions worldwide. Addressing the question of how women fare within the purview of Goddess worship requires extensive rethinking of women's history and Goddess traditions. Scholars have traditionally overlooked evidence of women's status and power, the existence and influence of Goddesses, and relationships between the two. This has been as true in the case of the study of Tantric Buddhism as in other fields. For example, scholars have downplayed the great Goddesses of Tantric Buddhism by identifying each female Deity simply as the spouse, wife, or consort of a male Deity, regardless of whether or not she appears with a male counterpart in a given context or even is typically paired with a male figure.[2] The women of Tantric Buddhism have been dismissed as marginal and peripheral members of Tantric circles or denounced as sluts, prostitutes, and witches.[3] Finally, any potential connection between the women and the female Deities is consistently and peremptorily denied.

This chapter analyzes previously translated materials as well as materials newly translated by me in order to provide a case study of women and Goddesses in a major Buddhist movement. The chapter looks first at the Goddesses of Tantric Buddhism in order to demonstrate their intended identification with human women and then introduces the main features of the worship of women as it is described in several classical Tantric texts. This form of worship has barely received passing mention in any scholarly literature on the subject. The practice has been ignored in modern scholarship because it directly contradicts accepted historical understandings of the roles of women and gender relations in this tradition, and thus there has been no interpretive category in which to locate it. The conclusion considers why this practice has been ignored in Buddhist studies and explores the significance of this case for the cross-cultural study of women in Goddess traditions.

Historically, the worship of women was part of the classical formulation of Tantric Buddhism from the seventh through at least the tenth century in India, at which point there is increasing evidence of a monastic appropriation of this tradition and a reinterpretation of Tantric symbols to make them compatible with a celibate lifestyle. Because of the inherent incompatibility between the life-affirming Tantric ethos and monastic renunciation, attempts to synthesize the two paradigms continued well into the fifteenth century in Tibet, where they occupied the great monk-scholars of the Tibetan renaissance. Although the energy of the Tantric tradition was diverted into the creation of male monastic institutions, the practices and symbols described here have survived as a living tradition in Tibet and throughout the Himalayan region. In my interviews with practitioners, I found that not all practitioners know about this tradition, but it does survive as a living strand within Tibetan and Nepalese Buddhism today. This tradition of yogis and yoginis is not as highly visible as the monastic institutions but is nonetheless vital and influential and has been a continuous source of teachers and leaders. Competition and mutual criticism between celibate and noncelibate factions have contributed to the dynamism and vitality of Himalayan Buddhism over the centuries.

WOMEN AS GODDESSES

Tantric Buddhism diverged from previous forms of Buddhism by filling its pantheon with female Deities, female spirit-beings of various types, and apotheosized women who had attained exalted spiritual states. Tantric Buddhism also departed from earlier practice by introducing the category of female Buddha, elevating female divinity to the highest echelon of the pantheon.[4] Scholars have denied even a potential connection between these female Deities, or Goddesses, and human women; this denial can be found in almost any work that interprets the female Deities of Tantra.[5] A recent contribution on the topic of gender in Buddhism includes the following pronouncement on Tantric female Deities: "Any valorization of the feminine is primarily of benefit to the male practitioner. . . . The feminine sky-dancers or *ḍākinīs* are a powerful representation of the repressed feminine aspects of the male psyche."[6] No argument or evidence is offered for this position, nor is the same line of reasoning used to argue that male Deities and figures serve only to empower women and to represent masculine aspects of the female psyche.

Unlike most of their Western interpreters, Tantric Buddhists themselves often make an explicit connection between women and Goddesses. Tantric Buddhism understands human women to be embodiments of the Goddesses and female Buddhas of the Tantric pantheon. These include Lady Perfection of Wisdom (*Prajñāpāramitā*), a Goddess of early Mahāyāna origin who embodies ultimate truth and continues to be honored in Tantra. Two of the major Goddesses are the green savior Tārā, a female Buddha whose sparkling emerald complexion evokes the lushness of plants, vines, and medicinal forests,[7] and Vajrayoginī, a coral red female Buddha who dances in a ring of fire and blazes with passion and intensity. These great Goddesses represent, in vivid iconographic form, the divine potentiality and innate divinity of all women.

The conviction that all human beings possess innate divinity, or Buddhahood, had emerged centuries earlier in the Mahāyāna doctrine that a seed of Buddhahood (*tathāgatagarbha*) resides in the heart of every person. The Tantric movement made the creative advance of linking this innate Buddhahood with gender. Thus, in the *Caṇḍamahāroṣaṇa -tantra* we find a male and female Buddha conversing, and the male Buddha announces:

> I am the son of Māyā [that is, Śākyamuni],
> Now in the form of Caṇḍamahāroṣaña;
> You are the exalted Gopā [that is, wife of Śākyamuni],
> Identical to Lady Perfection of Wisdom.
> All women in the universe
> Are your embodiments, and
> All men are my embodiments.[8]

The idea that men embody male Deities and women embody female Deities was absorbed from broader streams of Indian culture and resembles statements in Hindu Tantric literature of the same period.

One of the first appearances of this concept in Tantric Buddhism is in a statement by a woman:

> One must not censure women,
> In whatever social class they are born,
> For they are Lady Perfection of Wisdom,
> Embodied in the phenomenal realm.[9]

Here, Lakṣmīnkarā, one of the founding mothers of the Tantric movement, asserts the identity of all women as embodiments of Lady Perfection of Wisdom, thus offering a positive understanding of femaleness. The provision of divine counterparts ennobled women, in part because of the obvious implication that femaleness cannot be a liability for a human being if it is not a liability for a Buddha. Further, having a divine exemplar is essential for Tantric practice, and this metaphysical position effectively kept the doors of Tantra open to women.

The identification of human women and Goddesses is often voiced by a female Deity. For instance, in the *Caṇḍamahāroṣaṇa-tantra*, an important Tantric scripture, Vajrayoginī repeatedly states that she reveals herself in and through women. She claims that all forms of female embodiment (various supernatural beings, women of all castes and forms of livelihood, every category of female relative, and female animals) participate in her divinity and announces:

> Wherever in the world a female body is seen,
> That should be recognized as my holy body.[10]

She goes on to say that because all women and female beings in the universe are her embodiments (*rūpa*), they should all be respected, honored, and served without exception.[11]

This doctrine has different implications for men and women. For women, the relationship with Vajrayoginī is one of identity; for men, it is one of devotion. On the part of a woman it should inspire self-esteem, self-respect, and the confidence, or divine pride, necessary to traverse the Tantric path. Vajrayoginī herself states in the *Caṇḍamahāroṣaṇa-tantra* that she appears in bodily form so that women, seeing enlightenment in female form, will recognize their own innate divinity and potential for enlightenment.[12] On the part of a man, recognition of women's divinity should inspire respect, homage, and veneration. Devotion to Goddesses like Vajrayoginī should be expressed as respect for women, and respect for women provides a way of measuring devotion to a Goddess. Vajrayoginī dictated what a man should contemplate and recite in the presence of his female companion:

> Women alone are the givers of life,
> The auspicious bestowers of true bliss
> Throughout the three worlds.
> . . . .
> When one speaks of the virtues of women,
> They surpass those of all living beings.
> Whenever one finds tenderness or protectiveness,
> It is in the heart of a woman.
> Women provide sustenance to friend and stranger alike.
> A woman who is like that
> Is glorious Vajrayoginī herself.[13]

For men, meditating on women as embodiments of Vajrayoginī and transferring their reverence for Vajrayoginī to all women were ways to revise their ordinary views of women and purify their vision. This process was not an arbitrary exercise but a means of perceiving women accurately as embodiments of female divinity, inherently divine, and sacred in essence. Meditation was meant to lead to direct vision:

> A man should meditate intensely upon his female companion
> As an embodiment of your [Vajrayoginī's] form,
> Until the intensity of his yoga gives rise to
> Clear, direct vision.[14]

In Tantric Buddhism the man too is divine, and the woman sees him as a Buddha in certain ritual contexts, but she is not required to render him service in the same way he is required to serve her. His divinity is an ontological technicality, but it does not have the same religious and symbolic weight as the woman's divinity in this context. Thus, although technically men and women are of equal status in the Tantric worldview, women receive a greater degree of emphasis and veneration in the empirical realms of symbol, ritual, and social practice. This feature is shared with the Shākta and Hindu Tantric traditions of India. Adopting the Shākta worldview, Tantric Buddhism displays the conviction that all the powers of the universe flow through and from women. This affirmation of femaleness is a radical departure from the neutrality of Mahāyāna nondualism and is another feature imported directly from the Shākta milieu, which shared with Tantric Buddhists this view of women as possessors of a special spiritual potency or energy that gives rise to life and well-being on all levels. Buddhism also adopted the idea of the close relationship between women and the earth, the only two things in the universe capable of creating new life and nourishing living beings.[15]

In Tantric Buddhism, a female companion is seen as the foundation of a man's spiritual life. According to the *Pearl Rosary* (an eleventh-century Tibetan commentary), the yogini possesses spiritual qualities herself and can give spiritual sustenance just as the earth offers life-giving sustenance:

> Having recognized a yogini who will delight and transmit energy and power [*adhiṣṭhāna*] to him, and feeling passionately attracted to her, if the male aspirant does not worship that yogini, she will not bless the yogi, and his spiritual attainments will not arise.[16]

A man's attainment of enlightened qualities is dependent on his association with a female companion who can help him to generate these qualities in his stream of being.[17] Just as a Goddess blesses and benefits her devotees, and just as *shakti* vivifies all biological, cultural, and religious life, so the female Tantric channels this life force, or spiritual energy, to her devotee-consort. A woman is not depleted by contributing this religious nourishment any more than a mother is depleted by nursing a child or a candle flame is depleted by lighting many lamps.

Contrary to what is suggested in Western sources, this energy is not something a man extracts or steals from any woman who happens to fall prey to his designs. The woman chooses when and on whom to bestow her blessing. Her ability to enhance a man's spiritual development depends on her innate divinity as awakened and brought to fruition by her own religious practices, which include envisioning herself in the form of various Goddesses and imaginatively investing herself with all the features of their appearance, tender and wrathful expressions, and supernatural powers for liberating beings. By sharing her energy and power with a man, thereby blessing or empowering him (*adhiṣṭhāna*), she is not depriving herself, but sharing her energy at will with a man who has won her favor by meeting various requirements that she may impose, such as displaying ritual etiquette, using secret signs, and making offerings and acts of obeisance. Here the parallel with the divine-human relationship is clear. That is, the woman's beneficence is a gracious yet voluntary response to her devotee's supplication and devotion, homage and worship.

HOMAGE AND WORSHIP

> The Buddhas command that you must serve
> The delightful woman who will uphold you.
> A man who violates this is foolish and
> Will not attain enlightenment.[18]

The Tantric path outlines specific ways for a man to show honor and respect for a woman from the first moment of meeting her to the fruition of their journey. For example, when they first meet, he must approach her respectfully from the outset, acknowledging the spiritual qualities she possesses. He uses body language and secret signs to signal that he is a Tantric practitioner and aspires to join forces with her in a mutual pursuit of enlightenment. Through these behaviors, the man makes known his willingness and aspiration to become her companion. Having made his availability known, he must then await her invitation and initiative at every step. In this process, the woman remains the primary agent of her spiritual destiny. Retaining the right of initiative is a way for her to ensure that her actions proceed from her own intrinsic motives and primary purpose, which is to attain enlightenment.

The terms used to express the requisite attitudes and behavior of a man toward his female companion are drawn from the vocabulary of devotion. They include reliance and dependence on her as his religious refuge, honor and service, reverence and devotion, devotional servitude, and giving gifts, as well as ritual worship.[19] Although the man and woman recognize one another's divinity, implying complete reciprocity, the man is required to respond to the woman's divinity with numerous expressions of devotion. Physical acts of homage and a reverential, suppliant attitude are required of him. For the man, to see the woman as divine is part of a full devotional complex in which he makes offerings of gifts and traditional tokens of reverence, such as butter-lamps, incense, flowers, clothing, jewelry, and perfume, which he should apply to her with his own hands.[20] He should offer meat and various kinds of liquors, which have medicinal and sacramental value in the Tantric context. Regarding the woman as a living Goddess, or Goddess in human form, he should prostrate himself and circumambulate before her, both traditional ways of expressing respect in India.[21]

How the relationship between the man and woman parallels the relationship between a male devotee and a Goddess is elaborated in the *Caṇḍamahāroṣaṇa-tantra* where the female Buddha Vajrayoginī demands homage in the form of worship of women. Asked by *Caṇḍamahāroṣaṇa-tantra* how a man should honor Her Holiness, Vajrayoginī replies that he should make offerings to Her by worshiping her human embodiments:

> He should continuously worship Vajrayoginī
> With flowers, incense, and clothes and
> Honor her with speeches and ornate expressions,
> With palms pressed together.
> He should gaze, touch, and contemplate (her)
> And behave consistently with his speech.
> Kissing and embracing, he should always worship Vajrayoginī
> Physically if he can, or mentally and verbally if he cannot.
> The aspirant who satisfies me wins the supreme attainment.
> I am identical to the bodies of all women, and
> There is no way that I can be worshiped
> Except by the worship of women [*strīpūjā*].[22]

A man's attitude should match his behavior. He should be loving and worship with a cheerful attitude. Mere outward obeisance without a reverent, willing attitude is not meritorious or efficacious.[23] Tantric texts acknowledge the possibility of a negative or derogatory attitude toward a female companion and expressly forbid it, enjoining sincerity and pure motivation: "This worship is supreme, but if he is disrespectful, he will surely burn (in hell). . . . Thus, one . . . should worship with complete sincerity."[24]

Expressions of respect and reverence are not limited to the ritual setting but permeate daily life. In general, he "should speak with pleasant words and give a woman what she wants."[25] He must prostrate himself before her, massage her feet, cook for her, feed her, and wait until she has eaten to partake of her leftovers.[26] In Indian culture, a relationship in which the man prepares the food and eats only after the woman is a dramatic form of service and nurturance. It is also an expression of subordination in a hierarchical relationship. Touching and massaging her feet is another expression of humility and subordinate status. Further, he should observe a form of esoteric etiquette called "behavior of the left" as a way to show respect for a woman.[27] As the name indicates, this form of etiquette involves focusing on the left side in all interactions with women: walking to the left of a woman and taking the first step with the left foot, circumambulating her in a counterclockwise fashion, using the left hand to make the secret signs, and making offerings and feeding her with the left hand.[28] This behavior of the left is a way to make his actions pleasing to the woman. Further, he should regard every substance discharged by her body as pure and should be willing to touch and ingest it. For instance, he should be willing to sip sexual fluid and blood from her vulva and to lick any part of her body if requested to do so.[29] The following statement becomes his prayer of aspiration:

> I must practice devotion to women
> Until I realize the essence of enlightenment.[30]

There is some ambivalence in these texts regarding whether these exchanges are mutual. Sometimes a benefit for the woman is discussed, implying mutual gain, but more often the benefit for the man is emphasized. This again parallels human-divine relationships, in which the Deity is the benefactor and the human devotee is the beneficiary. Although the Deity may derive some gratification from the relationship, the devotee has much more to gain than does the sovereign object of devotion. What human devotees want from their Deities ultimately is supreme deliverance, or liberation, and this is what male Tantrics seek ultimately to gain in the context of a spiritual relationship with a woman. The texts reiterate that a man cannot gain enlightenment without respecting women and allying himself with a woman.[31] A man seeking enlightenment on this path is warned never to abandon, forsake, or even criticize women.[32] As the *Caṇḍamahāroṣaṇa-tantra* states, a man could kill one hundred Hindu priests and not be stained by sin, but criticizing or disparaging a woman will send him to hell.[33]

Although it may be tempting to interpret this ritual worship as evidence that men were exploiting women in an attempt to make spiritual progress at their expense, this interpretation ignores the overarching context of a devotional and hierarchical religious relationship patterned after, and expressed in terms of, the divine-human relationship between a devotee and a Goddess. The man deliberately cultivates the attitudes and behavior not of a dominator but of a devotee.

Women benefited from the worship in different ways than did men. The goal of Tantric practice is to cultivate a mode of awareness in which one comes to experience the world as perfect and oneself as divine, and anything that assists in that process is part of one's spiritual training. Therefore, being regarded and treated as a Goddess naturally offers spiritual as well as psychological benefits for the woman. Being treated and worshiped in that way would encourage a woman to experience and realize herself to be a Goddess and thus would have a direct bearing on her inner life, affecting her self-perceptions, self-esteem, meditations, dreams, and spiritual progress.

This practice also had an indirect but nonetheless tangible benefit for women in the way that it could reform a man's attitudes toward women, refining his emotions, perceptions, and behavior. One of the hallmarks of this movement is the conviction that men and women can enjoy relationships that are nonexploitative, noncoercive, and mutually liberative. Clearly, a man who underwent this kind of training would be a better companion and lover than a man schooled in misogyny, convinced of his superiority and divinely ordained right to dominate and exploit. Therefore, any progress that a man made on this path would immediately benefit his female companion and associates. Some of the Tantric relationships were of brief duration, and some lasted a lifetime. Unlike arranged marriages, the relationships were voluntary. Their basis was a passionate commitment to the same religious goals and ideals. A man's Tantric training prepared him to be an ideal companion for a woman who had a choice. Tantric texts emphasize what a man has to do to appeal to, please, and merit the attention of a woman, but there are no corresponding requirements that a woman has to fulfill.

When we turn to the final stages of the ritual worship, the intended benefits for the woman are more explicit. The benefits of the final offerings are, simply stated, pleasure and liberation.

THE OFFERING OF SEXUAL PLEASURE

The final stage of ritual worship begins with the man's offering of himself in the giving of sexual pleasure. Vajrayoginī insists that sexual satisfaction should be part of her worship. This is the ultimate method of worshiping the female partner and is sometimes described as worshiping the female organ. The female organ is referred to directly as a vulva (*bhaga*) or metaphorically as a lotus (*padma*), the Buddhist symbol of purity and enlightenment and a natural symbol for the vulva:

> Aho! I will bestow supreme success
> On one who ritually worships my lotus, bearer of all bliss.
> A wise one unites calmly and with patient application
> To the requisite activities in the lotus.[34]

In the *Caṇḍamahāroṣaṇa-tantra* Vajrayoginī describes how this Tantric worship is to proceed. A yogi and yogini should seclude themselves in a hermitage to practice together. After gazing at each other and attaining single-minded concentration, the woman should address the man, affirming that he is her son and husband, brother and father, and claiming that for seven lifetimes he has been her servant and slave, purchased by her and owned by her. He in turn should fall at her feet, press his palms together in a gesture of reverence, and declare his devotion and humble servitude to her, asking her to grace him with a loving glance. She will then draw him to her and kiss him, direct his mouth to between her thighs, and embrace and pinch him playfully. She guides him in how to make the offering of pleasure to her:

> Constantly take refuge at my feet, my dear . . .
> Be gracious, beloved, and
> Give me pleasure with your diamond scepter.
> Look at my three-petalled lotus,
> Its center adorned with a stamen.
> It is a Buddha paradise
> Adorned with a red Buddha,
> A cosmic mother who bestows
> Bliss and tranquillity on the passionate.
> Abandon all conceptual thought and
> Unite with my reclining form;
> Place my feet upon your shoulders and
> Look me up and down.
> Make the fully awakened scepter
> Enter the opening in the center of the lotus.
> Move a hundred, thousand, hundred thousand times
> In my three-petalled lotus
> Of swollen flesh.
> Placing one's scepter there, offer pleasure to her mind.
> Wind, inner wind, my lotus is the unexcelled!
> Aroused by the tip of the diamond scepter,
> It is red like a *bandhūka* flower.[35]

In this scriptural passage, a female Buddha demands pleasure for her embodiments, human women. She alternates between referring to the woman in the third person, as someone else, and in the first person, equating the woman with herself. This identification is an important part of the man's—and woman's—contemplation process when performing this practice. Instructions specify that the man should be free from lust and maintain a clear, nonconceptual state of mind. He is instructed not to end the worship until she is fully satisfied; only then is he allowed to pause to revive himself with food and wine—after serving the woman and letting her eat first, of course![36] Selfish pleasure-seeking is out of the question for him, for he must serve and please his Goddess.

Toward this salutary end, various texts describe the talents that a Tantric yogi would do well to develop, requiring that he employ an array of erotic techniques matching those described in the *kāmaśāstra*, or secular erotic manuals.[37] The *Caṇḍamahāroṣaṇa-tantra* describes an array of oral techniques and provides a catalogue of sexual positions to be used, such as the swing-rocking position, in which the couple interlace their arms like braids of hair and rock slowly,[38] and the thigh-rubbing position, in which the woman places the soles of her feet on the base of the man's thighs.[39] Reverse union, in which the man is supine and the woman takes the more active role, is highly recommended.[40] From the length of the list, one would imagine that Tantric couples enjoyed an erotic repertoire rivaling those of the amorous couples adorning Indian temple towers. The mood of delicacy, exuberance, and graceful sensuousness that characterizes the sculpted couples also suffuses the literary descriptions in the Tantric texts, which exult in an open and unashamed affirmation of sensuality in a religious context.

The offering of pleasure consists of sexual satisfaction for the woman in a spiritual companionship devoted to mutual liberation, and thus a relationship in which sexual exploitation has no place. The offering of pleasure is not an end in itself but a point of departure for an advanced Tantric yoga that uses the bliss of union as a basis for meditation. Thus, this offering to the female partner is ultimately an offering of the blissful pleasure necessary for Tantric contemplation.

This intimate offering, sometimes called the "secret offering," or "secret worship,"[41] proceeds in stages. One of the initial goals of erotic play is to stimulate the woman's flow of sexual fluid, the female equivalent of the man's seminal fluid.[42] This process is described with poetic delicacy in the *Hevajra-tantra*:

Having kissed and embraced, stroke the vulva.
The tip of the man, pressing (or kissing),
Drinks sweet nectar from the lips below.
The possessor of the diamond scepter
Should use his hands steadily to do
Activities that produce the musk of desire.[43]

This passage describes how the man distills nectar from the corolla of the woman's lotus, likening it to a mouth that sips sweet wine from a lotus flower. The woman's fluid is often called *madhu*, meaning "honey, nectar, wine, anything sweet."[44] Because it is a liquid that accompanies experiences of bliss and heightened awareness, it is sometimes called "musk of desire," or "musk of intoxication," referring to the woman's intoxication by pleasure.[45] Tsongkhapa, a Tibetan expert on the Tantric practices, shows how this fluid is an integral part of the woman's yogic experience:

> Practice with the great quality-possessing woman and she will become intoxicated by the sap of the elixir of union as it descends. Because of this, all the Buddhas will assemble in a sacred citadel [*maṇḍala*] in the aspirant's body, and likewise all the female divinities will assemble in a sacred citadel in the body of the great lineage consort, whom one visualizes as Sparśavajrī [a female Buddha]. Worship that woman.[46]

Tantric union requires a mixing of sexual fluids for the purpose of spiritual illumination rather than procreation. The man and woman mingle and then absorb small amounts of their combined fluids, a mixture that is generally referred to as a blend of camphor and red sandalwood, or of white drops and red drops.[47] The sexual fluids are considered to possess a special potency for nourishing the psychic or yogic anatomy and thus are reabsorbed and visualized as spreading through the body, accompanied by blissful sensations. This process is expressed poetically by Babhaha, one of the Tantric adepts who pursued enlightenment in the company of a woman also seeking enlightenment:

In the sacred citadel of the vulva of
A superlative, skillful partner,
Do the practice of mixing white seed
With her ocean of red seed.
Then absorb, raise, and spread the nectar—
A stream of ecstasy such as you've never known.
Then for pleasure surpassing pleasure,
Realize that as inseparable from emptiness.[48]

The exchange of fluids—white seed and red seed—on a physical level accompanies an exchange of breath and subtle energies on the psychic, experiential level. The combination of their energies adds the quality and quantity of each partner's energy to the other, thus heightening and accelerating the process of inner combustion. The advantage of this form of meditation over solitary contemplation is that the intensity and power of the meditation are heightened by the addition of the partner's energy.

The union of the two drops, red and white, begins a more interiorized yogic process in which the two partners direct their now combined energy in specific ways to produce subtle states of bliss and insight. Ultimately, the purpose of this esoteric yoga is to concentrate the inner breath, or wind, at a spot near the base of the spine and then make it ascend and descend in a psychic pathway, or channel, that traverses the body vertically.

Thus, the offering of pleasure is in essence an offering of the yogic experiences that this makes possible for the woman. Tsongkhapa describes this process as moving the veins in the lotus and waking them up, bringing the woman's attention to the lower end of the central channel, helping her to concentrate energy at the point where the energy and drops will be drawn into the central channel.[49] Stimulating that nexus of veins will unify her sensations and concentrate her attention at one point, which is near the lower opening of the central channel, allowing a woman who is trained in this process to draw the inner wind, or breath, into the central channel at that time. When the energies concentrated by that practice enter the woman's central channel, "that is the essence of worship of the woman."[50] At this point, the inner wind becomes a wisdom wind, that is, a vehicle of nondualistic Buddha-perception rather than dualistic thought. After inhaling this energy into the central channel and raising it up, the inner yoga practitioner exhales, or lets the energy descend again. Both the man and woman complete this process.[51] Having gathered the inner wind into the central channel, without thoughts or dualistic grasping, desire or attachment, the man and woman are now freed to meditate with complete clarity of mind. The fuel of their meditation is the passion and bliss of sexual union. The fire is the realization of emptiness, which consumes, purifies, and refines every form of consciousness and experience into a more rarefied, blissful form of experience.

Thus, in worship of the female partner, the offering substance is the man himself, which includes his respect and adoration, his own body in the form of the pleasure that he gives her, the sexual fluids that he blends with hers, and the breath and subtle energies that he mingles with hers. By virtue of being worshiped in this way, the woman brings her winds and drops into the central channel and stabilizes them there, bringing her to the threshold of nondualistic experience, or enlightened awareness.[52] In essence, this worship enables the woman to traverse the final stages of her journey to enlightenment.

Experientially, the worship of women has a distinctive psychological and affective content that will be missed by a secular, dualistic, or hierarchical interpretive framework. Ultimately, the partners do not seek to gain extrinsic benefits so much as to perfect a process that is seen to be transformative and liberating in itself. Their goal is an experience of the sacred, a vision of divine beauty, and a heightened mode of insight. The practice requires disidentification with the ordinary, conventional self and allows immersion in the blissful, enlightened core of being. The man and woman surrender their worldly identities as they assume the archetypal roles of devotee and Deity. Freed from the ordinary dynamics of interpersonal interaction, which inevitably mire a relationship in the painful shallows of value judgments, projections, and neurotic attachment, the partners can explore the deeper, impersonal ranges of spiritual experience. Ultimately, they can forget their bodies and minds and leave the world behind. The resultant loss of ego, or self-grasping, is a perennial Buddhist goal.

Thus released from worldliness, the partners are free to savor sublime and transcendent states of insight, purity, exaltation, rapture, and bliss. Having experienced their core identities as spiritual beings, the practitioners can go forth renewed, with a vastly expanded sense of purpose, vitality, and creativity. The woman has been honored, replenishing her emotional reserves and suffusing her with confidence, generosity, and radiant well-being. The man goes forth with an enhanced sense of his ability to give, nurture, respect, and appreciate others—a realization that is necessary for his wholeness and enlightened participation in life. The woman has been affirmed at the most profound level of her being, as a living Goddess—a spiritually beautiful, pristine, powerful being, while the man experiences the thrill, elation, and supreme satisfaction of directly seeing, worshiping, uniting with, and receiving blessings from a Goddess—present before him in visible, tangible, embodied form. Hypotheosized as a male and female Buddha, they interweave their energies so that together they can create a pattern of harmony, interdependence, and wholeness—with one another, their community, the world, and the cosmos.

CONCLUSIONS

This essay brings forward an important practice that has virtually been ignored in scholarly literature on Tantric Buddhism. Early in the twentieth century, Louis de la Vallée Poussin declared the worship of women to be the "most conspicuous topic" of Buddhist Tantra.[53] Despite the attention called to it by this leading Buddhist scholar, the practice of worshiping female Tantrics has met with almost total silence in the scholarly literature. Buddhist studies lags behind other fields in its attention to women and use of gender as an analytical category. It is still common to encounter dogmatic, simplistic, ahistorical assertions that Buddhism has always been a male dominant tradition.[54] There is an intense resistance to admitting women to the field of inquiry and to acknowledging women's participation as agents, subjects, and creators of Buddhist history, rather than as passive spectators of a male hegemonic enterprise. Therefore, the lack of attention to the worship of women does not imply its insignificance but rather reflects the fact that there has been no conceptual niche in which to locate this novel variation on gender relations. If it were a practice of worship of men, there would already be several monographs on the subject.

As part of the exploration of the relationship between Tantric Buddhist Goddesses and women, let us consider the iconography of these Goddesses and female figures (*ḍākinī, yoginī*). Their faces are variously fierce and ecstatic. They wear necklaces of skulls, brandish crescent-bladed knives and skull bowls, and step blithely through rings of flame. They epitomize freedom and power as they leap and fly, unfettered by clothing, encircled by billowing hair, their bodies curved in dynamic, vigorous poses. These exuberant, unrestrained damsels appear to revel in freedom of every kind. Most studies analyze the Goddesses of Tantric Buddhism only as they pertain to men. It is generally denied that these female figures bear any relationship with human women, either as their creators, referents, or users. One finds elaborate explanations, generally along Jungian or Freudian lines, of how these images symbolize male psychic processes and development. We are to believe that women never thought of themselves when they looked at these anatomically correct female figures and that men never thought of women when they looked at them. Rather, we are asked to believe that women and men alike did not associate these female images with women because it was clear to all of them that the images express the shape and drives of the male subconscious. In order to deny any possible connection with women, one author even recently stated that they are not really female![55]

Nonetheless, the claim that women never related these images to themselves and men never related them to women is directly contradicted by the scriptural sources of the Tantric tradition, such as the *Caṇḍamahāroṣaṇa-tantra* passages discussed here. I have shown that the written sources of the tradition are unambiguous regarding their intended identification between women and Goddesses, in both theory and practice.

Part of the strategy to dissociate these Goddesses from women has been the claim that these (and all) Buddhist symbols were created by men for their own use and that women never participated in this symbol-making process.[56] The claim, however, that these figures were the creations and religious media only of men is false. As active members of Tantric circles, women used and interpreted these symbols. Women also helped to create them. In addition to women's general participation in the groups that introduced them, several women introduced specific Tantric Goddesses, as I have documented elsewhere.[57] Thus, these Goddesses did not spring forth fully grown from the male subconscious, like Athena leaping from the forehead of Zeus. They emerged from the meditations, visions, and psychic explorations of women and men, and thus they express the insights and aspirations of women, as well as of men.

These Goddesses have been variously interpreted over the centuries and in the course of their geographical migrations. They admittedly functioned differently for men than for women. For a man, a Goddess may indeed be "other"—the energy and power of women and transcendental wisdom and everything that is greater than himself that he wishes to acquire by imagining that he unites with her. As one Western interpreter has suggested, "She is all that is not incorporated in the conscious mental makeup of the individual and appears *other-than and more-than himself*" [emphasis mine].[58] However, for a woman, to visualize herself as a Goddess is to affirm that power and wisdom within herself. For a woman, the Goddess is not "other" but "self" at the most profound level.[59] There is no doubt that women were empowered and inspired by the Goddesses, while the Goddesses drew credibility from their human counterparts. The portrayal of the female body in the iconography of enlightenment—as female Buddhas—supported women in their quest for liberation, especially in a movement that believes in enlightenment in the present lifetime and in the present body. These female figures represent a positive resource for identity formation for any woman in this tradition who chooses to adhere to the scriptural tradition and relate these Goddesses to herself.

One of the themes to be addressed is how women fared in Goddess-worshiping traditions, specifically in terms of how a specific Goddess affected the social reality of women. In the case of the tradition I am discussing, these images were *a vital, formative part of the social reality of women.* There is no dualism of society on one hand and religious images and practices on the other. Religious images and practices like the worship of women helped to shape personal and cultural identities and to configure and transact gender relations. There is no separate body of secular laws or norms that override those that are generated and transacted in the religious sphere. Membership in the loosely structured Tantric circles was voluntary, and the values and practices I have described here held sway in those circles. This was their communal social reality.

When we turn to the history of Tantric Buddhism, we find that the identification of women as Goddesses did correlate with the full participation of women in this movement. Women participated in this tradition at every level, from the practice of magic, ritual, yoga, and meditation through the attainment of enlightenment and assumption of the role of *guru.* Women served as *gurus* to other women and also to men. Further, women helped to shape the emerging movement by introducing meditations, doctrines, Deities (including some of the Goddesses), and practices. Therefore, these Goddesses correlated with positive roles for women and supported women in careers unsurpassed in the Buddhist tradition in their autonomy and spiritual attainment.

One may question whether the worship of women was meant to benefit or be liberating for women, in view of the extensive but not exclusive attention to the activities and attitudes of men in the textual sources. Buddhist scholars cite this general feature of Tantric literature as evidence that this movement functioned solely for the benefit of men. For about the first three years that I read the Sanskrit and Tibetan texts intensively, the theory of male dominance literally created a veil or screen in front of my eyes, preventing me from seeing what I was reading. I had a series of startled revelations as I realized that these sources record how anxious the men were to recognize and properly approach the female Tantrics. The texts inform men how to recognize and approach spiritually advanced women. The men hoped to gain admission to the women's rituals, receive initiation from them, and apprentice themselves to them. The Tantric women exacted specific forms of homage, esoteric etiquette, communication (a body language of secret signs), and obeisance before they would accept a male disciple or partner, and their requirements are all outlined in the *tantras.*

Perhaps the best way to understand the gender dynamics of the worship of women is to imagine that the situation were reversed. Imagine that the Tantric texts describe women's preoccupation with where to find men, how to approach them respectfully and communicate with them, and how to serve and worship them. We would accept at face value that the women worship men, and we would readily imagine the psychological benefits of this arrangement for the men, just as the laws of Manu that direct women to serve and worship their husbands as Gods are frequently cited as evidence of male dominance and female subordination in India. However, the idea that men could believe that respecting, serving, and worshiping women are essential to their religious progress is not readily accepted. Most Western readers have no conceptual niche in which to place the following statement from a Tantric text:

> The male aspirant, with all his possessions,
> Should worship the female partner.
> This worship is supreme, but
> If he is scornful, he will surely burn (in hell).[60]

Without the requisite interpretive framework, it remains difficult to understand this statement despite its clarion conviction and intent. In the West, with our prevailing cultural norm of male privilege and entitlement with regard to female identity and sexuality, it is difficult to concede and comprehend the degree of autonomy, agency, and affirmation enjoyed by women in the Tantric Buddhist context.

In the course of my research on the worship of women, I have come to believe that one of the reasons the man has to pay homage to the woman in numerous ways, although the woman does not have to show any particular deference to the man, is to symbolize concretely that their relationship will be devoted to mutual growth and liberation. That is, it will not be centered on the unenlightened ego needs of either person. It is necessary for a man to uproot any tendencies he may have to objectify his partner and initiate a dynamic of manipulation, exploitation, or abuse, a struggle that depletes the woman and deprives the man of vital energy he needs to attain enlightenment. His expressions of reverence betoken that he understands that she is devoted to her own spiritual growth and that he will not try to enlist her energies in the service of his own physical, psychological, emotional, or even spiritual well-being. Any attempt coercively to appropriate her energy will impede his spiritual progress. She is free to assist him on any level, but she does so completely freely and at her own initiative—not out of duty, obligation, or coercion.

For feminists and thealogians exploring the female imagery and gender arrangements of other cultures, the sexuality and sensuality of Goddesses like those of Tantric Buddhism may seem to threaten to reify female physiology, rather than to affirm women's full humanity. Any affirmation of women as gendered beings seems to threaten to diminish us or reduce us to a biological capacity. If women are to be affirmed as whole beings, however, sexuality and gendered embodiment are part of that whole. It may be deleterious to affirm women's biological capacities and sexuality in a system that sunders mind and matter, spirit and flesh; however, it is legitimate and even essential to affirm these aspects of embodied existence in a worldview that envisions the integral connectedness of body and spirit, eros and transcendence, passion and beatitude. One of the goals of feminism is to restore to women full access to our energies and capacities, including the erotic.[61] Women must reclaim the right to explore, express, and enjoy our erotic energy as it takes expression in sexuality, creativity, intellection, prophecy, and political zeal. The Goddesses and *ḍākinīs* present us with an iconography of femaleness that depicts Goddesses—and women—who have passion as well as crystalline clarity. They simultaneously embrace their sexuality and spirituality.

The identification of women as Goddesses and the practice of the worship of women emerged at a time of great creativity and change within Buddhism. Attitudes toward women and sexuality were uppermost in the minds of the reformers. In place of an ideal of detachment and monastic renunciation, Tantra offers a way to explore and use the erotic energy generated by intimacy and sexual pleasure as a path to enlightenment. This use of erotic power is the antithesis of control and domination; it is the essence of passionate and celebratory relatedness.[62] Here Tantric Buddhism shares a goal with feminist thinkers such as Mary Daly, Audre Lorde, Haunani-Kay Trask, and Rita Nakashima Brock in their attempts to reclaim eros and salvage the sacredness of sexuality from the desecration of phallic lust.[63] In Tantric Buddhism, the worship of women was an integral part of this reclamation, offering a discipline by which men can attempt to become capable of a higher octave of transforming, liberating intimacy. The men's efforts to reform themselves were of direct benefit to their female compatriots because the men's reform was (and is) essential to the formation of enlightened relationships and communities.[64] The worship of women served as a religious discipline whereby a man could become a worthy companion to a woman seeking enlightenment in Tantric Buddhism.

NOTES

1. These disciplines, introduced later in this article, and their female founders, are discussed at greater length in Miranda Shaw, *Passionate Enlightenment.*

2. The use of the term *Goddess* to refer to the female divinities of Tantric Buddhism is a departure from current practice in Buddhist studies. In most works on Buddhist art and iconography, one encounters the terms *female Deity* and *female consort*. Buddhist scholars generally avoid the terms *Goddess* and *God* in order to preserve a traditional Buddhist distinction between its own savior figures (Buddhas and Bodhisattvas) and those of Hinduism (*devī* and *deva*). I use the term *Goddess* deliberately to encourage comparison with other religions and to highlight the fact that Tantric Buddhism can be included among the Shākta traditions of India and the Goddess-worshiping traditions of the world. Further, the use of the term *Goddess* better conveys the role and importance of these figures in the devotional and religious life of the Buddhists who revere and meditate upon them. Narendra Nath Bhattacharyya also uses the term *Goddess* to refer to the female Deities of Tantric Buddhism and includes Tantric Buddhism among India's Shākta traditions; see *The Indian Mother Goddess,* 109-16, 178-91, 207-11.

3. See, for example, Havnevik, *Tibetan Buddhist Nuns,* 35; Siegel, "Bengal Blackie and the Sacred Slut," 52; Snellgrove, *Buddhist Himālaya,* 175; and Eliade, *Yoga, Immortality, and Freedom,* 261 n. 204.

4. Although previous forms of Buddhism had acknowledged that women could attain enlightenment, or Buddhahood, they did not believe that a supreme liberator could appear in female form. At least, no female Buddha has yet emerged in Mahāyāna iconography, and one finds explicit denials of the possibility of a female Buddha, but additional research may yet uncover a forgotten female Buddha or submerged Mahāyāna belief in her existence.

5. For example, see Guenther, *The Life and Teaching of Nāropa,* ix-x and x n. 1; Sierksma, *Tibet's Terrifying Deities,* 158, 197-98, 273, 275; Wayman, *The Buddhist Tantras,* 170-71; Dasgupta, *Obscure Religious Cults,* 99; Katz, "Anima and mKha'-'gro-ma," 13-43; and Willis, "Ḍākinī," 58.

6. Sponberg, "Attitudes toward Women and the Feminine in Early Buddhism," 28. Sponberg goes on to say that the *ḍākinīs* did not meet female psychological needs. He does not explain why, but seems to assume that female images cannot be meaningful for women, because he goes on to say that women need male Deities to meet their psychological needs (p. 28), although he does not explore how the male Deities might affirm and function for women.

7. One of the Tibetan terms for female Buddha is *sangs-rgyas-ma,* a title sometimes applied to Tārā in the Tantric context, although in the Mahāyāna context she remains a Bodhisattva.

8. *dPal gtum po khro bo chen poʾi rgyud kyi rgyal bo dpa bo gcig pa zhes bya ba* (Skt. *Ekavīracaṇḍamahāroṣaṇa-tantrarāja,* generally called the *Caṇḍamahāroṣaṇa-tantra*), sDe-dge 431, rGyud, NGA, fol. 319b.4-5.

9. Critical edition by Shendge, *Advayasiddhi,* 19, verse 21.

10. George, *The Caṇḍamahāroṣaṇa Tantra,* 32.

11. George, *The Caṇḍamahāroṣaṇa Tantra,* 81-83.

12. George, *The Caṇḍamahāroṣaṇa Tantra,* 121.

13. George, *The Caṇḍamahāroṣaṇa Tantra,* 28.

14. George, *The Caṇḍamahāroṣaṇa Tantra,* critical edition, 6.8-9, 27.

15. This comparison of women and the earth should not be mistaken for the Western equation of woman-as-nature versus man-as-culture that has been made explicit by Ortner, "Is Female to Male as Nature Is to Culture?" In the Indian context, the *shakti,* or life force, present in the earth and also in women vivifies culture and social institutions like the family, religious ritual, and kingship, as well as biological growth, the seasons, and cosmic rhythms; see Marglin, "Gender and the Unitary Self."

16. gNyan Phu-chung-pa, *Mu tig phreng ba,* vol. 1, 334.2.4-5. (This is a circa eleventh-century commentary.) Tantric texts use the term *adhiṣṭhāna* where Hindus would use *shakti* to express the power and energy that women can bestow upon men, strengthening them psychically. The term *adhiṣthāna* has a wide range of applications in the Buddhist context and is not always linked to gender, while *shakti* generally has a gender connotation.

17. gNyan Phu-chung-pa, *Mu tig phreng ba,* 334.3.3-334.4.1.

18. George, *The Caṇḍamahāroṣaṇa Tantra,* 56.

19. Terms used in Tantric Buddhist literature to express a man's reliance and dependence on a woman as his religious refuge are *niśraya, āśraya,* and *anubhava* (Tib. *brten-pa*). Honor and service is *sevā* (Tib. *bsten-pa*), reverence and devotion are *bhakti* and *śraddha* (Tib. *gus-pa, dad-pa, dad-mos*), devotional servitude is *upāsānā* and *upacāra* (Tib. *bsnyen-bskur*), giving gifts is *dāna* (Tib. *sbyin-pa*), and ritual worship is *pūjā* (Tib. *mchod-pa*).

20. Tsongkhapa, *sBas don kun gsal,* fol. 89.4-5.

21. *Caṇḍamahāroṣaṇa-tantra,* sDe-dge 431, chap. 10, fol. 318b.6-319a.1.

22. George, *The Caṇḍamahāroṣaṇa Tantra,* 123.

23. Tsongkhapa, *sBas don kun gsal,* fol. 307.4-5.

24. *Cakrasaṃvara-tantra, sDe-dge* 368, fol. 46a.4-5.

25. *Caṇḍamahāroṣaṇa-tantra, sDe-dge* 431, fol. 319a.1-2.

26. George, *The Caṇḍamahāroṣaṇa Tantra,* 74, 78.

27. The term for behavior of the left (*vāmācāra,* Tib. *g.yon-pai spyod*) is generally rendered in English as "left-handed path," in reference to the non-Vedic or heterodox nature of Tantra. Chattopadhyaya reads *vāma-ācāra* not as "practice of the left," implying an impure or reverse practice, but as *vāmā-ācāra,* meaning "practice centering on women," in *Lokāyata,* 65. The Tibetan translation, using the word *left,* suggests that Buddhist sources read *vāmācāra* as "practice of the left," but at the same time the Buddhist usage links the term solely to interactions with women and the symbolism of femaleness.

28. See *Cakrasaṃvara-tantra,* chap. 28 (and chap. 20 regarding the secret signs), and Tsongkhapa, *sBas don kun gsal,* fol. 275.5f., on the eight vows of mother-*tantra*. See also fol. 308.5-309.2 on behavior of the left.

29. George, *The Caṇḍamahāroṣaṇa Tantra,* 56, 73-79.

30. George, *The Caṇḍamahāroṣaṇa Tantra,* 56.

31. *Caṇḍamahāroṣaṇa-tantra,* sDe-dge 431, opening of chap. 10.

32. *Caṇḍamahāroṣaṇa-tantra,* sDe-dge 431, chap. 10, fol. 319a.1-2.

33. George, *The Caṇḍamahāroṣaṇa Tantra,* 79.

34. George, *The Caṇḍamahāroṣaṇa-tantra,* 104.

35. George, *The Caṇḍamahāroṣaṇa-tantra,* 27-28.

36. George, *The Caṇḍamahāroṣaṇa Tantra,* 78.

37. Secular Indian texts such as the *Kāma-sūtra* of Vātsyāyana were available to the Tantrics for study and reference, but the Buddhist Tantric sources seem to draw on or represent a different tradition, because they use a different vocabulary with only occasional overlap with the secular systems. The difference in intent between the secular and sacred arts of love is that in the secular context the goal is to enhance pleasure, while in the religious context it is to enhance meditation.

38. George, *Caṇḍamahāroṣaṇa Tantra,* 71.

39. George, *Caṇḍamahāroṣaṇa Tantra,* 71-72; for other positions, see 73-77.

40. For example, *Cakrasaṃvara-tantra,* sDe-dge 368, chap. 36, fol. 237a.2-3.

41. Skt. *guhyapūjā,* Tib. *gsang-bai mchod-pa.* The practice is also called "great worship," Tib. *mchod-pa chen-po.*

42. The same term, *śukra* (Tib. *khu-ba*), is used for both the male and female fluids. The usual translation of the term into English as "semen" has led to widespread misconception that only a male substance is designated, because of a late recognition in the West of the female effluviant and its corresponding anatomy.

43. Snellgrove, *The Hevajra Tantra,* vol. 2, 99.

44. Tib. *sbrang-rtsi.*

45. "Musk of desire," as a translation of *madana-anga,* retains the meaning of *madana* as "passion, love, a kind of embrace, or an intoxicating drink or liquor," and the meaning of the compound, confirmed by the Tibetan translation, as "musk."

46. Tsongkhapa, *sBas don kun gsal,* fol. 405.6-406.2. The title applied to Sparśavajrī as a female Buddha is *de-bzhin gshegs-ma.*

47. There is a common misconception that the red element contributed by the woman is menstrual blood. The term red in this case refers to an Ayurvedic medical theory that the mother's contribution to the fetus is the red elements of the body (blood, flesh, marrow, and so forth), while the father contributes the white elements (bone, brain, fat, and so on). Therefore, the term *red* refers to the endocrinal content of the female sexual fluid, not its color.

48. From the Tibetan edition reproduced in Robinson, *Buddha's Lions,* 353, fol. 167.4-168.1.

49. Tsongkhapa, *sBas don kun gsal,* fol. 96.3-4.

50. Tsongkhapa, *sBas don kun gsal,* fol. 96.4-5.

51. Tsongkhapa, *sBas don kun gsal,* fol. 409.3-4.

52. gNyan Phu-chung-pa, *Mu tig phreng ba,* 299, fol. 2.6-4.4.

53. de la Vallée Poussin, s.v. "Tantrism (Buddhist)," 196b.

54. This was reiterated in a recent volume entitled *Buddhism, Sexuality, and Gender.* The editor of this volume states that one of his guiding principles is the assumption that Buddhism has always been male-dominant; see Cabezón, "Mother Wisdom, Father Love," 181. The two woman-authored articles in this volume do explore the relationship between gendered imagery and women, but the rest of the volume is about men.

55. Willis, 72.

56. This claim was recently renewed by Cabezón, who first reminds the reader that Buddhism has always been male-dominated and states that the

female images of Tantric Buddhism were developed by men for their own use and that the men were indifferent or hostile to the interests of women and had no intention that women should use or benefit from the symbols; see Cabezón, "Mother Wisdom, Father Love," 181.

57. See Shaw, *Passionate Enlightenment*, chap. 5.

58. Guenther, *The Life and Teaching of Nāropa*, x.

59. An exploration of the significance of the femaleness of Vajrayoginī for a contemporary woman can be found in Rita Gross, "I will never forget," 77-89.

60. *Cakrasaṃvara-tantra*, Mal translation, fol. 20a.3-4.

61. For feminist theorists like Rita Nakashima Brock and Audre Lorde, women's reclamation of erotic power is of primary importance because it is the fundamental form of power from which other forms of power derive. According to Brock in *Journeys by Heart*, "all other forms of power emerge from the reality of erotic power" (p. 26), and "personal power grows out of erotic power" (p. 34).

62. For a contrast of these two forms of power, see Brock, *Journeys by Heart*, chap. 2, esp. 41-42.

63. See Daly, *Pure Lust;* Lorde, *Sister Outsider;* Trask, *Eros and Power;* and Brock, *Journeys by Heart.*

64. Ruether argues that if it is primarily men who have oppressed women, then a parallel but distinctive process of male conversion ideally should accompany women's liberation. This way, women's inner reality will be mirrored and supported by their relationships and social setting. See Ruether, *Sexism and God-Talk*, 17-18.

WORKS CITED

Bhattacharyya, Narendra Nath. *The Indian Mother Goddess*. 2d ed. New Delhi: Manohar, 1977.

Brock, Rita Nakashima. *Journeys by Heart: A Christology of Erotic Power*. New York: Crossroad, 1988.

Cabezón, José Ignacio. "Mother Wisdom, Father Love: Gender-Based Imagery in Mahayana Buddhist Thought." Pp. 181-99 in *Buddhism, Sexuality and Gender*, edited by José Ignacio Cabezón. Albany: State University of New York Press, 1992.

Chattopadhyaya, Debiprasad. *Lokāyata: A Study in Ancient Indian Materialism*. 6th ed. Delhi: People's Publishing House, 1985.

Daly, Mary. *Pure Lust: Elemental Feminist Philosophy*. Boston: Beacon Press, 1984.

Dasgupta, Shashibhushan. *Obscure Religious Cults*. Calcutta: Firma KLM, 1976.

de la Vallée Poussin, Louis, s.v. "Tantrism (Buddhist)." Vol. 12, p. 196b in *Encyclopedia of Religion and Ethics*, edited by James Hastings. New York: Charles Scribner's Sons, 1922.

Eliade, Mircea. *Yoga, Immortality and Freedom*. 2d ed. Princeton, N.J.: Princeton University Press, 1969.

George, Christopher, trans. *The Caṇḍamahāroṣaṇa Tantra, Chapters 1-8: A Critical Edition and English Translation*. American Oriental Series 56. New Haven, Conn.: American Oriental Society, 1974.

gNyan Phu-chung-pa. *dPal 'khor lo bde mchog gi rtsa ba'i rgyud kyi ṭīkā mu tig phreng ba, Sa skya bka' bum*. Vol. KA, *Complete Works of the Great Masters of the Sa Skya sect of the Tibetan Buddhism*, edited by Bsod nams rgya mtsho. Tokyo: Toyo Bunko, 1968.

Gross, Rita. "I will never forget to visualize that Vajrayoginī is my body and mind." *Journal of Feminist Studies in Religion* 3, no. 1 (1987): 77-89.

Guenther, Herbert. *The Life and Teaching of Nāropa*. 1963. Reprint, Oxford: Oxford University Press, 1975.

Havnevik, Hanna. *Tibetan Buddhist Nuns*. Oslo: Norwegian University Press, 1990.

Katz, Nathan. "Anima and mKha'-'gro-ma: A Critical Comparative Study of Jung and Tibetan Buddhism." *Tibet Journal* 2 (1977): 13-43.

Lorde, Audre. *Sister Outsider*. Trumansberg, N.Y.: Crossing Press, 1984.

Marglin, Frédérique Apffel. "Gender and the Unitary Self: Locating the Dominant When Listening to the Subaltern Voice." *International Journal of Indian Studies*, forthcoming.

Ortner, Sherry. "Is Female to Male as Nature Is to Culture?" Pp. 56–87 in *Woman, Culture, and Society*, edited by Michelle Rosaldo and Louise Lamphere. Stanford, Calif.: Stanford University Press, 1974.

Robinson, James B. *Buddha's Lions: The Lives of the Eighty-Four Siddhas*. (A translation of *Caturaśīti-siddha-pravṛtti* by Abhayadatta.) Berkeley, Calif.: Dharma Publishing, 1979.

Ruether, Rosemary Radford. *Sexism and God-Talk: Toward a Feminist Theology*. Boston: Beacon Press, 1983.

Shaw, Miranda. *Passionate Enlightenment: Women in Tantric Buddhism*. Princeton: Princeton University Press, 1994.

Shendge, Malati. *Advayasiddhi*. M. S. University Oriental Series 8. Baroda: Oriental Institute, 1964.

Siegel, Lee. "Bengal Blackie and the Sacred Slut." *Buddhist-Christian Studies* 1 (1981): 51-58.

Sierksma, Fokke. *Tibet's Terrifying Deities: Sex and Aggression in Religious Acculturation*. Rutland, Vt., and Tokyo: Charles E. Tuttle, 1966.

Snellgrove, David, trans. *Buddhist Himālaya*. Oxford: Bruno Cassirer, 1957.

———. *The Hevajra Tantra: A Critical Study*. London: Oxford University Press, 1959.

Sponberg, Alan. "Attitudes toward Women and the Feminine in Early Buddhism." Pp. 3-36 in *Buddhism, Sexuality, and Gender*, edited by José

Ignacio Cabezón. Albany: State University of New York Press, 1992.

Trask, Haunani-Kay. *Eros and Power—The Promise of Feminist Theory*. Philadelphia: University of Pennsylvania Press, 1986.

Tsongkhapa. *dPal 'khor lo sdom par brjod pa bde mchog bsdus pa'i rgyud kyi rgya cher bshad pa sbas pa'i don dun gsal* (from *rJe yab sras gsung 'bum*, bKra shis Lhun po edition). Vol. NYA, *The Collected Works of Tsong Khapa, rGyal Tshab, and mKhas Grub*. Delhi: Ngawang Gelek Demo, 1980.

Wayman, Alex. *The Buddhist Tantras: Light on Indo-Tibetan Esotericism*. New York: Samuel Weiser, 1973.

Willis, Janice. "Ḍākinī: Some Comments on Its Nature and Meaning." Pp. 57-75 in *Feminine Ground: Essays on Women and Tibet*, edited by Janice Willis. Ithaca, N.Y.: Snow Lion, 1989.

6

MIRIAM LEVERING

Stories of Enlightened Women in Ch'an and the Chinese Buddhist Female Bodhisattva/Goddess Tradition

Ch'an Buddhism is still practiced in China and the Chinese diaspora today. But it is best known in the West as the tradition from which Japanese Zen Buddhism, Korean Son Buddhism, and Vietnamese Thiên Buddhism took their sacred texts, lineages, teaching techniques, and models for ritual, architecture, and practice. Ch'an arguably began in China in the seventh century C.E., emerged as a distinctive school and produced great masters in the eighth and ninth centuries, and in the tenth, eleventh, and twelfth centuries took the fully developed shape in which it found new followers throughout East Asia.[1]

This Ch'an tradition is far from a Goddess tradition. Founding and continuing authority were vested in teaching lineages that began, mythically at least, with a series of six male "ancestors" (the term is usually translated "patriarch") and continued to be largely male, at least as far as we can tell from the records of the tradition. Sanctity and the sacred were imaged either in apparently genderless abstract terms ("the unity of intuitive wisdom and concentration"; "the One Mind of Enlightenment"; "true emptiness and marvelous existence"; "clarifying the mind and seeing the Nature") or in the image of the Buddha, the Awakened One. A goal of the school was "seeing the Buddha Nature" (that is, one's own Buddha Nature) and becoming a Buddha, who was never imagined as female. As in the case of the God of Western theology, sophisticated Buddhists knew that Buddhas were in some sense beyond gender, yet they said repeatedly that a male body presented him best to the human imagination, and many would certainly have been startled by a reference to the Buddha as female.[2]

Furthermore, Ch'an was predominantly a monastic tradition, and almost all of the training monasteries—including all the great ones—at which its sacred practices were formed and transmitted were male institutions—and all the officers were monks. So were the vast majority of the monastics who enrolled for training.[3] Their windows into the reality and power of the sacred were stories that recounted the circumstances and events of the enlightenment of their own ancestors, the patriarchs and their lineage heirs. To say that the ancestors in the story were all men would be only a very slight exaggeration.

Among the figures who were ritually honored or "worshiped" in these monasteries, the most prominent was the male Buddha familiar to most readers, Siddartha Gotama (known as Śākyamuni Buddha). At many monasteries Śākyamuni was enshrined in the "Buddha Hall," the great altar room in which all residents of the monastery came together to perform rituals of worship, including devotion and offerings.[4] Accompanying Śākyamuni (or possibly Vairoçana) on the main altar in the Buddha Hall were often Amitābha Buddha and Maitreya, the future Buddha of this world—both always represented as male.

An image of the male Bodhisattva Mañjuśrī, associated with Wisdom, was often enshrined in the center of the inner section of the Sangha Hall or Monks' Hall, where the monks doing Ch'an training lived and meditated. It is interesting that, according to T. Griffith Foulk, Mañjuśrī in the Sangha Hall setting "was not depicted in the conventional iconographic mode of a bejewelled Bodhisattva holding a sword (symbolizing the wisdom that cuts through all obstructions) and seated on a lion but was portrayed instead in monk's robes, seated in meditation. He was referred to as the Holy Monk and was treated in every respect as the most senior monk in the hall."[5] This important male symbol of transcendent wisdom was both a model and an object of rituals of devotion as a tutelary Deity for the monks in the hall.

Other Buddhas, Bodhisattvas, and Deities were given offerings at other altars in the monastic compound. Most of these were thought to protect the community and the practice as a whole, or to protect specific activities occurring in specific rooms and buildings. All of these were represented as male, with the possible exception of Kuan-yin (Avalokiteśvara), the Bodhisattva who in the best-known Buddhist sutras epitomizes compassion and rescue. An image of the Bodhisattva Mahāsattva Kuan-yin (generally a male image) was often found in the "Common Quarters" (*Chung-liao*) where monks read, wrote, drank tea, and rested when they were not in the Sangha Hall, where those activities were forbidden.[6] Foulk says that the Kuan-yin image in the Common

Quarters was treated in the same manner as the Holy Monk (i.e., the image of Mañjuśrī) in the Sangha Hall, that is, as the senior monk present. This certainly suggests that the image was not seen as female. There was probably also an image of Kuan-yin elsewhere in the compound, perhaps in combination with a set of *Arhats* (Ch. Lohan), who were "propitiated as supernatural beings who could use their magical powers to keep a monastery supplied with food and other necessities."[7] Although artistic representations of Kuan-yin in somewhat feminized or gender ambiguous form had been gaining in popularity since the T'ang dynasty, it is my hunch that in this role of monastic protector to whom offerings were given Kuan-yin was very likely represented most often in a form that would be read as male, as for example, in the case of the image of the Kuan-yin in the Common Quarters at the Japanese Zen monastery Sōjiji today.[8] Somewhat feminized but gender ambiguous images of the "White-Robed Kuan-yin" and "Water and Moon Kuan-yin" might well have appeared in Sung Ch'an monasteries in some other context—perhaps on the walls of the abbot's quarters as splendid pieces of art that would appeal to the monks and their gentry-scholar patrons.[9] But on the whole the fact that images of Kuan-yin were present and might occasionally be gender ambiguous or even possibly feminine did not mean that the later Kuan-yin as "Goddess of Mercy" was enshrined or present, that Kuan-yin was worshiped as a female Bodhisattva, or that feminine or somewhat feminized images of the sacred were a conspicuous part of the imaging of the sacred in the male-dominated monasteries, even in the Sung period.

Masculine imaging continued in the Ancestor Hall, where lineage ancestors and the founder and succeeding generations of abbots of the temple were honored as Buddhas; rituals were performed to them regularly. The *Gozan jissatsu zu* mentioned above gives a sketch plan of the arrangement of images in a Chinese Ch'an ancestral hall from the Sung or Yuan periods. The legendary Ch'an founder Bodhidharma is the central image, flanked by his Chinese dharma-heir, Hui-k'o, and by Pai-chang. The grouping is then filled out with images of nine generations of abbots of the temple, all enlightened Ch'an masters.[10] The present Ch'an master of each monastery, who was also the abbot, was also ritually treated as a Buddha, an Awakened One, equal to Śākyamuni and the great Buddhas of the past.[11]

In this setting quite a number of women studied, meditated, and supported monastery activities as donors and sponsors. A number of them went on to become abbesses and Ch'an teachers. By combing carefully the voluminous lineage records, I have found the names and brief biographies of thirty-five women who were recognized in Ch'an communities as fully enlightened women and full lineage heirs. By them the *dharma*, the truth, was fully realized; through them it was or could have been fully transmitted. And I have found quite a number of stories about these women and about other named and unnamed women whose accomplishments as students of Ch'an shine through the story. I have found sermons by some of these women and other indications that some them were active as Ch'an teachers (= Zen masters). I have found names and locations of monasteries at which some of these women served as abbesses. The records of a few women show that their primary teacher, that is, their link to the lineage and to enlightenment, was a woman.

So despite the overwhelming maleness of authority, symbol, text, and institution in this tradition, there were women who attained recognition of their enlightenment.[12]

I have asked myself how it was done. How could women have felt at home in this male-dominated milieu full of masculine symbols? All we can know for sure that they had to sustain them as women were the stories of the few women in the past who had attained recognition in the tradition—stories that some of the men told and to which I have found the women themselves alluded in their sermons. Thus a few of the historical myths, recounted by a few of the masters, told of the enlightenment of a woman.

When working on these stories about women in the historical records of the Chinese Ch'an Buddhist tradition, it became increasingly apparent to me that a number of these stories resembled each other and that the later ones might best be understood as textually related to the earlier ones. Then I began to notice that the group of stories forming in my mind included not only the stories in the Ch'an records but also stories in Buddhist Mahayana scriptures that a Chinese Buddhist audience, particularly a Ch'an audience, would have been very familiar with. Scriptures like the *Lotus Sutra*, the *Vimalakīrti-nirdeśa Sutra*, the *Sutra of the Dialogue of the Girl Chandrottarā* (*Candrottarā dārikavyākāraṇa sūtram*) and the *Avataṃsaka Sutra* (particularly the last section entitled the *Gaṇḍavyūha*). I formed the idea that to trace these lineages of stories, these interconnections, back to the sutras might help me to gain a fuller picture of how women, particularly women who sought Ch'an enlightenment, and gender itself were understood in the Chinese Ch'an tradition. It would make sense that women who participated in Ch'an and sought enlightenment there would understand themselves in terms of, and live out, narratives that were familiar to them, that made sense out of their quest. And the men who told their stories would also see those stories as conforming to culturally given narratives or would shape those stories so to as conform.[13]

One thing that soon became obvious is that although the Ch'an tradition, according to the picture it presents of itself in its records, was overwhelmingly male, the sutras were not male to the same degree. In them could be found many stories of women who had progressed far toward Buddhahood along the path of the Bodhisattva or even who were themselves Buddhas. If one could show that the stories about the Chinese women of the tenth, eleventh, and twelfth centuries were related to the stories of these enlightened women in the sutras, one might gain a better understanding of how the stories of the Chinese women were understood by their audiences, a fuller sense of how in Ch'an a woman could be understood to be enlightened.

I will argue that the sutras, peopled as they are with female as well as male Bodhisattvas and with Goddesses, offered a resource in the form of a partial Goddess tradition for Chinese Ch'an women and men. Chinese society and culture was overwhelmingly patriarchal. With the exception of the religious renunciant, all the roles women played were geared to dependence on men, marriage, and reproduction of the patriline. Even elite women had limited recognition, freedom, power, or agency outside the domestic sphere. In this context it must have seemed implausible, even radical, to claim that a woman could be fully enlightened and a Ch'an teacher.[14] I will suggest that, in a world in which women did not function as teachers or as public people in any other way, this socially radical claim would have been a lot less credible without the Goddess tradition of the sutras.[15] I propose to support this suggestion by demonstrating similarities that suggest what we might loosely call intertextuality between the most typical kinds of Ch'an stories about women and certain sutra stories about enlightened female figures.[16]

Does the imaginative world of the sutras constitute a Goddess tradition? My answer is, Not exactly, but more than you would think. The dominant figures in the sutras are Buddhas and Bodhisattvas, who are understood to be free of sexuality and to have transcended gender. They are almost invariably portrayed in male form, though sometimes they are shown with a lot of gender ambiguity and gender bending. But in some sutras, such as the *Gaṇḍavyūha* discussed below, there are a surprising number of Bodhisattvas who are portrayed as female. These female Bodhisattvas are close to at least one definition of Goddesses, that is, beings whose femaleness is recognized and thematized, and whose gnosis and conduct *are* the central reality—the undifferentiated "absolute" and the manifest differentiated world.[17]

The second point is that there is in the sutras a class of beings called Goddesses, *devī*. It is often said that although Goddesses exist in the Buddhist imaginative world, they are not important, because they are lower than Bodhisattvas—any enlightened being is more powerful and outranks any unenlightened being, even a God or Goddess. But whether or not they are as important as Bodhisattvas, they are there and are still allowed to tell us something about the world, namely, that important powers in the "world" (*lokadhātu*) are portrayed as female powers. Thus, while the Mahayana Buddhism of the scriptures most available to Chinese Ch'an Buddhist audiences in the tenth, eleventh, and twelfth centuries and beyond is not a Goddess tradition, it is also not a tradition without Goddesses, whether they be *devī* or female Bodhisattvas. And the construction of enlightened woman in Ch'an as Bodhisattvas or Buddhas, and thus in a sense as manifestations of Goddesslike power, may have made more sense to the hearers of the stories of enlightened women in Ch'an in the light of their knowledge of the scriptures.[18]

These women in the Ch'an tradition were in a tradition in which stories of female Bodhisattvas and Goddesses, as well as a few stories of previous women Ch'an masters, provided the only Buddhist models for how the category "enlightened women" was to be constructed, for how "enlightened women" were to be understood. Thus, in a sense, they stood in that part of their tradition that was a female Bodhisattva and Goddess tradition.

A Note on the Buddhist Universe

Before we begin to look at our stories from Ch'an literature and sutras, let us pause for some introductory notes, beginning with one on the Buddhist universe. The Buddhist universe of beings consists of forms in which one can be reborn and stages one can attain. The forms in which one can be reborn have been classified into six, as follows:

1. *deva/devī* (God and Goddess) —who live in special "heavens," *deva-lokas*.
2. *āsura* (anti-God, demi-God)
3. human
4. animal
5. *preta* (hungry ghost)
6. denizen of the hells

We get ten by adding four stages that one can attain:

7. *śravaka*
8. *pratyeka buddha*
9. *Bodhisattva*
10. *buddha*.[19]

These four kinds of enlightened beings are higher than any of the six forms and may be occupied by humans or *devas*. The occupants of the four stages are in one sense better candidates for functional equivalency with "Goddess" or "God" in our culture than occupants of the *deva* category. And because we are interested in beings with more than human powers, let us amplify our picture by citing another list of eight nonhuman forms that appear in the cosmos of the Buddhist sutras:

1. *devā* and *devī* (God and Goddess)
2. *nāgas* (serpents)
3. *yakśas* (spirits)
4. *gandharvas* (celestial males)
5. *āsuras* (antiGods)
6. *garudas* (demonic birds)
7. *kimnaras* (semihuman beings)
8. *mahoragas* (great serpents)[20]

In the stories behind our Ch'an stories, we find female humans, *devīs* (female Gods), and *nāga* (serpent) princesses. All of them are Bodhisattvas, that is practitioners of great insight and trance (*samādhi*) attainments, who have produced the thought of enlightenment and are far along the path to Buddhahood. As Bodhisattvas, they also have a certain freedom with respect to mundane forces, which they understand to be illusory, and certain powers to use those forces at will to enlighten other beings. More of that in a moment.

"WHY DON'T YOU CHANGE YOUR BODY?" STORIES

Ch'an collections contain several stories in which women are accused of possessing an inferior body, one that disqualifies them from being enlightened teachers, and they are challenged to prove their advanced Bodhisattvahood or Buddhahood by changing it. I have written elsewhere about the story of Mo-shan Liao-jan, the most famous of these stories.[21] Let us look at another of these stories, equally representative of the type:

The Nun and T'an-k'ung

> There was a nun who was studying with Lin-chi I-hsüan (?–866 C.E.). She wanted to become an abbess of her own convent (as a Ch'an teacher). T'an-k'ung looked her over and said, "You have the five hindrances, you are not allowed to become an abbess and teacher." The nun said: "The *nāga* [serpent, dragon] girl became a Buddha, how many hindrances did she have?" T'an-k'ung said, "The *nāga* girl manifested eighteen transformations. You try and see whether you can do one transformation!" The nun said, "I am not a wild fox spirit. What should I change into?"[22]

A Note about the Dragon Girl: What Is a *Naga*?

Diana Paul in *Women in Buddhism* gives a very good description of a *nāga:*

> *Nāgas* are "a species of serpentlike beings with human faces but having lower extremities resembling a snake. *Nāgas* were believed to inhabit aquatic paradises, namely, the depths of rivers, lakes, and oceans, residing in luxurious aquatic palaces. Not only were they the guardians of all the treasures of the seas, these serpentlike beings were also the protectors of the source of life, symbolized by the waters in which they resided and by their self-rejuvenation, illustrated in the shedding and replacement of the skin of a snake. They were viewed ambivalently as equally destructive and beneficial but always as mysterious and alluring."[23]

In south India *nāgas* are very popular Deities, and many non-Buddhist groups worship the *nāga* as their principal Deity. According to Mahayana tradition, the *nāgas* were entrusted with the Buddha's most precious teaching, the *Prajñāpāramitā.* The name of the greatest philosopher of early Mahayana Buddhism, Nāgārjuna, contains the element *nāga*.

> The *nāga* princesses were especially renowned for their beauty, wit, and charm and were claimed to be the female ancestors of some South Indian dynasties. They were delicate water-sprite creatures similar to mermaids. It was considered the highest compliment to say that one had the beauty of a *nāga* princess. Love stories between human heroes and *Nāga* maidens are common folklore and are also included in Buddhist literature."[24]

In Chinese the term *nāga* was translated as "dragon." There is also in Chinese elite and folk literature a considerable body of lore about dragon Deities, particularly dragon maidens, who are also associated with lakes, water, and rain.[25]

A Note About the Category "Bodhisattva"

What is a Bodhisattva? A Bodhisattva is one who has set out on the path to becoming a Buddha. She or he has given rise to the aspiration to attain the enlightenment of a Buddha, has made one or more great resolves, great vows, and has undertaken a multifold practice. In one formulation, the practice is threefold: wisdom, morality, concentration (*samādhi*); in another formulation, sixfold, the "six perfections": giving, keeping the moral precepts, patience, zeal to progress, *dhyāna* or mental concentration, and wisdom.

In the cultivation of wisdom, the aspirant will come to realize the illusory, insubstantial nature of all things. In the process, the person will attain certain higher states of *samādhi* and a state of irreversibility, where she or he is close to attaining Buddhahood and need never fear falling back to a less enlightened level. Some texts tell us that at a certain point, the person receives assurance of never again having to be reborn as a woman! At the higher stages of Bodhisattvahood, she or he was understood to be beyond gender and able to choose gender at will. The person would acquire "skill-in-means," abilities to enlighten other beings, as well as certain supernormal powers (*ṛddhi*). These include transformation into various shapes, and projecting a mentally created body.[26] Luis Gomez writes:

> According to Asanga, in his description of the various supernormal powers that result from the Bodhisattva's *samādhi*, these powers (*ṛddhibala*) are divided into two types: powers of transformation and powers of creation. The first group includes, among others, the power to produce fire and emit rays of light of many colors, the sight of which allays all suffering; the power to produce light that pervades every corner of the universe; the power to make everything visible anywhere in an instant; the power to change the form of things; the power to introduce any object, however large, into his own body; and the power to appear and disappear anywhere.[27]

In the class of powers of creation, one of the most important subtypes is the capacity to create or project bodies.

A Buddha or Bodhisattva can create illusory bodies, similar or dissimilar to the creator. These bodies are illusory, or, rather, "like magical creations, insofar as they exist for the sole purpose of being contemplated by living beings, yet they are real because they speak, drink, take food, etc."[28]

A Note on the "Five Hindrances"

Next a note about the "five hindrances," a doctrine mentioned in a number of sutras. It says that anyone born a woman in this lifetime cannot, by virtue of her woman's body, become in this lifetime any of the following five classes of beings: a Buddha, a universal monarch, a Śakra (or Indra) God, a Brahmā God, or a Māra. The universal monarch (*cakravartin*) and the Buddha are recognized by possessing on their bodies thirty-two major and eighty minor marks: anyone born with these marks may become either a univeral monarch or a Buddha. These marks include a sheathed penis. Śakra or Indra is the king of the Gods, a warrior God; Brahmā is the creator and lord of the Brahmā-worlds. These Gods were borrowed from the Brahmanic pantheon and made into adherents of the Buddha. Māra is the God who tempts and destroys, lord of love and death. In the Mahayana Buddhist tradition, none of the Gods is considered to be eternal, and the number of Śakras, Māras, and other beings is unlimited, so it is possible for anyone eventually to be reborn as one of these Gods.[29] The notion that, due to the five hindrances, possessing a female body limited the spiritual attainments that a woman could expect without "changing her body into that of a man" (normally, by being reborn as a man) is mentioned a number of times in the Ch'an literature and even more frequently in the literature of a number of Japanese Buddhist schools, which were greatly influenced by the *Lotus Sutra*.

Nancy Schuster Barnes and Diana Paul have written learned and illuminating discussions of the Mahayana literature in which women transform their bodies by an "act of truth" into male bodies, and I have written elsewhere about this idea as it appears in Ch'an literature,[30] so I will not go into this subject at length here. Let me add that it is not only physical appearance that must change. Diana Paul notes that in this literature, not only is a woman challenged to change her physical appearance, she is also challenged to change her "woman's thoughts," her nature, her mental attitude. She says that "being a male in mental attitude meant being unattached to sexuality and being responsible for one's actions, whereas being a female in Indian society did not entail such detachment and responsibility."[31] She also writes that in some Indian Buddhist texts it is stated that female physiology and female sexual "power" result physiologically in weakness of will. Thus, a woman who wants to advance on the spiritual path must seek rebirth in a male body *and* renounce and eradicate her woman's sexual power, which, because it ties her to sexual desire, is seen as inferior and an obstacle.

Once a woman's sexual power is eradicated, she can be reborn as a man, from which, if she can eradicate her male sexual power, she can become a Buddha.[32] As a Buddha, though, she retains her male form, for the male body was considered an image for the perfection of the mind. Transformation of sex represented a transition from the imperfection, impurity, and immorality of human beings (the female body) to the mental perfection of Bodhisattvas and Buddhas (the male body).[33]

Not all Mahayana sutras reflect these points of view, however, and some directly challenge them, as we shall see below.

Returning to our Ch'an story, there are stories in two different sutras about *nāga* princesses, daughters of the *nāga* King Sāgara, who offer precious pearls to the Buddha and demonstrate profound insight. Neither one mentions eighteen changes of form. But the issue of changing form is important in both. In only one of the stories does the *nāga* princess become a Buddha within her current lifetime and within the story, so it is almost certainly that story to which the nun refers. That story is found in the *Lotus Sutra*.[34] It goes as follows:

> The Bodhisattva Wisdom Accumulation questioned Mañjuśrī (who had just been preaching the *Lotus Sutra* in the *nāga* kingdom under the sea), saying, "That scripture is very profound and subtle, a gem among the scriptures, a thing rarely to be found in the world. Are there any beings who, putting this scripture into practice by the strenuous application of vigor, speedily gain Buddhahood, or are there not?"
>
> Mañjuśrī said, "There is the daughter of the *nāga* (dragon) king Sāgara, whose years are barely eight. Her wisdom is sharp-rooted, and well she knows the faculties and deeds of the beings. She has gained *dhāranī* (powerful verbal formulae). The profound treasure house of secrets preached by the Buddhas she is able to accept and to keep in its entirety. She has profoundly entered into *dhyāna*-concentration, and has arrived at an understanding of the *dharmas*. In the space of a moment she produced the aspiration to enlightenment, and has attained the point of nonbacksliding. Her eloquence has no obstructions, and she is compassionately mindful of the beings as if they were her babies. Her merits are perfect. What she recollects in her mind and recites with her mouth is subtle and broad. She is of good will and compassionate, humane and yielding. Her will and thought are harmonious and refined, and she is able to attain to enlightenment."
>
> The Bodhisattva Wisdom Accumulation said, . . . "I do not believe that this girl in the space of a moment directly and immediately achieved right, enlightened intuition."
>
> Before he had finished speaking, at that very time the daughter of the dragon king suddenly appeared in front [of them], and, doing obeisance with head bowed, stood off to one side and spoke a hymn of praise, saying:

"Having profoundly mastered the marks of sin and merit,
Universally illuminating all ten directions,
The subtle and pure *Dharma*-body
Has perfected the thirty-two marks,
Using the eighty beautiful features
As a means of adorning the *Dharma*-body.
The object of respectful obeisance for Gods and men
It is reverently honored by all dragons and spirits.
Of all varieties of living beings,
None fails to bow to it as an object of worship.
I have also heard that, as for the achievement of *bodhi*,
Only the Buddha can know it by direct witness.
I, laying open the teachings of the Great Vehicle,
Convey to release the suffering beings."

At that time Śāriputra spoke to the nāga girl, saying, "You say that in no long time you shall attain the unexcelled Way. This is hard to believe. What is the reason? A woman's body is filthy, it is not a Dharma-receptacle. How can you attain unexcelled enlightenment? The Path of the Buddha is remote and cavernous. Throughout incalculable aeons, by tormenting oneself and accumulating good conduct, also by thoroughly cultivating the perfections, only by these means can one then be successful. Also, a woman's body even then has five hindrances. It cannot become first a Brahmā God king, second the God Śakra (Indra), third King Māra, fourth a universal monarch, fifth a Buddha-body. How can the body of a woman speedily achieve Buddhahood?"

At that time the dragon girl had a precious gem, whose value was the [whole] thousand-millionfold world, which she held up and gave to the Buddha. The Buddha straightway accepted it. The dragon girl said to the Bodhisattva Wisdom Accumulation and to the venerable Śāriputra, "I offered a precious gem, and the World-Honored One accepted it. Was this quick or not?"

He answered, saying, "Very quick!"

The girl said, "With your supernatural power you shall see me achieve Buddhahood even more quickly than that!"

At that time, the assembled multitude all saw the dragon girl in the space of an instant turn into a man, perfect in Bodhisattva-conduct, straightway go southward to the world-sphere Spotless, sit on a jeweled lotus blossom, and achieve undifferentiating, right, enlightened intuition, with thirty-two marks and eighty beautiful features setting forth the Fine Dharma for all living beings in the ten directions...The Bodhisattva Wisdom Accumulation, as well as Śāriputra and all the assembled multitude, silently believed and accepted.[35]

For the nun in the Ch'an story, a meaning of the *Lotus Sutra* story is that the *nāga* girl definitively refuted the notion, so limiting to women, that a woman because of her body has "five hindrances" that prevent her from attaining Buddhahood. She did this by demonstrating that she could in the very lifetime in which she was born as a woman become first a Bodhisattva and then a Buddha. The male teacher T'an-k'ung in the Ch'an story has raised the notion that a woman shows by her woman's form and mind her lack of qualification for Buddhahood, and thus for the activity of Ch'an teacher, which is understood as the activity of one who is possessed of the Buddha's full enlightenment through direct mind-to-mind transmission. When the nun invokes the nearly instantaneous transformation of the *nāga* princess from lay girl to Buddha, the monk then challenges her to demonstrate her own Buddhahood. I will leave the reader to interpret whether or not her answer successfully does that.

In the story of the *nāga* princess, the princess defeats the notion of the five hindrances but does not challenge the notion that advanced, irreversible Bodhisattvas and Buddhas are characterized by male form, because, as her hymn of praise in the sutra passage avers, male form is the form in which perfect spiritual attainment represents itself and is worshiped in the world.

The nun's answer does seem to challenge that notion. She says: "I am not a fox-spirit." In Chinese folklore, female fox-spirits take female human form in order to lure young men into relationships with them. When recognized or challenged by superior spiritual power, they return to fox form.[36] I read the nun's answer to T'an-k'ung as saying: If I were a fox spirit, I would change back to fox form, for fox spirits are magically women but are essentially foxes—they have an essential form. But I am not, I am a Buddha. So there is no form for me to change into because Buddhas do not have essential forms, neither male nor female form is essential to an awakened mind of enlightenment. Buddhas are free of form and take forms for the sake of enlightening the unenlightened sentient beings.

Thus, though the nun and the monk in the Ch'an story apparently allude to the *Lotus Sutra*, it may be that the story with which this story has the closest intertextual connections is the story in the *Vimalakīrti nirdeśa sutra* of the Goddess (*devī*) and Śāriputra.

VIMALAKIRTI NIRDESA STORY

Vimalakīrti is a layman who is at the same time an advanced Bodhisattva, so advanced that his insight into emptiness is greater than that of any of the Buddha's monastic disciples. As the story opens, Mañjuśrī, the Bodhisattva most associated with wisdom, is asking

Vimalakīrti questions, and Vimalakīrti is answering wisely.[37]

A Goddess—she is not named, but rather referred to as "a certain Goddess" or "the Goddess"—who is living in Vimalakīrti's house and listening to the exchange, is so pleased that she manifests herself in a material body and showers all the "great spiritual heroes, the Bodhisattvas and the great disciples of the Buddha with heavenly flowers." The flowers do not stick to the bodies of the Bodhisattvas but do stick to the bodies of the great disciples, no matter how hard they try to shake them off.

Śāriputra, a great non-Mahayana disciple of the Buddha (male, of course), is the thick-headed non-Mahayana questioner in this story, as he is in the *Lotus Sutra* story above. Śāriputra questions the Goddess about why the flowers are sticking to him. She tells him the flowers only stick to those who have not eliminated their instincts for the passions. He then says to her:

> "Goddess, what prevents you from transforming yourself out of your female state?"
>
> She replies: "Although I have sought my female state for these twelve years, I have not found it. Reverend Śāriputra, if a magician were to incarnate a woman by magic, would you ask her, 'What prevents you from transforming yourself out of your female state?'"
>
> Śāriputra: "No! Such a woman would not really exist, so what would there be to transform?"
>
> Goddess: "Just so, reverend Śāriputra, all things do not really exist. Now, would you think, 'What prevents one whose nature is that of a magical incarnation from transforming herself out of her female state?'"
>
> Thereupon, the Goddess employed her magical power to cause the elder Śāriputra to appear in her form and to cause herself to appear in his form. Then the Goddess, transformed into Śāriputra, said to Śāriputra, transformed into a Goddess, "Reverend Śāriputra, what prevents you from transforming yourself out of your female state?"
>
> And Śāriputra, transformed into a Goddess, replied, "I no longer appear in the form of a male! My body has changed into the body of a woman! I do not know what to transform!"
>
> The Goddess continued, "If the elder could change out of the female state, then all women could also change out of their female states. All women appear in the form of women in just the same way as the elder appears in the form of women. While they are not women in reality, they appear in the form of women. With this in mind, the Buddha said, 'In all things there is neither male nor female.'"
>
> Then, the Goddess released her magical power and each returned to his ordinary form. She then said to him, "Reverend Śāriputra, what have you done with your female form?"
>
> Śāriputra: "I neither made it nor did I change it."
>
> Goddess: "Just so, all things are neither made nor changed, and that they are not made and not changed, that is the teaching of the Buddha."

The story continues with further one-way instructional dialogue between the two, in which the Goddess acquaints Śāriputra with Mahayana perspectives on birthlessness, the nonattainment of Buddhahood, and so forth, based on the notion of the emptiness of all things.

> Then the Licchāvi Vimalakīrti said to the venerable elder Śāriputra, "Reverend Śāriputra, this Goddess has already served ninety-two million Buddhas. She plays with the superknowledges (which include magical powers). She has truly succeeded in all her vows. She has gained the tolerance of the birthlessness of things. She has actually attained irreversibility. She can live wherever she wishes on the strength of her vow to develop living beings."

The *Vimalakīrti nirdeśa sutra* was immensely popular with educated people in China from roughly the fourth century on and remains popular today.[38] The great Sung literary figure Su Shih was one among many poets who wrote about or alluded to the story of Vimalakīrti.[39] One arena in which the popularity of this sutra among the elite is demonstrated is the art of the periods in which our Ch'an stories take place. Julia K. Murray notes that "while the theme of [Vimalakīrti's] debate with Mañjuśrī was totally ignored in Indian art, it was enormously popular in Chinese art from roughly the fourth through the tenth centuries and appeared occasionally thereafter."[40] In frontispieces to the sutra after the tenth century, the Goddess often appeared with Vimalakīrti.[41] Śāriputra and the Goddess "became standard figures in illustrations of the sutra, second only to the principals, Mañjuśrī and Vimalakīrti. himself."[42] The story of the Goddess and Śāriputra is one that all from the aristocracy or gentry-scholar classes in China who were active in Buddhist, artistic, and literary circles would have known well.

Note four things about this story. First, it pokes fun at Śāriputra, who, as a mere disciple (non-Mahayana) and not a Bodhisattva (Mahayana), is no match for the Goddess, who is a Bodhisattva and understands emptiness. In some ways most of the stories about successful enlightened women in Ch'an, like the stories of Mo-shan Liao-jan in the *Ching-te-ch'üan-teng lu* and the story of Wu-cho Miao-tsung below, are intertextually related to this story, for they all share the following structure: a woman who understands emptiness is challenged by a man who does not think her activities or her claim to teacherhood are appropriate for a woman. In a contest of wits the woman defeats the man, who challenges her because he does not understand emptiness as profoundly as she.

Second, we are told that the Goddess has attained irreversibility, which contradicts the notion apparently sustained by the *Lotus Sutra* story of the *nāga* princess that irreversible Bodhisattvahood is only open to those in male form, those who have overcome or abandoned their female sexual force. This Goddess takes any form she pleases and does not abandon or renounce female form once she becomes an irreversible Bodhisattva.

Third, the Goddess feels no need to change out of her female form, for all forms, female forms and male forms, are not "real" things and have nothing to do with Buddhahood. Her view connects this story with the several Ch'an stories in which women are challenged to change out of their female forms and reply that there is no need to do so.

Fourth, the Goddess has magical powers. Some magical powers no ordinary human would have belong to her as Goddess. But in the story Vimalakīrti emphasizes that she has these powers due to her attainments as an irreversible Bodhisattva who, as a Bodhisattva, now can exercise control over the illusory world for the sake of enlightening others. She can control this illusory world because she has now fully apprehended it as empty and she is now totally detached from it. Yet at the same time, in its ultimate nature as *Dharmadhātu,* as empty and nondifferentiated, yet differentiated and active for the sake of beings, she is now fully identified with it.

STORIES IN WHICH WOMEN TEACH OR DEBATE WITH THEIR BODIES

A second Ch'an story about a woman would remind the listener or reader, I am convinced, of a story in a famous sutra called the *Gaṇḍavyūha,* in which a number of Goddesses and other female Bodhisattvas appear prominently. It belongs to a class of Ch'an stories, more numerous in Japan, in which a woman presents herself naked, or a woman's female parts become the subject of Ch'an debate.[43] Here is the Ch'an story:

Wu-cho Tao-jen Miao-tsung Lodging in the Abbot's Quarters

The story occurs in a collection of verses about famous Ch'an masters, the *Wu-chia-cheng-tsung tsan,* the "Poems of Appraisal of the Correct Tradition of the Five [Ch'an] Schools," which dates from 1254 C.E. It is found in the preface to a poem of appraisal about the Ch'an master Wan-an Tao-yen, a dharma-heir of Ta-hui Tsung-kao (1089-1163).

> [Wan-an] relied on Ta-hui, and served as his Senior Monk (the head monk of the Sangha Hall in which the monks in Ch'an training lived and studied) at Ta-hui's monastery on Ching-shan.
>
> Before Wu-cho had become a nun [she used to visit Ta-hui at Ching-shan,

and] Ta-hui lodged her in the abbot's quarters. The Head Monk Wan-an always made disapproving noises.[44] Ta-hui said to him, "Even though she is a woman, she has strengths." Wan-an still did not approve. Ta-hui then insisted that he should interview her. Wan-an reluctantly sent a message that he would go.

[When Wan-an came,] Wu-cho said, "Will you make it a *Dharma* interview or a worldly interview?"

The Head Monk replied: "A *Dharma* interview."

Wu-cho said: "Then let your attendants depart." [She went in first, then called to him,] "Please come in."

When he came past the curtain he saw Wu-cho lying face upwards on the bed without anything on at all. He pointed at her and said, "What kind of place is this?"

Wu-cho replied: "All the Buddhas of the three worlds and the six patriarchs and all the great monks everywhere—they all come out from within this."

Wan-an said: "And would you let me enter, or not?"

Wu-cho replied: "It allows horses to cross; it does not allow asses to cross." ("It ferries [*tu*] [or transports] horses; it does not ferry asses.")

Wan-an said nothing, and Wu-cho declared: "The interview with the Senior Monk is ended." She then turned over and faced the inside.

Wan-an became embarrassed and left.

Ta-hui said, "It is certainly not the case that the old beast does not have any insight." Wan-an was ashamed.[45]

The phrase "old beast" is used to revile or scold people, particularly for lacking all human manners. Here it might refer to Wu-cho, because like an animal she violated etiquette by presenting herself naked to Wan-an. It also might refer to Ta-hui, because in lodging her in his quarters he violated monastic rules. The Japanese commentary tradition on which Leggett draws reads it as referring to Wu-cho.[46]

In the mind of the listener or reader, no doubt, would be the large body of stories in Chinese popular literature of monks who break their vows of celibacy. Certainly at issue is the fact that Wan-an Ta-hui is at least giving the appearance of belonging in such a story.[47]

But I think that also in the mind of the listener would be the story of the woman Vasumitrā found in the scripture called the *Gaṇḍavyūha*.

A Note on the *Gandavyuha*

Before I relate Vasumitrā's story, let me say a bit more about the *Gaṇḍavyūha*, because there is a lot of what I am loosely calling intertextuality between it and all of the stories in the Ch'an literature that feature wise, enlightened women. The *Gaṇḍavyūha* in China was the final book of the famous *Hua-yen ching (Avataṃsaka Sutra)*.[48] It tells the story of the pilgrimage of a youth, Sudhana, in search of enlightenment. The journey begins when the Bodhisattva who particularly symbolizes wisdom, Mañjuśrī, recognizes Sudhana's determination to seek supreme perfect enlighenment and sends him to the first of a series of teachers, a monk named Meghaśrī. Meghaśrī sends him on to another teacher, who sends him to the next, and so on. Each teacher describes how she or he first set out on the path, and her or his own means of progress on the path to supreme enlightenment. The teacher then describes the particular aspect of the practice of Bodhisattvas that she or he has come to understand, as well as the virtues and powers she or he has attained, and creates a display of magical power. Sometimes we are told this causes Sudhana to attain a new level of *samādhi* (concentration), which brings about in him this same understanding of the path, virtue, and powers. In all, Sudhana visits fifty-three teachers, all of whom should be considered Bodhisattvas, before his culminating interview with Maitreya, the next future Buddha of this realm, in which he realizes completely the nature of the *Dharmadhātu* (see below) and the Buddha's and Bodhisattva's conduct within it.[49]

This text was very popular with Buddhists in the Sung dynasty, particularly with Ch'an teachers. The latter often drew on it in their teaching, both because of its dramatic power and for the sake of its account of supreme perfect enlightenment.[50] There is even visual evidence of the popularity of this text in Buddhist circles still surviving from the Sung. There are two illustrated books of religious songs in which all of the visits to teachers in Sudhana's pilgrimage have been vividly represented in a series of woodcuts.[51] Another set of *Gaṇḍavyūha* illustrations is found carved on a wooden temple column scholars believe could well be from the Sung period.[52] A Ch'an audience at the time this story of Wu-cho and Wan-an was written would in all likelihood have been quite familiar with the stories in this text.[53]

Among the remarkable things about this scripture is the number of Sudhana's teachers who are female. He is taught by three laywomen;[54] by two girls;[55] by a nun, Simhavijṛmbhitā; by a woman who is possibly a courtesan, Vasumitrā; by an earth Goddess, Sthāvarā; by a series of eight "night Goddesses," beginning with Vāsantī and continuing through Sarvajagadrakṣāpraṇidhānavīryaprabhā; by a Goddess who lives in the thirty-three-fold heaven; by Śākyamuni Buddha's mother, Māyā, who is also the mother of countless other Buddhas; by Śākyamuni Buddha's wife Gopā; by the Goddess of the Lumbinī Grove who witnessed there the Buddha Śākyamuni's birth, as well as the birth of countless other Buddhas; and by a boy and a girl who are the ones to send Sudhana on to his final interview with Maitreya at his great tower called "Chamber of Adornments of Vairoçana." (City Goddesses, sky Goddesses, and others also appear, but not as members of the sequence of fifty-three teachers.) In other words, twenty-one of Sudhana's fifty-three teachers are female.

The array of teachers in this text depicts the social and cosmic world of Buddhist India as it could ideally be if those who occupied all the social and cosmic roles were advanced Bodhisattvas. Or another way of putting it is to say that in this sutra, the ideal world, the *Dharmadhātu*, which is the only reality and which is experienced by Bodhisattvas, is portrayed as identical with "the world," the *lokadhātu*, which is experienced by ordinary humans.[56] Lay householder women who are Bodhisattvas provide food to satisfy all beings in their tastes, including hungry ghosts.[57] Women make the contribution of giving birth, as in the case of Māyā, the Buddha's mother, who, as is true in the "ideal" reality of the *Dharmadhātu*, gives birth only to future Buddhas. A nun teaches splendidly; girls provide surpassing beauty that does not arouse lust; and a night Goddess, Vāsantī, protects and aids all those abroad at night, as well as all those in need, and brings into the light of truth all those in darkness.

In a sense all of these female figures are like Goddesses in that they have extraordinary powers they use to benefit and enlighten others. They are modeled in part on the best that can be found in women of the human realm, and yet they take those same activities and those same virtues (patience, devotion, giving, nurturing, beauty, giving birth, and so on) to a higher level because of their compassion and their detachment due to insight into the illusory nature of the world of manifestation.

At still another level, of course, some of these female teachers in the *Gaṇḍavyūha* are Goddesses in this birth, while others are not. Those who are Goddesses have some powers to protect and aid beings that are specific to them, in accordance with their cosmic roles. For example, there is a wonderful passage in which Sudhana meets Sthāvarā, the earth Goddess who is to be his teacher. She observes his arrival with a million other earth Goddesses:

> Then Sthāvarā and the million earth Goddesses shone forth a great light which illuminated the whole universe with its billions of worlds. They caused the earth(s) to tremble and roar everywhere at once. Jewels of all kinds, resplendent in every place, gave forth pure and flowing rays of brightness, each the more brilliant because it reflected back (mirrored) the radiance of all the others. All at once all the leafy trees grew, all

> flowering trees bloomed, the fruit of all fruit trees ripened, all rivers poured onward, all lakes and ponds filled their banks. Fragrant rains everywhere showered the earth(s), winds came and blew flowers all over its (their) surface. Numberless musics played, and celestial ornaments all emitted beautiful sounds. The king of bulls, the king of elephants, the king of lions and the like leaped for joy and roared, it was like the sound of giant mountains crashing together. Hundreds of billions of treasuries spontaneously surfaced.[58]

With what splendors of sound and sight do the earth Goddesses make their presence known, calling attention to all their features, which are also their gifts: mountains and rivers, vegetation, living creatures, and treasuries of jewels and precious metals!

But advanced Bodhisattvas also acquire powers regarded by the sutra as even more powerful and important than those that belong to the Goddess-Bodhisattvas in their role as Goddesses. This fact decreases the uniqueness of the Goddesses and supports my suggestion that we should see Bodhisattvas as analogous to Goddesses in other cultures. Vasumitrā, for example, who is not a *devī* in the cosmology of the *Gaṇḍavyūha*, emits a lovely, enrapturing light from her body and has the power to appear before all beings in the form of a female of their species.[59]

Sudhana's Visit to the Woman Vasumitra

It is the nun teacher who sends Sudhana to Vasumitrā. A passage that reminds one of the initial exchange between Wan-an and Ta-hui before Wan-an has met Wu-cho describes what happens when Sudhana begins to seek out Vasumitrā:

> When Sudhana reached the city of Ratnavyūha in the country of Durga, he sought everywhere for Vasumitrā. People there who did not know of Vasumitrā's virtues and wisdom thought to themselves: "Now this youth—with senses so calm and subdued, so aware, so clear, without confusion or distraction, his gaze focused directly right before him, his mind neither fatigued nor lazy, not clinging to appearances, his eyes gazing steadily without blinking, his mind so unmoved, as deep and broad as the ocean—what does someone like him have to do with Vasumitrā? He should not have any lust for Vasumitrā, his mind should not be turned upside down by thoughts of purity or by thoughts of desire. He should not be under the power of a woman's body. This youth is not bewitched, he does not enter the realm of temptation, he does not sink into the mire of sensuality, he is not bound by the snares of Māra, he does not do what should not be done. With what intention does he seek this woman?"

This passage supports the interpretation that Vasumitrā's general reputation was as a sexually enticing and sexually available woman. In what follows, Vasumitrā's own words support this picture:

> But there were those who knew that this woman had wisdom who said to Sudhana, "Good, Good! You have really made gain if you ask about Vasumitrā. You surely seek Buddhahood; you surely want to make yourself a refuge for all sentient beings; you surely want to extract the barbs of passion from all sentient beings; you surely want to destroy their notions of purity. Vasumitrā is in her house, north of the town square."

Sudhana then meets Vasumitrā and is delighted. She is transcendingly beautiful, has a beautiful voice, is learned in all the arts of communication, and has mastered the expedient means of the Bodhisattvas. Her beautiful body is described in some detail. Her face; the coloring of her skin and hair; the fullness, proportions, and modeling of her form—there are none in the realms of desire inhabited by men and Gods to equal her. Her body "was decorated with a myriad of jewelled necklaces, and covered with a mesh made of all kinds of precious substances. On her head was a tiara of wish-fulfilling *maṇi* gems."[60] Not exactly "without a stitch on," like Wu-cho, but not exactly covered up either—no cloth is mentioned, although the Chinese versions do not, as the Sanskrit version apparently does, make clear that the mesh with which she was covered was translucent.[61]

When Sudhana asks for instruction, Vasumitrā replies:

> "I have attained an enlightening liberation called 'departing from the realm of passion.' To all I appear in forms that accord with their desires and inclinations. To Gods I appear in the form of a Goddess of surpassing splendor and perfection; and to all other types of beings I accordingly appear in the form of a female of their species, of surpassing splendor and perfection. And to all who come to me with minds full of passion, I expound the *Dharma*. When they hear my teaching, they become free of passion and achieve an enlightening concentration called 'realm of non-attachment.'
>
> "Some attain dispassion as soon as they see me. . . . Some attain dispassion merely by talking with me. . . . Some attain dispassion just by holding my hand. . . . Some attain dispassion just by gazing at me . . . Some attain dispassion just by embracing me, and achieve an enlightening concentration called 'uniting all sentient beings constantly without rejection.' Some attain dispassion just by kissing me, and achieve an enlightening concentration called 'increasing the treasury of virtue of all beings.' All those who become intimate with me become established in dispassion, and enter the enlightening liberation in which all stages of wisdom manifest unimpeded."[62]

She then explains how she became a Bodhisattva lifetimes ago when she was the wife of a grandee. And she sends Sudhana on to the next teacher, without any description of whether or how he attains "ultimate dispassion" under her tutelage.[63]

Interpretation

What is the Vasumitrā story about? How do we interpret a story about a beautiful, sensual woman who displays her beauty and offers her favors to all comers, who is at the same time above all a Bodhisattva and a teacher? We might suggest that it is about passion and freedom from passion, dualism, and nondualism. Those who go to Vasumitrā, who are taught by her, learn freedom from passion—sometimes by embracing her. She challenges them by presenting them with an object of desire. If they respond with passion, then she is in a position to move them to dispassion *through* their passion. An initial dualistic opposition of passion/dispassion, which would advise avoiding the attractive, is not the method used here to produce dispassion. Vasumitrā's actions cause the subscribers to that method to hold her in ill repute. Passion plus nonattachment, or plus all-embracingness, yields dispassion. A nondualism between passion and dispassion yields dispassion. They learn what she knows—a *samādhi* called "uniting all sentient beings without rejection," and one called "increasing the treasury of virtue of all beings."

What is the logic of the Wu-cho story? Like Vasumitrā, Wu-cho too presents Wan-an with an object of desire, her female form, her private parts revealed. But unlike Vasumitrā, she is not proposing to teach by preaching nor to teach by physically embracing. She teaches by the methods of the Ch'an and Zen master. Those methods involve a contest in which her interlocutor is challenged not to fall into dualistic thinking. Wan-an can only manage this by not falling into the dualism of passion and dispassion.

Wan-an manages it on the first round. He turns the tables and challenges back: What is that? Can she now show her freedom from dualistic thinking by naming it nondualistically? She names it on two levels: on one level, the obvious biological fact that all Buddhas and teachers are born of woman's womb; on the other level, the question, What is the place from which all the Buddhas come into the world? is also answered by something like "emptiness," "suchness," or "Buddha nature," which her private parts in their essential purity and emptiness of all self-identity also manifest.[64] So she manages to come back with an answer that presents a nondualism of ultimate truth and phenomenonal truth, dispassion and passion.[65]

Wan-an challenges again: If Buddhas come out, it can only be because something else has gone in. Can she come up with a nondualistic answer to the question, Will you let me enter? Vasumitrā, after all, teaches dispassion, nondualism, by letting her visitors in, embracing them—embracing all, without rejecting any. But a mere yes or no will not do, because either falls into the dualism of passion and dispassion established by his question. (Remember that all Ch'an answers must avoid buying into any dualism suggested by the question—a yes or no answer to a yes-or-no question merely stays within the dualistic conceptual framework of the question.)

Wu-cho alludes to the "embracing all, without rejecting any" answer that she might have given by bringing up the crossing of horses and asses. This is a direct allusion to an old story in which Chao-chou, a famous master of an earlier generation, said of the bridge in his town, which stood for himself as a teacher, "It transports asses across, it transports horses across."

The dialogue in which this statement is embedded goes as follows:

> Another time a monk asked, "For a long time I aspired to see Chao-chou's stone bridge. Now that I am here, all I see is a log bridge."
>
> Chao-chou said, "You only see a log bridge. You do not see Chao-chou's stone bridge."
>
> The monk said, "What is Chao-chou's stone bridge?"
>
> Chao-chou said, "It transports asses across, it transports horses across."[66]

On one level Chao-chou's reply is based on a simple factual distinction: the stone bridge allows horses and asses to cross, while a log bridge, a single log across the stream, only allows people to cross. But many other dialogues in records of Chao-chou's sayings support the interpretation that "horses" refer to good students and "asses" to foolish students, students who do not understand anything yet. So one dominant line of interpretation of this reply is that Chao-chou is saying that he welcomes all who come.[67]

But there is more than that in the answer. The verb *tu*, "to ferry," which I am translating "to transport" because a bridge is the subject, is also the verb used in the Bodhisattva vow, "However innumerable sentient beings are I vow to ferry them all across [from "this shore," or *Samsāra*, to the "other shore," *Nirvana*]." Chao-chou says that his bridge "ferries asses, ferries horses." But on another level the verb used can add a shade of meaning: not only does it welcome both kinds, it (that is, the teacher Chao-chou) liberates them from *Samsāra*.

Wu-cho significantly leaves behind the verb of Wan-an's question, "to permit to enter," and changes to the verb "*tu*," "to ferry," placing herself in line with the Bodhisattva teaching activity of Chao-chou and Vasumitrā.

Wu-cho might simply have echoed Chao-chou's statement. Because the reference is her body, her answer would then have been, "I use my body, my sexual parts, to ferry all to the other shore of *Nirvana*." But to have taken that route would have stayed within the dualistic choice posed by the question. And it would have failed to challenge Wan-an back. Instead, she says, "Yes and no, depending on who you are." "With my body, like Vasumitrā, I ferry some to the other shore—providing they are horses, not asses." Thus she avoids the dualistic yes-or-no terms established by the question and puts Wan-an in the dilemma of having to avoid the dualism of having to say whether he is a horse or an ass.

Can he come up with a reply that shows his thinking is not being defined by that dilemma? His failure to do so suggests that his mind is not only not free, it is perhaps more specifically not free of passion, or of the idea that passion is bad and dispassion is good, or of defining women in terms of passion. One or more of these failures caused him to challenge Ta-hui's lodging of Wu-cho in his own quarters.

For Wu-cho's part, she portrays herself as Vasumitrā portrays herself, a sexually active woman, entrance into whose body can ferry a man to dispassion or *Nirvana*. In what could be a reference to the story of Vasumitrā's unusual method of teaching, she makes explicit reference to the idea that sexual embrace with her "saves" beings. Except for one major change—because the whole conversation is a contest in which he is challenging her and she is challenging him, she makes it clear that he cannot gain access to that body without winning the contest by showing that he is such a person already (unless, of course, *she* is not such a person already, in which case he might win even if he were not such a person; but in that case embrace with her would not liberate). So although she says her body is a bridge that allows horses to cross, in fact the verbal contest rather than her body becomes the liberating agent. In this regard, though she is casting herself as similar to Vasumitrā, she is also different from Vasumitrā.

Whether or not Wan-an learns "ultimate dispassion" from Wu-cho, who like Vasumitrā provides access to her beauty but unlike Vasumitrā refuses access to her person, Wan-an does come into the room seeing Wu-cho one way, as a female identified with sex, and leave seeing her in another, as a person more enlightened than he.[68] Perhaps in his final exchange with Ta-hui, Wan-an is also rebuked, as those who do not know Vasumitrā well would be, for his attachment to his monkish moralistic view of the female and her sexuality.[69]

PRAISE OF ENLIGHTENED WOMEN AS BODHISATTVAS AND BUDDHAS

A small number of records exist that show enlightened women of Sung dynasty Ch'an receiving praise for their accomplishment from their teachers. One instance is the following poem that Ta-hui Tsung-kao composed to honor his lay woman student who had attained enlightenment, Lady Ch'in-kuo. The occasion was her sponsorship of a meal for Ta-hui's monastery on her birthday, apparently not long after her enlightenment. Ta-hui told the assembled monastics and guests the story of how she had come to enlightenment and then offered this poem of praise:

Ta-hui's Praise of Lady Ch'in-kuo

Among womankind there is a great hero.
Manifesting her present form, she transforms her kind.
By means of precepts, *samādhi,* and wisdom, the liberating dharmas,
She pacifies greed, hatred and delusion;
Wherever she may be in their midst she does Buddha-deeds
As wind blows through the empty sky, depending on nothing.

The various Buddhas and Bodhisattvas,
Numerous as the Ganges river's sands,
With different mouths but the same refrain
They utter this speech:
"Excellent, extraordinary, rarely to be found in the world!"

Her mind is clean and pure, without distress or joy,
She does not even think of being without distress or joy.
Encountering a stage she puts on a play, suiting the worldly conditions,
But without becoming attached to any worldly condition.

In the sixth month clouds of fire burned the blue sky;
The sound of thunder suddenly shook the three thousand worlds.
The hot and vexatious are refined away, leaving the cool and pure.

This is that great hero's birthday celebration.
I compose this poem to add to its brilliance,
And present it as a gift to all the women in the universe.[70]

Had we read this poem without any knowledge of how Buddhas and Bodhisattvas are described in the sutras, its description of Lady Ch'in-kuo might have seemed ill-suited to a woman who had attained enlightenment in her old age and still remained quietly at home, not becoming a teacher or a nun.[71] But this is a poem in which a Ch'an master recognizes that the deep awakening experienced by his successful woman student means that now to be seen rightly she must be seen as a Buddha or an advanced Bodhisattva. This view is consistent with the claims members of the Ch'an lineage made for the transmission of the mind of enlightenment within their lineage: that it made a person as fully awakened as the Buddhas. This poem tells its hearers and readers that Lady Ch'in-kuo is, as a result of her enlightenment using a Ch'an meditational device, now detached and free within the *Dharmadhātu*, and showing herself master of its transformations.[72]

The stories and rhetoric used to describe and praise female Buddhas and Bodhisattvas in the sutras make it possible for twelfth-century Chinese Buddhist listeners to accept such a description of a woman contemporary. Lady Ch'in-kuo lived in a social world where women had very limited power or agency outside the domestic sphere. The sutra stories about and the sutra poems in praise of female Bodhisattvas were among the very few culturally available discourses on which Ta-hui could draw to enable his hearers to come to see Lady Ch'in-kuo or his other enlightened women students as manifesting in the world the wisdom, freedom, and authority of the awakened mind.

To make this point even clearer, I would like to present a note on the way the Bodhisattva and the *Dharmadhātu* are described in the *Gaṇḍavyūha*. Then I would like to offer from within that sutra a poem of praise by Sudhana to a night Goddess, which, though more complete as a praise of a Bodhisattva, is useful for purposes of comparison with Ta-hui's poem.

A Note on the Dharmadhatu and the Bodhisattva

In his article "The Bodhisattva as Wonder-Worker," Luis O. Gomez offers a nuanced and detailed exposition of the concept of the *Dharmadhātu* as adumbrated in the *Gaṇḍavyūha*, a concept he sees as drawing together into a single whole a number of fundamental doctrines in Mahayana Buddhism. Their relevance to the way in which Lady

Ch'in-kuo's newly enlightened state is described by Ta-hui will, I believe, immediately become clear. The Gaṇḍavyūha sees the world as "pure appearance, empty, and, as such, [as] like empty space." Enlightenment, which consists, as does the absolute, "in the fact and actuality of detachment," "consists in traversing this emptiness as birds glide through the sky, clinging to nothing, leaving no trace upon the essentially pure firmament."[73] "'As birds do not leave a path in space, thus do Bodhisattvas awaken to the true nature of Awakening. The sky is said to be ungraspable, in it there is nothing to grasp. This is the true nature of *dharmas,* ungraspable like the sky.'"[74] The realization, acceptance and mastery of this very ungraspability is enlightenment, perfect freedom.

> "The ontological equivalent for the empty space of the simile, the sphere of action for the Bodhisattva's wonder-working (that is to say, his conduct aimed at enlightenment and the salvation of all living beings) is [what is] called the *Dharmadhātu.*"[75]
>
> "The *Dharmadhātu's* original purity corresponds to the Bodhisattva's pure mind, which discerns illusion from reality, yet patiently conforms to the former. The *Dharmadhātu* . . . is the whole range of the Bodhisattva's knowledge and skill as a wonder-worker (in this sense the Bodhisattva, though one with the *Dharmadhātu,* works *within* the *Dharmadhātu*). The difference between the Bodhisattva and the common wonder-worker is two-fold: (1) his [or her] magical creations are not merely apparitions within the 'reality' of our everyday world, rather they are that very reality as manifested to the enlightened, therefore, ultimately one with the *Dharmadhātu.* (2) [Her or] his creations, though conforming to the delusion of her audience, are presented in order to reveal the true nature of the delusion, unlike the magician who rests content with the success of his deception.[76]

Lady Ch'in-kuo too is described in the poem as doing Buddha-deeds wherever she may be, "as wind blows through the empty sky, depending on nothing." The Bodhisattva's pure mind, we are told, discerns the difference between illusion and reality yet conforms to illusion for the sake of beings. Of Lady Ch'in-kuo it is said, "Encountering a stage she puts on a play, suiting the worldly conditions, but not becoming attached to any worldly conditions." And like the Bodhisattva, she is a wonder-worker. She is not to be identified with her present female form, in which she chooses to be revealed for the sake of transforming (that is, teaching or enlightening) her kind. She is in essence "a great hero," a Buddha or a Bodhisattva.[77]

SUDHANA'S PRAISE OF THE NIGHT GODDESS PRASANTARUTASAGARAVATI

Instructed by a spiritual benefactor,
I came to you, O Goddess;
I see you sitting on your seat
You whose body is of infinite height.

Those whose minds are on appearances,
Who cling to existence or conceptualize being,
And the low-minded with false views,
Cannot know this realm of yours.

No worldly or celestial beings can know
The features of your appearance and form,
Even if they were to observe you for endless eons—
So limitless is your form and hard to imagine.

You are free from dependence on the body-mind clusters [the *skhandhas*]
And you do not rest on the sense-media either;
Gone beyond the world for the sake of sentient beings,
You display in the world all varieties of magical powers.

You have attained immovability, faultless and unattached,
You have clarified the eye of highest wisdom;
In every atom you see as many Buddhas as all atoms
Magically transforming.

Your body is the storehouse of truth,
Your mind is made of wisdom unhindered.
Illumined by wisdom's light,
You illumine all beings.

You produce endless deeds from the mind,
So all worlds are adorned by your deeds;
Knowing that worlds are mental in nature,
You manifest yourself in bodies
Equal to beings.

Knowing this world is like a dream
And all Buddhas are like reflections
And all phenomena like echoes, empty,
You follow your mind and appear everywhere.

In each moment you show yourself
To the beings of past, present and future,
Yet there is no inclination to dualism in your mind,
And thus do you expound the Teaching in all realms.[78]

CONCLUSION

By pursuing these clues of the relation between sutra stories and Ch'an stories, what have we been enabled to see more clearly about how enlightened women have been evaluated and appreciated in Ch'an Buddhism? The story of the *nāga* princess and stories about other changers of form have provided the men in the tradition a rhetoric and a cosmology, an ideology of gender difference, with which to challenge women to prove their claim to enlightenment. But the tradition has recorded stories in which women have succeeded by invoking their profound understanding of the emptiness of forms and denying any need to change their form. They have had the model and support provided by sutra stories like that of the Goddess of the *Vimalakīrti Nirdeśa*. The *Lotus Sutra* story of the *nāga* girl is used to cut both ways.

We have seen that the tradition can tell a story that affirms that a woman who is a sexual being—sexually active like Vasumitrā or in a sexually active status like Wu-cho—can nonetheless be enlightened herself and can enlighten others. She can even use her sexual attractiveness and the propensity of men like Wan-an to see her as exclusively a sexual being as a powerful teaching situation. The story suggests that even though she is not a man or a monk but rather a woman, she need not be identified with or attached to sex. (This is particularly striking in the Sung Chinese social context, in which all but one of the roles for women were closely tied to marriage, sexuality, and reproduction, and in which the meaning of a woman's life was seen as lying in her reproductive success.) At the same time we have seen that the tradition tells stories that suggest that devaluing passion and valuing purity is not the route to ultimate dispassion. Both the Vasumitrā story and the story of Wu-cho suggest that the dualistic thinking that categorizes sex as wrong is profoundly unenlightened.

Finally, we have seen that an enlightened woman like Lady Ch'in-kuo can be praised as free in perfect purity and detachment, yet carrying out the activity appropriate to advanced Bodhisattvas, transforming others into Buddhas in the *Dharmadhātu*. That is to say, she can be evaluated very highly. And the evaluation is made plausible because enlightened female Bodhisattvas are so praised and evaluated in the sutra's Goddess tradition.

NOTES

1. I follow John McRae here, who locates the beginning of Ch'an in the seventh century communities of Tao-hsin (580–651 C.E.) and Hung-jen (574–674). (McRae, "The Story of Early Ch'an," 130–32). The distinctive teaching style that characterizes the Ch'an that has flourished throughout Asia apparently emerged under Ma-tsu in the eighth century.

2. Cf. the *Mahāprajñāpāramitā śastra* (Ch. *Ta-chih-tu-lun*), *chüan* 2, and Chan-jan, *Chih-kuan pu-hsing chüan hung chüeh, chüan* 2, section 2, T. vol. 46, 196a.

3. Although both the Buddhist tradition and Sung government prescribed safeguards against close contact between monks and nuns, in Sung China some monastic institutions for monks where Ch'an was taught apparently had a dormitory for nuns. See, for example, the sketch in the *Gozan jissatsu zu* of the groundplan of the monastic compound of the Ching-te Temple on Mt. T'ien-t'ung, which was made in the early thirteenth century and preserved in Japan. The Ching-te temple on Mt. T'ien-t'ung had been exclusively headed by abbots of the Ch'an lineage since 1007 (Mochizuki, *Bukkyō Daijiten*, vol. 4, 3812c). According to this groundplan, the monastery includes a *ni-liao*, a dormitory for nuns. The *Gozan jissatsu zu*, in two *chüan*, is preserved in the Daijō Temple in Kanazawa, Japan. A photograph of this plan from this text is found in *Zengaku Daijiten* (hereafter *ZGDJ*), vol. 3, 12. Another monastery plan with a nuns' dormitory is that of the Wan-nien Monastery on Mt. T'ien-t'ai (*ZGDJ* 3, 13). (Contra Foulk, "Myth, Ritual, and Monastic Practice," 167, the Wan-nien Monastery was headed by a Ch'an teacher in the thirteenth century at the time of Dogen's visit there, as reported in his *Hōkyōki*. Thus it probably was a Ch'an monastery at the time the sketch of the groundplan included in the *Gozan jissatsu zu* was made in the thirteenth century. Thus Foulk's argument that the layout and buildings of T'ien-t'ai monasteries looked just like that of Ch'an monasteries at this time will have to rest on other evidence.) In addition, our stories tell us of nuns and laywomen who studied for extended periods with Ch'an masters at Sung Ch'an monasteries for extended periods of time as personal disciples of the master who could "enter his room" for individual instruction. Where they stayed overnight we cannot tell from the stories, except in the case of the story of Wu-cho given below.

4. The main image might also be Vairoçana. On the subject of this paragraph, see the important essay by Foulk, "Myth, Ritual and Monastic Practice." On the subject of what Buddhas, Bodhisattvas, Deities, and lineage ancestors were enshrined or given offerings in the Sung Ch'an monasteries, see esp. pages 169–72.

5. Foulk, "Myth, Ritual, and Monastic Practice," 183.

6. Foulk, "Myth, Ritual, and Monastic Practice," 186. On the presence of Kuan-yin images in the monasteries: There are three architectural sketches related to common quarters in Sung Ch'an monasteries in the thirteenth century preserved in the *Gozan jissatsu zu* (reproduced in *ZGDJ*, 10, 11, and 23). Two contain the words "[Bodhisattva] Mahāsattva Kuan-yin (Kuan-yin Ta-shih)" in a location that suggests an image was present. The third, at Gold Mountain, contains a sketch that might be of Kuan-yin in a relaxed pose.

7. Foulk, "Myth, Ritual, and Monastic Practice," 170. One of the *Gozan jissatsu*

zu sketches shows a Kuan-yin Pavillion as part of the monastery compound at Ching-te ssu at Mt. T'ien-t'ung (*ZGDJ*, 12).

8. Cf. *ZGDJ*, vol. 3, 24. Masculine images of Kuan-yin by no means disappeared or lost favor in the Sung: a case in point is Su Shih (Tung-p'o)'s account of the circumstances surrounding the construction of the Pavilion of the Great Compassionate [One] in Ch'eng-tu and the accompanying hymn describing the image, a Thousand-Armed Thousand-Eyed Kuan-yin. Nothing in this hymn indicates that this image had any feminine associations for him (Grant, *Mount Lu Revisited*, 86–90).

9. On the feminized or feminine forms of Kuan-yin that appeared in the Sung in elite paintings that might have found a place in the Sung dynasty monasteries, and the popular noncanonical stories and pilgrimages that they probably reflect, see Yü, "Guan-yin," 151–81, and Stein "Avalokiteśvara." Mu-ch'i's famous thirteenth-century large painting of Kuan-yin in a white robe in the Daitokuji triptych seems to me to be a feminized, but not completely feminine image. There is certainly a good chance not only that it played some role in monastic life in Lin-an (Hang-chou) in the thirteenth century but that it responded to an already established interest in a somewhat feminized Kuan-yin in elite society since the Northern Sung and especially in Lin-an, where we know that stories were told in the Sung about Kuan-yin appearing in female form (Cf. Grant, *Mount Lu Revisited*, 60, Stein, "Avalokiteśvara," 22–23; Yü "Guan-yin," 171) and where at least at the Upper T'ien-chu Monastery Kuan-yin was worshiped in female form (cf. Yü, "Guan-yin," 171). (For a reproduction of the Mu-ch'i painting, see Hisamatsu, *Zen and the Fine Arts*, plate 60, 166. Cf. Fontein and Hickman, *Zen Painting*, 28–32, for a good discussion of Mu-ch'i's life.) Likewise, images of the white-robed Kuan-yin by the T'ang artist Wu Tao-tzu were popular in the southern Sung at the time of these stories, and the important northern Sung painter Li Kung-lin is said to have painted the white-robed Kuan-yin. (Cf. Amy McNair in Weidner, *Latter Days*, 244, on the existence in the Sung of Wu Tao-tzu Kuan-yins.) Judging by a later copy reproduced in Weidner, *Latter Days*, 243, Wu Tao-tzu's image could have been at least somewhat feminized. Fontein and Hickman also include an unsigned thirteenth century painting of water and moon Kuan-yin looking at least somewhat feminized or ambiguous, that is thought to be a copy of a twelfth-century Chinese original (Fontein and Hickman, *Zen Painting*, 48). A clearly feminine image to my eye is the Water and Moon Kuan-yin in the Nelson-Atkins Museum, published in Weidner plate 21, which is dated to the Sung or Yüan dynasties. (I would say that the fourteenth-century white-robed Kannon by the Japanese artist Ryōzen included in Fontein and Hickman, *Zen Painting*, 80, unlike the earlier ones discussed above, could not have been read as anything but a feminine image.) This whole subject of when images of Kuan-yin began to be feminine is a vexed one, though many would say the tenth or eleventh centuries. Part of the problem is that the dress, jewels, headdres, and other iconography of the feminine-appearing Kuan-yin images are not exclusively feminine, so that much depends on the eye of the beholder. And there is very little textual evidence on how the Five Dynasties or Sung dynasty beholder read the gender of the images that appear feminine or ambiguously feminine to the modern viewer.

10. This is reproduced in *ZGDJ*, vol. 3, 28. On this subject see Foulk, "Myth,

Ritual, and Monastic Practice," 172–76, and Jorgenson, "The Imperial Lines," 109–11. Also see Foulk, Horton, and Sharf, "The Meaning and Function."

11. Cf. Foulk, "Myth, Ritual, and Monastic Practice," 176–77.

12. These historical findings are summarized in part in Levering, "Enlightened Women"; for full details see my book entitled *The Zen of Women*.

13. One should not forget, of course, that men and women might hear these stories quite differently.

14. I cannot in the scope of this paper provide the detailed information about women's place in the social world of tenth-, eleventh-, and twelfth-century China that would place the stories I am about to discuss in their full context. Please see my forthcoming book. It will have to suffice for the moment to say that although Sung dynasty elite women seem to have been somewhat less restricted in their actions than their counterparts in late imperial China and could even under some circumstances dispose of property, women studying anywhere but in the home and women acting as teachers or heading institutions were all unheard of outside the monastic institutions of Buddhism and Taoism. For a book-length study of marriage and the lives of women in the Sung period, see Ebrey, *The Inner Quarters*.

15. I am not claiming that any of these female figures in the scriptures were worshiped by the Ch'an women; we do not know whether that happened or not.

16. I am using the term "intertextuality" very loosely here, I am afraid. I seem to be using it to mean three different things.

In the case of all the stories that challenge women to change their form from female to male, the parallels seem to me to be so striking and consistent that one cannot imagine a later author setting down his tale in ignorance of the earlier stories, including the earlier sutra stories. The sutra stories are not simply alluded to: they provide the structure, the tone, even some of the dialogue.

In the case of the Ch'an and Zen stories that are similar to that of Wu-cho given below, later ones parallel earlier ones in a striking way in structure, tone, dialogue. The parallels between the Ch'an stories and the sutra story of Vasumitrā are not so tight—one can imagine the Wu-cho story developing without the Vasumitrā story in the background. Here perhaps it would be better to speak of the Vasumitrā story as being in the background, forming the hearer of the story rather than the story itself.

Yet another kind of similarity obtains in the final case, the poem praising Lady Ch'in-kuo. Here the concept and imagery of this poem is clearly largely taken from that of poems of praise in the sutras. One cannot imagine that Ta-hui could have developed this poem without knowledge of the body of similar sutra poems. What we cannot argue, of course, is that Ta-hui modeled his poem on a specific sutra poem, or that he had a specific sutra praise poem in mind as he composed his poem.

17. In her essay included in this volume, Rita Gross writes: "Though Saṃbhogakāya Buddhas and Bodhisattvas look like Deities, they are non-theistic or mythic. Inherent existence would never be attributed to them, for they arise out of the emptiness of *Dharmakāya* and return to that emptiness." (cf. 412) I agree completely with her characterization of the Buddhas and Bodhisattvas in the sutra stories—the degree to which they are identified with *Dharmakāya* or *Dharmadhātu* and thus are ontologically "empty" is evident in the sutra stories I will

narrate below. But to my mind it is that very identification with *Dharmakāya* or *Dharmadhātu* that makes them in an important respect like Goddesses, even though they may not be conceived in exactly the same way as theistic Deities. A tougher objection for my position to answer would be that though presented as female, these Bodhisattvas and Buddhas are not "essentially" female, though they may have begun their Bodhisattva path as females, have been repeatedly reborn as females, and are now choosing to manifest female form. And the message, as we will see below, is that their human counterparts are also not "essentially" female. All are empty of any essentialistic, deterministic gender. I still would argue that their representation as female in the sutras is a powerful representation that might affect Buddhist women in ways that female representations of the divine might do in other traditions. Their lack of "essential" femaleness only improves them as female "Deities" from the postmodern point of view!

18. In the Ch'an school an enlightened woman who became a teacher may have been, like an enlightened man, ritually treated as a Buddha and considered at the very least an advanced Bodhisattva, but we do not know for sure. Likewise the texts do not make totally clear whether a women, when enlightened and a dharma heir, was ever referred to with the term "Buddha," as masters who were men were.

19. See the discussion in Hurvitz, *Scripture*, xix–xx.

20. Paul, *Women*, 215 n. 40.

21. Levering, "The Dragon Girl."

22. This story is found in *Yün-chou Ta-yü Chih Ho-shang yü-lu*, in *Ku-tsun-su yü-lu*, *chüan* 25, *Dainihon Zoku Daizōkyō* (hereafter "*Zokuzōkyō*") no. 1315, vol. 68, 165c–166a; also in a slightly different version in the *Ching-te ch'üan-teng lu*, *chüan* 12. This is a translation of the *Yün-chou Ta-yü Chih Ho-shang yü-lu* version; I translated the *Ching-te ch'üan-teng-lu* version in Levering, "The Dragon Girl."

23. Paul, *Women* 185.

24. Paul, *Women* 185.

25. Cf. Schafer, *The Divine Woman*.

26. Schuster, "Changing the Female Body," points out that there is an assumption common to Indian thought that the attainment of extraordinary levels of understanding of reality naturally entail the attainment of extraordinary powers. On these powers as discussed in the *Visudhimagga*, see the discussion in Schuster; Gomez, "The Bodhisattva"; and Buddhaghosa, *The Path of Purification*, 414–20.

27. Gomez, "The Bodhisattva," 230; I have deleted some Sanskrit terms.

28. Gomez, "The Bodhisattva," 230; I have deleted some Sanskrit terms.

29. Schuster, "Changing the Female Body," 59.

30. Schuster, "Changing the Female Body"; Barnes, "Buddhism"; Paul, *Women*; Levering, "The Dragon Girl."

31. Paul, *Women*, 186–87.

32. Paul, *Women*, 171–73.

33. Paul, *Women*, 175.

34. There are a number of versions of the *Lotus Sutra* in Chinese, as well as a text in Sanskrit. Because the nun in my Ch'an story would probably have known the story as it appears in the text that circulates as Kumarajiva's translation into Chinese, I will present a synopsis of that version, in the English

translation by Leon Hurvitz. I have made Hurvitz's translation slightly more "reader friendly."

35. Hurvitz, *Scripture*, 199–201.

36. On fox spirits, see Huntington, "Tigers, Foxes and the Margins."

37. A Chinese translation of the *Vimalakīrti Nirdeśa* is found in *Taishō* vol. 14; I am using here Robert Thurman's translation, *The Holy Teaching*, beginning on p. 58.

38. Cf. Ch'en, *The Chinese Transformation*, 253.

39. Cf. Grant, *Mount Lu Revisited*, 45–49 and *passim*. See also the colophon in Weidner, *Latter Days*, 349–51, in which a number of Su's poems are quoted.

40. Murray, "Evolution," 147 n. 52. see Bunker, "Early Chinese," and Ho, "The Perpetuation." Note that Su Shih wrote in response to a portrait of Vimalakīrti by Shih K'o (Grant, *Mount Lu Revisited*, 47).

41. Cf. Murray, "Evolution," 137, and Fong, *Beyond Representation*, 330–33.

42. Weidner, *Latter Days*, 353, in the catalog entry for the 1308 painting "Vimalakīrti and the Doctrine of Non-duality" by Wang Chen-p'eng. The colophon by the artist on this painting tells the story of the Goddess's scattering flowers that stick to Śāriputra and not to the Bodhisattvas and her explanation to Śāriputra that "it must be because you have not renounced your mundane desire that the flowers cling to your body." (This is no doubt the part of the story that would be easy to illustrate!) The colophon is translated in full by P'an An-yi in this catalog entry, pp. 349–51. In an early twelfth-century frontispiece made in the Da-li kingdom in present-day Yunnan Province, "the Goddess is portrayed as a key figure, on a par with Mañjuśrī, while Śāriputra is reduced to a subservient role" (Karen Mack in Weidner, *Latter Days*, 299).

43. One story that could be included in this group is the story of Mr. Ma's Wife. A Sung work called *Tsung-lin sheng-shih* says, "The Painting called 'Bodhisattva of the Golden Sand Beach' has an Indian monk carrying a staff with a skeleton on his shoulder while looking back at Mr. Ma's Wife behind him. There are many eulogies on this painting. But the best is written by Ssu-ming Tao-ch'uan nicknamed Ta-t'ung. It goes like this: 'She looks at everyone equally with compassion. She entices people to her with desire. One uses a wedge to knock out another wedge and fights one type of poison with another type of poison. While the thirty-two [manifestations in] response [to the needs of beings to be ferried to Nirvana by certain types of beings as teachers] [by Kuan-yin] are found in completion in the Universal Gate chapter [of the *Lotus Sutra*], this one steals the eyes of a thousand sages (that is, is the most impressive of all)'" (*Zokuzōkyō*, vol. 148, 45b). I have not identified this monk. There are several monks named Tao-ch'üan but none in Suzuki's index named Ssu-ming Tao-ch'uan. This passage is also translated by Yü somewhat differently ("Guan-yin," 179 n. 32) though I think our translations agree on the overall meaning. On Mr. Ma's wife, see Sawada, "Yuiran Kannon," 37–43; Stein, "Avalokiteśvara," 54–57; and Yü, "Guan-yin," 166–69. Stein cuts off the verse after "P'u-men chu tzu."

44. The Head Monk was second in command to Ta-hui with respect to the training of the monks.

45.*Wu-chia cheng-tsung tsan, chüan* 2, *Zokuzōkyō* 2b, 8, 475a-b. This story is given as *kōan* #51 in a Japanese text of 1545, the *Shōnan kattōroku*, which Trevor

Leggett has translated as *The Warrior Koans;* this story is on pp. 106–107 of his translation. The text says that this story is taken from the *Wu-chia cheng-tsung-tsan,* [which was printed in Japan in 1349], became a *kōan* used by the Japanese nun teacher *Shōtaku,* who became the third teacher at the famous nunnery Tokeiji. I have consulted Leggett's translation in producing my own.

46. Leggett, *The Warrior Koans,* 109.

47. With regard to Ta-hui's reputation, we should note that the events that are narrated in the story are not otherwise attested, and, if they did take place, would have occurred in the twelfth century (probably around 1140), a hundred years earlier than the text in which they are found.

48. *The Avataṃsaka sutra,* including the *Gaṇḍavyūha* as its last chapter was translated twice in China—first between 418 and 421 C.E. by Buddhabhadra in 60 *chüan,* then in 699 C.E. in 80 *chüan* by a team led by Śikṣānanda. In both cases the Sanskrit manuscripts were imported from Khotan. Between 796–98 C.E. a monk named Prajñā translated the *Gaṇḍavyūha* only in 40 *chüan* from a manuscript presented to the Chinese emperor by the king of Orissa. A Sanskrit text exists today.

49. It has been suggested that we only have part of the text and that the original plan was to have 108 teachers. Cf. Frances Wilson in Paul, *Women,* 96.

50. See Levering, "Ch'an Enlightenment."

51. See Fontein, *The Pilgrimage,* 24.

52. Fontein, *The Pilgrimage,* 76. The column is now in the Honolulu Academy of Arts. All of the surviving Chinese illustrations are discussed by Fontein in detail on pp. 23–77.

53. A complete but not scholarly translation of this text from Chinese into English exists now (see Thomas Cleary, *Entry;* see my review in *Parabola,* 1990). This translation is readable and engaging but not reliable as a faithful translation of any of the extant Chinese versions. Therefore, in the passages translated below, I have begun with Cleary's versions but have changed them substantially to render them faithful to either the 40 *chüan* or the 80 *chüan* Chinese texts. It is unfortunate that Cleary's version is not more reliable for scholarly purposes. Frances Wilson has published translations of the sections of the Sanskrit *Gaṇḍavyūha* relating to the nun, the laywomen Āśā and Prabhūtā, and the Bhāgāvatī Vasumitrā in Paul, *Women.* Because the Chinese Ch'an communities that are the subject of this essay would not have had access to any Sanskrit version, I felt it necessary to make translations from the Chinese versions that they would have known.

54. Āśā, wife of King Suprabha (T.10.693); also Prabhūtā (T.10.706); also Bhadrottamā (T.10.805).

55. Maitrāyaṇī (T.10.701) and Acalā (T.10.722).

56. Cf. Wilson in Paul, *Women,* 95–96; 136–37.

57. This is Prabhūtā, who satisfies sentient beings with food, and of whom it is said that all who saw her, whether human or celestial beings, thought of her as a teacher (T.10.706).

58. *Ta-fang-kuang, fo-hua-yen-ching, chüan 68, Taishō* 10.279.368c.4–12. [Śikṣānanda translation in 80 *chüan.*]

59. Why then do the authors of the sutra have some Bodhisattvas take birth as Goddesses? Their number and prominence in the sutra, where they out-

number Gods 11 to 1, suggests that Buddhist communities in India participated in the great wave of enthusiasm for Goddesses that swept over India at the time. Thus Goddesses made up a rather large part of the imagined cosmos in which Buddhist communities functioned, and were thus incorporated into the Buddhist cosmos. Because the sutra sets out to describe the cosmos as essentially the field of activity of the Bodhisattva (the *Dharmadhātu*), all elements of the cosmos must be shown to be areas in which Bodhisattvas carry out distinct parts of their multiform activities. Another reason might be an actual valuing of the feminine contribution in the universe of manifestations represented by the Goddesses.

60. *Ta-fang-kuang fo-hua-yen-ching, chüan* 15, *Prajñā* trans. in 40 *chüan, Taishō* 293.10.731b.8–9.

61. F. Wilson, in Paul, *Women,* 159. It is also interesting that the two Chinese representations of this scene published in Fontein, *Zen Painting*, plates 26a and 26b, following p. 68—a woodcarving on a "Pilgrimage Column" owned by the Honolulu Academy of Arts, which may date from the thirteenth century (end of Sung or beginning of the Yüan) and the woodblock illustration in the book "*Wu-hsiang chih-shih sung*," a work which may be from the eleventh century (northern Sung dynasty)—show her robe as opaque.

62. *Ta-fang-kuang fo-hua-yen-ching, chüan* 68, Śikṣānanda trans. in 80 *chüan, Taishō* 10.279.365a–366a.

63. It is a significant point that with only one exception, all of the female teachers whom Sudhana meets were also female when they first became Bodhisattvas, that is, in the "how it all started in my former birth" stories narrated in the sutra.

64. Wu-cho's "this is the place from which all Buddhas, patriarchs and esteemed monks come" reminds me, as it might other readers of the *Gaṇḍavyūha* of the figure of Māyā, mother of Śākyamuni Buddha and all other Buddhas; and of Prajñāpāramitā, the Perfection of Wisdom, who is also called "mother of all the Buddhas" in the *Prajñāpāramitā* sutras.

65. Wu-cho is referring here to a famous *kōan* found in the record of Yun-men Wen-yen (864–949): "Someone asked: 'What is the place from which all the Buddhas come?' Master Yun-men said, '[Where] the East Mountains walk on the river.'" Cf. App, *Master Yunmen*, 94. App comments: "A key to this exchange may lie in a poem by Buddhist layman Fu Dashi: [Where] the East Mountains float on the river and the West Mountains wander on and on, in the realm [of this world?] beneath the Great Dipper: just there is the place of genuine emancipation."

66. Omori, et al., "Hekiganroku," in *Zenkegoroku* II, 263. This version is given in the *Blue Cliff Record* of 1128 and later in the *Record of Chao-chou* (*Chao-chou lu*).

67. Cf. Hoffmann, *Radical Zen*, 106. The story is included in the *Ching-te ch'üan-teng lu* of 1004 and the *Pi-yen-lu* (*Blue Cliff Record*) of 1128. Both were texts that were well known in Wu-cho's and Wan-an's time. The English translation from the *Ching-te ch'üan-teng lu* of 1004 by Chang Chung-yuan in *Original Teachings of Ch'an Buddhism*, 170, reads: "What is the Chao-chou bridge? The Master said, "'Horses pass over it, donkeys pass over it.'" But the *CTCTL*, Chen-shan-mei edition, *chüan* 10, 179, and all subsequent texts that include the story have: *Ju-ho shih chao-chou ch'iao*? *Shih yun*: *tu-lu tu-ma*. Thus: "ferry asses, ferry horses." The unnamed subject and agent is the bridge, which ferries or transports asses and horses.

68. Note that she has met an outrage with an outrage and succeeded in disarming it. It was surely an outrage on Wan-an's part to suggest that Ta-hui and Wu-cho were committing improprieties or transgressions of monastic rules. Wu-cho meets this outrage with another outrage—she presents herself naked to Wan-an.

69. Another possible reading would be that Ta-hui's defense of his behavior is not that he is not having sex with Wu-cho in violation of the rules but that because Wu-cho like himself is enlightened the rules have ceased to apply. Either sex is a different matter once one has become enlightened, or it ceases to be an obstacle to religious self-mastery.

70. *Ta-hui p'u-chüeh Ch'an-shih yü-lu* (T.47.872c).

71. I myself made this mistake earlier; see Levering, "Enlightened Women," where I wrote disparagingly about the rhetorical effect of this poem.

72. A second piece of evidence that Ta-hui sees Lady Ch'in-kuo as a Bodhisattva is found in another sermon about her, this time a memorial sermon after her death, in which he compares her to the Bodhisattva Avalokiteśvara (Kuan-yin), and closes with a question to his audience of Ch'an students: "Are Lady Ch'in-kuo and Avalokiteśvara the same or different?" *Ta-hui P'u-chüeh Ch'an-shih p'u-shuo* (in 4 *chüan*), *Zokuzōkyō* 2, 31, 5, p 416a.

73. Gomez, "The Bodhisattva," 225.

74. *Samādhiraja*, quoted in Gomez, "The Bodhisattva," 225–26.

75. Gomez, "The Bodhisattva," 227.

76. Gomez, "The Bodhisattva," 229.

77. On the term "great hero" as used in the Ch'an tradition, see Levering "Lin-chi Ch'an."

78. Gomez translates half of this poem from the Sanskrit text into English, "The Bodhisattva," 232. Cleary translates the whole poem, *Entry*, 213–15, sticking for the most part to the Śiksānanda translation in the 80 *chüan* version, but putting in a couple of lines that are found only in the Prajñā translation in 40 *chüan*. What follows is Cleary's version with substantial changes. I have followed Cleary's practice of blending the two versions, a practice I did not follow in the other translations from the *Gaṇḍavyūha* above. The reason is that in this case Śikṣānanda's version uses a shorter line and thus omits some details preserved in *Prajñā's* version that I would like to include.

WORKS CITED

App, Urs. *Master Yunmen*. New York: Kodansha International, 1994.

Barnes, Nancy Schuster. "Buddhism." Pp. 105–33 in *Women in World Religions*, edited by Arvind Sharma. Albany, N.Y.: State University of New York Press, 1987.

Buddhaghosa. *The Path of Purification*. Translated by Bhikkhu Nyanamoli. Berkeley, Calif.: Shambala, 1976.

Bunker, Emma. "Early Chinese Representations of Vimalakirti." *Artibus Asiae* 30 (1968): 28–52.

Chang Chung-yuan, trans. *Original Teachings of Ch'an Buddhism*. New

York: Vintage Books, 1971. (Selections from *Ching-te-ch'üan-teng-lu*, by Tao-yüan, 1004.)

Ch'en, Kenneth. *The Chinese Transformation of Buddhism*. Princeton: Princeton University Press, 1973.

Cleary, Thomas. *Entry into the Realm of Reality: The Text*. Boston and Shaftesbury: Shambala (Gandavyuha), 1989.

Ebrey, Patricia Buckley. *The Inner Quarters*. Berkeley, Calif.: University of California Press, 1993.

Fong, Wen. *Beyond Representation: Chinese Painting and Calligraphy, 8th-14th Century*. New York: Metropolitan Museum of Art; New Haven, Conn.: Yale University Press, 1992.

Fontein, Jan. *The Pilgrimage of Sudhana*. The Hague: Mouton, 1966.

Fontein, Jan, and Monty L. Hickman. *Zen Painting and Calligraphy*. Boston: Museum of Fine Arts, 1970.

Foulk, T. Griffith. "Myth, Ritual and Monastic Practice in Sung Ch'an Buddhism." Pp. 147–208 in *Religion and Society in T'ang and Sung China*, edited by Patricia Ebrey and Peter N. Gregory. Honolulu: University of Hawaii Press, 1993.

Foulk, T. Griffith, Elizabeth Horton, and Robert Sharf. "The Meaning and Function of Ch'an and Zen Portraiture," a paper given at the College Art Association annual meeting, February 17, 1990.

Gomez, Luis O. "The Bodhisattva as Wonder-worker." Pp. 221–61 in *Prajnapuramita and Related Systems: Studies in Honor of Edward Conze*, edited by Lewis R. Lancaster. Berkeley, Calif.: University of California Press, 1977.

Grant, Beata. *Mount Lu Revisted: Buddhism in the Life and Writings of Su Shih*. Honolulu: University of Hawaii Press, 1994.

Hisamatsu Shin'ichi. *Zen and the Fine Arts*. Tokyo and Palo Alto: Kodansha International Ltd, 1971.

Ho, Judy. "The Perpetuation of an Ancient Model." *Archives of Asian Art* 41 (1988): 32–46.

Hoffmann, Yoel. *Radical Zen*. Brookline, Mass.: Autumn Press, 1978.

Huntington, Rania. "Tigers, Foxes and the Margins of Humanity in Tang Chuanqi Fiction." Pp. 40–64 in *Papers on Chinese Literature* (vol. 1.) Cambridge, Mass.: Fairbank Center for East Asian Research, Harvard University, 1993.

Hurvitz, Leon. *Scripture of the Lotus Blossom of the Fine Dharma* (*The Lotus Sutra*). New York: Columbia University Press, 1976.

Jorgenson, John. "The 'Imperial' Lineage of Ch'an Buddhism; the Role of Confucian Ritual and Ancestor Worship in Ch'an's Search for Legitimation in the Mid-T'ang Dynasty." Pp. 89–133 in *Papers on Far*

Eastern History, no. 35. Canberra: The Australian National University, March, 1987.

Leggett, Trevor. *The Warrior Koans*. (A translation of the *Shonan kattoroku* of 1545 as reconstructed by Imai Fukuzan.) London and New York: Arkana (a division of Routledge & Kegan Paul), 1985.

Levering, Miriam L. "Ch'an Enlightenment for Laymen: Ta-hui and the New Religious Culture of the Sung." Ph.D. Diss., Harvard University, 1978.

———. "The Dragon Girl and the Abbess of Mo-shan: Gender and Status in the Ch'an Buddhist Tradition." *The Journal of the International Association of Buddhist Studies* 5, no. 1 (1982): 19–35.

———. "Enlightened Women in Ch'an Buddhism: A Preliminary Report on the Record." Unpublished manuscript, 1992.

———. "Lin-chi (Rinzai) Ch'an and Gender: The Rhetoric of Equality and the Rhetoric of Heroism." Pp. 137–56 in *Buddhism, Sexuality and Gender*, edited by Jose Ignacio Cabezon. Albany, N.Y.: State University of New York Press, 1992.

———. Review of Thomas Cleary, trans., *Entry into the Inconceivable* in *Parabola* 15.1 (1990), 133-39.

McRae, John R. "The Story of Early Ch'an." Pp. 125-39 in *Zen: Tradition and Transition*, edited by Kenneth Kraft. New York: Grove Press, 1988.

Mochizuki Shinko, ed. *Bukkyō Daijiten*. Tokyo: Bukkyō daijiten hakkōjo, 1931–36.

Murray, Julia K. "The Evolution of Buddhist Narrative Illustration in China after 850." Pp. 125–49 in *Latter Days of the Law: Images of Chinese Buddhism, 850-1850*, edited by M. Weidner. Spencer Museum of Art, University of Kansas; Honolulu: University of Hawaii Press, 1994.

Omori, Sogen, et al., trans. "Hekiganroku." In *Zenkegoroku II*, edited by Nishitani Keiji, and Yanagida Seizan. Tokyo: Chikuma Shobo, 1974.

Paul, Diana Y. *Women in Buddhism*. Berkeley, Calif.: Asian Humanities Press, 1979.

Sawada Mizuho. "Yuiran Kannon." *Tenri Daigaku gakuho*. 30 (1959): 37–51.

Schafer, Edward H. *The Divine Woman: Dragon Ladies and Rain Maidens in T'ang Literature*. Berkeley, Calif.: University of California Press, 1973.

Schuster, Nancy. "Changing the Female Body: Wise Women and the Bodhisattva Career in some *Maharatnakutasutras*." *The Journal of the International Association of Buddhist Studies* 4, no. 1 (1981): 24–69.

Stein, Rolf A. "Avalokitesvara/Kouan-yin, un exemple de transformation d'un dieu en déesse." *Cahiers d'Extreme Asie*, no. 2 (1986): 17–80.

Tao-yüan. *Ching-te-ch'üan-teng-lu.* Taipei: Chen-shan-mei ch'u-pan-she, 1967.

Thurman, Robert A. F., trans. *The Holy Teaching of Vimalakirti: A Mahayana Scripture.* University Park and London: The Pennsylvania State University Press, 1976.

Weidner, Marsha, ed. *Latter Days of the Law: Images of Chinese Buddhism, 850–1850.* Spencer Museum of Art, University of Kansas; Honolulu: University of Hawaii Press, 1994.

Yü Chun-fang. "Guan-yin: The Chinese Transformation of Avalokiteshvara." Pp. 151-81 in *Latter Days of the Law: Images of Chinese Buddhism, 850-1850*, edited by Marsha Weidner. Spencer Museum of Art, University of Kansas; Honolulu: University of Hawaii Press, 1994.

Zengaku Daijiten. Tokyo: Taishukan, 1978.

PART TWO

THE ANCIENT MEDITERRANEAN

7

SUSAN ACKERMAN

The Queen Mother and the Cult in the Ancient Near East

I

A search of the scholarly literature[1] reveals that one topic that has generated a steady stream of discussion among biblicists over the past forty years is the function of the queen mother or *gĕbîrâ* in ancient Israel.[2] Studies have primarily discussed what social and political role the queen mother might have played in the Israelite and Judaean monarchies, with most concluding that the queen mother had an official position as counselor in her son's court, her advice being sought especially in matters concerning the royal succession.[3] Relatively few scholars, however, have considered whether there might also have been a religious role within the state cult for the *gĕbîrâ*, and those who have addressed this issue either have rejected the notion that the queen mother could have had an official place within the state religion[4] or have proposed theories that have proven unconvincing to the scholarly community as a whole.[5] In a recent article,[6] however, I have proposed—in the light of archaeological discoveries of the past two decades and also in the light of revised exegeses of the biblical text—that we address the question of the *gĕbîrâ* and the cult anew. My conclusion there was that, contrary to the majority of commentators, the queen mother, especially in the Southern Kingdom of Judah did play an official role in Israelite *religion*: that role was to devote herself to the worship of the mother goddess Asherah.

Several pieces of evidence converged to support this conclusion. First, while the biblical texts rarely tell us anything about a queen mother other than her name, materials in Kings and Chronicles do hint that at least four queen mothers—Maᶜacah, queen mother of Abijam/Abijah[7] and also of Asa (1 Kgs 15:1-2, 9-10); Jezebel, queen mother of Ahaziah and Jehoram (1 Kgs 22:51; 2 Kgs 3:1; 10:13); Athaliah, queen mother of Ahaziah (2 Kgs 8:25-26); and Nehushta, queen mother of Jehoiachin (2 Kgs 24:8)—can be associated with the worship of Asherah. These queen mothers, however, in devoting themselves to the goddess Asherah, appear not to abandon the state religion of Yahwism. Rather, their children all bear Yahwistic names, and the cult object for Asherah that Ma^{c}acah is said to have built (1 Kgs 15:13) stood in all likelihood in Yahweh's temple in Jerusalem. Such evidence is consistent with the thesis that many scholars have proposed in the past fifteen years:[8] that Asherah could be worshiped side by side with Yahweh in ancient Israel and Judah, both as a part of the so-called popular religion[9] and as a part of the religion of state.[10] The queen mothers who worshiped Asherah, in short, may have done so concomitant with their official obligations to the Yahwistic cult.

Another piece of evidence crucial to my thesis was the fact, often noted by commentators, that the office of the queen mother was more important in the Southern Kingdom of Judah than it was in the Northern Kingdom of Israel. Archival notices in the books of Kings, for example, routinely preserve for us the names of Judaean queen mothers, whereas we know the name of only one Israelite queen mother, Jezebel. Jezebel, moreover, serves as queen and later queen mother in a court much more characterized by the southern model of dynastic kingship rather than by the "charismatic" monarchy that A. Alt has described for the north.[11]

My paper concluded by suggesting that if the office of the queen mother was a more typically southern institution, then, by inference, the queen mother's devotions to Asherah are to be associated more with the religious traditions of the south than with those of the north. I deemed this latter datum significant due to the well-known southern ideology of divine sonship, which regards the king in Jerusalem as the adopted son of Yahweh.[12] If the Judaean monarch is considered the adopted son of Yahweh, I argued, and if many southerners, including both devotees of popular Yahwism and of the state cult, regard Yahweh and Asherah as consorts, then would it not follow that the king of Judah would be perceived not only as the adopted son of Yahweh, the divine father, but also of Asherah, the divine mother? And if this were so, would not that king's biological mother, the queen mother, be understood as the earthly counterpart of Asherah? It is, I suggested, unsurprising, and it is indeed even proper, that the queen mothers whose religious devotions are described for us in the Hebrew Bible dedicated themselves to the cult of Asherah. Such worship is perfectly consistent with the royal ideology that defined their sons' courts.

II

Admittedly, this conclusion as offered in my earlier paper was speculative, hampered by the lack of evidence, both textual and archaeological, that so often plagues historians of Israelite religion. Nor is there significant comparative material from elsewhere in the ancient Near East that can prove conclusively the validity of my reconstruction. Still, I intend to suggest below that if the thesis that the Judaean queen mother served in her son's court as the human surrogate of Asherah were adopted, it would help explain certain biblical texts that have heretofore been imperfectly understood by scholars. Similarly, I intend to argue that the Judaean paradigm of queen mother as devotee of Asherah held in other monarchies in the west Semitic world, and I will propose that certain evidence from these monarchies, evidence that is both written and iconographical, is better illuminated if my thesis is accepted.

Let us turn first to this evidence from elsewhere in the west Semitic world, and, in particular, to evidence from Late Bronze Age Ugarit. We may begin our discussion by recalling what many studies have already shown: that Ugarit does share with the Southern Kingdom of Judah an ideology of sacral kingship.[13] This is most thoroughly indicated in a literary composition, the Kirta Epic.[14] In that epic, language identifying King Kirta as the adopted son of the Canaanite high god El is frequent: thus Kirta in the first two tablets of the text (*KTU* 1.14-15) is repeatedly called the "lad of El" (*ġlm il, KTU* 1.14.1.40, 61-62; 14.6.299-300, 306 [restored]; 15.2.20), and El is almost as often referred to as Kirta's father (*ṯr abh il, KTU* 1.14.1.59, 14.4.169; *ṯr abh, KTU* 1.14.1.41; *ṯr abk il, KTU* 1.14.2.76-77). Even more telling is the scene with which the third tablet of the Kirta Epic opens (*KTU* 1.16). There, Kirta has been struck by some unspecified illness, and his family gathers around him. Their reaction to his sickness can only be described as one of shock, as they cannot believe that Kirta might die as mortals do. "Shall gods die?" his son Ilihu[15] asks, "Shall the offspring of the Kindly One [a well-known epithet of El] not live?" (*u ilm tmtn // špḥ lṭpn lyḥ: KTU* 1.16.1.22-23; see also 16.2.105-106). Ilihu also in the same speech refers to his father's immortality (*lmtk,* literally "your not dying," *KTU* 1.16.1.15). Clearly what is assumed here is an ideology of divine sonship through which Kirta has been adopted into the family of the immortal gods. Not insignificantly, it is in this part of the epic that Kirta is explicitly called the "son of El" (*bn il* and *bnm il, KTU* 1.16.1.10, 20; 16.2.110 [restored]) and "the offspring of the Kindly and Holy One" (*špḥ lṭpn wqdš, KTU* 1.16.1.10-11, 21-22; 16.2.111 [restored]); "the Holy One," *qdš*, like "the Kindly One," *lṭpn*, is well known as an epithet of El.[16]

The Kirta Epic, however, is a mythological text, and it thus can be questioned whether it reflects accurately the actual royal ideology of Ugarit. Evidence demonstrating that it does includes the verso of the so-called "Ugaritic King List" (*KTU* 1.113), where can be read a list of fourteen royal names, each with the divine determinative (the *il* sign) preceding it. To be sure, all the kings named are deceased, probably an indication that a monarch could assume the title *ilu*, "divine one," only upon his death.[17] Still, I would argue that in order to be given the title "divine one" at death, the recipient most likely had to have had some extraordinary relationship with the divine during life. Thus the fact that dead Ugaritic kings are called "divine one" after their deaths suggests that an ideology of sacral kingship similar to that found in first-millennium Judah did function in Late Bronze Age Ugarit.[18]

The presence of this type of royal ideology, of course, was crucial to my earlier proposals concerning the cultic role of the queen mother in the Judaean court. This suggests that inherent in the Ugaritic monarchy is the same potential I found in Judah for the queen mother to function in the court as the earthly representative of Asherah. Equally significant in this regard is evidence suggesting that the city-state of Ugarit is willing to ascribe to its queen mothers the same kind of political power that previous commentators have described for the queen mothers of Judah. A letter (RS 11.872; *KTU* 2.13) published in 1940 by Ch. Virolleaud,[19] for example, and then subsequently discussed by H. N. Richardson[20] contains the words of a king who pays homage to the authority and power of his queen mother by bowing at her feet (*lpᶜn umy qlt*, lines 5-6) and by invoking the gods, asking them to guard (*nǵr*) his mother and bring her peace (*šlm*, lines 7-8).

As Virolleaud and Richardson point out,[21] the language of this letter closely parallels that of two other letters from Ugarit published in 1938.[22] The first (RS 9.479; *KTU* 2.12), like the letter discussed by Richardson, is addressed *lmlkt*, "to the queen" (line 1). Unlike the Richardson letter, however, the sender here is not specifically identified as the son of the queen, the reigning king, but only by the name *tlmyn*, described further as "your servant" (*ᶜbdk*). This means it is impossible to determine from this letter alone whether the "queen" addressed is the royal wife or the royal mother. The second letter of comparison (RS 8.315; *KTU* 2.11), however, makes clear that the "queen" in question is in fact the queen mother. That letter is also written by *tlmyn*, although this time in conjunction with *aḫ•tmlk*, who is probably *tlmyn's* wife. The recipient, the "queen" of the previous letter, is here called *umy*, "my mother." The addressee of the two letters, therefore, is both a "queen" and a "mother." She is the queen mother.[23] From *KTU* 2.16 (RS 15.09), another letter from *tlmyn* to his queen mother, we learn that the mother's name is *ṯryl*; any doubts that remain concerning *ṯryl*'s status as queen mother are assuaged by *KTU* 2.34 (RS 17.139), a letter addressed to *ṯryl* from her son, the "king" (*mlk*, line 1).

Several data within this collection of "queen mother" letters are significant. First, in both *KTU* 2.11 and 2.12, as in *KTU* 2.13, the first letter discussed above, the writers acknowledge the queen mother's authority and power by bowing at her feet; in *KTU* 2.12, indeed, *tlmyn* describes prostrating himself some fourteen times before his mother (*sbᶜ wsbᶜid,* lines 8-9). This motif is found also in several letters I have not yet had occasion to mention: *KTU* 2.24.5-7 (RS 16.137), a letter to "the queen" (to be understood as the queen mother, based on the parallels presented above) from *illḏr,* "your servant" (*l mlkt . . . rgm tḥm illḏr ᶜbdk,* lines 1-4); *KTU* 2.33.3-4 (RS 16.402), a letter to "the queen" (again, surely, to be understood as the queen mother) from *irrṯrm,* "your servant" (*l mlkt . . . rgm tḥm irrṯrm ᶜbdk,* lines 1-2); and *KTU* 2.30.4-5 (RS 16.379), a letter to "the queen, my mother" (*l mlkt umy,* line 1) from "the king, your son" (*mlk bnk,* line 3; there can be no doubt here that the "queen" in question is the queen mother).

In addition to paying homage to their queen mothers by bowing before them, reigning kings also, in four of the letters cited above (*KTU* 2.11, 2.12, 2.24, and 2.33), acknowledge the queen mother's authority by repeatedly addressing her as *adt* (*KTU* 2.11.1, 5, and 15; *KTU* 2.12.2, 7, and 12; *KTU* 2.24.2, 5, and 10; *KTU* 2.33.1, 3, 4), best analyzed as a feminine form of *adn*, "lord."[24] Of further note is an argument advanced by M. Heltzer,[25] who has proposed that these various "queen mother" letters were missives concerning administrative and political issues, sent by the king when he was absent from Ugarit to the queen mother, who had remained behind at the palace. Thus when the king was away, the responsibility concerning the day-to-day functioning of the Ugaritic court seems to have resided in the hands of the queen mother.

Another political responsibility the Ugaritic queen mother seems to have assumed, as is indicated in a text concerning Aḫat-milki, wife of King Niqmepa and queen mother of their son, Ammištamru II (RS 17.352; *PRU* IV, pp. 121-22), is a role in determining the royal succession.[26] Ammištamru II was a younger son of Niqmepa, yet his mother exerted enough authority to have him crowned king after the death of his father. She also seems to have served as regent on behalf of Ammištamru, who, it appears, ascended the throne while still a minor.

An Akkadian text that describes the terms of a divorce between the same Ammištamru II and the daughter of Bentešina, king of Amurru (RS 17.159; *PRU* IV, pp. 126-27), further attests to the political powers of the queen mother at Ugarit.[27] As in modern divorce cases, much of the settlement concerned the disposition of the children, especially the crown prince Utrišarruma. Utrišarruma is told he will remain his father's heir after the divorce only if he allies himself with his father; if he sides with his now-divorced mother, the king, Ammištamru, will appoint an alternate heir. Moreover, according to the agreement, even after Utrišarruma becomes king subsequent to his father's death, he cannot reestablish ties with his mother. More specifically, under the terms of the divorce, the son is told that should he bring his mother back to Ugarit as queen mother (*SAL.LUGAL-ut-ti*), he will be forced to abdicate. What is crucial to note for our purposes is the implicit assumption that the queen mother holds a position of power within the royal court.

Finally, Heltzer has assembled data attesting to the economic power of the Ugaritic queen mother.[28] She owned land and also, according to *Ugaritica* V, Nos. 159-61 (RS 17.86 + 241 + 208; 17.102; 17.325), was able to buy property throughout her tenure in order to supplement her holdings. She had her own storage facilities: Heltzer cites *KTU* 4.143, lines 1-2, which speaks of the 250 measures of oil housed in the queen mother's *gt*, a warehouse used for agricultural products. These holdings in land and agricultural produce seem to have been managed by administrative personnel under the authority of the queen mother. Heltzer notes that she counted among her household a *šākinu*, who served as a chief administrative official, a *mudu*, a sort of chief counselor, and several *mārê šarrati*, a term that literally means "sons of the queen" but in reality refers to certain officials of high rank rather than actual biological descendants. Also in the queen mother's entourage were the *bunušū* (Akkadian) or *bnšm* (Ugaritic), her "dependents."

Certain biblical materials are strikingly similar to these Ugaritic data. In 1 Kgs 2:13-25, for example, Bathsheba, now after David's death the queen mother of Solomon, approaches her son bearing a petition from the recently deposed Adonijah. Solomon, to be sure, hardly receives with favor this petition, which asks for David's concubine (tantamount to asking for David's kingdom; see 2 Sam 3:6-11). But this does not affect the respect the king accords Bathsheba as queen mother. He rises and, as in *KTU* 2.11, 2.12, 2.13, 2.24, 2.30, and 2.33, bows down to her (*wayyištaḥû*), then has a seat placed for her at his right hand (1 Kgs 2:19). Ps 110:1, where the king is described as sitting at the right hand of God, suggests that the chair assigned to Bathsheba is, next to the throne of the monarch himself, the place of highest honor on the royal dais.[29]

This text in 1 Kgs 2:13-25 thus attests to an exalted position for Bathsheba, the queen mother, in Jerusalem, similar to the exalted position held by queen mother in Ugarit; it also demonstrates that one of her chief responsibilities within this exalted position is to serve as an adviser to her son Solomon, bringing to him requests from supplicants like

Adonijah and counseling the king concerning his response. But this was not Bathsheba's only responsibility, it seems: equally, or perhaps more important, was securing for Solomon the throne at the time of David's death. That story, as told in 1 Kgs 1:5-40, describes how the prophet Nathan wanted David to name Solomon as his heir rather than Adonijah, who was the oldest surviving son. To effect this, Nathan went to Bathsheba, who in turn persuaded the king to declare Solomon his successor. The final decree, to be sure, is David's. But it is Bathsheba who, practically speaking, determines the royal succession. Her power in deciding the king's heir is further alluded to in Cant 3:11:

> Look, O daughter of Zion,
> At King Solomon,
> At the crown with which his mother crowned him
> On the day of his wedding,
> On the day of the gladness of his heart.

We may compare to 1 Kgs 1:5-40 and Cant 3:11 the role of the Ugaritic queen mother Aḫat-milki and the part she played in promoting the succession of her son, Ammištamru II. Overall, moreover, we may conclude that as Ugarit and Judah share an ideology of sacral kingship, they also demonstrate a shared understanding concerning the rights and responsibilities of the queen mother in the royal court. If, then, my thesis stated earlier concerning the queen mother and the cult in Judah is correct, we should similarly expect to find the queen mother in Ugarit associated with the cult of Asherah.

Three pieces of evidence, two literary and the other artistic, are particularly suggestive in this regard. The first is an episode, again from the Kirta Epic, that has caused much confusion among scholars. The scene in question comes at the midpoint of the first tablet. Kirta has just awakened from his dream visioning El; he proceeds to undertake those tasks that El in the dream has commanded in order to procure the Lady Ḥurriya as a wife. He offers sacrifices, musters an army, and marches forth to do war in the land of Udm. Kirta, however, deviates in one significant aspect from El's instructions. On the third day of his march, he and his forces come to a shrine of Asherah, and there Kirta makes a vow to the goddess: he will dedicate gold and silver to her if he is successful in his quest for Ḥurriya (*KTU* 1.14.4.194-206).

Critics have puzzled over this vow.[30] It appears unnecessary, indeed superfluous, for Kirta to seek divine succor from Asherah, because success in his mission has already been promised by El. In fact, although the text becomes fragmentary at a crucial point, it seems that Kirta's vow ultimately brings him harm rather than good. The king fails to dedicate the promised riches to Asherah, and, at the end of *KTU* 1.15.3, she vows revenge. The next complete scene in the epic describes Kirta's illness, the result, most commentators presume, of Asherah's curse.[31]

Why, then, does Kirta enter into this unnecessary and even foolish vow?[32] The context of his mission, I would suggest, provides a clue. The crisis with which the Kirta Epic opens, which brings El down in a dream and which sends Kirta to war against Udm, is the king's lack of a wife and, more important, his lack of an heir. "Grant that sons I might acquire," Kirta begs El, "Grant that children I might multiply" (*[tn b]nm aqny // [tn nᶜ]rm amid, KTU* 1.14.2.57-58). What Kirta needs is a queen who will mother for him a royal son; he needs a woman who will eventually assume the role of queen mother. And that queen mother, I have argued, will function in her son's court as the earthly counterpart of Asherah. I therefore suggest that Kirta is described as deviating from El's instructions because the epic tradition recognizes that, even though El is the high god of the pantheon and the one who determines destinies, matters concerning queen mothers appropriately fall within the province of Asherah. Kirta, when seeking a mother for his royal heir, dare not ignore the mother goddess. If, then, I am correct in positing a special relationship at Ugarit between the queen mother and Asherah, Kirta's otherwise puzzling vow becomes a perfectly comprehensible part of the epic's plot.

Even more significant in this regard is a scene later in the Kirta Epic, after Ḥurriya has been procured as wife. There, at a banquet that celebrates the marriage, El blesses Kirta by saying that upon the birth of Yaṣṣib, the king's son and heir (*KTU* 1.15.2.26-28):

> *ynq ḥlb a[ṯ]rt*
> *mṣṣ ṯd btlt [ᶜnt]*
> *mšnq[t ilm]*
> He will suckle the milk of Asherah,
> Suck at the breasts of Virgin Anat,
> The two wet-nurses of the gods.

Most commentators cite here parallel traditions from elsewhere in the ancient Near East that describe a royal child being suckled by a goddess: thus J. Gray notes that "the Sumerian King Lugalzaggisi was also said to be 'fed with holy milk by Ninḫarsag'";[33] H. L. Ginsberg and J. C. L. Gibson draw attention to Enuma Elish 1.85, where Marduk nurses at the breasts of goddesses;[34] S. B. Parker writes, "Rulers claim to have been suckled by a goddess as early as the presargonic royal inscriptions from Lagash."[35] I agree with Gray, Ginsberg, Gibson, and

Parker concerning the stereotypical nature of language describing the divine wet-nurses of royal sucklings; I am not convinced, however, that reference only to other ancient Near Eastern comparative material fully explicates the Kirta passage. More specifically, I would suggest that the naming of Anat and, in particular, Asherah as the wet-nurses in the cliché is not accidental. Elsewhere in the Kirta epic, Anat's partner in parallelism is Astarte (*KTU* 1.14.3.145-46; 14.6.291-93). Why here do we find Asherah instead? I have argued that a Ugaritic audience would expect Ḥurriya as queen mother to serve as an earthly surrogate of Asherah. That same audience should then find it appropriate that Yaṣṣib's metaphorical nurse be none other than the mother goddess. The language of the poetry alludes to the Ugaritic belief that Yaṣṣib's mother, Ḥurriya, the queen at whose breasts the child actually nurses, is the earthly designate of Asherah in the royal court.

John Gray,[36] among others, has compared the poetic allusion to Asherah as a divine wet-nurse to an ivory relief found by excavators at Ugarit and published by C. F. A. Schaeffer.[37] The plaque, which according to the excavators dates from about 1350 B.C.E., shows a woman suckling two male children, one at each breast. There can be no question that the nurse is divine: she has two pairs of wings, one extending upward from her shoulders and the other downward from her waist; from her forehead sprout two horns. I would argue further that this goddess is Asherah, for she wears the Egyptian Hathor-style headdress that R. Hestrin has demonstrated is typical in representations of Asherah from throughout the ancient world.[38]

Less definite but also, I think, probable is that the two male children the goddess suckles are meant to be human. Certainly there is nothing in the representation of the two that suggests divinity. Moreover, I believe it can be argued that these two human children are royal.[39] The context of the find is pertinent here; the relief was carved as a decorative panel for the headboard of a bed. At a minimum, this ivory bed would have belonged to an aristocratic family and more likely to a royal one. One is reminded here of the ivory furniture that decorated Ahab's palace in Samaria (1 Kgs 22:39; see also Amos 3:15; 6:4).[40] That the panel depicts a suckling motif may further indicate that this royal bed was meant for a child, and I would be so bold as to suggest that the royal child whose bed would have merited such an elaborate and exquisitely carved panel would have been the crown prince.[41] And, if my thesis concerning the queen mother and Asherah at Ugarit is correct, what more appropriate decoration could there be for the bed of the Ugaritic heir presumptive?[42]

Asherah, the divine mother, is depicted here as fulfilling the duties of her alter-ego, the queen mother, in giving suck to the royal son.[43]

J. B. Pritchard,[44] along with several other scholars, has compared to the Ras Shamra ivory another piece of iconographical data, an eighth-century basalt relief from the Phoenician city of Karatepe.[45] This is significant, for I intend to argue that because Phoenician culture shared with Ugarit and Judah an ideology of sacral kingship and also a similar description of the kind of political power the queen mother was able to wield, the three cultures likewise shared an understanding of the queen mother's cultic role as devotee of Asherah.

That the Phoenician city-states shared with Judah and Ugarit an ideology of sacral kingship is particularly well illustrated by Ezek 28:2, where the king of Tyre is said to claim, *ʾēl ʾānî*, "I am a God" (similarly, in Ezek 28:9, *ʾĕlōhîm ʾānî*). Elsewhere in the same chapter that king is described as thinking himself "as wise as a God" (*wattittēn libbĕkā kĕlēb ʾĕlōhîm*, 28:2; *tittĕkā ʾet-lĕbābĕkā kĕlēb ʾĕlōhîm*, 28:6) and as believing he sits on the throne of a god (*môšab ʾĕlōhîm*, 28:2). This Tyrian ideology seems also to hold elsewhere in the Phoenician world. At Pyrgi, for example, G. Knoppers has convincingly drawn on multiple ancient Near Eastern parallels (from the Hebrew Bible, Hittite culture, Emar, Nuzi, Old and Middle Babylonian, and Ugarit) to demonstrate that the phrases in that inscription describing "the burial of the god" (*qbr ʾlm*, lines 8-9) and "the god in his temple/tomb"[46] (*ʾlm bbty*, lines 9-10) refer not to a deity, but to a recently dead member of the royal family.[47] (Knoppers believes the deceased to be the crown prince; I would suggest instead that the tomb is that of the recently dead king, the father of Thebariye Velinas, who is the author of the inscription and now the reigning monarch.)

In addition to these materials demonstrating a Phoenician ideology of sacral kingship, there also comes from that culture evidence suggesting that, as in Judah and at Ugarit, the queen mother commanded significant political power. Most telling is the Sidonian inscription of Ešmunazor (*KAI* 14), which dates from about 500 B.C.E. Lines 3 and 12-13 of that inscription, which describe Ešmunazor as "an orphan" (*ytm*) and "the son of a few days" (*bn msk ymm*), indicate that Ešmunazor succeeded his father Tabnit on the throne of Sidon while still a child. Line 1, which states that Ešmunazor died in the fourteenth year of his reign (*bšnt ʿsr wʾrbʿ 14 lmlky*), and lines 2-3 and 12, in which Ešmunazor describes how he was "snatched away before my time" (*ngzlt bl ʿty*),[48] suggest that Ešmunazor was still a minor upon his death. Notably for our purposes, the regent who seems to have guided the reign of this boy king was Amoaštart, Tabnit's widow and Ešmunazor 's queen mother.

Thus in lines 14-18 of the inscription, in which some of the accomplishments of Ešmunazor's reign are listed, it is said that *we* (Ešmunazor and Amoaštart) built temples for the gods, for Aštart, for Ešmun, and for other gods of the Sidonians. Similarly, in lines 18-20 the inscription reads that *we* (again, Ešmunazor and Amoaštart) annexed Dor and Joffa as part of Sidonian territory. The queen mother of Ešmunazor thus seems to rule side by side with her son, exercising the same kind of political power that characterized the queen mother in Judah and in Ugarit.

My thesis would next propose that we should find in Phoenicia, as in Judah and at Ugarit, a cultic role for the queen mother as devotee of Asherah. The Ešmunazor inscription, however, gives pause, for there the Sidonian queen mother Amoaštart, as her name suggests, is a devotee of the goddess Astarte. Her devotion to Astarte is in fact made explicit in line 15 of the inscription, where Amoaštart is labeled a "priestess of Astarte" (*khnt ᶜštrt*). Two points need to be kept in mind here, however. First, the Ešmunazor inscription is relatively late (about 500 B.C.E.) and thus comes from a period when the identities of the three great Canaanite goddesses—Asherah, Astarte, and Anat—have become quite fluid. Indeed, this tendency toward fusion begins quite early, as is evidenced, for example, in the Winchester College plaque published by I. E. S. Edwards.[49] This plaque, dated by Edwards to the Egyptian Nineteeth or Twentieth Dynasty and by J. Černy to the reign of Ramesses III,[50] shows a naked goddess who wears a Hathor-style headdress and stands astride a lion, holding a lotus plant in her right hand and a serpent in her left. The Hathor headdress, as I have already noted, suggests a depiction of Asherah; so, too, do the lion imagery and the presence of a serpent.[51] Yet the goddess is in fact identified by the ancient scribe as a composite deity, Qudšu-Astarte-Anat (Qudšu being a well known epithet of Asherah); there has been a conflation, that is, of the three great Canaanite goddesses.

The evidence of the Sarepta inscription, which is roughly contemporary with Ešmunazor (seventh century B.C.E.) and like Ešmunazor is Phoenician, is of even greater significance.[52] The inscription reads *ltnt ᶜštrt*, suggesting that the epithet *tnt* is a title of Astarte. Yet a compelling argument can also be made for identifying *tnt* with Asherah.[53] In fact, it is necessary to side neither with those who would argue *tnt* is Astarte nor with those who would identify her with Asherah. Instead, given the Canaanite propensity to conflate the three great goddesses, *tnt* is appropriately understood as Astarte, as Asherah, and as a syncretism of both.[54] Thus, for Amoaštart to worship Astarte in the fifth century is, in some sense, to worship also Asherah.[55]

A second point that needs to be kept in mind concerning the religious devotions of Amoaštart is evidence that the patron goddess of Sidon was originally Asherah and that only secondarily was there a syncretism with Astarte. Thus in Ugaritic texts, it is Asherah who is called the "goddess of Sidon" (*ilt ṣdynm, KTU* 1.14.4.199, 202), but by the time of the Hebrew Bible that title can also be applied to Astarte: *ʾĕlōhê sidōnîm* (1 Kgs 11:5; see also 11:33; 2 Kgs 23:13).[56] Again, this would argue for conflation of the two goddesses. Amoaštart's devotion to Astarte in Ešmunazor is thus for the most part devotion also to Asherah.

Moreover, in the Karatepe relief mentioned above, I find compelling evidence associating Phoenician queen mothers with the cult of Asherah. The relief shows a nude male child nursing from the breasts of an adult female. Both the figures are arguably human; neither, at least, shows any features that would characterize it as divine. The male figure, I would further suggest, is in all likelihood the crown prince. Certainly the archaeological context in which the relief was found (the monumental gateway on the southwest side of the royal citadel) indicates that those pictured are members of the royal family. That the suckling is to be identified specifically as the crown prince is more speculative but is suggested by comparing certain Egyptian paintings and reliefs from the New Kingdom that depict a nursing male known from accompanying inscriptions to be the pharaonic heir. Most significant is a painting that shows Thutmose III standing beside a sacred tree from whose branches extend a large breast and one arm (the left).[57] The arm is crooked, reaching up to support the breast; Thutmose III stands facing the tree, holding its arm and suckling from its teat. The iconography at Karatepe is amazingly similar: the mother figure at Karatepe holds her left arm crooked, using it to support her breast, while the nursing male, who faces her, reaches out to touch her elbow. Moreover, like Thutmose III, the suckler at Karatepe is shown standing with his feet on the ground, as if almost full grown, rather than being depicted as an infant. These parallels should indicate that the nursing male at Karatepe holds the same rank in society as does Thutmose III in the Egyptian painting: he is the heir presumptive. The woman who suckles this crown prince is thus the queen mother-to-be (or her designated wet-nurse).

The difference, of course, between the painting of Thutmose III and the Karatepe relief is that the Egyptian heir sucks at the breast of a tree, whereas the Karatepe nurse is a human. But there is a tree elsewhere on the Karatepe relief: a date palm tree that stands immediately to the right of the queen mother and is equal to her in height. One could, of course, regard this tree as merely decorative, but the absence of any other ornamental iconography on the relief mitigates such an interpretation. Moreover, the Egyptian parallels, which identify the tree of the suckling scene as Isis (as in the case of the Thutmose III painting) or (in other exemplars) as Nut[58] or Hathor, the mother goddess and nurse of the king of Egypt,[59] indicate that the Karatepe tree should likewise be considered "sacred" and should be identified, as are its Egyptian counterparts, with some deity.

Of course, to identify such sacred trees, ubiquitous in Semitic art, with one specific god or goddess is not always possible. Still, scholars are increasingly coming to realize how often the sacred tree serves as a symbol of Asherah. The biblical tradition is quite emphatic in making this identification. In the Hebrew Bible, the *ʾăšērâ* understood by almost all as the cult object of the goddess Asherah,[60] is surely to be understood as a stylized wooden tree. Most explicit is Deut 16:21: "You shall not plant [*nātaʿ*] for yourself as an *ʾăšērâ* any tree beside the altar of Yahweh, your God." Elsewhere the *ʾăšērâ* is said to be "made" (*ʿāśâ*) or "built" (*bānâ*), "stood up" (*ʿāmad*) or "erected" (*hiṣṣîb*). When destroyed, the cult symbol is "burned" (*biʿēr* or *śārap*), "cut down" (*kārat*), "hewn down" (*gādaʿ*), "uprooted" (*nātaš*), "overturned" (*nātaṣ*), or "broken" (*šibbēr*).[61] The Septuagint most commonly translates Hebrew *ʾăšērâ* by *alsos*, "grove," and twice by *dendra*, "trees."[62] Similarly the Latin reads *lucus*, "grove," or *nemus*, "wood," "grove," for Hebrew *ʾăšērâ*.[63] I also might note Gen 2:4b-3:24, for it has been suggested that the way Eve is described in that narrative mimics in some respects the goddess Asherah.[64] If so, then the role of the tree of life/tree of knowledge in the Eden story is significant.

To be paired with this textual data demonstrating the association of Asherah with sacred trees is glyptic evidence assembled in two articles by R. Hestrin.[65] From the Canaanite world of the Late Bronze Age comes the Lachish Ewer (late thirteenth century). The images on the ewer, while damaged by the ravages of time, clearly depict several pairs of animals, each pair flanking a stylized tree. Hestrin, following E. D. van Buren, argues that trees that are flanked by animals in this way are, in the conventions of ancient Near Eastern art, "sacred."[66] The question, "Sacred to whom?" is answered by the inscription on the ewer,[67] which marks it as an object dedicated to Elat, an epithet of Asherah known from both Ugaritic and Phoenician sources. (Not coincidentally, this epithet comes into Hebrew as a common noun, *ʾēlâ*, meaning "terebinth," further indicating Asherah's association with sacred trees.)[68]

Hestrin cites other Canaanite iconography that she believes

demonstrates the association of Asherah with sacred trees, including several gold and electrum pendants from Ugarit and other sites in the northern Levant. These pendants vary somewhat but all can be said to depict a goddess who often wears a Hathor headdress and "in at least three cases [is] standing on a lion; in one plaque snakes curl behind her back."[69] As discussed above, the Hathor headdresses, lion imagery, and presence of serpents suggest that the icons are meant to represent Asherah. It is notable in this regard that on each pendant there is etched in Asherah's navel a stylized branch or tree.

Hestrin's articles also discuss Iron Age images that suggest the association of Asherah with sacred trees. Most important is the tenth-century Taᶜanach cult stand. The stand is made of terra-cotta and is some sixty centimeters high; the sixty centimeters are divided into four registers of almost equal height. The bottom register depicts a nude female standing between two lions; this female is surely to be understood as the goddess Asherah, who, I note once more, is the "Lion Lady" in the mythology of the west Semitic world.[70] In the third register, the two lions appear again, but here, instead of an anthropomorphic figure, they stand flanking a sacred tree. Arguably, what we have here are alternate images of the "Lion Lady" Asherah—her anthropomorphic form in the bottom register and her symbolic representation as a sacred tree in the third register of the stand.

There is, moreover, evidence that associates Asherah not just with sacred trees but particularly with the date palm, the species of tree depicted on the Karatepe relief. R. A. Oden[71] has proposed that the caduceus imagery associated in a later period with Phoenician-Punic Tannit, whom Oden identifies primarily with Asherah,[72] has its origins in a depiction of a date palm tree that, over time, became increasingly stylized and abstracted. While Oden does not comment specifically on the Karatepe date palm, according to his thesis it should represent an earlier, more realistic representation of this specific species as a tree sacred to Asherah.

Recall once more the composition of the Karatepe relief on which the male child (the crown prince, I have argued) is flanked on one side by a sacred date palm tree and on the other by a woman, identified here as the queen mother, who gives him suck. Recall also that the queen mother and the tree are the same height. They stand almost as if they are mirror images of one another. Indeed, in the ideology of the royal cult, mirror images is precisely what they are: both represent the goddess Asherah. The date palm thus depicts Asherah in the form of her common symbol, the sacred tree; the queen mother, according to my thesis, serves as the earthly surrogate of Asherah in the royal court.

III

Let us turn now to consider certain data from the Bible, one piece of evidence from the Hebrew Bible and the rest from the New Testament. The Hebrew text in question is short: 2 Kgs 23:7 describes how Josiah as part of his massive reforms "broke down the houses[73] of the *qĕdāšîm* that were in the temple of Yahweh where the women wove garments [*btm*] for the *ʾăšērâ*." Commentators have generally focused here on two points: the translation of *btm* as "garments" and the reference to the *qĕdāšîm*, traditionally understood as male cult prostitutes.

While Hebrew *btm* was vocalized by the Masoretes as *bāttîm*, the plural of *bayit*, "house,"[74] there is among scholars widespread agreement, following A.Šanda and G. R. Driver,[75] that we should revocalize to read *battîm*, cognate with Arabic *batt*, "woven garment." This revocalization is supported by the Lucianic recension of the LXX, which reads *stolas*, "garment, robe."[76] As for the nature of the garments woven for the *ʾăšērâ*, there is general consensus that the referent is to clothing that would have been draped over a cult statue dedicated to the goddess Asherah.[77] The practice of clothing cult statues is known from the Bible (Jer 10:9; Ezek 16:16)[78] and throughout the Semitic and eastern Mediterranean worlds.[79] It is also interesting to note that among the archaeological discoveries at Kuntillet ʿAjrud, where inscriptional evidence has indicated the presence of some sort of Asherah worship,[80] were many textile fragments.[81]

The problem of the *qĕdāšîm* in 2 Kgs 23:7 is somewhat more complex. Traditionally, it has been assumed that syncretistic forms of Israelite religion, under the influence of Canaanite and Babylonian customs, included a form of sacred prostitution in which participants engaged in sexual intercourse with certain cultic personnel (*qĕdāšîm, qĕdāšôt*) in order to "emulate and stimulate the deities who bestowed fertility"[82] and thereby to ensure fruitfulness in the land.[83] Recently, however, more and more scholars have been questioning this traditional assumption. J. G. Westenholz,[84] for example, has suggested that while the *qĕdāšîm* and *qĕdāšôt* are certainly depicted in the Bible as cultic functionaries, there is no firm evidence that their cultic function was sacred sexual intercourse. Nor is there conclusive evidence from Canaanite (Ugaritic) or Mesopotamian (Sumerian, Akkadian, and Assyrian) sources that the role of the *qdšm* and *qdšt* (Ugaritic) or the *qadištu* (Akkadian) was sexual. Only Herodotus presents a picture of Mesopotamian sacred prostitution, but as Westenholz, E. J. Fisher, and especially R. A. Oden cogently argue, Herodotus as a source is on this issue tendentious and therefore unreliable.[85]

It has thus become increasingly difficult to understand the *qĕdāšîm* of 2 Kgs 23:7 as male cult prostitutes; instead they seem simply to be some class of cultic personnel who are housed in and presumably supported by the temple. This last datum is significant, for their presence in Yahweh's temple suggests a group perceived in at least some periods as an accepted part of the Yahwistic cult.[86] Josiah, to be sure, like the Deuteronomistic agenda that inspires him (Deut 23:18 [English: 23:17]), rejects the *qĕdāšîm* (and, presumably, the *qĕdāšôt*) as inappropriate in Yahwism. But evidently there had previously been those within the state cult who felt differently.

Who were those who had thought otherwise? Biblical evidence suggests that among them were Josiah's royal predecessors. The temple stood adjacent to the palace in Jerusalem and essentially functioned as a private chapel for the court.[87] Kings of Judah were the titular heads and chief patrons of the temple cult and as such reserved for themselves the right to appoint temple personnel, as David had appointed Abiathar and Zadok to administer to the ark in its tent shrine when it was brought to Jerusalem,[88] and as Josiah himself had attempted to establish the levitical priests whom he had removed from the outlying *bāmôt* as cult functionaries in the Jerusalem sanctuary (2 Kgs 23:8-9). Similarly, the *qĕdāšîm* of 2 Kgs 23:7, while they clearly did not have the support of the reformer King Josiah, at some point must have been introduced into the temple under royal patronage.

This brings us to the women who wove garments for Asherah in the houses of the *qĕdāšîm*. The text, unfortunately, does not assign a title to these women, although they may well have been *qĕdāšôt*, the female equivalents of the male cult functionaries in whose houses they wove. Certainly, however, even if not *qĕdāšôt*, we can assume the women were some sort of religious personnel: that they could spend their days weaving on behalf of the goddess Asherah must indicate that the temple economy was providing their support. In addition, as religious personnel, we can assume that they, like their male counterparts, were appointed either directly or indirectly by the crown. Is it too far-fetched to suggest that the royal patron of these women cult officials would have been female? Moreover, if male cult functionaries were appointed by the most powerful male in the royal court, the king, is it not likely that female cult functionaries would have been appointed by the most powerful female within the monarchy, the queen mother? And, finally, if these female cult personnel were appointed by the queen mother, then is it not significant for my thesis that the women religious functionaries the queen mother chose to appoint were dedicated to the service of Asherah, the goddess I have posited was identified in ancient Judah with the queen mother?

To be sure, such a proposal is highly conjectural. But there are supporting data that suggest that Judaean queen mothers did have some influence in the disposition of temple accouterments and personnel. Most significant is the fact that the *ʾăšērâ* Ma^{c}acah is said to have made (1 Kgs 15:13) stood in all likelihood in the Jerusalem temple, because the temple, as noted above, is in essence a private chapel for the monarchy and thus is the obvious place for a member of the royal family to erect a religious icon. Also of importance is the fact that Ma^{c}acah as queen mother, when she chooses to assert herself in matters concerning the temple cult, asserts herself on behalf of the worship of Asherah. I propose that some unnamed queen mother asserted herself in a similar fashion to appoint the women devotees of Asherah described in 2 Kgs 23:7.

I submit, in short, that as queen mothers like Ma^{c}acah would devote themselves to the goddess Asherah by erecting her cult statue in the Jerusalem temple, they would also see to the maintenance of that cult statue by appointing cult functionaries to weave garments for it and also possibly to offer sacrifices. (Note that the reference in 2 Kgs 23:4 to vessels made for Asherah indicates a functioning sacrificial cult.) 2 Kgs 23:7, that is, seems to indicate again the intimate link I have posited between the queen mother and the mother goddess in Judaean religion.

The royal ideology I have argued fueled in Judah the cultic association of the queen mother with Asherah—namely, the belief that the king was the adopted son of Yahweh, the divine father, and Asherah, the divine mother—ceased to function in the political life of the nation in 586 B.C.E., when the Jerusalem monarchy fell to the Babylonians. But even though the ideology ceased to have meaning after 586 in the historical present, it remained a vibrant aspect of the tradition as a vision projected into the future—an eschatological description of an ideal king, descended from David, who would rule in a new age in a new Jerusalem. Such a vision is found already in the protoapocalyptic works of the exilic and postexilic periods (for example, Ezek 37:24-25; Zech 9:9-10); in the full-blown apocalyptism of Qumran (for example, 1QS 9.11; 1QSa 2.11, 14, 20; 1QSb 5.20-29; CD 12.23; 14.19; 19.10; 20.1; 1QM 5.1; 4QPBless 1.3; 2.4; 4QFlor 1.11-13) and also elsewhere in intertestamental Judaism (Dan 9:25; Pss. Sol. 17:21-44; 18:6-9); and in certain of the eschatological tradents of the New Testament, especially in the gospels of Matthew and Luke.

That Matthew's Christology has as an essential component an understanding of Jesus as the new David, the fulfillment of Jewish messianic hopes, is made evident already in the first verse of the Gospel, where Matthew introduces Jesus' genealogy by announcing that Jesus is the "son of David, son of Abraham" (Matt 1:1). The genealogy follows, tracing three periods in Jesus' family tree: from Abraham to David (1:2-6a), from Solomon to Jechoniah (1:6b-11), and from Shealtiel to Jesus (1:12-16). The first and second of these periods consist of fourteen generations each, as the gospel itself points out (1:17); Matt 1:17 erroneously counts fourteen generations (instead of thirteen) in the third period as well. From a historical point of view, however, such a tripartite chronology is highly problematic, which suggests that the primary meaning of the genealogy's structure is not historical but symbolic. Several scholars have noted in this regard that the numerical value of *dwd*, the name of David in Hebrew, is fourteen ($d = 4$; $w = 6$; $d = 4$).[89] The very structuring by "fourteens" in the genealogy thus may reflect Matthew's overarching concern to portray Jesus as the new David.

Matthew's understanding of Jesus as the new David manifests itself also in 2:2-6, where the evangelist insists on Jesus' birth in Bethlehem, the town where David was born (1 Sam 17:12) and also the town from which, according to Mic 5:1 (English: 5:2), the ideal Davidic ruler will come. Matthew's Jesus fulfills other eschatological expectations associated with the new David, especially in the story of the entry into Jerusalem (Matt 21:1-11; see Zech 9:9). For Matthew, in short, no matter how mockingly Herod (Matt 2:2) and the Romans (Matt 27:11, 29, 37) use the title, Jesus really is the "King of the Jews."

The Gospel of Luke is also rich in the ways it describes Jesus as the new David. Luke 24:21 (see also Acts 1:6) speaks of Jesus as the redeemer of Israel; similarly, in 2:38, Jesus is described as the redeemer of Jerusalem. Like Matthew, Luke insists on Jesus' birth in Bethlehem, "because he was of the house and the lineage of David" (2:4). Luke's description of the annunciation to Mary is particularly replete with language of the Davidic monarchy, especially in 1:32-33, where the angel Gabriel promises to Mary a child who will be called Son of the Most High, who will sit on the throne of David, who will reign over the house of Jacob, and whose kingdom will be without end (see also 2 Sam 7:12-16; Isa 9:5-6 [English: 9:6-7]; Ps 89:26-29; Dan 2:44; 7:14, 27). This stress in Luke, as in Matthew, on Jesus as the royal Messiah is significant for our purposes because H. Cazelles has suggested that we posit in these two Gospels a role for Mary, Jesus' mother, that corresponds to that of her son: if Jesus is characterized as the royal Messiah, Israel's new king, then Mary, at least figuratively, is depicted as queen mother.[90]

Certain data, especially in Matt 1:1-25, suggest precisely such an understanding of Mary as a queen mother. For example, as is often noted, a peculiar feature of Matthew's genealogy of Jesus (1:1-17) is the fact that it includes four women: Tamar, Rahab, Ruth, and Bathsheba (called in Matt 1:6 "the wife of Uriah").[91] Commentators usually assume these four women are included because their characters bear some relation to Mary's: like her, they are all said to participate in some extraordinary or irregular marital union, scandalous in the eyes of outsiders yet essential in the preservation of the messianic line; like her, they are instruments through which God works the divine will.[92] I would add that like her they either are queen mothers (Bathsheba) or adumbrate that office in the premonarchic period: thus Tamar bears Perez through Judah, to whom is already assigned, in Gen 49:10, the "scepter" and the "ruler's staff" as emblems of monarchy; Rahab, through Salmon, is the mother of Boaz, and Ruth, through Boaz, is the mother of Obed, both of whom are important in biblical tradition because they are immediate ancestors of David, the founder of the Judaean royal dynasty.[93]

Even more notable parallels between Mary and the queen mothers of old are found in Matthew's story of the virgin birth (Matt 1:18-25). As is well known, Matthew in that birth narrative quotes the great Immanuel prophecy of Isa 7:14, or, more specifically, Matthew quotes the LXX translation of Isa 7:14, which uses *parthenos*, "virgin," rather than reflecting Hebrew *ʿalmâ*, "young woman" (Matt 1:23). Contrast Luke, who, although he does recount the story of the virgin birth, does not cite the Isaiah passage. As R. E. Brown has pointed out, this suggests that the virgin birth narrative did not emerge because of the Isaiah prophecy (the prophecy, that is, as it was understood in its Greek manifestation), but instead the tradition of the virgin birth circulated in early Christianity independent of the Isaianic text.[94] What, then, inspired Matthew but not Luke to quote the prophecy in order to illustrate the virgin birth narrative?

The answer to this question, of course, simply could be coincidence—Matthew thought to cite the passage, Luke did not—or it could be that we should explain Matthew's quote as yet another example of his propensity to quote the Hebrew Bible whenever any potential parallel, no matter how distant, comes to mind. But I am intrigued by the original context of Isa 7:14. In Isaiah 7, the prophet Isaiah confronts King Ahaz, urging him to resist a foreign alliance with Assyria. The child Immanuel, whose name means "God is with us," is to be for Ahaz a sign that foreign alliances are unnecessary and that Israel should rely on God alone. The child is born to an *ʿalmâ*, a "young woman," who most commentators now understand to be Ahaz's wife.[95] The child in question is thus Hezekiah, the royal heir, and the child-bearing woman of 7:14 should therefore be Abi, Hezekiah's queen mother (1 Kgs 18:2).[96] It is, of course, impossible to say whether Matthew realized that the original prophecy applied to a queen mother. But if he did, this may explain why he, given his concern to portray Jesus as the new David, chose to quote Isa 7:14.

What finally of Mary as queen mother and the thesis that is our concern: that the queen mother served as the earthly representative of Asherah or, to speak in post-Canaanite terms more appropriate to the period of early Christianity, that Mary as the figurative queen mother of Jesus would have been perceived within the cult as the earthly representative of the mother goddess? Certainly in the rather unrelenting patriarchy of the New Testament there is no suggestion of this. But can we see in later Mariology the tendency we found already in second-millennium Ugarit to identify queen mother and a mother goddess? Note in this regard that in the earliest attestation of an emerging cult of Mary, the second-century *Infancy Gospel of James,* Mary is said to be dedicated by her parents to a life of service in the temple, and as part of her service she is chosen to be one of seven virgins who weaves a new curtain for the sanctuary.[97] It is not hard here to hear echoes of the weaving women of 2 Kgs 23:7, which describes, I argued above, women appointed to cultic service by the queen mother in order that they might tend to the cult statue of the queen mother's divine patron, Asherah. Mary, that is, within a century of Jesus' death, is described by the author of the *Infancy Gospel of James* as participating in a type of temple service that in an earlier period in Israel's history was a part of the cult of Asherah. Also worthy of mention is the *Gospel of Philip*, a collection of Valentinian Gnostic meditations with its roots in the second century,[98] in which Mary is interpreted simultaneously both as Jesus' mother and as a female heavenly power, the Holy Spirit (55:23; 59:6;[99] see also the *Gospel of Thomas*, logion 99).[100] Mary, in short, is said to correspond to a mother figure in the heavens, a mother figure who in an earlier period was the goddess Asherah. I conclude, then, with this possibility: that even within the radical religious transformation that was early Christianity, the old mythic paradigm that linked the queen mother and the mother goddess still reverberated in the emerging Marian cult.

NOTES

1. Major articles include Ben-Barak, "Status and Right," 23-34; and "Queen Consort," 33-40; Andreasen, "Role of the Queen Mother," 179-94; Donner, "Art und Herkunft," 105-45; Molin, "Die Stellung der Gᵉbira," 161-75. Discussions in monographs include Ishida, *Royal Dynasties,* 155-60; de Vaux, *Ancient Israel* 1,117-19; Ahlström, *Aspects of Syncretism,* 57-88.

2. The term *gĕbîrâ/gĕberet* is used fifteen times in the Hebrew Bible. In Gen 16:4, 8, and 9 it means "mistress" (describing Sarah's relationship with Hagar), and this translation is also required in 2 Kgs 5:3; Ps 123:2; Prov 30:23; and Isa 24:2; 45:5, 7. In 1 Kgs 1:19 *gĕbîrâ* should be translated "queen," referring to the wife of the Egyptian pharaoh. Elsewhere in Kings, Chronicles, and Jeremiah (1 Kgs 15:13; 2 Kgs 10:13; 2 Chr 15:16; Jer 13:18; 29:2), the term means "queen mother."

3. See, however, Ben-Barak, "Status and Right."

4. For example, Andreasen, "Role of the Queen Mother," 186-88.

5. Terrien, "Omphalos Myth," 315-38; Ahlström, *Aspects of Syncretism,* 57-88.

6. Ackerman, "Queen Mother," 385-401.

7. The variant names Abijam and Abijah are most probably the result of textual confusion. See Noth, *Die israelitischen Personennamen,* 234, #117.

8. See especially Olyan, *Asherah.*

9. As seems indicated, for example, by the Khirbet el-Qom inscription found in the Southern Kingdom of Judah and by the Kuntillet ᶜAjrud inscriptions associated with the northern capital of Samaria.

10. Asa (1 Kgs 15:13), Hezekiah (2 Kgs 18:4), and Josiah (2 Kgs 23:6)—the reformer kings of Judah—all remove an *ʾăšērâ* from the temple in Jerusalem, suggesting that the presence of an *ʾăšērâ* was the norm in the state cult of the Southern Kingdom in the ninth, eighth, and seventh centuries. In the north, the *ʾăšērâ* Ahab erected as part of the state religion in Samaria (1 Kgs 16:33) was let stand during the purge of Jehu (2 Kgs 13:6), and a similar *ʾăšērâ* stood in "the temple of the kingdom" (Amos 7:13) dedicated to Yahweh in Bethel (2 Kgs 23:15).

11. "Das Königtum in der Reichen Israel und Juda"; English translation, "The Monarchy in the Kingdoms of Israel and Judah," 321-26.

12. The debate concerning the "divine" character of Judaean kingship is, of course, an extensive one. The most radical position is that advanced by British and Scandinavian proponents of the "myth and ritual" school, who have argued for a Jerusalem ideology of a "god-king" and for associated cultic rituals involving the king's symbolic death and rebirth, followed by a *hieros gamos.* Most scholars, however, while acknowledging that the British and Scandinavian schools correctly have drawn our attention to the special place of the king in the Israelite cult, tend to prefer a more moderate description of the Judaean monarchy, one that would characterize Jerusalem kingship not so much as "divine" but rather as "sacral." The sacral king is not truly a "god" but has instead a unique filial relationship with Yahweh. This divine sonship is perhaps described best in Cross, *Canaanite Myth,* 241-65. For bibliography and for the history of the debate on "divine" versus "sacral," see Miller, "Israelite Religion," 218-20; more fully but less up-to-date, the survey of Johnson, "Hebrew Conceptions of Kingship," 204-35, and "Living Issues," 36-42.

13. Again, as in n. 12 above and in contradistinction to the British and Scandinavian "myth and ritual" schools, it is crucial not to overstate the nature of the "divinity" ascribed to Ugaritic kings. See the cautions of Merrill, "House of Keret," 5, 7.

14. For sacral kingship in Kirta, see Gray, *The KRT Text,* 5-9; "Canaanite Kingship," 193-220; and "Sacral Kingship," 289-302; and Merrill, "House of Keret," 5-6.

15. For the identity of the speaker, see Parker, *Narrative Tradition,* 179.

16. See, however, Parker, "Historical Composition," 174 n. 59, on the use of epithets in Kirta.

17. Lewis, *Cults of the Dead,* 49-52.

18. To be sure, it is not only kings who can have a special relationship with the divine while alive. In Israel, at least, such a relationship is also presumed for prophets, and thus Samuel after his death can be called an *ʾĕlōhîm* (1 Sam 28:13).

19. Virolleaud, "Lettres et Documents," 250-53.

20. Richardson, "Ugaritic Letter," 321-24.

21. Virolleaud, "Lettres et documents," 251; Richardson, "Ugaritic Letter," 322, note on lines 1-2.

22. Virolleaud, "Textes alphabétiques," 127-31; Dhorme, "Nouvelle lettre," 142-46.

23. See further Molin, "Die Stellung der Gᵉbira," 168; Gordon, "Ugaritic *RBT/RABĪTU,*" 127.

24. So Aistleitner, *Wörterbuch,* 8 (s. v. *ʾdn*); see, however, Gordon, *Ugaritic Textbook,* 351 (s. v. *ad* [#71]).

25. Heltzer, *Internal Organization,* 182.

26. Lipínski, "Aḫat-milki," 79-115; see also Ben-Barak, "Queen Consort," 34, 37; Drower, "Ugarit," *CAH* 2, part 2, chap. XXI (b), 141-42; Ishida, *Royal Dynasties,* 155; Rainey, "Kingdom of Ugarit," 84-85; Seibert, *Women,* 48.

27. Yaron, "Royal Divorce," 21-31; see also Seibert, *Women,* 15.

28. Heltzer, *Internal Organization,* 182-83.

29. Gray, *I and II Kings,* 104.

30. Representative are the comments of Parker, *Narrative Tradition,* 159: "This raises the question in the mind of the audience, why, in a long narrative in which Keret is clearly acting out El's instructions to the letter, he should now initiate this unanticipated act with reference to another deity?" and 172, "the vow is intrusive in the account of Keret's expedition . . . the vow actually has no function in the tale of El's response to Keret's need of a family."

31. See Parker, *Narrative Tradition,* 176; idem, "Historical Composition," 163; Coogan, *Ancient Canaan,* 53.

32. See also the comments of Trible concerning the unnecessary and even foolish vow of Jephthah in Judg 11:29-40 (*Texts of Terror,* 96-97).

33. Gray, *KRT Text,* 59; see also idem, "Sacral Kingship," 295-96.

34. Ginsberg, *King Keret,* 41; Driver, *Myths and Legends,* 91 n. 7.

35. Parker, *Narrative Tradition,* 162.

36. Gray, *KRT Text,* 59.

37. Schaeffer, "Les fouilles," 54-56, and pl. VIII; also idem, *Reprise des fouilles,* pl. VIII. A photograph is easily accessible in Pritchard, *Ancient Near East in Pictures,* pl. 829.

38. Hestrin, "Lachish Ewer," 215-20; see, however, Schaeffer, "Les fouilles," 54-55, and Ward, "La déesse nourricière," 229-30, who argue that the goddess is Anat.

39. Similarly, see the suggestion of M. Dussaud, as reported in Schaeffer, "Les fouilles," 55. (Schaeffer, on the other hand, considers the sucklers to be divine.) Also see Ward, "La déesse nourricière," 230-31.

40. See Crowfoot, et al., *Early Ivories.*

41. Similarly, see Gray, "Sacral Kingship," 296 n. 31.

42. E. F. Beach has pointed out to me (in private communication) that the ivory beds attested at many west Semitic sites may never have been intended for sleeping but were used only for ritual feasting and other ceremonial purposes. Beach's point is compelling, although my thesis about the special iconography of the crown prince's bed holds, I think, regardless of whether the couch is one upon which the child actually slept. Beach also has suggested to me the intriguing possibility that the king's bride, the queen mother-to-be, may have brought such an ivory bed as part of her dowry. The iconography the queen brings with her to her husband's court, that is, might suggest already at the time of marriage the woman's eventual identification with the winged, horned goddess of the Hathor headdress, Asherah.

43. S. A. Wiggins, in his recently completed doctoral dissertation *Athirat, Asherah, Ashratu: A Reassessment According to the Textual Sources* (New College, Edinburgh, 1992), has pointed out two other pieces of evidence from Ugarit that suggest a connection between the earthly queen mother and the goddess Asherah. The first is an incident from the Baal cycle, *KTU* 1.6.1.39-55, where the goddess Asherah at the request of El proposes in the face of Baal's death to make Aṯtar, her son, king on Mount Saphon. Asherah, that is, undertakes in El's heavenly court the responsibility for determining the royal succession, a responsibility assumed on earth by Ugaritic queen mothers. Wiggins further notes that the title that seems to be used for queen mothers at Ugarit, *rbt* (see further C. Gordon, "Ugaritic *RBT/RABĪTU*," 127-32), is also a title used of Asherah in her standard Ugaritic epithet *rbt aṯrt ym*, "Lady Asherah of the Sea."

44. In Pritchard, *Ancient Near East in Pictures,* note on pl. 798 (p. 375).

45. First published by Bossert, *Die Ausgrabungen,* pl. 14, no. 71; a photograph is easily accessible in Pritchard, *Ancient Near East in Pictures,* pl. 798.

46. For *bt* meaning "tomb," see Dahood, *Ugaritic-Hebrew Philology,* 65, and the discussion by Knoppers, "The God in His Temple," 118.

47. Knoppers, "The God in His Temple," 105-20; see also Dahood, *Ugaritic-Hebrew Philology,* 65 (pointed out by Knoppers, 105 n. 3).

48. On this idiom and its meaning, see Greenfield, "Scripture and Inscription," 259-60.

49. Edwards, "Relief of Qudshu-Astarte-Anath," 49-51.

50. As noted by Edwards, "Relief of Qudshu-Astarte-Anath," 51.

51. See Ackerman, "Queen Mother," 396-98, on Asherah's association with lions and serpents; idem, *Under Every Green Tree,* 190-91, for further materials concerning Asherah's connections with lions.

52. Pritchard, *Recovering Sarepta,* 104-5.

53. See Cross, *Canaanite Myth,* 28-35.

54. See Oden, *Lucian's De Syria Dea,* 98.

55. See further Dever, "Asherah, Consort of Yahweh?" 28.

56. Further on Asherah at Sidon, see Betlyon, "The Cult of ᵓAšerah/ᵓĒlat," 53-56; Betlyon assembles significant evidence associating Asherah with Sidon during the time of Ešmunazor, but his overall conclusions contrasting a flourishing Asherah cult with a more minimal Astarte cult are, to my mind, overstated.

57. See Mekhitarian, *Egyptian Painting*, 38; conveniently reproduced in Hestrin, "Lachish Ewer," pl. 29:C; idem, "Cult Stand," fig. 6 (p. 70); Keel, *Symbolism*, fig. 253 (p. 186).

58. See, for example, Piankoff and Rambona, *Egyptian Religious Texts* 3, pt. 2, papyrus no. 9 (discussed in pt. 1, "Texts," 105-6); conveniently reproduced in Keel, *Symbolism*, fig. 255 (p. 187). Similarly see Bruyere, *La tombe N° 1*, pl. 24; conveniently reproduced in Hestrin, "Lachish Ewer," fig. 5 (p. 219) and in Keel, *Symbolism*, fig. 254 (p. 186). Also Wild, *La tombe de Néfer-Hotep (I)*, II, pl. 23.

59. See Wildung and Schoske, *Noferet die Schöne*, pl. 151 (p. 113), which pictures a sycamore goddess giving nurture; also Wild, *La Tombe de Néfer-Hotep (I)*, II, pl. 21. For the sycamore as the tree of Hathor, see Buhl, "Egyptian Tree Cult," 86, 91, 94-95; Moftah, "Uralte Sykomore," 40-47.

60. See, however, Lipínski, "The Goddess," 112-16; Smith, *Early History*, 80-94; see also the useful survey of scholarly positions found in Day, "Asherah," 398-404.

61. For a complete survey of the verbs used with *ᵓăšērâ* in the Hebrew Bible, see Reed, *Asherah*, 29-37.

62. Twice (2 Chr 15:16 and 2 Chr 24:18) the Greek reads Astarte (*Astarte, Astartais*) due to textual confusion.

63. Once (Judg 3:7) the Latin reads *Astaroth* due to textual confusion.

64. Wallace, *Eden Narrative*, 111-14, 158.

65. Hestrin, "Lachish Ewer," "Cult Stand."

66. Hestrin, "Lachish Ewer," 214.

67. Cross, "Proto-Canaanite Alphabet," 20-21; " Origin and Early Evolution," 16*.

68. Albright, *Gods of Canaan*, 189; Oden, *Lucian's De Syria Dea*, 154.

69. Hestrin, "Lachish Ewer," 216.

70. See also in this regard Hestrin, "Cult Stand," 70-71.

71. Oden, *Lucian's De Syria Dea*, 149-55.

72. Although see n. 54 above.

73. Greek *oikon* (singular).

74. So, for example, F. Brown, S. R. Driver, and C. A. Briggs, *A Hebrew Lexicon of the Old Testament* (Oxford: Clarendon, 1980), 109a, s. v. *bayit*, which understands the verse as referring to tent-shrines woven for Asherah.

75. Šanda, *Die Bücher der Könige 2*, 344 (pointed out by Day, "Asherah," 407); Driver, "Supposed Arabisms," 107 (pointed out by Gray, *I and II Kings*, 664 n. b, and by Cogan and Tadmor, *II Kings*, 286).

76. Beyond the Lucianic recension, the Greek has become corrupt, reading *chettiein* or *chettieim*, possibly an error for *bettieim*, a transliteration of the original Hebrew *battîm* (so Day, "Asherah," 407; Montgomery, *Books of Kings*, 539), or possibly a Greek attempt to reflect Hebrew **kuttōnîm*, "tunics" (so Gray, *I and II Kings*, 664 n. b, but, as Day notes ["Asherah," 407], this is unlikely, because the attested plural forms of *kuttōnet/kĕtōnet*, "tunic," are feminine: *kuttŏnôt and kotnôt*).

77. See n. 10 and cf. n. 60 above.

78. Gressmann, "Josia," 325-26 (pointed out by Cogan and Tadmor, *II Kings*, 286).

79. Oppenheim, "Golden Garments," 172-93 (pointed out by Cogan and Tadmor, *II Kings*, 286).

80. Above, n. 9; I have discussed the significance of the ᶜAjrud materials more thoroughly in the companion paper to this chapter (Ackerman, "Queen Mother," 393-94); also available there is an extensive bibliography (n. 28).

81. Meshel, *Kuntillet ᶜAjrûd;* Dever, "Asherah, Consort of Yahweh?" 29.

82. The words are those of Pope, "Fertility Cults," 265a.

83. For a good summary of the traditional view, see Oden, *Bible without Theology,* 131, although note that Oden himself provides this summary only to critique it.

84. Westenholz, "Tamar, Qĕdēšā, Qadištu," 245-65.

85. Westenholz, "Tamar, Qĕdēšā, Qadištu," 261-63; Oden, *Bible without Theology,* 144-47; Fisher, "Cultic Prostitution," 225-26.

86. See Bird, "Place of Women," 419 n. 41.

87. See Albright, *Archaeology,* 139, and the references there; also Pedersen, *Israel* III-IV, 429.

88. On David's "choice" of Zadok and Abiathar, see Cross, *Canaanite Myth,* 208, 215 n. 74, and 232. 1 Kgs 2:26-27, which describes Solomon's expulsion of Abiathar from the Jerusalem priesthood, further attests to the king's right to appoint, or in this case depose, temple personnel.

89. E.g., Brown, *Birth of the Messiah,* 80, and n. 38 on that page; Perrin, *New Testament,* 275; see further the references listed in Johnson, *Biblical Genealogies,* 192 nn. 1-8.

90. Cazelles, "La Mere du Roi-Messie," 39.

91. See Johnson, *Biblical Genealogies,* 152-79; Brown, *Birth of the Messiah,* 71-74.

92. Brown, "Genealogy," 354a-b; idem, *Birth of the Messiah,* 73-74; see also Brown, et al., *Mary,* 78-93.

93. The Bible itself makes explicit this connection between the royal line as descended from Judah to Perez and as descended from Boaz to Obed and then to Jesse, David's father: see Ruth 4:12.

94. See further Brown, et al., *Mary,* 91-95, 119-25.

95. E.g., Cazelles, "La Mere du Roi-Messie," 40, 51-53; Hayes and Irvine, *Isaiah,* 132, 135-36; see, however, Gottwald, "Immanuel," 36-47; Roberts, "Isaiah," 198.

96. Vawter ("The Ugaritic Use of *GLMT,*" 319) and later Wyatt ("'Araunah the Jebusite,'" 45) point out that in *KTU* 1.14.4.204 the term *ǵlmt,* the Ugaritic cognate of *ᶜalmâ,* is used of Ḥurriya, Kirta's prospective wife and, as I have discussed above, the eventual queen mother.

97. *Infancy Jas.* 10.1-2; for the text, see Miller, *Complete Gospels,* 388; for discussion, see Brown, et al., *Mary,* 247-49, 258-60.

98. Brown, et al., *Mary,* 245, 269-70.

99. Isenberg, "The Gospel of Philip," 134, 135-36.

100. Brown, et al., *Mary,* 265, and the references there; for the text of the *Gospel of Thomas,* see Lambdin, "The Gospel of Thomas," *Nag Hammadi,* 128.

WORKS CITED

Ackerman, S. "The Queen Mother and the Cult in Ancient Israel." *JBL* 112 (1993): 385-401.

———. *Under Every Green Tree: Popular Religion in Sixth-Century Judah.* HSM 46. Atlanta: Scholars Press, 1992.

Ahlström, G. W. *Aspects of Syncretism in Israelite Religion.* Horae Soederblomianae 5. Lund: C. W. K. Gleerup, 1963.

Aistleitner, J. *Wörterbuch der ugaritischen Sprache.* Berlin: Akademie Verlag, 1974.

Albright, W. F. *Archaeology and the Religion of Israel.* 2d ed. Baltimore: Johns Hopkins, 1946.

———. *Yahweh and the Gods of Canaan: A Historical Analysis of Two Contrasting Faiths.* Winona Lake, Ind.: Eisenbrauns, 1968.

Alt, A. "Das Königtum in der Reichen Israel und Juda." *VT* 1 (1951): 2-22. Reprinted in *Kleine Schriften zur Geschichte des Volkes Israel* 2. Munich: C. H. Beck, 1959. English trans., "The Monarchy in the Kingdoms of Israel and Judah." Pp. 321–36 in *Essays on Old Testament History and Religion.* Garden City, N.Y.: Doubleday, 1967.

Andreasen, N.-E. A. "The Role of the Queen Mother in Israelite Society." *Catholic Biblical Quarterly* 45 (1983): 179-94.

Ben-Barak, Z. "The Status and Right of the *Gĕbîrâ*." *JBL* 110 (1991): 23-34.

———. "The Queen Consort and the Struggle for Succession to the Throne." Pp. 33–40 in *La femme dans le Proche-Orient antique.* Compte rendu de la XXXIIIe Rencontre assyriologique internationale (Paris, 7-10 juillet 1986), edited by J.-M. Durand. Paris: Recherche sur les Civilisations, 1987.

Betlyon, J. W. "The Cult of ᵓAšerah/ᵓĒlat at Sidon." *JNES* 44 (1985): 53-56.

Bird, P. "The Place of Women in the Israelite Cultus." Pp. 397–419 in *Ancient Israelite Religion: Essays in Honor of Frank Moore Cross,* edited by P. D. Miller, P. D. Hanson, and S. D. McBride. Philadelphia: Fortress Press, 1987.

Bossert, H. Th., et al. *Die Ausgrabungen auf dem Karatepe, Erster Vorbericht.* Ankara: Türk Tarih Kurumu Basimevi, 1950.

Brown, R. E. *The Birth of the Messiah: A Commentary on the Infancy Narratives in Matthew and Luke.* Garden City, N.Y.: Doubleday, 1977.

———. "Genealogy (Christ)." Pp. 354 a-b in *The Interpreter's Dictionary of the Bible, Supplementary Volume.* Nashville: Abingdon, 1996.

———. K. P. Donfried, J. A. Fitzmeyer, J. Reumann, eds. *Mary in the New Testament.* Philadelphia: Fortress Press; New York: Paulist Press, 1978.

Bruyere, B. *La tombe N° 1 de Sen-Nedjem à Deir el Médineh.* Cairo: L'Institut français d'archéologie orientale, 1959.

Buhl, M. L. "The Goddesses of the Eygptian Tree Cult." *JNES* 6 (1947): 80-97.

Cazelles, H. "La Mere du Roi-Messie dans l'Ancien Testament." Pp. 39–56 in *Maria et ecclesia 5: Acte Congressus Mariologici-Mariani in civitate Lourdes anno 1958 celebrati.* Rome: Academie Mariana Internationalis, 1959.

Cogan, M., and H. Tadmor. *II Kings.* Anchor Bible 11. Garden City, N.Y.: Doubleday, 1988.

Coogan, M. *Stories from Ancient Canaan.* Philadelphia: Westminster, 1978.

Cross, F. M. *Canaanite Myth and Hebrew Epic: Essays in the History of the Religion of Israel.* Cambridge, Mass.: Harvard University Press, 1973.

———. "The Evolution of the Proto-Canaanite Alphabet." *BASOR* 134 (1954): 15-24.

———. "The Origin and Early Evolution of the Alphabet." *Eretz Israel* 8 (Sukenik volume; 1967): 8*-24*.

Crowfoot, J. W., G. M. Crowfoot, and E. L. Sukenik. *Early Ivories from Samaria.* London: Palestine Exploration Fund, 1938.

Dahood, M. *Ugaritic-Hebrew Philology.* Rome: Pontifical Biblical Institute, 1965.

Day, J. "Asherah in the Hebrew Bible and in Northwest Semitic Literature." *JBL* 105 (1986): 385-408.

de Vaux, R. *Ancient Israel. Vol. 1. Social Institutions.* New York: McGraw-Hill, 1965.

Dever, W. G. "Asherah, Consort of Yahweh? New Evidence from Kuntillet ᶜAjrûd." *BASOR* 255 (1984): 21-37.

Dhorme, Ed. "Nouvelle lettre d'Ugarit en écriture alphabétique." *Syria* 19 (1938): 142-46.

Dietrich, Manfried, Oswald Loretz, and Joaquin Sanmartin. *Die Keilalphabetischen Texten aus Ugarit.* Abhandlungen zur Literatur Alt-Syrien-Palestinus und Mesopotamiens 8. Neukirchen-Vluyn: Neukirchener Verlag, 1976.

Donner, H. "Art aund Herkunft des Amtes de Königinmutter im Alten Testament." Pp. 105–45 in *Festscrift Johannes Friedrich zum 65. Geburtstag am 27. August gewidmet,* edited by R. von Kienle, et al. Heidelberg: Carl Winter, 1959.

Driver, G. R. *Canaanite Myths and Legends.* 2d ed. Rev. J. C. L. Gibson. Edinburgh: T & T Clark, 1978.

——— "Supposed Arabisms in the Old Testament." *JBL* 55 (1936): 101-20.

Drower, M. S. "Ugarit." Vol. II, Part 2, chap. XXI(b), pp. 130–60 in *Cambridge Ancient History.* 3d ed. Cambridge: Cambridge University Press, 1975.

Edwards, I. E. S. "A Relief of Qudshu-Astarte-Anath in the Winchester College Collection." *JNES* 14 (1955): 49-51.

Fisher, E. J. "Cultic Prostitution in the Ancient Near East? A Reassessment." *Biblical Theology Bulletin* 5 (1976): 225-36.

Ginsberg, H. L. *The Legend of King Keret: A Canaanite Epic of the Late Bronze Age.* BASOR Supplementary Studies 2-3. New Haven, Conn.: *ASOR,* 1946.

Gordon, C. H. "Ugaritic *RBT/RABĪTU.*" Pp. 127–32 in *Ascribe to the Lord: Biblical and Other Studies in Memory of Peter C. Craigie,* edited by L. Eslinger and J. G. Taylor. Journal for the Study of the Old Testament Supplement 67. Sheffield: JSOT Press, 1988.

———. *Ugaritic Textbook.* Rome: Pontifical Biblical Institute, 1965.

Gottwald, N. "Immanuel as the Prophet's Son." *VT* 8 (1958): 36-47.

Gray, J. *I and II Kings: A Commentary.* London: SCM, 1964.

———. "Canaanite Kingship in Theory and Practice." *VT* 2 (1952): 193-220.

———. *The KRT Text in the Literature of Ras Shamra: A Social Myth of Ancient Canaan.* 2d ed. Leiden: E. J. Brill, 1964.

———. "Sacral Kingship in Ugarit." Pp. 289–302 in *Ugaritica VI.* Paris: Mission Archéologique de Ras Shamra; Librairie Orientaliste Paul Geuthner, 1969.

Greenfield, J. C. "Scripture and Inscription." Pp. 253–68 in *Near Eastern Studies in Honor of William Foxwell Albright,* edited by H. Goedicke. Baltimore and London: Johns Hopkins, 1971.

Gressman, H. "Josia und das Deuteronomium." *ZAW* 44 (1924): 313-37.

Hayes, J. H., and S. A. Irvine. *Isaiah: The Eighth-Century Prophet—His Times and His Preaching.* Nashville: Abingdon Press, 1987.

Heltzer, M. *The Internal Organization of the Kingdom of Ugarit.* Wiesbaden: Reichert, 1982.

Hestrin, R. "The Cult Stand from Taᶜanach and Its Religious Background." Pp. 61–77 in *Studia Phoenicia 5: Phoenicia and the East Mediterranean in the First Millennium B. C,* edited by E. Lipínski. Orientalia Lovaniensia Analecta 23; Leuven: Uitgeverij Peeters, 1987.

———. "The Lachish Ewer and the ᵓAsherah." *Israel Exploration Journal* 37 (1987): 212-23.

Isenberg, W. W. "The Gospel of Philip." Pp. 131–51 in *The Nag Hammadi Library in English,* edited by J. M. Robinson. San Francisco: Harper and Row, 1977.

Ishida, T. *The Royal Dynasties in Ancient Israel: A Study on the Formation and Development of the Royal-Dynastic Ideology.* Beiheft zur ZAW 142. Berlin: De Gruyter, 1977.

Johnson, A. R. "Hebrew Conceptions of Kingship." Pp. 204–35 in *Myth, Ritual, and Kingship: Essays on the Theory and Practice of Kingship in the Ancient Near East and in Israel,* edited by S. H. Hooke. Oxford: Clarendon, 1958.

———. "Living Issues in Biblical Scholarship: Divine Kingship and the Old Testament." *Expository Times* 62 (1950-51): 36-42.

Johnson, M. D. *The Purpose of the Biblical Genealogies with Special Reference to the Setting of the Genealogies of Jesus.* 2d ed. Cambridge: Cambridge University Press, 1988.

Keel, O. *The Symbolism of the Biblical World: Ancient Near Eastern Iconography and the Book of Psalms.* New York: Seabury, 1978.

Knoppers, G. "`The God in His Temple': The Phoenician Text from Pyrgi as a Funerary Inscription." *JNES* 51 (1992): 105-20.

Lambdin, T. O. "The Gospel of Thomas." Pp. 118–30 in *The Nag Hammadi Library in English,* edited by J. M. Robinson. San Francisco: Harper and Row, 1977.

Lewis, T. J. *Cults of the Dead in Ancient Israel and Ugarit.* HSM 39. Atlanta: Scholars Press, 1989.

Lipínski, E. "Aḫat-milki, reine d'Ugarit, et la guerre du Mukiš." *Orientalia Lovaniensia Periodica* 12 (1981): 79-115.

———. "The Goddess Atirat in Ancient Arabia, in Babylon, and in Ugarit." *Orientalia Lovaniensia Periodica* 3 (1972): 101-19.

Mekhitarian, A. *Egyptian Painting.* New York: Skira, 1954.

Merrill, A. L. "The House of Keret: A Study of the Keret Legend." *Svensk Exegetisk Årsbok* 37 (1968): 5-17.

Meschel, Z. *Kuntillet ᶜAjrûd: A Religious Center from the Time of the Judaean Monarchy.* Israel Museum Catalogue 175; Jerusalem: Israel Museum, 1978.

Miller, P. D. "Israelite Religion." Pp. 201–37 in *The Hebrew Bible and Its Modern Interpreters,* edited by D. A. Knight and G. M. Tucker. Philadelphia: Fortress Press; Chico, Calif.: Scholars Press, 1985.

Miller, Robert J. (ed.) *The Complete Gospels.* Sonoma, Calif.: Polebridge Press, 1994.

Moftah, R. "Die uralte Sykomore und andere Erscheinungen der Hathor." *Zeitschrift für ägyptische Sprache und Altertumskunde* 92 (1966): 40-47.

Molin, G. "Die Stellung der Gᵉbira im Staate Juda." *Theologische Zeitschrift* 10 (1954): 161-75.

Montgomery, A. *A Critical and Exegetical Commentary on the Books of Kings*. International Critical Commentary. New York: Scribner's, 1951.

Noth, M. *Die israelitischen Personennamen im Rahmen der gemeinsemitischen Namengebung*. Hildesheim: Georg Olms, 1980.

Oden, R. A. *The Bible without Theology: The Theological Tradition and Alternatives to It*. San Francisco: Harper and Row, 1987.

———. *Studies in Lucian's De Syria Dea*. HSM 15. Missoula, Mont.: Scholars Press, 1977.

Olyan, S. M. *Asherah and the Cult of Yahweh in Israel*. Society of Biblical Literature Monograph Series 34. Atlanta: Scholars Press, 1988.

Oppenheim, A. L. "The Golden Garments of the Gods." *JNES* 8 (1949): 172-93.

Parker, S. B. "The Historical Composition of KRT and the Cult of El." *ZAW* 89 (1977): 161-75.

———. *The Pre-Biblical Narrative Tradition*. Society of Biblical Literature Resources for Biblical Study 24. Atlanta: Scholars Press, 1989.

Pedersen, J. *Israel*. London: Oxford University Press; Copenhagen: Branner og Korch, 1940.

Perrin, N. *The New Testament: An Introduction*. 2d rev. ed. by D. C. Duling. New York: Harcourt Brace Jovanovich, 1982.

Piankoff, A., and N. Rambona. *Egyptian Religious Texts and Representations 3: Mythological Papyri*. Bollingen Series 40.3. New York: Pantheon Books, 1957.

Pope, M. H. "Fertility Cults." Vol. 2, p. 265 in *Interpreter's Dictionary of the Bible*. Nashville: Abingdon, 1962.

Pritchard, J. B. *The Ancient Near East in Pictures Relating to the Old Testament*. Princeton: Princeton University Press, 1954

———. *Recovering Sarepta, a Phoenician City*. Princeton, N.J.: Princeton University Press, 1978.

Rainey, A. F. "The Kingdom of Ugarit." *Biblical Archaeologist Reader* 3. Sheffield: Almond, 1970.

Reed, W. L. *The Asherah in the Old Testament*. Fort Worth, Tex.: Texas Christian University Press, 1949.

Richardson, H. N. "A Ugaritic Letter of a King to His Mother." *JBL* 66 (1947): 321-24.

Roberts, J. J. M. "Isaiah and His Children." Pp. 103–203 in *Biblical and Related Studies Presented to Samuel Iwry*, edited by A. Kort and S. Morschauser. Winona Lake, Ind.: Eisenbrauns, 1985.

Šanda, A. *Die Bücher der Könige*. Münster: Aschendorff, 1912.

Schaeffer, C. F. A. "Les fouilles de Ras Shamra-Ugarit quinzième, seizième et dix-septième campagnes (1951, 1952 ET 1953), Rapport sommaire." *Syria* 31 (1954): 14-64.

———. *Reprise des fouilles de Ras Shamra-Ugarit, campagnes XII à XVII (1948-1953).* Paris: Librairie orientaliste Paul Geuthner, 1955.

Seibert, I. *Women in the Ancient Near East*. New York: Abner Schram, 1974.

Smith, M. S. *The Early History of God: Yahweh and the Other Deities in Israel.* San Francisco: Harper and Row, 1990.

Terrien, S. "The Omphalos Myth and Hebrew Religion." *VT* 20 (1970): 315-38.

Trible, P. T*exts of Terror: Literary-Feminist Readings of Biblical Narrative.* Overtures to Biblical Theology 13. Philadelphia: Fortress Press, 1984.

Vawter, B. "The Ugaritic Use of GLMT." *Catholic Biblical Quarterly* 14 (1952): 319-22.

Virolleaud, Ch. "Lettres et Documents Administratifs Provenant des Archives d'Ugarit." *Syria* 21 (1940): 247-76.

———. "Textes alphabétiques de Ras-Shamra provenant de la neuvième campagne." *Syria* 19 (1938): 127-41.

Wallace, H. N. *The Eden Narrative.* HSM 32. Atlanta: Scholars Press, 1985.

Ward, W. A. "La déesse nourricière d'Ugarit." *Syria* 46 (1969): 225-39.

Westenholz, J. G. "Tamar, *Qĕdēšā, Qadištu,* and Sacred Prostitution in Mesopotamia." *Harvard Theological Review* 82 (1989): 245-65.

Wild, H. *La tombe de Néfer-Hotep (I) et Neb-Néfer à Deir el Médina [N° 6] et autres documents les concernant* 2. Cairo: L'Institut français d'archéologie orientale, 1979.

Wildung, D., and S. Schoske, eds. *Nofret—Die Schöne. Die Frau im Alten Ägypten.* Cairo: Ägyptische Altertümserwaltung; Mainz: Verlag Philipp von Zabern, 1984.

Wyatt, N. "`Araunah the Jebusite' and the Throne of David." *Studia Theologica* 39 (1985): 39-53.

Yaron, R. "A Royal Divorce at Ugarit." *Orientalia* 32 (1963): 21-31.

8

SUSAN TOWER HOLLIS

Queens and Goddesses in Ancient Egypt

Millennia of fascination with Egypt have evoked much interest in the study of royalty—masculine royalty—but relatively little in feminine royalty save Cleopatra VII (69-30 B.C.E.), at least until very recently. Thus the study of Egyptian queenship is in its infancy, lacking the long scholarly history of Egyptian kingship.[1] The present paper is derived from studies about the Goddesses Neith and Hathor, especially in the late fourth and third millennia B.C.E., and about the nature of the queen in ancient Egypt and her relation to Goddesses and to the king.

NEITH

Beginning at the beginning, one finds that the dominant documented Deity of Egypt's Early Dynastic Period (about 3000-2647 B.C.E.) is the Goddess Neith. Her presence surpasses even that of Horus, the titular Deity of the king, in the published corpus of theophoric names (that is, names incorporating the name of a Deity) of royal officials and other people of rank dating from this time,[2] appearing at least 107 times or in nearly 40 percent of known cases. Of the thirty-nine or so other Deities attested in these names, no other Deity comes even close to Neith in the number of occurrences.[3] One surmises that the populace of well-to-do officials and nobles of whom evidence remains perceived some specialness that caused them to relate more closely to her than to other Deities.

Because by definition a theophoric name makes a statement about the Deity or Deities incorporated in it, one might expect that a close look at names containing Neith would elucidate her nature and characteristics. I have classified her names into a number of categories:

those suggesting cult; those expressing her beneficent behavior; those relating her to a geographical location; those bespeaking her martial or warrior spirit; those attesting to her spiritual relationship with the individual; those making a statement about Neith herself; and finally those affirming the individual's attitude or action toward her. Except for the one name incorporating a geographical location, "the Libyan Neith is her *ka*,"[4] multiples and variations exist within each category. The most prominent category comprises the names attesting Neith's beneficent attitude toward the individual and includes such names as "Neith is satisfied (with me),"[5] "Beloved of Neith,"[6] and "One whom Neith protects."[7] Names such as "Neith is her *ka*"[8] and "Neith is mistress of my *ka*"[9] point to the individual's spiritual life in relation to Neith, because a person's *ka* is his or her double or life force. The individual's attitude toward the Goddess is expressed in names like "My house is grounded in the *ka* of Neith,"[10] "Neith is my mistress,"[11] and "She loves Neith,"[12] while a cultic relation might be seen in names such as "One who has seen the wide hall of Neith,"[13] "One who is in the following of Neith,"[14] and "Beautiful is the bark of Neith."[15] Perhaps the most anomalous of these categories is the one I have designated "warrior." This group includes names such as "Great is the anger of Neith,"[16] "Neith is victorious,"[17] and "Neith fights."[18] When one thinks about the symbols of Neith, however, the crossed arrows with or without the so-called shield[19] and the double bow, the warrior aspect should not be surprising. In fact, Egyptologists have commonly called her the hunting or war Goddess,[20] although she participates in no mythology that supports this appellation. Perhaps, as has been suggested, she originated among a fighting group, possibly in Libya to the west,[21] and these signs are what remains of those times.

Because of her femaleness as well as her dominant position, it is tempting to see in her something of a mother Deity, even a primordial Mother Goddess, but given the knowledge that people lived in the lands bordering the Nile for millennia[22] before they became a unified people, an event that occurred around 3000 B.C.E.,[23] without clear evidence of Neith or any other Deity in such a role, to draw this conclusion would be speculative at best and blatantly erroneous at worst. In later times, however, she clearly appears in the role of creator and maintainer of the cosmos. In "Contendings of Horus and Seth," a Twentieth Dynasty (1186-1070 B.C.E.) tale found on Papyrus Chester Beatty I, recto, Neith, in response to a letter from the ruling company of Gods about a divine dispute, threatens that if her will is not followed, she "will be angry and the sky will meet the ground" (3,3).

The implication here that she controls the cosmos—for she must if she can cause its demise—points to a role as a cosmic Deity. Later in the Ptolemaic temple at Esna this role is expressed most explicitly, as, for example, in a text that instructs the worshiper:[24]

(242,25) To adore Neith, say:
You are the mistress of Saïs,
that is to say Tanen,[25]
of whom two parts are masculine
and one part feminine;[26]
original Goddess, mysterious and great,
who began to be at the beginning
and inaugurated everything(?).
You are the celestial vault (252,26),
in which . . .
the one who bore the stars, all that are,
and raised them on their mats(?);
the wind which burned the land by the flame of her eyes,
of the heat gone out from her mouth;
the divine mother of Re, who shines in the horizon,
the mysterious one who radiates her own light(?).
You are the serpent Goddess, who occurs before all those,
the protectress of the whole land,
who began to be
before those who came to be,
those who had become after she had first been,
the one who . . . under her authority[27]
. . . .
You are the one who made the Netherworld
in her form of Goddess who reaches (252,27) the limits of the universe,
in her material form from the liquid surface,
in her name of "enduring without end."
Mistress of the oil of unction
as well as the pieces of cloth,
Goddess who divided the comb of her loom (?) into the five … who
inhabit the sky and the earth. [28]
You are the expanse of water,
who made Tanen and who made Nun, [29]
and of childbirth, from whom goes out all which is;
(the one) who makes gush forth the inundation in its time,
and also gives a new youth with the water-of-renewal in its season;
(the one) who makes sprout the vegetation
and creates the tree of life for the living; . . .

It is possible, indeed probable, given her dominance in the early period, that ancient Egyptians viewed Neith as a creator Deity in earliest times, but definitive evidence for this idea is lacking. Deities in ancient

Egypt tended to appear prominently and in creator roles when their city or town rose to importance and, correspondingly, they declined in visibility when their city diminished in power. One sees this pattern with the rise of Amun, God of Thebes in Upper Egypt, in the Twelfth and again in the Eighteenth Dynasties. Neith's city was Saïs in the western Delta, a city that apparently lacked political importance in the early period. On the other hand, it is possible that her early strength derived in part from the importance Saïs carried in the early mythology of the mortuary realm,[30] and we know that her strength from the Twenty-sixth Dynasty on relates to the prominence of that Delta city, which began then and continued into Greco-Roman times. It is important to note, however, that the reference in "Contendings" appears at a point when Saïs is not prominent in the Egyptian political world. This fact might suggest that we simply lack information due to the very chancy nature of the finds and evidence available to us about ancient Egypt.

FIRST DYNASTY QUEENS

In light of Neith's early dominance, one can understand the possible significance of the Neith-related names borne by four royal women of the First Dynasty, two of them clearly queens. Neith-hetep, "Neith is peaceful/satisfied," belonged to a woman associated with kings Narmer, Hor-Aha (the first king of unified Egypt), and Djer; Her-Neith, "the face of Neith," was associated with Djer; and Meret-Neith, "Beloved of Neith," was also related to Djer as well as Djet (or Wadj) and Den. Finally Nekhet-Neith, "Neith is strong/the strength of Neith," was associated with Djer.[31]

The major significance of two of these queens, Neith-Hetep and Meret-Neith, lies in the appearance of each of their names in a *serekh*. Commonly used for kings' names in the early dynasties, the serekh represents iconographically the special relation the Egyptian ruler plays relative to the world of the divine and the world of humanity.[32] It consists of a palace façade surmounted by a rectangle in which is written the royal name, itself topped by a falcon (fig. 15), though near the end of the Second Dynasty, a falcon along with a mythical form of canid or even this latter figure alone appeared.[33] The falcon is identified as the falcon-God Horus, despite its lack of a name, and the canid, when it appears, is identified with his brother Seth. Whatever Deity surmounts the *serekh,* that Deity stands for the world of the Gods, the heaven that arches over all the world. The palace façade represents the earth, and of course the name of the ruler, written in the space between the two sections of the cosmos, speaks to the mediating role filled by this individual. Taken as a whole, the *serekh* signifies the king as the bridge between the sky and its powers—embodied in the Deity—and the earth, visualized in the façade.

A First Dynasty comb (fig. 16), on which is incised a *serekh,* treats the teeth of the comb as the plant life of earth, similar to the building. The flying falcon, with the sun boat spread across the very top, parallels the imagery of the Deity on the top of the *serekh.* Taken as a whole, one finds a reduplication of meaning in the comb's symbolism. It is not that the ruler is solely divine (the ruler is under the God), yet neither is the ruler wholly of the earth (the ruler is over the earthly residence). Rather the ruler seems to partake of both divine and human, of the Gods as well as of humankind. In addition the *serekh* represents the ruler "in the unusual position of being both worshiper and the object of veneration ."[34]

When the names of the queens Neith-hetep and Meret-Neith appear in *serekhs* similar to that of the king, the Deity on top of the figure is Neith, symbolized by her sign of the crossed arrows (fig. 17),[35] rather than Horus, Seth, or a combination. The two queens' use of the *serekh* suggests that these women actually ruled.[36] Neith-Hetep probably ruled, or at least acted as regent, for less than a year following Hor-Aha's reign,[37] and Meret-Neith seems to have done the same, maybe late in the reign of her husband Djer or more likely following.[38] Each is presumed to have ruled alone, thus allowing, if not demanding, the use of the *serekh.* But using the Neith *serekh* rather than the Horus *serekh* reflects her special relation with and her source of power from the Goddess.

Interestingly, one example of Meret-Neith's *serekh* is paired with that of Djer, suggesting that she filled the role of ruler or coruler with him.[39] Her importance is further demonstrated by the location of her burial in the midst of the kings at Abydos.[40] Indeed, the presence of the female's name within a symbol that so clearly delineates its possessor in relation to Deities (through the Deity surmounting the structure) and to the earth (represented by the palace façade) suggests very strongly a role parallel to that of the male ruler. On this basis, one might say that rulers could be either men or women, even both together, and whether male or female, the ruler's position was depicted by means of the *serekh.* The only difference iconographically was the identity of the Deity with whom that ruler identified.[41] The Djer-Meret-Neith sealing would further suggest that one can speak of kings and queens together as the ruling power in this early period, rather than queenship as an aspect of kingship as Lana Troy has suggested.[42]

Royal Titularies: Kings and Queens

Both kings and queens carried extensive and distinctive titularies relating to their roles in the divine, mythic, and human worlds of ancient Egypt. In the case of kings, this titulary had been fixed by the end of the Old Kingdom, but that of queens evolved over a much longer period and, as Sabbahy has noted, was "never as standardized or constant" as that of the king.[43] She suggests the reason for its slow development was the lack of a single, separately established role for the queen.[44] In fact, she could and did fill at least three different major roles in Egypt: She was the king's wife, the mythologically significant king's mother, and finally, as seen above, actually the ruler in at least a few cases. Each of these roles carried its own titulary, which tended not to be mixed with the others, particularly in the Old Kingdom.[45]

The queen as *ḥmt nsw*, "wife of the king," carried a varied set of titles. Among them are *m33.t Ḥr [Stš]*,[46] "she who sees Horus [and Seth]"; *wrt ḥst*, "great of praise";[47] and *wrt ḥts*, "the great one of the *ḥts*-scepter,"[48] titles of the king's wife, which are rarely shared with the mother of the king. The first of these, "she who sees Horus [and Seth]," refers particularly to the intimacy of the queen and the God Horus [and Seth],[49] generally considered to be the king. Even Edmund Meltzer's suggestion to me that the title *m33.t Ḥr [Stš]* could alternatively mean "she whom Horus [and Seth] see,"[50] points to the same kind of intimacy.

As *mwt nsw*, "mother of the king," the queen was also *s3t-nṯr*, "daughter of the God," that is, of the deceased king,[51] and thus responsible for the God's (that is, the king's) renewal.[52] In addition to *mwt nsw*, she also bore the epithet *ḏdt ḫt nbt ir.tw n.s*, "all things that are said are done for her."[53]

As mother of the king and daughter of the God, one sees her defined in relationship to a king, while the third title speaks to her exalted royal position.[54] Significantly kings' mothers were highly venerated, even receiving cult, as did several queen-mothers, for example, Khenetkawes of the Late Fourth/Early Fifth Dynasties[55] and Ahmose-Nefertary, who spanned the Seventeenth and Eighteenth Dynasties. The latter was also divinized.[56]

The third set of titles a queen might bear consisted of the usual king's titulary and certainly excluded the other sets. The only exceptions occur with Neith-hetep and Meret-Neith in the first dynasty. Although their names appear within the *serekh*, so characteristic of the early kings' presentation of their Horus names, and evidence exists that each of them ruled as regent or sole ruler for a short period of time,[57] they do not seem to have assumed any of the rest of the royal titulary developing at that time. In fact, Neith-hetep bears the title "one who is joined to the Two Lords,"[58] that is, "consort of the Two Lords,"[59] a title also carried by Her-Neith, whose name does not appear in a *serekh*. Later this title appears as *sm3wyt nbty*, "consort of the Two Ladies."[60] Both titles define the queen in relation to the king, who embodies the Two Lords, that is Horus and Seth, and carries the *nbty* or Two Ladies name as part of his titulary. Finally, both ruling queens in the first dynasty bear the enigmatic epithet *ḥnty*, "the foremost (of women?)."[61]

In contrast to these early ruling queens, later ruling queens assumed the usual fivefold king's titulary, for example, Hatshepsut. These women, rather than being queens and gaining their definition as rulers by means of Neith, became "female Horuses" with all the attributes—regalia, names, inscriptions, and so forth—of male Horuses,[62] even to donning the ceremonial royal beard, as did Hatshepsut,[63] although they, like their First Dynasty counterparts, were originally ordinary queens, wives of kings.

FEMININE ASPECTS OF RULERSHIP

After Meret-Neith, one does not find a queen, even a ruling queen, using the Neith *serekh*. In fact, Neith's appearance in connection with the names of royal women, although not limited to the First Dynasty, loses its dominance in later dynasties, appearing only very occasionally.[64] Nevertheless, the feminine aspect of rulership persists in numerous ways, most notably in the so-called *nbty* or "Two Ladies" title in the royal titulary and in the use of the cobra Goddess on the king's brow as the uraeus. The "Two Ladies" name appears as the second name in the king's five-part titulary and incorporates Wadjet, the cobra Goddess of Lower Egypt, and her Upper Egyptian counterpart, the vulture Goddess Nekhbet (fig. 18). The pairing appears first with Hor-Aha at Naqada[65] and continued to play a part in the designation of rulership throughout Egyptian history.

The cobra Goddess Wadjet or Uto appears in a number of forms from the predynastic period on,[66] but her appearance as the uraeus, the hooded cobra rising from the royal forehead, concerns us most here. In this form, she is both dangerous and protective: dangerous to the royal enemies and protective of the king. As the sun's eye,[67] she plays a part in the creation of the world, and she also functions as the sun's mother, wife, sister, or daughter,[68] sometimes in several roles simultaneously. Significantly, the cobra not only appears as the king's uraeus but also as that of the queen, at least by the time of the Sixth Dynasty.[69] Before that time, the only females who wore the uraeus were Goddesses.

Even before assuming the uraeus, the queen appeared wearing a vulture headdress, recalling the appearance of a flying protective vulture above the king as early as the late predynastic Narmer macehead.[70] This headdress appears on some queens during the Fifth Dynasty, although some fragments from Khafre's Fourth Dynasty tomb complex suggest the possibility of its use even earlier.[71] The vulture headdress had become a regular part of the queen's iconography by the time of the second queen of the Sixth Dynasty.[72] This headdress shows the bird's head rising from the Goddess's or queen's forehead (rather like the rising cobra), while the bird's body stretches along the top of her head with its wings folded down the sides of her head behind her ears (fig. 19). A relief from the Fifth Dynasty temple of Niuserre shows the cobra Goddess Wadjet in anthropomorphic form wearing the combined cobra-vulture headdress (fig. 20),[73] while the Sixth Dynasty queen Neith wears a similar head covering,[74] possibly showing the appropriation of divine iconography by the queen or even perhaps relating the queen to the world of the divine, as does the *serekh*. The persistent presence of the uraeus on the ruling king, and eventually the queen, even when she is not formally acknowledged as ruler, along with the vulture, either flying above the king or as a headdress on the queen, suggests a strong female element in royalty.

THE GROWTH IN THE KING'S DOMINANCE

Rainer Stadelmann's discussion of the queens' tombs and the pyramid precinct[75] provides interesting and provocative archaeological evidence about the queen's position relative to the king and about the royal ideology during the Early Dynastic and Old Kingdom periods. This evidence might be supported by or support the meaning of the queens' names in the Neith *serekh* and some of the epithets gained by the queens as these periods progressed. He observes that from the near parity of the size of queens' tombs in the First Dynasty,[76] the queens' tombs later move away geographically from the kings' precincts to the edges of or outside the pyramid area[77] and become smaller. He suggests that the change derives from the increased thrust of the kingship to a divine or an approximately divine position, leading to a progressive subordination of the queen,[78] a development emphasized by the queen's titles, suggesting her dependence on the king. In other words, an increasing emphasis on the king's divinity occurs at the expense of that of the queen, leading to a greater emphasis on her humanity. This movement continues on through the Third Dynasty, and by the Fourth, it is established enough that a small pyramid appears for a queen of Khufu. According to Stadelmann, this granting of a pyramid to the queen does not express her emancipation or equality or a move toward it, but rather it represents the loss of the symbolic value of the form.[79] Perhaps an appropriate analogy lies in the appropriation of the royal mortuary texts by nonroyal people during the First Intermediate Period and in the Middle Kingdom for use on their coffins. One could argue, however, that the clear establishment of the king's dominance by this time, especially regarding the Gods, may permit the closer proximity of the queen.[80]

One might see a similar movement in the diminished use of the *serekh* by the king after the early dynasties. With the adoption of the cartouche for the king's birth name at the end of the Second and beginning of the Third Dynasties[81]—and a change in the manner by which the ruler was identified, from the Horus name to names such as *nsw-bit*, "King of Upper and Lower Egypt," and *s3 R*ᶜ, "son of Re,"—the sense of the king as bridge between the realms of the Gods and humanity gave way to an emphasis on the ruler's relation to the land, on the one hand, and to the Deity as son, on the other. With the cartouche established, the *serekh* could again be used as desired, as occurred on Menkaure's throne base, now in the Boston Museum of Fine Arts, where one finds both the *serekh* and the cartouche.

HATHOR

Contemporaneous with the rise of the pyramid form, the exclusion of queens' tombs, and the conscious striving to establish kingship as divine or approximately divine came the rise in prominence of the Goddess Hathor, along with that of the sun God Re. Concurrently, evidence of Neith and her symbols diminishes greatly. From her dominant position in the corpus of theophoric names on the Early Dynastic seals,[82] vases, and palettes[83] in the Old Kingdom, Neith seems to appear most commonly in the context of an individual serving as a priestess of Neith and Hathor, rarely of just Neith.[84] Thus, aside from the religio-political shifts in the rulership during these years, as evidenced in the male royal titulary, the loss of the Neith queens' power, and hence their use of the *serekh*, is not surprising.

Hathor's rise to dominance is thought to derive from her relation to Re. According to Wolfgang Helck, in the course of the Third Dynasty as the sun God began to supersede the king as world God, his wife is called Hathor.[85] Certainly a great number of Old Kingdom seals show the two paired[86] or as a triad with the king between them.[87] In this latter form, he is their son, as the establishment of the king's name "Son of Re" suggests. Of particular interest is Pepi I's use of the name "Son of Hathor" in the Sixth Dynasty, referring to Hathor, Mistress of Dendera, rather than the now-expected name "Son of Re."[88] This title is also used by Mentuhotep II in the Eleventh Dynasty.

THE QUEEN IN THE OLD KINGDOM

The king's designation as "Son of Re" shows no parallel in the queen's titulary during the course of the Old Kingdom, but rather, moving from the implied divinity of the queen seen in the *serekh*,[89] one finds Fourth Dynasty queens bearing titles like *mwt njswt-bity*,[90] "mother of the King of Upper and Lower Egypt"; *ḥmt njswt mrt.f*, "wife of the king whom he loves"; and the old title, *m33t Ḥr Stš*, "she who sees Horus and Seth"; along with various forms of the words *tist* ("companion"), *smrt* ("friend"), and *ḥt Ḥr* ("possession or follower of the king").[91] According to this terminology, the queen's significance lies in her relation to the king rather than in her own person. If one could find a corresponding epithet or title for the contemporary king, that is one placing him in relation to his queen, it would then be possible to speak truly of an equality between the two. Apparently none exists,[92] and so it has been concluded that, in general, an equality of divinity between the king and the queen did not exist or at least is not publicly manifested after the First Dynasty.

Other Old Kingdom evidence of the queen's relation to the king appears in various sculptures. Fragments of a statue of Djedef-Re, third king of the Fourth Dynasty, show the king with his wife, presumably Khentetenka, sitting or squatting beside her husband's left leg (fig. 21). Depicting a configuration common in later statues and reliefs,[93] this piece suggests a true subordination of the queen to the king in accordance with the principle that the dominant figure or figures in a group are portrayed much larger than the accompanying figures.[94] According to Heinrich Schäfer, such scaling emphasizes power and authority rather than physical strength but does not normally appear in depictions of Gods or with the chief wife of her husband.[95] Thus the presentation of Djedef-Re and his wife appears anomalous. Might one suggest that this presentation is analogous to Ramesses II's representations of himself as a colossus with his miniature family, including his wife, about him at Abu Simbal?[96] Because various pieces of evidence witness to Ramesses's self-deification during his lifetime,[97] perhaps one should see in Djedef-Re's statue an emphasis on the divine nature of the king as contrasted with the humanity and mortality of the queen, in accordance with Stadelmann's thinking.[98] One might also see Djedef-Re's depiction as related to the increased emphasis on the divine relations of the king at the expense of his earthly roots.

A different view appears in the slate statute of Menkaure and his queen Khamerernebty (fig. 22, a little later in the Fourth Dynasty,[99] one that illustrates Schäfer's understanding of parity of size between the king and his chief wife.[100] This remarkable piece sets the second pattern for later pair statues, presenting the husband and wife on a par with each other.[101] Simply garbed and coiffed, the king and queen stand shoulder to shoulder, lacking even an allowance for the expected size differential of male and female.[102] The position of the bodies of the pair provides particular interest, for they are not just standing side by side, but rather she is embracing him, even protecting him, with her right hand around his back and her left hand on his left arm. Schäfer states that this position means that the man is his wife's support, that is, he is her protector.[103] Surprisingly and with no discussion, Schäfer then describes the reverse situation in which the man has his arm about his wife, a position that first appears in the New Kingdom, as *meaning the same thing*.[104] While one can dispute exactly what each position means, it is hard to accept that reversed positions carry an identical meaning.

Furthermore, the depiction of Menkaure in the famous triads, also from the Valley Temple, belies Schäfer's suggestion. These triads, four of which are complete,[105] depict the king accompanied by Hathor and a nome Deity.[106] The triad with the Deity from the Hare nome (fig. 23) shows the king with Hathor's arms about him as in the pair statue, while that with the Cynopolite nome depicts the king with the arms of both Deities around him. The other two complete triads show mere body proximity. In one, the Goddesses—Hathor and the nome Goddess of Diospolis Parva—stand shoulder to shoulder with the king, arms touching him. Curiously, in the second triad, the Theban nome Deity, a male, appears considerably smaller than the king, a size relation also suggested, though not to such an extreme degree, in a fifth, fragmentary triad. Assuming that Hathor is minimally the mother of the king, as is suggested by the triadic presentation on Old Kingdom seals where the king is between the Goddess and his father Re,[107] the position Schäfer describes as the male protecting the female would appear to be the reverse: the female figure, perhaps the mother, is protecting the male. Thus, the position of the Goddess's arm around the king suggests she plays a protective role.

Some hard thinking about these sculptures raises other questions, to which there are no clear answers but that appear worth considering. Returning again to the pair of the king and queen, one would assess them as equals. Here one should pay particular attention to the headdress of each. The tripartite coiffure with long hair characterizes Goddesses and queens at this time.[108] Correspondingly the king wears the *nms*-headdress, a form of head covering, linking him more to his nonruling, therefore nondivine person than the more formal crown does.[109] Each wears very simple clothing, she a plain sheath of the type characteristically worn by females through the beginning of the New Kingdom[110] and he the plain *šnḏyt*-kilt with the triangular middle piece, dress that is characteristic of great men of the Old Kingdom.[111] In sum, one sees in the dyad a humanization of the royal pair[112] that belies the move to divinity suggested by the pyramids and male titulary. It might be possible to argue, however, that the pairing emphasizes the humanity of the king in light of the presence of the queen.

When one turns to the triads and focuses on the king and Hathor, one sees a replication of the pair statue *except* in the headdress. Now the king wears the White Crown, the insignia of his divine ruling role as Horus or King of Upper Egypt. The Hathor figure resembles the queen of the pair except she wears the cow's horns surmounted with the sun disk that becomes so characteristic of Hathor beginning in the Fifth Dynasty.[113] Indeed, Reisner has suggested that in these triads, the face of the queen appears as that of Hathor and the accompanying female nome, and the face of the king appears as the face of the nome God when the third member is a God,[114] an idea reiterated by numerous subsequent commentators.[115] While the idea may be valid, implicit in these comments lies a belief in portraiture as the modern Western world perceives it. Because modern Western portraiture, itself controversial in definition, and what is commonly called portraiture in ancient Egypt are questionably related, if at all,[116] such an idea seems dubious at best. Nevertheless, it is not impossible that there does exist some relationship between the queen of the slate pair and Hathor of the triad.

INSIGNIA AND REGALIA: INFLUENCE OF THE FEMININE

Such a relationship revolves around the power inherent in insignia and particular dress. The modern cliché "the clothes make the man [*sic*]" is most apt here, but from an anthropological view, this idea is not a cliché at all. Instead, it speaks to a significant reality. The dress donned on a particular occasion or an insignia used or bestowed in a specific situation greatly affects the status of the participating individuals. Putting this concept in Egyptological terms, in his study of the significance of particular features of early Egyptian depictions of kings, Helck states, "Through the placement of the (animal's) horns (on his head), the leader disguised himself and became the animal referred to and thereby possessed its power."[117] Hornung, referring to the same phenomenon, suggests that when the king clothed himself with the royal insignia, he thereby took on the role of the creator God, though he was not a God.[118] These examples, two of many, show that the garb, including the headdress, of the king signifies his state or mode at that time. Thus in the triads, the king fills the position of Horus or ruler of Upper Egypt by wearing the White Crown. The significance comes by changing *only* his headgear from that seen on the slate pair, for the shift from the unpleated to the pleated *šnḏyt*-kilt is of no apparent significance.[119]

Might a similar change carry parallel significance for the queen, given that she also carries specific insignia?[120] Before dismissing the question out of hand, especially if one accepts the idea of a progressive diminution of the apparent early equality of the queen with the king during the course of the first four dynasties, one must recall that a cow Deity, probably Bat rather than Hathor,[121] occurs at least as early as the late predynastic period.[122] With time and the rise of Hathor,[123] whom the Egyptians eventually saw as a cow Goddess, the cow's horns came to represent an attribute of Hathor, alluding to part of her nature or manifestation.[124] Thus, to wear this headdress is to identify with Hathor, in fact, to become her, even as in the presentation of the ornamental *menat*,[125] a priestess becomes a Hathor, who herself is the Great Menat.[126] Under these circumstances, the individual takes on the Goddess's identity.

One can see the same phenomenon with the vulture headdress mentioned previously. Originally specific to Goddesses, it was assumed by the queens in the Fifth and Sixth Dynasties, and in the Sixth Dynasty combined with the uraeus. The association of the queen with these female Deities, all very much a part of the rulership of ancient Egypt from earliest times, suggests that the queen continued to represent the feminine divine in the rulership. Indeed, as implied by the total femaleness of the symbols of the queen in addition to the female symbols related to the king, namely the uraeus and the Two Ladies name, there was more of the female in Egyptian rule than male—if one wants to weigh the elements.

THE QUEEN AND THE DIVINE IN NARRATIVES

Available narrative materials further support the significant position of the queen in relation to Egyptian rule. In the Middle Kingdom story of Sinuhe, one finds several references to the queen that reflect associations with the world of the Deities in general and with Hathor in particular. The story relates the adventures of a self-exiled man who had close connections to the queen before his departure and who returned, in part, because of his love for his queen. In a letter enticing him back, the king describes the queen as "your heaven which is in the palace,"[127] "heaven" being a term referring to Deities. In the next sentence, the king writes that the queen "covers her head with the rulership of the Two Lands (Egypt),"[128] by which one may understand the combined vulture-cobra headdress. Combined, these phrases strongly imply that the queen shares the power of the king in ruling the land, participating, as he does, in the divinity that legitimizes the ruling power of ancient Egypt. This sense appears even more dramatically in the hymn sung by the royal children to the king following Sinuhe's return to the palace. Here the queen is referred to as "the mistress of heaven" with the classic Egyptian phrase, *nbt pt*,[129] determined by the cobra, a hieroglyph that frequently determines the names of Goddesses. Thus, what appears to be an ambiguous presentation of the queen in the hymn may not be so ambiguous in light of the foregoing discussion.

Another Middle Kingdom narrative[130] relates a narrative placed in the early years of the Fourth Dynasty, about a millennium earlier, telling of the wife of a priest of Re giving birth to the first three kings of the Fifth Dynasty. Their procreation by Re provides an explicit example of a God's intervention in the human world to produce a divine king through a human woman.

A later but perhaps even more dramatic example of this same theme appears on the walls of Hatshepsut's temple at Deir el Bahri.[131] The text tells of Amun going in to the queen in the form of the ruling king to beget the heir with her, followed by the eventual birth of the child and his presentation to and recognition by the God as the king-to-be. It is illustrated by as many as fifteen vignettes showing the Deities and humans involved. Significantly, the New Kingdom saw an increasing visibility in the queen's activities, perhaps representing an increased strength of the feminine aspect of the ruling power. One modern scholar has ventured to suggest that the vicious treatment of women in three later New Kingdom tales, "The Tale of Two Brothers," "Truth and

Falsehood," and "The Contendings of Horus and Seth," results from a reaction to the queens' use of power.[132]

Perhaps the most prominent of these queens was Hatshepsut, the wife of Tuthmosis II. She became queen regnant for the very underage Tuthmosis III at his father's death, and within a short time moved from this position to that of actual ruler, accepted as such by her subjects. While the extent of her power was suppressed in the records from late in Tuthmosis III's independent reign and following, that she was a strong and effective ruler goes without question. In fact, as the young Tuthmosis grew, the stability of the rulership was such that he, as co-regent, could venture further up into the Syro-Palestinian area to establish Egyptian power than any previous or subsequent ruler. The Egyptian empire was the result.

Besides Hatshepsut, a number of other New Kingdom queens, both before her and following her, exerted great influence. For example, following the Seventeenth Dynasty, highly regarded queen Teti-Sheri, Ahhotep, mother of Ahmose, the first king of the Eighteenth Dynasty, seems to have actually ruled while her husband was on campaign.[133] As noted above, her successor, Ahmose-Nefertari, was divinized, receiving cult, while Queen Tiye, the commoner wife of Amenhotep III, likewise divinized, also enjoyed the king's confidence regarding state affairs.[134] And there is currently much lively discussion about Nefertiti, the famous wife of Akhenaten, who may well have wielded considerable power during her husband's reign and who certainly appears in iconographic depictions in poses similar to and even identical with those of the king. In the Nineteenth Dynasty, before the time of the tales mentioned above, Nefertari, beloved queen of Ramesses II, was honored with her own temple at Abu Simbal, significantly with Hathor as the titulary Deity, and with a beautiful tomb, one of the loveliest, in the Valley of the Queens in West Thebes.

During this same time and later, royal women served as the so-called God's Wife of Amun,[135] a role that combines the divine with the human in her person. Finally, one finds strong, even ruling queens, among the Greek and Roman rulers following Alexander.[136] Of course, the legendary Cleopatra VII dominates this group of women, but in fact she was only the last, albeit the most dramatic, of the line. The traditional, historic strength of Macedonian queens and the divinity of Egyptian queenship combined in the earlier Ptolemaic queens eventually to make possible a Cleopatra VII.[137]

In conclusion, it is clear that queenship in ancient Egypt is closely related to the world of the divine in the form of several specific

Goddesses, most notably Neith and Hathor along with Wadjet and Nekhbet, though the exploration of the extent of this relation is just beginning. It is also clear that Hathor, Wadjet, and Nekhbet also play very significant roles with regard to the kingship, a concept to which one might more properly refer with the nongendered term rulership, because queens could and did rule with impunity. Much remains to be researched, especially in light of the long history of the civilization and the changes that took place in its course. Thus, this discussion represents only a beginning that needs development, alteration, and refinement.

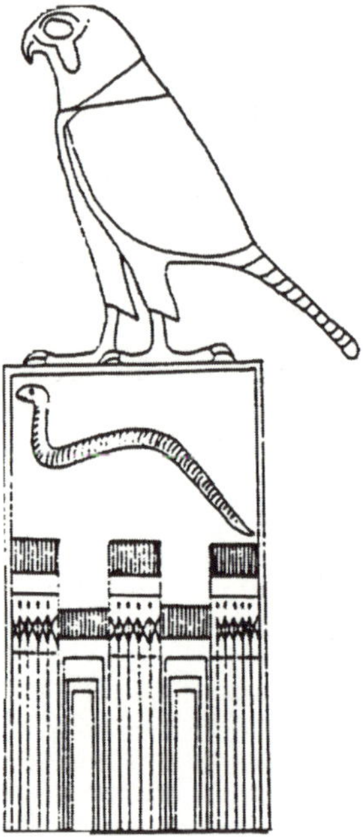

Fig. 15

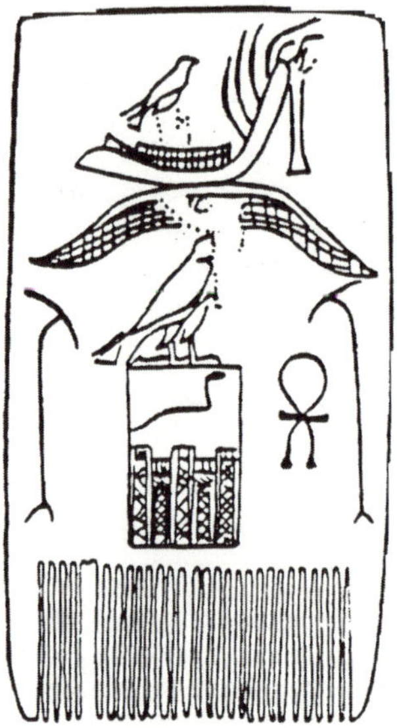

Fig. 16

Fig. 17

Fig. 15 Serekh of King Djet, Dynasty 1
Fig. 16 Djet's comb
Fig. 17 Serekh of Meret-Neith, Dynasty 1
Fig. 18 Nbty hieroglyphs

Fig. 18

Fig. 19

Fig. 20

Fig. 19 Queen Iput I in vulture crown, Dynasty 6
Fig. 20 The Goddess Wadjet with King Niuserre, Dynasty 5
Fig 21 Fragment of statue of Djedef-Re and his wife, Dynasty 4

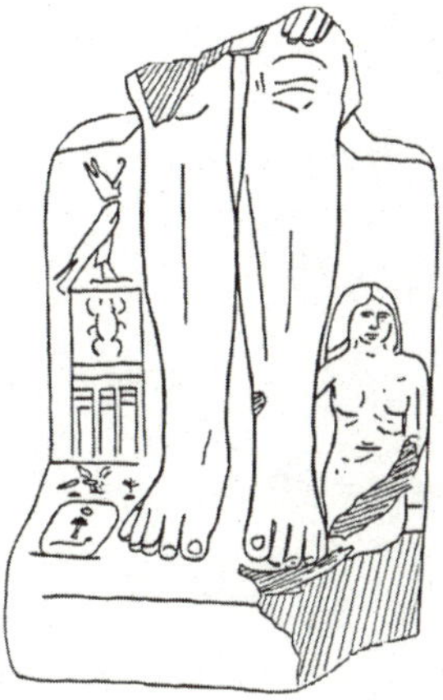

Fig. 21

Fig. 22

Fig. 22 Menkaure and his queen, Dynasty 4
Fig. 23 Menkaure, Hathor, and the Goddess of Hare Nome (Hermopolis, Upper Egypt), Dynasty 4

Fig. 23

NOTES

1. Since 1980, however, at least five dissertations on the subject have appeared (Seipel, Robins, Sabbahy, Troy, and Green), although only two (Seipel and Troy) have actually been published, one of them in German (Seipel). One more, unpublished, appeared in 1952 (Mertz). In addition, Christiane Desroches-Nobelcourt, *La femme*, and Barbara Lesko, *The Remarkable Women*, include sections on queens in their recent books, while Sarah Pomeroy presents a discussion of queens in Hellenistic Egypt in yet another publication (*Women in Hellenistic Egypt*). While Lisa Kuchman Sabbahy discusses the relationships between queens and Goddesses to some degree, only Lana Troy's study makes a concerted attempt to relate the two worlds, as the title of her book, *Patterns of Queenship in Ancient Egyptian Myth and History*, suggests.

2. Kaplony, *Die Inschriften*.

3. Hollis, "The Roles." Interestingly Khnum, the God with whom Neith is closely associated in the Ptolemaic temple at Esna, is the Deity mentioned the next most frequently, appearing twenty-seven times.

4. Sayed, *La Déesse Neith*, doc. 12.

5. Sayed, *La Déesse Neith*, doc. 105.

6. Sayed, *La Déesse Neith*, doc. 8, 85.

7. Sayed, *La Déesse Neith*, doc 67.

8. Sayed, *La Déesse Neith*, doc. 17.

9. Sayed, *La Déesse Neith*, doc. 10.

10. Sayed, *La Déesse Neith*, doc. 23.

11. Sayed, *La Déesse Neith*, doc. 30.

12. Sayed, *La Déesse Neith*, doc. 16.

13. Sayed, *La Déesse Neith*, doc. 5, 11.

14. Sayed, *La Déesse Neith*, doc. 61.

15. Sayed, *La Déesse Neith*, doc. 106.

16. Sayed, *La Déesse Neith*, doc. 3.

17. Sayed, *La Déesse Neith*, doc. 91.

18. Sayed, *La Déesse Neith*, doc. 98.

19. Hollis, "Neith's Standard."

20. Bonnet, *Reallexicon*, 513; Schlichting, "Neith," col. 392.

21. Wainwright, "The Red Crown"; Bonnet, *Reallexikon*, 517.

22. Shaw, "The Black Land."

23. For the most recent discussion of the complexities of the unification of ancient Egypt, see Baines, "Origins of Egyptian Kingship," and also the index of O'Connor and Silverman, *Ancient Egyptian Kingship*.

24. Translation from Sauneron, *Les Fêtes*, 110-19. This hymn dates to the time of Hadrian (118-38 C.E.).

25. Tanen, or Tatenen, is the God of the primordial earth, bedrock. This God is not known in the Old Kingdom, appearing first in the Middle Kingdom. Most frequently he is met as Ptah-Tatenen, although he is syncretized to other Gods as well.

26. Andrea Nash, a student of mine at Scripps College in 1987, suggested that this formula reflects the world as represented by the sky Goddess Nut, the earth God Geb, and the air God Shu, thus resulting in the two-thirds male, one-third

female of the text. Such a concept raises some fascinating possibilities for study of the distinctions between female and male primordial creators. Can one say that female creators, like Neith, incorporate the creation within themselves, as women do in the procreation of a child, while male creators use external materials like clay, mud, spittle, and so on? The idea demands research.

27. Perhaps, "the sovereign is crowned under her authority."

28. The reference here is to Neith as the inventor of weaving, and "the five," refer to the five cosmogonic Deities according to the Heliopolitan scheme of creation: Atum, Sh, Tefnut, Geb, and Nut.

29. The primordial waters from which all emerged. It is thought that the image derives from the land emerging as the yearly Nile flood recedes.

30. Settgast, *Untersuchungen*, 65-74.

31. Seipel, *Untersuchungen*; Troy, *Patterns of Queenship*, 152.

32. The publication in 1995 of *Ancient Egyptian Kingship*, edited by David O'Connor and David P. Silverman, provides the most recent current thinking about ancient Egyptian kingship and has been utilized where possible in the revision of this paper. It is important to note, however, that there is no mention of "queen" in the index of this volume and very few citations for any queens by name.

33. Beckerath, *Handbuch*, 7ff.

34. Green, "Queens and Princesses," 442. For a fuller discussion of the nature of Egyptian kingship, see Silverman, "The Nature of Egyptian Kingship." For a fuller discussion of the *serekh*, see Baines, "Origins of Egyptian Kingship," 2.3, 121-25.

35. The meaning of the arrows or the other signs (the crossed arrows on some kind of figure-eight device and an interlinked double arc), often referred to as a bow, is frequently discussed but with no firm conclusion. Most recently see Hollis, "Neith's Standard."

36. Seipel, *Untersuchungen*, 12-15, 35-36.

37. Seipel, *Untersuchungen*, 14-15.

38. Seipel, *Untersuchungen*, 35-36; Baines, "Origins of Egyptian Kingship," 131.

39. Emery, *Great Royal Tombs*, 169; Seipel, *Untersuchungen*, 28-35, esp. 35.

40. Seipel, *Untersuchungen*, 35.

41. In relation to the pre-Incas, Irene Silverblatt (*Moon, Sun, and Witches*) has shown a parallel descent of kings and queens from a God and Goddess respectively. Her discussion has strongly influenced the present interpretation regarding Egyptian kings and queens.

42. Troy, *Patterns of Queenship*, 3.

43. Sabbahy, "Development," 357.

44. Sabbahy, "Development," 357. Although Sabbahy notes that queens had a different mythological basis from that of kings, unfortunately she does not discuss this topic further.

45. Sabbahy, "Development," 42, 372.

46. The oldest form of this title is simply *m33.t Ḥr,* but by the Fourth Dynasty, Seth was included in its articulation (see Troy, *Patterns of Queenship*, 189).

47. Sabbahy, "Development," 358.

48. Troy, *Patterns*, 189. Sabbahy translates the epithet "great of affection(?)" noting that the exact meaning of *ḥts* in this context is uncertain ("Development," 358).

49. Sabbahy, "Development," 53; Green, "Queens and Princesses," 282.

50. Personal conversation. This suggestion highlights the continuing problem of the translation of participles (and other grammatical forms) in Egyptian. We cannot be certain whether the verbal form here is active or passive. The idea is also presented by Ward ("Non-Royal Women," 42, n. 45). Quite possibly it meant one thing at one time and another at a different time, reflecting changing dynamics in the perception of the masculine and the feminine in rulership. See below for further discussion.

51. Sabbahy, "Development," 317.

52. Troy, *Patterns of Queenship*, 61, 99.

53. Sabbahy, "Development," 228; Troy, *Patterns of Queenship*, 88.

54. Kuchman, "Titles," pl. II.

55. Sabbahy, "Development," 80.

56. She was the wife of Ahmosis, the founder of the Eighteenth Dynasty and mother of Amenhotep I, a king who was also divinized following his death. Ahmose-Nefertary was one of several dominant women in the latter years of the Seventeenth Dynasty and the early years of the Eighteenth (see James "Egypt," 305-8).

57. Seipel, *Untersuchungen*, 12-15, 35-36.

58. Following the possibilities mentioned in note 50 above, one might translate this epithet as "one who joins the Two Lords." Such a translation raises some interesting ideas about feminine influence with the king not yet explored. One might also question why the passive participle rather than the active has been the usual choice in the translation of this and other epithets. From a critical feminist viewpoint, the possibility arises that such translations reflect modern patriarchal assumptions of the scholar.

59. Seipel, *Untersuchungen*, 10; Sabbahy, "Development," 27; Troy, *Patterns of Queenship*, 106, 116, 152, 183.

60. Troy, *Patterns of Queenship*, 183.

61. Seipel, *Untersuchungen*, 36; Troy, *Patterns of Queenship*, 152, 185.

62. Sabbahy, "Development," 37.

63. Hayes, *Scepter of Egypt*, II, fig. 53.

64. Troy, *Patterns of Queenship*, Register A:6.9; 11.9; 26.7; GW.7; Edwards, et al., *Cambridge Ancient History*, 995.

65. Beckerath, *Handbuch*, 13-17.

66. Fischer-Elfert, "Uto"; Johnson, *Cobra Goddess*.

67. Johnson, *Cobra Goddess*, 6.

68. Johnson, *Cobra Goddess*, 11.

69. Troy, *Patterns of Queenship*, 120.

70. The protective position of the vulture is identical to the falcon, interpreted as Horus, flying above the king's head, as in the relief of the Third Dynasty King Djoser (Smith, *A History*, pl. 31a). The falcon also appears positioned behind the king's head in several royal statues, e.g., Khafre (Aldred, *Egyptian Art*, 71), Pepy I (Smith, *Art and Architecture*, 144), and Tuthmosis III (Vandersleyen, *Das alte Ägypten*, 245 and fig. 177).

71. Sabbahy, "Development," 313-14, but see Troy, *Patterns of Queenship*, 17.

72. Troy, *Patterns of Queenship*, 117.

73. Johnson, *Cobra Goddess*, 131.

74. Troy, *Patterns of Queenship*, 120; Johnson, *Cobra Goddess*, 177.

75. Stadelmann, "Königinnengrab."

76. Stadelmann, "Königinnengrab," 252, includes the Second Dynasty despite lack of finds.

77. Stadelmann, "Königinnengrab," 251.

78. Stadelmann, "Königinnengrab," 251.

79. Stadelmann, "Königinnengrab," 260.

80. Because Khufu (Cheops) built the largest pyramid and his successors continued to build pyramids, the form being used in one way or another for at least another millennium, one might question the idea that the queen's gaining a small pyramid represents a loss in its symbolic value. I rather suspect that the king's greater security of dominance permitted it.

81. Kaplony, "Königsring," 610.

82. Kaplony, *Die Inschriften*.

83. Sayed, *La Déesse Neith*, 209-38.

84. Sayed, *La Déesse Neith*, 239-75; Galvin, "Priestesses," 56-57, 66, 69, 73; Kaplony, *Die Rollsiegel*, Tafel 85,3; 85,4; 97,29.

85. Helck, "Herkunft," 976. Fischer states that the earliest evidence for an association of Hathor and Re dates to the sun temples of the early Fifth Dynasty (*Dendera*, 34). In contrast, Kaplony (*Die Rollsiegel*, 71-72) argues that *nṯr* in expressions with the *dw3* mark on Old Kingdom seals stands for and is interchangeable with Re's name, dating to the Second Dynasty. There is a certain sense to his argument in that some kings begin to use Re as part of their names beginning with Neb-Re, the second king of the Second Dynasty (see Beckerath, *Handbuch*).

86. Kaplony, *Die Rollsiegel*, 78.

87. Kaplony, *Die Rollsiegel*, 79.

88. Allam, *Beiträge*, 12; Fischer, *Dendera*, 37 and n. 152; Beckerath, *Handbuch*, 57, 184.

89. Even when it is linked with the title of "consort of the Two Lords" as well as the enigmatic designation of "foremost," perhaps of women (see Troy, *Patterns of Queenship*, 185 [B1/2]), borne by Neith-Hetep and Meret-Neith.

90. *njswt-bity* is an alternative transliteration, equivalent to *nsw-bit*. In the former I am quoting Troy, *Patterns of Queenship*.

91. Troy, *Patterns of Queenship*, 152-56 and Register B.

92. Beckerath, *Handbuch*, 11, 46.

93. Smith, *A History*, 32; Aldred, *Egypt*, 114, 115.

94. Schäfer, *Principles*, 230-34.

95. Schäfer, *Principles*, 233.

96. Freed, *Ramesses*, 66-67.

97. Habachi, *Features*.

98. Stadelmann, "Königinnengrab," 251.

99. Seipel (*Untersuchungen*, 165) argues that the woman with Menkaure is not Khamerernebty. He does not offer an alternative, however.

100. Schäfer, *Principles*, 233.

101. Smith, *A History*, 38; Aldred, *Egypt*, 114-15.

102. Schäfer, *Principles*, 233.

103. Schäfer, *Principles*, 74, see also 318. Against this position, see Aldred, *Egypt*, 114.

104. Schäfer, *Principles*, 174.

105. Although Reisner, *Mycerinus*, and others following him suggest that originally a triad of the king, Hathor, and a nome Deity existed for every nome, Wendy Wood, "A Reconstruction," has made a cogent argument for the existence of only eight such triads. Hawass ("Programs," 232-37), noting that "a complete set of ... royal estates is never seen in wall reliefs of the temples" (235), suggests, "It is impossible to know for certain how many triads were originally in the court" (235).

106. Reisner, *Mycerinus*, 109-10; pls. 38-46.

107. Kaplony, *Die Rollsiegel*, 304.

108. Staehelin, *Untersuchungen*, 180-81.

109. Abubakr, *Untersuchungen*, 68.

110, Staehelin, *Untersuchungen*, 166-70.

111. Staehelin, *Untersuchungen*, 5.

112. Aldred, *Egypt*, 115.

113. Fischer, *Dendera*, 33 and n. 140; Wood, "A Reconstruction," 86-87. Fischer uses for his source Berlin cylinder seal 16955 in a copy showing no disk between the Goddess's horns, while Kaplony's drawing of the same seal (*Die Rollsiegel*, Tafel 50, #4; see also 140ff.) shows a clear sun disk between the horns. It seems to me that Fischer's statement needs to be reexamined in light of the work done by Kaplony.

114. Reisner, *Mycerinus*, 127.

115. Westendorff, *Painting*, 144 and n. 29 for others; Aldred, *Egypt*, 113.

116. Spanel, *Through Ancient Eyes*, 1-39.

117. Helck, "Herkunft," 969.

118. Hornung, *Conceptions*, 142.

119. Staehelin, *Untersuchungen*, 5-6.

120. Sabbahy, "Development," chap. 8; Troy, *Patterns of Queenship*, index.

121. Fischer, "The Cult," 7 ff., and "*Ba.t* in the New Kingdom," 50-51.

122. Arkell, "An Archaic Representation," *JEA* 1955 and 1958.

123. Neither Allam (*Beiträge*, 5) nor Daumas ("Hathor," 1024) speaks of her origins, and Moftah ("Die uralte Sykomore," 40) specifically avoids the subject.

124. Hornung, *Conceptions*, 113.

125. The *menat* was an ornament related to Goddesses, most especially Hathor, and carried by the priestesses in the Goddesses' service.

126. Blackman, *Middle-Egyptian Stories*, 14; Galvin, "Priestesses," 215.

127. Sinuhe, 185. The hieroglyphic text reads: "this your heaven which is in the palace endures and flourishes today" (Blackman, *Middle-Egyptian Stories*).

128. Sinuhe 186. The hieroglyphic text reads: "She covers (?) her head with the rulership/kingship of the Two Lands" (Blackman, *Middle-Egyptian Stories*).

129. The hieroglyphic text reads: "jewels of the mistress of heaven" (Blackman, *Middle Egyptian Stories*). See Seipel (*Untersuchungen*), who clearly states that this reference is to the queen where one might think it refers to Hathor, particularly because the next phrase, "the God (an epithet of Hathor) gives life to your nostrils," explicitly mentions the Goddess.

130. This one is found on the Papyrus Westcar dating from the Hyksos period (middle of the second millennium B.C.E.) according to Lichtheim, *Ancient Egyptian Literature*, I, 215.

131. With similar versions from the temple at Luxor (Amenhotep III), Medinet Habu (reused blocks from Ramesses II's Ramesseum), and in the mammises of various Ptolemaic temples and the precinct of Mut at Karnack (ruler undetermined). Brunner, *Die Geburt*, presents a full discussion of the texts and iconography of these examples. See Assmann, "Die Zeugung," for a more recent discussion making special use of mythic concepts.

132. Lesko, "Three Late Egyptian Stories," 102-3.

133. James, "Egypt," 306.

134. James, "Egypt," 344, 350.

135. Robins, "The God's Wife"; Troy, *Patterns of Queenship*, 177-78.

136. His birth narrative, as related by Pseudo-Callisthenes, borrows strongly from the Egyptian (see Wolohojian, *The Romance*).

137. Pomeroy, *Women in Hellenistic Egypt*.

WORKS CITED

Abubakr, A. el M. J. *Untersuchungen über die ägyptischen Kronen*. Glückstadt: Verlag J. J. Augustin, 1937.

Aldred, C. *Egypt to the End of the Old Kingdom*. New York: Thames and Hudson, 1982.

———. *Egyptian Art in the Days of the Pharaohs 3100-320 BC*. New York and Toronto: Oxford University Press, 1980.

Allam, S. *Beiträge zum Hathorkult (bis zum Ende des Mittleren Reiches)*. Berlin: Verlag Bruno Hessling, 1963.

Arkell, A. J. "An Archaic Representation of Hathor." *JEA* 41 (1955): 125-26.

———. "An Archaic Representation of Hathor." *JEA* 44 (1958): 5 and plates VIII and IX.

Assmann, J. "Die Zeugung des Sohns. Bild, Spiel, Erzählung und das Problem des ägyptischen Myth." Pp. 13–61 in *Funktionen und Leistungen des Mythos: Drei altorientalische Beispiele*. Freiburg and Göttingen: Universitätsverlag Vandenhoeck & Ruprecht, 1982.

Baines, J. "Origins of Egyptian Kingship." Pp. 95–156 in *Ancient Egyptian Kingship*, edited by David O'Connor and David P. Silverman. Probleme der Ägyptologie 9. Leiden: E. J. Brill, 1995.

Beckerath, J. *Handbuch der ägyptischen Königsnamen*. Munich and Berlin: Deutscher Kunstverlag, 1984.

Blackman, A. M. "On the Position of Women in the Ancient Egyptian Hierarchy." *JEA* 7 (1921): 8-30.

———. ed. *Middle-Egyptian Stories*. Bibliotheca Aegyptiaca. Brussels: Édition de la Fondation Égyptologique Reine Élisabeth, 1972.

Bonnet, H. *Reallexikon der ägyptischen Religionsgeschichte*. Berlin: Walter de Gruyter & Co, 1952.

Brunner, H. *Die Geburt des Gottkönigs: Studien zur Überlieferung eines ägyptischen Myth*. Wiesbaden: Otto Harrassowitz, 1964.

Daumas, F. "Hathor." Pp. 1024–33 in *Lexikon der Ägyptologie*. Wiesbaden: Otto Harrassowitz, 1977.

Desroches-Noblecourt, C. *La Femme au temps des pharaons*. Paris: Stock/Laurence Pernoud, 1986.

Edwards, I. E. S., C. J. Gadd, and N. G. L. Hammond. *Cambridge Ancient History*. Vols. 1, 2. Cambridge: Cambridge University Press, 1971.

Emery, W. *Archaic Egypt*. Harmondsworth and Baltimore: Penguin Books, 1961.

———. *Great Royal Tombs of the First Dynasty*. London: Egyptian Exploration Society, 1954.

Faulkner, R. O. *The Papyrus Bremner-Rhind (British Museum No. 10188)*. Brussels: Édition de la Fondation Égyptologique Reine Élisabeth, 1933.

Fischer, H. G. "*Ba.t* in the New Kingdom." *Journal of the American Research Center in Egypt* 2 (1963): 50-51.

———. "The Cult and Nome of the Goddess Bat." *Journal of the American Research Center in Egypt* 1 (1962): 7-23.

———. *Dendera in the Third Millennium B.C.* New York: J. J. Augustin, 1968.

Fischer-Elfert, H.-W. "Uto." Pp. 906–11 in *Lexikon der Ägyptologie*. Wiesbaden: Otto Harrassowitz, 1985.

Freed, R. *Ramesses the Great: An Exhibition in the City of Memphis*. Memphis, Tenn.: City of Memphis, 1987.

Galvin, M. "The Priestesses of Hathor in the Old Kingdom and the 1st Intermediate Period." Ph.D. diss., Brandeis University, 1981.

Green, L. "Queens and Princesses of the Amarna Period: The Social, Political, Religious and Cultic Role of the Women of the Royal Family at the End of the Eighteenth Dynasty." Ph.D. diss., University of Toronto, 1988.

Habachi, L. *Features of the Deification of Ramesses II*. Glückstadt: Verlag J. J. Augustin, 1969.

Hawass, Z. "The Programs of the Royal Funerary Complexes of the Fourth Dynasty." Pp. 221–62 in *Ancient Egyptian Kingship*, edited by David O'Connor and David P. Silverman. Probleme der Ägyptologie 9. Leiden: E. J. Brill, 1995.

Hayes, W. C. *The Scepter of Egypt. Part II: The Hyksos Period and the New Kingdom*. New York: Metropolitan Museum of Art, 1959.

Helck, W. "Herkunft und Deutung einiger Züge des frühägyptische Königsbildes." *Anthropos* 49 (1954): 961-91.

Hollis, S. T. "The Roles of Two Third Millennium BCE Egyptian Goddesses, Hathor and Isis." Unpublished manuscript, 1989.

———. "Is the Figure on Neith's Standard a Shield?" Unpublished manuscript, 1991.

Hornung, E. *Conceptions of God in Ancient Egypt*. Ithaca, N.Y.: Cornell University Press, 1982.

James, T. G. H. "Egypt: From the Expulsion of the Hyksos to Amenophis I." Pp. 289–312 in *The Cambridge Ancient History*. 3d ed. Cambridge: The University Press, 1973.

Johnson, S. B. *The Cobra Goddess of Ancient Egypt: Predynastic, Early Dynastic and Old Kingdom Periods*. London and New York: Kegan Paul International, 1990.

Kaplony, P. *Die Inschriften der ägyptischen Frühzeit*. Wiesbaden: Otto Harrassowitz, 1963.

———. *Die Rollsiegel des Alten Reichs I: Allgemeiner Teil mit Studien zum Königtum des Alten Reichs*. Brussels: Édition de la Fondation Égyptologique Reine Élisabeth, 1977.

———. *Die Rollsiegel des Alten Reichs II: Katalog der Rollsiegel: A. Text, B. Tafeln*. Brussels: Édition de la Fondation Égyptologique Reine Élisabeth, 1981.

———. "Königsring." Pp. 610–26 in *Lexikon der Ägyptologie*. Weisbaden: Otto Harrassowitz, 1979.

Kuchman, L. "The Titles of Queenship: Part I, the Evidence from the Old Kingdom." *Newsletter of the Society for the Study of Egyptian Antiquities* 7.3 (1977): 9-12 and pl. II.

Lesko, B. S. (ed.) *The Remarkable Women of Ancient Egypt*. Providence, R.I.: B. C. Scribe Publications, 1987.

Lesko, L. H. "Three Late Egyptian Stories Reconsidered." Pp. 98–103 in *Egyptological Studies in Honor of Richard A. Parker*. Hanover and London: University Press of New England, 1986.

Lichtheim, M. *Ancient Egyptian Literature: A Book of Readings. Volume I: The Old and Middle Kingdoms*. Berkeley, Calif.: University of California Press, 1973.

Mertz, B. "Certain Titles of the Egyptian Queen and Their Bearing of the Hereditary Right to the Throne." Ph.D. diss., University of Chicago, 1952.

Millet, Nicholas. "Figures for 'The Narmer Macehead and Related Objects." *Journal of the American Research Center in Egypt*. 27 (1991): 223-25.

Moftah, R. "Die uralte Sykomore and andere Erscheinungen der Hathor." *Zeitschrift fur Ägyptische Sprache* 92 (1965): 40-47.

O'Connor, D., and D. P. Silverman, eds. *Ancient Egyptian Kingship.* Probleme der Ägyptologie 9. Leiden: E. J. Brill, 1995.

Pomeroy, S. *Women in Hellenistic Egypt from Alexander to Cleopatra.* New York: Schocken, 1984.

Reisner, G. *Mycerinus: The Temples of the Third Pyramid at Giza.* Cambridge, Mass.: Harvard University Press, 1931.

Robins, G. "Egyptian Queens in the 18th Dynasty Up to the Reign of Amenhotpe III." Ph.D. diss., Oxford University, 1981.

———. "The God's Wife of Amun in the 18th Dynasty in Egypt." Pp. 65–78 in *Images of Women in Antiquity.* Detroit: Wayne State University Press, 1983.

———. *Women in Ancient Egypt.* Cambridge, Mass.: Harvard University Press, 1993.

Sabbahy, L. K. "The Development of the Titulary and the Iconography of the Ancient Egyptian Queen from Dynasty One to Early Dynasty Eighteen." Ph.D. diss., University of Toronto, 1982.

Sauneron, Serge *Les Fêtes religiouses d'Esna aux derniers siècles du paganisme.* Esna V. Le Caire: Institut Français d'Archéologie Orientale du Caire, 1962.

Sayed, R. el. *La Déesse Neith de Saïs.* Caire: Institut Français d'Archéologie Orientale du Caire, 1982.

Schäfer, H. *Principles of Egyptian Art.* Oxford: Clarendon Press, 1974.

Schlichting, R. "Neith." Pp. 392–93 in *Lexikon der Ägyptologie.* Wiesbaden: Otto Harrassowitz, 1980.

Seipel, W. "Königin." Pp. 464–69 in *Lexikon der Ägyptologie.* Wiesbaden: Otto Harrassowitz, 1978.

———. "Untersuchungen zu den Ägyptischen Köninginnen der Frühzeit und des Alten Reiches: Quellen und historische Einordnung." Ph.D. diss., University of Vienna, 1980.

Settgast, J. *Untersuchungen zu Altägyptischen Bestattungsdarstellungen.* Abhandlungen des Deutschen Archäologischen Instituts Kaire, Ägyptologische Reihe, Band 3. Glückstadt: Verlag J. J. Augustin, 1963.

Shaw, I. "The Black Land, the Red Land." Pp. 13–25 in *Egypt: Ancient Culture, Modern Land,* edited by Jaromir Málek. Norman, Okla.: University of Oklahoma Press, 1993.

Silverblatt, I. *Moon, Sun, and Witches: Gender Ideologies and Class in Inca and Colonial Peru.* Princeton, N.J.: Princeton University Press, 1987.

Silverman, D. P. "The Nature of Egyptian Kingship." Pp. 49–92 in *Ancient Egyptian Kingship,* edited by David O'Connor and David P. Silverman. Probleme der Ägyptologie 9. Leiden: E. J. Brill, 1995.

Smith, W. S. *Ancient Egypt as Represented in the Museum of Fine Arts, Boston*. Boston: Museum of Fine Arts, 1960.

———. *The Art and Architecture of Ancient Egypt*. Harmondsworth, U. K.: Penguin Books, 1981.

———. *A History of Egyptian Sculpture and Painting in the Old Kingdom*. Boston: Museum of Fine Arts, 1949.

Spanel, D. *Through Ancient Eyes: Egyptian Portraiture*. Birmingham, Ala.: Birmingham Museum of Art, 1988.

Stadelmann, R. "Königinnengrab und Pyramidenbezirk im Alten Reich." *Annales de Service des Antiquités de l'Égypt* 71 (1987): 251-60.

Staehelin, E. *Untersuchungen zur ägyptischen Tracht im Alten Reich*. Berlin: Verlag Bruno Hessling, 1966.

Troy, L. *Patterns of Queenship in Ancient Egyptian Myth and History*. Uppsala: Almquist and Wicksell, 1986.

Vandersleyen, C. *Das alte Ägypten*. Berlin: Propyläen Verlag, 1985.

Wainwright, G. A. "The Red Crown in Early Prehistoric Times." *JEA* 9 (1923): 26-33 and plate XX,3.

Ward, W. "Non-Royal Women and Their Occupations in the Middle Kingdom." Pp. 33–43 in *Women's Earliest Records from Ancient Egypt and Western Asia*. Atlanta: Scholars Press, 1989.

Westendorf, W. *Painting, Sculpture, and Architecture of Ancient Egypt*. New York: H. N. Abrams, 1969.

Wolohojian, A. M., ed. *The Romance of Alexander the Great by Pseudo-Callisthenes*. New York and London: Columbia University Press, 1969.

Wood, W. "A Reconstruction of the Triads of King Mycerinus." *JEA* 60 (1974): 82-93.

9

ELEANOR FERRIS BEACH

Transforming Goddess Iconography in Hebrew Narrative

The preliminary title of this paper was "Transformations of Goddess Iconography in Hebrew Narrative," a phrase that signaled the biblical narrators' appropriation of visual imagery for their literary purposes. The present title is meant to convey a more complex dynamic in the interactions between image and word:

1. A key feature of the iconography and textual adaptations is a Goddess's role in transforming claimants into legitimate kings;
2. The narrators transform the visual depictions of Goddesses into literary characterizations of human women; and
3. Visual allusion transforms interpretation of the text.

I suspect that textualized Goddess imagery may set in motion further transformations of an ancient or modern audience that may take this dynamic beyond the text's control and my description.

ISSUES AND METHODS

The overarching question addressed in this volume is, How are women's social realities affected in various cultures and at particular historical moments by articulations of the female divine—in myth, ritual, art, music, dance, and the structural organization of religious life? My investigations center on the relations between visual representations of Goddesses and the biblical texts authored, edited, and transmitted by Yahweh-worshiping elements in ancient Israel. The specific question I will address in this chapter is, If, as I argue in two cases, some biblical accounts of supposedly "real" women are shaped by Goddesses' depictions in art and literature, how can we use these texts to examine Israelite women's social realities?

A first question is how to recognize Goddess imagery in Hebrew narrative. Attempts to relate ancient Near Eastern materials about Goddesses to biblical studies have produced extensive and methodologically confused debates.[1] Documenting the course of that enterprise would be a major investigation in itself, so I offer only a few observations. Behind many of the works, one finds theological presuppositions driving the issues into dualistic oppositions: If the God of Israelite religion is held to be singular, invisible, described principally by male analogies, revealed more through word and deed than by sight, then evidence of female divine imagery is the antithesis of this dominant symbolic set, for the texts and artifacts introduce plural, often blatantly corporeal, sometimes exaggeratedly female, and frequently visual manifestations. Within the archaeological record, the visual evidence leads to reconstruction of an Israelite religious environment with significant and legitimate female presence, although until recently the biblical texts, if taken alone or given priority, had yielded an opposite impression.

Attempts to deal with these dichotomies produce several schemes that replicate the dualisms. One may attempt to distinguish, for example, between an aniconic Yahwistic Israelite religion and the visually expressive "Canaanite" cults, but then one must account for the approved embellishments of Solomon's temple as being under foreign influence.[2] Or, one may posit a significantly different "popular" religion, especially women's local worship, not governed by the same visual restrictions as the Yahwistic establishment and its literary products.[3] Theological and political evolution or revolution may be invoked to account both for an increasing apprehension of visual images as threatening and for the religious and nationalistic reforms that periodically purged the Jerusalem temple, countryside sanctuaries, and venerated literary works of inappropriate representations.[4] As scholars increasingly recognize the complexity of Israelite Yahwism evidenced in the diversity of archaeological and literary artifacts, these dualisms are understood to reflect modern biases toward postexilic interpretations more than ancient Israelite realities.

Of special note has been debate about several recently discovered votive inscriptions in the ninth to eighth centuries that invoke the blessing of Yahweh and his Asherah. Do the inscriptions refer to Yahweh and a Goddess consort, or Yahweh and a cultic object? Are they genuinely Israelite and Yahwistic formulations, especially given that they appear on painted pottery at the Sinai desert installation of Kuntillet ʾAjrûd with drawings of mixed origins?[5] I find it interesting that these inscriptions are forcing logocentric scholarship to take seriously what visual evidence has long suggested.

My method for investigating how visual description and plot in a narrative about women can be based on Goddess iconography is comparable to feminist examinations of other biblical patterns. When one knows comparative folklore or mythological motifs, for instance, of a young male offending a Goddess, one may recognize that pattern in Sarah's rejection of Ishmael and Hagar.[6] Narratives of a young woman's sacrificial death in Greek etiologies for women's rites of passage provide a comparative basis for understanding the death of Jephthah's daughter and the associated women's observance.[7] The comparisons I make arise primarily from a regional visual base rather than from a literary one, but the thematic connection suggested by one thing looking like another is not sufficient by itself to establish the relationship.

As in the literary studies, a cluster of (in this case, visual) features, an analogous situation, and the probability that both authors and audience were aware of the images and their connotations are all significant factors for establishing that a pattern is based on historical as well as thematic associations.[8] To be most effective, a visual allusion may refer not only to a single representation but also to associated images and their connotations. Especially if one tries to establish that biblical authors were overtly calling attention to a visual symbol in order to invoke its connotations, one must employ multiple criteria—features common to both image and word at several levels—the overlapping of which reduces the possibility that the resemblance is coincidental. To use archaeological terminology, one should compare one assemblage with another, not only examine the individual artifacts.

The following studies of Jezebel in 2 Kgs 9:30-37 and Tamar in Gen 38 present what I believe are examples of biblical writers' intentionally adopting Goddess iconography as the antecedent for a human female character, calling to mind the Goddess as a foil for understanding the woman's role. I should offer (as the autobiographical statement that usually opens a feminist presentation) that in each case I was looking for something else when I found a Goddess. With Jezebel, I was looking for the connections between ivory carvings excavated from Samaria and the depiction of Jezebel's death at a window. For Tamar, I was looking for the royal iconographic background of the ring, staff, and cord that Judah gives her in pledge for future payment. I suspect that after one develops "eyes to see," one may recognize similar manifestations in other passages.

2 KINGS 9:30-37

> When Jehu came to Jezreel, Jezebel heard of it; and she painted her eyes, and adorned her head, and looked out of the window. And as Jehu entered the gate, she said, "Is it peace, you Zimri, murderer of your master?" And he lifted up his face to the window, and said, "Who is on my side? Who?" Two or three eunuchs looked out at him. He said, "Throw her down." So they threw her down; and some of her blood spattered on the wall and on the horses, and they trampled on her. Then he went in and ate and drank; and he said, "See now to this cursed woman, and bury her; for she is a king's daughter." But when they went to bury her, they found no more of her than the skull and the feet and the palms of her hands. When they came back and told him, he said, "This is the word of the LORD, which he spoke by his servant Elijah the Tishbite, 'In the territory of Jezreel the dogs shall eat the flesh of Jezebel; and the corpse of Jezebel shall be as dung upon the face of the field in the territory of Jezreel, so that no one can say, This is Jezebel.'"
>
> —2 Kgs 9:30-37

I am not the first to point out the resemblance between Iron Age ivory carvings of Phoenician style that feature a woman at the window and the description of the Israelite queen mother Jezebel. (See fig. 24) Even before archaeological excavations revealed in 1932 that the motif was present among the ruins of Ahab and Jezebel's ivory house at Samaria (later to be Jehu's), Herbig had proposed that the 2 Kings passage should be examined in light of other examples of the image, although not many took his suggestion.[9] He identified the female figure as an Aphrodite/Astarte or hierodule of the Goddess, found at her window on a thirteenth-century bronze Cypriote incense stand, on Iron Age Phoenician ivory carvings from Nimrud, and on a stone wall relief at Nineveh showing Ashurbanipal's ritual couch in a garden banquet. Almost everyone who comments on this motif posits a sexual motivation for the figure's appearance at the window, and both Goddess and hierodule are regularly described as "sacred prostitute." These accounts follow the lead of several ancient sources that designated the Cypriote version as Aphrodite Parakyptusa (leaning or glancing out the window) or that describe a Babylonian counterpart, Kililu, whose epithets are interpreted as referring to windows and implying "prostitution." In both cases, ritual defloration is reported as a feature of this Goddess's cult.[10]

The biblical description of Jezebel in a situation identical to that on the ivory carvings from her family's and their successors' palace can be seen as an attempt to connect her with the connotations of the image. Commentators interested in Jezebel's adornments explain them as an attempt to save her life by seducing Jehu, as dignified preparation for certain death by donning her full womanly accoutrements, or more sympathetically as the queen mother's attire in what should have been a ceremonial welcome for a returning king or legitimate successor.[11] Recognition of the visual allusion to a Goddess brings a more sophisticated analysis of the literary character, as in Peter Ackroyd's treatment.

> I am well aware that I have said something about Jezebel and something about Goddesses, but not much about women. But in part this has been implied by what amounts not to a defence of Jezebel but to an attempt to understand the projection into her figure of antagonism to the worship of a Goddess as consort to Israel's God. It is possible here to wonder whether one of the details of that vivid description of the last scene of her life means more than is at first sight clear: when she paints her eyes and dresses her hair and looks down from the window, she appears rather like the portrayal of the "woman at the window," a familiar symbol of ancient Near Eastern art, and held to represent the Goddess as sacred prostitute (ANEP, 131). It is almost as if she is being presented, and rejected, as the Goddess herself. The projection of antagonisms into female figures is to be found not only here but also in the opening chapters of Genesis and in the portrayal of "dame folly," the seductress, in the opening chapters of the book of Proverbs (e.g. Prov. 5:7).[12]

Ackroyd's association of Jezebel with antagonism to a Goddess/prostitute is at least an attempt to deal with the narrative's symbolic dimension. By concentrating on archaeological and art historical studies, my investigations have unearthed, as it were, a somewhat different set of symbolic associations for the woman at the window and a clearer understanding of the visual allusion's role in the text.[13]

The woman at the window design was found on ivory plaques excavated in three Mesopotamian sites (Nimrud, Arslan Tash, Khorsabad) as well as in Israelite Samaria.[14] When considering carvings found in the same limited archaeological locus as these plaques, one observes that the motif occurs regularly with a small repertoire of designs. Although Phoenician ivories were applied to many objects, from horse trappings to cosmetic dishes, and although they were found in many locations—tombs, temple deposits, women's residential quarters, and royal warehouses—the cluster that includes the woman at the window is rather restricted in number of designs and location of finds, leading to its identification as the conventional iconography for ceremonial furniture located in rooms and hallways adjacent to royal courtyards. Other motifs in the set are the cow nursing its calf, an infant on a lotus, human-headed sphinxes, grazing stag, and standing, winged guardians saluting a central element. Like much Phoenician art, several of these designs resemble Egyptian models. Art historians formerly made the judgment that Phoenician art was derivative and imitative, borrowing Egyptian designs favored by royal clients for decorative purposes without regard to religious or political significance. In this case, I disagree.

Egyptian influence here seems to apply not only to individual designs but also to the choice of what appears together in funerary designs. Lotiform faience chalices from the Tûna el-Gebel cemetery near Hermopolis (Twenty-second Dynasty, 945-715 B.C.E.) display cow and calf, infant on a lotus, a number of other designs also found on Samaria's ivories, and frontal Hathor head.[15] Several of the chalices depict royal military victories featuring horses and chariots and banquet scenes. Although one must be cautious in ascribing funerary significance to Egyptian art simply because so much of it was found in burial contexts, these chalices are shown in painting only as cult vessels in the ritual of the dead, never as common drinking cups.[16] The symbolic cluster corresponds well to this function. The cow with calf is sometimes explicitly Hathor nursing a pharaoh, the wild Cow of the West who greets the deceased and nurtures the living ruler as she did Horus. The infant on a lotus derives from New Kingdom depictions of a very young pharaoh (Akhenaten, Tutankhamen, Ramesses II) and develops the identification of the king with the daily rebirth of the sun(God). Hathor's presence in bovine form is reinforced by instances of her framed frontal head.

The ivory and chalice designs are closely paralleled by Phoenician bronze and silver bowls from the late eighth to early seventh centuries, recovered from two principal contexts throughout the Mediterranean area: sanctuary offerings (in Greece and Cyprus) and grave deposits, thought to be of a warrior aristocracy (Italy, Cyprus, Crete, Rhodes, Near East).[17] Military engagements and banquets are commonly engraved on these products of a Cypro-Phoenician centered craft. Again, the frontal Hathor head, infant on a lotus, cow and calf, and sphinx are recurring motifs of the iconography.

If these were simply the most frequently occurring designs in the Egyptian and Phoenician art of the period, it would be inaccurate to call them a cluster with special significance. The most popular motifs—sphinx, sacred tree, cow and calf—were well traveled throughout the Levant. But the solar infant on a lotus and the frontal woman's head are much more limited in geographic and temporal distribution, suggesting they were used on the ivories for more than general beneficence.

What did the woman at the window represent? Her resemblance to the frontal Hathor head may be explained by the meeting of conventional Hathor iconography with the influence of Minoan frescoes showing women at windows, combined in Cypro-Phoenician art.[18] The female head was featured in Cypriote masks and stone or terra-cotta stele displayed at sanctuary doors and windows in a Hathor-related cult. By the sixth century models of these sanctuaries with figures at the front door and side windows were used as domestic shrines or votive pieces and grave deposits to invoke the Goddess's blessings of vitality upon living and dead. Ovid's etiological tale of such a stone carving in the Salamis sanctuary reports that Aphrodite petrified a Greek princess who displeased the Goddess by smiling coldly upon the funeral procession of her rejected and despairing Phoenician suitor, who had killed himself.[19] Was the lesson that a woman ought to be more warm-hearted? Or did the Greek version misrepresent a Phoenician Goddess's attributes in the cultural mixture of Cyprus?[20]

The sexual preoccupation of ancient and modern interpreters ignores what may be the more important *funerary* aspect. In the region's literature, Goddesses at windows regularly confront their own or another's death. Ugaritic myths record the storm God Baal's initial reluctance to open a window in his palace, lest his dewy lasses be seen by rival Yamm. After the window is installed and Baal is swallowed by Mot (literally, Death), the lasses must descend after Baal into Mot's sterile realm.[21] Jeremiah may be referring to similar associations in his call to the mourning women (9:20-22): "Teach to your daughters a lament, and teach to her neighbor a dirge; for death has come up into our windows, it has entered our palaces, cutting off the children from the streets and the young men from the squares." In Egyptian Pyramid texts, a deceased pharaoh climbing the ladder to the sky encounters Anubis's daughter, "who is in the windows of the sky," and whose permission is required for passage.[22] This is not to deny that sexual affirmation may have a role in confronting death, but to ignore the latter is to misunderstand the former. As Robertson aptly summarizes:

> Nothing in the stories hints at temple prostitution; the lady at the window is either a princess (as at Salamis) or a queen (Jezebel) or a seeming Goddess (Helen of Tyre) or a member of Baal's household, whether wife or daughter (for the matter is in doubt). In sum, whatever our lady was doing at the window, she was not soliciting.[23]

To return to the ivory-inlaid furniture, the Hathor-based woman at the window design and her sister cow with calf share connotations with the other motifs of chalices and bowls. These images center on life-death transformations, on particularly sensitive moments of transition for royalty and their noble entourage. The vulnerable moment may have been a funeral or memorial event or succession. The ivory symbols—carrying the mixed signals of birth, death, rebirth—probably supported a victorious occasion, a festive legitimation of continuity in the face of acknowledged loss.

I believe that the biblical authors were aware of this funerary symbolism. In Amos 6:4-7 ivory furniture is mentioned in the prophet's condemnation of a particular ceremonial occasion, a *marzeaḥ*.

> Woe to those who lie upon beds of ivory,
> and stretch themselves upon their couches,
> and eat lambs from the flock
> and calves from the midst of the stall;
> who sing idle songs to the sound of the harp,
> and like David invent for themselves instruments of music;
> who drink wine in bowls,
> and anoint themselves with the finest oils,
> but are not grieved over the ruin of Joseph!
> Therefore they shall now be the first of those to go into exile,
> and the revelry [*marzeaḥ*] of those who stretch themselves
> shall pass away.[24]

Elsewhere in the Hebrew scriptures, Jeremiah is forbidden to participate in the functions of the *beit marzeaḥ*, a place for marriage and mourning (Jer 16:5-9).

The *marzeaḥ* is also mentioned in Ugaritic texts and in Phoenician, Elephantine, Nabatean, and Palmyrene sources. The term seems to apply to both a religious association and its gatherings. As defined by Marvin Pope, a *marzeaḥ* is:

> a social and religious institution which included families, owned property, houses for meetings and vineyards for wine supply, was associated with specific deities, and met periodically, perhaps monthly, to celebrate for several days at a stretch with food and drink and sometimes, if not regularly, with sacral sexual orgies.[25]

It may also be linked to a Mesopotamian rite, the *kispu*, at which communal eating, drinking, and remembering the ancestral dead were featured, sometimes as a special event in a coronation.[26]

Now the pieces of the puzzle—art, ceremony, and text— begin to fit. The encounter between Jehu and Jezebel takes place at the vulnerable moment of succession, or rather, of usurpation. Jezebel stands between Jehu and the kingship, and the account of his trampling her with horse and chariot, of his entering the palace to feast, is reported by reversing the *marzeaḥ's* symbols. He does not want ritualized continuity with the Omride house, having just murdered two kings and a queen mother. He claims legitimacy by quoting prophetic oracles, not by memorializing his predecessors. In Jezebel, the literary Jehu encounters the personified visual image of the *marzeaḥ* couch and shatters her, quite physically, as the last obstacle to the throne. During his banquet, he mockingly calls for the proper disposal of the foreign princess, only to learn that there is not enough left of her to bury. Her dismemberment allows him to boast, "that no one can say, 'this is Jezebel.'"

Yet the visual image had its own subversive power, fulfilling the *marzeaḥ's* role of remembrance contrary to Jehu's claim and the narrators' intention. By invoking the woman at the window under Jezebel's name, the text reincarnated the Goddess as queen and launched her new career as a powerful literary manifestation of religious initiative, political influence, and sexual energy. Jezebel *is* remembered, albeit as idolatress, manipulator, and harlot. A New Testament prophetess (Revelation 2:19-23) and European queens were branded with her attributes. Protestant reformer John Knox blasted the English and Scottish Catholic Marys as Jezebels,[27] and Spanish Jews are reported to have labeled Queen Isabella of Spain "the Catholic Jezebel."[28]

But even Jehu fails to escape the reversal for long. Amos does not condemn the *marzeaḥ* but those—the nobility of the Jehuite dynasty—whose revelry is not true mourning for the house of Jacob. Hosea, too, withdraws the supposed prophetic endorsement for Jehu and proclaims judgment upon his house for the blood of Jezreel (Hosea 1:4-5). One may wonder if Jehu truly had prophetic license in the first place, for, unlike David who spared Saul's life and killed one who claimed to have killed him, Jehu actively sought the downfall of the one whom he was anointed to succeed. I can find no other instance of a biblical agent of fulfillment self-consciously justifying action on that basis.

To return to the original issue, after having identified the transformation of Goddess symbols in a narrative about a human queen, what does this have to do with women's social realities? As a contribution to the new quest for the historical Jezebel, this study has succeeded only in questioning one of the episodes about her as a source for direct historical investigation. Was Jezebel a participant in *marzeaḥ* rituals and succession rites? Did she actually create the allusion by self-consciously appearing at the window in a pose adopted earlier for legitimate successors to accuse Jehu of usurpation and regicide, or is the entire report a manipulation of *marzeaḥ* symbolism, molded to suit the usurper's needs? Which came first, Amos's condemnation of Jehu's descendants by alluding to *marzeaḥ*, or their literary self-defense by mocking the Omrides with the imagery of the same occasion? These realities lie beyond the evidence.

What emerges are the dynamics of visual, literary, and theological processes. The visual depiction of a Goddess in the empowering ritual of *marzeaḥ* was naturalized and applied to a "real" woman's confrontation with death. The imagery of dynastic legitimation and continuity was parodied to support usurpation with Yahwistic approval. Would these tactics have been artistically successful with the ancient audience unless the Goddess and the ritual maintained some active standing? Four generations after Jehu, his successors were still practicing the *marzeaḥ*, according to Amos. Perhaps it was only between dynasties that the discontinuity was appropriate, while the Jehuites continued the occasion to ensure their own memorials. If so, we may have evidence that in royal practice, at least, the Hathor-related functions of legitimating and renewing monarchy through a Goddess were still honored by a court that claimed initial support from Yahwistic prophets and the fundamentalist Rechabite clan.[29] These observations lead to the hypothesis that Jehu's successors and literary apologists were flexibly opportunistic and self-serving in their treatments of the Goddess—they could "revel" for the benefit of their own dynasty on furniture that symbolically represented her powers while naturalizing and smashing the same features in writing when it was expedient to dishonor their predecessors.

Jezebel's case is so compelling because after the initial jolt of visual recognition, one finds the allusion sustained at so many levels. There may be a far vaster topic lurking here—the levels of analogy operating subconsciously for both narrator and audience in the visual-verbal interaction. How well can one "translate" the nondiscursive presentation of visual image into its verbal equivalent? What kinds of cognitive patterning are common to both?

I have observed a structural similarity deeper than my original criteria of image, situation, and historical context. The narrative in 2 Kings 9:30-37 is divided into three parts, each opening with Jehu's movement into the scene; he comes into city (v. 30), into royal precinct (v. 31), and into palace (v. 34) with repetitions of the verb, only to confront Jezebel at the center of each movement in her preparation, the encounter, and attempted burial. The woman at the window plaques uniformly feature a three-tiered frame progressively moving the viewer's gaze to the confrontational frontal view of the face. One may say that the conceptual, almost physical, structures of image and text are comparable, both in design (three-part frame) and in the affective quality (confrontation) conveyed by it. If, as I believe, the visual artifact preceded the text, then one may say the affective structures of the Goddess iconography appear to have influenced, consciously or not, the "shape" of the text.

But one can recognize a mythic pattern in the narrative without claiming that the human characters are really scaled-down Deities, as Jo Ann Hackett "will not argue that Sarah and Abraham were Deities in some early form of the story.... [R]ather, we can simply say that several authors have made use of a typical or formulaic scene within several oral narrative traditions."[30] The humans are simply acting in roles made familiar by stories about Deities. Should the same be said for human women characters in literary situations shaped by Goddess iconography? Is the narrative pattern simply transferred without the cultic implications?

In Jezebel's case, the narrative's inclusion of so many visual details seems intended to make the allusion very graphic and specific. Window, adornments, horse and chariot, banquet, and (non)burial and (non)naming direct the audience's attention to the *marzeaḥ* symbolism through the whole episode. The point of reversing the symbolic impact would be lost if the antecedent did not retain some impact of its own. One cannot totally separate "mere" royal convention—the public symbolic forms adopted by Israelite monarchy as part of contemporary royal cultus—from the Yahwistic practice of the population. As Solomon's temple with its cherubim and bulls at the laver, named pillars, and sometimes an Asherah was the version of Yahwism legitimated by the southern state, so the calves at Dan and Bethel, the Samaria Asherah, and apparently, *marzeaḥ* on beds of ivory, were manifestations of northern royal Yahwism. There is no record of a Jehu zealous for Yahweh having abolished any of these. He recognized and pointedly denied the Omrides the ritual regard that was their due, or so the story goes.

So although a reading of 2 Kgs 9:30-37 through the lens of the later Yahweh-alone deuteronomistic theology might lead to Ackroyd's earlier quoted statement ("It is almost as if [Jezebel] is being presented, and rejected, as the Goddess herself"), that is not the only possible reading. Jezebel and her murdered son were denied the honor of memorial rites in which a Goddess was portrayed at least on the furniture, if not by the roles of the celebrants—rites still practiced by Jehu's offspring. More than a mythic pattern is being evoked. The Goddess's role seems still important for the kings of Jehu's line to establish continuity and to honor their predecessors.

The thought that neither Goddess nor iconography is the target of rejection by Jehuite apologists may be amplified by briefly examining other examples for adaptation of Goddess elements. In two other passages I am studying, there is the strong possibility of a similar dynamic between image and text.

JEREMIAH 31:16-20

I believe that the Goddess's roles in *marzeaḥ* remained active for some time, eventually to be co-opted by Yahweh along with her symbols. For example, Jeremiah's reference in 31:16-20 to Yahweh's compassionate yearning for the penitent Ephraim calf may be an allusion to the cow and calf as *marzeaḥ* symbols. The allusion appears in poetry rather than narrative, and the Goddess's features are attributed to Yahweh, not a woman.

The context for this passage is chapters 30-31, the "Book of Consolation" thought by some to have been addressed initially to the dismembered Northern Kingdom during the Judean King Josiah's reforms and expansions, and later edited for application to Judah. The funerary dimension is explicit throughout Jeremiah's writings in calls to lament, descriptions of mourning, quotation of complaint (when help is still anticipated) and of lament (when it is too late for help). The prophet is explicitly barred from participating in the *marzeaḥ* as a sign that the rites will be futile for comfort or continuity in the face of Yahweh's overwhelming punishment (16:5-9).

As in other sections of the Book of Consolation, reversal of the funerary darkness typifies the passage 31:15-22. Mother Rachel's opening lament (v. 15) is reversed by Yahweh's salvation oracle (vv. 16-17), and Ephraim's confession of guilt as "an untrained calf" (31:18-19) is answered by Yahweh's tender promise: "Is Ephraim my dear son? Is he my darling child? For as often as I speak against him, I do remember him still. Therefore my heart yearns for him; I will surely have mercy on him" (v. 20).

Phyllis Trible's analysis of the unit identifies a chiastic structure according to which words of a female voice and to a female addressee frame the confession of the male Ephraim calf.[31]

Word of a woman: Rachel cries in mourning for her children (15)
    Words to a woman: Yahweh consoles her (16-17)
        Words of a man: Ephraim confesses (18-19)
    Words of a woman: Yahweh contemplates (20)
Words to a woman: Jeremiah commands (21-22)

This language of maternal grief from both Rachel (v. 15, whose name means "ewe") and Yahweh, combined with the explicit reference to the nation-prince Ephraim as calf, evokes the connotations of the Egyptian Hathor cow and pharaoh calf, and of the Ugaritic expression describing Anath's grieving for Baal: "Like the heart of a cow for her calf, like the heart of a ewe for her lamb, so's the heart of Anath for Baal."[32] Jeremiah thus depicts Yahweh's words and care as encircling and renewing the life of the Northern Kingdom, which had been as good as dead for a hundred years. (See figs. 25 and 26)

As with structural correspondence of art and text in 2 Kings 9, visual and verbal elements in this passage share an almost physical pattern. Trible's analysis convincingly visualizes the literary chiasmus, the encircling of the male Ephraim calf by speeches of a woman and to a woman. The ivory carving of the *marzeaḥ* designs shows the suckling calf parallel to its mother and enclosed by her legs, while her head is turned back to lick the newborn's rump. The most abstract visual rendering of the cow and calf motif reduces the pair's relation to an asymmetrical encircling pattern, a small oval (calf's body) with dot (eye) held within a larger oval with dot (cow). Thus both the verbal and visual art display the most fundamental structures of intimacy and dependence expressed in circles and centers. Again, the conceptual designs of image and text are comparable in conveying the affective quality of enclosure.

Whether naturalized into a human queen in 2 Kings or poetically coopted as a metaphor for Yahweh in Jeremiah, the *marzeaḥ* Goddess has become almost invisible in her own right, but her contribution remains. The biblical accounts show diverse practices and ambivalent attitudes toward death. Regularized activities involving necromancy and other contacts with the deceased certainly do not get approbation in the received text, whether legislative (Lev 18:10-12), narrative (Saul and the medium of Endor, 1 Sam 28), or prophetic (Is 8:19-22).[33] By adopting *marzeaḥ* symbols, the biblical authors may have redefined the range of activity for Yahweh, who now claimed the ability to cross death's borders to seek the guilty (Amos 9:2), as Anath vengefully sought Mot, and to restore long-dead Israel as a newborn calf and kingdom in Jeremiah. They could not have conceived it, maternal pun intended, without Her.

What effect did this co-opting of language and concept have on women who were the chief participants in other mourning rites? Did the women celebrants deserve Amos's taunting epithet, "You cows of Bashan" (4:1)? Did Yahweh's arrival on Death's threshold displace female symbols and women's ceremonial functions?

GENESIS 38

Genesis 38 offers an example in which Goddess elements survive another form of narrative adaptation, positive yet trimmed with wit.[34]

While Jezebel is the antecedent for a prophetess condemned by the New Testament, Tamar is implicitly praised by her inclusion as one of only four women in Matthew's genealogy from Abraham to Jesus (Matt 1:1-17). How did she contribute to the movement of promise?

Women in Genesis are often depicted as working to achieve patriarchal priorities, even if their means sometimes run counter to patriarchal control. Cooperating in a scheme of sister-brother deceit of a king (Sarah, Rebekah), offering a maid to the husband (Sarah, Rachel, Leah), disguising oneself (Tamar) or another (Rebekah-Jacob), rivalry in childbearing (Hagar and Sarah, Rachel and Leah)—all are modes of furthering the promise of offspring, land, and prosperity.

The themes familiar from other Genesis stories are abundant in chapter 38: that the desired male offspring is unborn or unblessed creates the narrative tension, developed through a dramatic situation of risk or intrigue initiated by a woman, to a dénouement at odds with plans of the chief male character (and contrary to primogeniture) but apparently in accord with divine intention. In this instance, Tamar—widowed and childless by Judah's two sons and promised to a third whom he keeps from her—takes the initiative to conceive offspring for her father-in-law's line by making herself available to him in the guise of a prostitute. Her unborn children, momentarily jeopardized by Judah's death sentence for her harlotry, are acknowledged when he claims the pledge of ring, cord, and staff that he left with the "prostitute." One of her twin sons is David's ancestor, Perez (whose manner of birth gives his name, "breach").

This account is a sophisticated literary composition, employing tribal legends, legal elements, and mythical motifs in a narrative unified by skilled and self-conscious verbal wordplay and cross-reference. The historical value of the chapter has long been called into question by recognition of several strands of ancient Near Eastern mythical motifs: the woman or Goddess who brings death to her lovers;[35] father-daughter unions;[36] the birth and conflict of twins;[37] the fertility implications of sheep shearing festivities;[38] and the frequent identification of goat and palm tree with "fertility Goddesses" in ancient Near Eastern art (hence the cleverness of Tamar's name, "palm," and the fee of a kid for services rendered).[39]

My contribution to the symbolic dimension is an iconographic investigation of the ring, cord, and staff—the unredeemed pledge upon which the plot's dramatic turn hinges.

Most commentators on this passage since Gunkel have cited Herodotus's observation that Babylonians carried a seal ring and carved staff for identification and authority in transactions.[40] In this tale, too, they are mentioned as literal objects, given away too easily by Judah perhaps, but used like other objects in Genesis as the vehicles for disguise or recognition (Jacob wearing Esau's clothes, Joseph's bloodied coat, Joseph's hidden cup). In the iconographic vocabulary of ancient Near Eastern kingship, however, the ring and staff (and cord) do have significance as royal emblems from at least the late third millennium in the Egyptian Old Kingdom and the Sumero-Akkadian period in Mesopotamia. The ring appears in art as a large bound circlet, not a finger ring, and the staff varies from walking-stick size to a shorter rod.[41] Four examples will serve to illustrate the connotations. (See fig. 27)

Ring, staff, and looped cord appear together in the extended hand of a seated male Deity usually identified as Nanna (moon God) on the stele commemorating Ur-Nammu's temple construction (ca. 2050 B.C.E.).[42] Standing before the God, the king pours a libation into an altar vase from which extends a palm frond or emblem. To the right of this scene, the king repeats the libation before a seated Goddess. The image is near the top of the stele, above several registers showing the king himself as builder, ceremonially laying bricks. There had been general agreement that the instruments proffered by the Deity represent the physical surveying tools invested in the king as the God's earthly contractor. These architect's tools were thought to symbolize the "measurement" of justice and order also delegated to the king as the God's representative. In later art, the looped cord was omitted, leaving only rod and large ring as symbols of the king's divine commission.

Bikai presented reasonable alternative evidence that "the origin of the rod and the ring can be found in the taming stick and the nose rope with a ring at the end. Thus the later meaning of victory [and] divine power had its roots in early animal domestication. Ultimately, in representational art, these symbols came to demonstrate that the recipient of them is a true king."[43] The pastoral connection may be seen on the next example—Hammurabi's stele—in which the king is called shepherd in the text as well as receiving the rod and ring in the pictorial heading.[44] (See fig. 28)

Although Hammurabi's representation omits the altar and palm frond of Ur-Nammu's picture, other examples continue the motif. A contemporary early second-millennium wall painting at Mari uses several palm trees to frame the main scene, in which a standing Ishtar has become the divine commissioner who inaugurates the king with the emblems.[45] (See fig. 29) In this period, the glyptic art of Syria adopted much of its repertoire from Babylonian monumental art, including the extended rod-and-ring as a symbol of authority on cylinder seals, thus miniaturizing and transmitting the motif to the Mediterranean coast.[46]

Among first-millennium specimens that occur in a great variety of media and contexts, one example deserves special notice. (See fig. 30) On an inscribed tablet from Nabuapaliddin (885-850 B.C.E.), an enthroned Shamash is shown in relief extending the rod and ring toward three approaching figures—priest, king, and accompanying female Deity.[47] Above Shamash and beneath the canopy that covers him are three astral symbols—moon, sun, and star—labeled in cuneiform as Sin, Shamash, and Ishtar. The canopy is supported by a palm tree/column, topped by two male Deities called by the inscription "the twins" (!) Kittu and Misharu, Justice and Righteousness.[48] The reverse of the tablet describes the king's rebuilding a temple.

The ingredients in these scenes of royal investiture are not identical, but the visual elements of rod and ring, palm and Goddess, when combined with the thematic elements of temple building and administration of justice, constitute a cluster of associations quite appropriate for Genesis 38. The chapter is often attributed to J, a biblical author thought to have written during Solomon's reign or shortly afterwards. Through Tamar's mediation, Judah's patriarchal insignia and lineage, which appeared lost, are restored and transformed into the inaugural symbols and ancestor of Israel's greatest temple builder and administrator of justice—Solomon.

This symbolic inauguration of the Judean monarchy would also help to explain the chapter's position as a seeming digression in the middle of the Joseph story. Just when Joseph, soon-to-be savior of the Israelites and father of the northern tribes, is enslaved and carried to Egypt, kingship is being invested by ironic circumstances in the southern house of Judah. Joseph will regain prominence as a temporary leader, but the dynasty of Judah's heirs is already legitimated, not by Samuel's anointing David but by Tamar's waylaying Judah.[49] This would be an apt account at a later period redefining north-south relations.

Theologically, then, Israelite kingship is seen as a divine prerogative, delegated to Judah by Yahweh's loyalty to the covenant promise and not awarded for Judah's competence. The mediating Goddess/woman redirects legitimacy, presumably with approval of the hidden divine judge who has not been mentioned since Onan's death. As is so often the case in Genesis, female initiative transforms misdirected male intention and inadvertence into productive results for the covenant. Understood as the deceitful actions of "real women," these initiatives have been interpreted to show women's lack of social and political power, necessitating indirect action and manipulation, though ultimately fulfilling divine and patriarchal purposes. On the surface, Tamar's case also fits this model. Does recognition of the Goddess imagery change this assessment?

Modern readers' long-faced seriousness in biblical interpretation may dampen our ability to recognize the comic ingredients so prevalent in Hebrew narrative—the love of irony, paradox, reversals, and double entendre. In feminist earnestness we may take Tamar as an example of the least powerful of Israelite women—a childless widow—and applaud the text's expression of her subversive courage, even for patriarchal social and political goals. In light of the iconographic allusion, how are we to understand the text's self-conscious juxtaposition of legal widow and mythic Goddess? Has the Goddess's symbolism lost its specific royal and religious impact to become a typical pattern in the narrative tradition? I think, rather, that the paradox of her disguise as the least powerful woman is part of the literary wit. Trying unsuccessfully on Judah's behalf to deliver the promised kid to a *zônah,* a common prostitute, Judah's friend is told, "No *q*ᵉ*deshah* has been here," no sacred/consecrated one. But that is precisely who was there!

REFLECTIONS

As in 2 Kings 9, the Goddess imagery in Genesis 38 belongs to a cluster of motifs concerning royal legitimacy transformed into a complex narrative. One could say that rather than demythologizing or historicizing, as is popularly credited to the Hebrew writers, this text appears to remythologize Solomon's royal origins, albeit with a naturalism that transforms highly symbolic elements into narrative props. I call this *an artistic strategy of "naturalizing,"* which encodes the still active divine symbolism in "realistic" description. How would it have registered with Israelite audiences, women and men? What is left for our use in studying Israelite women's social reality?

We should be sensitive to the fact that both of these texts originated in royal circles. In the process of inventing Hebrew monarchy, Jerusalem and Samaria adopted some of the ideologies and visual symbols of neighboring Egyptian and Mesopotamian empires. That this appropriation included practices opposed by the deuteronomistic school of Yahwism can be seen in the repeated condemnation of foreign and feminine elements—of Solomon's sharing in his wives' worship, of queen mothers Jezebel's and Athaliah's leadership in cult and kingdom—but this does not preclude that other strands of Yahwism, especially the royal one, did endorse them. If we subscribe to the presupposition that texts do not exhort against a practice or co-opt a tradition unless it has active influence, then we have increasing evidence for the role of Goddess imagery and women's participation in the legitimating ideology and practice of Israelite monarchy.[50] The narrators did not invent this role; they depended on widespread recognition of it for the effectiveness of their allusions.

To develop this line of thought, inquiries need to be pursued at several levels of study. (1) If the re-vision of textual exegesis could include visual elements, one may find other manifestations of female presence that have been rendered almost invisible. (2) This approach may contribute to reexamination of Israelite religious history, showing the diversity and complexity of female Deities and symbols, especially in royal contexts. (3) Recovery of feminine aspects of divinity in the biblical tradition—whether separately deified, personified, or co-opted, whether approved or condemned—will necessitate new models of biblical thealogy/theology. (4) By rendering visible some of the theological choices made in the development of Israelite religion and its more limited biblical expressions, this enterprise may offer new resources for modern feminist critique and feminist spirituality.

Fig. 24

Fig. 25

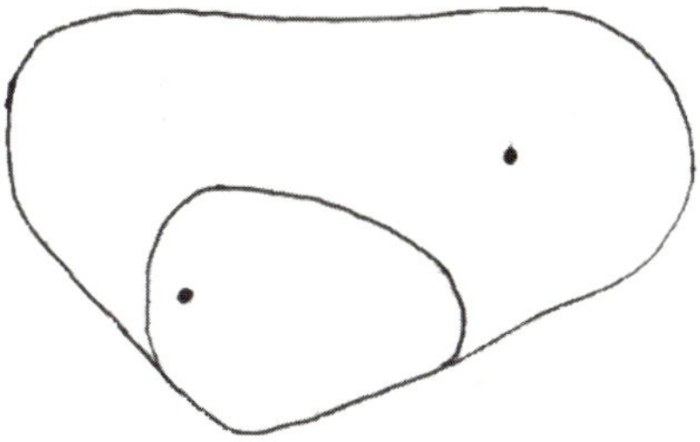

Fig. 26

Fig. 24 Woman at the window design in carved ivory, from Northwest Palace at Nimrud
Fig. 25 Cow and calf design in carved ivory, from Fort Shalmaneser at Nimrud
Fig. 26 Abstracted structure of cow and calf design, conveying enclosure
Fig. 27 Section of Ur-Nammu's stele

Fig. 27

Fig. 28

Fig. 29

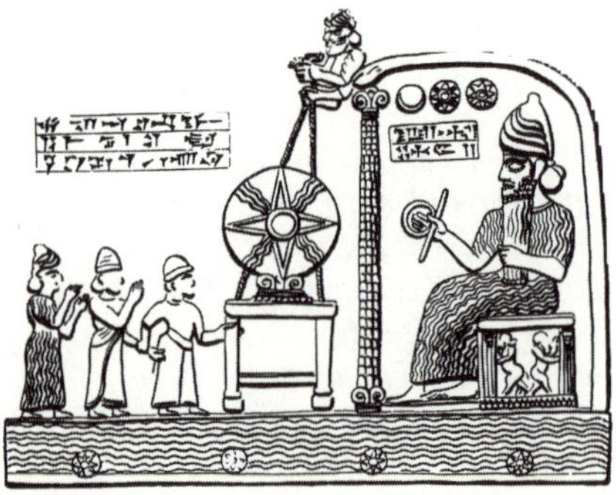

Fig. 28 Section of Hammurabi's stele
Fig. 29 Wall painting from court 106, Mari
Fig. 30 Nabuapaliddin's inscribed stone tablet

Fig. 30

NOTES

1. For one recent work that tries to untangle the literary, artistic, and interpretive threads for one Goddess, Asherah, see Olyan, *Asherah*. Interestingly, the visual evidence is treated in a chapter entitled "Epigraphic sources," seeming to subordinate iconographic remains to literary ones.

2. The *Encylopaedia Judaica*'s 1971 article by Cecil Roth is a good example of this strategy (vol. 3, col. 506). He writes: "It is not easy to discern the development of what may be termed native Hebrew art in the period of the Monarchy. Indeed, there is explicit information that the expert craftsmen employed in the construction of the Temple were Phoenicians from Tyre. The relatively few relics that have been preserved in Eretz Israel from this period, such as the not uncommon Astarte figurines, are mainly Canaanite in character. On the other hand, the plaques from the "House of Ivory" built in Samaria by King Ahab (876-853 B.C.E.), which show great taste and sensitivity, are under the influence of Phoenician art and were possibly executed by craftsmen introduced by Queen Jezebel from her native Sidon. Similarly, the admirably executed Israelite seals of the period are Egyptian or Assyrian both in character and in execution."

3. For example, in describing a great rectangular trench at Samaria where hundreds of clay figurines were found datable to the eighth and seventh centuries, the excavators said, "To this sanctuary, we may imagine, the country folk brought their gifts and pottery vessels, probably of their own making and sometimes marked with their names." See pp. 137-39 in Crowfoot, Crowfoot, and Kenyon, *The Objects from Samaria*.

4. See for instance Saul Olyan's argument that Asherah was a long-standing and legitimate figure in Yahwistic circles except for minority deuteronomistic opposition, which has so strongly shaped biblical editing that it has become the seemingly original and dominant position in the texts. *Asherah*, 3-22.

5. See Olyan, *Asherah*, 23-33, and bibliography.

6. Hackett, "Rehabilitating Hagar," 12-27.

7. Day, "From the Child Is Born the Woman," 58-74.

8. I believe archetypal theories are very useful for adapting ancient symbols to modern spiritual practice. In this case, however, I am trying to investigate more direct and self-conscious connections in antiquity.

9. Herbig, "Aphrodite Parakyptusa," 917-22.

10. For a summary, see Barnett, *Catalogue*, 149-51.

11. For examples of these lines of interpretation, see the following passages: as seductress, see Barnett, *Catalogue*, 147; as dignified preparation, Ellul, *Politics of God*, 105; as queen mother, Robinson, *Second Book of Kings*, 90, and Fauth, *Aphrodite Parakyptusa*, 47-48.

12. Ackroyd, "Goddesses, Women, and Jezebel," 245-59. Professor Ackroyd kindly sent me an offprint of his article in acknowledgment of his having earlier heard my similar view in my paper "The Death of Jezebel: Art, Theology and Politics in 2 Kings 9:30-37," presented to the Form Criticism Section of the Society of Biblical Literature's annual meeting, New York, 1979.

13. This research is described and illustrated in Beach, "The Samaria Ivories, *Marzeaḥ*, and Biblical Text," 94-104.

14. The principal publications for the ivories from each site are the following:

for Nimrud, Barnett, *Catalogue*; for Arslan Tash, Thureau-Dangin, *Arslan-Tash*; for Khorsabad, Loud and Altman, *Khorsabad*; for Samaria, Crowfoot and Crowfoot, *Early Ivories from Samaria*.

15. Tait, "The Egyptian Relief Chalice," 93-139.

16. Tait, "The Egyptian Relief Chalice," 99.

17. Markoe, *Phoenician Bronze*.

18. This connection is demonstrated in a series of articles. See Caubet, "Héraclès ou Hathor," 1-6; Caubet and Courtois, "Masques," 43-49; Caubet, "Les maquettes," 94-118; Caubet and Pic, "Un culte hathorique," 237-49.

19. Ovid, *Metamorphoses* 14.696-761.

20. For fuller discussion of several ancient versions of the story, see Robertson, "Ritual Background," 313-59, esp. 315.

21. See "Poems about Baal and Anath," trans. Ginsberg, esp. IIAB, vi-vii and I*ABv in Pritchard, ed., *Ancient Near Eastern Texts*.

22. Utterance 304, in Faulkner, *Ancient Egyptian Pyramid Texts*, 93.

23. Robertson, "Ritual Background," 321.

24. For the physical elements of *marzeaḥ* in Amos, see King, "The *Marzeaḥ* Amos Denounces," 34-44, and also chap. 6 of his book, *Amos, Hosea, Micah*.

25. Pope, "A Divine Banquet at Ugarit," 193.

26. Greenfield, "Un rite religieux Araméen," 46-52.

27. *First Blast* [Arb.] 39, 1558

28. Farrar, *The Second Book of Kings*, 124 n. 2.

29. For the possibility that this Goddess was Asherah in the official cult of Samaria for both Omride and Jehuite dynasties, see Olyan, *Asherah*, esp. 6-8, and Ackerman, "The Queen Mother and the Cult," 385-401.

30. Hackett, "Rehabilitating Hagar, " 22.

31. Trible, *God and the Rhetoric of Sexuality*, 50.

32. Pritchard, *Ancient Near Eastern Texts*, Ugaritic text I AB ii, 140.

33. For an excellent study of these conventional practices, see Ackerman, *Under Every Green Tree*.

34. A fuller discussion of Genesis 38 appears in Beach, "An Iconographic Approach."

35. Skinner. *Commentary on Genesis*, 452.

36. Astour, "Tamar the Hierodule," 185-96, esp. 195-96, and Wright, "Positioning of Genesis 38," 523-29.

37. Skinner,"Positioning of Genesis 38," 455-56.

38. Haran, "zebah hayyamim," 11-22, esp. 22.

39. Gray, *I and II Kings*, 350, and Hartmann, "Zu Genesis 38," 76-77.

40. Gunkel, *Legends of Genesis*, 416.

41. A major survey of this symbol, "The Rod and the Ring," was presented by Bikai at the 1990 Society of Biblical Literature annual meeting. See 1990 SBL Abstracts, paper S136, 329.

42. This is a limestone stele found at Ur, now at the University Museum of the University of Pennsylvania, Philadelphia. See Pritchard, *Ancient Near East in Pictures*, ill. 306 and p. 285.

43. Bikai, "The Rod and the Ring."

44. Prologue of "The Code of Hammurabi," in Pritchard, *Ancient Near Eastern Texts*, 163-80. The diorite stele was discovered at Susa in 1901-02 and is now

in the Louvre. See Pritchard, *Ancient Near East in Pictures,* ill. 246, 515, and p. 277.

45. Wall painting was excavated in 1935-36 season at the Palace Court 106. See Pritchard, *Ancient Near East in Pictures,* ill. 610 and pp. 322-23.

46. For the artistic influence of Hammurabi's dynasty, see Frankfort, *Cylinder Seals,* 155. For examples of Western cylinder seals with this motif, see Parrot, *Studia Mariana,* fig. 5 and pp. 17-19.

47. The stone tablet and two clay impressions of the relief were preserved in a clay box found at Abu Habbah in 1881 and are now in the British Museum. See Pritchard, *Ancient Near East in Pictures,* ill. 529 and p. 313.

48. For general description, see Langston, *Semitic Mythology,* 150-51. For discussion of the twins, see Rosenberg, "The God Ṣedeq," 161-63.

49. Matthew's genealogy includes David's other notable foremother, Ruth, who likewise had to take extraordinarily bold measures to get the attention of her levirate mate, Boaz.

50. See Ackerman, "Queen Mother," for a similar conclusion from different evidence.

WORKS CITED

Ackerman, Susan. "The Queen Mother and the Cult in Ancient Israel." *JBL* 112 (1993): 385-401.

———. *Under Every Green Tree: Popular Religion in Sixth-Century Judah.* HSM 46. Atlanta: Scholars Press, 1992.

Ackroyd, Peter R. "Goddesses, Women, and Jezebel." Pp. 245-59 in *Images of Woman in Antiquity,* edited by A. Cameron and A. Huhrt. Beckenham, Kent: Croom Helm, 1983.

Astour, Michael. "Tamar the Hierodule: An Essay in the Method of Vestigial Motifs." *JBL* 85 (1966): 185-96.

Barnett, R. D. *A Catalogue of the Nimrud Ivories, with Other Examples of Ancient Near Eastern Ivories in the British Museum.* London: Trustees of the British Museum, 1957.

Beach E.F. "An Iconographic Approach to Genesis 38." In *Feminist Companion to Biblical Methodologies, Strategies, and Approaches,* edited by A. Brenner and C. Fontaine. Sheffield: Sheffield Academic Press, forthcoming.

Beach, Eleanor Ferris. "The Samaria Ivories, *Marzeaḥ,* and Biblical Text." *Biblical Archaeologist* 56 (1993): 94-104.

Bikai, Pierre M. "The Rod and the Ring." Unpublished manuscript, 1990. See *SBL Abstracts* S136. Atlanta: Scholars Press, 1990.

Caubet, Annie. "Héraclès ou Hathor: orfèvrerie chypriote." *La revue du Louvre* 23 (1973): 1-6.

———. "Les maquettes architecturales d'Idalion." Pp. 94–118 in *Studies*

Presented in Memory of Porphyrios Dikaios, edited by V. Karageorghis, et al. Nicosia: Lions Club, 1979.

Caubet, A., and J.-C. Courtois. "Masques chypriotes en terre cuite du XIIe S. av. J.C." *Report of the Department of Antiquities, Cyprus* (1975): 43-49.

Caubet, A., and M. Pic. "Un culte hathorique à Kition-Bamboula." Pp. 237–49 in *Archéologie au Levant: Recueil à la mémoire de Roger Saidah.* Lyon: Maison de l'Orient Méditerranéen, 1983.

Crowfoot, J. W., and G. M. Crowfoot. *Early Ivories from Samaria.* London: Palestine Exploration Fund, 1938.

Crowfoot, J. W., G. M. Crowfoot, and K. M. Kenyon. *The Objects from Samaria.* London: Palestine Exploration Fund, 1957.

Day, Peggy. "From the Child Is Born the Woman: The Story of Jephthah's Daughter." Pp. 58–74 in *Gender and Difference in Ancient Israel,* edited by Peggy Day. Minneapolis: Fortress Press, 1989.

———, ed. *Gender and Difference in Ancient Israel.* Minneapolis: Fortress Press, 1989.

Ellul, Jacques. *The Politics of God and the Politics of Man.* Translated by J. W. Bomiley. Grand Rapids, Mich.: Wm. B. Eerdmans Publishing Co., 1972.

Farrar, F. W. *The Second Book of Kings.* The Expositor's Bible 10. New York: Funk & Wagnalls, 1900.

Faulkner, R. O. *The Ancient Egyptian Pyramid Texts.* Oxford: Clarendon Press, 1969.

Fauth, Wolfgang. *Aphrodite Parakyptusa: Untersuchungen zum Erscheinungsbild der vorderasiatischen Dea Prospiciens.* Wiesbaden: Franz Steiner Verlag, 1967.

Frankfort, Henri. *Cylinder Seals: A Documentary Essay on the Art and Religion of the Ancient Near East.* 1939. Reprint, London: The Gregg Press, Ltd., 1965.

Gray, John. *I and II Kings: A Commentary.* 2d rev. ed. Philadelphia: Westminister Press, 1970.

Greenfield, Jonas C. "Un rite religieux Araméen et ses parallèls." *Revue Biblique* 80 (1973): 46-52.

Gunkel, Hermann. *The Legends of Genesis.* Translated by W. H. Carruth. Chicago: Open Court Publishing Co., 1907.

Hackett, Jo Ann. "Rehabilitating Hagar: Fragments of an Epic Pattern." Pp. 12–27 in *Gender and Difference in Ancient Israel,* edited by Peggy Day. Minneapolis: Fortress Press, 1989.

Haran, Menahem. "zebah hayyamim." *VT* 19 (1969): 11-22.

Hartmann, Richard. "Zu Genesis 38." *ZAW* 33 (1913): 76-77.

Herbig, R. "Aphrodite Parakyptusa (Die Frau im Fenster)."

Orientalistische Literaturzeitung 30 (1927): 917-22.

King, Philip J. *Amos, Hosea, Micah—An Archaeological Commentary.* Philadelphia: Westminster Press, 1988.

———. "The *Marzeaḥ* Amos Denounces." *Biblical Archaeology Review* 14 (1988): 34-44.

Langston, Stephen Herbert. *Semitic Mythology.* The Mythology of All Races 5. Boston: Marshall Jones Co., 1931.

Loud, Gordon, and Charles B. Altman. *Khorsabad, Part II: The Citadel and the Town.* University of Chicago, Oriental Institute Publications 40. Chicago: University of Chicago Press, 1938.

Markoe, G. E. *Phoenician Bronze and Silver Bowls from Cyprus and the Mediterranean.* University of California Publications, Classical Studies 26. Berkeley, Calif.: University of California Press, 1985.

Olyan, Saul M. *Asherah and the Cult of Yahweh.* SBL Monograph Series 34. Atlanta, Ga.: Scholars Press, 1988.

Parrot, A., ed. *Studia Mariana.* Leiden: E. J. Brill, 1950.

Pope, Marvin H. "A Divine Banquet at Ugarit." Pp. 170–203 in *The Use of the Old Testament in the New and Other Essays: Studies in Honor of William Franklin Stinespring,* edited by James M. Efird. Durham, N.C.: Duke University Press, 1972.

Pritchard, James B., ed. *The Ancient Near East in Pictures Relating to the Old Testament.* 2d ed. with supp. Princeton, N.J.: Princeton University Press, 1969.

———, ed. *Ancient Near Eastern Texts Relating to the Old Testament.* Princeton, N.J.: Princeton University Press, 1969.

Robertson, Noel. "The Ritual Background of the Dying God in Cyprus and Syro-Palestine." *Harvard Theological Review* 75 (1982): 313-59.

Robinson, Joseph. *The Second Book of Kings.* The Cambridge Bible Commentary on the New English Version. Cambridge: Cambridge University Press, 1976.

Rosenberg, Roy. "The God Ṣedeq." *Hebrew Union College Annual* 36 (1965): 161-77.

Skinner, John. *A Critical and Exegetical Commentary on Genesis.* 2d ed. International Critical Commentary. Edinburgh: T&T Clark, 1930.

Tait, G. A. D. "The Egyptian Relief Chalice." *Journal of Egyptian Archaeology* 49 (1963): 93-139.

Thureau-Dangin, F. A., et al. *Arslan-Tash.* Bibliothèque archéologique et historique 16. Paris: Librairie Orientalist Paul Geuthner, 1931.

Trible, Phyllis. *God and the Rhetoric of Sexuality.* Philadelphia: Fortress Press, 1978.

Wright, G. R. H. "The Positioning of Genesis 38." *ZAW* 94 (1982): 523-29.

10

HAL TAUSSIG

Wisdom/Sophia, Hellenistic Queens, and Women's Lives

The Mediterranean knew some of the most powerful queens in the ancient world. In the Hellenistic period (fourth to first centuries B.C.E.) these queens were often the primary monarchs of their empires, and they regularly exerted great political influence. During the same period, Judaism elaborated its most articulate expression of female divinity in the figure of Wisdom/Sophia. Here in a consistently patriarchal tradition, a powerful divine female persona made a dramatic appearance. This essay will explore the relationships between these two developments and their implications for women of that period.

WISDOM/SOPHIA AS DIVINE QUEEN

Wisdom/Sophia becomes a much more powerful figure in the literature of later Hellenistic Judaism than she was in the earlier portraits of her in Proverbs. She is much more clearly and definitively divine, more cosmic in her activity, and more explicit in her claims and demands on individuals. This chapter will examine the particular shift toward royal images for Wisdom/Sophia after 200 B.C.E.

Royal Images of Wisdom/Sophia in Sirach

In the first chapter of Sirach, the Job 28 theme of God searching for her is taken up again, but with a monarchical twist. Here the question "Her resourceful ways, who knows them?" is answered "Only one is wise, terrible indeed, seated on his throne, the LORD" (1:6, 8). The "LORD's" revealing of her (1:6) has to do with his proximity to her on the throne.

In 1:18 we read of "the crown of Wisdom/Sophia" and how "she makes peace and health flourish." Although Sirach regularly takes pains to secure the Lord's prerogatives, the next verse makes it clear that the Lord's closeness to her crown makes it possible for the Lord to "shower down knowledge and intelligence" and "exalt the renown of those who possess her" (1:19). The Lord and Wisdom/Sophia seem to be imaged, albeit implicitly, as king and queen, royal consorts.

This theme is picked up in the introduction to Wisdom/Sophia's self-presentation in chapter 24 where

> Wisdom[1] praises herself
> and tells of her glory in the midst of her people.
> In the assembly of the Most High she opens her mouth,
> and in the presence of his hosts she tells of her glory. (24:1,2)

Here she is clearly pictured as a part of the heavenly court with a special role of glorying in herself in the presence of the heavenly king.

Curiously, however, the speech of Wisdom/Sophia that follows does not make reference to the heavenly court or use any royal images for her. This highly exalted language about her is full of rich imagery but none that seems to refer to queenship or monarchy.

One other passage in Sirach uses monarchical imagery in relationship to Wisdom/Sophia but with a different twist. In chapter 6 the result of the sage putting on her "fetters" and "yoke" is that "her yoke is a golden ornament, and her bonds a purple cord. You will wear her like a glorious robe, and put her on like a splendid crown" (6:30, 31).

Here the queenly imagery makes Wisdom/Sophia into royal garb for the sage. The sage wears her rather than encounters her as a persona. There seems to be an objectification of her in the eyes of the sage, which tends to make her less an agent and more the object of the sage's search. It is true that this still could be seen as somewhat consistent with the picture of Wisdom/Sophia as divine royalty in that the relational appropriation of her by the sage is the wearing of her crown and royal garb. In a certain sense the human sage learning of the divine is captured in the metaphor of wearing her as royal garb. But even so in this passage for the sage she is something to possess or wear, not a divine persona to encounter.[2]

Royal Images of Wisdom/Sophia in the Wisdom of Solomon

The royal metaphors in the Wisdom of Solomon are much more pervasive. Much of the book is organized around the fictional authorship of the wise king Solomon. The book is consistently addressed to "rulers" (1:1), "kings" (6:1), and "monarchs" (6:21), although they too are probably fictional. So the royal metaphors provide a kind of frame for the work itself.

Wisdom/Sophia plays a central role in the elaboration of the royal metaphors. She is the *paredron* of both the sage/king in 6:14 and God in 9:4. This term is rarely used to mean exactly "queen" (the common words for "queen" are *basileia* and *basilissa*, to which *paredron* is not a frequent parallel). The most common meaning of *paredron* is "coadjutor" or "assessor." The meaning then connotes a close associate of an important official nature. It is used also to designate divine rule and judgment.[3] James Reese translates *paredron* as "throne partner"[4] and the New Jerusalem Bible calls her "a consort" of the throne in the translation of 9:4. The translation of "throne partner" does justice to the literary frame in Wisdom of Solomon, as is evident from the texts that follow.

This double queenly partnership is also clear in the sequence of 8:2, 3. That sequence is framed by the mythical Solomon in 6:22, 24, 25:

> I will tell you what wisdom is and how she came to be . . .
> A sensible king is the stability of any people.
> Therefore be instructed by my words, and you will profit.

Then he outlines Wisdom/Sophia's double queenly relationship to himself and the "Lord of all":

> I desired to take her for my bride,
> and became enamored of her beauty.
> She glorifies her noble birth by living with God,
> for the Lord of all [*panton despotes*] loves her. (8:2, 3)

In fact, it is this double queenly relationship that makes her so crucial, as 6:21 summarizes:

> Therefore if you delight in thrones and sceptres, O monarchs over the peoples, honor wisdom, so that you may reign forever.

"King Solomon" charts his royal relationship to her in 8:9-16:

> Therefore I determined to take her to live with me,
> knowing that she would give me good counsel
> and encouragement in cares and grief.
> Because of her I shall have glory among the multitudes
> and honor in the presence of the elders, though I am young.
> I shall be found keen in judgment,
> and in the sight of rulers I shall be admired.
> When I am silent they will wait for me,
> and when I speak they will give heed;
> if I speak at greater length,
> they will put their hands on their mouths.
> Because of her I shall have immortality,
> and leave an everlasting remembrance to those who come after me.
> I shall govern peoples

and nations will be subject to me;
dread monarchs will be afraid of me when they hear of me;
among the people I shall show myself capable and courageous in war.
When I enter my house, I shall find rest with her;
for companionship with her has no bitterness,
And life with her has no pain, but gladness and joy.

Immortality, ease, and honor come to the one who acknowledges her as queen, both in relationship to the "God of my ancestors" (9:1) and to one's self.

QUEENS AS GODDESSES IN HELLENISM

Actual queens in the Hellenistic period are associated with Goddesses in a number of ways. These queens are often more involved in the governance of their domains than in either previous or subsequent periods of Mediterranean history.[5] The following survey may elucidate the character of the associations between actual queens and Goddesses in the Mediterranean during the period in which Jewish wisdom literature about Wisdom/Sophia developed.

Queens in Cultic Activities and Sites

Olympias of Macedon in the mid-fourth century was a very powerful monarch[6] whose activities spanned the cultic and the political. Plutarch reports her to have introduced Dionysian rites into Macedonia. Around this activity a number of stories developed about the appearance of Dionysius to her in the form of a snake, although Plutarch ascribes these to her own fascination with the animals themselves.[7] Plutarch explicitly associates Olympias' assertive political acts with her Bacchic activity.[8]

This cultic and political activity of Olympias herself occasioned Alexander, her son, to promote her to be honored as Goddess. This was in strong tension with Macedonian resistance to considering their kings and queens as divine.[9] That Alexander associated Olympias in cultic activity with a Goddess despite Macedonian tradition seems to verify the historical connection between her own political and religious influence.

Probably around the turn of the century in the Ptolemaic empire, Bernice I was honored with the building of temples. In Alexandria there was a temple devoted entirely to her as Goddess, and Theocritus writes of another temple where she and Ptolemy were worshiped together, she as Aphrodite and he as Zeus.[10] If the characterization of Bernice by Theocritus is accurate, she herself encouraged her own association with the Goddess.[11]

Although many of the Ptolemaic queens were of Macedonian lineage, their Egyptian context made their association with Goddesses much easier. There was none of the Macedonian inhibition on this score, and millennia of Egyptian association between royalty and the Deity propelled these powerful queens into a divinized image.

A Fayum papyrus witnesses to a temple for Queen Arsinoe II in which she is associated with "Aphrodite of the western shore."[12] This temple, according to Callimachus, was built near Alexandria. According to Pliny, her husband Philadelphus wanted to create a magnetized chapel for worship of her in which the iron statue was to float in the air.[13]

At about the same time but in the Seleucid milieu, Queen Stratonice's own activity at the shrine of Delos led to her being worshiped at Smyrna as Aphrodite Stratonikis. Although she herself may not have been influential politically, her cultic activity in association with her royal position deified her in the eyes of some, including perhaps herself.[14]

Around 120 B.C.E. Cleopatra III was worshiped as Isis and "the twin of Osiris Euergetes" in the Ptolemaic realm. In contrast to Stratonice, she was pro-active in both the political and cultic frame and actively promoted her own royal cult.[15]

Cleopatra VII, of course, did all of this and more. She is said to have worn the sacred costume of Isis in public, and her name appears on the temple at Denderah where her Goddess form was that of Hathor.[16]

Queens in Divine Marriages

The king and queen as divine partners were common images in Hellenism. Some queens during this period married their brothers as an assertion of their divine status and political power. These marriages were meant to associate the brother-sister monarchs with either Zeus and Hera or Isis and Osiris, two divine sibling pairs who also were sexual partners.

Arsinoe II married her brother Ptolemy around 270 B.C.E., most likely as a way of solidifying her political power among the Egyptian priests, for whom the divine marriage of Isis and Osiris should be mirrored by the royalty.[17] Because the Greeks did not approve of such marriages, Theocritus seems to have been called on to justify Arsinoe's act. He compares their marriage then to the "one bed for the sleep of Zeus and Hera."[18]

The names of Cleopatra I and Ptolemy, husband and wife, are inscribed on the temple at Philae as "King Ptolemy and Queen Cleopatra, Gods of Epiphanes."[19] Cleopatra also kept the divine title of "sister" from Arsinoe II. [20]

In 173 Cleopatra II married her fourteen-year-old brother, and they were hailed as divine sexual partners and siblings and worshiped as "mother loving Gods." After his death she married another of her brothers, Ptolemy VII. [21] These two marriages exemplify the dual empowerment of politics and theology so typical of the Ptolemaic queens. The sequence of marriages makes it clear that she was the primary political figure and that she actively promoted herself as divine.

Cleopatra III captured the throne from her mother, in part through her marriage to Ptolemy VIII, her uncle. This marriage signaled the divine presence in Cleopatra III and allowed her to reign afterwards with her two sons as well.[22]

This divine marriage of brother and sister served Cleopatra Tryphaena (VI) and Ptolemy well in 79 B.C.E., for in the face of Roman objection they were declared "father loving Gods and brother and sister loving Gods."[23]

Queens Divinized on Coinage

Throughout the Hellenistic period, monarchs' images were put on coins as signs of their immortality. In the Syrian and Macedonian milieu queens were regularly put on coins after their deaths to signify their attainment of immortal status.[24] But certain queens of this period also appear on coins during their own lifetimes and at their own initiative. A series of Ptolemaic coins picture Arsinoe II wearing the divine diadem. Other coins call her and her brother "divine siblings."[25]

Two queens struck coins in only their own names during their reigns. Cleopatra Thea in 125 B.C.E. issued a tetradrachma with the inscription "Queen Cleopatra, Goddess [*thea*] of Plenty." The other queen to strike a coin in her own name was the Hasmonean Queen Salome Alexandra, who ruled Israel as sole monarch from 76 to 67 B.C.E. Alexandra, of course, did not explicitly call herself Goddess, but her coin image was in an Isis-like pose.

Cleopatra VII also struck coins in her name, mostly paired with Antony. Her coins immortalized her in Greek and Latin as "the new Goddess"[26] and "queen of kings." Her daughter, Cleopatra Selene, although under Roman control, also issued coinage picturing herself as Isis.[27]

Queens Divinized in Inscriptions

A variety of writings, pottery, temple monuments, and political annals also give indication that the Hellenistic queens were considered divine. In the Boston Museum of Fine Arts is a chalcedony gem of a queen portrayed as Isis. McCurdy proposes that this gem is of Ptolemaic Bernice I, who, as we have seen earlier, was also honored culticly as Aphrodite.[28]

In a salute to Arsinoe II, a stele dated around 270 describes her death as "this Goddess departed to the sky."[29] In the British Museum's oenochoe collection a blue enamel piece is inscribed with the name Arsinoe

Philadelphus, and the image of the piece is of a Goddess with the horn of plenty in her left hand and a libation in her right.[30]

Cleopatra III's titles included savior, the saving one, Isis, great mother of the Gods, mother loving Goddess, and justice.[31] Inscriptions hailed Bernice II with her father as "the savior Gods" at the death of her father.[32]

Cleopatra VII and her son Caesarion were called "father loving Goddess" and "father loving, mother loving God" respectively in the inscriptions from the time of her ascendance to power.[33] The later inscriptions near the time of her partnership with Antony are like the coinage in that they hail her as the "new Goddess" and the "new Isis."

Summary

The breadth of association of a variety of queens with a variety of Goddesses in the Hellenistic period demonstrates that this association was not an obscure notion. Rather, the queen as Goddess seems to have been more the rule than the exception during this period. It probably should not be overlooked that the development of this divine queen notion is paralleled by increased political, military, economic, and cultural power of the same queens.

Given the predominance of this queen/Goddess association in the Mediterranean world at this time, it is difficult to believe that the queenly imagery for Wisdom/Sophia in Hellenistic Judaism was not referring to these historical queens. Queen Salome Alexandra's reign and coin in Hasmonean Israel demonstrate that Judaism in Israel knew about politically powerful queens who "gloried in" themselves (Sir 24:1, 2). That the apogee of these queens' political power and divine claims occurred in Egypt corresponds directly with the predominance of the image of Wisdom/Sophia as queen in the Wisdom of Solomon, a work written in Alexandria.

But confirming such references and correspondence does not really say how the images of queen as Goddess functioned for women within the frame of Sirach and Wisdom of Solomon. This issue needs closer attention.

WISDOM/SOPHIA, HELLENISTIC QUEENS, AND WOMEN'S LIVES

Sarah Pomeroy has made a strong case that these queens had a major effect on the lives of women in the Hellenistic era. These "queens served as new paradigms for Greek women," according to Pomeroy. "Not only were they instrumental in the social, political, and cultural changes that transformed the Classical era into the Hellenistic, but they themselves embodied the new Hellenistic woman."[34]

To connect the portrait of divine Wisdom/Sophia in the later Jewish scriptures with the queens of that era would then be, according to Pomeroy, to associate Wisdom/Sophia with "the new Hellenistic woman." Wisdom/Sophia to one extent or another, inasmuch as her portrait is drawn from the consciousness of the divinized queens, would herself serve as one of the "new paradigms for Greek women."

On the other hand, Claudia Camp has proposed that the elevation of Wisdom/Sophia in Sirach and Wisdom of Solomon in fact represents an alienation of women from power:

> It is widely recognized in women's studies, however, that idealized female imagery does not always support women's equality. Indeed, the higher the pedestal and the further removed from the life of real women, the more likely such an image is to be used to repress women through negative comparison.[35]

In a pioneering study Camp has successfully demonstrated that Wisdom/Sophia (or as she calls her, "Woman Wisdom") is an important divine image in Proverbs who connects wise women of Israel to the divine.[36] But when she examines the later exalted Wisdom/Sophia whose parallels with Hellenistic queens we have been noting, Camp concludes: "The memory of the connection of powerful, politicized and faithful women with the (Wisdom/Sophia) tradition is not lost entirely, but its transformation into the idealized figure of Woman Wisdom ultimately ensures that it will remain just that—a memory."[37]

Camp acknowledges that the queens were known in this period and even quotes Pomeroy's appreciation of the advances made by upper-class women.[38] But in relationship to the lives of women in general, Camp's conclusion about the elevated Wisdom/Sophia is as categorically negative as Pomeroy's is positive about the elevation of the queens.

Although at first glance these two analyses seem to be mutually exclusive, I think they are mutually elucidating as well. Some careful attention to both Sirach and Wisdom of Solomon can serve this mutual elucidation well.

Sirach, Women, and Queens

Camp attends carefully to a whole series of texts in Sirach whose aim is to "keep an erring wife at home" (42:5), protect patrilineage from interfering women, keep the lusty daughters under control (7:24, 25; 22:3-5; 26:10-12; 42:9-14), and keep men from looking at women (9:7-9; 41:21).

Her list seems to overlook some of the most misogynous passages (for example, "Better a man's spite than a woman's kindness; women give rise to shame and reproach" in 42:14), but her point is eloquently made.[39]

Camp's assertion that the elevated status of Wisdom/Sophia in Sirach is, in fact, a sign of antagonism toward women is born out by Sirach's consistent and explicit campaign against women in society and the home.

What then do we make of the relatively clear references to real queens as images for Wisdom/Sophia in Sirach? It is important to note that the elevation of one part of a social group can be used to continue the oppression of that same group (in this case, Hellenistic women).

Such was the case, for instance, with regard to the economic status of African Americans in the 1980s. During the 1980s wealthy African Americans were more visible and more lauded than in any other decade in American history. This, however, happened at the same time as a higher percentage of African Americans slid into the depths of the economic underclass. Those who criticized the lack of equality for African Americans in the 1980s were often met with citations of how the 1980s saw the elevation of a number of African Americans to great wealth and privilege in the entertainment world. The visibility of a few wealthy African Americans shielded the public from awareness of the growth of a vast new underclass of African Americans. We need not disagree with Pomeroy that the Hellenistic queens were in fact impacting women in general in a positive way (any more than one could dispute that Oprah Winfrey and Arsenio Hall impact African Americans in a positive manner). The power and influence of the Hellenistic queens did almost certainly effect a whole series of positive changes for women in Israel[40] and the Mediterranean.

The basic truth of Camp's thesis about Sirach remains, however: the elevation of Wisdom/Sophia in Sirach seems to be a part of a consistently misogynous work. Sirach's use of the royal Wisdom/Sophia reinforces patriarchal privileges and the oppression of women. This point can be stated even while maintaining Pomeroy's insight that these same images in Sirach also probably connected to the overall positive effect of the divinized queens on women. That Sirach appeals to the queen imagery for Wisdom/Sophia much less than the Wisdom of Solomon tends to bear out both authors' insights. The reference points for Sirach's elevation of Wisdom/Sophia are less the historical phenomenon of divinized queens and more the Torah (24:23), the tree (24:12-22), and the royal garments (6:29-31).

Wisdom of Solomon, Women, and Queens

I believe that the situation is different in the Wisdom of Solomon. Here Pomeroy's case can be made in a more thoroughgoing manner, and here perhaps Camp's critique cannot be sustained as comprehensively. Closer attention to the way Wisdom of Solomon refers to actual women helps here, as well. In the case of this work of Egyptian Hellenistic Judaism, there are not the attacks or even limitations on women that Trenchard and Camp found in Sirach.

In fact, Camp's criticism of Wisdom of Solomon's treatment of women is limited to one verse, which itself is an odd praise of them. She says, "Real women are mentioned only in the eschatological adulation of those who remain childless rather than transgressing the marriage bed" (3:13).[41]

It is striking that the program of limiting women's public and family power in Sirach is completely missing from the Wisdom of Solomon. And the verse cited by Camp concerning the lauding of childless women is followed by a parallel praise of eunuchs: "Blessed too the eunuch, whose hand commits no crime" (3:14), indicating that eschatological praise of independence from the family is directed at both men and women.

Camp's criticism of the Wisdom of Solomon's treatment of women is that "the quest for Woman Wisdom seems, rather, to turn the sage's focus away from home and family, resulting in the devaluation of this arena."[42] It does seem true that the Wisdom of Solomon does not focus on the home and family, which was for earlier Israelite wisdom the locus of power for women. But the Wisdom of Solomon, as we have seen from the above quote about childless women and eunuchs, seems to propose another locus for women's power.

This shift is consistent with the royal metaphors and the emphasis of the queenly images for Wisdom/Sophia. It also concurs with a growing appreciation of asceticism in Hellenism. The invitation to the sage, the childless woman, and the eunuch to become royal in their control over their world also fits. The fictional monarchs of the work could well be women and men whose focus was more in arenas inspired by the queenly Sophia as she comes to meet her *paredron* at the gates (6:14). The political, economic, and cultural modeling of the queens that Pomeroy asserts for Hellenistic women in general is quite congruent with the queenly Wisdom/Sophia in Wisdom of Solomon.

That the Wisdom of Solomon was written in Alexandria during the apogee of the Ptolemaic queens—Camp notes that it could have even been during Cleopatra VII's reign[43]—also must be taken into consideration. The impact of the queens on ordinary women had to be much greater in

Alexandria than in Jerusalem, where Sirach was written. Pomeroy has shown that the women of Alexandria were lively participants in many economic, political, and cultural arenas and that the societal, familial, and marital controls over women were drastically loosened.[44]

The Wisdom of Solomon integrates this complex and new social situation for Jewish men and women into the earlier Israelite story about being a minority in Egypt by making the divine agent of salvation the queenly Wisdom/Sophia rather than the Lord:

> It was Wisdom/Sophia who delivered a holy people, a blameless race, from a nation of oppressors. She entered the soul of a servant of the Lord, and withstood fearsome kings with wonders and signs. To the holy people she gave the wages of their labors; she guided them by a marvelous road, herself their shelter by day—and their starlight through the night. (10:15-17)

Here divine Wisdom/Sophia clearly images power that real Hellenistic queens and many other Hellenistic women began to exercise in new ways.

This does not completely eliminate the truth of Camp's observations. For some social milieus, this focus on the public domain over against the familial meant a disenfranchisement of women.[45] Even though the Wisdom of Solomon's Wisdom/Sophia complements Pomeroy's "new Hellenistic woman," the focus on the public arena certainly also meant that "this orientation removes itself from the daily arena of common sense wisdom, which is the typical woman's main hope for authority in a patriarchal society."[46] Although "new Hellenistic women" were developing roles of political, economic, and cultural power, other women were being squeezed out of their traditional places of social direction. We can recognize the validity of Camp's observations here, but it is important not to miss the striking correspondence between the divine queen Wisdom/Sophia of Alexandrian context and the emerging powerful women of that same milieu.

CONSTRUCTS OF DIFFERENCE AND SAMENESS RELATIVE TO GENDER DEFINITION

This proposal, that both authors' perspectives on the relationship between the divinized royal persona and the broader sweep of Hellenistic women are helpful even in their tension, points toward a larger methodological issue.

In examining Wisdom/Sophia in these later texts alongside the divinized Hellenistic queens and the larger pool of Hellenistic women, the questions about difference and similarity among them have been crucial.

The work of Rachel T. Hare-Mustin and Jeanne Marecek concerning gender constructs in psychology may be helpful in both the literary and social analysis of these three phenomena (Wisdom/Sophia, divinized queens, and the larger pool of Hellenistic women).[47] Hare-Mustin and Maracek propose a framework of two analytic biases. The "alpha bias is the exaggeration of differences." The beta bias is "the inclination to ignore or minimize differences." [48] Application of this framework to the socio-literary analysis of these three historical phenomena indicates an exaggeration, an alpha bias, when one characterizes the issue in terms of difference between the phenomena. To define the issue in terms of the sameness of queens, Wisdom/Sophia, and/or Hellenistic women would be the beta bias. In their approach to gender constructs Hare-Mustin and Maracek challenge "positivist paradigms" and propose to accept "multiplicity, randomness, incoherence, indeterminacy, and paradox." Such an approach avoids both exaggerating and minimizing differences (the alpha and beta biases) by critiquing both and accepting the multiplicity and indeterminacy of the phenomena.

In the case of this socio-literary analysis, neither the differences nor the similarities among Hellenistic queens, Wisdom/Sophia in the later literature, and women can be allowed to assert a positiv(e/ist) answer. Rather, both the relative differences and similarities need to be factored into an ongoing analytical process. To stop with the recognition of differences between Sirach's or Wisdom of Solomon's Goddess and some Hellenistic women obviously misses the extraordinary connective power between Wisdom/Sophia, the queens, and other women. On the other hand, to be satisfied with noticing the similarity between the Wisdom/Sophia of later Hellenistic Judaism and the queens obviously ignores both the manipulation of Sirach and the differences between queens and other women in patriarchy.

The ease with which Hare-Mustin's and Maracek's categories apply to the socio-literary analysis of these genderful historical texts reveals the larger gender issues at stake in the interpretation of them. The ways that the categories of difference and sameness so easily become final in the examination of these texts reveal the epistemological inadequacies of Western society's readings of gender.

Why is there a tendency to halt the interpretive process when a pattern of difference or sameness is noted? Why do we tend to base our analyses on some definitive difference or sameness between Wisdom/Sophia, the queens, and Hellenistic women? For Hare-Mustin and Maracek,

> [the] alpha and beta bias have similar assumptive frameworks despite their diverse emphases. Both take the male as the standard of comparison. . . . The issue of difference is salient for men in a way that it is not for women. Those who are dominant have an interest in emphasizing those differences that reaffirm their superiority and in denying their similarity to subordinate groups. By representing nonsymmetrical relationships as symmetrical, those who are dominant obscure the unequal social arrangements that perpetuate male dominance.[49]

According to Hare-Mustin and Maracek,

> gender is not a property of individuals but a socially prescribed relationship, a process, and a social construction. . . . The riddle of gender is presumed to be solved when heterogeneous material is reduced to the homogeneity of logical thought (Gallop, 1982). To establish a dichotomy is to avoid complexity. The idea of gender as opposites obscures the complexity of human action and shields both men and women from the discomforting recognition of inequality.[50]

Interpretation of later Wisdom/Sophia in relationship to the queens and Hellenistic women must be a process that includes the multiplicity of relatedness among a Goddess-like Wisdom/Sophia, Isis, Aphrodite, the various queens, upper-class women in Alexandria, and poorer women in Jerusalem. Stopping with one set of differences or similarities hinders a more complex understanding of the material and of gender itself.

NOTES

1. In my own text I have chosen to call this figure "Wisdom/Sophia." Most of scholarship (e.g., James M. Robinson, Burton Mack, Elisabeth Schüssler Fiorenza) refers to her as "Sophia," taking their cues from both the Greek word for "wisdom" and the clear persona in the texts. Some other scholars refer to her as "Wisdom," (e.g., von Rad), "Woman Wisdom" (Claudia Camp), or "Lady Wisdom" (Virginia Ramey Mollenkott). In order to cover both the literal base and the literary persona, I have combined the two basic terms. In the biblical quotations only "Wisdom" is used in order to observe the standard use of the New Revised Standard Version.

2. Here Margaret Miles's observations about male representation of women seem to be particularly helpful. She says, "Overlapping cumulative representations of 'women' select certain characteristics to 'stand for' women, enabling men to 'handle' the women to whom they must relate. The social function of representations, then, is to stabilize assumptions and expectations relating to

the objects or persons represented" (*Carnal Knowing,* 10). The result, according to Miles, is that "men usually have created representations of women out of their fears and fantasies" (169).

3. Liddell and Scott, *A Greek-English Lexicon,* 1332.

4. In "The Wisdom of Solomon," *Harper's Bible Commentary,* 825. Unfortunately, Reese understands God to be the throne partner in both verses, even though chapter 6 charts the relationship to the wise king.

5. See McCurdy's classic study, *Hellenistic Queens,* for an overview.

6. See McCurdy, *Hellenistic Queens,* 23-46. Olympias's power is so striking that it occasions the threatened characterization of her by Hogarth as "Jezebel of a Queen" (*Philip and Alexander of Macedon,* 137).

7. See the E 253 amphora in the British Museum and McCurdy's discussion, *Hellenistic Queens,* 27-29.

8. *Alexander* 2, 9.

9. Beloch, *Griechische Geschichte,* 372-75, charts the Macedonian resistance. Plutarch, *Alexander* 26, 27 discusses Alexander's effort.

10. Theocritus, *Idyll* 17; and Callixenus, *Athenaios,* 196-204.

11. Sarah Pomeroy (*Women in Hellenistic Egypt,* 37, 38) seems to lend this account credence.

12. Papyrus Berlin 13417. See also the discussion of Longega, *Arsinoe II,* 133-35.

13. *Natural History* 36, 37

14. See also the honorific inscriptions to Stratonice, *I Hell Paphos,* number 41, P. Pt. 15939, published in Mitford, "The Hellenistic Inscriptions of Old Paphos."

15. See Dittenberger, *Orientis Graeci,* I. 103, 106, 109, 111, 115. See also Bouche-Leclercq, *Histoire des Legides,* III, 57.

16. Strabo 17, *Rerum Geographicarum,* 794-99.

17. McCurdy, *Hellenistic Queens,* 116.

18. Theocritus, *Idyll* 2, 14, 15.

19. Papyrologica. Lugduno.-Batava. XV, in Pestman, *Chronologie egyptienne.*

20. Kornemann, "Die Ehe der Theoi Philometores," 9.

21. Samuel, *Ptolemaic Chronology,* 139-48.

22. Papyrologica. Lugduno.-Bateva. XXIIA, 66, in Pestman, *Chronologie egyptienne.*

23. Papyrologica. Lugduno.-Batava. XV, 76, in Pestman, *Chronologie egyptienne.* See also Preisigke, *Die Prinz Joachim Ostraka,* 1,22,21, and Skeat, *The Reigns of the Ptolemies,* 37-39.

24. McCurdy, *Hellenistic Queens,* 18-20.

25. Thompson, *Ptolemaic Oinochoai,* 56; Kyrieleis, *Bildnisse der Ptolemaeer,* pls. 72, 75, 79, 80. Also important in evaluations of Arsinoe II is the discussion of her relative and actual influence according to the Greek and Egyptian sources in Pomeroy, *Women in Hellenistic Egypt,* 21-40.

26. Plutarch, *Antiquities,* 54.

27. Karstedt, *Frauen auf antiken Muenzen,* X, 301.

28. McCurdy, *Hellenistic Queeens,* 104.

29. Callimachus, *The Deification of Arsinoe,* repeats this description.

30. The extensive comparison between Arsinoe II and Aphrodite in Hellenistic literature is surveyed in volume 1 of Frazer, *Ptolemaic Alexandria.*

31. Fraser, *Ptolemaic Alexandria*, 122-25, and McCurdy, *Hellenistic Queens*, 168.
32. Appian, *Bellorum Civilium Liber Quintus* I, 102.
33. Edgar, "Zeno Papyri," 221.
34. Pomeroy, *Hellenistic Women*, 3.
35. Camp, "Female Sage," 22, 23.
36. *Wisdom and the Feminine in the Book of Proverbs.*
37. Camp, "Female Sage," 22.
38. Camp, " Female Sage," 23, 24.
39. Camp, "Female Sage," 14-24. She also cites and agrees with the negative judgment of Trenchard in *Ben Sira's View of Women* that Sirach's "glowing regard for dame Wisdom stands in astounding contrast to his reflections on women in the flesh." Camp does qualify her agreement with Trenchard in that she sees some positive valuation of the wise woman still extant in Sirach.
40. The effects of Queen Salome Alexandra on equal rights in Israel in fact were substantial, especially in areas such as women's ability to own property and women's rights in divorce. In particular the reforms of the *ktubba* under Salome "made it very difficult for the husband to pay the marriage settlement and thus be rid of his wife" (Klausner in "Queen Salome Alexandra," 251). Under Salome, Simeon ben Shetah, who was "very close to the Pharisee queen" (Klausner, "Queen Salome Alexandra," 248), also obliged the husband to the *ktubba* and the wife in terms of his entire holdings and not just some symbolic holding. Under important Greek influence, "the general attitude towards women took a turn for the better in Hasmonean Judea. The position of Queen Salome constitutes further proof of this," according to Klausner ("Queen Salome Alexandra," 252).
41. Camp, "Female Sage," 27.
42. Camp, "Female Sage," 26.
43. Camp, " Female Sage," 23.
44. *Goddesses, Whores, Wives, and Slaves* and the more recent and already cited *Women in Hellenistic Egypt.*
45. See the analysis Torjesen in *Excavations*. Her analysis concentrates on our period, and she seems to be theoretically indebted to Lerner's *The Creation of Patriarchy*.
46. Camp, "Female Sage," 27
47. Hare-Mustin and Maracek, *Making a Difference.*
48. Hare-Mustin and Maracek, *Making a Difference*, 34.
49. Hare-Mustin and Maracek, *Making a Difference*, 54, 55.
50. Hare-Mustin and Maracek, *Making a Difference*, 54.

WORKS CITED

Beloch, K. *Griechische Geschichte.* Berlin: Walter de Gruyter and Co., 1927.

Bouche-Leclercq, A. *Histoire des Legides*. Paris: Ernst Leroux, 1907.

Cady, Susan; Marian Ronan; Hal Taussig. *Wisdom's Feast: Sophia in Study and Celebration*. San Francisco: Harper and Row, 1988.

Camp, Claudia. "The Female Sage in Ancient Israel and the Biblical Wisdom Tradition." Unpublished manuscript, 1987.

———. *Wisdom and the Feminine in the Book of Proverbs*. Sheffield: Almond Press, 1985.

Dittenberger, W. *Orientis Graeci inscriptiones selectae I*. Munich: C. H. Beck, 1903-1905. Reprint, 1960.

Edgar, C. C. "Zeno Papyri." *Annales du Service des Antiquites de l'Egypte* 20 (1920), 219-23.

Fraser, P. M. *Ptolemaic Alexandria*. Vol. 1. Oxford: Clarendon Press, 1972.

Hare-Mustin, Rachel, and Jeanne Maracek. *Making a Difference: Psychology and the Construction of Gender*. New Haven, Conn.: Yale University Press, 1990.

Heyob, Sharon Kelly. *The Cult of Isis among Women in the Graeco-Roman World*. Leiden: E. J. Brill, 1975.

Hogarth, D. G. *Philip and Alexander of Macedon*, London: John Murray, 1897.

Karstedt, U. "Frauen auf Antiken Muenzen." *Klio* 10 (1910): 297-307.

Klausner, J. "Queen Salome Alexandra." *The World History of the Jewish People* 6. New York, 1972.

Kornemann, E. "Die Ehe der Theoi Philometeres." *Klio* 9 (1909): 2-16.

Kyrieleis, Helmut. *Bildnisse der Ptolemaeer*. Berlin: Mann Verlag, 1975.

Lerner, Gerda. *The Creation of Patriarchy*. New York: Oxford University Press, 1986.

Liddell, H. G., and R. Scott. *A Greek-English Lexicon*. Oxford: Clarendon Press, 1968.

Longega, Gabriella. *Arsinoe II*. Rome: L'erma di Bretschneider, 1968.

Mack, Burton *A Myth of Innocence: Mark and Christian Origins*. Philadelphia: Fortress Press, 1988.

McCurdy, Grace. *Hellenistic Queens: A Study of Woman-Power in Macedon, Seleucid Syria, and Ptolemaic Egypt*. Baltimore: Johns Hopkins Press, 1932.

Miles, Margaret. *Carnal Knowing: Female Nakedness and Religious Meaning in the Christian West*. Boston: Beacon Press, 1989.

Mitford, T. B. "The Hellenistic Inscriptions of Old Paphos." *Bulletin de la Societe Archeologique d'Alexandrie* 56 (1961):1-41.

Mollenkott, Virginia Ramey. *The Feminine Dimension of the Divine*. Philadelphia: Westminster Press, 1979.

Neumer-Pfau, Wiltrud. *Studien zur Ikonographie und gesellschaftlichen Funktion hellenistischer Aphrodite-Statuen*. Bonn: R. Habelt Verlag, 1982.

Pestman, P. W. *Chronologie egyptienne d'apres les textes demotiques 332 avant Jesus Christ -453 apres Jesus Christ*. Leiden: E. J. Brill, 1967.

Preisigke, F., and W. Spiegelberg. *Die Prinz Joachim Ostraka*. Strasburg: Schriften der wissenschaftlichen Gesellschaft in Strasburg, Heft 19, 1914.

Pomeroy, Sarah. *Goddesses, Whores, Wives, and Slaves: Women in Classical Antiquity*. New York: Schocken Books, 1975.

Pomeroy, Sarah. *Women in Hellenistic Egypt*. Detroit: Wayne State University Press, 1990.

Reese, James. "The Wisdom of Solomon." Pp. 820-35 in *Harper's Bible Commentary*, edited by James L. Mays. San Francisco: HarperCollins, 1988.

Robinson, James M. "Very Goddess and Very Man: Jesus' Better Self." Pp. 113–27 in *Images of the Feminine in Gnosticism*, edited by Karen L. King. Philadelphia: Fortress Press, 1988.

Samuel, A. E. *Ptolemaic Chronology*. Munich: C. .H. Beck, 1962.

Schüssler Fiorenza, Elisabeth. *In Memory of Her. A Feminist Reconstruction of Christian Origins*. New York: Crossroad, 1983.

Skeat, T. C. *The Reigns of the Ptolemies* Munich: C. H. Beck, 1969.

Torjesen, Karen J. *Excavations in the Deep Structure of the Theological Tradition*. Claremont, Calif.: Institute for Antiquity and Christianity Occasional Papers, 1989.

Thompson, Dorothy Burr. *Ptolemaic Oinochoai and Portraits in Faience: Aspects of the Ruler Cult*. Oxford: Clarendon Press, 1973.

Trenchard, Warren. *Ben Sira's View of Women: A Literary Analysis*. Chico: Scholars Press, 1982.

Von Rad, Gerhard. *Wisdom in Israel*. Nashville: Abingdon, 1972.

11

SAVINA J. TEUBAL

The Rise and Fall of Female Reproductive Control as Seen through Images of Women

When Yahweh proposed that he should be the sole God of the Israelites (Exod 20:3), he not only decried the worship of other Gods and Goddesses, he also condemned their sculptured likeness (Exod 20:4). But according to Meyers, "pure, widespread Yahwism, without graven images was a relatively late development in Israelite history."[1]

Graven images, figurative representations of divinity, were a fundamental component of ancient religions, and Yahwism[2] was no exception. Whether they were perceived as housing the spirit of the Deity or merely as artistic renderings of supernatural beings, these images were categorized as sacred.

In this chapter I will argue that, viewed in sequence, there is archaeological evidence, both artistic and architectural, for women's separate practices, both religious and social, that were maintained in varying degrees over the millennia, including much of the Yahwistic era! Female images depicting women's reproductive capabilities and their discovery in specific locations used as menstruation or birthing centers indicate that, traditionally, reproductive control was in the hands of women. Reproductive control governs the quality of life. This information reflects important changes in the perception of women and their attributes, changes that do not benefit women in the present as they seemingly did in the past.

The biblical graven image prohibition (Exod 20:4) helped to erase the female link with the divine and opened the way for literary characterization to absorb all former female traits into Yahwism.

Women in the Bible have been viewed as being allotted restrictive roles as conventional mothers, concubines, or whores, typical of female roles in patriarchy. What seems to have been left out of this evaluation is that biblical women's stories belong to *sacred* texts and must therefore contain specific religious dimensions uniquely theirs. I submit, therefore, that biblical references to menstruation, pregnancy, birth, and lactation derive from a long tradition regarding reproduction that can be traced back to figurative art in the Upper Paleolithic.

In the ancient Near East, gender was not initially a significant category in the divine pantheon, whereas in Israel, the rise of the one male God was correlated with a deep concern for gender as a central determinant of appropriate behavior in both cult and society, and with the exclusion of women from religious life.[3] Women are given no authoritative role in the cult of Yahweh; rather, it is men who serve as officiants and men to whom the conventional regulations are addressed.[4] Setel, commenting on the numerous associations between women and non-Yahwistic worship in the Hebrew Bible, suggests that because of this exclusion, women may have sustained earlier Canaanite practices separately, at least until the Babylonian conquest and the exile in the sixth century B.C.E.[5] Canaanite practice, like that of the rest of the ancient Near East that informed our ancestors, included making and venerating sacred images.

Female iconography, reaching as far back as the Upper Paleolithic and continuing through to the Iron Age, supports the concept of a separate religious practice for women that may or may not have included men but in which males were not central. Throughout this period, men organized their own separate practices, parallel to those of women and initially related to hunting and defense. These became more dominant as populations grew and more elitist as warrior classes took control, finally culminating in Israel and Judah in Yahwism, which absorbed all the female properties and practices. Nevertheless, parallel to the almost universal rise in the status of male Gods, images of females persistently outnumbered those of their male counterparts. Many arguments have been proposed and as many interpretations made about the essence of prehistoric female figures: seeing them as "Venus" figurines, Mother Goddess representations, or being employed as teaching aids, votive offerings, or for sympathetic magic.[6]

Although interpretations are difficult without written records, I would argue that such an unfailing *focus* on the female over such a vast period of time does indicate an interest or consciousness surrounding the mystery of female reproductive capabilities. A strong underlying female-centered tradition that honored the enigma of life-giving and nurturing implies an understanding that the female of the species had particular (supernatural?) attributes that males did not.

Prehistoric female representations, whether stone or bone carvings, rock reliefs, paintings, engravings, or clay models, range from Western Europe to the Baltic, through Asia Minor to the Fertile Crescent and Africa—a vast geographical area, indeed. Add to this the enormous span of time covered, from the Upper Paleolithic (commencing about 35,000 years ago) to the Iron Age (about 587 B.C.E.), and generalization seems impossible.

As mentioned above, archaeological remains not associated with written records are difficult to interpret. Margaret Ehrenberg tells us that "nearly every idea put forward by archaeologists is theory or hypothesis, rather than firm fact,"[7] and to a certain extent this applies to biblical scholars also. Theories tend to be subjective. If archaeologists are from middle-class elite backgrounds, schooled in Greek classics and history, their conjectures would certainly be limited to that experience. So, on the one hand, archaeology needs interpretation. Archaeology nevertheless can have its advantages. Assuming the archaeologist is able to adopt an unbiased attitude, archaeological data can furnish us with a much more ample view of the society that left the evidence than do the written records of a small elite.

Relatively recently archaeology has merged with other disciplines—anthropology, history, and so on. Because archaeology, anthropology, and related disciplines come from a male-dominated society, however, it is not surprising to find a focus on male interests, which color the research. As pointed out by Carol Meyers,[8] until the last decade or so, archaeologists working in Palestine at sites dating from the biblical period have suffered from the same urban, elite bias that characterized the document, the Bible, which in nearly every case determined their choice of sites, [choosing those] which possessed the greatest likelihood for yielding monumental architecture and distinctive artifacts,[9] thereby virtually excluding from the archaeologist's purview the investigation of villages and hamlets, of farmsteads and country estates,[10] which more likely include the domestic realm pertaining to women.

Written records do not fare much better. Written language is relatively young when measured in the context of human history: barely 4,000 years out of a span of 40,000.[11] In other words, only 10 percent of human experience is available in written form. This leaves 90 percent for archaeological evidence to interpret as best we can. To compound the problem, the vast majority of written records were composed by a relatively small number of privileged men, mainly interested in trade and military exploits, male ventures in which, they claim, women usually took no part. In written form, then, little if anything is chronicled about the lives of ordinary people, men or women, before the third millennium B.C.E.

Nevertheless, despite the enormous time frame (or perhaps because of it), looking at the cycles of female art as a whole rather than investigating chunks of it out of this wider context can give us insight into the enduring tradition of ancient women's interests and persuasions.

Let us first consider the data. Archaeological testimony of *homo sapiens sapiens* (that is, modern humans, with the same physique and brainpower as ours) began to appear on the shores of the Mediterranean and northern Spain about 40,000 years ago. These people are perhaps best known for what is referred to as Ice Age art, cave paintings and figurines. Archaeologically speaking, these people belong to the Upper Paleolithic, their economy is based on gathering and hunting, but little is known of their social lives. They used stone implements such as cooking devices, blades, and tools, and made ornaments from shells, bone, and ivory. They also created human and animal images. Of the former, the plastic image of the human female predominates during the entire period—almost 30,000 years!

Prehistoric female figurines belong to two phases, the Paleolithic and the Neolithic. Those from the Upper Paleolithic (ca. 34,000-12,000) come from Europe, are carved in stone or bone, and were found in cave wall crevices or in dwellings. Despite the length of time and huge geographic area involved, the figures show marked similarities. They are often corpulent or pregnant. In design they are faceless and lacking full extremities. The Venus of Willendorf (fig. 31) is a good example.

Whether reproductive faculty implied innate or supernatural power at any given point during this period is a matter of conjecture. It is therefore unrealistic to theorize that all representations of humans (or animals, for that matter) are necessarily associated with the realm of the divine or sacred.

Ice Age art falls into three categories reflecting different patterns of thought and behavior: home or portable art, rock art, and cave art.[12]

Home or portable art consists of small unpainted objects, engravings, carvings, and some modeling, always found in living sites and therefore associated with daily life. It is by far the most common and most widespread category. The most interesting and distinctive form of home art is the human female figurine, the Venus type.

Rock art consists of bas-reliefs, engravings, and drawings on walls and ceilings of rock shelters and cave mouths and in corridors leading off from them, or on slabs of rock or large stream pebbles. These are adjacent to living areas. Stylistic kinship of some of the reliefs to the Venus figurines is obvious, and the function may have been the same (see below).

Recently a category, art *sur bloc,* has been added that refers to stone blocks, usually limestone, with engraving or sculpting that could, in theory, have been moved around within the locale.[13]

Unlike the first three categories, cave art is not associated with living sites and seems to be a later development, about 16,000. These occur in the innermost galleries of caves, always in total darkness, and are often difficult to access. Because the portrayals in these inner caves are mostly of animals and hunting implements, we will not be concerned with them here.

We will examine the art in the first three categories, examining representative illustrations typical of each era: Upper Paleolithic, Neolithic, Bronze Age, and Iron Age.

UPPER PALEOLITHIC EVIDENCE (34,000–7500)

A Cave of Her Own

Remarkable images of Upper Paleolithic women have been found in and over the entrance to cave shelters. Representations of women in this period are inaccurately referred to as "Venus." Archaeologists, historians of prehistory, and biblical scholars tend to label ancient female figurines solely as mother or fertility Goddesses, and Venus or concubine figurines, the two roles assigned to women in patriarchy: the reproductive vessel and the sex object.

Two reliefs from about 25,000-20,000, carved on limestone slabs displaying female figures, were found at the site of Abri Laussel in the French Dordogne Valley. The best known of these, designated Venus of Laussel (fig. 32), is housed in the Musée d'Aquitaine, Bordeaux, France; a smaller relief (fig. 33) is in the Staatliche Museen of Berlin.[14] An almost identical image, known as the Venus of Grimaldi, was found at the Italian site of Balzi Rossi.

The larger Venus of Laussel was placed dramatically over the shelter's entrance. It represents the figure of a naked woman, about eighteen inches (forty-four centimeters) high with one hand on her protruding belly and the other held shoulder high, to one side. In both reliefs the figure holds a crescent or bison horn in her raised hand; the horn in the larger relief has thirteen lines notched on it. The face is turned toward the raised hand and, characteristically of this period, the face is featureless. These reliefs are typical of many Paleolithic representations of women, with small heads atop imposing bodies, large hanging breasts, huge buttocks, but small or nonexistent hands and feet. When the reliefs were discovered, there were still traces of red ocher present on the figures. Red ocher associated with skeletons and burials predates even the Laussel women. Lumps of red ocher have been found in Neanderthal and other Mousterian burials.[15] On the inner walls of the Laussel shelter were carvings of several female figures, two animals (a doe and a horse), a fragment of a male figure, and a "curious double image that appears to be a copulating couple."[16]

There are many conjectures as to what the Laussel Venus figure represents. Elinor Gadon believes the shelter itself was probably a place of ritual.[17] Marija Gimbutas suggests that women shown with their hand or hands on their bellies indicate pregnant women.[18] She also proposes that the thirteen lines on the horn may symbolize the waxing days of the moon.[19]

We do not know what calendric devices were used by our Upper Paleolithic forebears or the calendars' functions, but many conjectures are possible. For example, an ancient Mayan calculation of the Venusian cycle of 260 (lunar) days was divided into thirteen twenty-day sections.[20] Furthermore, 260 divided by 9 (gestation months) = 28.888 days, the average length of a woman's menstrual cycle. The link between women's menstrual cycles and moon phases is universal, and a great deal of significance has been attached to it.

The Laussel figure is anything but static. The head turned toward the notched horn raised in one hand to the height of the shoulder suggests communication (or teaching?) on the part of the woman who holds it. The other hand, resting on her abdomen, has the fingers pointing toward her vulva, which gives the impression that there is a relationship between the horn and the vulva. The red pigment, a symbol of blood (life force) highly associated with women, would signify menstruation or birth.

The presence of three almost identical images in similar settings would suggest the function of the shelters was analogous. The outdoor reliefs may have indicated special land rights or shrine rights to particular seclusionary shelters. The makers of these reliefs were foragers, gatherers, and hunters; these people lived in small nomadic groups, moving as the various food resources determined.[21] Seasonal and astronomical cycles were part of the natural order, as were female menstrual cycles, a connection bound to have been made. I suspect the ties between the moon, the evening star, and menstrual cycles were obvious to women of this period, as were seasonal cycles. Menstruating females would have noted the increased danger from predators drawn to the smell of their menstrual blood and would have taken precautionary measures to safeguard themselves and their community by secluding themselves in hard-to-reach areas.[22] Females living in close quarters often find their menstrual cycles become synchronized, and they would therefore go into menstrual seclusion, several at a time, with older female caretakers.[23] Because menstruants were perceived as dangerous, a variety of taboos restricting their activities grew up around them. Their hands and feet could not touch anything; mouth, eyes, and hair all came to exude ominous powers.[24]

In view of the widespread attention given to women and girls at the time of their menstruation, the hazard inherent in regular monthly bleeding, and the rituals and taboos that arose because of it, we may surmise that similar attitudes were held by various groups very early on. The bloated bodies and red coloring of the figures could certainly indicate the condition of the menses, whereas the obvious lack of feet, hands, and face would represent the areas of taboo. Even the gaze of the menstruant came to be understood as perilous, so she had to keep her head lowered, for she had the eye of death as well as of life.[25] Unlike the reliefs, the faceless heads on the three figurines from Willendorf, Menton, and Lespugue (figs. 31, 32, 33) are all bent forward. Rather than Goddesses, I suggest these figures may depict menstruants.

It is possible that menstruating women may have produced some of the art on the inner walls of shelters when they spent their days segregated from communal activities, particularly in view of the possible calendric connection. Furthermore, it is believed[26] that the painted or imprinted hands, found in abundance from 30,000 to 10,000 and then again in the Neolithic, were imprinted or were painted by women. In at least one cave, Pech-Merle, the size of handprints and footprints found there fit the skeletal remains of women,[27] although these may also belong to children.

There is nothing to indicate that the relief figures were envisioned as Goddesses by their prehistoric artists, but red ocher does suggest a relationship to the power of the spirit world.

The Spirit within Her

An affinity exists between the reliefs and the portable art in that they have similar characteristics. Over sixty Paleolithic female figurines have been found in widespread locations in Europe,[28] among which are the baked clay figurines from Dolni Vestonice in Czechoslovakia, the earliest evidence of clay firing.[29] Most figurines are associated with houses or home bases, and they are usually found singly among assemblages of flint tools and debris.[30]

As in the shelter reliefs, the small female figurines display substantial bodies with large breasts and bellies; they are topped by small, faceless but covered heads, small or spindly arms, and tapering legs with no feet. The most famous, from Willendorf (fig. 31), like the Laussel reliefs, is also carved from limestone. Others, however, like the Austrian Venus of Menton (fig. 32) are fashioned from soapstone. And perhaps the most common are carved in ivory, as is the beautiful Venus of Lespugue, France (fig. 33). Traces of red ocher are also found on some of them.

NEOLITHIC EVIDENCE (10,000–4000)

A Shrine of Her Own

A larger and more diverse group of female representations belongs to the Neolithic and is found around the Mediterranean basin of Eastern Europe, Asia Minor, and the Near East. These female images are carved, incised, or molded. Unlike those of the Paleolithic, many figurines of this period have distinctive features; this may be due to the advent of clay modeling. Although most of these figurines are of human females, there are some animals and some male figures, in that order of frequency. Many other figurines appear to be sexless.

The Upper Paleolithic themes of menstruation, pregnancy, and birth, which take place in specific separate quarters, and their association with blood (red ocher) are also apparent in the Neolithic period. But from now on we begin to see significant social changes in shorter periods of time.

Stone Age art, as mentioned above, is the work of hunter-gatherer communities living on the edge of glacial ice sheets in which meat and fish would be more abundant than grain. People of the Neolithic, however, belong to simple agricultural societies in which women play a key role in food production. Unlike the nomadic hunting and food gathering of the Paleolithic, Neolithic farming and animal domestication require sedentary living.

The best example of a Neolithic site was found in Anatolia (*Ana-dolu*, "[land of] many mothers," Turkey), which produced a remarkable series of early Neolithic female figurines. Ehrenberg points out that "this area is particularly important because it is one of the few areas in which fertility cults and a 'Mother Goddess' are historically attested at a later period."[31] Çatal Hüyük is also the largest Neolithic site (only thirty-two acres of the site have been excavated to date) and was continuously inhabited for 850 years, from 6250 to 5400 B.C.E. The time span is more impressive when compared to the average life span of only thirty years,[32] that is, about eighty-five generations (as compared to about twenty-eight modern generations over a similar period).

In the early levels of Çatal Hüyük, as in the caves of the Upper Paleolithic, wall decorations show abstract patterns and various animals. Felines, in particular, were closely associated with women in Çatal. As in earlier eras, the women's bodies are full, their heads small, and their legs tapering.

A baked clay figure (fig. 36, about 5,750) of a corpulent woman sitting on a massive thronelike chair with her arms resting on felines (female lions or leopards) standing on either side of her was found in a grain bin close to a shrine. It is perhaps one of the most impressive objects found at Çatal Hüyük. James Melaart, excavator of the site, presumed the woman was in the process of giving birth[33] because of what looks like a protruding head between her feet. On closer examination, however, the object between the woman's feet may not be a human head, particularly as she herself seems to be enthroned rather than being in a birthing position. Furthermore, each of her hands rests on the head of the feline flanked at her sides, which gives the impression of power over animals (or nature?) or an affinity with them.

Melaart believes that Çatal Hüyük gives a unique picture of Neolithic religion in Anatolia. He also suggests the figure of the woman with felines is that of a Goddess and that the leopard was her sacred animal.[34] Indeed, the figure, now in the Anatolian Museum at Ankara, is not surprisingly labeled "Cybele" (Kybele, Kubele, Kubaba) by present-day Turks. The worship of Cybele was later centered in Phrygia (central Asia Minor, 1200-585), where she was also represented seated on a throne flanked by two female lions.[35] Cybele was a mountain-dwelling Goddess who was responsible for creating and maintaining the wild things of the earth.

Females with felines are a common motif in Çatal Hüyük and in coexistent Hacilar, where women were sculptured wearing leopard skins or standing next to a leopard.[36] There is also a figure of a seated male wearing a leopard-skin cap and a boy riding on a leopard.[37] One intriguing grouping from Hacilar has a woman sitting on a leopard holding a leopard cub[38] (fig. 37). The ability to tame wild animals may relate to the domestication of animals; the Cybele figure may represent this transition.

Control over food production by manipulating the female of the species, whether plant or animal was, plausibly, initiated by women. It seems probable that it was women who made the first observations of plant behavior and worked out, presumably by long trial and error, how to grow and tend crops.[39] Storage bins were built into the floor of houses,[40] a precursor perhaps of the *giparu*: "the storehouse [like that] of Inanna in which the 'sacred marriage' rite took place."[41]

Taming wild animals, such as leopards (for protection or sympathetic magic for healing) or sheep, goats, and cattle (as livestock), would more likely have initially been in the hands of the women who bore and reared their own young.

From Spirit Within to Spirit Without

It is generally thought that the relationship between intercourse and procreation was not understood until the Neolithic. Elinor Gadon,[42] however, interprets a relief at Çatal Hüyük as a symbolic representation of this concept: four figures are carved in bold relief on a plaque in which a couple on the left embrace, and on the right a mother holds a child. Moreover, in view of the prior 20,000 years of images describing women's reproductive faculties, it seems unbelievable to me that the male role in conception was not understood.

Initially, women may have raised orphaned cubs. This would have symbolized the power and strength of the mountain-dwelling Goddess, the abode of the felines. Due to the particular needs of a growing sedentary population, sheep and goats were also tamed and eventually domesticated, that is, forced to breed, by both men and women. Not procreation, I would argue, but rather the innovation of controlled breeding was the major event in the Neolithic "revolution."

Power and control over the reproductive forces of nature (both plant and animal) during the Neolithic would have diminished the innate awe with which people of the Paleolithic had viewed the magical nature of females, because men must certainly have taken a part in capturing the familiar but dangerous wild bovines and in controlling their breeding. The transition from spirit within to supernatural power over was inevitable. Women would still have been held in high regard due to the uniqueness of their biological functions, but now their role was perceived not as innate but rather as having been endowed from without. Thus was born the conception of Goddess(es), personified nature, and her abode: the shrine.

Melaart distinguishes shrines from houses by their superior decoration and contents[43] (fig. 38). Forty shrines or sanctuaries distributed over nine building levels at Çatal Hüyük were unearthed by Melaart.[44] The shrines were evidently the scene of a fertility cult, he surmises, "the main aim of the religion being the procreation of life, the assurance of its continuity, and abundance in both this life and the next."[45]

Nevertheless, Melaart was bewildered by the immense variety of the shrines: "no two are alike," he tells us.[46] Dorothy Cameron, a woman on his research team, however, identified one room as a birthing room.[47] Red and black seem to be the predominant colors in Çatal Hüyük, but in this particular shrine the walls and floor, platforms, and benches are all painted red, with red gutters running alongside a raised platform bed. Gadon suggests that the long red runnels carried plentiful water needed during confinement and that the floor was burnished and hardened for easy cleaning.[48]

Shrines and models of shrines from the Neolithic era have also been unearthed in Old Europe.[49] One rectangular shrine (seventy square meters) discovered at Sabatinovka II in the valley of Southern Bug, Western Ukraine (fig. 39) and described by Gimbutas caught my attention. In all, thirty-two female figurines were found in this sanctuary. On a raised platform at the far end of the sanctuary, sixteen of these figurines were seated, leaning backwards on reclining horned thrones, which seem to have been designed for the comfort of menstruating or pregnant women (fig. 40). All the figures are schematically portrayed with snake-shaped heads and no arms, and they may be in various stages of pregnancy.

Alongside the raised platform or altar stood a large thronelike horned chair. Its seat, one meter wide, was originally covered with split planks. Gimbutas suggests it was for a priestess or priest overseer.[50] Under the circumstances it was just as likely for a midwife shaman, or even for the women who gave birth, a kind of ritual chair. Horns, associated with women in the Paleolithic, are not only abundantly displayed in Çatal Hüyük, they are also found in Minoan Crete and crown the heads of the Egyptian Goddesses Hathor and Isis.

Prominent in the sanctuary was a large oven, at the base of which a female figurine was found, and close to it was a group of five saddle querns and a row of five terra-cotta figurines.[51] The association of quern and grindstones with figurines portrayed in seated position suggests magical grinding of grain and then perhaps baking of sacred bread.[52] The baking of sacred bread (which rises like a menstruating or pregnant woman?) and cakes for the Queen of Heaven was common to cultic offerings in the Fertile Crescent, and these offerings were often associated with pregnancy.[53]

What struck me about the figurines (although Gimbutas does not mention this) is their similarity to the Paleolithic figures: large bellies and buttocks, featureless faces, and tapering legs with no feet. The lack of arms and the large breasts on these figurines emphasize the pregnancy. Separate areas designated for the particular use of women, whether described as shelters or shrines, suggest specific ritual activity by and for women.

BRONZE AGE EVIDENCE (4000–1200)

A Tent of Her Own

The Bronze Age is distinguished by the introduction of copper and its combination with smelted alloys, chiefly tin, that produce bronze. It is the era that also brings with it monumental buildings, temples, palaces, and fortified towns. Egypt and Mesopotamia become the dominant regions in the ancient Near East. Trade becomes extensive and with it comes the need for recording: writing is invented. It is the Bronze Age that ushers in what we herald as "civilization."

The uniformity of the imposing figures with large hanging breasts of the Upper Paleolithic and early Neolithic periods gives way to more varied examples, giving the impression of an amalgamation of cultural differences. Some figures retain the imposing bodies but lack the huge breasts (fig. 41) and acquire a pronounced pubic triangle, the small breasts are often cupped in the woman's hands, and others figures are slender even when they are pregnant (fig. 42). Figures giving birth are rare.

Monumental buildings (that is, temples and palaces) do not appear in Canaan during the Bronze Age as they do in Egypt and Mesopotamia; rather, household shrines and images are the norm. Neighborhood shrines are visited by our biblical ancestors on their journeys, where they build altars (Gen 1:7-8; 12:8; 22:9; 26:25; 35:1) and plant trees (Gen 22:33; 26:23-25). Public shrines may have been serviced by males, but anthropological research shows that important aspects of religious activity take place in domestic settings. According to Meyers, "Such a context often constitutes the core of women's religious experience and also the major part of their participation in religious life."[54]

Veiled references to the biblical matriarchs' associations with home-based religious practices can be found in the Genesis narratives. Goddesses, though not mentioned openly, are symbolically present in the stories: Sarah lives in a grove of terebinths[55] sacred to Asherah;[56] Rebekah consults an oracle concerning her difficult pregnancy (Gen 25:22); Rachel takes the household "Gods" that her father claims are his (Gen 31:19). Some of these *teraphim*, in the form of plaque impressions of the nude figure of Astarte (fig. 43), are, according to Albright,[57] the most "common religious objects discovered in the Late Bronze Age levels" (twenty-first to thirteenth centuries B.C.E.) in Palestine, particularly in the town of Devir (Tell Beit Mirsim). Devir is southwest of Hebron, close to where the biblical Sarah lived.

Despite cryptic references to any association of the matriarchs of Genesis with ceremonies and rituals, it is impossible to imagine these Bronze Age women taking no part in religious culture, particularly in view of the influential religions that surrounded them and the importance of the household as a religious center.

Furthermore, the joint perception of real and unreal as described in the Genesis stories implies a close association between Deities and humans. From Adam and Eve conversing with Yahweh in Eden (Gen 3:12, 13), to Sarah and Abraham discussing her pregnancy with Yahweh at Mamre (Gen 18:13-15), to Jacob's struggle with an angel after crossing the Jabbok River (Gen 32:25), examples of personal relationships with supernatural beings abound. The perceptions, if not the actual accounts, are real enough.

Some events reported in Genesis, Exodus, and Judges presumably occur in this Bronze Age period, when a pronounced change begins to take shape in the religious sphere of the early Hebrews. Household ceremonies and rituals slowly begin to give way to the creation and leadership of a priesthood in premonarchic Israel, corresponding to similar developments already in place in the religions of neighboring countries.

Yahweh's Public Shrine Overshadows Women's Personal Shrines

In premonarchic Canaan, the personal tent is the focal point for cultic expression and ritual: Noah was "uncovered" in his tent (Gen 9:21); the tent is central to the annunciation of Sarah's pregnancy (Gen 18:9-10); it is in Sarah's tent that Isaac consummates his marriage to Rebekah (Gen 24:67); Rachel is in her tent during her menstruation (Gen 31:34); and so on.

During the Israelite exodus from Egypt, however, an important modification occurs. Whereas regional Deities are paid respect in their local shrines by native devotees and foreign travelers, Yahweh attaches himself to a people rather than a locale. The thought that the people of Israel were the personal possession of Yahweh belongs to the oldest traditions of Israel.[58] Because Yahweh journeys with the Israelites, Moses creates a portable shrine for Him. He pitches a tent some distance from the camp; when Moses enters the tent, a pillar of cloud descends and stands at the entrance of the tent and stays there while Yahweh speaks to him face to face, as one person speaks to another (Exod 33:9). In this tent was placed the Ark of the Covenant contracted at Sinai. Anyone inquiring of Yahweh, that is, anyone requesting an oracle, would go to the designated tent of meeting (Exod 33:7). Presumably the household shrines, serviced by women as well as men, were estranged. It took incredible vision to bind divinity to a people rather than to a locale. The vision, whether intentional or not, disenfranchised women and their sacred traditions.

In both Exodus and Numbers, the main protagonists are Moses and Aaron. The few references to Miriam imply that she plays an important role in the story, from the birth of Moses to her death in Kadesh. Kadesh, Rita Burns has suggested, may have been the historical Miriam's home, where she officiated as a priestess in a pre-Yahwistic religion.[59] If Burns is correct, it would explain why Miriam is not mentioned in connection with the tent of meeting as were other women (Exod 38:8; 1 Sam 2:22). This tent, and the ark it housed, was to become the great sanctuary built by King Solomon for Yahweh in Jerusalem and is known to us as the first temple.

The Divine Son, A Warrior's Challenge

Most important for our purposes, however, is the advent of centrally controlled religions in the urban centers surrounding Canaan, in which unattached Goddesses acquire husbands and sons who eventually take over their power.

The imposing female of the Paleolithic who acquired divine attributes in the Neolithic is challenged in the Bronze Age. Although she remains the creatrix of all that lives, including Gods and humans, she now acquires a husband, father of her divine children. We begin to see the establishment of the patriarchal royal family in heaven as it is on earth. But in heaven, father and mother Goddesses are challenged by a divine son. In Babylon, Marduk kills his mother, Tiamat, mother of all the Gods, and forms out of her body heaven and earth. Once this is accomplished, the other Gods and Goddesses turn over to him all their functions and epithets—becoming merely aspects of the one God Marduk.[60] In Egypt, Osiris, brother-husband of Isis, "shut in his father Seb together with his mother Nut on the day of the great slaughter."[61] The Ugaritic El takes his sisters Asherah and Astarte to wife and emasculates his father,[62] as later does the Greek Kronos. Zeus goes to war against his parents (Rhea and Kronos) and defeats them, casting them into the nether world.[63] In Ugarit, the young Baal attempts to take over the functions of El but succeeds only in northern Canaan. The biblical Yahweh can be recognized as originally a cultic name of El, subsequently "ousting El from his place in the divine council, and eventually condemning the ancient powers to death."[64] At any rate, "many of the traits and functions of El appear as traits and functions of Yahweh in the earliest traditions of Israel."[65] Significantly they both acquire the epitaph "Bull," claimed by many Gods since the Neolithic and in evidence even in the Paleolithic. Yahweh's greatest rival, however, is Baal. Yahweh-El usurps Baal's functions just as Baal had usurped El's in the north.[66]

Despite the incursion of the upstart warrior Gods, not all Goddesses lose their devotees. Inanna/Ishtar of Babylon, Isis and Hathor of Egypt, and Asherah of Ugarit and Canaan and her daughter Astarte remain influential.

Asherah (fig. 46) was perhaps the most favored Goddess among the early Hebrews and Israelites prior to the monarchy; she was the supreme Goddess of ancient Canaan, *qaniyatu ilima*, "creatrix of the Gods," seventy in all,[67] a mother par excellence. Asherah is also an ancient Mesopotamian Goddess; she is mentioned in an eighteenth-century Sumerian inscription and other contemporary documents as "Ashratum, the bride of Anu."[68] Among her many titles, an ancient epithet of the Goddess describes her as *labi't(u)*, "one of the lion" or "lion lady,"[69] a feature of the more ancient Goddesses of Asia Minor. As *Qudshu*, "holiness," Asherah is portrayed on reliefs as a nude Goddess standing on a (female) lion, holding one or more serpents.[70] In Ugarit, Asherah was perhaps best known as *'atiratu yammi*, "she who *treads the sea*," or "the *sea dragon*."[71] Saul M. Olyan, in his monograph on Asherah and Yahweh, suggests a possible connection between the dragon (serpent) aspect, *dat batni* ("the one of the serpent," epithet of Asherah), and the removal by King Hezekiah of Nehushtan, the serpent presumably made by Moses, together with the *asheras* (symbols of the Goddess; 2 Kgs 18:4).[72] Olyan goes on to say that the cumulative evidence associating the serpent with the Goddess Asherah makes it possible that the "bronze serpent Nehushtan of the Jerusalem temple" was an Asherah cult symbol.[73]

Temples and monuments are built in urban centers as abodes for Deities, but in rural areas shrines in the home or on the "high places" still serve most of the population.

Toward the end of the Bronze Age, and despite the increasingly forceful presence of Gods and the priests who represent them, depictions of Goddesses still preserve many of the exclusively female characteristics emphasized in the Paleolithic and Neolithic eras. Goddesses are still closely associated with plants and animals; in many areas they retain their impressive body size but seem to lose their large breasts.

Now Deities acquire specific insignia and headdresses that

distinguish them individually. Isis, whose Egyptian name *Au Set* means "she of the throne," for example, sometimes wears a throne on her head (in the shape of an L, as is a component of the hieroglyph of her name), although she is usually depicted with a crown of horns between which is a solar disk[74] (fig. 45). The useful great birthing chair and the comfortable reclining seats of yore (fig. 44) have been traded for the upright seat of the royal warrior and the mystery of birth exchanged for the divine son (fig. 45).

THE IRON AGE EVIDENCE (1200–536)

A Sanctuary of His Own

It is in the Iron Age (ca. 1000) that the Israelite monarchy was established in Jerusalem by King David and the temple to Yahweh built by his son Solomon. It is a period, too, in which portions of the Bible began to be transcribed, though that process was not completed until after the Babylonian exile (sixth century B.C.E.).

The extended female tradition that we have been following through iconography becomes more problematic in the Israelite period in view of the edict against "graven images." Nevertheless, we will see that the tradition continues in the Bible in literary form.

Asherah, and her daughters, Astarte and Anat (and under their various manifestations as Elat, Athirat/Yam, Qudshu, Tannit, and others), modeled and sculptured in gold, stone, or clay, have been discovered in sites ranging from Syria to Israel to Egypt. Figurines and plaques of a nude woman wearing a Hathor wig or horns, standing on a female lion, or wearing a lion mask are thought to be representations of Astarte. Her figure is slender with small breasts and delineated pubic triangle; her arms are hanging by her sides or may be raised, holding flower stalks (fig. 43). Sometimes she is flanked by snakes or holds them in her upraised hands. Plaques and figurines from Canaanite realms in Syria Palestine conform to the Qudshu (holy women) representations in Egypt.

The biblical Eve reflects the close connection between Goddesses and animals dating back to the Upper Paleolithic. She replaces animals as a fitting mate for Adam (Gen 2:18-20), and Yahweh links her childbearing to the snake (3:15).

Iconography of Asherah, or her cult symbol the *asherah,* is more difficult to describe, because most *asherim* seem to have been made of perishable wood. According to Olyan, biblical and extrabiblical evidence seems "to indicate that the *asherah* was not a living tree but rather a stylized tree [probably a date palm or a pole]."[75]

The pole, or pillar, is frequently mentioned in the Bible in language analogous to that of the *asherim* (Exod 34:13 and Deut 7:5 are good examples), where Yahweh exhorts the Israelites to tear down altars, smash pillars (*masseboth*), and cut down or burn sacred posts (*asherim*). In fact, before the reforming kings of Judah, the *asherah* seems to have been entirely legitimate.[76] Although it cannot be ascertained who the figures represented, the matriarch Rachel carried sacred images (*teraphim*) with her from her homeland in Mesopotamia to Canaan (Gen 31:19). Rachel died in childbirth on her journey (35:19), and Jacob set up a pillar (*massebah*) over her grave. Shortly before she died, Jacob buried the *teraphim* under a sacred tree (35:4) and turned to El/Elohim (35:3), the God who had appeared to him when he was fleeing from his brother Esau at a site he named Beth-El ("House of El," 28:19) and set up a pillar (*massebah*) there (29:22). The *massebah*, like the *asherah*, is condemned by the deuteronomistic school as a "Canaanite" fertility symbol.[77]

That the Goddess Asherah lost her distinction in Israel and was eventually reduced to being represented solely by her symbol alone, it seems to me, obscures the intent of the Kuntillet Arjud and Khirbet el-Qom inscriptions[78] in which Asherah is paired with Yahweh.[79] Just as the Yahweh of Exod 6:3 took upon himself the identity of the "other Gods," so the deuteronomistic school, in editing the Bible in the eighth century, fused Yahweh with the nurturing elements of Asherah/*asherah*. The inscriptions, with the enigmatic references to Asherah/*asherah* and dating from the same period (Late Iron Age), are evidence of this transition.

Evidence of the Figurines in Biblical Lore

Many figurines have been found in Israel from the Iron Age. These are figurines of females; male figures are practically nonexistent.[80] According to Frymer-Kensky, there is a distinct development occurring at this time. Images of upright female figures with divine symbols, "which were very common in the Late Bronze Age, disappear in Israelite times"[81] and are exchanged for plaques of women lying on beds. These in turn "disappear from Judah by the time of the monarchy" (ca. 1000).[82] A new type of figurine, commonly referred to as the Asherah figurine and molded in the round with a flared pillar base, becomes prominent in the eighth century (fig. 46). Like their Upper Paleolithic counterparts, these figurines have seemingly no overt divine insignia. This setting suggests that the powerful tradition of female figurines associated with reproduction persisted among the women of Israel, even though their nurturing attributes were slowly being transferred to Yahweh, who opens the womb (Gen 29:31) and rewards women with children (Gen 18:10; 25:21; 30:6; 29:17, 18).

Despite the literary conviction of Yahweh's life-giving intercessions as recorded in the Bible, the stories themselves paint a different picture. *Teraphim*, sacred images, are not mentioned in relation to women only in the Bronze Age, as with Rachel, but also in the Iron Age: David's wife Michal owned at least one (1 Sam 19:13), despite Frymer-Kensky's implication that only plaques existed in Israel at that time.[83]

What ramification does the possession of sacred images by only two biblical matriarchs have for our contention that women in biblical times enjoyed control of their reproductive functions? The attestation is literary. The matriarchs regulated their own pregnancies, as well as the sexual activity between their *sh'phahot* ("companions") and the patriarchs. Rachel and Leah negotiate over some mandrakes, a root believed to cause fertility, for a night with Jacob (Gen 29:14). The *sh'phahot* Hagar, Bilhah, and Zilpah have sexual relations with the patriarchs only at the behest of the matriarchs (16:2; 30:3; 30:9). The sons of these women became heirs of the matriarchs, not of their own mothers. This pattern implies that the women had children for each other and that the function of the mother-companion was childbearing for the matriarch (fig. 42), not the patriarch (an indication of descent in the female line).

Judging by the many figurines of females with their hands cupped under their breasts, lactation seems to have been a primary concern among women. This is evident in the story of Sarah. When Sarah's son Isaac is weaned, Abraham makes a great feast for him. Presumably Abraham would have made a feast for the son's circumcision, but obviously Isaac's weaning took precedence. It is Sarah's joy at the weaning (21:6) that is associated to her son's name.[84]

The naming of children can also be viewed as an aspect of reproductive control, because in Hebrew thought a name is inextricably bound up with existence. Nothing exists unless it has a name. More often than not it is the mother (or the matriarch as social mother) who names the child.

The name Cain, Ilana Pardes observes,[85] "derives from the root *qyn* (not *qnh*), meaning 'to shape or to fashion,'" and appears in the title of Asherah: *qnyt 'ilim*, "the creatress/bearer of the Gods." This title implies that Eve, the primordial biblical mother "claims to have generative powers that are not unlike God's."[86] Asher, the name of Leah's son, was most probably derived from Asherah.[87] In the Book of Ruth, Naomi takes Ruth's child to her bosom and becomes a nurse to him (4:16), and she and her neighbors, rather than Ruth, name him. Naming, then, can be seen as an important ingredient in the birthing process: in biblical times naming is understood as conferring life on the child.

CONCLUSION: A ROOM OF HER OWN

We have seen that over the millennia women enjoyed separate space and artifacts for their distinctive physical and spiritual needs. Although there is no archaeological evidence to support this view for the biblical matriarchs, the biblical record justifies the proposition.

Ancient images of women fall into two categories: those whose status cannot be classified and those that can be identified as Goddesses. Images in the first category are found predominantly in the Upper Paleolithic and belong to nomadic cultures, in which these figures may have been used as demarcation signs or teaching aids in menstruation, pregnancy, or parturition rituals, or to demonstrate pertinent behavior. Goddess figures bearing or wearing distinctive insignia, on the other hand, come from a later period in which societies and religion were far more complex.

Çatal Hüyük is a good example of a more intricate social system, but this is the only sample of its kind (to date) from the Neolithic, and it may indicate the transitional period from a previous domestic cult.

There is a much closer link between ideology and behavior in egalitarian than in hierarchical societies, where inequality and exploitation are deliberately veiled by ambiguous and contradictory ritual and rhetoric.[88] Female images in the more egalitarian nomadic communities may represent a status for their women that is preferable to those in the Late Bronze Age and subsequent societies in which the representations indicate a supernatural status. The appearance of Goddess figures may imply a diminishing status for the women of that period, as the perceived magical nature of females was transposed to the supernatural power in nature, personified by a Goddess.

One explanation does not suffice for all the figures. Rock art on shelters, which could be seen by everyone, made public statements or gave particular messages. Home or portable art was more likely to be individual or belong to a small segment of the community. The use of female figurines in sympathetic magic is attested in many ethnographic examples[89] and may have been perceived to assure easy delivery or a child's future prosperity. The many sexless samples, rather than being images of young women, as Melaart suggests, seem to me more like effigies of aborted fetuses.[90]

The buildings discovered by Melaart in Late Neolithic Çatal Hüyük have every indication of being for ritual use, with one apparently for ritual births. Likewise, the Proto or Early Cucuteni structural remains found in the site of Sabatinovka II need not be viewed as a temple or shrine, as Gimbutas suggests, but rather as a menstruation or birthing center.

Representations of both human female figurines and those of Goddesses (usually with identifying headdress) appear side by side in the Neolithic and subsequent periods in the ancient Near East. In these periods, too, female figurines far outnumber those of males, and representations of pregnant women, Goddesses, or mother Goddesses with child continue into the Iron Age.

The abundance of female representations throughout prehistory and history makes the biblical invective "Thou shalt not make . . . any graven image" (Exod 20:4) even more poignant. There are at least forty-five references to graven images in the Hebrew Bible, most of them an indictment against those who made them or worshiped them. The very fact that their condemnation was deemed necessary attests to the popularity of the images; they were obviously not easily eradicated—and their purpose as blessing and support for women's reproductive functions, not easily obliterated.

Yahweh's sanctuary would slowly come to challenge all the local and household shrines in both Judah and Israel, which included the Canaanite Gods and Goddesses whom the Israelites had embraced. The great struggle to eradicate the influence of local Deities and their religious observances permeates the Hebrew Bible.

I question whether stories such as those of the biblical matriarchs did not derive from a tradition that was ancient even to them. Did the stories about the matriarchs become a part of our sacred lore because they were originally traditional tales of ancestors or supernatural beings with a long illustrated legacy reaching back into prehistory? Or, to put it differently, were illustrations of pregnancy and birth over a period of tens of thousands of years forbidden by a male clergy, so that later written records of the same theme could be applied to a male Deity, thus confining women's mysteries to the secular sphere?

OUR MOST PRECIOUS MYSTERIES

Have we sacrificed our most precious mysteries to Yahweh and his followers?

The subsequent "biology is destiny" paradigm confined women's roles to that of sex object and reproductive vessel. In an effort to distance themselves from this limitation, contemporary women have too often strived to follow roles that honor men *at the expense* of their own unique fulfillment. We have, it would seem, willingly given our functions over to Yahweh and scientists.

In the past four thousand years the profound mystery of life-giving, the potential of the female to re-create herself in her own image, has been denigrated to such a degree that now, at the apex of Western civilization, control over all aspects of the birthing process is mostly in the hands of a group of elite males. We depend on government legislation to provide us with authorization over the functions of our own bodies; we count on representatives of male Gods to guide our spiritual lives, and we rely on the prototypical male medical establishment's techniques for the supervision and resolution of pregnancy and birth—to say nothing of women being sexual trophies at home and abroad, in peace and in war. Has the sacred become profane?

Women's traditions die hard, though. I would argue that the stories of perhaps all the conceptions, pregnancies, and births recorded in the sacred biblical texts reflect a literary compromise to women for the loss of their sacred images, images that must have been hallowed to the biblical women themselves, who inherited this long, long tradition, a tradition that included separate spiritual space for women, whether in the cave shelter, the tent, or the household shrine.

It is encouraging to speculate that the broken link is being repaired. Temples and churches may be decrying their loss of membership, but women are making spiritual room for themselves separate from official centers, in their own homes, creating autonomous religious practices in common with their very ancient ancestors. It is for women to reclaim their heritage: divinity in their own image, their separate spiritual/ritual space, and control of their own bodies. In time, the association between women's religious empowerment and reproductive control will be strengthened, allowing for a reign of peace at home as well as abroad.

Fig. 31

Fig. 32

Fig. 33

Fig. 34

Fig. 31 Venus of Willendorf, Limestone, Austria
Fig. 32 Venus of Menton, Limestone, Austria
Fig. 33 Venus of Lespugue, Ivory, Haute Garonne, France.
Fig. 34 Venus of Laussel, Dordogne Valley, France.

Fig. 35

Fig. 36

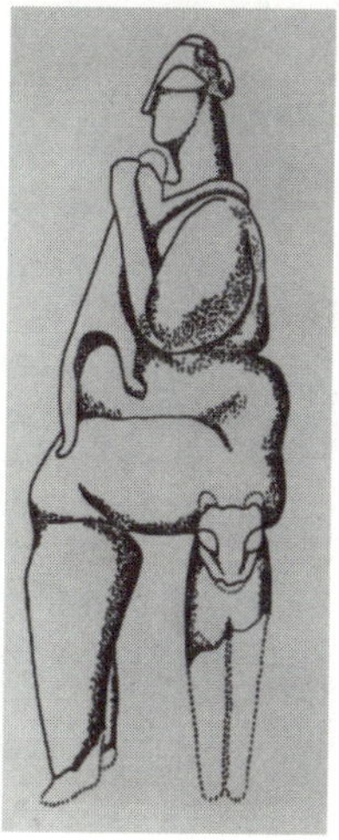

Fig. 37

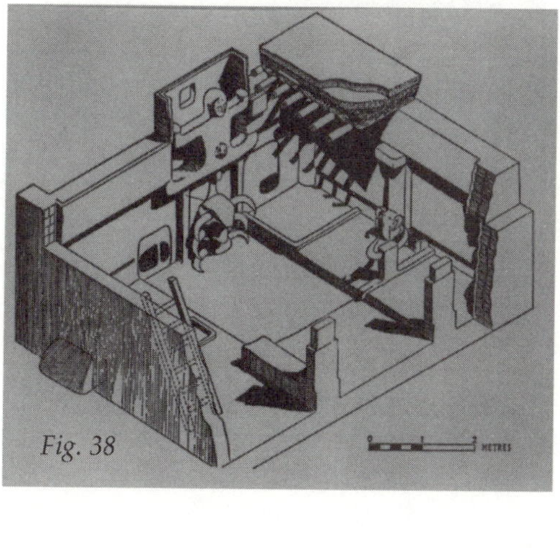

Fig. 38

Fig. 35 Venus of Laussel, Dordogne, France
Fig. 36 Cybele, Çatal Hüyük, Turkey
Fig. 37 Woman sitting on leopard holding leopard cub, Hacilar, Turkey
Fig. 38 Çatal Hüyük shrine (reconstruction)

Fig. 39

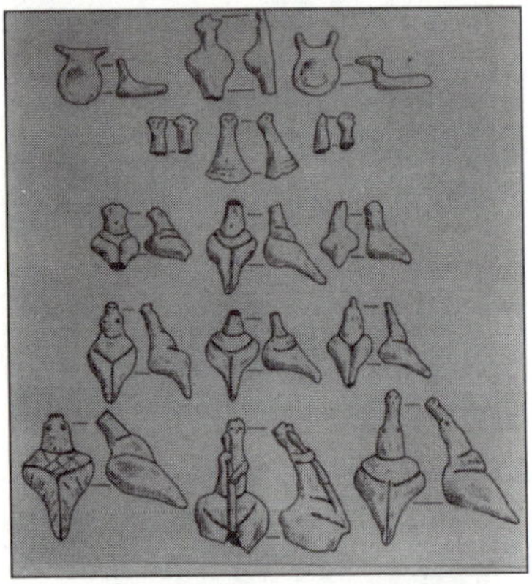

Fig. 40

Fig. 41

Fig. 42

Fig. 39 Shrine, Sabatinovka II, Early Cucuteni, Southern Bug Valley, Soviet Moldavia
Fig. 40 Sabatinovka II (detail of figures)
Fig. 41 Female figure, Susa, 2nd millenium
Fig. 42 Ivory statuette, "Beer-sheva Venus," Beer Safad, Israel

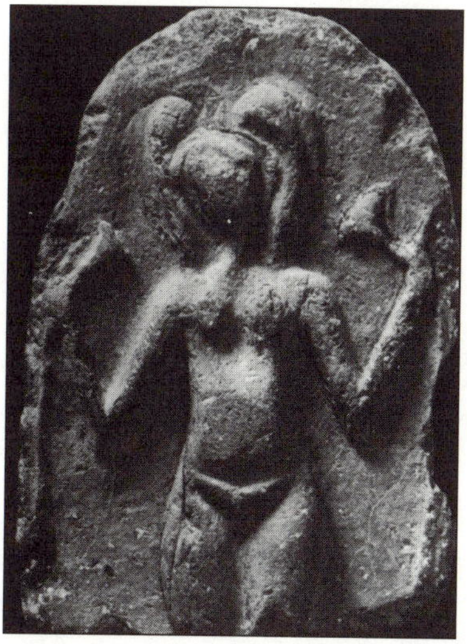

Fig. 43

Fig. 45

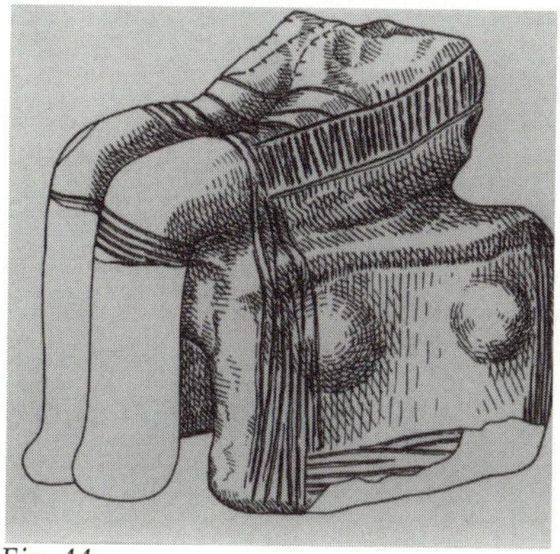

Fig. 44

Fig. 43 Astarte holding flowers, Beth Shemesh, Israel
Fig. 44 Birthing or reclining chair, Naroden Muzey, Belgrade
Fig. 45 Isis suckling Horus
Fig. 46 Asherah. Lachish, Israel, seventeenth century B.C.E.

Fig. 46

NOTES

1. Meyers, *Discovering Eve*, 161.
2. Biblical premonarchic period.
3. Plaskow, *Standing Again*, 125.
4. Setel, "Exodus," 33.
5. Setel, "Exodus," 34.
6. Ehrenberg, *Women in Prehistory*, 73-75.
7. Ehrenberg, *Women in Prehistory*, 13.
8. Meyers, *Discovering Eve*, 17.
9. Meyers, *Discovering Eve*, 16.
10. Meyers, *Discovering Eve*, 17.
11. The history of *homo sapiens sapiens* beginning with the Upper Paleolithic as registered from Europe to Russia is the period and geographical area we are concerned with here.
12. Chard, *Man in Prehistory*, 180.
13. Conkey, "Humans," 97.
14. This is a copy. The original was lost during World War II.
15. Fisher, *Woman's Creation*, 153.
16. Gadon, *Once and Future Goddess*, 12.
17. Gadon, *Once and Future Goddess*, 12.
18. Gimbutas, *Language of the Goddess*, 141-42.
19. Gimbutas, *Language of the Goddess*, 288.
20. Aveni, *Conversing with Planets*, 79.
21. Ehrenberg, *Women in Prehistory*, 39-40.
22. Grahn, *Blood, Bread, and Roses*, 52-53.
23. Grahn, *Blood, Bread, and Roses*, 54.
24. Grahn, *Blood, Bread, and Roses*, 74.
25. Grahn, *Blood, Bread, and Roses*, 74.
26. Gimbutas, *Language of the Goddess*, 305.
27. Johnson, *Lady of the Beasts*, 62.
28. Ehrenberg, *Women in Prehistory*, 66.
29. Ehrenberg, *Women in Prehistory*, 68.
30. Ehrenberg, *Women in Prehistory*, 67.
31. Ehrenberg, *Women in Prehistory*, 70.
32. Fisher, *Woman's Creation*, 225.
33. Melaart, *Çatal Hüyük*, 183, 184.
34. Melaart, *Çatal Hüyük*, 166.
35. Gurney, *The Hittites*, 138.
36. Melaart, *Earliest Civilizations*, 94; *Çatal Hüyük*, 181.
37. Melaart, *Earliest Civilizations*, 94; see illustrations 70, 71.
38. Melaart, *Earliest Civilizations*, 108; see illustration 94.
39. Ehrenberg, *Women in Prehistory*, 78-80.
40. Ehrenberg, *Women in Prehistory*, 86.
41. Jacobsen, *Towards an Image*, 376.
42. Gadon, *Once and Future Goddess*, 36.
43. Melaart, *Earliest Civilizations*, 89.
44. Melaart, *Earliest Civilizations*, 89.

45. Melaart, *Earliest Civilizations*, 96.
46. Melaart, *Earliest Civilizations*, 97.
47. Cameron, *Symbols*, 22.
48. Gadon, *Once and Future Goddess*, 32.
49. Gimbutas, *Gods and Goddesses*, 67-74; *Language of the Goddess*, 132-33.
50. Gimbutas, *Gods and Goddesses*, 73.
51. Gimbutas, *Gods and Goddesses*, 72.
52. Gimbutas, *Gods and Goddesses*, 73.
53. Teubal, *Hagar the Egyptian*, 91-98.
54. Meyers, *Discovering Eve*, 161.
55. Teubal, *Sarah the Priestess*, 18.
56. Teubal, *Sarah the Priestess*, 88.
57. Albright, *Archaeology of Palestine*, 104-5.
58. De Moor, *Rise of Yahwism*, 165, n. 294.
59. Burns, *Has the Lord*, 125-28.
60. De Moor, *Rise of Yahwism*, 58.
61. Budge, *Gods*, vol. 2, 99.
62. Cross, *Canaanite Myth*, 41.
63. Cross, *Canaanite Myth*, 41.
64. Cross, *Canaanite Myth*, 71.
65. Cross, *Canaanite Myth*, 72.
66. De Moor, *Rise of Yahwism*, 106.
67. Patai, *Hebrew Goddess*, 32.
68. Patai, *Hebrew Goddess*, 33.
69. Cross, *Canaanite Myth*, 33.
70. Cross, *Canaanite Myth*, 33.
71. Cross, *Canaanite Myth*, 31.
72. See Olyan, *Asherah*, 71-72.
73. Olyan, *Asherah*, 71.
74. Budge, *From Fetish*, 199.
75. Olyan, *Asherah*, 1.
76. Olyan, *Asherah*, 73.
77. Olyan, *Asherah*, 5 n. 15.
78. For two recent views see Olyan, *Asherah*, chap. 2, and Frymer-Kinsky, *In the Wake*, 156-59.
79. Olyan, *Asherah*, xiv.
80. Frymer-Kinsky, *In the Wake*, 158.
81. Frymer-Kinsky, *In the Wake*, 158.
82. Frymer-Kinsky, *In the Wake*, 159.
83. Frymer-Kinsky, *In the Wake*, 159.
84. Teubal, *Hagar the Egyptian*, 107-9.
85. Pardes, *Countertraditions*, 43.
86. Pardes, *Countertraditions*, 46.
87. Patai, *Hebrew Goddess*, 294, n. 15.
88. Ehrenberg, *Women in Prehistory*, 75.
89. Ehrenberg, *Women in Prehistory*, 75.
90. For illustrations, see Ehrenberg, *Women in Prehistory*, 69.

WORKS CITED

Albright, W. F. *The Archaeology of Palestine*. Glouster, Mass.: Peter Smith, Publisher, 1971.

Aveni, A. *Conversing with Planets: How Science and Myth Invented the Cosmos*. New York: Times Books, 1992.

Budge, E. A. W. *The Gods of the Egyptians: Studies in Egyptian Mythology*. Vol. 2. New York: Dover Publications, 1969.

———. *From Fetish to God in Ancient Egypt*. London: Oxford University Press, 1934,

Burns, R. J. *Has the Lord Indeed Spoken Only Through Moses: A Study of the Biblical Portrait of Miriam*. SBL Dissertation Series 84. Atlanta: Scholars Press, 1987.

Cameron, D. *Symbols of Birth and Death in the Neolithic Era*. London: Kenyan-Deane Ltd., 1981.

Chard, C. S. *Man in Prehistory*. New York: McGraw-Hill Book Company, 1969.

Conkey, M. "Humans as Materialists and Symbolists: Image Making in the Upper Paleolithic." In *The Origin and Evolution of Humans and Humanness*, edited by D.T. Rasmussen. Boston, Mass.: Jones and Bartlett, Publishers, 1993.

Cross, F. M. *Canaanite Myth and Hebrew Epic: Essays in the History of the Religion of Israel*. Cambridge, Mass.: Harvard University Press, 1973.

De Moor, J. C. *The Rise of Yahwism: The Roots of Israelite Monotheism*. Louvain, Belgium: Leuven University Press, 1990.

Ehrenberg, M. *Women in Prehistory*. Norman, Okla.: University of Oklahoma Press, 1989.

Fisher, E. *Woman's Creation: Sexual Evolution and the Shaping of Society*. Garden City, New York: Anchor Press/Doubleday, 1979.

Frymer-Kensky, T. *In the Wake of the Goddess: Women, Culture and Biblical Transformation of Pagan Myth*. New York: The Free Press, 1992.

Gadon, E. *The Once and Future Goddess*. San Francisco: Harper and Row, 1989.

Gimbutas, M. *The Language of the Goddess*. San Francisco: Harper & Row, 1989,

———. *The Gods and Goddesses of Old Europe 7000-3500 BC: Myths, Legends and Cult Images*. Berkeley, Calif.: University of California Press, 1974.

Grahn, J. *Blood, Bread, and Roses: How Menstruation Created the World*. Boston: Beacon Press, 1993.

Gurney, O. R. *The Hittites*. London: Penguin Books, 1954.

Jacobsen, T. *Towards an Image of Tammuz and Other Essays on Mesopo-*

tamian History and Culture. Cambridge, Mass.: Harvard University Press, 1970.

Johnson, B. *Lady of the Beasts: Ancient Images of the Goddess and Her Sacred Animals*. San Francisco: Harper & Row, 1988.

Mellaart, J. *Earliest Civilizations of the Near East*. New York: McGraw-Hill, 1965.

Meyers, C. *Discovering Eve: Ancient Israelite Women in Context*. New York: Oxford University Press, 1988.

Newsom, Carol A., and Sharon H. Ringe, eds. *The Women's Bible Commentary*. Louisville, Ky.: Westminster John Knox Press, 1992.

Olyan, S. M. *Asherah and the Cult of Yahweh in Israel*. Society of Biblical Literature Monograph Series 34. Atlanta: Scholars Press, 1988.

Pardes, I. *Countertraditions in the Bible: A Feminist Approach*. Cambridge, Mass.: Harvard Univ. Press, 1993.

Patai, R. *The Hebrew Goddess*. New York: KTAV Publishing House, Inc., 1967.

Plaskow, Judith. *Standing Again at Sinai: Judaism from a Feminist Perspective*. San Francisco: HarperCollins, 1990.

Setel, D. O. "Exodus." Pp. 26–35 in *The Women's Bible Commentary*, edited by Carol A. Newsom and Sharon H. Ringe. Louisville, Ky.: Westminster John Knox Press, 1992.

Teubal, Savina J. *Hagar the Egyptian: The Lost Traditions of the Matriarchs*, San Francisco: Harper & Row, Publishers, 1990.

———. *Sarah the Priestess: The First Matriarch of Genesis*, Athens, Ohio: Swallow Press/Ohio University Press, 1986.

12

CLAUDIA V. CAMP

The Strange Woman of Proverbs: A Study in the Feminization and Divinization of Evil in Biblical Thought[1]

The figures of female personified wisdom and her counterpart, the "Strange Woman," in the Book of Proverbs provide a rare locus for analyzing elevated female imagery in the biblical tradition. Whereas elsewhere in the Bible Goddesses are simply condemned, if not ignored, here both positive and negative traits of powerful female symbols are rhetorically limned. This paper will focus on the Strange Woman, asking questions about the rhetorical value of the term *strange*; possible implications of this rhetoric for reconstructing the social context of this figure, the relationship of this figure to Goddess worship in the postexilic period, and its implications for the shifting theology of the period. I argue against certain scholarly views that the Strange Woman reflects directly either a foreign Goddess or a foreign woman who, in a mixed marriage, might lead her Israelite husband into such worship. Instead, the figure operates at a more abstract level of symbolism, consolidating a variety of images of evil and, indeed, beginning to carry the burden of theodicy, providing a means to shift responsibility for evil from Yahweh.

THE STRANGE WOMAN IN THE POSTEXILIC PERIOD

Scholars have reached a certain level of agreement in the past few years that Proverbs' Strange Woman is the product of a post-exilic Judean setting, particularly of the temple elite. The motivation for this figure has, however, remained in debate, largely because the imagery used to construct her is so rich with varied implications. The most obvious images are those of sexual indiscretion, including a peculiar combination of accusations of adultery and prostitution. The Strange Woman "forsakes the partner of her youth" (2:17) and allures her lover with the assurance that her husband "has gone on a long journey" (7:19), yet she also walks the streets "decked out like a prostitute" (7:10), which would not, presumably, be the most usual way for a married woman to seek alternative sexual partnership.

In addition, certain features of the imagery seem to link the Strange Woman with post-exilic prophetic polemic against Goddess worship, with its presumed sexual rituals for fertility.[2] She is located "at the high places" (9:14); she sits by a doorway, with all its sexual implications (9:14); her bed is the focus of her attraction (7:17); and it is associated with her participation in a sacrificial cult (7:14). Similar imagery, including the overloaded adulterer/whore calumniation, is used by Third Isaiah (chap. 57) to construct the picture of idolatrous Israel. In both cases, moreover, the female image is associated with Sheol, the realm of the dead (Prov 2:18; 7:27; 9:18; Isa 57:9).

The question of the significance of this variegated imagery is further complicated by the fact that the two terms in the word-pair used to refer to this female figure are themselves multifaceted. *Zār* and *nokrî* can refer to persons of foreign nationality, to persons who are outsiders to one's own family household, to persons who are not members of the priestly caste, and to Deities and practices that fall outside the covenant relationship with Yahweh. The recognition that neither *zār* nor *nokrî* necessarily refers to a foreigner (in the literal sense of that word) has led to diverse scholarly conclusions about the sense of the terms. One scholar takes the rather minimalist perspective that in many cases they simply refer to another person; hence the *ʾiššâ zārâ*, the "strange woman," in Proverbs is "the wife of another," that is, an adulteress.[3] Another scholar, on the other hand, finds a broad sense of deviation, faithlessness, and the unknown: the *ʾiššâ zārâ* represents all one must utterly avoid.[4]

Attention to the post-exilic setting in Proverbs helps in part to resolve these ambiguities, though questions of emphasis still remain. Let me sketch both the consensus and the remaining disagreements by comparing some work of my own with that of Joseph Blenkinsopp. The upshot of this will be to suggest yet a new direction for analysis.

In post-exilic Palestine, I have argued,[5] the figure of the Strange Woman functioned symbolically, synthesizing several of the meanings of "strangeness" as they related to the ethos and worldview of the time. Two major issues were at stake for the returned exiles. One was the need for family stability, in both the material and symbolic senses of that phrase: a functional family household was needed to accomplish the tasks of survival in a rebuilding society, and clear evidence of family identity was needed to establish claims to land and political power in a divided and contentious community. The second issue was the need to promulgate pure and proper worship of YHWH, unadulterated by foreign cultic practice. The two issues were closely linked, and indeed reached moments of crisis, because of the practice by some members of the *gōlah* (the community of returned exiles) of marrying into foreign families. Foreign marriage (we shall consider in a moment whether it was always a question of wives) not only brought the danger of foreign Gods but also threatened the stability of the authority structure: intermarriage for the sake of upward mobility could bring outside challenges to the power of this group aspiring to leadership, and, further, call into question whether this group could maintain power over the generations if inheritances passed out of the families of "pure Israelites." Especially relevant here are the railings of Ezra and Nehemiah against "foreign women" (*nāšîm nokrîyôt*; Ezra 10:2, 10-11, 17-18, 44; Neh 13:26-27). The punishment called for by these men was exclusion from the community, with its attendent forfeiture of property and civic status, a fate similar to that expressed by Prov 5:7-14 for assignation with the Strange Woman.

There is also post-exilic prophetic material that helps locate the Proverbs poems in the early post-exilic period and, specifically, ties the problem of exogamy to the problem of the foreign worship. In addition to the material cited from Isa 57, Zech 5:5-11 also contains a vision of a woman with a name sounding much like Asherah (*hāriš*ᶜ*â*, "Wickedness"), flown to Babylon in an ephah. And, in terms reminiscent of Prov 2:17, Mal 2:10-12 enjoins against men divorcing the wives of their youth in favor of "the daughter of a foreign God."

Given this background, I suggested, the Strange Woman of Proverbs could be understood as a multivalent symbol. She is strange both in the sense of being an adulteress, whose breaking of social boundaries disrupts the stability of the family household, and in the sense of being a foreign national, who introduces the dangers of foreign worship and of ramifications of power and wealth outside the community. The imagery of the adulteress predominates, however, in Prov 1–9, and thus I concluded that this connotation was the dominant and originary one in the figure's history, that it was the aspect of deviant sexuality that gave her the power to function as "an archetype of disorder at all levels of existence."[6] The interpretation of the *zārâ* as a "foreign woman" was, then, secondary, emerging significantly in the course of Nehemiah's and Ezra's marriage reforms.

In a recent article, however, while arguing again forcefully for a post-exilic *Sitz im Leben* for the Strange Woman, Joseph Blenkinsopp puts almost exclusive emphasis on the problem of exogamy as it relates to foreign worship as the *raison d'etre* for this figure. In addition to the biblical evidence already noted, Blenkinsopp also cites the attribution of the Proverbs' instructions to Solomon, whose single sin was "his addiction to foreign women" (*nāšîm nokrîyôt*, 1 Kgs 11:1-8).[7] These led him to violate the deuteronomic law against intermarriage and to fall prey to the inevitable consequence of syncretism (Deut 7:3-4). Prov 1–9 is thus formulated as "a cautionary instruction of Solomon based on his own experience."[8] In Blenkinsopp's view, moreover, the prophetic material mentioned above not only points to intermarriage and syncretism as Proverbs' motivating concern but also identifies the idolotrous practice as that of Goddess worship, with its attendent symbolism of sexual allure and practice. The description of the Strange Woman was, then, influenced by such language and themes. This fact, plus the analogy of the Proverbs instructions to Solomon's problem with foreign women, indicates to Blenkinsopp that foreign worship, not "sexual irregularity," is the primary issue of the poems of chapters 1–9.

There are a number of problems with limiting the meaning of *zārâ/nokrîyâ* to "foreign woman" in Proverbs, some of which may be adduced from the summary of my own argument for multivalence and others to which I shall draw attention below. There are, however, two larger critical issues at stake here that may call into question not only aspects of Blenkinsopp's argument but some of my own previous work as well. The first is the problem of dating this material in the early post-exilic period.[9] If this dating is correct, then I think Blenkinsopp's emphasis on the exogamy/foreign worship issue is indeed *á propos*, and there is no reason to assume, as I have done, that adultery was the originary and dominant connotation of the Strange Woman's strangeness. I should now like to suggest, however, that I am seeing a concatenation of evidence that may force us toward an even later date for the Proverbs poems, to a time when intermarriage and idolatry were not the overriding concerns they were early on, as evidenced by Ben Sira's lack of attention to them. Although the evidence is not conclusive, it bears consideration as an alternative socio-historical reconstruction. Central to such a reconstruction is a revised understanding, which I shall offer below, of the purported cultic activity of Woman Stranger in Prov 7.

A second difficulty lies in the fact that neither my own nor Blenkinsopp's analysis has been sufficiently critical with respect to the imagery of sexuality. Thus, the full ideological range of the figure of Woman

Stranger has yet to be articulated. An analysis of this figure as a metaphor, "woman is a stranger," will extend and refine both Blenkinsopp's and my own previous attempts at interpretation.

THE STRANGE WOMAN AND HER "CULT"

Two recent studies on sacred prostitution help to clarify the identity of the woman in Prov 7. Phyllis Bird's examination of harlotry as a metaphor in the Hebrew Bible[10] establishes conclusively that the *zônâ* ("harlot"; cf. 6:26; 7:10; 23:27) is never associated with cultic activity and that even *qĕdēšâ*, usually translated "sacred prostitute," means simply "consecrated woman" ("hierodule," in Bird's terminology), among whose varied functions may or may not have been ritual sex. Thus, she concludes, the association of sex and foreign cult in the Hebrew Bible is polemical, not necessarily descriptive, a piece of rhetoric initiated by Hosea.

Although Bird does not discuss Prov 7, extension of her argument allows us to draw two corollary inferences. This poem has been the source of much interpretive debate because of its apparent linkage of sexual activity with cultic ritual: a woman "dressed as a prostitute" seeks a sexual partner as some sort of culmination to her offering of sacrifices in payment of vows. The passage has almost always been assumed to refer to ritual sexual activity associated with the cult of a Goddess of fertility and/or love. Bird's analysis relieves us of any necessity to interpret this language literally. On the other hand, given the fact that Hosea's polemical rhetoric became increasingly naturalized over time in Israelite thought,[11] we cannot deny the possibility that the illicit sexuality rendered in Proverbs functioned, in part, as a cipher for the breaking of covenant faith with Yahweh. The question of whether ritual sex associated with a Goddess cult was involved remains open to investigation.[12] Bird's careful analysis of the mixture of literal and allegorical sex-language in Hosea provides a model for interpreting the multivalence of the Strange Woman: not only must references to human sex acts be distinguished from theological rhetoric, but polemic that hurls accusations of illicit sex must be distinguished from descriptions of actual activity.

In another recent article, Karel van der Toorn independently argues against the existence of sacred prostitution in ancient Israel.[13] He proposes a novel interpretation of the strange woman in Prov 7 as a basically honest Israelite matron who turns in desperation to an isolated act of harlotry in order to raise money to pay a vow to the temple. Although I find this particular thesis implausible and his argumentation for it unpersuasive, van der Toorn's work does provide a clue that might explain the woman's reference to her sacrifices and vows in 7:14. As part of her invitation to the young man, she says:

> Sacrifices of peace offerings (*zibḥê-šĕlāmîm*) are upon me;
> today I fulfill (*šillamtî*) my vows.

The question of how to translate the tense of *šillamtî* has been a crux for interpreters, the assumption being that if she has already offered her sacrifice (14a) but has yet to "fulfull her vows" (14b), then the implication is that she has made a vow of ritual sex in honor of the Goddess, which she plans to fulfill with the young man.

The significant move made by van der Toorn is to associate the vow instead with a typical act of *Israelite* piety[14] that is, however, being funded by extraordinary means. Although, as I have noted, the scenario of a proper Israelite matron picking up some pocket change with a little harlotry on the side seems improbable, his instinct to associate Prov 7:14 with biblical rather than foreign ritual is attractive. Indeed, further investigation reveals that, in spite of widespread acceptance of some sort of fertility-worship theory,[15] this aspect of the Strange Woman's speech can be easily and well explained by reference to the biblical laws.

C. H. Toy noted long ago that the "sacrifices of peace offerings" (*zibḥê-šĕlāmîm*) alludes to the sacrificial feasts described in Lev 7:11-21. "In the present instance its occasion is a vow which has just been fulfilled,"[16] that must be eaten on the day of the offering or the next (Lev 7:16). Unmentioned by Toy is the fact that the levitical law also requires that the flesh of the sacrifice be eaten by people in the state of ritual cleanness (7:19-20). Thus, when the Strange Woman invites the young man for sexual activity to take place either the night before the sacrifice or the next night, between the two days of feasting, she invites him to commit with her a crime whose penalty is that "that person shall be cut off from his or her people" (*wĕnikrĕtâ hannepeš hahîʾmē ʿammêhā*, Lev 7:20).[17] Proverbs describes a similar fate for the man who associates with Woman Stranger (Prov 2:22; 5:14). As one of the wicked, he will be "cut off" (*yikkārētû*), in this case "from the land" (2:22), and in "utter ruin in the *qāhāl* (assembly) and *ʿēdâ*" ("congregation"; 5:14), that is alienated from the people.[18]

The concept of ritual uncleanness associated with sexual activity—

though here with a quite different motivation—is also found in the deuteronomic legislation, where the payment of a vow to the temple with "the hire of a harlot (*ʾetnan zônâ*) or the wages of a 'dog'" is regarded as an abomination to YHWH (*tô ʿăbat* YHWH, Deut 23:19 [English:18]).[19] In Leviticus, it is the act of sex itself that ritually defiles, while in Deuteronomy the problem lies in the people's deviance from prescribed socio-sexual roles.[20] The overlap and distinction between what might be seen as two primary symbols—that of "stain" in the former text and "deviation" in the latter—would be an interesting object of scrutiny.[21] That particular investigation of sexual cultics lies mostly outside our present scope, though I shall suggest at least one implication of it below. Of significance for this moment is the fact that both of these pieces of legislation apply to the vow of Woman Stranger in Prov 7:14. We have already seen that she proposes to defile—ultimately defile—both herself and the young man with sex during the period of feasting. But now we also see that she has paid or will pay her vow to the temple (the sequence matters nowhere near as much as past commentators have fretted) with the "hire of a harlot."

With these two links between the Strange Woman's words and biblical cultic regulations rather firmly established, another somewhat more tenuous one may be suggested. The sensual attraction in the woman's speech is enhanced, in 7:17, with the allure of a bed perfumed with "myrrh (*mōr*), aloes (*ʾăhālîm*), and cinnamon (*qinnāmôn*)." Although, on the one hand, this is typical love-talk such as that found in Ps 45:9 (the royal lover's robes are "fragrant with myrrh and aloes and cassia") and Cant 4:14 (the beloved is compared to a garden of spice and fruit, including "myrrh and aloes"), the background of cultic violation already invoked suggests another allusion as well. In Exod 30:22-33, a recipe is provided for the "holy anointing oil" to anoint the cultic objects and to consecrate the priests, "Aaron and his sons." The oil is to be made of myrrh, cinnamon, aromatic cane, cassia, and olive oil, that is, with two of the Strange Woman's three ingredients. The connection might seem stretched but for the following line that concludes the legislation on oil:

> Whoever compounds any like it or whoever puts any of it on an outsider [*zār*] shall be cut off from his people [*wĕnikrat mē ʿammāyw*].

Here, as elsewhere in the priestly writings, our variegated term *zār*, when applied to people, means "outsider to the priesthood, layperson."[22] The penalty for disobedience, being "cut off from one's people," clearly connects this law, however, with the levitical legislation on peace offerings and, hence, with the *zārâ* of Prov 7.

If Prov 7:14 is related not to foreign worship but to defilement of the Israelite cult, an unexpected twist is added to our mysterious Strange Woman, and the question of her socio-historical setting is further complicated. Whatever the merit of the argument that interprets this figure as a foreigner and Goddess worshipper, we now find that she is also a violator of not just one but a whole series of Israelite cultic laws as well. In this reading, then, she appears not as a foreign woman but as an Israelite, though a peculiarly and intentionally deviant one. The "foreign worship" interpretation is, moreover, undercut, insofar as 7:14 had provided the only explicit reference to such presumed practices in Prov 1–9.

Now, if the Strange Woman poems are dated in the fifth to early fourth century, it may well be the case that intermarriage and its attendant possibility of syncretism are the underlying issues in Proverbs, even if the references are allegorical rather than explicit. But this revised interpretation of Prov 7:14 puts a hitch in that proposed dating, as well as in the ethnicity of the female figure. The poet of chapter 7 clearly assumes that readers will be familiar with both deuteronomic and priestly legislation and, indeed, see them as pieces of a single fabric that can be wrapped around this female figure. Thus, we see an author who is a student and interpreter of Torah and, more specifically, one with a special investment in pieces of legislation dealing with cultic purity. It is unlikely, then, that Prov 7 can be dated before the time of Ezra, and it may be considerably later. More than ever the editor of Proverbs appears as a prototype for Ben Sira, by whom the interlocking of Torah, cult, and wisdom will be finally, fully expressed.

WOMAN STRANGER AS METAPHOR

A fuller understanding of the function of the Strange Woman figure may be available by analyzing it as a metaphor. The metaphor can be expressed as "woman is a stranger," wherein the "system of commonplaces" or "metaphorical paradigm" associated with each term, woman and stranger, interact to produce a new semantic entity.[23] We must be clear, however, that "woman" is defined in quintessentially male terms, namely, as "one with whom one has some form or another, socially sanctioned or not, of sexual relationship." The question of what makes the Strange Woman strange centers around the sexual behavior of her and her partner. Although the significance of sexuality is not entirely a literal one in this material, I shall suggest that it functions far more complexly and powerfully than as a mere allegory for faithless worship. Because of the repeated scholarly emphasis on this aspect of the metaphor, it is worth beginning with a reevaluation of the relationship of strangeness to exogamy and foreign cults.

A cursory overview of Israelite thought on this matter in fact reveals a wide variety of dynamics among these ideas. In Deut 7:2-5, and likewise in 1 Kgs 11, although the *functional* connection between intermarriage and religious syncretism is made, the *symbolic* connection between marriage to foreign women and worship of a foreign Deity is not. Because marriage is fundamentally a mechanism for control of women's sexuality, however, even this seemingly gender-neutral act already overdetermines sexuality in a peculiar way: the sort of sexual activity that would normally be legitimate, sex within marriage, is delegitimated when it occurs with the "wrong" women, namely, strange (=foreign) ones.

It would seem at first glance that the concern for exogamy in Malachi and Ezra-Nehemiah does no more than reiterate that of Deuteronomy. However, even their seemingly literal reference to sexuality, in the form of social regulation, already shows evidence of a gender bias that casts it in the direction of the ideological symbol it will become: unlike Deut 7:2-5, which legislates against any sort of spousal exchange ("giving your daughters to their sons or taking their daughters for your sons"), the post-exilic material is concerned primarily with foreign *wives*.[24] There are several possible explanations for this shift. In general, because wives become part of the husband's family, there is more danger in this situation of foreign religious practices being imported into the community than when an Israelite daughter leaves her father's household. This fact does not explain, however, the difference between Deuteronomy and the later material. More specifically, the focus on wives in the post–exilic literature may represent a sociological situation in which Judean men were marrying foreign women but not giving their daughters as brides to foreign men, perhaps because the foreign brides brought as dowries actual land holdings titularly claimed by members of the community of returned exiles. A third possibility, which does not exclude either of the first two, is that we are already finding at work the presence of a gender ideology in which woman *qua* woman has become the symbol of the strange.

If this conceptual move has not been made (or has been made only implicitly) in Ezra and Nehemiah, it is certainly obvious in Proverbs, where the "strange women" of the two former writers are poetically condensed into *the* Strange Woman. Along these lines I would reevaluate Blenkinsopp's important reference to the sin of Solomon as a basis for the Proverbs instructions, an allusion also made in Neh 13:26. While

1 Kgs 11 makes the causal connection between foreign women and foreign worship, thus reinforcing a crucial division between what is proper to Israel and what is not, Proverbs makes the metaphorical connection between woman and the strange, thus identifying woman as that which is not proper to Israel. Ethnic distinction has been assimilated to and named by gender distinction.

A comparison of Proverbs with the pre- and post-exilic prophets must also be made to appreciate the variety of metaphorical linkages between sex, strangeness, and idolatry. In the pre-exilic prophets and in Third Isaiah (chap. 57), an act of illicit sexuality, wanton adultery, serves as an allegory for religious infidelity. Accusation of actual human sexual activity as part of this foreign cultic practice is, however, a polemical move whose validity cannot be determined.[25] It is important to bear in mind that, with our new understanding of Prov 7:14, the book of Proverbs gives no clear indication of such activity.

We must also be clear that the form of the sex/worship relationship in both Malachi and Proverbs departs drastically from its appearance in the pre-exilic prophets. For the earlier prophets, the female figure did not represent either a foreign woman or a foreign Goddess. To the contrary, Gomer can only be understood as an Israelite, and, thus, as an allegory for the people of Israel, who join themselves with a foreign Deity (indeed, as in the case of Malachi, a male Deity). The people are thus represented in female form (perhaps a derogatory comment in itself), and a wanton one at that, but intermarriage is not an issue (even though it may have been a causal force!).

In Malachi, both the gender dynamic and the symbolic dynamic change. Here the people are imaged as male, rather than as female.[26] This shift in the gender dynamic is presumably due to a social situation in which literal Judean men were marrying literal foreign women, a practice that had to be stopped. Foreign worship is still presumably an issue, but the focus is as much on the cause—intermarriage—as it is on the effect. Indeed, except for the allusion to one's foreign wife as "the daughter of a foreign God," the problem of foreign worship is nowhere explicit in Malachi. I would suspect, in fact, that the basis of the concern for syncretism in both Malachi and Ezra-Nehemiah is their perception of a more pervasive cultural danger than simply the foreign cult. The concern is for maintaining family and community identity, and rights to inheritance and power, at least as much as it is for pure worship of Yahweh. It is undoubtedly too cynical to say that the theological motive functions solely as an ideological justification for more material interests, but it certainly is no more than one part of the mix. In any case, no longer do we have an act of socio-sexual deviance, adultery, functioning as a *symbol for* religious deviance. Rather, we have an act of communal deviance, intermarriage, functioning as a *cause of* religious deviance. We have thus returned at this point to the logic of the "sin of Solomon": the thread from 1 Kgs 11 to Malachi is clear, but it is not that of the other prophets.

The female imagery in Proverbs creates a different dynamic yet. It is still the case, as in Malachi, that the Israelite addressee is imaged as male rather than as female. It may also still be the case that the exogamy that leads to polytheistic worship is at issue. There is a significant difference, however, between the portrayal of women's alien status in Malachi and that in Proverbs. Whereas the prophet's "daughter of a foreign God" is no more than a woman, even if she is seen to represent a foreign cult,[27] Woman Stranger of Proverbs is a full-blown force of evil, an evil that manifests death in sexual form. Unlike the earthly daughter of a strange God, who awaits the pleasure of her prospective husband, Woman Stranger accosts, deceives, and seduces.

In this regard, the shift in subject in the otherwise similar imagery in Mal 2:14 and Prov 2:17 is instructive. In Malachi, the active partner is the man, who is condemned for being faithless to "the wife of your youth" (*ʾēšet nĕ ʿûrêkā*) who is "your companion and your wife by covenant" (*ḥăbertĕkā wĕʾēšet bĕrîtekā*). The contextual connection of this judgment with the preceding one against those who marry daughters of a foreign God, and thereby are "faithless to one another, profaning the covenant of our fathers" (2:10), makes clear that the prophet (or at least his editor) viewed faithlessness to one's wife as a form of covenant infidelity, given its motivation (a foreign wife) and its consequence (foreign worship) in this particular social setting. The same train of thought occurs in Prov 2:17, but the gender dynamic shifts. Here it is the *ʾiššâ zārâ*, not her partner, who forsakes the "companion of her youth" (*ʾallûp nĕʿûrêhā*) and forgets "the covenant of her God" (*bĕrît ʾĕlōhêhā*).[28]

How should we understand the gender and symbolic dynamics in Prov 2? It seems, first of all, an exercise in irrelevance to imagine the Judean poet castigating a foreign woman who forgets her marital vows and/or her devotion to her (foreign) Deity. Alternatively, taken out of context, it is possible to construe this verse allegorically, with the woman forgetful of her marital covenant representing the Israelite community acting in covenant faithlessness. Such an understanding is hard to square with the context, however, which assumes a male listener who is being persuaded against a future liaison with a female who has forgotten (in parallel) her youthful companion and the covenant of her God. Although the identification of marital and religious faithlessness is similar to that in Malachi, Proverbs' focus on female agency, rather than male, suggests that decisions about exogamy—over which women had little control—are not the main concern. In sum, it is difficult to construe this particular text as representing anything other than an Israelite wife who is faithless to her husband. The issue at stake here is not marriage to the proper wife or even faithfulness to one's wife. Rather, the issue is social control of women's sexual behavior.

We are forced, then, to consider a second of the connotations of *zār/nokrî*, that of the outsider to the family household, which is, in fact, the dominant imagery in Prov 1–9. The woman is depicted as *zārâ* because, as an adulteress and prostitute, she acts in ways that are alien to the family structure, a structure that itself is a fundamental defining feature of what is "our own," not-strange.[29] If we eliminate Prov 7:14 as evidence for a foreign cultic practice, all the language of sexuality in Prov 1-9 has socio-sexual deviance—prostitution and adultery—as its primary referent.

One could argue, as Blenkinsopp does, that the allusion to Solomon in Prov 1:1, as well as the allegorical use of sexuality in the pre-exilic prophets and Third Isaiah, should lead us to the conclusion that, in the wisdom book too, religious fidelity, not sex, is at issue. The problem with such a conclusion is that, unlike in those prophets, Proverbs never makes explicit the association with foreign worship while, to the contrary, faithfulness to one's wife, adultery, and harlotry are discussed in literalistic (if not fully literal) ways (see especially the poem on marital fidelity [5:5-19]; the contrast between the prostitute and the adulteress [6:26]; and the description of the consequences for "going in" to the "wife of another" [6:27-35]). Perhaps we might assume that an Israelite of this day would "naturally" make the connection between these images and foreign worship. But we must also assume that an Israelite of this day would have been concerned with such matters as establishment and preservation of the family name and inheritance rights, and of status and power within the community, all of which are threatened by deviant sexual activity by the women in a man's household.

In Prov 7, strangeness, not of nationality but of gender, is given its fullest expression. We must be clear, however, that neither Prov 2 nor 7 is attempting to describe the actions of a particular woman. The language of deviant sexual behavior *is* being used symbolically but not as a mere cipher for deviant worship. Rather, it is a symbol of the forces deemed destructive of patriarchal control of family, property, and society. Because control of women's sexuality is the *sine qua non* of the patriarchal family, it is no accident that the forces of "chaos" are embodied in a woman who takes control of her own sexuality.

Indeed, it would seem that the purpose of this poem is to project into a single figure the greatest evil imaginable, even at the expense of realistic description, by portraying an improbable combination of sexually deviant activities. It seems clear that the Strange Woman in Prov 7 (cf. 2:17) is about to commit an act of adultery against her own husband, an act which in itself is bad enough. But this is adultery of the worst kind: no passionate love affair (however improbable that may have been in any case) but calculated, anonymous sex with a stranger, and an innocent lad at that. Indeed, we learn of her marital status only at the end of her speech; it is with her wantonness that we are first impressed. Notice, however, that she is not a professional prostitute but is only "dressed" as one.[30] Had she been a "pro," the sage's depiction of utter evil would have been undercut, for the professional prostitute does have a place in a patriarchal world, even if it is a liminal one. Not protected by any man, she is also not obligated to any man; she is the "institutionally legitimated 'other woman.'"[31] Far more dangerous is the woman who exists within the boundaries of male-controlled sexuality but who decides for herself to opt out of them. Such is the wife *šît zônâ* in Prov 7.[32]

There is yet one more piece to the puzzle of sexuality and strangeness that will complete our picture of woman embodied in the full paradigm of sexual evil. The one who is *zār* can be not only foreign, not only outside the family, but also outside the priesthood. In a general sense, of course, all women are *zārôt* on this level. Once again, however, the Strange Woman is portrayed as an active creator of her own alien status, engaging in sex during the feast of her peace offering, bringing her harlot's hire to the temple to pay her vows, and compounding the priestly anointing oil to perfume her illicit sexual encounter.

Given how fully the meanings associated with sexuality and strangeness are articulated and interwoven in Prov 1–9, it becomes important to ask to what extent and in what manner any of these represent a socio-historical "reality." I have already suggested the possibility that, whatever concerns our poet-editor has for exogamy and foreign worship, they may not reflect the same sort of immediate crisis as that confronting the writers of the fifth and very early fourth centuries. Given the shift in imagery from the "real" foreign women of Malachi and Ezra-Nehemiah to the almost mythical figure in Proverbs, it seems possible that the latter book may express less of a current situation and much more of an increasingly mythicized *memory* of a time when, as it were, the bad women were really bad. Because of the chronological telescoping effected by myth, however, one era of the past becomes conflated with another and with the present as well. Thus, "memories" of the foreign women who led our ancestors astray at Baal Peor, the foreign women who turned Solomon's heart from God,[33] and the "daughter of a foreign God" who caused Malachi to castigate our fathers' (grandfathers'?) generation meld into an image of all that is dangerous to us in the present and future. In such an interpretation of Proverbs, it is not so much a matter of illicit sex serving as an allegory for dalliance with strange Gods (or Goddesses), but rather of a female image that evokes this metonymic memory and thus functions as a symbol for every danger that threatens the well-being of the community (as defined, of course, by those in charge).

The socio-historical veracity of the association of strangeness with adultery and harlotry must be assessed in an analogous way. Against van der Toorn, I think it is unlikely that we should imagine a social situation in which married women regularly engaged in acts of harlotry. Although it is certainly true that laws are often enacted to counter some existing practice, what information we have about the post-exilic period suggests to me that in Prov 7 we are confronting not a social reality of wanton wives but rather a socio-psychological reality of men threatened by a multiply-stressed social situation, including internal religio-political power struggles, economically oppressive foreign rule, and the pressures of cultural assimilation. We might describe the psychological dynamics in this way: The need to maintain familial and social stability in the face of enormous disruptive forces created in the male leaders and thinkers of the community a fear of chaos that was projected into an external, but nonetheless imaginary, object of fear, the woman who goes strange in the sense of deciding to stand outside the family structure as defined by its sexual roles and restrictions.

Finally, the sage's close association with, if not membership in, the priestly caste completes the linkage of woman, strangeness, and sex. Precisely because all women are *zārôt* to the sons of Aaron, woman becomes a "natural" target on which to project evil. But, just as Woman Stranger's vile adultery is not a depiction of women's actual activities, so also her deliberate violations of cultic regulations do not represent the acts of a flesh-and-blood woman. Rather they represent the worst forms of defilement our priestly sage can imagine. Along with the accusations of wanton adultery, this depiction of the cultic violator must be taken as polemical, not descriptive, an expression of male anxiety as one generation attempts to pass its ideology of control to the next.[34] Although in the biblical laws defilement can come in many forms, from both men and women, here woman—particularly in her sexual nature—becomes the embodiment of defilement. The metaphor has now been fully realized, but also reified: "Woman is Strange."

DEATH, YHWH, AND THE STRANGE WOMAN

One final step is necessary to reveal the depth and significance of this ideological move, and that is to suggest its theological dimensions. We must consider the relationship of Woman Stranger to death and Sheol in light of their connection to YHWH. A rather unexpected connection—of Isa 28 to Prov 1–9—provides the basis for our reflection. This chapter of Isaiah is notable for its concentration of wisdom vocabulary, most obviously its reference to "teaching knowledge" (v. 9) and its description of YHWH as "wonderful in counsel, and excellent in wisdom" (v. 29). More specifically, however, Isa 28 contains a series of images and vocabulary that are later used in connection with the strange woman and strange man[35] of Proverbs. YHWH's message is said to come "on jabbering lips and in another tongue" (*bĕla ᶜăgê śāpâ ûbĕlāšôn ᵓaḥeret,* Isa 28:11). In Proverbs, YHWH does not need to speak in an alien language, for Woman Stranger's smooth lips and tongue offer a quite comprehensible message.[36] The imagery of the snare is also prominent in both pieces of material. Because of the people's failure to listen to YHWH's warnings, Isa 28:13 claims that the divine word will cause them to "go, and fall backward, and be broken, and baited (*wĕnōqĕšû*) and snared (*wĕnilkādû*)." In Proverbs, the word-pair *yqš/lkd,* both in the niphal, is repeated exactly in a reference to the effect of going surety for a strange man (6:2; cf. 6:5), but the imagery of bond (*môsēr*, emended) and snare (*pāḥ*) also helps to create one of the sage's most powerful warnings against the strange woman (7:22-23).

The most important point for our purposes is that Isa 28 contains one of the few scattered places outside Proverbs where the word-pair *zār/nokrî* occurs.[37] The chapter describes a situation in which the leaders of Ephraim, likened to drunkards (vv. 1, 3, 7–9),[38] make "a covenant with death, an agreement with Sheol" (vv. 15, 18). Because of this, YHWH will rise up

> to do his deed—strange [*zār*] is his deed!
> to work his work—alien [*nokrîyâ*] is his work! (28:21)

It is not only this word pair that anticipates the Proverbs poems; so also does Isaiah's mythicized death-Sheol language that is so similar to its use in Prov 2:18; 5:5; 7:27; and 9:18, where the house of Woman Stranger—who forgets "the covenant of her God"—is imaged as in the maw of Mot.[39]

The continuity of imagery between Isaiah and Proverbs helps to call our attention, however, to a very significant difference between them. In

Isaiah it is YHWH who speaks a fatal word in a foreign tongue, while in Proverbs this word issues from the enticing mouth of Woman Stranger. Similarly, Isaiah portrays the Deity doing the strange deed and working the alien work in response to the people's covenant with death and Sheol, while Proverbs moves the burden of strangeness to the Deadly One herself. I would suggest, then, that we see in Proverbs manifestation of a pattern of post-exilic theological thought in which evil, whether in the form of strange deeds or deadly words, is removed from the character of the Deity, and responsibility is ascribed to a quasi-human, quasi-mythical incarnation of evil. The language of death, shades, and Sheol, which may have had its origin in the cult of a Goddess (so Blenkinsopp) or some other chthonic Deity (so McKane), is transformed in Proverbs to articulate a force—defined here as female—that will ultimately split the religious cosmos of Judaism and Christianity into a dualistic moral system in which female images can represent only absolute good or absolute evil. Thus are defined the categories with which real women will have to contend for centuries to come.

NOTES

1. This is a slightly revised version of a paper that originally appeared under the title "What's So Strange about the Strange Woman?" in *The Bible and the Politics of Exegesis,* D. Jobling, et al., eds. Cleveland, Ohio: Pilgrim, 1991. I thank Pilgrim Press for permission to reprint it here.

2. Blenkinsopp, "Social Context," 464-65.

3. Humbert, "La femme étrangère," "Les adjectifs 'zār' et 'nokrî.'"

4. Snijders, "*The Meaning of zār.*"

5. *Wisdom and the Feminine,* 112-20.

6. *Wisdom and the Feminine*, 119. See Snijders, "The Meaning of *zār*"; Aletti, "Séduction et Parole"; and Yee, "'I Have Perfumed My Bed'" for similar opinions. Boström, *Proverbiastudien*, and McKane, *Proverbs*, on the other hand, have emphasized the woman's status as a foreigner, while Newsom sees a movement between these ascriptions ("Woman and the Discourse of Patriarchal Wisdom").

7. Blenkinsopp, "Social Context," 457.

8. Blenkinsopp, "Social Context," 457.

9. I had originaly argued for a very early date, in the fifth century shortly after the return from exile. Blenkinsopp alludes to the Persian period in general, but his biblical sources date no later than the very early fourth century or earlier, depending on when one dates the arrival of Ezra in Judah. Second Temple studies have continued to analyze the issue of mixed marriages in connection with Ezra-Nehemiah, and the argument for relating this issue to Proverbs' Strange Woman has recently been reinforced by Washington ("Strange Woman"). Although my paper raises the possibility of a later date for this material, my central argument does not finally hinge on dating. Even if the Strange

Woman is to be associated with Ezra-Nehemiah, the rhetorical and theological force of the figure cannot be limited to the mixed-marriage debate as it played out in that period.

10. "'To Play the Harlot.'"

11. That is, religious faithlessness came to be understood, by virtue of a dying metaphor, to be an almost literal referent of the language of sexual deviance. See Camp, *Wisdom and the Feminine*, 265-71, and Archer, "The 'Evil Women.'"

12. It is worth noting, for example, that, although the vocabulary in Mal 2:10-15, which clearly does refer to exogamy and foreign worship, is very similar to that of Prov 2:16-17, the prophet's concern is with a God (*ʾēl nēkār*), not with a Goddess, and does not allude to ritual sex.

13. Van der Toorn,"Female Prostitution."

14. Van der Toorn, "Female Prostitution," 194-97. He suggests that vow making is particularly a form of female devotion. That women make vows is clear; whether they do so more frequently than men remains unproven, but neither his argument nor mine depends on this point.

15. See van der Toorn, "Female Prostitution," 197-201, for a recent review of literature.

16. Toy, *Book of Proverbs*, 151.

17. This interpretation of the passage removes much, if not all, of the burden long carried by the tense of the poor verb *šillamtî*. Because the ultimate fulfillment of the "peace offering" vow involves two days of feasting, it seems clear that this process is not yet in every sense complete at the time the woman accosts the young man. It is possible that she has already offered her sacrifice (though the lack of a verb in v. 14a leaves the phrase temporally ambiguous) and that the moment of the sacrifice constituted a technical completion, thus making appropriate a translation of the perfect verb in 14b with the English past tense. On the other hand, the "today" (*hayyôm*) of v. 14b may refer to the twenty-four-hour period beginning that night (cf. 7:9) and ending the following evening, in which case the act of sacrifice has yet to take place and a translation of *šillamtî* with modal force (so Böstrom and van der Toorn) is appropriate. In any case, all we need to know for our purposes is that sometime "today" the act has been or will be complete; hence, my choice of the present tense, "fulfill," rendered with the force of a perfect verb.

18. In Blenkinsopp's view ("Social Context," 468) the warning in Prov 5:10 that "strangers [*zārîm*] will take their fill of your wealth and your labors will go to the house of an alien [*bêt nokrî*]," which immediately precedes the reference to ruin in the *qāhāl wĕ ʿēdâ*, is a further indication that the *ʾiššâ zārâ* is a foreign woman (see the actions taken by Ezra against men with foreign wives). The Hebrew Bible also shows evidence, however, for the *zār* as one who is outside of one's family household. Thus, the beneficiaries of the young man's profanation of the cult could as well be construed as other members of the community to whom his goods would be distributed when he is "cut off." Our interpretation of chapter 5 should perhaps be guided, however, primarily by the poem on marital fidelity in vv. 15-19. In this case the crime is adultery, but the punishment—loss of status and property to fellow citizens who are nonetheless *zār* with respect to one's patrimony—is still the same.

19. It is in interpreting passages like Deut 23:19 that van der Toorn's argument, in my view, runs astray. He sees this verse as evidence that "among

Israelites, the custom of paying vows by means of prostitution was a known phenomenon" ("Female Prostitution," 200). I have offered here what seems to me a far more natural interpretation, namely, that prostitutes sometimes made vows and then attempted to pay them with the proverbial wages of sin.

20. Recent studies on sex and cultic impurity include Wenham, "Sexual Intercourse," 432–34, and Milgrom, "Rationale." For a functionalist approach to socio-sexual deviance, see Frymer-Kensky, "Law and Philosophy."

21. For an analysis of symbolic modalities related to the human experience of evil, see Ricoeur, *The Symbolism of Evil,* esp. p. 18.

22. Snijders, "The Meaning of *zār*," 127.

23. See Camp, *Wisdom and the Feminine*, 71–75, for a fuller elaboration of the theory of metaphor applied here.

24. The one questionable text is Neh 10:31 (English: 10:30), which uses the full reciprocal formula: "give our daughters/take their daughters." Toni Craven, in oral communication, has suggested that Nehemiah's policies were in general more egalitarian and inclusive of women as members of the people than were Ezra's (see, for example, Neh 5:1-13), a possibility that deserves further exploration.

25. Van der Toorn raises the interesting possibility that a (quite secular!) prostitution service was run by temple personnel for the purpose of enhancing temple revenues ("Female Prostitution," 202–4). Similarly, Bird finds that Hos 4:11-14 suggests "that prostitutes found the rural sanctuaries an attractive place to do business, quite possibly by agreement with the priests" ("'To Play the Harlot,'" 88). Both scholars caution against taking evidence for such activities as sign of authorized sexual ritual.

26. With respect to gender, then, Malachi makes literal and univocal what had been tensive and disturbing. In Hos 2 and 4, in Num 25:1 (the story of Baal-Peor), and in Isa 57, the authors waver in their depiction of Israel's faithlessness between the image of the wanton female and language about lustful men. Bird ("'To Play the Harlot,'" 75) notes the special incongruity of Num 25:1: "While Israel dwelt at Shittim the people began to play the harlot with the daughters of Moab."

27. So Glazier-McDonald, "Intermarriage."

28. The choice of alternative words for "companion" (*ḥăbertĕkā* in Mal 2:14 and *ʾallûp* in Prov 2:17) can be explained by the needs of alliteration and assonance. See Camp, *Wisdom and the Feminine*, 319 n. 5.

29. See Snijders, "The Meaning of *zār*," 68, 78, 88-104, and Wright, "The Israelite Household."

30. Bird's analysis of Gomer reveals that the various modes of sexual deviance are interrelated in a similar manner in the prophetic text: Gomer is not a professional prostitute but rather a wanton woman; only gradually does the context move us to understand her as an adulteress.

31. Bird, "'To Play the Harlot,'" 79; Niditch, "The Wronged Woman Righted," 147.

32. The point is reaffirmed in Prov 6:26 by the negative comparison between the *ʾiššâ zônâ*, who may be had for a loaf of bread, and an *ʾēset ʾîš*, who "stalks a man's very life."

33. That such "memories" of the dastardly foreign female were held in high

regard by members of the wisdom tradition is evident in the fact that Ben Sira's hymn to the ancestors contains allusions both to Phineas's mighty deed against Cozbi, the daughter of Midian who married an Israelite at Baal Peor (Num 25; Sir 44:23-25), and to the demise of Solomon, who gave women (here, no longer even qualified as "foreign") dominion over his body (1 Kgs 11; Sir 47:19).

34. See Newsom's analysis of the intergenerational aspects of Proverbs' discourse, "Woman and the Discourse of Patriarchal Wisdom."

35. The relationship of the figure of the Strange Man in Proverbs to the Strange Woman is the subject of a study currently in progress by this author.

36. Prov 5:3; 6:24; 7:21; cf. 2:16, and for the strange man, 6:2.

37. Other references include Isa 61:5; Jer 5:19; Obad 11; Ps 69:9; 81:10; Job 19:15; Lam 5:2.

38. See Prov 23:33, where drunkenness is said to cause one's eyes to see *zārôt*, presumably an abstraction ("strange things"), but in a grammatical form that could be construed "strange women."

39. McKane, *Proverbs*, 287-88.

WORKS CITED

Aletti, Jean-Noël. "Séduction et Parole en Proverbes I-IX." *VT* 27 (1977): 129–44.

Archer, Léoni "The 'Evil Women' in Aprocryphal and Pseudepigraphical Writings." Pp. 239–46 in *Proceedings of the Ninth World Congress of Jewish Studies. August 4–12, 1985. Division A: The Period of the Bible.* Jerusalem: World Union of Jewish Studies, 1986.

Bird, Phyllis. "'To Play the Harlot': An Inquiry into an Old Testament Metaphor." Pp. 75 –94 in *Gender and Difference in Ancient Israel*, edited by P. L. Day. Minneapolis: Fortress Press, 1989.

Blenkinsopp, Joseph. "The Social Context of the 'Outsider Woman' in Proverbs 1–9." *Biblica* 72 (1991): 457–73.

Boström, Gustav. *Proverbiastudien: die Weisheit und das Fremde Weib in Sprüche 1–9*. Lund: C. W. K. Gleerup, 1935.

Camp, Claudia V. *Wisdom and the Feminine in the Book of Proverbs*. Bible and Literature 11. Sheffield: Almond; Decatur JSOT, 1985.

Frymer-Kensky, Tikva. "Law and Philosophy: The Case of Sex in the Bible." In *Thinking Biblical Law*, edited by D. Patrick. *Semeia* 45 (1989): 89–102.

Glazier-McDonald, Beth. "Intermarriage, Divorce, and the *Bat-ʾēl Nēkār*: Insights into Mal 2:10–16." *JBL* 106 (1987): 603–11.

Humbert, Paul. "La femme étrangère du livre des Proverbes." *Revue des études sémitiques* 6 (1937): 40–64.

——— "Les adjectifs 'zār' et 'nokrî' et la femme étrangère." Pp. 259–66 in *Mélanges syriens offerts à M. René Dussaud I.* Bibliothèque

Archéologique et Historique 30. Paris: Librairie Orientalist Paul Guenther, 1939.
McKane, William. *Proverbs: A New Approach*. Philadelphia: Westminster, 1970.
Milgrom, Jacob. "Rationale for Cultic Law: The Case of Impurity." in *Thinking Biblical Law*, edited by D. Patrick. *Semeia* 45 (1989): 103–09.
Newsom, Carol. "Woman and the Discourse of Patriarchal Wisdom: A Study of Proverbs 1–9." Pp. 142–60 in *Gender and Difference in Ancient Israel*, edited by P. L. Day. Minneapolis: Fortress Press, 1989.
Niditch, Susan. "The Wronged Woman Righted: An Analysis of Genesis 38." *HTR* 72 (1979): 143–49.
Ricoeur, Paul. *The Symbolism of Evil*. Boston: Beacon Press, 1967.
Snijders, Lambertus A. "The Meaning of *zār* in the Old Testament." *Oudtestamentische Studien* 10 (1954): 1–154.
Toy, Crawford H. *A Critical and Exegetical Commentary on the Book of Proverbs*. International Critical Commentary. Edinburgh: T.&T. Clark, 1899.
van der Toorn, Karel. "Female Prostitution in Payment of Vows in Ancient Israel." *JBL* 108 (1989): 193–205.
Washington, Harold. "The Strange Woman of Proverbs 1–9 and Post-Exilic Judaean Society." Pp. 217–42 in *Second Temple Studies*. Vol. 2, edited by T. C. Eskenazi and K. H. Richards. Sheffield: JSOT, 1994.
Wenham, Gordon J. "Why Does Sexual Intercourse Defile (Lev 15:18)?" *ZAW* 95 (1983): 432–34.
Wright, Christopher J. H. "The Israelite Household and the Decalogue: The Social Background and Significance of Some Commandments." *Tyndale Bulletin* 30 (1979): 101–24.
Yee, Gale. "'I Have Perfumed My Bed With Myrrh': The Foreign Woman (*ʾiššâ zārâ*) in Proverbs 1–9." *Journal for the Study of the Old Testament* 43 (1989): 53–68.

13

AMY RICHLIN

Carrying Water in a Sieve: Class and the Body in Roman Women's Religion

> . . . and as she sat there weeping a most curious image, born perhaps from that other image of the spilt milk, arose in her mind. She saw herself as a cup of clear water, which she herself was somehow bearing through a crowd, and which she should have carried carefully, steadily, losing not a drop, so that when *he* asked for it the cup was still full and unpolluted. But instead of that she had let anyone drink who wished. . . . And the strange image grew, till Julia saw all the race of women bearing their vessels of water and passing to and fro among the thirst-tormented race of men: and in the forefront she saw her daughter, carrying a cup of crystal, and holding it high over her head.
>
> —Margery Sharp, *The Nutmeg Tree*, 248-49

When people talk about "Goddess worship" today, they often have in mind a cultural formation in which femaleness enjoys a high cultural value, and women benefit thereby. The Goddesses of the ancient Mediterranean world are still familiar names in the West, and it might be expected that Greek and Roman women's religion would have been focused on these Goddesses and that the presence of Goddess worship would have influenced, and for the better, not only their lives but their whole culture. To test this idea, it is important to take a close look at the cultures of the ancient Mediterranean—distinct, various, and many. Of these, Rome is too often lumped in with Greece, but it had, in fact, a fascinating and peculiar set of religions all its own, as well as many borrowings. In Roman religion can sometimes be seen practices that would be transformed into Christian festivals and cults of saints. Yet while the beginning of the Roman Empire, of course, is roughly contemporary with the beginning of Christianity, Rome had existed as a republic by that time for five hundred years and more. Our fragmentary sources thus allow us to see something of Roman women's religion over a long span of time, a span that also in some respects extends to modern-day Italy. And what we see, I would argue, is a decidedly phallocentric culture in which femaleness is valued only insofar as it is connected with fertility and governed by chastity. As in Julia's vision in the epigraph to this chapter, Roman women must have viewed their bodies as vessels borne through life, not only precariously but competitively.

The study of Roman women's religion is in its infancy, and in this chapter I can only hope to suggest some issues for discussion.[1] I will be considering both the historical circumstances of some aspects of women's religious experience and the symbolic meaning of women's cult in the larger culture. I would like, someday, to establish for Rome the relation of women and the sacred to women and the monstrous. In particular, I want to understand some negative stereotypes that pervade Roman culture (and many others)—stereotypes in which women monsters, or witches, do things like eat babies, poison people, and transform people into animals. One of my hypotheses is that this kind of thing can be understood as a symbolic inversion of what was normative behavior for real Roman women, and of the female, with respect to religion and ritual. Apart from culturewide festivals (for example, the Saturnalia) and foreign imports (for example, Magna Mater, the Bacchanalia), Roman women's cults show a preoccupation with the female body—with chastity, lactation, childbirth, the nurturing of children, marriage—and with the class divisions relevant to the female body: *matrona,* slave, prostitute. The same concerns are shown in household cult and ritual, in medico-religious beliefs associated with the female body (for example, beliefs in the curative or harmful uses of menstrual blood and women's milk),[2] and in state rituals like the Fordicidia that enacted beliefs about birth and fertility using animals' bodies. Where the monstrous female kills (and sometimes eats) children, feeds people poison, and breaks boundaries, the sacred female values the bearing and nurturing of children and reinforces boundaries.

Such questions about symbolic meaning can only be asked after inquiry into the varieties of Roman women's religious experience. What was it? How was it structured? Did the worship of Goddesses in a coed pantheon correspond with an elevation of the female in Roman symbolic systems? Any examination of Roman women's rituals raises issues about the way in which these women may have accepted, and defined themselves by, rituals that gravely limited them—in which they looked at themselves from a male perspective; and about how these rituals may have been used by one class of women to express their power over another class of women, in a culture in which both classes were in the power of men. This in turn raises overall issues of women's complicity in patriarchy. On the other hand, the extant sources also raise the definite possibility of female solidarity and group identification in Roman culture; it is probably of a sort not uncommon in societies with strong gender differentiation, and it can simply reinforce the oppression of women, but it can also be a source of women's strength and female consciousness.[3] John Winkler, in "The Laughter of the Oppressed," analyzed Athenian women's rituals in such a positive light and compared them with similar rituals of modern Arab women. Indeed this whole problem ties in with current concerns about ethnography and epistemology: how can we, as outside observers, evaluate the experience of Roman women?[4]

In framing answers to these questions, I am following in the footsteps of feminist historians of religion, whose projects have made scholars aware of whole new ways of looking at religion in culture: Bernadette Brooten's recovery of women leaders in the ancient synagogue; Karen Torjesen's of women in the early church; Ross Kraemer's treatment of the ancient Mediterranean as a world full of women visibly active in religion, which Greeks, Romans, Jews, and Christians inhabit together. Where Kraemer[5] asks what it meant for Roman women to be priests, Mary Beard[6] asks what it meant for any Roman to be a priest. Chava Weissler, in her study of Jewish women in the early modern period, points out that

> making gender a category of analysis enables us to understand Ashkenazic Judaism as a *total* social system in which both men and women participated. . . . [I]t leads . . . to the investigation of the distribution of domains of the religious life between women and men.[7]

Their work made this chapter thinkable and informs my efforts to imagine real Roman women as active participants in an intelligible cultural system.

In what follows, the reader may feel, with dismay, that I am here leaving out the most familiar faces in the world of Roman religious culture: Christian, Jewish, and imperial cults receive no attention here, and I give short shrift to weddings and funerals, which of course played important roles in Roman women's lives. The day-to-day or "folk" aspect of women's religious practice could also be much more fully documented than the scope of this chapter allows; I have dealt elsewhere with women's use of magico/medical rituals and amulets,[8] and there is more to be said about women's involvement in "magic" generally,[9] as well as about daily observance associated with the home and women's duties. The Vestals[10] show up here only intermittently, as do the more familiar Goddesses in the Roman pantheon and the notorious Gods and Goddesses of imported cults: Bacchus, Isis, Magna Mater, all popular with women. Here I want to focus mainly on those aspects of Roman women's religious life that were most peculiarly Roman.

SOURCES

The religion of Roman women, and Roman women in Roman religion—which are two different things—have been very imperfectly known, dependent as they are on scattered data that have yet to be assembled in full.[11] The extant Roman sources for women and religion are like tattered lacework: the original Roman treatises on the subject, such as they were, are lost, and even the testimonia of them are fragmentary. We must depend on Roman anecdote collectors, encyclopedists, and cultural historians, sometimes fleshed out by Ovid's *Fasti*.[12] What we have from them is tantalizing—for example, the source usually known as Paulus ex Festo.

One of the obscure characters on the edges of a classical education, Paulus is even blocked from the general reader by his peculiar name: "ex Festo" is clearly not a cognomen, but because the book that bears the name consists of lists of definitions, most scholars just dip into him and leave with a feeling of relief, still wondering who he is. He turns out to be three people: Verrius Flaccus, who put together a marvelous dictionary of Roman lore in the early first century C.E.; Pompeius Festus, who epitomized this dictionary in the late second century C.E.; and Paulus Diaconus, who excerpted from Festus in the eighth century C.E. (hence the name Paulus ex Festo). The Teubner text obligingly prints the fragments of Festus interspersed with the excerpts from Paulus, so in some places we have both Festus's original and Paulus's excerpt. Then there are places where there are shreds of Festus, partly reconstructed from Paulus's excerpt. And, unfortunately, there are long runs where we have only Paulus. And here before our eyes we see the process by which women get erased from history.

First, it is clear that Verrius Flaccus drew on several books about rituals involving substantial participation by women. Festus gives long runs of entries about women and mourning, or wedding customs, or women in ritual generally.[13] And it is clear that, just as Paulus excerpted from Festus and Festus from Verrius, so Verrius was copying out of something like "The Big Book of Roman Weddings." Such sources are all lost.[14] Second, although Paulus does keep a lot of items about women, we can see, when we have both the passage from Festus and the excerpt from Paulus, that sometimes he did not. For example, Festus records[15] a taboo on wearing footgear made from the skin of a dead cow, for the *flaminicae,* high priestesses at Rome; in Paulus,[16] Festus's *flaminicis* has become *flaminibus,* so that the priestesses are replaced by priests.[17] So when we have long runs of Paulus and Festus is lost, we know that a lot about women is lost, too. I dwell on the case of Paulus ex Festo here to emphasize that the state of our knowledge of Roman women's participation in cult may well mislead us as to the original attitude toward this phenomenon in pre-Christian Roman culture. When it has been pieced together, the evidence suggests that Roman women participated actively in cult at all levels.

A different sort of lacy data, more directly attached to real women, is available from Latin inscriptions from all over Italy. It shows, roughly, that there were priestesses and precincts of dedication special to women in numerous places. But, though it is useful to have the map of Italy dotted with these points of light, each individual case brings with it only the sketchiest context. Moreover, the way in which the *CIL* (the "Corpus of Latin Inscriptions") was assembled means that we have a deceptively large sample. In the late nineteenth century, a team of energetic German classicists began scouring Italy and the former Roman Empire for inscriptions, most of them religious dedications and tombstones. They not only examined stones themselves—Theodor Mommsen climbed up a ladder to look through a spyglass at an inscription incorporated into a church tower—but collected reports of stones, some long vanished, that had been turned up by eighteenth-century plows. The resulting enormous collection, assembled in huge volumes with meticulous reproductions—organized geographically, town by town, province by province—gives the impression of comprehensiveness. In fact, what we often get is ten stones from one village, a hundred or so from a big town, all spread over a period of five hundred years or so. The resulting picture could be called "suggestive," no more. Thus, although my preferred goal would be a picture of religious life throughout the Italian peninsula, I am forced, as usual, to depend for my main narrative on textual sources based in the city of Rome. At least sometimes these sources indicate that they describe life in the countryside or in other towns.[18]

PRIESTESS TERMINOLOGY

H. S. Versnel begins his recent essay on Roman women's worship of Bona Dea with an apposite quotation from the elder Cato (second century B.C.E.) describing the duties of the slave housekeeper (*vilica*) on a plantation:

> She must visit the neighbouring and other women very seldom, and not have them either in the house or in her part of it. She must not go out to meals or be a gad-about. She must not engage in religious worship herself or get others to engage in it for her without the orders of the master or the mistress; let her remember that the master attends to the devotions for the whole household.[19]

Versnel goes on to base his otherwise convincing and lively argument on a putatively strict division of the Roman religious sphere by gender à la Cato: ritual is a male thing, not for women. And this is the impression one would get from most accounts of Roman religion; the Vestals are the exception that proves the rule. Perhaps the real situation, however, was not so clear-cut, just as (we might assume) Cato's housekeeper was doing something that prompted him to say no. Indeed, Cato himself goes on to suggest that the *vilica* should garland the hearth on holidays and pray to the *Lar familiaris* ("household God") for plenty.[20] There is, moreover, textual evidence that women were indeed involved in public rituals, sometimes as priestesses or sacrificers. At the Liberalia, old women sat selling cakes, each one with a little grill (*foculum*) on which she sacrificed for each buyer.[21] Old women were also important during the rites of the Feralia, when the ghosts of the dead were placated.[22] And a woman called the "Petreia" used to lead processions in the provincial towns and imitate a drunken old woman.[23] More vaguely, we hear that there were some rites that had to be performed by women, so the wives of the priests were assigned these.[24]

Sources like Paulus give us the words for types of women involved in ritual: he tells us that an *armita* was a maiden sacrificing with the fold of her toga thrown back over her shoulder,[25] and that a *simpulum* was a little cup used for libations, so women dedicated to religion were called *simpulatrices*.[26] Festus says that a public chorus of maidens sang a special hymn during the second Punic War[27] and that there were Salic maidens, like the Salic priests,[28] who made sacrifices.

Women who were expert in religion, or who carried out sacrifices, were called *sagae, piatrices, expiatrices,* or *simulatrices*.[29] Women priests were usually just called *sacerdotes,* the same word used for men, but sometimes were called *sacerdotulae* (diminutive ending) or *antistitae* (feminine ending).[30] They wore a special head-shawl called a *rica* when sacrificing.[31] The wife of the *flamen Dialis* (the priest of Jupiter at Rome) had the title of *flaminica* and had all the same bizarre taboos as he did, plus a few more. She had her own bizarre outfit, including the *rica,* which Festus describes as "square, fringed, and purple."[32] She also had a special tall headdress called a *tutulus,* tied onto her hair by a purple ribbon.[33] She had to wear a dyed (*venenato*) dress and a twig from a fruitful tree (*de arbore felici,* literally "from a lucky tree") in her *rica.* She could not climb higher than three rungs up a ladder, except for a certain kind called a "Greek ladder." And she could neither smile, bathe, comb her hair, nor fix her hairdo when she went to the festival of the Argei.[34] The *flamen* had to resign if she died, perhaps because of the fact that some rites could not be performed without her.[35] There was a *regina* who made sacrifices as well as a *rex*; she wore a twig of pomegranate on her head.[36] Priestesses used the same sacrificial knife as priests—and *virgines.*[37] And some Goddesses had their own priestesses: Bona Dea's was called the *damiatrix,*[38] and Ceres had special ones.[39]

PRIESTESSES FROM ROMAN ITALY

The *CIL* leaves us in no doubt that women were active in public cult throughout Italy. This took several forms: (1) priestesshoods in imperial cult, almost always the cult of a female relative of the emperor, (2) priestesshoods in the cult of various Goddesses, (3) participation as worshipers involving large or small dedications (gifts to God or Goddess).[40]

Several titles indicating that a given woman holds a priestesshood recur in inscriptions (see appendix A). Most commonly found is *sacerdos;* evidence is extant of at least eighty-four women from all over Italy who held this title, of whom twenty-four—only about 29 percent—were involved in imperial cult. In contrast, the title *magistra* is found thirty-six times and is never, or perhaps once, associated with imperial cult. *Ministrae* are sometimes found accompanying *magistrae,* occasionally alone; there are ten of these, none of them associated with imperial cult. Both of these terms have male equivalents, *magister* and *minister;* these titles are of great antiquity and are used in a range of contexts from politics to the army to education, and might be translated "superior officer" and "inferior officer." In a religious context, they are normally used of officers in a religious association.[41] The last commonly found title is *flaminica,* a term best known as applied to the wife of the *flamen Dialis* at Rome (above). Extant from all over Italy, however, are the names of at least twenty-five *flaminicae,* of whom ten (40 percent) served in the imperial cult. A couple of rare titles that describe groups of female worshipers exist: a group of *cultrices* from the *collegium* of the small town of Fulginiae[42]; and a group of *consuplicatrices,* "fellow women suppliants" of Mater Matuta from Cora in Latium just south of Rome.[43]

Outside of imperial cult, the terms *sacerdos, magistra, ministra,* and *flaminica* are associated with a wide range of particular Goddesses. Of the fifty nonimperial *sacerdotes,* thirty were involved with the worship of Ceres or Venus; the public priestesshood of Ceres and Venus was a major municipal honor in the area around the Bay of Naples. Numerous examples survive from Pompeii, including the benefactress Eumachia, whose statue is a familiar figure to students of women in antiquity.[44] Other *sacerdotes* were in charge of the rites of Magna Mater (eleven examples), Juno Populonia (three), Minerva (two), Isis (two), Fortuna Redux (one), and Jovia Veneria of the people of Abellae (one). The Goddess most commonly served by *magistrae* was Bona Dea (nine), followed by Mater Matuta (three); *magistrae* of some other Goddesses are attested only singly: Dea Obsequens ("Goddess Obedient"), the spirit of Diana Augusta, Ceres Augusta, Minerva, Fortuna Melior ("Better Luck"), and Juno. A pair of *magistrae* served Proserpina at Vibo in the toe of Italy,[45] and Venus seems to have been served by teams of *magistrae* at Furfo in the hills northeast of Rome and at Cupra Maritima, a small town on the Adriatic coast.[46] *Ministrae,* who occur more rarely, naturally show a narrower range: three for Bona Dea, one for Magna Mater, one for Salus, one for Juno Populonia, and four unspecified. *Flaminicae* outside imperial cult are often unspecified (twelve of fifteen), and there is a chance that some of these are really in imperial cult, the connection being implicit. Of the remaining three, one represents Feronia, while the other two are described only by place name, the *flaminica pagi Arusnatium* up in Cisalpine Gaul[47] (Italy north of the Po) and the *flaminica* of Pisaurum and Ariminum, neighboring towns on the Adriatic coast.[48] One woman is described as both *sacerdos* and *flaminica* of Julia Augusta, Mater deum ("Mother of the Gods," that is, Magna Mater), and Isis Regina,[49] showing how the worship of the empress could blend with the worship of Goddesses.

Tombstones quite often give age at death and other biographical information about the person commemorated, and we might hope to find out from inscriptions something about the age at which a woman might become a priestess or how long she might serve; the Vestals, for example, had well-known rules about this.[50] The available information, however, is disappointingly sparse, although it is still better than nothing. A tombstone from the thinly settled coast between Barium and the mouth of the river Aufidus,[51] set up by an unhappy mother to her daughter, tells us that Petilia Secundina, daughter of Quintus (Petilius), was priestess of Minerva and lived for nine years, seven months, and eighteen days; her mother commemorates her *infatigabilem pietat(em)*, her "tireless sense of duty." So from this backwater we get a glimpse of something almost unattested elsewhere: a child priestess, and one seemingly engaged in religious activity. Another woman, *ministra* of Salus in the hilly countryside near Amiternum, died at the age of thirty, having served as priestess for thirteen years.[52] Here we have something that looks more familiar, a woman becoming active in religion around the age at which she would be taking on the role of *matrona*. And a woman who held the high-ranking job of *sacerdos publica* of Ceres at Puteoli on the bay of Naples died at the age of ninety-three, according to her tombstone.[53]

We have much better luck with the question of class. For present purposes, I will begin with a crude division of these women into freeborn (certain and uncertain), freed (certain and uncertain), and slave. Roman nomenclature makes this fairly easy to do: freeborn men and women were entitled to give their "filiation," their father's name, but slaves and freed slaves (who legally had no parents) were not. Instead, freed slaves gave their former owner's name in the "libertination" formula "freedwoman of So-and-so," and slaves gave their owner's name. Guesswork comes in when there is no filiation or libertination, and you have to go by the name itself, hence the category "uncertain." Of the 147 priestesses whose names are readable, 81 are certainly freeborn women, and 38 are uncertain freeborn. Of this group of 119 freeborns, which constitutes over 80 percent of the whole, 45 (38 percent) have some definite marker of elite status, in the form of money, other rank markers, or rank markers of their kin.

Freedwomen are obviously much rarer, but they are there. Ten priestesses also identify themselves clearly as freed slaves, and another fifteen are likely to have been so. There are even three priestesses definitely identified as slaves.[54] So we might assume that becoming a priestess was something a freeborn woman might expect and a freed slave might aspire to.

The freeborn/freed division here may be quite misleading, however. Even for the elite women, it is not always clear that they come from an aristocratic family or even from a family that has always been free. Most of the members of one honor-laden family have the Greek cognomina characteristic of freed slaves;[55] we can occasionally see the move from freed slave to town bigwig in a series of inscriptions. One set of probably linked inscriptions from Ovid's home town of Sulmo outlines the following family tree:[56]

C. Satrius Dexter = Cae(i)dia Ionice (3092)
sevir Augustalis | *sacerdos* of Ceres and Venus (3087)

C. Satrius Secundus = Hortensia
sacerdos of Isis (3091)

(3092) C. Satrius Secundus, quattuorvir and aedile — C. Satrius Hortensianus

Dexter's office of *sevir* marks him as a successful freedman, and his wife's Greek cognomen makes her a probable freedwoman. Their son marries a woman with a very high-class name, and their grandson holds a respectable junior magistracy.[57] The tombstone of one freeborn priestess, Ninnia Primilla, daughter of Quintus (Ninnius), bears a touching poem explaining that she sprang from humble origins: "I was born of freed parents, both of them, poor people in terms of their income, but of freeborn character."[58] She became priestess of Ceres in the small town of Pinna Vestina. On the other hand, of the twenty-five certain or uncertain freedwomen priestesses, eleven (44 percent) have some definite tie to money or public prestige. Ninnia Primilla's tombstone reminds us, if we needed a reminder, that slavery put a stigma on the person. Still, it was not an insuperable barrier to social success.

The inscriptions also give us fascinating insights into women acting together, sometimes across status boundaries. A stone from Aquileia, in the far eastern reaches of Cisalpine Gaul, commemorates a gift or gifts from four women:

> To Bona Dea Pagana ("of the village"?)
> Rufria Festa daughter of Gaius [Rufrius]
> Caesilia Scylace freedwoman of Quintus [Caesilius]
> *magistrae*
> with their own money;
> Decidia Pauli(na) daughter of Lucius [Decidius]
> and Pupia Peregrin(a) freedwoman of Lucius [Pupius]
> *ministrae*
> of Bona Dea
> built this temple
> with their own money.[59]

I should note that "with their own money" is a formula in this sort of inscription, not at all unique here.[60] It does underscore that aspect of Roman religion that has more to do with conspicuous consumption than with spirituality. This inscription also hints, however, at a priestessly hierarchy about which I yearn to know more. Why does each rank include one freeborn and one freedwoman? Was this a necessity or an accident? Clearly here being a freed slave is not what separates the *magistrae* from the *ministrae,* and all the women have "their own money," as this durable witness has been telling all viewers for two thousand years.[61]

A similar group from Furfo, northeast of Rome, lists two freeborn women, two freedwomen, and a slave woman, all *magis(trae)* of Venus. (They seem to be listed in descending status order.[62]) And a group from Tridentum, back in the far north of Italy, suggests another possible criterion for division in rank[63]:

Mag(istrae)
Cassia Marcella
Iuentia Maxsuma
Firmidia Modesta
Numonia Secunda
Min(istrae)
Iuentia Secunda
Manneia Pupa
Loreia Prima
Vettia Secunda

Two of these women—Iuentia Maxsuma and Secunda—are very likely sisters, and, in the quaint convention of old-fashioned Roman naming in which all sisters in a family have the same name with some numerical marker, they would be an older and a younger sister. Three of the *ministrae* in fact have such markers: Vettia is also "Number Two," and Manneia is "Doll" (that is, "Baby"?). One of the *magistrae* is a "Number Two," too, but it seems at least possible that women moved up in rank with age. What cult these women served is unspecified here. More than anything, they present a marked display of Roman naming in a part of Italy where a lot of the inscriptions are bilingual in Latin and the local Celtic dialect.

Most priestess groups, like this one, are made up of women of the same class.[64] Likewise, women make dedications within status boundaries: "the *matronae*" at Interamnia put up a statue together to honor a woman,[65] and so did the *matronae* of Surrentum.[66] Three probable freeborn women made a dedication to Bona Dea together at Tuder.[67] Sometimes priestesses are buried together[68] (possibly part of a larger burial ground). Very occasionally, we find female kin engaged on a religious project together: a freeborn woman and her mother who set up and ornamented a statue to Venus Augusta;[69] a pair of freeborn sisters who contributed generously to the temple of Demeter at Cumae around C.E. 7.[70] Some mother-daughter pairs hold the same priestesshood,[71] but a mother and her daughter-in-law hold different ones.[72] At Veii, her "most pious sisters" set up a major inscription in honor of Caesia Sabina, *sacerdos* of Fortuna Redux: "she alone of all women gave a banquet to the mothers of the magistrates and to [their] sisters and daughters and her fellow-townswomen of every rank, and during the days of the games and banquet of her husband she gave a bath [that is, admission to the baths] with free oil."[73]

But women also act with men. There are several priest/priestess pairs;[74] several kin groups (husband and wife);[75] the two sisters noted above, acting with their male kin;[76] and some women acting with men presiding or helping.[77] Where extended families are visible in inscriptions, we can sometimes see how priesthoods and similar offices run in families.[78] Women who were priestesses would be very likely to have male kin who held priesthoods and were likely to have seen religious activity as something men and women had in common, not something that separated them.[79]

It has become almost a commonplace to say that the municipal aristocracy defined itself through officeholding.[80] The main function of cult often seems to have been as a status marker in small towns and cities. The upper ranks of the local bourgeoisie would be honored by rank in a cult and would in turn express their gratitude by substantial grants to the town in the form of buildings, public banquets, gladiatorial games, or simple bundles of cash.[81] Or vice versa: giving the cash might result in a priesthood. (We must bear in mind that we have records only of people who could afford to have an inscription made.) As seen above, the correlation between holding a priestesshood and other elite markers is very high.

There also was a well-established connection between freed slaves' upward mobility and priesthoods. A freedman who made enough money could aspire to be a *sevir Augustalis*, a member of the board of six men annually appointed to oversee the cult of the emperor, and freedmen are conspicuous in the inscriptions as public-spirited members of the community. In many honorific decrees we see the sevirs and the priestesses bowing and curtseying to each other,[82] and indeed the female kin of *seviri* might well be priestesses.[83] As seen in the case of the *magistrae* and *ministrae* of Aquileia above, this might give a freed slave woman the chance to hobnob with the freeborn ladies, to be invited, as it were, to join the Ladies' Saturday Afternoon Society. Being a priestess was above all a way in which women became visible in public: thanked by groups of men, their names put up in large letters (sometimes carefully larger than other names),[84] giving multiple gifts "with their own money."

It would be a mistake, however, to think that this nexus of public service, status, prestige, and piety necessarily implies hypocrisy or lack of religious feeling. The separation of church and state is not a new idea, but when Christ said to render unto Caesar what is Caesar's and unto God what is God's, it was in direct contravention of the Roman idea of being a good citizen. A good citizen was, among other things, active in the temples—as indeed is the case in some modern communities. How can we document spiritual feeling, so long gone? The inscriptions are a sort of fossil, the stony remainder of an impulse strong enough to make someone spend money on a commemorative plaque to mark an action now lost to us. Another study might consider women's votive offerings, replicas of body parts and babies, which seem somehow more affect-laden. But the question of priestesses' actual involvement in religious cult is perhaps addressed by a small group of inscriptions that foreground sacrifice. A *magister* and *magistra* of Ceres set up an inscription on the "day of the sacrifice," April 19, 18 C.E.[85] The *ordo* of Capena, outside Rome, set up a stone to a *sacerdos* of Ceres "to honor the ceremonies most respectably provided."[86] A tombstone commemorating a *sacerdos* of Ceres and Venus at Sulmo, commissioned by her, has reliefs of a torch, an altar, a woman sacrificing, and a child holding an animal.[87] On the tombstone of a *sacerdos* of Ceres at Atina in southern Italy is carved a *culter,* the sacrificial knife, and a sow.[88] As Versnel notes, women did carry out blood sacrifices in the rites of Bona Dea;[89] as seen in Festus, priest and priestess used the same knife. And in an impassioned dedication to Venus Proba, one male worshiper gave her the epithet of *sacrificatrix.*[90]

Women's devotion to Goddesses (and some Gods) can also be seen in dedicatory inscriptions (see appendix B). The inscriptions surveyed include twenty-seven major donations, from Forum Vibii in the Ligurian Alps to Campania (but not further south), many of them statues and altars but also including temples, porticos, whole temple complexes, a fishpond, and a silver dish weighing one pound seven ounces. More humble (but not cheap) dedications seem to consist largely of the inscription itself, possibly with an ephemeral offering attached or made during an accompanying ritual. The dedications to Magna Mater provide a good illustration of this tie between writing and ritual, because they are often made *ob taurobolium,* "on the occasion of a taurobolium," and we know what this was: a ritual in which the initiate stood in a pit with a grating above him or her and bathed in the blood of a bull slaughtered above the grate. It seems safe to say that some religious feeling accompanied this experience.[91] Of the forty-one moderate offerings documented here, Bona Dea receives the largest number, five major and ten minor; Magna Mater is second, with ten offerings; and Juno, in various manifestations, and Mater Matuta are tied for third, with six each. Other well represented recipients include Venus and Ceres with four each, and the Matronae with three. A long list of other Deities with one or two dedications from women completes the roster—mostly, but not exclusively, Goddesses: Fonio (evidently an adjunct of Bona Dea),[92] the Parcae, Minerva, Fortuna, Demeter, Dea Obsequens, Diana Loch(ia?), Isis—and also Saturn, Silvanus, and Jupiter Optimus Maximus.

Some geographical patterns are discernible. The Matronae and Junones, singly or together, are popular in Cisalpine Gaul, probably due to the influence of nearby Celtic peoples.[93] Dedications to Mater Matuta come only from Campania, with one notable exception, while the dedications to Bona Dea come from every part of Italy. Two dedications to the Matronae are made by a woman for the sake of another woman.[94] Similarly, a freedwoman makes a dedication to Bona Dea "for the wellbeing of our (A)tel(li)a," evidently her former mistress.[95] A mother makes a dedication to Venus Aug(usta) in memory of her daughter.[96] A freedman, with his wife (a *flaminica*) and four children, sets up an elaborate dedication to Juno to honor his *patrona*.[97]

Most intriguing of all are what appear to be two cult sites in which women played an important role: a shrine of Minerva Memor ("Remembering") near Travi in Etruria,[98] and a women's shrine at Pisaurum with dedications to at least ten different Goddesses,[99] possibly dating to the second century B.C.E. The dedications at the shrine of Minerva Memor, in fact, include more by men (eleven) than by women (seven), though two of the men are there on behalf of female relatives. Several dedications indicate what was special about this manifestation of the Goddess:

> To Minerva Memor, Coelia Iuliana, freed from a serious illness by the grace of her medicines, placed this gift.[100]

> To Minerva Memor, Tullia Superiana, on the restoration of her hair, made good on her vow willingly and deservedly.[101]

> To Minerva Medica Cabardiacensis, Valeria Sammonia from Vercellae made good on her vow willingly and deservedly.[102]

This Minerva is a doctor to whom women and men came to be cured; the alternate cult title in the last dedication makes Minerva's function here explicit. (What had happened to Tullia's hair? We will never know.) Valeria Sammonia, like others who visited the shrine, has come a long way to see the Goddess; Vercellae is in Cisalpine Gaul.

The shrine at Pisaurum is attested by a group of thirteen plain stones in the shape of truncated pyramids, found in a field about a mile from Pisaurum in 1738, with "a quantity of votives of metal and terra cotta, large statues of terra cotta, mountains of offerings … and more than four thousand coins," as the *CIL* editor relays to us from the original report. Most of the stones hold only the name of a Deity, usually a Goddess: Fides, Juno, Juno Loucina, Mater Matuta (twice), Salus, Diana, Feronia, Juno Regina. Three women's names are given as dedicators—Cesula Atilia,[103] and Mania Curia and Pola Livia[104]—and one stone seems to indicate that the dedicators are the *matronae* of Pisaurum as a group.[105] The attestation of cult centers like this, however sketchy, fills out the picture suggested by better-known cults like that of Diana at Aricia or of Mater Matuta at Satricum—and here she is in Pisaurum on the Adriatic coast. Women might, then, have both a special local place, perhaps a grove or rural shrine, at which to worship, and a reason for travel to well-known cult centers, where they might meet and mix with women from all over Italy.

But the gender balance at the shrine of Minerva Memor reminds us that many cults mixed men and women together. The worship of Magna Mater involved an elaborate and coed hierarchy, as seen best in a series of inscriptions from Beneventum.[106] The officers include a *cymbal(istria) loco secundo,* a male *augur* and *sacerdos,* and two female *sacerdotes xv vir(ales),* one of whom shows up in two other inscriptions, where she has become *sac(erdos) prima;*[107] a female *sacerdos;*[108] a male *sacerdos* and his female *consacerdos;*[109] a male *primarius* and a female *sacerdos secundo loco xv vir(alis);*[110] and a *tympanistria.*[111] A priest and a *ministra* of Magna Mater made a joint dedication at Corfinium;[112] the "inferior officer" paid for a new statue of Bellona and one of the Goddess and had the Goddess gilded, along with the hair on the statue of Attis. Two women (one probably freed, one a slave) who celebrated their *taurobolia* at Puteoli were supervised by the same priest, Tiberius Claudius Felix, one in 134 C.E., one in 144 C.E.[113]

And many men set up dedications to Goddesses, especially to the Iunones and Matronae in the north. In so doing, they in turn were sometimes supervised by priestesses.[114] Men also served as priests of Goddesses: there is a group of *magistri* of Venus Iovia at Capua in 107 B.C.E.[115]

and a *magister* of the shrine of Juno at nearby Cubulteria.[116] Such a mix of genders is familiar from many aspects of religion in the city of Rome: the *pontifex maximus* and the Vestals, the *flamen* and the *flaminica,* the *flamines* of various Goddesses.[117] What is startling is the evidence of men's involvement in the cult of Bona Dea, the one Goddess whose cult at Rome was strictly off-limits to men.[118] There was a male priest of Bona Dea at Puteoli in C.E. 62, a freedman, Claudius Philadespotus, freedman of the emperor,[119] and a "*collegium* of male worshipers of the heavenly Bona Dea" at Venafrum.[120] One man set up a dedication to Bona Dea in Cubulteria,[121] ornamented with carvings of a man and a woman carrying baskets of fruit. All these sites are in Campania or on the road north of it. Perhaps the importance of Ceres and Venus on the Bay of Naples and of Mater Matuta at Satricum[122] and Cales (where she and Juno had temples)[123] somehow attracted some men to women's cults. But well to the north, at Spoletium, a grove of Bona Dea was "dedicated so that it might be permitted to be cleaned up again by men," though the names given in the inscription are those of the presiding priestess and of a woman, a centurion's wife, who dedicated an altar there.[124]

This fragmentary survey of some remnants of women's cult practice serves as a useful reality check. It reminds us that women held the title of "priestess" all over Italy. It suggests a relationship between status and religious office, with freeborn women predominant but freedwomen forming an important minority and sometimes participating alongside freeborn women. It confirms that public, high-prestige priestesshoods were indeed one way in which women were active in public, but it also shows that not all priestesshoods were like that and that priestesses can be found in some very small towns. As objects of devotion, Bona Dea and Mater Matuta are as well represented as Juno and Minerva. Women gave large sums of money to support cults. They also traveled to the country, or to far-off towns, in order to carry out their worship. And they worshiped often with other women but not infrequently alongside men.

There is one major absence, however. In all this testimony of women's worship, there is almost no trace of slave women. The only references are to one *ministra* of Bona Dea at Tuder, Quieta slave of Atia Pieris;[125] one *magistra* of Venus at Furfo, Sperata, slave of Aulus Munatidius, among a group of free *magistrae;*[126] one *magistra* at Grumentum who gave a chest and candelabrum to Juno and (because of Juno's relation to marriage?) identifies herself as "Pietas, slave-wife of Secundus."[127] A worshiper of Magna Mater, Thalame slave of Hosidia Afra, commemorates her *taurobolium.*[128] What religions did slave women practice? Some, especially the field slaves who had no hope of being freed, would have been captives who brought their religion with them. Many others would have been born in Italy, or bought from Greece or Asia for the household, positioned as outsiders who might someday move inside—but as slaves, they were literally outsiders inside the house. To understand their part of and in Roman women's religion, we must return to texts.

ROMAN WOMEN'S GROUPS

Texts can give us more of a story about women's religious practice, and we have nowhere else to turn if we want to ask further questions, such as, How can we interpret the inscriptions? What did Roman women think they were doing? What did other people think the women were doing? What was the meaning of women's cults? Unfortunately, these texts bring with them problems of their own. Not only do they provide pretty meager information, they are uniformly written by Roman and Greek men, who may well have their own axes to grind in the account they give of women's cults. For instance, Ross Kraemer usefully suggests that the recurring focus on chastity cults in some accounts may have more to do with the political agenda at the time they were written than with women's actual preferences and practices.[129] But these texts can at least attest to the attitudes of elite male writers toward women's cult, and sometimes they seem to provide us with plain statements of fact: what a priestess wore, where a temple was.

In order to talk about Roman women's religion meaningfully, we need to look for further evidence that Roman women thought of themselves as a group. It seems that some did, but the word "some" here is important. It is a common pitfall of scholarship on ancient women that we find ourselves saying "Roman women" or "Greek women" when what is meant is "freed or freeborn women of the citizen class"—as if slaves, of course, did not count or were not "women." This is a clear example of students of a society picking up that society's biases. So when I mean "free women of the citizen class," I will use the word "matronae," and I will say "Roman women" only when I mean "all female people living in Rome." As shown above, inscriptions conventionally indicate the status of people relative to slavery, and we have to keep slaves in mind.

Matronae first of all were clearly marked, like all inhabitants of the Roman world, by their dress. Paulus defines them as "those who had the right of wearing *stolae*,"[130] and we read elsewhere what this *stola* was like: a long dress—with a sort of flounce at the bottom, the *instita*—that thoroughly covered the woman, even to her feet. Satirists remarked on what a bad idea it is to chase after married women, because you can never see what you are getting; much better to go for a slave or freedwoman, who (they claim) wore clothes you could see through.[131] Matronae also had folkways of their own—a preferred drink, for example. Paulus, when talking about the wine called *murrina,* says "women [*mulieres*] call this *muriola,*" which is a diminutive form, like a nickname.[132] We read elsewhere that older women drank *passum,* raisin wine, and other sweet drinks.[133] And Pliny tells us that women (*mulieres*) chewed gum.[134] Aristocratic matronae of the early first century B.C.E. apparently kept an old-fashioned way of speaking.[135] Matronae rode around the city of Rome in special kinds of carriages, called *pilenta* or *carpenta,*[136] a right that was given them because as a group they gave gold to ransom the city from the Gauls.[137] In Nero's theater, women seem to have sat together—and among the poorer spectators.[138]

They had other special rights that had to do with their bodies. The reconstructed text of Festus tells us: "Matronae were not moved aside by magistrates, lest they should seem to be pushed or handled, or pregnant women be jostled."[139] And Valerius Maximus, who is something of an extremist on female chastity, says: "They did not permit one carrying out a summons to touch a matrona with his body; so that the *stola* should be left unviolated by the touch of an alien hand."[140]

The specialness of the matrona's body again comes into play when the title itself is being defined. Aulus Gellius, arguing against Aelius Melissus, quotes him as saying, "A 'matrona' is a woman who has given birth once; one who has done this more often is called a 'materfamilias'; just as a sow which has given birth once is called a *porcetra,* and one who has done it more often, a *scrofa.*"[141] Now Gellius heaps scorn upon this, suggesting that Aelius has made it all up, at least the part about women, but he goes on to say that it is more likely, as most authors he has consulted say: "that 'matrona' is a married woman, even if she has no children; and she is so called from the name *mater,* not yet achieved, but with the hope and omen of soon achieving it, whence *matrimonium* itself is named."[142]

So we see that, on the one hand, matronae have some group definition, and, on the other, that it is biologically determined; that is, it relates to their reproductive function.

We do have some specific instances of the matronae acting as a group, as the *ordo matronarum*—not always in a reproductive context.[143] One of the most interesting is one of the latest instances, in which Hortensia, daughter of the famous orator Hortensius (first century B.C.E.), pleaded the case of the *ordo* with the triumvirs, when they were being heavily taxed.[144] Hortensia's action has mythic justification going back to Rome's foundation myths: the Sabine women, Rome's first women, acted as a group to intercede between their fathers and their new husbands. Traditionally they were led by a woman called Hersilia,[145] and there is a further tradition that, in gratitude, Romulus named the thirty neighborhoods of Rome after the thirty women on the embassy.[146] A story told by Valerius Maximus takes the *ordo* back to the earliest Republic,[147] in the context of the story of Coriolanus's wife and mother, Volumnia and Veturia, and how the senate rewarded them for turning him back and protecting the city from invasion. The senate at this time supposedly gave the *ordo* signs to distinguish itself by: men should yield to them on the sidewalk; they could wear *vittae* as well as gold jewelry, purple clothing, and gilded flounces; and they also set up the temple and altar to Fortuna Muliebris. The matronae most famously acted jointly to lobby for the repeal of the Oppian law, which limited female practice of conspicuous consumption. Phyllis Culham interestingly ties in this sumptuary regulation of women with "increased religious activity and displays of wealth by women," possibly linked, during the Hannibalic wars. She also suggests that women were able to organize to resist the law through "contacts and skills" acquired through cult participation.[148] Again, we should ponder here not just the story but what our sources make of it. Valerius Maximus comments as follows: "But why do I speak further of women? Whom both the weakness of their intellect, and the denied pursuit of the more serious sort of work, encourages to bestow every effort on the more painstaking cultivation of themselves. . . ."[149]

But Valerius's obsession also leads him to comment on how the matronae voted for Sulpicia as the chastest matrona:

> Deservedly is Sulpicia, daughter of Servius Paterculus, wife of Q. Fulvius Flaccus, brought to the commemoration of men. When the senate had decreed, the Sibylline books having been inspected by the decemviri, that a statue of Venus Verticordia ("Who Turns the Heart") should be consecrated, so that the will of maidens and women might be turned more easily from lust to chastity; and from all the matronae one hundred, from one hundred again ten, having been selected by lot, passed judgment about the most holy woman [*sanctissima*], she was picked out of all [women] for her chastity.[150]

This supposedly happened in 112 B.C.E., fairly late in the Republic—a time when women were supposedly leaving behind their traditional restrictions.

Once again it is hard to know how thrilled to be with this story.[151] On the one hand you get women, together, apparently in large numbers, voting, and about something with which they are credited with expertise. They are being consulted about the state religion, by the men's legislative body, about Goddess worship. So far, so good. But then we get the casual equation of *castitas* ("purity, chastity") with *sanctitas* ("holiness"). And this degree of co-optation seems to be on a par with the Miss America pageant: look who approves (Valerius Maximus) and look what kind of Goddess this is. It seems to me that stories like this should be enough to make people think twice about the significance of Goddess worship to women. Not all Goddesses imply women's autonomy.

So what can be said about this evidence for Roman women's self-perception as a group? (1) Our evidence, as testimony to women's groups, is just terrible. Scholars who work in more modern periods have the benefit of first-person testimony from women, and it is overwhelming to realize that such evidence is almost entirely lacking for pre-Christian Rome, with the exception of inscriptions, which are necessarily limited in scope. Moreover, it is almost impossible to trace changes in Roman women's groups over time, because the evidence is so fragmentary that we have to pick up a piece here and a piece there. (2) What we seem to be seeing is that matronae at Rome did have the sort of network, extending over at least several centuries, that did enable them to act in groups on occasion, but that such groups were heavily enmeshed in an ideological system that was always ready to belittle them, that approved of them only insofar as they ratified the social assessment of themselves as the property of individual men for the production of children, and that saw them as always prone to lapses into unchastity. (3) Moreover, we must now be on the lookout for the practical implications of the classism built into this system. What about all the Roman women who did not count as matronae? Did they have any group unity? Did they feel solidarity with matronae? How did they fit into the ideological system in which the matronae were enmeshed?

One answer to these questions may be summed up in a brief story of a pair of women, both from Capua, who helped the Romans out during the Punic Wars. One was a materfamilias, and one was a *meretrix,* a prostitute; one "sacrificed daily for the safety of our army," the other gave food to the captured Roman soldiers. The senate, after the Romans won, rewarded these women. Valerius Maximus, typically, comments: "How marvelous that the fathers [that is, the senators] took the time, during such rejoicing, to thank two humble women."[152] But we note the way their labor is divided: the sacrifice belongs to the matrona.

The complexity of Roman cultural co-optation of women through religion may further be illustrated by a deceptive passage from Petronius's *Satyricon,* the Roman novel about the escapades of three young men in Neronian Italy. During a dinner party held at the home of the vulgar, nouveau-riche freed slave Trimalchio, one of the guests complains that things are not what they used to be:

> Why, nobody thinks that heaven is heaven, nobody fasts, nobody gives a rap for Jupiter, but everybody is counting up their goods when their eyes are covered [in prayer]. In the old days women used to go in their *stolae,* barefoot, to the hill, with their hair hanging down, and their minds pure, and pray to Jupiter for water. And so just like that it rained buckets, then or never, and they all went home like drowned rats.[153]

This picture of married women's good behavior in the good old days comes not from some Cato-like Roman aristocrat but from a freed slave with a Greek name, Ganymedes—perhaps a hint at his employment as cupbearer and sex toy by a former master. By his own account, he arrived in Italy as a boy from Asia Minor,[154] an origin widely associated in Roman elite texts with effeminacy and cultural degeneracy. Moreover, he is not a real freed slave but one imagined by Petronius, who was probably a Roman noble at Nero's court. Can we believe that his speech represents a real social attitude among freed slaves in Roman Italy? It does not seem impossible. The epigraphic evidence surveyed above suggests that some freedwomen were indeed involved alongside matronae in public cult. So, alongside the class *divisions* to be examined below, we might also keep in mind an ongoing system of class *transition,* in which women formerly slaves moved up in the religious world, while their husbands, perhaps, urged them on.[155]

WOMEN'S INDIVIDUAL CULT PRACTICE AT ROME

As we move now into looking at evidence for Roman women's religion, we are on our guard. We have already seen that Goddess worship is hardly a guarantee of feminist consciousness. As we look at the circumstances of ritual in which Roman women would have gotten to know each other, we need to consider ways in which the centrality of the body in women's religion ties in with problems of class. On the one hand, the evidence is abundant that we have in Rome a society with extended networks of kin, stretching not only all over the city but across the Italian countryside, reinforced by all sorts of political and economic obligations.[156] On the other, this coexisted with and depended on another society, made up of slaves and freed slaves and characterized by broken kinship, cultural, and ethnic bonds. Religious rites would have meant very different things to women in the two groups. Sandra Joshel[157] shows how slave child nurses might have experienced lopsided and painful affective ties to an owner/child, with comparisons to the situation in American slavery. Certainly slave women might have had good reason to fear or distrust free women as well as men in their households, and, in a system in which their bodies were the sexual property of the master, would have experienced their own bodies very differently from the way free women did.[158]

I look first here at evidence on individual women's participation in ritual.

A story in Valerius Maximus testifies to a rite of passage for Roman citizen girls that also suggests a special intergenerational bond:

> But Caecilia, wife of Metellus [this probably dates the story to 212 B.C.E.], while she sought wedding omens for her sister's daughter, a grown maiden, in the traditional manner [*more prisco*], by an all-night vigil, made the omen herself. For when she had been sitting in a certain shrine for this reason for some time, and no utterance relevant to the purpose had been heard, the girl, tired out by the long delay of standing, asked her aunt (*matertera*, "mother's sister") that she give her a place to sit down for a bit; the aunt replied to her: "Truly, I willingly leave my seat for you." Which statement, made out of kindness, turned out to be a sure sign: since Metellus, not much after this, when Caecilia had died, married the maiden of whom I am speaking.[159]

The epigraphic evidence occasionally shows us sisters or mother-daughter pairs engaged in cult activity together. This story suggests further that there was a tradition at Rome that bound together each (citizen) woman with her sister's daughter, at least in that the two of them participated together in an important rite of passage for the young woman. Roman citizen women were expected to marry, and their first marriage would normally take place at or soon after puberty.[160] Thus, this ritual would help to mark the girl's movement into adulthood.[161]

The concern with marriage is reflected in the stories about Deities worshiped especially by women. The temple of Fortuna Muliebris, at the fourth milestone outside of Rome on the via Latina, supposedly marked the occasion when Coriolanus was talked out of attacking Rome by his mother and wife.[162] Festus says that it was a *nefas* ("sin") for the cult statue there to be touched except by a *univira*—a woman who had only ever had one husband.[163] Likewise, in the temple of patrician Pudicitia in the Forum Boarium, along with the temple of plebeian Pudicitia in the Vicus Longus, it was a *nefas* for any woman to sacrifice who had either never been married or had been married more than once.[164] The shrine of Dea Viriplaca specialized in a sort of couples counseling[165]—one-sided, judging by her name, "Goddess Husband-Pleaser."

Livy tells the tale of the founding of the cult of plebeian Pudicitia[166] as the story of a patrician woman who marries down, is barred from the cult by the other matronae, and goes off and starts her own shrine at home. He also says the cult has lapsed due to being "made common by polluted [*pollutis*] women, not only matronae but women of every order." Writing under Augustus, Livy is looking back three hundred years, to a time when "patrician" and "plebeian" were still meaningful class divisions. To him, the divided cult means the marking of a division between levels of women. When the process of division is pursued, however, it results in the breakdown and disappearance of the cult itself, which must exclude in order to have meaning. "Polluted," then, means "insufficiently chaste."[167]

Women also are said to have sacrificed especially to Goddesses of childbirth. At one point, when Aulus Gellius is talking about breech births at some length, he quotes Varro as saying:

> Since . . . women then labor with more difficulty, for the sake of praying to avert this danger, altars have been set up at Rome to the two Carmentae, of whom one is called "Postverta," the other "Prorsa," from the power and name of straight and backward birth.[168]

Paulus says that pregnant women sacrificed to the nymph Egeria—Numa's friend—according to him, because of her name: *e-gerere* means "push out" in Latin.[169] Three statues in front of the shrine of Minerva on the Capitol were called the *nixi di*, the "straining Gods," and they were thought to preside over the labor of pregnant women, though Festus thinks their odd posture was derived from their former location in Greece, where they had been seated at a table. Here Romans superimpose on borrowed Gods a meaning having to do with childbirth.[170]

Of course Juno was the chief Goddess of all these things. Here we pick up another bit of information about class distinction in religious practice:

> "*Paelices*" is a name indeed now given to those who lie under those not belonging to them, not only women, but even males. The ancients properly called a woman a *p(a)elex*, who married a man who (already) had a wife. For this class of women indeed a penalty was established by Numa Pompilius in this law: "Let a *paelex* not touch the altar of Juno; if she does, let her sacrifice a female lamb to Juno with her hair let down."[171]

Now a *paelex* was a concubine, a mistress, a kept woman, and the word is often construed in Latin with the name of the wife depending on it in the genitive; for example, Philomela, in Ovid, describes herself as *paelex sororis*, "my sister's *paelex*."[172] It has connotations of rivalry, of "the other woman." But normally the *paelex* is a slave, or a freedwoman, not a threat to the wife. Why can she not touch Juno's altar? I think two things are operating here. (1) If we focus on the words "not belonging to them," we can suppose the *paelex* takes the blame for the lack of symmetry in the couple's monogamy. In literature, Juno was always depicted as resentful of Jupiter for his affairs. (2) The *paelex* is contaminated by her status, by the very "lying under someone." In Roman sexuality, it is a commonplace that slaves are thought less of, de-grad-ed, not only for their lower social status, but because they have been sexual common property. The one penetrated ("not only women, but even males") is thereby stained.[173] Certainly one of the few first-person women's voices we have from Rome, that of the elegist Sulpicia, includes a protest against her lover's betrayal of her, a citizen woman, with a female slave, a "slut with a wool-basket."[174]

Juno was worshiped at Rome as Iuno Iuga because she joined (*iug-*) marriages.[175] A street was named for her altar, and matronae worshiped her as Opigena, because she gave help (*ops*) to women in labor.[176] And she was especially worshiped as Juno Lucina, the main Goddess of childbirth. Paulus says that matronae celebrate the first of March, the Matronalia, because it is the anniversary of the opening of the shrine of Juno Lucina.[177] The explanations of her name, Lucina, produce some oddities. Varro says:

> . . . the moon is called "Noctiluca" on the Palatine, because from there her temple shines at night. . . .[178] But she is also called, by the Latins, Juno Lucina; either because she is also the earth, and shines (*lucet*); or because from her light in which conception occurs to the one in which she has brought forth into the light (*produxit in lucem*), the moon helps (*luna iuvat*) until she has brought [the child] into the light (*lucem*), and the name "Juno Lucina" is thus made up from *iuvando* and *luce*. From this fact women in childbirth invoke her; for the moon is the guide of those being born, because hers are the months. It is clear that the women of old times saw this, because women gave credit for their eyebrows most of all to this Goddess.[179]

Festus[180] also has this: apparently the idea is that the eyebrows protect the eyes, we see light through eyes, and Juno Lucina protects light. The younger Pliny[181] provides instances of mirrors as the kind of gifts given by women in particular, to Juno in particular, and perhaps we might connect this with Juno Lucina and light.

WOMEN'S FESTIVALS

We move now from women's individual worship to festivals that were special to women. The Roman year was, of course, defined by the procession of days marked by religion,[182] and women played a part in many of the general festival days. Indeed, Roman women should be imagined like women in Orthodox Judaism, their lives patterned by carefully observed ritual—though the pattern could be expanded. Outside of Rome, each town might have celebrated some of these festivals and would presumably also have had some of its own. A list of only those festivals that would have had a special significance for women would include:[183]

January 11, 15, Carmentalia. Carmenta or Carmentis, a Goddess of childbirth, had a temple at the foot of the Capitol, near the Porta Carmentalis, and her own *flamen.* Her altars and her powers over breech births have been noted above, though for Varro she is a double Goddess.

February 1, Juno Sospita. In a girls' ritual at Lanuvium, blindfolded girls feed cakes to the snake in the sacred grove; their proven virginity ensures a good crop.

February 15, Lupercalia. Young aristocratic men run naked through the streets of Rome, flogging the bystanders, especially women,[184] with thongs of bloody goatskin from the goat they have just sacrificed.

February 21, Feralia. Old women and girls propitiate the Silent Goddess, the mother of the Lares.[185] This was part of a three-festival period of placating the dead that took up most of February.

March 1, Matronalia. Sacred to Juno Lucina; this is the date on which her temple on the Esquiline was dedicated by the matronae. Husbands pray for the health of their wives and give them presents; the wives get dressed up, pay visits, probably go to the temple, and entertain their slaves and serve them food.

March 17, Liberalia. This is the festival of the God Liber, sometimes associated with the Greek Dionysus; in the town of Caere, his female counterpart Libera is worshiped as well. At Rome, old women sit selling sweet cakes and sacrificing on small altars. At Lavinium, according to Augustine, a matrona garlands the large phallus that represents Liber.

April 1, Veneralia. Upper-class and lower-class women worship the Goddess Fortuna Virilis in separate groups, some in the men's baths. They also bathe the cult statue of the Goddess. This is also the festival of Venus Verticordia.

April 23, Vinalia. During this wine festival, prostitutes sacrifice to Venus Erycina.

April 27, Floralia. Games are held, including theatrical shows at which prostitutes dance naked.

May 1, Bona Dea. This temple cult festival includes the offering of a sow; rituals involving wine; and wreathing the Goddess's head with vine leaves.

June 9-15, Vestalia. Barefooted matronae bring offerings to the temple of Vesta.

June 11, Matralia. Rites are held at the temple of Mater Matuta in the Forum Boarium, where only *univirae* can decorate her statue. Matronae bake special cakes.[186] Matronae gather in the temple, a slave woman is let in, and the matronae drive her out by slapping her. They then pick up and cuddle the child of a sister.

July 6, Fortuna Muliebris. *Univirae* decorate the cult statue (?).

July 7, Nonae Caprotinae ("Fig-tree Nones"). Slave women hold a feast and mock battle outside the city, commemorating a time when Roman slave women saved the matronae from being raped by an invading enemy force by standing in for them. Matronae and slave women worship Juno Caprotina.[187]

August 13, Diana on the Aventine. Processions of women march out from Rome to Diana's cult center at Aricia, holding burning torches, to thank the Goddess for answering prayers. Votive offerings at Aricia include "models of reproductive organs and women with infants." Slaves have the day off. Women wash their hair.

November 13, Feronia. Freedwomen make an expiatory gift to the Goddess Feronia, a patron of slaves, at her temple in the Campus Martius. Matronae make a gift to Juno Regina on the Aventine.

December 3, Bona Dea. A ritual is held in the home of the wife of one of the consuls or praetors, attended by Vestals, matronae, and female musicians (probably slaves). Men are strictly barred from the ceremonies, which involved drinking unwatered wine. (The location in a private house must have limited the number of attendees.)

This calendar emphasizes the degree to which Roman women, like Roman men, must have measured their lives from festival to festival. The rhythms of the women's year synchronize with those of the culture as a whole, with a preponderance of activity in the late winter through early summer. Combined with household cult and personal religion, this program must have kept women busy and conscious of religion as a factor in their lives.

Living through the calendar also would have contributed greatly to Roman women's sense of who belonged where. As Richard Gordon says of municipal cult, "divisions of the local society are repeatedly rehearsed."[188] Juvenal in his sixth satire[189] describes the Bona Dea rites as bestial orgies in which women get drunk, dance lewdly, and finally cry out for men to be brought in to service them sexually. There is the same prurient curiosity as in Aristophanes' *Women at the Thesmophoria,* a need to know what it is that women do when they are alone together. But Juvenal gives one suggestive detail: He describes a competition in dancing between the aristocratic women and prostitutes.[190] And slave "women" form part of the transvestite imitation of the Bona Dea cult in his second satire as well.[191] Such a two-class distinction shows up in several other women's rituals—most notably, the Matralia (matronae slap slave woman) but also at the Matronalia (matronae serve slaves), at the cult of Fortuna Virilis at the Veneralia (matronae and lower-class women worship in different places), on the Nonae Caprotinae (legend of the substitution of slaves for matronae), and in the offering to Feronia (matronae offer to Juno instead). That is, six of seventeen festivals involving special women's rituals include a marked element in which women are divided into classes (seven, counting Bona Dea twice). Moreover, several more festivals depend on class identity: The Vinalia is just for prostitutes, Diana's day off is just for slaves, and the cult of Fortuna Muliebris is just for *univirae.* No prostitutes walk to the temple on the Vestalia (they could not go near the Vestals anyway); no matronae dance at the Floralia. The only festivals that seem to cross these boundaries are the Carmentalia (for all women who give birth) and the Lupercalia (the goatskin-thong treatment seems to be for everyone), and it seems that any woman could march in the procession to Diana at Aricia.

Putting the calendar together with textual accounts, however biased, begins to give a body to the scattered bones of the inscriptions. The remarkable description of the cult of Mater Matuta—surely connected with the ritual whereby aunts and nieces wait together for an omen of marriage—suggests what events may have accompanied the dedications to her. Archaeological work on her temple in Satricum has recovered terra-cotta votive offerings like those for Diana at Aricia, along with mother-child statuettes. There are over ninety of them in the museum at Capua, and many of these show a seated woman with multiple babies—as many as a dozen.[192] In the Roman material on witches and negative stereotypes of women, there is great anxiety over fostering of children by women other than their mothers. Surely this women's ritual is aimed at affirming kin ties, while emphasizing class barriers. Where there is no mother, aunts are good, nurses are bad.[193] The need of matronae to mark their superiority to slave women determines the shape of Roman women's religion.

In large part these festivals remind us of the way women were marked off into classes, by their dress and so on, according to the degree of access they allowed to their bodies. Roman women's rituals insist on the danger of the permeability of women's bodies, and the high price to be paid for wrongful openness. Perhaps the best instance of this idea comes in a story about one of the Vestal Virgins, who for ordinary women must have served as a constant reminder of the possibility of a completely closed body and the very high price to be paid for its breach.

The worst crime for a Vestal Virgin was to be unchaste; they were punished for this by being buried alive. So, naturally, if a Vestal was accused of unchastity, she took it seriously. Valerius Maximus tells the story of one who did, the Vestal Tuccia:

> By the same sort of aid the chastity of Tuccia, the Vestal Virgin, accused of the crime of unchastity, emerged when obscured by the cloud of slander. She, with the consciousness of her certain purity, dared to seek hope of her safety by a dangerous proof. For she took up a sieve [a ritual implement in Vesta's cult],[194] and said, "Vesta, if I have always moved chaste hands to your rites, let it be that I may take up water from the Tiber in this, and carry it to your temple." Boldly and rashly the vow of the priestess was cast; the very nature of things gave way.[195]

It seems to me that this story of a holy woman sets up the model for all Roman women; they are permeable yet must be impermeable, they must carry water in a sieve. That matronae accepted this symbolic logic, enacted it in their rituals, and enforced it on girls and on nonmatronae seems amply attested. This suggests further that the negative images of the monstrous female may well have been fostered by women. The two systems are complementary not only in terms of their symbolism but in terms of their social function.

What, then, is the bottom line for Roman women's religion? The focus on chastity always reminds me of values within some modern Italian cultures, as seen, for example, among the Sicilian townspeople in Maureen Giovannini's study.[196] This may well be a useful analogy, in that it is hard to doubt that the townspeople have internalized the values their code imposes on women. We need not doubt that Roman women—probably from household slaves on up—shared ideals, though we might see the Roman state as using their bodies to think with.[197] Thus, when we see women proudly connecting religious leadership with affluence and upward mobility, we must also realize that the religion itself was ambivalent about femaleness. Still, when women put their cult titles on a tombstone or dedication along with their names, they were claiming that title as part of their identity, as Sandra Joshel has shown for freed slaves' identification with their labor. The name of priestess is, as we say, written on their grave.

NOTES

I am embarrassed to thank the editors for patience beyond what anyone should expect. Their encouragement was truly Goddesslike. This chapter depends on research carried out under a grant from the even more patient National Endowment for the Humanities in 1987-88, for which I am still extremely grateful. Audiences at Haverford College, Princeton University, Rollins College, Texas Tech University, the Huntington Library, Occidental College, and the Annenberg Institute in Philadelphia, as well as at the Goddess Conference at Claremont, made helpful comments. Special thanks to Daniel Boyarin, Howard Eilberg-Schwartz, Ross Kraemer, Joseph Russo, Chava Weissler, to Sheryl Conkelton for aid nobly rendered, and most of all to Karen King, again and always.

Translations throughout are my own except as noted.

1. Notable recent contributions to the problem include Brouwer, *Bona Dea*; French, "Cult of Mater Matuta"; Stehle, "Venus, Cybele and the Sabine Women"; Versnel, "Festival for Bona Dea." Ross Kraemer's overviews in *Her Share of the Blessings* (chapters 5 and 7) provide an invaluable orientation and cover far more ground than can this more narrowly focused study. Gagé's *Matronalia* was far ahead of its time and constitutes the most important study of Roman women's cult, but is naturally not informed by feminist theory. The most recent handbook on Roman religion (Latte, *Römische Religionsgeschichte*) says very little about women. Latte's index includes a total of two entries under "Frauen" ("women" were excluded from the cult of Silvanus; and of Hercules). On the experience of slave women in the Matralia, his only comment is: "Sklavinnen waren, wie selbstverständlich, von einem Fest ausgeschlossen, das der legitimen Weiterführung der Familie galt" ("As is obvious, slave women were excluded from the celebration, since it had to do with the continuation of the family," pp. 97-98). Compare the discussion of the Matralia below. In *Roman Festivals*, Warde Fowler has much more to say and is especially interested in women's cult as related to the Earth Mother and fertility. The index of Ferguson in *Religions of the Roman Empire* contains no entry under "Women," "Mater Matuta," or "Bona Dea." Oddly, both Beard ("Priesthood in the Roman Republic") and Gordon ("From Republic to Principate" and "Veil of Power") make little mention of women in religious office.

For a general introduction to Roman women, including religion, see Fantham, et al., *Women in the Classical World*, 216-42, with illustrations.

2. See Richlin, "Pliny's Brassiere."

3. See, for comparison, e.g., du Boulay, "Women"; Giovannini, "Woman";

Buckley and Gottlieb, "Critical Appraisal," 13, on the enjoyability of menstrual seclusion.

4. On the postmodernist ethnographer's dilemma, see Rosaldo, "From the Door of His Tent"; for feminist precursors, critiques, and updates, see Abu-Lughod, "Can There Be a Feminist Ethnography?"; Mascia-Lees, et al., "Postmodernist Turn in Anthropology"; and Shapiro, "Anthropology and the Study of Gender." For an overview of this issue from the perspective of ancient history and feminism, see Richlin, "Ethnographer's Dilemma."

5. Kraemer, *Her Share of the Blessings*, 80-92.

6. "Priesthood in the Roman Republic," 41-47.

7. "Religion of Traditional Ashkenazic Women," 86-87.

8. See Richlin, "Pliny's Brassiere."

9. Faraone and Obbink, *Magika Hiera*, passim, give an idea of what might be said.

10. See Beard, "Sexual Status of Vestal Virgins."

11. Some can be found in Kraemer, *Maenads*.

12. Sources referred to below include: the remains of the book *On the Latin Language* by M. Terentius Varro, an upper-class Roman of the first century B.C.E.; Dionysius of Halicarnassus, a Greek rhetorician at Rome whose *Roman Antiquities* began to appear in 7 B.C.E.; Valerius Maximus, who put together a collection of *Memorable Deeds and Sayings* for the use of orators in the early first century C.E.; the *Roman Questions* of the Greek biographer and moral philosopher Plutarch (before 120 C.E.); and Aulus Gellius, whose *Attic Nights*, a collection of brief ruminations on topics of interest, came out around 180 C.E. Ovid's *Fasti*, written very early in the first century C.E., was a long poem on the Roman religious calendar, complete only through the end of June.

13. For example, 282-84L.

14. See Gordon, "From Republic to Principate," 184-91, esp. 189 n. 29, for another perspective on the intellectual climate that produced books like Verrius's, which he sees as part of a process of "institutionalizing unintelligibility" (189), the information purveyed by these books being mostly "obsolescent" (188). Festus and Verrius seem to have felt this themselves; see Festus 242L. References to Paulus ex Festo herein are to pages in the Teubner text edited by W. M. Lindsay, hence "282L" for "Lindsay, page 282." This text has not been translated into English.

15. See 152L.

16. See 153L.

17. For other examples, see: *Manare solem*, 150L vs. 151L (reference to Matuta gone); *Nothum*, 182L vs. 183L; *Pietati*, 228L vs. 229L; *Propius sobrino*, 260L vs. 261L (female kin disappear); *Plebeiae pudicitiae*, 270L vs. 271L; *Praebia*, 276L vs. 265L; *Probrum virginis Vestalis*, 277L (gone in Paulus); *Pudicitiae signum*, 282L vs. 283L; *Praefericulum*, 292L vs. 293L (reference to Ops Consiva gone); *Redimiculum*, 336L (gone in Paulus); *Strittavum*, 414L vs. 415L (female kin disappear); *Salias virgines*, 439L (gone in Paulus); *Tutulum*, 484-86L vs. 485L; Tarpeia's statue, 496L (gone in Paulus). For Paulus importing (male-male) homophobia into an "excerpt," see 284L vs. 285L, *puer quem quis amabat* vs. *puer qui obscene ab aliquo amabatur*.

18. The present study is also limited in its epigraphic scope: I have surveyed all inscriptions from Roman Italy (*CIL* volumes 5, 9, 10, 11, 14) but not from the

city of Rome itself (*CIL* 6) or Ostia (*CIL* supp.). And I have used only the *CIL*, without searching more recent sources of inscriptions. Compare the sample in Forbis, "Women's Public Image," which uses sources beyond the *CIL* but omits *CIL* 5.

19. *De Agri Cultura* 143.1, in Versnel, "Festival for Bona Dea," 31. Versnel is here using the translation of William Davis Hooper and Harrison Boyd Ash in the Loeb Classical Library edition of *De Agri Cultura* (Cambridge, Mass.: Harvard University Press, 1960).

20. Cato, *De Agri Cultura*, 143.2.

21. Varro, *De Lingua Latina* 6.14, cf. Ovid, *Fasti* 3.763-67.

22. Ovid, *Fasti* 2.571-82.

23. Paulus 278L, 280L.

24. Dionysius of Halicarnassus 2.22.

25. Paulus, 4L.

26. See Paulus 455L.

27. See Festus 446L.

28. See Festus 439L.

29. See 232L, 303L, 426L.

30. On the meaning of *sacerdos*, see Beard, "Priesthood in the Roman Republic," 43-47.

31. Varro, *On the Latin Language*, 5.130.

32. See Festus 152L, 342L, 368L.

33. Festus 484L.

34. Aulus Gellius 10.26-30; Plutarch, *Roman Questions*, 285a.

35. Plutarch, *Roman Questions*, 276e.

36. Paulus 101L.

37. Paulus 472L.

38. See 60L.

39. Valerius Maximus 1.1.1.

40. On epigraphic evidence for women's participation in public life during the empire, see MacMullen, "Women in Public"; Van Bremen, "Women and Wealth"; and Forbis, "Women's Public Image." For priestesses, see MacMullen, op. cit., 211-12, 213, 215; Forbis, op. cit., 500, 501-2.

41. The old standard Latin dictionary, Lewis and Short, gave no indication of the commonness of the female forms of these titles in the context of religion. The new *Oxford Latin Dictionary* gives a fair account of *magistra* but relies on textual instances of *ministra*. For *magistrae* and *ministrae* in the *collegia* of Bona Dea, see Kraemer, *Her Share of the Blessings*, 88, following Brouwer, *Bona Dea*, 280-81.

42. *CIL* 11.5223.

43. *CIL* 10.6518.

44. *CIL* 10.810, 811, 812, 813; see MacMullen, "Women in Public," 209, for a quick description of Eumachia's activities. For illustration of her statue see Fantham, et al., *Women in the Classical World*, 335, fig. 12.4.

45. *CIL* 10.39.

46. *CIL* 9.3518, 5295.

47. *CIL* 5.3928.

48. *CIL* 11.6354.

49. *CIL* 9.1153.

50. Plutarch, *Life of Numa* 10.1-2; Aulus Gellius 1.12.
51. *CIL* 9.307.
52. *CIL* 9.4460.
53. *CIL* 10.1829.
54. *CIL* 9.3518, 10.202, 11.4635.
55. *CIL* 10.4790.
56. *CIL* 9.3087, 3091, 3092.
57. On the sevirate, see Gordon, "Veil of Power," 205 ("freedman [*sic*] aping their social superiors"), 208. In Petronius's *Satyricon*, both Trimalchio and his friends Hermeros and Habinnas are *seviri* (30.2, 57.6, 65.5, 71.12).
58. *CIL* 9.3358.
59. *CIL* 5.762.
60. For the same phrase in Greek inscriptions, see MacMullen, "Women in Public," 216.
61. On this inscription, see Brouwer, *Bona Dea*, 116-17, 281. The inscription is only poetically durable, because it is now lost. Brouwer found a preponderance of freed slaves in the worship and priesthood of Bona Dea across the Roman Empire. This is markedly at odds with the proportions in the overview of women's worship presented here.
62. *CIL* 9.3518; cf. 5.757, from Aquileia, one freeborn and two uncertain freed *magistrae* of Bona Dea.
63. *CIL* 5.5026.
64. Priestess groups: *CIL* 5.4458 (one certain and two probable freeborn); 9.3167 (both probable freeborn); 9.5295 (both certain freed); 10.39 (both certain freeborn); 10.5192 (all uncertain freed); 10.6511 with 6518 (two certain freeborn).
65. *CIL* 9.5071.
66. *CIL* 10.688.
67. *CIL* 11.4636.
68. *CIL* 10.4789-91, possibly part of a larger burial ground.
69. *CIL* 5.835.
70. *CIL* 10.3685, 3688.
71. *CIL* 9.1153 and 1154; probably 10.1074.
72. *CIL* 9.3087, 3092, seen above.
73. *CIL* 11.3811. Reading *matribus c vir* as "mothers of the *centumviri*." The *centumviri* were judicial magistrates at Rome and in some towns, of which Veii was one (*CIL* 11.3801, 3805).
74. *CIL* 5.3922, 3923, both at pagus Arusnatium; 9.3146; 11.3196.
75. *CIL* 5.6514, 10.1549.
76. *CIL* 10.3685.
77. *CIL* 5.6412.
78. *CIL* 5.3926-28, 3962, 7788.
79. On women's public activities with their male kin, see Forbis, "Women's Public Image," 502-4, and in general Hallett, "Women as *Same* and *Other*."
80. See MacMullen, "Women in Public," 211-12; Gordon, "Veil of Power," 224-31.
81. *CIL* 9.1153, 14.2804.
82. *CIL* 10.51, 10.54, 11.5752, 11.6172.
83. *CIL* 5.3438, 10.3087, 3092.

84. *CIL* 5.4458, 9.5841, 10.1074.
85. *CIL* 11.3196.
86. *CIL* 11.3933.
87. *CIL* 9.3089.
88. *CIL* 10.5073; cf. similar carvings, 10.129, 10.1812, both also priestesses of Ceres.
89. See "Festival for Bona Dea," 32, 43, 48.
90. *CIL* 10.3692.
91. See Ferguson, *Religions of the Roman Empire*, 104-6, for a full description. Women's *taurobolia* and *criobolia* (ram sacrifice) are commemorated in *CIL* 9.1538, 1539, 1541, 1542; 10.1596, 1597, 6075.
92. *CIL* 5.757, 758.
93. See Ferguson, *Religions of the Roman Empire*, 16-17 and fig. 8, for a brief description and illustration.
94. *CIL* 5.4134, 4137.
95. *CIL* 9.5421.
96. *CIL* 5.836.
97. *CIL* 5.7811.
98. *CIL* 11.1292-1309.
99. *CIL* 11.6294-6302.
100. *CIL* 11.1297.
101. *CIL* 11.1305.
102. *CIL* 11.1306.
103. *CIL* 11.6298.
104. *CIL* 11.6301.
105. *CIL* 11.6300.
106. *CIL* 9.1538-42.
107. *CIL* 9.1538; cf. 1541, 1542.
108. *CIL* 9. 1539.
109. *CIL* 9.1540.
110. *CIL* 9.1541.
111. *CIL* 9.1542.
112. *CIL* 9.3146.
113. *CIL* 10.1596, 1597.
114. *CIL* 10.39, 6640.
115. *CIL* 10.3776.
116. *CIL* 10.4620.
117. See chart in Beard, "Priesthood in the Roman Empire," 20-21.
118. So also Kraemer, *Her Share of the Blessings*, 53, following Brouwer, *Bona Dea*, 258; also in Warde Fowler, *Roman Festivals*.
119. *CIL* 10.1549.
120. *CIL* 10.4849.
121. *CIL* 10.4615.
122. See Bettini, *Anthropology and Roman Culture*, 77-78.
123. *CIL* 10.4650, 4660.
124. *CIL* 11.4767.
125. *CIL* 11.4635.
126. *CIL* 9.3518.

127. *CIL* 10.202.

128. *CIL* 10.1597.

129. Kraemer, *Her Share of the Blessings*, 55, 58-60.

130. See 112L.

131. On Roman women's dress, see Sebesta and Bonfante, *World of Roman Costume*. For *vittae* (fillets, or hair ribbons) and *instita* as the symbol of a chaste Roman matrona, see Ovid, *Ars Amatoria* 1.31-32. For satirical advice to avoid covered-up matronae, see Horace, *Satires*, 1.2.69-95.

132. See Paulus 131L.

133. See Varro in Non. 551M.

134. *Natural History* 22.45.

135. Cicero, *De Oratore* 3.45.

136. Paulus 225L, Festus 282L.

137. See Festus 138L.

138. Calpurnius Siculus, *Ecl.* 7.

139. See Festus 142L.

140. Valerius Maximus 2.1.5.

141. Aulus Gellius 18.6.4.

142. Aulus Gellius 18.6.8.

143. On the powers, duties, and privileges of Roman matronae, see, above all, Gagé, *Matronalia*; also Dixon, *Roman Mother*; Hallett, *Fathers and Daughters*, "Women as *Same* and *Other*"; Treggiari, *Roman Marriage*.

144. Valerius Maximus 8.3.3.

145. Aulus Gellius 13.23 records the supposed wording of her prayer.

146. Dionysius of Halicarnassus 2.45, 47.3.

147. Valerius Maximus 5.2.1.

148. Culham, "*Lex Oppia*," 791.

149. Valerius Maximus 9.1.3.

150. Valerius Maximus 8.15.12.

151. See Kraemer, *Her Share of the Blessings*, 57; Stehle, "Venus, Cybele," 153.

152. Valerius Maximus 5.2.1.

153. Petronius, *Satyricon*, 44.17-18.

154. Petronius, *Satyricon*, 44.4, 6.

155. For a discussion of freed slaves' movement into Roman-ness through work, see Joshel, *Work, Identity, and Legal Status at Rome*.

156. See Bradley, *Discovering the Roman Family*; also Hallett, *Fathers and Daughters*; Dixon, *Roman Mother*.

157. See "Nurturing the Master's Child."

158. Labor historians and anthropologists have mapped and documented tensions between modern-day women employers and women domestic workers; see Gill, "Painted Faces," with bibliography.

159. Valerius Maximus 1.5.4.

160. See Hopkins, "Age of Roman Girls at Marriage."

161. See Kraemer, *Her Share of the Blessings*, 55, on girls dedicating their togas; background and sources in Flory, "*Sic Exempla Parantur*," 314.

162. Valerius Maximus 1.8.4.

163. See Festus 282L; also Williams, "Some Aspects of Roman Marriage."

164. Festus 282L; Valerius Maximus 2.1.3

165. Valerius Maximus 2.1.6.

166. Livy 10.23.3-10; see Kraemer, *Her Share of the Blessings*, 58.

167. See Flory, "*Sic Exempla Parantur*," for an excellent overview of the rich array of cults celebrating chastity and "family values" connected with Augustus's religious revival, under the leadership of his wife, Livia.

168. Aulus Gellius 16.16.4.

169. Paulus 67L.

170. Paulus 182L.

171. Paulus 248L; compare Aulus Gellius 4.3.3.

172. *Metamorphoses* 6.537.

173. On slaves' sexual degradation, see Joshel, *Work, Identity and Legal Status*, 28-32; and in general, see Richlin, *Garden of Priapus*, 26-31, 58-59, 66-70; and "Invective against Women." On Roman rules regarding adultery, see Richlin, "Approaches to the Sources"; Gardner, *Women in Roman Law and Society*, 127-32.

174. Tibullus 3.16.3-4.

175. Paulus 92L.

176. Paulus 221L.

177. Paulus 131L.

178. Varro, *On the Latin Language*, 5.68.

179. Varro, *On the Latin Language*, 5.69, partly paraphrased.

180. Festus 396L.

181. Pliny, *Epistle* 95.48.

182. See Latte, *Roemische Religionsgeschichte*; Scullard, *Festivals and Ceremonies*; Warde Fowler, *Roman Festivals*.

183. The following is based on general descriptions in Scullard, *Festivals and Ceremonies*.

184. Varro, *On the Latin Language*, 6.13; Paulus 49L.

185. Ovid, *Fasti* 2.571-80.

186. Varro, *On the Latin Language*, 5.106.

187. See Versnel, "Festival for Bona Dea," 41, for a brief analysis of this festival in comparison with elements in the Athenian Thesmophoria; Stehle, "Venus, Cybele," 147-48, for analysis of its symbolic meaning.

188. Gordon, "Veil of Power," 228.

189. Juvenal, *Satires*, 6.314-51.

190. Juvenal, *Satires*, 6.320-23, cf. 350-51.

191. Juvenal, *Satires*, 2.83-116, esp. 90, 98.

192. See Bettini, *Anthropology and Roman Culture*, 77-78; French, "Cult of Mater Matuta."

193. Dumézil, *Camillus*, 175-209, provides Vedic parallels. The connection between the Matralia and the story of Caecilia Metella is also made by Gagé, *Matronalia*, 225-43; Hallett, *Fathers and Daughters*, 183-89; and most thoroughly by Bettini, *Anthropology and Roman Culture*, 67-99. For connections between the Matralia and other women's cults, see Flory, "*Sic Exempla Parantur*," 313-14; note especially the close physical proximity of the temple to the site of girls' dedication of their togas.

194. Paulus 94L.

195. Valerius Maximus 8.1.absol.5.

196. "Woman."

197. See Joplin, "Ritual Work on Human Flesh"; Joshel, "Body Female and the Body Politic."

198. See, for example, Brouwer, *Bona Dea,* for a complete list for Bona Dea.

WORKS CITED

Abu-Lughod, Lila. "Can There Be a Feminist Ethnography?" *Women and Performance* 5 (1990): 7-27.

Beard, Mary. "The Sexual Status of Vestal Virgins." *Journal of Roman Studies* 70 (1980): 12-27.

———. "Priesthood in the Roman Republic." Pp. 17–48 in *Pagan Priests,* edited by Mary Beard and John North. Ithaca, N.Y.: Cornell University Press, 1990.

Bettini, Maurizio. *Anthropology and Roman Culture: Kinship, Time, Images of the Soul.* Translated by John Van Sickle. Baltimore: Johns Hopkins University Press, 1991.

Bradley, Keith R. *Discovering the Roman Family.* New York and Oxford: Oxford University Press, 1991.

Brouwer, H. H. J. *Bona Dea: The Sources and a Description of the Cult*. Leiden: E. J. Brill, 1989.

Buckley, Thomas, and Alma Gottlieb. "A Critical Appraisal of Theories of Menstrual Symbolism." Pp. 3–50 in *Blood Magic: The Anthropology of Menstruation,* edited by Thomas Buckley and Alma Gottlieb. Berkeley, Calif.: University of California Press, 1988.

Culham, Phyllis. "The *Lex Oppia.*" *Latomus* 41 (1982): 786-93.

Dixon, Suzanne. *The Roman Mother*. Norman, Okla.: Oklahoma University Press, 1988.

du Boulay, Juliet. "Women—Images of Their Nature and Destiny in Rural Greece." Pp. 136–68 in *Gender and Power in Rural Greece,* edited by Jill Dubisch. Princeton, N.J.: Princeton University Press, 1986.

Dumezil, Georges. *Camillus.* Berkeley, Calif.: University of California Press, 1980.

Fantham, Elaine, Helene Peet Foley, Natalie Boymel Kampen, Sarah B. Pomeroy, and H. Alan Shapiro. *Women in the Classical World.* New York: Oxford University Press, 1994.

Faraone, Christopher A., and Dirk Obbink, eds. *Magika Hiera: Ancient Greek Magic and Religion.* Oxford: Oxford University Press, 1991.

Ferguson, John. *The Religions of the Roman Empire.* Ithaca, N.Y.: Cornell University Press, 1970.

Flory, Marleen Boudreau. "*Sic Exempla Parantur:* Livia's Shrine to Concordia and the Porticus Liviae." *Historia* 33 (1984): 309-30.

Forbis, Elizabeth P. "Women's Public Image in Italian Honorary Inscriptions." *American Journal of Philology* 111 (1990): 493-512.

French, Valerie. "The Cult of Mater Matuta." Paper presented at the Berkshire Conference on Women's History, 1987.

Gagé, Jean. *Matronalia: essai sur les dévotions et les organisations culturelles des femmes dans l'ancienne Rome.* Brussels: Collection Latomus (60), 1963.

Gardner, Jane. *Women in Roman Law and Society*. Bloomington, Ind.: Indiana University Press, 1986.

Gill, Lesley. "Painted Faces: Conflict and Ambiguity in Domestic Servant-Employer Relations in La Paz, 1930-1988." *Latin American Research Review* 25, no. 1 (1990): 119-36.

Giovannini, Maureen J. "Woman: A Dominant Symbol within the Cultural System of a Sicilian Town." *Man* n.s. 16 (1981): 408-26.

Gordon, Richard. "From Republic to Principate: Priesthood, Religion and Ideology." Pp. 177–98 in *Pagan Priests,* edited by Mary Beard and John North. Ithaca, N.Y.: Cornell University Press, 1990.

———. "The Veil of Power: Emperors, Sacrificers and Benefactors." Pp. 199–232 in *Pagan Priests,* edited by Mary Beard and John North. Ithaca, N.Y.: Cornell University Press, 1990.

Hallett, Judith P. *Fathers and Daughters in Roman Society.* Princeton, N.J.: Princeton University Press, 1984.

———. "Women as *Same* and *Other* in the Classical Roman Elite." *Helios* 16 (1989): 59-78.

Hopkins, Keith. "The Age of Roman Girls at Marriage." *Population Studies* 18 (1965): 309-27.

Joplin, Patricia Klindienst. "Ritual Work on Human Flesh: Livy's Lucretia and the Rape of the Body Politic." *Helios* 17 (1990): 51-70.

Joshel, Sandra R. "Nurturing the Master's Child: Slavery and the Roman Child-Nurse." *Signs* 12 (1986): 3-22.

———. "The Body Female and the Body Politic: Livy's Lucretia and Verginia." Pp. 112–30 in *Pornography and Representation in Greece and Rome,* edited by Amy Richlin. New York: Oxford, 1992.

———. *Work, Identity, and Legal Status at Rome.* Norman, Okla.: University of Oklahoma Press, 1992.

Kraemer, Ross S[hepard]. *Maenads, Martyrs, Matrons, Monastics.* Philadelphia: Fortress, 1988.

———. *Her Share of the Blessings: Women's Religions among Pagans, Jews, and Christians in the Greco-Roman World.* New York: Oxford University Press, 1992.

Latte, Kurt. *Römische Religionsgeschichte.* Munich: C. H. Beck, 1967.

Lindsay, W. M. *Sextus Pompeius Festus De Verborum Significatione.* Leipzig: Teubner, 1913.

MacMullen, Ramsay. "Woman in Public in the Roman Empire." *Hermes* 29 (1980): 208-18.

Mascia-Lees, Frances E., Patricia Sharpe, and Colleen Ballerino Cohen. "The Postmodernist Turn in Anthropology: Cautions from a Feminist Perspective." *Signs* 15 (1989): 7-33.

Richlin, Amy. "Approaches to the Sources on Adultery in Rome." Pp. 379–404 in *Reflections of Women in Antiquity,* edited by Helene P. Foley. New York: Gordon and Breach Science Publishers, 1981.

———. "Invective against Women in Roman Satire." *Arethusa* 17 (1984): 67-80.

———. *The Garden of Priapus: Sexuality and Aggression in Roman Humor.* Rev. ed. New York: Oxford University Press, 1992.

———. "The Ethnographer's Dilemma and the Dream of a Lost Golden Age." Pp. 272–303 in *Feminist Theory and the Classics,* edited by Nancy Sorkin Rabinowitz and Amy Richlin. New York: Routledge, 1993.

———. "Pliny's Brassiere." In *Roman Sexualities,* edited by Judith P. Hallett and Marilyn B. Skinner. Princeton, N.J.: Princeton University Press, 1997.

Rosaldo, Renato. "From the Door of His Tent: The Fieldworker and the Inquisitor." Pp. 77–97 in *Writing Culture,* edited by James Clifford and George E. Marcus. Berkeley, Calif.: University of California Press, 1986.

Scullard, H. H. *Festivals and Ceremonies of the Roman Republic.* Ithaca, N.Y.: Cornell University Press, 1981.

Sebesta, Judith Lynn, and Larissa Bonfante, eds. *The World of Roman Costume.* Madison, Wis.: University of Wisconsin Press, 1994.

Shapiro, Judith. "Anthropology and the Study of Gender." Pp. 110–29 in *A Feminist Perspective in the Academy,* edited by Elizabeth Langland and Walter Gove. Chicago: University of Chicago Press, 1981.

Sharp, Margery. *The Nutmeg Tree.* New York: Grosset & Dunlap, 1937.

Stehle, Eva. "Venus, Cybele and the Sabine Women: The Roman Construction of Female Sexuality." *Helios* 16 (1989): 143-64.

Treggiari, Susan. *Roman Marriage: Iusti Coniuges from the Time of Cicero to the Time of Ulpian.* New York: Oxford University Press, 1991.

Van Bremen, Riet. "Women and Wealth." Pp. 223–42 in *Images of Women in Antiquity,* edited by Averil Cameron and Amélie Kuhrt. Detroit: Wayne State University Press, 1983.

Versnel, H. S. "The Festival for Bona Dea and the Thesmophoria." *Greece & Rome* 39 (1992): 31-55.

Warde Fowler, W. *The Roman Festivals of the Period of the Republic.* London: Macmillan & Co., Ltd., 1916.

Weissler, Chava. "The Religion of Traditional Ashkenazic Women: Some Methodological Issues." *AJS Review* 12 (1987): 73-94.

Williams, Gordon. "Some Aspects of Roman Marriage Ceremonies and Ideals." *Journal of Roman Studies* 53 (1963): 16-29.

Winkler, John J. "The Laughter of the Oppressed: Demeter and the Gardens of Adonis." Pp. 188–209 in *The Constraints of Desire: The Anthropology of Sex and Gender in Ancient Greece.* New York and London: Routledge, 1990.

APPENDIX A: PRIESTESSES FROM THE *CIL* FOR ITALY

The following list divides priestesses according to title and follows the numerical order of the *CIL.* The volumes of the *CIL* cover various geographical regions: volume 5 covers Cisalpine Gaul; volume 9 covers the east coast of Italy; volume 10 covers the west side of southern Italy, Sicily, and Sardinia; volume 11 covers Italy north of Rome and south of the Po; volume 14 covers Latium. Each "s" on this list means "one *sacerdos,*" each "m" means "one *magistra,*" and so on.

sacerdos

5.520, Usia L. fil. Tertullina, s. divarum
5.2829, Asconia C. f. Augurini, s. divae Domitillae
5.3438, Veronia Trofime, s. Matris deum
5.4387, Aemilia C. f. Aequa, s. divae Plotinae
5.4400, Caecilia Procula, s. xv viralis
5.4458, (P)ostumia P. f. Paulla, Avidia Procula, Rutilia Proba, s(ss?). div(a)i August
5.4485, Clodia Q. fil. Procilla, s. divae Plotinae
5.5647, Caesia P. f. Maxima, s. divae Matidiae
5.5862, Gei(inia . . .) C. Var(i) Elpidephori, s. Matr Magn deum Ideae
5.6412, Petilia Q. f. Sabina, s. Minervae
5.7617, [no name extant], s. (di)vae Plotinae (P)ollentiae divae Faustinae Taurinis divae Faustinae Maioris Concordiae
9.307, Petilia Q. f. Secundina, s. Minervae
9.1100, Eggia Sabina Bast . . ., s. M.D. Mag
9.1153, Cantria P. f. Longina, s. and flam divae Iuliae Aug et Matr deum . . . et Isidis Regin
9.1154, Cantria P. fil. Paulla, s. Augustae Aeclano

9.1538, Servilia Varia and Terentia Elisuiana, ss xv vir; . . . Ianuaria, cymbalistria
9.1539, Mummeia C. f. Atticilla, s.
9.1540, Cosinia Celsina, consacerdos Matri deum
9.1541, Terentia Flaviana and Servilia Varia, s. secundo loco xv vir; [s prima (same woman in 1538)]
[9.1542, Servilia Varia, s. prima (same woman in 1538)]
9.2569, Helvia Mesi f., s. Vener
9.2670, Suellia C. f. Consanica, s. Cerialis deia libera
9.3087, Caeidia . . ., s. Cereris et Veneris
9.3089, Helvia G. l. Quarta, s. Cere(ris et Veneris)
9.3090, Mamia V. f., s. Cereris et Veneri(s)
9.3091, Hortensia, s. Isidis
9.3166, Acca Q. f., s. Veneris
9.3167, Accia and Modia, ss. Veneris
9.3170, Attia Mirallis, s. Cereris
9.3358, Ninnia Q. f. Primilla, s. Cereria
9.3429, Nummia Varia C. f., s. Veneris Felicis
9.4200, Tamudia M. f. Severa, s. public Cerer
9.5068, Attia P. fil. Maxima, s. Augustar
9.5428, Antonia Cn. fil. Picentina, s. divae Fau(sti)nae
10.51, Latia P. f. (and ?) Auleia Avirna, s(s?). Aug
10.54, . . . Quinta . . .a, s. per(petua) (divi Fausti)nae
10.129, Bovia Maxima, s. xv viral, to Ceres
10.343, Lucia M. l., s.
10.680, . . .a L. f. Magna, s. public (Vene)ris et Cereris
10.688, [no name extant], (s) public Vener (et Cereris?)
10.810, Eumachia L. f., s. publ [also 811, 812, 813]
[10.811, same as 810]
10.812, Eumachia L. f., s. publ; Aquuia M. f. Quarta, s. Cereris publ; Heia M. f. and (Ru)fula L. f., ss. Cereris publ
[10.813, Eumachia, s. publ]
10.816, Mamia P. f., s. public [also 10.998]
[10.998, Mamia P. f., s. publicae]
10.999, Istacidia N. f. Rufilla, s. publica
10.1036, Alleia M. f. Decimilla, s. publica Cereris
10.1074, Clodia A. f. and Lassia M. f., ss. publica Cereris
10.1207, Avillia Aeliana, s. Ioviae Veneriae Abellanorum
10.1798, Faltonia Procula, s.
10.1812, Sabina, s. Cereris public
10.1829, . . .na Mun. . ., (s. public)ae Cereris

10.3911, Herennia M. . ., s., to Ceres
10.3926, Icuria M. f., s. Cerialis mundalis
10.4673, Aria C. f., s.
10.4789-91, Flavia Coelia Annia Argiva, s. Iunonis Populonae; Nonia Prisca, s. Iunon Populon; Vitellia Virgilia Felsia, ministra sacrorum publ (p)raesidis Iu(n)onis Populo(n)
10.4794, Staia M. f. Pietas, s. Cerer(is) publ prima
10.4889, Tillia Eutychia, s.
10.5073, Munnia C. f., s. Cer
10.5144, . . . asennia, (s) (Vene)ria
10.5191, Agria Sueia N. f., s. Cerer et Veneris
10.5201, Pompeia Cn. f. Phoebe, s. divarum
10.5413, Dentria L. f. Polla, s. divae Augustae
10.5414, Floria C. f. Posilla, s. publica
10.5656, Saenia Cn. f. Balbilla, s. divae Faustinae
10.6018, Pompeia Q. f. Catulla, s. August
10.6074, Decimia C. f. Candida, s. M. D.
10.6075, Helvia Stephanis, s. M. M. I., a *taurobolium*
10.6103, Caesia No f., s. Cereri(s)
10.6109, Sallustia Saturnina, s. deae Cereris
10.6640, Iulia Procula, s. [Cereris] (presides over dedication)
10.7352, Antia M. f. Cleopatra, s.
10.7501, Lutatia C. f., s. Augustae imp perp, wife of flamen of Livia's cult; dedication to Ceres Iulia Augusta
11.407, Cantia L. f. Saturnina, s. divae Plotin
11.3810, (Caesia) Sabina, s. Fortunae Reducis
11.3933, Flavia Ammia, s. Cereris
11.6172, Curtilia C. f. Priscilla, s. divae Augustae
11.6520, Cetrania P. f. Severina, s. divae Marcian
14.2804, Agusia T. f. Priscilla, s. Spei et Salutis Aug

magistra

5.757, Aninia M. f. Magna, Seia Ionis, and Cornelia Ephyre, mmm. B.D.
[5.758, Seia Ionis, m. (B.D.? to Fonio)]
5.759, Petrusia Proba . . . Galgesti Hermerot(is), m. to B.D.
5.762, Rufria C. f. Festa and Caesilia Q. l. Scylace, mm. to B.D. Pagana (with *ministrae*)
5.814, Leuce Anspaniae l. (and?) Occusia Venusta, mm? to dea Obsequens
5.5026, Cassia Marcella, Iuentia Maxsuma, Firmidia Modesta, Numonia Secunda, mmmm (with min)

5.7633, Valeria Epithusa, m., to numen Dianae Aug
9.805, Vergilia Prisca, m. Bonae (Deae?)
9.3518, Salvidia T. f. Secunda, Quinctia Sex. f. Secunda, Casnasia Q. l. Rufa, Casnasia G. l. Sperat(a), Sperata Munatidi A(uli) ser, mmmmm(?) Vene
9.5295, Veidia T. l. Auge and Iulia C. l. Urbana, mm. Veneri(?)
10.39, Helvia Q. f. and Orbia M. f., mm of Proserpina
10.202, Pietas Sec(un)di contuber(nalis), m. to Juno
10.5192, Fabia Philema(tium?), Baionia Philema(tium?), and Graecina Myrinna, [mmm?]
10.6511, Cervaria Sp. f. Fortunata, m. Matri Matutae
11.3196, Bennia Primigenia, m., with mag(ister) pagi, to Ceres August
11.3246, Servilia Felix, m., to Minerva
11.4391, Iulia M. f. Felicitas, m. Fortunae Melioris
11.4767, Pom(p . . .), com(magi)str(a), in dedication to B.D. by wife with husband
11.6185, Rufellia L. l. Tych(e), m
14.2997, Publicia L. f. Similis, m. Matris Metut
14.3006, Sulpicia Sergi filia, m. Matris Matutae
14.3437, Iulia Athenais, m. Bonae Deae Sevinae

ministra

5.762, Decidia L. f. Pauli(na) and Pupia L. l. Peregrin(a), mm. to B.D.
5.5026, Iuentia Secunda, Manneia Pupa, Loreia Prima, Vettia Secunda, mmmm
9.3146, Acca L. f. Prima, m. Matris Magnae, on altar w/ priest
9.4460, Plaetoria Secunda, ministra salutis
[10.4791, m. sacrorum publ . . . (see above under s.)]
11.4635, Quieta Aties Pieridis, m. Bone Die, (and ?) proma[gistra?]

flaminica

5.3916, Cusonia Maxima, f., to Saturn, with a man (her husband?)
5.3922, Pomponisia Ponti fil. Severa, f., with a man
5.3923, Cassia P. f. Iustina, f., with a man
5.3928, Octavia M. f. Magna, f. (pa)gi Arusnati(um)
5.3930, Tullia Tul. f. Cardelia, f.
5.6365, Catia M. f. Procula, f.
5.6514, Albucia M. f. Candida, f. (di)vae Iuliae No(var) and f. (d)ivae Sabinae Ticini, with her husband
5.6840, Octavia Elpidia, f.
5.6954, Tullia C. f. Vitrasi(?), flaminicia [*sic*] Iulia August

5.7345, . . . a M. f. Secunda Aspri, (flam)inica divae Drusillae
5.7629, Tullia C. (f.), f. Iulia Augusta
5.7788, . . . nia M. f. Mar . . . and . . . a A. f. Sabina, ff. divae Aug
5.7811, Metilia Tertullina, f., with husband and four children, to Juno regina, for *patrona*
[9.1153, see under *sacerdotes*]
[9.1155, f. divae Aug—same woman as in 9.1154 under *sacerdotes*]
9.1163, Neratia Betitia Procilla, f. Faustinae Aug
9.4881, Egnatia A. f. Aul(ina), f. in colonia provinciae Narbon
9.5534, Vitellia C. f. Rufilla, flamen [*sic*] salutis Aug
9.5841, Vibia L. f. Marcella, flamina [*sic*] Aug
10.5924, Flavia Kara Gentia, f.
10.6978, Messia Prisci fil. Crispina, f. divae Aug
10.7602, Iulia Vateria Vateri fil., flamen [*sic*]
10.7604, Titia Flavia Blandina, f. perpetua
11.5711, Camurena C. fil. Celerina, f. Feron
11.5752, Avidia C. f. Tertullia, f.
11.6354, Abienia C. f. Balbina, f. Pisauri et Arimini

cultrix
11.5223, cc collegii Fulginiae

consuplicatrices
10.6518, Paul(a) Toutia M. f., with c.

hymnetria
10.7426, Nicarin Munatiae L. l. Zosimae filia, h. a s(acris?)

APPENDIX B: DEDICATIONS BY WOMEN

The following dedications by women are cited or discussed in the text above. This does not by any means constitute an exhaustive list of such dedications.[198]

MAJOR DONATIONS

5.412, temple, statue, and portico to Juno Feronia
5.757, temple to Fonio
5.761, temple to Augusta Bona Dea Cereria
5.762, temple by *magistrae* of Bona Dea
5.781, temple, statues, porticos with markets and kitchen to Iunones

5.835, statue and ornaments to Venus Augusta
5.7345, fishpond by *flaminica* of Drusilla
5.8242, altar to Parcae, silver dish to Bona Dea
9.3146, altar commemorating restoration and gilding of statues of Magna Mater, Attis, and Bellona
9.5428, statues for theater by *sacerdos* of Faustina
9.5071, statue to Feronia (or to a woman named Feronia?)
10.810, buildings attached to the temple of Concordia Augusta
10.3685, 3686, 3688, 3689, temple and portico, etc., to Demeter; and dedications by the same people
10.3817, statue to Mater Matuta
10.3818, statue to Mater Matuta
10.3819, statue to Mater Matuta
10.4635, temple to Magna Mater
10.5192, steps and *epimedia* by three *magistrae*
10.6074, (statue of ?) Attis by a *sacerdos* of Mater deum
10.6640, statues in shrine of Ceres
10.8416, statue of Jupiter to Mater Matuta
11.574, site for temple of Isis
11.1291-1306, shrine of Minerva Memor
11.4767, altar in grove of Bona Dea
11.6290-6302, shrine at Pisaurum
14.3437, temple pavement and roof repair by *magistra* of Bona Dea

ORDINARY DONATIONS

5.758, to Fonio by *magistra* of Bona Dea
5.759, earrings (?) for the statue of Bona Dea by a *magistra*
5.814, to Dea Obsequens by a freedwoman (or women?)
5.836, to Venus Augusta
5.3240, to the Iunones by a *sacerdos* and a man
5.3264, to the Matronae
5.3916, to Saturn by a *flaminica* and a man
5.4134, to the Matronae
5.4137, to the Matronae
5.5647, to Jupiter Optimus Maximus by a *sacerdos* of Matidia
5.6829, two vessels and a mirror to Jupiter, Juno, and Minerva
5.7811, to Juno, from a family, to honor *patrona*
9.684, to Bona Dea
9.1538, *criobolium* by a *cymbalistria*

9.1539, *taurobolium*
9.1541, *taurobolium*
9.1542, *taurobolium*
9.1552, to Silvanus Staianus on behalf of a son
9.3518, to Venus, group of five *magistrae*
9.5295, to Venus, two *magistrae*
9.5421, to Bona Dea
10.129, to Ceres
10.202, chest and candelabrum to Juno by *magistra*
10.467, to Ceres
10.816, to the Genius of Augustus by *sacerdos*
10.1549, to Bona Dea
10.1555, to Diana Loch(ia?)
10.1596, *taurobolium*
10.1597, *taurobolium* by a slave
10.3911, to Ceres by a *sacerdos*
10.5383, to Bona Dea
10.5384, by the same woman to Fortuna Sancta
10.6075, *taurobolium* by *sacerdos* of Magna Mater Idaea
10.6511, to Mater Matuta by a *magistra*
10.6518, to Mater Matuta, woman with *consuplic(atrices)*
10.6595, to Bona Dea
11.3246, to Minerva by *magistra*
11.4636, to Bona Dea
11.6185, to Bona Dea by *magistra*
11.6304, to Bona Dea
11.6305, to Bona Dea

PART THREE

CONTEMPORARY GODDESS THEALOGY

14

JUDITH OCHSHORN

Goddesses and the Lives of Women

In the United States, contemporary interest in Goddess traditions is embedded in the reemergence of feminism. The radical assertion of the full personhood of women helped illuminate the profound androcentrism in Jewish and Christian sacred texts, rituals, and commentaries on them, often articulated as profound ambivalence toward women. On this basis, feminist theologians and others engaged in re-visioning their spirituality mounted challenges to the "maleness" of the biblical God and its legitimation of male dominance on earth.

The broad areas of agreement that developed on these issues by no means masked areas of disagreement, which tended to cluster around whether and how much traditional Jewish and Christian beliefs and practices are redeemable from sexism, and on what grounds. Thus, almost twenty years after Valerie Saiving's groundbreaking essay, "The Human Situation: A Feminine View," Carol Christ's "Why Women Need the Goddess" resonated deeply, particularly among those who no longer could or would struggle to transform these religious traditions. Forcefully responding to the social and religious denigration of the minds and bodies of women, and with scant biblical models of female power and autonomy, Christ's argument was part of a search undertaken for nonoppressive spiritual alternatives, in many cases for Goddess traditions in other times and places.

Undoubtedly, this search was motivated in part by a desire to look to the past in order to assess whether male domination and female subordination were, indeed, "natural," caused by our genes or our stars, as accepted scholarship contended. If, however, the origins of male dominance could be traced to specific times and places,[1] if it had not prevailed in all societies, then one might envision a future without it.

Hence, while some attempted to expand or reform Judaism and Christianity considerably to include women's experiences,[2] for others the lure of a past era when Goddesses were revered and women ruled or exercised real power proved almost irresistible.

A number of studies published in the past two decades made just those kinds of claims about a "golden age" in the prehistoric or ancient past, when "the reign of the Goddess" produced, or at least was concomitant with, an era of justice, peace, artistic creativity, high status for women, and sexual egalitarianism.[3] Emphasizing the high value placed on the female in conceptions of divinity and the socially constructed character of gender, they tended to expand our imagination of the humanly possible and purported to explain the origins of patriarchy. Importantly, among other things, they helped to relativize the universalism of the male God of Judaism and Christianity, as well as that of patriarchal social and religious structures.

Those explanations, however, may forever remain in the realm of the historically possible but ultimately undemonstrable. For example, it has been argued that the possible meanings of Paleolithic and Neolithic sculptures, like the Venus figurines, often used as evidence for Goddess worship, dating back to 25,000 B.C.E. and extending up to the Neolithic period, are not necessarily self-explanatory and might, indeed, have had varied meanings at different times in different locales.[4] In addition, the use, alone, of physical artifacts in their material contexts as evidence, even if one accepts Marija Gimbutas's translation of their decorations as "the language of the Goddess," suggests a number of underlying epistemological problems.

First, in the absence of independent corroborative evidence left by contemporaries of those who produced the artifacts, there is disagreement over what they can disclose about their meanings to the people of their own times, or whether they alone can serve as the basis for reconstructing the religious and social beliefs and practices of vanished cultures.[5] Second, there is disagreement among scholars of antiquity over whether the outlook of ancient societies was "mythopoeic," fundamentally different from that of later times—for example, from the rationalism of classical Athens (though one wonders about the "rationalism" of theories promoted then about women's nature)—or whether similar concerns over the meaning of mortality, the existence of gratuitous evil in the world, and the need to feel a measure of control over the future have all been concerns of people whenever they lived, and served as the heart of most religious beliefs and rituals including the prehistoric. Third, there is the question of who produced the surviving artifacts or sacred texts. Did they express the views of a priestly elite, in historic times a male elite whose experiences were shaped by conventions of gender and class,[6] or were they rather representative expressions of their communities? These are hardly trivial questions if, as Christ maintains, human experience provides insights about the divine, and if religion itself evolves from and is revealed in the stories we tell about our lives.[7]

It seems to me that important as physical artifacts are and as much as they may enable us to avoid male biases in the interpretations of women's history,[8] those that remain from 7,000—much less 27,000—years ago probably cannot by themselves disclose what they meant to the people who created or valued them. Gimbutas argues that the decorative symbols repeatedly found on prehistoric sculptures and figurines are associated with specific aspects of the Old European Goddess, but even if true, that is a far cry from using them to reconstruct a religious and social system that endured for thousands of years, particularly when so much of what we know about those societies must remain conjectural.

Furthermore, to say that motifs are repeated does not *necessarily* mean that they have religious significance or are associated with the Goddess.[9] For instance, rather than the repeated use of symbols associated with birds, snakes, or fish representing the regenerative powers of the Goddess, as Gimbutas asserts, their use might have symbolized people's awe at the sight of living things in their close environment flying, shedding their skins, or living in water—and surviving. To cite another example, it is puzzling that some assert that the depictions of bulls' heads in ancient tombs and temples were intended to symbolize human uteri and fallopian tubes, or were symbols of the Goddess in her regenerative capacity simply because of similarities in their shapes, particularly in those cultures that practiced excarnation.[10] In short, some of the evidence for the universal reign of the Goddess seems rather equivocal.

With regard to the mythopoeic mentality of these early cultures, while respecting the integrity of cultural differences and alert to the dangers of ethnocentrism, I tend to agree with Samuel Noah Kramer that, if I were to meet a schoolteacher from third-millennium Sumer, we would likely have much to discuss together.[11] And on the possibly privileged status or nonrepresentative perspectives of ancient creators of artifacts and sacred texts, if that standard were to be a determining one for judging authenticity, given the widespread educational deprivation of most women and lower-class persons at least in historic times, we might well have to discount most of our information from the past.

Given these uncertainties, I shall (1) reconsider the importance of the past to us and discuss why we probably cannot simply slough off its oppressive parts and start virtually anew, as some have attempted; (2) briefly reexamine, both on their own terms and for their possible promise and pitfalls for women's spirituality today, some of the more influential current scholarly theories about the allegedly golden age of Goddess worship and its social ramifications, exemplified in the work of archeologist Marija Gimbutas and theologian and historian of religion Mary Condren, as well as the earlier, more popularized argument for the femaleness of God by sculptor Merlin Stone that captured the imagination of many women; and (3) propose that knowledge of the content of Goddess worship and social arrangements in the ancient Near East, from which we have both physical remains and written documents, might yield some new ways of articulating social and religious issues that could prove liberating and empowering to women in the present and future.

These issues, in turn, suggest a number of questions, including: To what extent and in what ways did ancient Near Eastern conceptions of the divine reflect and affect women's experiences? What appear to have been the cultural conditions minimally required for the worship of powerful, autonomous Goddesses rather than male-constructed female divinities such as the Olympic Athena? By implication, are any feminist theoretical perspectives consonant with what appears to be required for imaging of the divine as both female and powerful? Finally, why not break free from the past with its multiple restrictions and injustices, begin over, and fashion our own traditions? Why insist on grounding our identities in our histories? Certainly we do not need to clone the past.

There have been a few efforts in that last direction. In *Les Guerilleres*, for instance, Monique Wittig writes about the women who come together from all over the world to bear witness to their lives. As former slaves, their past has been stolen from them. In an act of empowerment, the narrator, Wittig, exhorts them, in the inevitable failure of their memories, to invent their pasts. Similarly, with considerable poetic license, some currently engaged in Wicca have appropriated as models their versions of the lives of lower-class peasant women denounced as witches in sixteenth- and seventeenth-century Europe (though we have only the Inquisitors' descriptions of them and their experiences, beliefs, ordeals, and "rituals"). Cast by those allegedly continuing in their path as powerful and wise midwives, healers, and practitioners of "the old religion" that presumably threatened Christendom,[12] they are barely recognizable as the same women who, in their powerlessness, were arrested, interrogated, tortured for the good of their souls, and, usually, then publicly humiliated, imprisoned, exiled, or killed.

This kind of romanticism is inadequate to counter our real legacies from the past, that is, the many faces of male dominance. Beyond Santayana's warning about the cost of forgetting our past and the responsibility to commemorate its victims and understand the misogyny they suffered that endures into the present, there is also a need to look for models of strength, both sacred and profane, that can project us into a different kind of future. Feminism may be grounded in analysis and theory, but it is also activist and transformative, pointing toward an altered world. It *is* likely that patriarchy in its many cultural guises has not always been with us and instead originated at different times in history, but it is not clear that what preceded it was the universal rule of the Goddess, either symbolically or literally. Indeed, despite the marginalization of women in the telling and interpretation of that history, it is equally likely, even in male-dominated societies, that women, like men, were on a daily basis at the center of their history's creation.

What we must use is something like Elisabeth Schüssler Fiorenza's subversion of the male historical enterprise when she writes:

> History is not written today for people of past times but for people of our own times. The antiquarian understanding of history is not only epistemologically impossible but also historically undesirable. What needs to be rediscovered is the understanding of history not as artifact but as "historical consciousness" for the present and the future.[13]

It is of course the case, as has been endlessly pointed out by postmodernists and others, that knowledge is the union between the knower and that which is known, contoured by all the assumptions and values of the former. But while this theoretical stance is a healthy antidote to reification of "the truth" and "objective reality," it is also the case that things *did* happen in the past that set the course for what later transpired and from which we can learn. Not everything, particularly our evaluation of those events relating to moral issues, is nor should be made relative, because the development of what Schüssler Fiorenza calls "historical consciousness" requires our conviction that there were *real* events that shaped it. Therefore, what we learn from the past should be subject to the same kinds of scrutiny that inform our encounters with ideas and events in contemporary life, namely our tendency to understand and evaluate them based not only on what we agree we know but also on common sense and logic.

In the claims made for Goddess worship in Old Europe and the ancient Near East, which provides one dimension of a "historical consciousness" that asserts the primacy of the female as divine and as a social being, there is a fair degree of consensus by proponents of these claims about how female divinity was perceived in terms of attributes, powers, and the social and religious consequences of both. As described best by Gimbutas, Paleolithic and Neolithic sculptures and visual representations, found in the Near East, southeastern Europe, around the Mediterranean, and in central, western, and northern Europe, all "indicate the extension of the same Goddess religion to all of these regions as a cohesive and persistent ideological system."[14] This universal ideology, according to Gimbutas, continues from its earliest appearance to the present. Great Goddess-referents on physical artifacts from the Paleolithic can be traced, long after patriarchal incursions and even today, by their recurrence on other artifacts and in folklore, linguistics, and myths, stretching over a wide area in peripheral (that is, relatively untouched) parts of Europe, for example, in Basque, Welsh, Irish, and Scandinavian countries. Belief in the Goddess persists up to the present, "passed on by the grandmothers and mothers of the European family," surviving the Indo-European and Christian mythologies, and "leaving an indelible imprint on the Western psyche."[15] Reminiscent of Lovejoy's Great Chain of Being, in which symbols, metaphors, images, and ideas have identical meanings in widely disparate times and places,[16] one of the cornerstones of Gimbutas's argument for the universal reign of the prehistoric Goddess is this continuity of symbolism and content into historic times, presumably signifying the same thing to Neolithic and contemporary believers.[17]

This view is related to other beliefs about the Great Goddess. One is that she was supreme. Gimbutas is the only one who deals in any meaningful if cursory way with the significance of excavated male and asexual figurines, though they never challenge the supremacy of the Goddess.[18] Another is that her worship emerged from an essentially "mythopoeic," "holistic" world view whose images and symbols articulated the supremacy of the parthenogenetic Goddess. Participants in the culture of the Goddess delighted in nature, in *this* world, lived without weapons or fortifications, though they had the technology to produce both; built beautiful tombs, shrines, and temples in human-scale villages; and created lovely pottery and sculptures. "This was a long-lasting period of remarkable creativity and stability, an age free of strife. Their culture was a culture of art."[19] This near-idyllic characterization of thousands of years of Goddess-worshiping Old Europe seems to suggest how inaccessible so much of our prehistoric origins are, or the degree to which all of us tend to find what we desire in the past.

Another attribute of the Great Goddess is her oneness. In her survey of scholarly work on the ancient Near East, Stone sees her various names and diverse characteristics in many periods and parts of the world as descriptive of the "various titles of the Great Goddess." Indeed, "the female Deity in the Near and Middle East was referred to as Goddess—much as people today think of God."[20] Some, for example, Carol Christ and Christine Downing, personally identify with one Goddess or another at particular stages of their lives,[21] and Gimbutas discusses a number of zoomorphic Goddesses as well as various cosmic roles filled by female divinities in her *Civilization of the Goddess.*[22] It is also the case, however, that though Gimbutas portrays the Goddess as complex, she nevertheless concludes: "It seems more appropriate to view all of these Goddess images as aspects of the one Great Goddess."[23] Further, she asserts, "The multiple categories, functions, and symbols used by prehistoric peoples to express the Great Mystery are all aspects of the unbroken unity of one Deity, a Goddess who is ultimately Nature herself."[24]

The monotheistic heritage of many U.S. feminists preconditions us to assume that ultimately, and despite contrary evidence, the divine must by definition be unitary. What we "see" through the lens of that conditioning distorts and trivializes several thousand years of complex and densely tapestried polytheistic conceptions of the divine in, for example, the ancient Near East. These religious beliefs lasted for a much longer time than Judaism or Christianity has been in place. They apparently retained their attraction for people in both polytheistic and monotheistic societies long after the latter evolved, as is attested in the prophetic books of the Hebrew Bible and the Book of Revelation in the New Testament.

Gimbutas sees the symbolism of the Great Goddess emerging from the "celebration of life . . . the leading motif in Old European ideology and art." The main subject of this symbolism is "the mystery of birth and death and the renewal of life, not only human but all life on earth and indeed in the whole cosmos."[25] The important regenerative function of the Goddess in this cycle of life and death is portrayed in physical forms associated with female generative organs—vulva, pubic triangle, uterus, fetuses.[26] The images of the Great Goddess as "the single source of all life," "birth-giver," "fertility-giver," "life- or nourishment-giver," all can be detected as early as 25,000 B.C.E. (and traceable, in turn, to an even earlier time) when sculptures appeared bearing their symbols—"vulvas, triangles, breasts, chevrons."[27]

In her emphasis on what she believes is the pandemic religious symbolism in prehistoric Europe, Gimbutas writes:

> The primordial Deity for our Paleolithic and Neolithic ancestors was female, reflecting the sovereignty of motherhood. . . . Paleolithic and Neolithic symbols and images cluster around a self-generating Goddess and her basic functions as Giver-of-Life, Wielder-of-Death, and as Regeneratrix.[28]

According to Gimbutas, in an agricultural society she becomes sacred as the Pregnant Goddess or Mother Earth.[29] Indeed, the Goddess's functions are based on the bodily or reproductive functions of real women. Though she describes the gynocentric, Goddess-worshiping religion and culture of Neolithic Europe by linking the sexual identity of the supreme Deity with the sexual identity of the head of the family and kinship group, or grounds the worship of Goddesses in preexisting social relations and most often deals with symbolic representations of the Goddess, Gimbutas ultimately grounds her powers in the bodies of real women:

> The Paleolithic Goddess was typically a macrocosmic extension of a woman's body. Her essential parts—vulva, breasts, buttocks, belly—were endowed with the miraculous power of procreation. These symbols continued into the Neolithic and can later be explained as a reflection or memory of a matrilineal system in which paternity was considered unimportant and difficult to establish. The Goddess was a cosmic Creatrix, Life- and Birth-giver, while the father is not known to Paleolithic or Neolithic art.[30]

She played her role as Goddess of Death and Regeneration: "For Old Europeans, the tomb was a womb. Symbols of regeneration—the egg and the regenerative organs of the Goddess [pubic triangle, vulva, uterus, belly, buttocks]—are the basis of Old European tomb shapes."[31] Megalithic tombs are portrayed as "the body of the Goddess," even as "the universe *is* the body of the Goddess, within whom all death and rebirth takes place."[32] Thus, even after death, the consequences of Great Goddess worship were only benign and life affirming, promising regeneration to the dead who returned to her womb.

Unlike Stone, who tends to think male Deities usurped power from the Great Goddess whenever they met her, Gimbutas, referring to a somewhat earlier period, describes the presence of a small number of male figurines recovered from Neolithic settlements as representations of male Deities. Though in her view fatherhood was unknown in those early times and therefore men were not regarded as a source of life, their social and physical powers were valued as somehow magically enlarging women's life-giving force, and their union, in almost mystical fashion, created the energy needed to infuse nature itself with "life powers." Just as the polarization of the sexes was unknown on earth during the Neolithic era, so male Deities at this time were regarded as "partners, consorts and brothers of Goddesses."[33]

Both Gimbutas and Stone describe the status of women as high wherever the Great Goddess was worshiped. Stone links matrilineal kinship systems in the ancient Near East, in which women held high status, with the worship of Goddesses.[34] In fact, she conflates the functions of Goddesses and the roles of women. For example, she describes how the worship of female healing Deities in many parts of the world led to the assignment of roles as physicians to the priestesses who officiated at their worship.[35] Gimbutas describes Old Europe as a matrilineal, theacratic, communal temple society in which females held high status as Great Mothers of the clan along with their brothers or served as members of governing councils, and in which succession to leadership roles and inheritance passed through females.[36]

The invasion of the Near East by patriarchal, militaristic Indo-Europeans from the north, and the invasion of Old Europe by patriarchal, militaristic pastoralists from the eastern steppes beginning about 4300 B.C.E., precipitated the overthrow of Goddess cultures. Gimbutas writes that with the Kurgan invasions, Old Europe changed from a "matrilineal to patrilineal order, from a learned theacracy to a militant patriarchy, from a sexually balanced society to a male dominated hierarchy, and from a chthonic goddess religion to the Indo-European sky-oriented pantheon of Gods."[37] In short, from this perspective, the introduction of patriarchy meant the decline of civilization, the power of the Goddess, and the status of women.[38]

In like fashion, in her study of ancient Ireland and the overthrow of the Goddess-dominated old order by both the invading Celts and the proselytizers of Christianity, Mary Condren locates the essential differences in the experiences and consciousness of women and men in their different bodily reproductive functions. She seems to identify maternity as the core experience in the shaping of women's consciousness and tends to align the characteristics of Goddesses with those of women as actual or potential mothers. Condren terms "war Goddesses" one of the distortions of patriarchal scholarship, an oxymoron. She maintains: "Unlike the male Gods . . . weapons are not their province. The symbols of the Goddess were likewise opposed to battle."[39] She describes the Celtic invaders as coming to a matrifocal society in which "the relationship to the mother formed one of the central principles of social organization" and where "the primary focus of cultural unity is the Goddess."[40]

She considers motherhood in a warrior society a "handicap" rather than "a source of strength."[41] Moreover, in her view, the differing consequences of reproduction for women and men, the "rootedness" that actual or potential maternity gives women's consciousness and the opposite effect of paternity on men's, created a need for the latter to keep proving their manhood. She writes:

> For men, meaning has had to be achieved or imposed upon reality. The natural cycle of birth and death simply condemns them to what they consider to be a "meaningless" existence. Unlike women, whose identity has been tied up with the visibility of childbearing, men have needed to externalize themselves by means of achievements, visible edifices, acting almost as a counterpart to women's natural functions. At the same time women's natural functions were denigrated by the extent to which men succeeded in carving out for themselves a sacred space not accessible to women.[42]

What do all these theories about the nature and social implications of Goddess worship in antiquity have to do with women today? I suspect that most of us have known women who feel that Goddess worship and a focus on the "Goddess within all of us," especially when experienced in a community of women, is healing and empowering. There is no question that women's spirituality groups or covens or whatever their names—with diverse kinds of participants, at times a cross between consciousness-raising and survivors' groups—have been experienced as helpful for a variety of reasons, perhaps not least among them that they make some women who suffer low self-esteem feel better. There are, after all, costs to oppression, and low self-esteem is unfortunately one of them, though obviously it does not afflict all women. Also, ours is an age marked by alienation and a belief in the efficacy of therapy, and many women have described their groups as experientially therapeutic. Feelings of belonging and the effects of participating in communal observances, the basis of all ritual, are very significant, and many women apparently find it both less oppressive and more authentic, more consonant with their own experiences, to identify with a female divinity. Certainly the interest of women's spirituality groups in divine immanence is of enormous value for a planet that threatens to destroy its life-sustaining environment. And obviously the work of theorists like Gimbutas, Condren, and Stone have touched a responsive and deep chord in many women, offering an intellectual and emotional grounding for modern Goddess worship.

While some women of color have written about the rich Goddess traditions of their own cultures,[43] a number of others have expressed anger over the proliferation of new, nature-venerating, Goddess-worshiping groups on the ground that they coopt and diminish the sanctity of their own cultural traditions.[44] Still others, working out of their own diverse cultural traditions, have increasingly discussed how, with their commitments to both feminism and spirituality, they should relate to one another across lines of class, ethnicity, race, religion, sexual orientation, and the like.[45] It is apparent that an emphasis by U.S. white feminists on female experience alone, without explicitly dealing with issues of commonalities and differences, is too hegemonic.

In addition, without disparaging the empowerment reported by some women who participate in these womanspirit groups or discounting the social activism of some involved in them, for example, the feminist witch Starhawk,[46] it seems to me that what is being promoted as empowering for women is seriously flawed, misleading, and does not attend to the many things that cause their denigration or exclusion. Although there might be some changes in the psyches of individual women (no small thing), what seems lacking is a political analysis of the sources of power and powerlessness. Indeed, everything is left essentially unchanged.

Fixing the distant origins of Great Goddess worship in the female's ability to reproduce is biological reductionism at its most pernicious. This has been one of the major ways in which women worldwide have been stereotyped, devaluing all of our other human traits, and it does not take into account the varied contributions of women to culture, including those who cannot or choose not to reproduce. While childbirth probably was seen as awesome in cultures in which paternity was unknown, as was women's periodic bleeding without dying from it in cultures that did not connect menstruation and maternity, to suggest that those physiological functions alone accounted for the supremacy of the Great Goddess is to beg the question of whether there is ever anything new under the sun. Furthermore, the *veneration* of maternity sounds very much like a male invention.

Childbearing and childrearing may indeed be wonderful for many of us, but for some, for example, in the absence of enough food or the presence of untreatable disease, they have been mixed blessings. While women might have gladly borne the children needed by their tribe or clan, particularly if that was an honored role and particularly at a time when the good of the kin group, tribe, or community took precedence over that of the individual, there is much contrary evidence, at least in historic times, to suggest that childbirth also has been feared by women because of its death-dealing possibilities.[47] Complications of pregnancy, breech births, and puerperal infections have been killers of women, and maternal and child mortality are still high in some parts of the world. Unless it can be shown that Paleolithic Europe developed the technology to remedy such devastating conditions, it is difficult to believe that women themselves always welcomed or celebrated maternity.

And what of the patriarchal, militaristic Indo-European invaders? Did the Kurgan pastoralists not see their women give birth? Did female Indo-Europeans reproduce differently than Goddess-worshiping women? Why didn't Indo-European men translate the mystery of that event to Goddess worship as, presumably, Western European and ancient Near Eastern men did? One might argue that observation of animal copulation and birth taught these patriarchal pastoralists about the male role in reproduction, but, interestingly, Gimbutas and others do not make that claim. Moreover, Goddess worshipers in Old Europe also had much contact with animals. Indeed, Gimbutas identifies sheep as "the most important meat supply from the earliest Neolithic."[48] In other words, why and how did patriarchy arise in one culture but not another?

It also is difficult to believe, as Gimbutas and others assert, that death was viewed by Paleolithic and Neolithic Goddess worshipers as only part of the cycle of life (and perhaps inferior to it?), but that it was not seen as the opposite of life, simply because the Goddess was celebrated as the source of regeneration after death. It is one thing to say that there were explanations of what happened after death—all religions offer those in one way or another, and some are more comforting than others—but except when people have had the strongest religious and ideological revulsion to what they were compelled to submit to in order to live, we do not have many examples of people who were sanguine in the face of death, even in cultures like ancient Egypt that promised an eternity of bliss to the virtuous. Christian martyrs died rather than renounce their faith and pay allegiance to the Roman emperor as an incarnation of divinity, and Jews died rather than give up their religion and convert to Christianity, but we do not otherwise know of Christians or Jews who, wholesale, thought life and death equally appealing or who chose death over life. One might surmise that Christians and Jews made these choices in patriarchal cultures in which, Gimbutas claims, life and death were seen as binary opposites,[49] but the same cannot be said of ancient Egypt.

We really do not know what prehistoric people thought about death. Excavations of excarnated human remains might unearth evidence that people practiced a burial ritual to unite the dead more closely with the Goddess, as Gimbutas contends, or the remains might just as easily have meant something else. And it will not do simply to attribute a cyclical view of life, death, and regeneration to a mythopoeic mentality that, in circular reasoning, did not, therefore, produce fear of death. At times, scholars have used a "mythopoeic" (that is, nonrational) designation to cover what they saw as alien. For example, that term has frequently been used to describe the outlook of ancient Near Eastern, highly advanced cultures even though they invented writing; produced beautiful art, poetry, and sacred literature; developed irrigation; conducted business and trade; initiated schools; built temples; and erected pyramids without the use of pulleys in ways we do not yet fathom.

If women as mothers may not have always felt neutral about death or welcomed it as a return to the womb of the Goddess, the absolutely benign nature of her reign is problematic in other ways as well. Are we to believe that in this thousands-of-years era of cooperative, peaceful, egalitarian, artistic, one-with-nature living, no bad things ever happened? There were never any storms or droughts, no sickness, pain, or rotten behavior? No quarreling siblings, disappointed lovers, imperfect humans? There was no dark side to human nature, none of the complex, irrational forces, along with life-enhancing impulses and struggles we know as part of the ambiguity of being human? Can we make the claim that the rule of the Goddess, linked to the leadership of women in human societies, yielded a four-thousand-year-long Neolithic idyll *because* it was based on female preeminence both symbolically and in real life? Is there something intrinsically nurturant of life in women? In Goddesses? Valuable as nurturance is, do we come by it naturally or through socialization? Is nurturance in our genes as potential reproducers, and is this the only kind of power we aspire to? Are all women alike, and will nurturance free us of male dominance? What *do* we really know about the thinking of Neolithic people?

The recent embrace of Goddess worship by many sorts of women and the growing popularity of work on Goddesses by scholars and nonscholars alike, bridging many disciplines, cultures, and periods of history, have elicited a number of critiques and commentaries. Among the most perceptive, it seems to me, are those that raise concerns about the over-simplification and essentialism of the contemporary resurrection of the Goddess.

For example, screenwriter Donaleen Saul and therapist Jean Napali analyze their own discomfort in terms of the need Goddess worship appears to fill. In their view, in the face of innumerable problems in the world and in our homes, at the center of interest in ancient Goddess civilizations today is a "nostalgic yearning" for a simpler, better, trouble-free golden age.

Given the horrific state of our planet—war, starvation, injustice, environmental disaster—it is understandable that people would long for a more innocent time, that they would search for an ideal that could somehow alleviate (or at least buffer them from) the suffering of this world. The Goddess has been accorded all of the qualities that make up such an ideal—strength, beauty, fertility, love, harmony, peace. Characterizing the spread of interest in Goddesses as a "New Age ideology—not truly interested in real female power because accessing such power would mean having to experience those parts of ourselves that are wounded, destructive, and painful beyond words,"[50] they see the women's spirituality movement as essentially harmless in that it does not really change the status quo. It simply projects all negative qualities onto men as the Other. They conclude that there is much that must be transformed but that "the Goddess will not do it for us."[51]

Writer Catherine Madsen extends the argument further to address the issues of essentialism and the utility to women of a benign Goddess. While agreeing that revelations about women's place in patriarchal religions have "left many women profoundly in need of comfort . . . it has left them in even greater need of truth." To project all the good qualities absent from the Father God onto the Goddess "is to maintain a dependent and docile relationship to God, and to assert that gender is the factor which makes dependency on the Father God intolerable and dependency on the Goddess permissible." Indeed, feeling comfortable with the Goddess can be infantilizing, "a kind of invasion of one's authority." She continues: "But why is it necessary (and how is it possible?) to have a God one trusts and approves of? I say this not as someone who has known only the Father God, but as someone who has known the world."[52]

By detailing the unavoidable mix of pleasure and pain in being human, Madsen hits on one of the key issues in contemporary conceptions of the Goddess.

> To establish a Goddess in place of the Father God accomplishes nothing if we try to make her good. To substitute feminine virtues for masculine powers is impossible, either in divine or in human terms; in the world, virtues and powers are entirely mixed, so that no good act takes place (even nurturance, even comfort) without its undercurrent of danger; and no evil act takes place but through the intermediary of the body, the physical reality we love. If we are made in the divine image, *that* is what we are up against: the inseparability of good and evil.[53]

In short, romanticizing the Neolithic Goddess and her analogues does not do justice to the anxieties, complexities, imperfections, and ambiguities of the human existence out of which conceptions of the divine emerge, just as romanticizing and sentimentalizing the lives and deaths of accused witches in early modern Europe does not sufficiently acknowledge their unspeakable suffering, nor explain how the ideology of the witch hunts was integral to the High Renaissance and Reformations, nor counter the characterization of women in those and other times as morally weaker than men—evil, sexual predators diverting men from the pursuit of righteousness, but simultaneously powerless. In addition, then, to whether the claims for the benign and enduring reign of the Goddess in antiquity are demonstrable, there is the question of whether such a past would necessarily be desirable, whether it ought to be appropriated by women.

Underlying the gender-based hierarchy in the West—the dichotomy between the superior soul/spirit/male and the inferior body/nature/female, early identified by Rosemary Ruether as our legacy from ancient Greece via Christianity and subsequently elaborated by many others—is the persistent belief among many educated men, in modern times especially since about the thirteenth century, that the natures of women and men are irrevocably different.[54] Faced with our designation as the Other, with the male defined as the norm for the fully human, the valorization of femaleness explicit in Goddess worship is comprehensible and probably psychologically healthy. It does not, however, confront the issues of gender polarity or gender hierarchy and, indeed, may affirm them, only substituting the female for the male.

If hierarchy, domination, and subordination based on sex are unjust and oppressive, how will worshiping a female divinity in or out of our selves deal with all of that? And how can we understand the claims of Gimbutas that a supreme Great Goddess was worshiped by societies that, on the one hand, were led by women as clan mothers, through whom inheritance and political leadership were transmitted, but that, on the other hand, simultaneously were sexually egalitarian with no hierarchy based on gender? If the latter were the case, why were the clan leaders and divinities only female? For thousands of years, were all women genetically nonexploitative and men nonobservant about who was really in charge?

There are other models of female agency available to our "historical consciousness" based on more than our awesome power to produce and reproduce life. Polytheistic cultures, which existed in the ancient Near East for several millennia before the Common Era, have left us a body of literature encompassing myths, descriptions of sacred rituals, conceptions of the divine, and accounts of their beliefs about moral behavior. These cultures were very far from perfect, marked as they were by wars, class stratification, slavery, and, at times, human sacrifice. Nevertheless, some of their beliefs and practices—principally their conceptions of divinities, in their immanence and anthropomorphism expressive of the ambiguities and complexities of human existence, and their attitudes toward the significance of gender and gender differences, female sexuality, and the linkage of gender to power—might serve as constructive resources and models for us today.

In general, their worldview was based on the conviction that the individual was part of a social group embedded in the natural world, and that the survival and prosperity of both the group and individual depended on the survival and prosperity of the natural world. Though their divinities were anthropomorphically conceived, they were also transcendent, greater than humans, and not only immanent but omnipresent in nature and interventionist in human affairs. In contrast to ways of thinking prevalent in monotheism dominated by male imagery and metaphors, the sex of the divine was relatively so unimportant that it sometimes changed as the worship of specific Deities spread geographically. What mattered to worshipers was the satisfaction of community and, later, individual needs.

Creators of the universe were female or male, but mythic portrayals of the divine from Egypt and Mesopotamia describe some of these creator-Deities as bisexual. Honoring creation itself, however, was not the sole preoccupation of the human community. Not infrequently, emerging out of a rather pragmatic worldview, creator Deities came to be elevated to almost honorific status, while younger, more active divinities of both sexes came to be seen as organizing, structuring, and maintaining the ongoing business of the created universe by, for example, judging, punishing, and rewarding the behavior of both other Deities and humans. Creation was bodily, and the organization of the universe was often portrayed as the result of divine sexual unions, or there was no divine body-spirit dichotomy and, therefore, no denigration of divine sexuality and bodily processes.

In contrast to a monotheistic view, the divine was conceived of as plural. Each Goddess and God had several attributes that were most often not linked to their sex: there were Gods and Goddesses of fertility, justice, war, wisdom, social order, death, and the like, frequently sharing these attributes in rough equivalence within the same pantheon. No Deity had all-encompassing power. Perhaps most striking, gender was not the locus of divine good and evil, power and powerlessness, virtue and vice, beneficence, malevolence, and capriciousness.

Some understand this as the period in which the provenance of the Great Goddess was overshadowed and eclipsed by the male Deities of the invading patriarchal Indo-Europeans.[55] Others maintain that ancient Near Eastern polytheistic religions and thought can be understood only in terms of the nature, actions, and relationships of both Goddesses and Gods, but that the sexual identities of those divinities determined much about the provenance of their authority and powers.[56] Another way of reading the situation, however, is that for several thousand years, the variety, complexity, anxieties, and triumphs of women and men were embodied in the attributes of the Goddesses and Gods they worshiped in ways that did not establish gender hierarchies constructed on sexual polarities.

In fact, struggles for power did not always involve Goddesses and Gods. The battle between male Deities for kingship of the Gods runs like a recurrent theme through ancient Near Eastern myths. But when Goddesses and Gods fought, the latter were by no means always victorious. For example, long after its society had become male-dominant, the Assyrian palace library at Nineveh contained the most complete text of the Babylonian version of a Noah-type flood story. The God Enlil, with the collaboration of the council of the Gods, lets loose a deluge on earth to quiet the noise of humans. After the Goddess Ishtar realizes *her* people are endangered by the flood, she regrets her consent to it, blames Enlil for it, and "lifting her [lapis lazuli] necklace with the jewels of heaven that once Anu [the supreme sky-God] had made to please her," she punishes Enlil for his destructiveness by decreeing that he alone of all the Goddesses and Gods was forbidden to enjoy the sacrifices offered by the surviving humans.[57]

In the broad range of divine activities, some divinities, such as the Egyptian Goddess Maat, acted alone. Some collaborated with other divinities, either male or female; for example, the Egyptian Goddess Isis worked with Nephthys, and Isis with the Egyptian Gods Osiris and Thoth. Some, for example, the Sumerian Goddesses Inanna and Ereshkigal, were enemies. Divine power did not reside in nor was it defined by the sex of the divinity, and the great power of Goddesses did not rest solely on veneration of their maternity. To cite but a few examples, if the Egyptian Deity Thoth was the God of wisdom, the Goddess Isis, among her many other attributes, was his counterpart. The myth "The God and His Unknown Name of Power" (ca. 1350-1200 B.C.E.) describes the Goddess Isis' successful attempt to discover the

God Ra's secret name, his source of personality and power, thereby obtaining power for herself. The Goddess is described as "a clever woman . . . choicer than a million Gods. . . . There was nothing she did not know in heaven and earth, like Ra, who made the content of the earth."[58]

A Sumerian myth, "Inanna and Enki: The Transfer of the Arts of Civilization from Eridu to Erech" (inscribed about 2000 B.C.E.), recounts how the *Me,* the divine decrees fundamental to the organization and functioning of Sumerian civilization, were transferred from their guardian Enki, the great God of wisdom and sweet water, to Inanna, the great Goddess of fertility and the judge of humanity, after she encourages him to get drunk. Nowhere in that telling is gender mentioned as the reason one divinity rather than the other is the more appropriate custodian of the decrees. Nor is Enki shown as willing (or perhaps able) to confront the Goddess himself and regain control of those decrees. In fact, by relinquishing them to Inanna, Enki guarantees the primacy of her city at that time. Significantly, here the sex of the divine is a non-issue.[59]

Similarly, "Nergal and Ereshkigal," a more complete neo-Assyrian version of an earlier myth from about 1300 B.C.E., tells us how the God Nergal came to share dominion over the dead with the chthonic Goddess Ereshkigal. In contrast with the earlier version in which Nergal physically browbeats her into sharing her rule with him, in this later version when her lover Nergal abandons her to return to the domains of the supreme Gods—Anu, Enlil, and Ea—Ereshkigal threatens to raise the dead so they would outnumber the living. The Goddess invokes the laws of the underworld that forbade anyone simply to leave, and, in acknowledgment of her great power, those three ruling Gods accede to her demand, and Nergal is returned to her as her husband.[60]

Divine motherhood was not worshiped in and of itself once the requisite number of Deities to do the work of the world was provided. For instance, when the worship of Isis spread throughout the Mediterranean and she came to be viewed as a universal Goddess, it was popular piety that transformed her character into a maternal one.[61] And though the Greek Goddess Demeter was strongly maternal toward her daughter—her two sons barely figure in myth or ritual—she did not only weep after the abduction of her daughter Kore, but in her bereavement she stopped doing her job as the Goddess of cultivated grain. The barrenness of the earth threatened to extinguish all life, and her brothers, the Gods Zeus and Hades, were forced to bow to her power and autonomy. They returned Kore to her but had to use trickery to call her back to the underworld for half the year as its august Queen Persephone, without whom Hades might not have been able to rule and to assure the cycle of seasons. No wonder Demeter was hardly present on male-dominated Olympus.

Many of the greatest Goddesses did not endlessly reproduce. At times the social and spiritual ends of divine maternity, once the necessary functions of the universe were attended to, were served by one or two mighty offspring. Isis had only one son, Horus, but he with his mother defended his father, the God Osiris, and guaranteed legitimate succession to the throne of Egypt. The Sumerian Goddess Nammu parthenogenetically gave birth to only two Deities, the God An and and the Goddess Ki, but they were heaven and earth. At a time when the role of men in reproduction was understood, the fathers of some of these divinities, for example, the Greek Kore, were insignificant in myth and cult, and some Goddesses, for example, the Egyptian Hathor, had no male partners.[62] Even when the Canaanite Goddess Asherah mothered seventy Deities and the Greek Gaia bore many, maternity did not prevent their participation in the power struggles for supremacy by the Gods Baal, Cronos, and Zeus, nor were the Goddesses limited in any way by their physiology. In fact, divine female sexuality and reproduction (which did not always go together) were often portrayed as active and beneficial to the human community, as, for example, when Isis impregnated herself with Horus from the dead body of Osiris, and when people gathered around the temples of Inanna and Ishtar to celebrate the sacred marriage described in two thousand years of Sumerian poetry.

Goddesses were not all alike, nor did the status of real women inevitably depend upon the nature of Goddesses. Condren may be right about Irish Goddesses not being warlike, but that certainly was not the case in the ancient Near East. Similarly, mortal women as mothers—for instance, Spartan women, upper-class women in imperial Rome, and noblewomen in feudal Europe—did not always suffer handicaps in warrior societies, contrary to Condren. While scholars like John Bright may be confounded by the "surprising polarity" when fertility Goddesses are also depicted as "bloodthirsty Goddesses of war,"[63] it is because he does not appreciate the full range of meaning and power ascribed to them. Fertility Goddesses were conceived of as providing for some of the most basic needs of human communities. They not only created divine offspring, they also guaranteed the fertility of the soil, legitimated the rule of the king, guaranteed victory in battle, themselves fought (like, for example, the Canaanite Goddess Anath), and, like the Goddesses Inanna and Ishtar, judged the human community and gave it its "just desserts."[64] One might argue that it was precisely their active engagement in the multifaceted concerns of the community, including victory in war, that gave them their powers. Fertility Goddesses were perceived not only as mighty wombs that generated all life, welcomed it back after death, and then regenerated it. They, like Gods, by their power also assured the continuation of the human community in the face of possible disasters and chaos, such as droughts and storms, crop failures, defeats by enemies, social instability, and so on.

While Christ is right about religion being revealed in the stories we tell about our lives, there was no universal, linear, causal connection between the worship of great Goddesses and the status of women. For one thing, like Goddesses, women were not all alike. As classicist Sarah Pomeroy pointed out in her work on women in ancient Greece and Rome, it depended on which women were telling their stories. That is, were they slave or free, upper or lower class, members of the conquered or conquering culture?[65] For another, while religious views undoubtedly have always reflected in many ways the cultures of which they were a part, the relation of Goddesses to the status of some classes of women has been extremely complicated, marked by inconsistencies and conflicting evidence. For instance, the presence and power of Goddesses in third-millennium Sumer and second-millenium Mari apparently were matched by the high status of upper-class women.[66] In imperial Rome, however, at the same time that the worship of Isis spread widely, well beyond the devotion accorded to other Roman Goddesses and seriously competing with Christianity for the allegiance of Rome, upper-class women had won some *de facto* rights through Augustan legislation designed as incentives for them to bear more patrician children. They also had virtually no political rights, however, because of their allegedly frivolous nature, and, while better off than the wives of Athenian citizens of the classical period, they lived under a thoroughgoing double standard.[67] Clearly, Juvenal's *Sixth Satire* was not anomalous for those times.

Given the rough equivalence in the power of Goddesses and Gods, and given the fact that the status of certain classes of women fluctuated over the course of three millennia despite the persistent worship of great Goddesses in the ancient Near East, it is difficult to argue that the worship of great Goddesses always mirrored women's status in society, as for instance in late second-millennium Assyria. All one might conclude is that the prevalence of polytheism probably accounted for the widespread and enduring involvement of women as well as men in many capacities and aspects of cult, both official and popular—for example, in first-millennium mystery cults—and for their probable prominence in the cult of the dying young Gods Dumuzi, Tammuz,

Adonis, or Baal.[68] Rather, reversing the assertion, one might say that among the factors that might have accounted for the worship of powerful, autonomous Goddesses in the ancient Near East was the real or remembered public prominence of some classes of women in social as well as cultic life.

For example, until well into the first millennium, though Egyptian women of all classes were not absolutely equal to Egyptian men, they enjoyed equal legal safeguards and, like men, had public rights and responsibilities to the state.[69] In the first half of the second millennium, in the Old Babylonian period, at a time when temples and temple personnel reached their long arms into the economic and political affairs of surrounding communities, there are records of women being involved in all kinds of public, religious, and economic activities.[70] The royal archives of Mari indicate that King Zimri-Lin's armies marched on the advice of female and male ecstatics and oracles, even as a woman administered his kingdom.[71] In Sumer, prior to the development of male military leadership to meet military crises and the emergence of a male priestly elite, royal women helped legitimate the king's ascension to the throne, and some queens, not all of them of royal origin, managed their own estates, conducted their own diplomatic negotiations, held their own courts, and, in earliest times, were named along with their husbands in the king lists.[72] In sum, the belief that powerful, independent Goddesses, like Gods, could and did keep nature and the human community running did not seem to rest on awe of female reproductive potential alone but instead might have been consonant with the visible or recollected agency and influence of real women. Put another way, the later stereotypes associated with gender polarity and hierarchy had not yet solidified.

By way of example, the myth "Inanna's Descent to the Netherworld," inscribed about the beginning of the second millennium, was the prototype for the myth "Ishtar's Descent to the Netherworld," recorded a thousand years later. During the interval, Sumer had been conquered by Babylonia, and, by the end of the second millennium, women's status had declined precipitously. In the first myth, the threat of the powerful Goddess Inanna to reduce the civilized world to its primitive state convinces the God of wisdom to rescue her from the netherworld and restore her to life. When her consort, King Dumuzi, refuses to pay her proper homage, she consigns him to the netherworld in her place, and only the intervention of his gifted sister persuades Inanna to let them both share the penalty she decrees. In the second and later myth, the Goddess Ishtar is restored to life by the God of wisdom, not in response to her threats but because, in her absence, animals and humans stop reproducing. When Ishtar returns to life, she does not consign her consort Tammuz to death for showing disrespect toward her, and when he mysteriously appears in the netherworld anyway, compassionate Ishtar provides him with courtesans to ease his death.[73]

In addition, there was a less dogmatic, more inclusive attitude toward religious beliefs and practices in the ancient Near East than has been true of later societies in the West. There were popular, often home-based religious practices that are believed to have preceded and surely coexisted with temple-based worship and, eventually, with the evolution of national Deities. As Babylonia, Assyria, and other cultures became more male-dominant and militaristic during the second millennium, women increasingly were shut out of any but priestly roles in the temples. They apparently moved into and often assumed primacy in cults devoted to the young dying Gods of vegetation (Dumuzi, Tammuz, Adonis, Baal). In some of the most widespread first-millennium mystery cults (for example, the Eleusinian and Isaic), women were priestesses, celebrants, and initiates. The worship of Demeter/Kore was the popular religion of Greece for all classes, and, by the time of the Roman Empire, the worship of Isis had so many devotees among women and men of all classes that it strongly competed with Christianity to become the official religion of Rome.[74]

The elements that might be profitably appropriated as our "historical consciousness" of this period are not reprehensible and inhumane social practices like slavery, human sacrifice, and propensity for war. These practices alone did not define the period any more than the entire classical period of Athens can be defined by its slave-system and wars or the Renaissance and Reformations only by the witch hunts. The presence of these elements is part of what Madsen meant by the inextricableness of good and evil. Rather, we might profit by considering the religious and social implications of the radically different attitudes toward the significance of gender, gender differences, and female sexuality in the ancient Near East, certainly in the divine sphere and at times in the earthly. The powerful, often autonomous, Goddesses and Gods, whose attributes and activities reflected the complexities, anxieties, and imperfections of the human community, all of which were evident in the changing face of nature, provide images and models, otherwise absent from solely male images of monotheistic traditions, of sexual egalitarianism and female as well as male agency and strength, based on the attributes rather than the gender of the divine.

Divine power and attributes were not exclusively identified with either sex; the sexuality of Goddesses and Gods was treated as normal, neither denigrated nor restricted for either sex; and there was no dichotomy between divine body and spirit. In short, Goddesses and Gods appeared to share divine responsibilities for the ongoing existence of the human community and nature. And for long periods of time in the ancient Near East, gender-neutral attitudes toward the efficacy of divinities apparently spilled over into cult. Women as well as men were relied upon to propitiate Goddesses and Gods and to attend to their affairs on earth on behalf of the entire community.

If it is truly to empower us, the women's spirituality movement must move beyond taking its inspiration from the Great Goddess as great source of life, death, and regeneration. Those alone are not liberating images for us, because we have often suffered from them and always been more than that. They do not deal with the sources of our oppression, and not to take a position on those sources is in itself taking a position. If the Goddess is to liberate us, once we acknowledge her presence within and our worth as persons, she will turn our energies and talents outward to struggle with all forms of oppression—poverty, racism, homelessness in the midst of affluence, destruction of rain forests, and the like. It is not only because as women we belong to many classes, ethnic groups, races, and cultures. It is also because if rights to justice and freedom from oppression are not recognized as universal entitlements for *all* people, women, in justice, will never be free of oppression. Indeed, if we as feminists commit ourselves to such struggles, we just might provide the kind of female public presence and influence that will enable the reemergence of the Goddesses.

NOTES

1. See Lerner, *Creation of Patriarchy.*

2. See Ruether, *Sexism and God-Talk;* Plaskow, *Standing Again at Sinai.*

3. See Gimbutas, *Language of the Goddess,* 321.

4. Ehrenberg, *Women in Prehistory,* 66-76; Nelson, "Diversity."

5. Based on a conversation between Sumerian scholar Samuel Noah Kramer and biblical archeologist James Strange at the University of South Florida, 1983, in which the two held opposing views, and personal conversation with archeologist Nancy White, 1993.

6. See Ruether, *Womanguides,* 3–4

7. Christ, *Laughter of Aphrodite.*

8. See Brooten, "Early Christian Women," 89-90.

9. See Barnett, "Language of the Goddess"; Fagan, "Sexist View."

10. Gimbutas, *Civilization of the Goddess,* 244-46.

11. Personal conversation with Samuel Noah Kramer, 1983.

12. See Starhawk, "Witchcraft and Women's Culture"; Adler, *Drawing Down the Moon,* 57, 65, 81; Gimbutas, *Civilization of the Goddess,* 244.

13. Schüssler Fiorenza, "Remembering the Past," 51.

14. Gimbutas, *Language of the Goddess,* xv.

15. Gimbutas, *Language of the Goddess,* xvii.

16. Lovejoy, *Great Chain of Being.*

17. Gimbutas, *Language of the Goddess,* 318-20; *Civilization of the Goddess,* viii, 222-23, 230, 235, 238, 243, 249, 251, 294, 305, 342, 344-45.

18. Gimbutas, *Civilization of the Goddess,* 243.

19. Gimbutas, *Language of the Goddess,* 321.

20. Stone, *When God Was a Woman,* 22, 9-29.

21. See Christ, *Laughter of Aphrodite;* Downing, "Artemis."

22. Gimbutas, *Civilization of the Goddess,* pp. 223-48.

23. Gimbutas, *Language of the Goddess,* 316; see also *Civilization of the Goddess,* 225-26, 230-40.

24. Gimbutas, *Civilization of the Goddess,* 223.

25. Gimbutas, *Language of the Goddess,* 321, xix; *Civilization of the Goddess,* 222-305, 399-400.

26. Gimbutas, *Civilization of the Goddess,* 242, 244, 281, 304, 399-401.

27. Gimbutas, *Language of the Goddess,* xix; *Civilization of the Goddess,* 352.

28. Gimbutas, *Civilization of the Goddess,* x.

29. Gimbutas, *Civilization of the Goddess,* 228.

30. Gimbutas, *Civilization of the Goddess,* 342.

31. Gimbutas, *Civilization of the Goddess,* 281.

32. Gimbutas, *Civilization of the Goddess,* 305.

33. Gimbutas, *Civilization of the Goddess,* 249.

34. Stone, *When God Was a Woman,* 30-61.

35. Stone, *When God Was a Woman,* 3.

36. Gimbutas, *Civilization of the Goddess,* 324, 336, 349.

37. Gimbutas, *Civilization of the Goddess,* 401.

38. Gimbutas, *Civilization of the Goddess,* 352-401.

39. Condren, *Serpent and the Goddess,* 35.

40. Condren, *Serpent and the Goddess,* 60.

41. Condren, *Serpent and the Goddess,* 42.

42. Condren, *Serpent and the Goddess,* 38.

43. See Allen, "Grandmother of the Sun"; Anzaldua, "Entering into the Serpent."

44. See Springer, "Whose Goddesses Are They?"; Smith, "For All Those Who Were Indian"; Kasee, "Identity, Recovery and Religious Imperialism."

45. Eugene, et al., "Appropriation and Reciprocity."

46. Starhawk, *Dreaming the Dark.*

47. See Leavitt, "Under the Shadow of Maternity," 129-54.

48. Gimbutas, *Language of the Goddess,* 317.

49. See Gimbutas, *Civilization of the Goddess,* 243.

50. Saul and Napali, "Goddess Worship," 4.

51. Saul and Napali, "Goddess Worship," 4.

52. Madsen, "Roundtable Discussion," 104.

53. Madsen, "Roundtable Discussion," 104.

54. Stuard, "Dominion of Gender," 154.

55. For example, Gimbutas and Stone.

56. Frymer-Kensky, *In the Wake of the Goddess,* 9-80.

57. Sandars, *Epic of Gilgamesh,* 107-9.

58. Wilson, "The God," 12.

59. Kramer, *Sumerian Mythology,* 64-68.

60. Grayson, "Akkadian Myths," 507-12.

61. Bleeker, "Isis and Hathor," 31.

62. Bleeker, "Isis and Hathor," 48.

63. Bright, *A History of Israel,* 118-19.

64. See Enheduanna, *Exaltation of Inanna.*

65. Pomeroy, *Goddesses.*

66. Kramer, "Poets and Psalmists," 12–16; Batto, *Studies on Women at Mari;* Dossin and Finet, *Archives Royales.*

67. Pomeroy, *Goddesses,* 149-89, 205-26; Cantarella, *Pandora's Daughters,* 135-70.

68. See Ochshorn, *Female Experience,* 107-15, 124-26.

69. Lesko, "Women of Egypt," 44-58.

70. Harris, *Ancient Sippar.*

71. Cited in Ochshorn, *Female Experience,* 112-14.

72. Lesko, "Women of Egypt," 61-62.

73. Enheduanna, *The Exaltation of Inanna;* Speiser, "Descent of Ishtar," 106-8; Ochshorn, *Female Experience,* 82-87; Ochshorn and Cole, *Women's Spirituality,* 23-24.

74. Pomeroy, *Goddesses,* 217-25.

WORKS CITED

Adler, M. *Drawing Down the Moon: Witches, Druids, Goddess-Worshippers, and Other Pagans.* 2d rev. ed. Boston: Beacon Press, 1986.

Allen, P. G. "Grandmother of the Sun: The Power of Woman in Native

America." Pp. 22–28 in *Weaving the Visions: New Patterns in Feminist Spirituality,* edited by Judith Plaskow and Carol Christ. San Francisco: Harper and Row, 1989.

Anzaldua, G. "Entering into the Serpent." Pp. 77–86 in *Weaving the Visions: New Patterns in Feminist Spirituality,* edited by Judith Plaskow and Carol Christ. San Francisco: Harper and Row, 1989.

Barnett, W. "The Language of the Goddess." *American Journal of Archaeology* 96 (1992): 170-71.

Batto, B. F. *Studies on Women at Mari.* Baltimore: Johns Hopkins University Press, 1974.

Bleeker, C. J. "Isis and Hathor: Two Ancient Egyptian Goddesses." Pp. 29–48 in *The Book of the Goddess Past and Present,* edited by C. Olson. New York: Crossroad Publishing, 1983.

Bridenthal, R., C. Koonz, S. Stuard, eds. *Becoming Visible: Women in European History.* 2d rev. ed. Boston: Houghton Mifflin, 1987.

Bright, J. *A History of Israel.* 3d ed. Philadelphia: Westminster Press, 1981.

Brooten, B. "Early Christian Women and Their Cultural Context: Issues of Method in Historical Reconstruction." Pp. 65–91 in *Feminist Perspectives on Biblical Scholarship,* edited by A. C. Collins. Chico, Calif.: Scholars Press, 1985.

Cantarella, E. *Pandora's Daughters: The Role and Status of Women in Greek and Roman Antiquity.* Translated by M. Fant. Baltimore: Johns Hopkins University Press, 1987.

Christ, C. "Why Women Need the Goddess: Phenomenological, Psychological and Political Reflections." Pp. 273–87 in *Womanspirit Rising: A Feminist Reader in Religion,* edited by C. Christ and J. Plaskow. San Francisco: Harper & Row, 1979.

———. *The Laughter of Aphrodite.* San Francisco: Harper & Row, 1987.

Christ, C., and J. Plaskow, eds. *Womanspirit Rising: A Feminist Reader in Religion.* San Francisco: Harper & Row, 1979.

Collins, A. C., ed. *Feminist Perspectives on Biblical Scholarship.* Chico, Calif.: Scholars Press, 1985.

Condren, M. *The Serpent and the Goddess: Women, Religion, and Power in Celtic Ireland.* San Francisco: Harper & Row, 1989.

Dossin, G., and A. Finet *Archives Royales de Mari: Correspondence Feminine.* Paris: Librairie Orientaliste Paul Guenther, 1978.

Downing, C. "Artemis: The Goddess Who Comes from Afar." Pp. 119–27 in *Weaving the Visions: New Patterns in Feminist Spirituality,* edited by Judith Plaskow and Carol Christ. San Francisco: Harper and Row, 1989.

Enheduanna. *The Exaltation of Inanna.* Translated by W. W. Hallo and J. J. A. Van Dijk. New Haven, Conn.: Yale University Press, 1968.

Ehrenberg, M. *Women in Prehistory*. Norman, Okla: University of Oklahoma Press, 1989.

Eugene, T. M., A. M. Isasi-Diaz, Kwok Pui-lan, J. Plaskow, M. Hunt, E. Townes, E. Umansky. "Appropriation and Reciprocity in Womanist/Mujerista/Feminist Work." *Journal of Feminist Studies in Religion* 8 (1992): 91-124.

Fagan, B. "A Sexist View of Prehistory." *Archaeology* 45 (1992): 14–66.

Frymer-Kensky, T. *In the Wake of the Goddesses*. New York: The Free Press, 1992.

Gimbutas, M. *The Language of the Goddess.* San Francisco: Harper & Row, 1989.

———. *The Civilization of the Goddess.* Edited by Joan Marler. San Francisco: Harper & Row, 1991.

Grayson, A. K. "Akkadian Myths and Epics." Pp. 507–12 in *Ancient Near Eastern Texts Relating to the Old Testament,* edited by J. B. Pritchard. 3d ed., with supp. Princeton, N.J.: Princeton University Press, 1969.

Harris, R. *Ancient Sippar: A Demographic Study of an Old Babylonian City (1894-1595 B.C.).* Istanbul: Historische-Archeologische Institut, 1975.

Kasee, C. R. "Identity, Recovery and Religious Imperialism: Native American Women and the New Age." In *Women's Spirituality, Women's Lives,* edited by J. Ochshorn and E. Cole. New York: The Haworth Press, 1995.

Kramer, S. N. *Sumerian Mythology: A Study of Spiritual and Literary Achievement in the Third Millennium* B.C.. Rev. ed. Philadelphia: University of Pennsylvania Press, 1972.

———. "Poets and Psalmists: Goddesses and Theologians; Literary, Religious and Anthropological Aspects of the Legacy of Sumer." Vol. IV, pp. 112–16 in *The Legacy of Sumer,* edited by D. Schmandt-Besserat. Malibu, Calif.: Undena Publications, 1976.

Leavitt, J. W. "Under the Shadow of Maternity: American Women's Responses to Death and Debility Fears in Nineteenth-Century Childbirth." *Feminist Studies* 12 (1986): 129-54.

Lerner, G. *The Creation of Patriarchy.* New York: Oxford University Press, 1986.

Lesko, B. "Women of Egypt and the Ancient Near East." Pp. 41–77 in *Becoming Visible: Women in European History,* edited by R. Bridenthal, C. Koonz, and S. Stuard. 2d rev. ed. Boston: Houghton Mifflin, 1987.

Lovejoy, A. O. *The Great Chain of Being: A Study of the History of an Idea.* 1936. Reprint, Cambridge: Harvard University Press, 1964.

Madsen, C. "Roundtable Discussion: If God Is God, She Is Not Nice." *Journal of Feminist Studies in Religion* 5 (1989): 103-17.

Nelson, S. M. "Diversity of the Upper Paleolithic 'Venus' Figurines."

Powers of Observation: Alternative Views in Archeology. Archeological Papers of the American Anthropological Association 2 (1990): 11-22.

Ochshorn, J. *The Female Experience and the Nature of the Divine.* Bloomington, Ind.: Indiana University Press, 1981.

———. "Ishtar and Her Cult." Pp. 16–28 in *The Book of the Goddess Past and Present,* edited by C. Olson. New York: Crossroad Publishing, 1983.

Ochshorn, J., and E. Cole, eds. *Women's Spirituality, Women's Lives.* New York: The Haworth Press, 1995.

Olson, C., ed. *The Book of the Goddess Past and Present.* New York: Crossroad Publishing, 1983.

Plaskow, J., and C. Christ, eds. *Weaving the Visions: New Patterns in Feminist Spirituality.* San Francisco: Harper & Row, 1989.

Plaskow, J. *Standing Again at Sinai: Judaism from a Feminist Perspective.* San Francisco: Harper & Row, 1990.

Pomeroy, S. *Goddesses, Whores, Wives, and Slaves: Women in Classical Antiquity.* New York: Schocken Books, 1975.

Pritchard, J. B. *Ancient Near Eastern Texts Relating to the Old Testament.* 3d ed., with supp. Princeton, N.J.: Princeton University Press, 1969.

Ruether, R. R. *Sexism and God-Talk: Toward a Feminist Theology.* Boston: Beacon Press, 1983.

———. *Womanguides: Readings toward a Feminist Theology.* Boston: Beacon Press, 1985.

Saiving. V. "The Human Situation: A Feminine View." Pp. 25–42 in *Womanspirit Rising: A Feminist Reader in Religion,* edited by C. Christ and J. Plaskow. San Francisco: Harper & Row, 1979.

Sandars, N. K., trans. *The Epic of Gilgamesh.* Middlesex, England: Penguin Books, 1960.

Saul, D., and J. Napali. "Goddess Worship: Toxic Niceness?" *New Directions for Women* July/August 1991, 4.

Schmandt-Besserat, D., ed. *The Legacy of Sumer.* Vol. 4. Edited by G. Buccellati. Bibliotheca Mesopotamica: Primary sources and interpretive analyses for the study of Mesopotamian civilization and its influences from late prehistory to the end of the cuneiform tradition. Malibu, Calif.: Undena Publications, 1976.

Schüssler Fiorenza, E. "Remembering the Past in Creating the Future: Historical-Critical Scholarship and Feminist Biblical Interpretation." Pp. 43–63 in *Feminist Perspectives on Biblical Scholarship,* edited by A. C. Collins. Chico, Calif.: Scholars Press, 1985.

Smith, A. "For All Those Who Were Indian in a Former Life." *Ms.,* November/December (1993): 44-45.

Speiser, E. A., trans. "Descent of Ishtar to the Netherworld." Pp. 106–09 in *Ancient Near Eastern Texts Relating to the Old Testament,* edited by J. B. Pritchard. 3d ed., with supp. Princeton, N.J.: Princeton University Press, 1969.

Springer, C. "Whose Goddesses Are They?" *New Directions for Women* July/August (1990): 4.

Starhawk. "Witchcraft and Women's Culture." Pp. 259–68 in *Womanspirit Rising: A Feminist Reader in Religion,* edited by C. Christ and J. Plaskow. San Francisco: Harper & Row, 1979.

———. *Dreaming the Dark.* Boston: Beacon Press, 1982.

Stone, M. *When God Was a Woman.* New York: The Dial Press, 1976.

Stuard, S. "The Dominion of Gender: Women's Fortunes in the High Middle Ages." Pp. 153–72 in *Becoming Visible: Women in European History,* edited by R. Bridenthal, C. Koonz, and S. Stuard. 2d rev. ed. Boston: Houghton Mifflin, 1987.

Wilson, J. A. "The God and His Unknown Name of Power." Pp. 12–14 in *Ancient Near Eastern Texts Relating to the Old Testament,* edited by J. B. Pritchard. 3d ed., with supp. Princeton, N.J.: Princeton University Press, 1969.

Wittig, M. *Les Guerilleres.* Translated by David Le Vay. New York: The Viking Press, 1969.

15

RITA M. GROSS

Some Buddhist Perspectives on the Goddess

For several reasons, Buddhism is not a well-known resource to those interested either in Goddess spirituality or in culturally unfamiliar resources for Goddess imagery, mythology, and ritual. First, Buddhism has a reputation as simply another version of Asian patriarchal religion, a view that meshes with the general reluctance of Western feminist theology to deal seriously with non-Western religions. (Even those who delve into premonotheistic resources tend to work mainly with *Western* antiquity.) Second, those forms of Buddhism—Mahayana, and especially Vajrayana, or Tantric, Buddhism—that are the most fertile ground for those interested in resources for Goddess spirituality are less well-known to Western scholars than are earlier forms of Buddhism that have almost no feminine (or masculine) imagery of an anthropomorphic ultimate or myth-model. Finally, for those not well-versed in Buddhist thought, and even for many who are, Buddhism seems to be characterized by its philosophical abstractness and the rigor of its meditation disciplines but to lack almost completely the symbols, myths, and rituals that would be characteristic of a religion that devotes serious attention to Goddesses.

These impressions do not hold up well in the perspective of Buddhist feminist thought or in the experiences of someone with long-term involvement in both Buddhist spiritual disciplines and Goddess theology. In this paper, I will seek to address this topic as someone with long-term, significant experience with Buddhism, at both the theoretical and the practical levels, but also as someone who addressed the issue of male God-language in the monotheistic context early in the development of feminist theology[1], and who tried early in the development of feminist theology to introduce Indian resources into the discussion.[2] In summary, my conclusions will be that Buddhism is exemplary in some of its ways of incorporating feminine imagery and meditation rituals, but that other aspects of traditional Buddhist approaches to the divine feminine are less exemplary and need feminist reconstruction.

Because Buddhism is a nontheistic religion, the first issue to be discussed in any commentary on Buddhist perspectives on the Goddess must be the interface between nontheism and Goddess symbolism. Building upon the base of Buddhist nontheism, I will discuss late Mahayana Buddhist understandings of Buddhahood and ultimate reality contained in *trikaya* ("three bodies of Buddhahood") theory, which is the matrix within which Buddhist examples of the divine female find their symbolic and mythic existence. I will present two important Buddhist myth-models, Tara and Vajrayogini. I will discuss how *trikaya* theory has traditionally been brought into the human realm, pointing out positive and negative uses of this resource, from a feminist point of view. Some feminist reconstructions of traditional but inadequate applications of *trikaya* theory will be suggested.

THE RESOURCE OF BUDDHIST NONTHEISM

In my book *Buddhism after Patriarchy: A Feminist History, Analysis, and Reconstruction of Buddhism,* I titled the section in which I dealt with Buddhist nontheism "Count Your Negative Blessings: Battles We Don't Have to Fight." I meant every word of that title. In my judgment, Buddhist nontheism offers feminists two vital resources. The first is the lack of a male Absolute that must be deconstructed before meaningful feminist discourse can occur. The second is the example provided by nontheistic traditions of how one can construct and utilize nonabsolute mythic, symbolic female and male personifications of enlightenment.

It may be helpful first to define briefly what Buddhists mean by nontheism. At the simplest level, nontheism has meant that Buddhism does not posit an Ultimate Other who can create or redeem the phenomenal world, stands outside the phenomenal world in any way, or has any kind of dualistic relationship with that world. Lacking the categories of "creation" and "redemption," Buddhism is thoroughly nondualistic. There is no one or nothing to whom to appeal or complain about the state of affairs, no one or nothing who can be blamed for the situation or who can do anything about it except oneself and one's community. (Traditional Buddhists might not include one's community as responsible for the situation; my Buddhist feminist interpretation of the classic Buddhist concept of interdependence (*pratityasamutpada*) leads me not simply to say that one creates one's situation solely by one's own *karma*, but to include the whole community as creator of the *status quo*.)

Defining nontheism as the lack of a creator or redeemer is somewhat dependent on the contrast Buddhism presents with more common spiritualities, whether Western or Indian. It attempts to define nontheism in theistic terms. At a deeper level, nontheism implies that there is no formula, no practice, nothing that one can borrow and imitate that will launch the seeker into spiritual realization. All the philosophy or meditation in the world can only work up to a certain extent to clarify the nature of reality; after that it is completely a matter of insight and intuition. Not only is there no Ultimate Other upon whom one could rely; there is not even an ultimate formula that has captured the essence of truth for us. Fluidity, open-endedness, and nongraspability always turn out to be the last words in this nondualistic, nontheistic spirituality.

Therefore, Buddhism includes a view of language and truth that is relatively unfamiliar to Western theologians, but that is quite helpful to those trying to construct or reconstruct Goddess imagery. Put most simply, for Buddhism, ". . . religious doctrines have utility rather than truth; . . . their importance lies in the effects they have upon those who believe in them."[3] According to Mahayana Buddhism, the goal of religious practice is to develop simultaneously and to balance *prajna* and *upaya*. *Prajna* is often translated as "wisdom," but this wisdom is not an accumulated body of truth claims that one believes one can verify empirically or analytically. It is wisdom as a skill or an ability, the ability to think on one's feet, to hone words to fit the context, to take appropriate action in a unique and nonrepeatable situation. *Upaya* is often translated "method" or "skillful means." Method has an impact or promotes certain results. For example, some methods are effective in promoting a desirable goal, such as the development of *prajna*. Thus, religious doctrines, as verbal attempts to grasp and communicate intuitive insight, belong to *upaya*, rather than to *prajna*; they are judged by their effectiveness rather than by truth or accuracy. The same principle would apply to mythic and anthropomorphic imagery of Ultimate Reality.

Nontheism, understood both superficially as the absence of a dualistic Supreme Being and nonsuperficially as the recognition that doctrines and images have utility rather than truth, is a wonderful resource for feminist discourse. First, Buddhist feminists do not face the burdens of recognizing the destructiveness of exclusively male symbolism God-language, reconstructing that imagery, and struggling to convince their religious communities to accept those reconstructions. Although it remains completely obvious to me that from the theistic and monotheistic point of view, male monotheism is patently idolatrous, and although I remain convinced that its idolatry is easily overcome by feminist reconstruction, I was extremely relieved to leave that particular battle behind when I took up the nontheistic path of Buddhism. At first, I simply regarded the resource of nontheism as my freedom from the battle to reconstruct the Deity of male monotheism.

Understanding that religious symbols and doctrines possess utility rather than truth, however, is much more freeing than simple freedom from a traditional doctrine. Because this is a subtle point that goes against the grain of Western thought, though, it took quite a while for it to sink in. When we understand that religious symbols and doctrines are important more for their utility than for their truth, our analysis could move in two directions. On the one hand, to evaluate religious images and doctrines on the basis of their utility enormously fuels the feminist critique of male monotheism. Because it is completely clear that the effect of male God-language has been to reinforce and justify male dominance in society and religion, and because it is equally clear, at least to feminists, that such an effect is completely undesirable, therefore, as *upaya* (and no doctrine is ever more than a method), male monotheism is completely bankrupt. If utility, rather than truth, were the principle by which monotheists evaluated God-talk, perhaps it would be easier to exorcise the Deity who lacks femaleness as part of his transcendence.

On the other hand, seen in its own context, free of polemical implications vis-à-vis theism of any variety, the nontheistic principle that religious symbols and doctrines contain utility rather than truth is radically freeing. The recognition that religious symbols and doctrines never possess truth but only utility frees human spirituality immensely, rather than dampening the impulse to construct religious symbols and doctrines. One can freely play with symbols and doctrines, exploring their impact without worrying about the metaphysical status of their referents. Or, more precisely, in terms of Buddhist understandings, there is nothing "behind" these images, because they arise out of Emptiness and dance in that void. Because no inherent nature or own-being adheres to these mythic and symbolic entities, idolatry can never arise. Idolatry can arise only when one fixates on such a symbol, attributing to it an ultimacy it does not and cannot have. Instead, all images and doctrines are seen as essentially mythic, that is to say, neither true nor false, but sacred. As sacred stories that are neither true nor false, doctrines, images, and symbols should be evaluated on the basis of their utility. Do they promote human wholeness, or do they promote alienation and oppression?

Thus, manifold and varied symbols and doctrines could be expected to flourish. This is exactly what eventually happened in nontheistic Buddhism, much to the surprise of those who see nontheism only in its more superficial sense. The vast pantheons of Mahayana and especially of Tantric Buddhism were created in this fashion and continue to move practitioners because of their utility. The resource base of Mahayana and Tantric Buddhism includes powerful and provocative female representations of enlightenment—"Goddesses," in popular parlance, but nontheistic Goddesses. Their presence is the most surprising and compelling twist in the resource of Buddhist nontheism. When one moves from theism to nontheism, one expects to be free of a Supreme Being imaged as male but not female. Usually one does not expect when taking up the path of nontheism to meet Goddesses who might prove helpful on one's spiritual journey. Like the sword of *prajna*,[4] Buddhist nontheism is two-edged. On the one hand, it frees us from having to deconstruct a male absolute before we can begin meaningful discourse. On the other hand, it provides us with meaningful but nonreified images of a divine feminine, a myth-model for our own living in the world. As someone who is very wary of spiritualities invented out of present need without deep immersion in traditional resources, these nontheistic Buddhist "Goddesses" were an unexpected blessing for me.

TRIKAYA THEORY, MYTHICAL BUDDHAS, AND LIVING BUDDHAS

Feminist theology consistently concerns itself with two important questions: What is the relationship between abstract, neuter, nongynemorphic language about Ultimate Reality, on the one hand, and personal, gynemorphic images and stories of Ultimate Reality, on the other hand? What is the relationship between either kind of language about Ultimate Reality and human beings? Buddhism has linked all three levels—the neuter abstract, the personal gynemorphic, and the human—in its concept of the *trikaya*, usually translated as "triple body." Developed relatively late in the history of Buddhist thought, this concept gives theoretical underpinnings to the widespread Mahayana devotion to various popular "celestial" Buddhas and Bodhisattvas, at the same time as it explains the possibility of human spiritual realization. This Buddhist concept is relatively obscure, however, even to many in the Buddhist world, and it is almost completely misunderstood in most Western presentations of Buddhism. I remember it being one of the most obscure and incomprehensible of Buddhist concepts when I was attempting to learn Buddhism from the Western academic accounts that were standard in the late sixties and early seventies. In this discussion, I follow an interpretation of *trikaya* prevalent in some varieties of Tibetan Buddhism but not universally followed, even by Mahayana Buddhists.

Misunderstanding begins when *trikaya* is interpreted as "the triple body of the Buddha," a common translation that I have, and will continue carefully to avoid. When one hears of "the triple body of the Buddha," one immediately thinks that Siddartha Gautama, the historical Buddha of our world epoch, has somehow taken on two other bodies, and from there the confusions get worse. Siddartha Gautama, the historical Buddha, however, is not the equivalent of a Deity or an incarnation. The *trikaya* does not begin with him; it ends with him and others who are his equivalents and equals. The *trikaya* is really about three levels or manifestations of Buddhahood: the abstract, the mythic, and the human (*dharmakaya, sambhogakaya,* and *nirmanakaya*). Early Buddhism talked of the abstract and the human levels of Buddhahood and largely limited the human manifestation of Buddhahood to the work of Siddartha Gautama. Mahayana and Tantric Buddhism expanded Buddhahood to include an intermediate mythic manifestation of Buddhahood and also expanded greatly the scope and incidence of human manifestations of Buddhahood.

In Mahayana Buddhism, *dharmakaya* is one of many names for the Ultimate, which cannot, of course, really be named or grasped (which is why it is called by so many names). Sometimes translated as "truth-body," it is the source of Buddha-activity in the mythic and phenomenal realms. But that source is not different or separate from Emptiness (*sunyata*) or "Suchness" (*tathata*). Little more can be said about that matrix; it is impersonal and neuter, nondual, and highly abstract. Because so little can be said about it, what is said is both accurate and extremely abstract; there are few hooks for imagery or conceptualization. In this sense, it is akin to Mary Daly's Verb of Verbs or other abstract ultimates found behind the male Deity deconstructed by feminist theology. The greatest difference is perhaps that in Buddhism such discourse is the foundation for a more concrete imagery of Buddhas and Buddha-activity, rather than the distillation from a critique of more conventional language.

Dharmakaya as source takes form in *sambhogakaya* and *nirmanakaya. Sambhogakaya* is usually translated as "bliss-body" or "enjoyment-body," but these literal translations convey almost nothing in English. I would argue that the term is more accurately, if less literally translated as "mythic manifestation of Buddhahood," if the term "myth" is understood as "sacred presence" about which neither truth nor falsity is at issue and that has utility as model and inspiration for human Buddha-activity. These "sacred presences" are much more tangible than is the abstract *dharmakaya.* They are somewhat human in form, though they can have anatomical features, such as multiple heads and such, not usually sported by mortals. Traditionally, the *sambhogakaya* Buddhas cannot be seen by ordinary human beings but are visible to highly realized human beings. Fortunately, their mythic form has been captured for us ordinary human beings in art and, thus, can readily be contemplated. Their form can also be seen esoterically in visualization meditations, common in Tantric Buddhism. In such visualization meditations, they can be the model for one's own enlightened being, which slowly emerges as one identifies with a specific *sambhogakaya* Buddha. If one does not have the energy to engage in visualization practices, one could also approach these mythic Buddhas and Bodhisattvas through ritual and veneration, though that technique will probably not result in human Buddha-activity as quickly as will visualization meditations.

For feminist theology, two generalizations about *sambhogakaya* Buddhas are important. First, they are imagined in both female and male sexes. (Because these *sambhogakaya* Buddhas do not observe gender roles, I emphasize their anatomical maleness and femaleness.) Buddhism bears out the generalization that whenever "anthropomorphic" imagery is used about Ultimate Reality, both feminine and masculine images are commonplace unless something has gone wrong. Thus, even nontheistic symbol systems bear out this generalization. Second, though these *sambhogakaya* Buddhas and Bodhisattvas look like Deities, they are nontheistic or mythic. Inherent existence would never be attributed to them, for they arise out of the Emptiness (*sunyata*) of *dharmakaya* and return to that Emptiness. Yet such mythic beings have carried both an esoteric and an exoteric religious system of great popularity and depth. Such information is important to feminists struggling to reconstruct a vibrant and compelling set of symbols on the base of a deconstructed abstract Ultimate. If even a nontheistic religion like Buddhism constructs anthropomorphic and gynemorphic models of enlightenment, feminist theology, growing out of a theistic base, will undoubtedly also need such mythic images. On the other hand, Buddhism clearly shows that it is possible to celebrate such myth-models without reifying them, which has always been the pitfall of theistic anthropomorphism and sometimes seems to overtake feminist theology as well.

VAJRAYOGINI AND TARA: TWO BUDDHIST "GODDESSES"

To see, in practical concrete terms, how the *sambhogakaya* forms are used in Vajrayana Buddhism, let us look at two important and popular female *sambhogakaya* forms, one of them exoteric, the other esoteric. It is important to remember that neither of these "Goddesses" were found in early layers of Buddhist tradition; that they each patronize a complete myth, ritual, and meditation system for those who practice their *sadhanas* as their spiritual discipline; and that the assertion of their independent, reified existence apart from Emptiness would be incomprehensible in the context of traditional Buddhist thought and practice.

Tara, the Saviouress, is certainly one of the two most popular meditational Deities of Tibet. According to Beyer,[5] one seldom finds a Tibetan shrine that lacks her icon, though it may be surrounded by many other more esoteric *yidams*.[6] She is widely prayed to and contemplated by practitioners of every level and lifestyle, and her *mantra*[7] is one of the best known and most widely used. Initiation to practice her *sadhana* (spiritual discipline) is widely available and its practice is encouraged for virtually anyone.

Her well-known story is told on two levels. Though she is said now to be both an advanced Bodhisattva and a fully enlightened Buddha, like all such beings, she was once an ordinary human who aroused the "thought of enlightenment" (*bodhicitta*) and practiced the various disciplines for many eons. In 1608, Taranatha, an important Tibetan teacher, wrote the text that has become a standard "history" of Tara. He relates that eons ago, a princess named Moon of Wisdom made extensive offerings for a long time to the Buddha of that eon and to his entourage. Finally, for the first time, *bodhicitta* arose in her. Then the monks present suggested, "If you pray that your deeds accord with the teachings, then indeed on that account, you will change your form to that of a man, as is befitting." After a long discussion, she told them, "In this life, there is no such distinction as 'male' and 'female' . . . and therefore attachment to ideas of 'male' and 'female' is quite worthless. Weak-minded worldlings are always deluded by this." Then follows her vow:

> There are many who wish to gain enlightenment in a man's form, and there are but few who wish to work for the welfare of sentient beings in a female form. Therefore, may I, in a female body, work for the welfare of beings right until Samsara has been emptied.[8]

It is also said that she originated from the tears of Avalokitesvara, the male Bodhisattva of compassion who appears as the female Kuan-yin in East Asia. It is said that Avalokitesvara wept when he saw that no matter how many beings he saved, countless more still remained in *samsara*. A blue lotus (also held by Tara) grew in the water of his tears and Tara was born on that lotus.[9]

Her appearance and activities, frequently described in Sanskrit and Tibetan poetry, are well known and widely contemplated. The best known set of descriptions is the "Praise in Twenty-One Homages." It gave rise to several traditions of *thangka* paintings in which a central figure of Tara in her most familiar form is surrounded by twenty-one smaller figures of Tara representing all the activities she undertakes. This set of praises is found in *sadhanas*, composed for meditation on Tara as one's *yidam* (Deity contemplated in meditation practices) and has been widely commented upon.[10] Rather than trying to summarize these praises or even to summarize a complete description of Tara, I will quote two verses from one of the many devotional poems composed in her honor. This description includes some of her most important features and explains their symbolic meaning, important to the *yidam's* form or appearance. Though this quotation is not from a *sadhana*, the description is congruent with the form that would be used for self-visualization of one's self as Tara when meditating using her *sadhana*.

> On a lotus seat, for pure understanding of emptiness,
> Emerald-colored, one-faced, two-armed girl,
> In full bloom of youth, right leg out, left drawn in,
> Uniting Method and Wisdom—homage to You!
>
> Prominent, full breasts, treasures of undefiled bliss,
> Face with a brilliant smile like a full moon,
> Mother with calm-mannered, wide, compassionate eyes,
> Beauty of Khadira Forest—to You I bow![11]

Not explained in the text is Tara's green color. Though there are Taras in other colors as well, the Green Tara is the most popular. In Tantric symbolism, green is the color of the action family, of those Buddhas and Bodhisattvas who specialize in the Wisdom of All-Accomplishing Action. This color is consonant with Tara's constant activity to help and save beings. Thus, it is often explained at a Green Tara initiation that her *sadhana* is especially recommended for active people who have major projects underway.

Much of the devotional poetry written to Tara praises her for her many activities. A standard repertoire of activities attributed to her includes saving people from the eight great dangers. Though there are some variants in some lists, or sometimes more than eight dangers from which Tara rescues, a standard list of the eight includes: fire, water, prison, bandits, elephants, tigers (or lions), snakes, and evil spirits.[12] One can appreciate these as troublesome mundane dangers that would worry anyone in the environment of ancient India. Tara is very accessible; she helps people with these everyday worries and does not confine her help to so-called spiritual matters. If one wishes, one can interpret any of the eight dangers in a spiritual way, as was sometimes done by devotees singing her praises.[13]

Among the many stories of how Tara rescued her devotees, I find two narrated by Taranatha especially appealing and whimsical. She saved a devotee from bandits in the following fashion. She appeared in a dream to the master Sanghamitra, telling him to study Mahayana teachings. He set out to go to Kashmir, but on the way he was captured by bandits who said that they needed to worship Durga (a popular Hindu Goddess) by offering her warm human blood. They took him to a Durga temple "like a charnel ground." He prayed to Tara, and the Durga image spontaneously split into many pieces. The bandits became frightened and ran away from him. How she saved living beings from tigers is even more intriguing. Master Buddhadasa traveled through an empty town with many tiger dens. When he enquired, he was told that the tigers ate humans every day. "Therefore, great compassion arose in him." He walked toward the tigers, prayed to Tara, and sprinkled water over which he had recited *mantras.* "Through this, the tigers became of peaceful mind; thereafter they did no harm to living creatures but stopped eating and passed away." Things ended well for the tigers, who were reborn in a more fortunate existence in which, presumably, they could subsist as vegetarians.[14] The gentleness of Tara, the peaceful *yidam,* could not be more graphically demonstrated.

The red, semi-wrathful Vajrayogini or Vajravarahi, sow-headed, dancing on a lotus, corpse, and sun disk, is much more esoteric. She is undoubtedly the most important female *yidam* of the *anuttarayoga* tantras, the highest and most esoteric class of *tantras* according to most classification schemes. In these *tantras,* she is celebrated both as the central *yidam* of her own extensive *sadhana* and as the consort of major male *yidams,* such as Cakrasamvara and Hevajra. Her initiation is much more difficult to receive than is Tara's and her practice much more restricted because, as a semi-wrathful *yidam,* she can arouse emotions that may overwhelm a student not ready to take on her wild, untamed, fierce energy or her "transcendental lust." Therefore, commentaries about her are more restricted to the oral tradition.

Thangkhas and line drawings of Vajravarahi are relatively standard.[15] In the *sadhana* text itself, as is always the case, the meaning of each aspect of her form is explained, because the meditator visualizing herself as

Vajrayogini is not especially trying to become a red sixteen-year-old but to take on and manifest the qualities implicit in her form. Thus, for example, she wears a garland of fifty-one freshly severed heads, which represents wearing out the habitual patterns of grasping and fixation. She also carries a hooked knife and a skullcup filled with blood or *amrta* ("deathless"—a liquid much used in Tantric ritual liturgies). She holds the *khatvanga* staff in the crook of her arm. She is naked and wearing bone ornaments. She dances on a corpse, sun, and lotus.[16] She is surrounded by four *dakinis* almost identical to her in form, but in appropriate colors (blue, yellow, red, and green) for the sphere of the *mandala*[17] they embody. Thus her practice involves a complete universe in which all five of the basic energies so important to Vajrayana Buddhism are roused and transmuted.

Because practicing with Vajrayogini as one's *yidam* is considered relatively advanced and dangerous, she is not usually regarded as a savior and one does not do her practice for relative benefits, but for the ultimate *siddhi*—enlightenment. Therefore, her praises talk of her as promoting, often in terrifying fashion, the states of mind that overcome confusion and clinging. A number of these praises have been translated and ably commented upon in an illuminating article by Chogyam Trungpa. A few of them will suffice to connote Vajrayogini's immensely compelling, highly charged, and provocative iconography. They also communicate well her activities to promote enlightenment. One praise comments on the meaning of her sow's head as well:

> Your sow's face shows nonthought, the unchanging *dharmakaya,*
> You benefit beings with wrathful mercy
> Accomplishing their welfare with horrific accouterments,
> I prostrate to you who benefit beings in nonthought.

The efficacy of her wrathful actions is evoked in many praises.

> Naked, with loosed hair, of faultless and terrifying form
> Beyond the vice of the *klesas,* you do benefit for sentient beings.
> You lead beings from the six realms with your hook of mercy,
> I prostrate to you who accomplish Buddha-activity.

A concluding praise links her with Prajnaparamita, the mother of all Buddhas. This certainly sums up the meaning and purpose of her fierce form and activity, which summons primordial energies in the practitioner, familiarizes the practitioner with them, tames them, and harnesses their energy— quickly and effectively, it is hoped.

Prajnaparamita, inexpressible by speech or thought
Unborn, unceasing, with a nature like sky
Which can only be experienced by discriminating awareness wisdom,
Mother of the victorious ones of the three times,
I praise you and prostrate.[18]

Both of these anthropomorphic representations of enlightenment are central to Vajrayana Buddhism. As anthropomorphic representations that can be visualized and related with, they demonstrate more readily than does philosophy the nature of enlightened mind, which, according to Vajrayana Buddhism, is always there waiting to be realized. If gentle Tara's smile does not push one over the brink from confusion to enlightenment, perhaps Vajrayogini's fang-filled grimace will. But clearly, in consonance with the command not to denigrate women,[19] Vajrayana tradition claims that these wonderful female *yidams* demonstrate to the seeker the nature of her or his own mind in its unfettered form as readily as their male counterparts might.

SAMBHOGAKAYA AND *NIRMANAKAYA*

The *nirmanakaya* is seemingly the most immediate and ordinary manifestation of Buddhahood. Usually translated as "transformation" or "apparition" body, it is commonly understood as Buddhahood in human form, an "enlightened one." All forms of Buddhism recognize that there has been and will be a series of *nirmanakayas,* but most forms of Buddhism expect them to be rather rare and, in a certain sense, regard them as another variety of mythical Buddha, an earthly rather than a heavenly mythic Buddha. Tibetan Vajrayana Buddhism does not. A realized human being or recognized teacher is understood to be a *nirmanakaya* Buddha. While some forms of Buddhism invoke a heavily docetic mode when telling stories of the *nirmanakaya* Buddhas, as if they were literally apparitions, Tibetan Buddhism stresses the human[20] birth, life, education, accomplishments, teaching, and death of a *nirmanakaya.*

Accomplishing the *nirmanakaya,* which is possible for any being possessing the "precious human birth,"[21] brings the energy of *dharmakaya* and *sambhogakaya* down to earth, so to speak. The way in which human potential for spiritual realization is connected with the abstract, neuter, nonpersonal *dharmakaya* and the sacred presence of *sambhogakaya* Buddhas is instructive for those concerned with Goddess theology. Following *trikaya* theory, a "Goddess" could be either the myth-model or her human embodiment, and both arise from and dissolve into *dharmakaya.*

Dharmakaya is conceptualized as all-pervading and found in all phenomena. This concept is the source of the common Mahayana Buddhist statement that Buddha is present in a grain of sand and that virtually any human activity can be the trigger for enlightenment. *Dharmakaya* is present in human beings as *tathagatagarbha,* often translated as "Buddha-nature," the "Buddha within,"[22] or the "enlightened gene."[23] Therefore, when the focus shifts from the historical Buddha to the nonpersonal, neuter source of enlightenment, the emphasis shifts from one historical person to the potential of each and every embodied human being. Buddhahood ("Buddha" simply means "awake" or "enlightened") is not the possession of one quasi-mythical person who lived a long time ago, but the potential of each human being and the resource coursing through all of experience and the phenomenal world, linking them all and us all in our most primordial and essential characteristic. That resource is activated by the sacred presence of *sambhogakaya* Buddhas and Bodhisattvas. They are myth-models in the sense that they are not external beings to be worshiped but the anthropomorphic or gynemorphic form of *dharmakaya* and, hence, of one's own enlightened experience. As such, one identifies with them in a series of powerful meditations and contemplations, gradually interfusing their form into one's own. Therefore, according to *trikaya* doctrine, mythical manifestations of Buddhahood help in training and encouraging human beings, endowed with inherent Buddhahood, to manifest as *nirmanakaya* Buddhas.

It is interesting and instructive to consider the links between gender symbolism associated with the mythical Buddhas and Bodhisattvas and the sex and gender of the Buddhist practitioners who take them as myth-models. As has already been made clear, *sambhogakayas* take both female and male forms, but these myth-models themselves do not conform to gender roles, either divine or human. That is to say, as is typical of symbol systems that include Goddesses, Goddesses are not confined to the human female gender role. (The label "Mother Goddess" as the generic label for all female personifications of divinity could not be further from the mark.) There is little, if any, gender-linked specialization associated with female and male *sambhogakayas.* Nor is there any link between the sex of a myth-model and the sex of the human being who is assigned to contemplate a specific *yidam* in his or her *sadhana* (spiritual discipline). Men are often assigned to visualize themselves as a female Buddha and women to visualize themselves as male; the reverse of each practice is equally common. In the system with which I am most familiar, everyone, woman or man, first identifies with a powerful female *sambhogakaya.* That visualization is followed by a practice involving a couple in sexual union, but along the way, male myth-models are also introduced to both women and men, without regard for the physiological sex of the meditator.

Gender symbolism is utilized in the Tibetan Vajrayana Buddhist symbolic universe, but because neither myth-models nor their human emulators are thought to be limited by their physiological sex to gender-linked symbolic traits,[24] such symbolism need not be discussed in detail in this context. The phenomenal and psychological universes are divided into elements that represent the feminine and the masculine principles, which have a relationship of complementarity and dyadic unity. Leading examples of the feminine and masculine principles are *prajna* (feminine) and *upaya* (masculine), discussed at the beginning of this paper. The interdependence and dyadic unity of *prajna* and *upaya* are indicative of the relationship between the masculine and feminine principles in the phenomenal world, at least in the abstract and the ideal. When humans seek to embody the qualities contained in the masculine or feminine principles, obviously physiological sex is not relevant. Both qualities need to be developed in an enlightened individual, whether she is male or female.[25]

NIRMANAKAYA AND *GURU*: SOME FEMINIST ASSESSMENTS

As already has been made clear, the point of *trikaya* theory and the meditations involving *sambhogakaya* Buddhas is their ability to serve as *upaya,* as tool and technique that enables those endowed with the "enlightened gene" to realize the *nirmanakaya* and to develop their human potential. Those humans who are recognized as having done so are honored by their communities as "living Buddhas" and as *gurus.* Because Vajrayana Buddhism depends heavily on oral tradition and a direct student-teacher relationship, the *guru* is extremely important in this form of Buddhism. In fact, the *guru* is so important that he or she is sometimes considered to be the fourth object of refuge—in addition to the Buddha, the Dharma ("teachings") and the Sangha ("community")[26]—and to be the avenue of access to the three major objects of refuge.

The *guru* has this position of honor because, according to Vajrayana Buddhism, spiritual truth cannot be captured in words, so that reading or memorizing the Dharma that has been written in books is no guarantee of realization and insight. The scholar may have all the right words but may have totally missed the sense of those words, to use a distinction familiar to Vajrayana Buddhism. A *guru* is someone who has not only mastered the words of the tradition but has thoroughly incorporated their meanings into her or his being; because of that she is competent to guide the spiritual search of her students. Because her understanding reduplicates that of the Buddha, in essence, not necessarily in form or content, she is a lineage holder whose job it is to keep the teachings not only pristine but up to date. The lineage holder must interpret the teachings in the idiom of the day, perhaps crossing cultural frontiers to do so. The lineage holder also trains the next generation of students and certifies those whose level of spiritual understanding is sufficient to make them lineage holders as well.

From the student's side, this relationship is extremely intense and personal, though not necessarily in conventional ways. Devotion is the proper attitude with which to regard the wondrous *guru.* The importance of these *gurus* is explicitly recognized in Buddhist meditation liturgies and religious art. Daily chants include an invocation to and a recitation of the lineage of *gurus,* from one's own *guru* back to sect founders and the Buddha. *Gurus,* like *yidams* and Buddhas, are frequently the subject of Buddhist religious art and meditation. The lineage is sometimes portrayed in the form of a lineage tree, a great tree in whose branches sit all the *gurus* of the lineage, surrounded by the Buddhas, Bodhisattvas, *yidams,* and protectors, with the sacred books also supported by the tree. Prostrations are done before this lineage tree containing all the objects of refuge. Given the centrality of the *guru* in the spiritual life of the student and the intensity of the devotion that is cultivated and recommended, it is provocative to suggest that, in the forms of Buddhism that regard the *guru* so highly, the *guru* is a nontheistic, functional equivalent of the Deity of theistic religions.

If society followed symbolism, one would expect that about equal numbers of women and men would be recognized as such leaders and *gurus.* But this has not been the case throughout Buddhist history. A woman such as Yeshe Tsogyel can be recognized and venerated as a *guru.* Vajrayana Buddhism places no theoretical limits on those humans who achieve the female form of the "precious human body." But, however many women may have activated their "enlightened gene" and manifested Buddha-activity, few of them have been recognized and honored as *gurus* by their contemporaries. As a result they have had few students and little impact on the shaping and articulation of their tradition.

That *gurus* and teachers throughout Buddhist history and currently are almost always men is thoroughly androcentric and completely disempowering for women, in the same way as is the male monopoly on images of Deity in monotheism. The lack of female presence in the lineage supplications, on the limbs of the refuge tree,[27] and on the teaching throne from which living teachers teach, reinforces and drives home the shame of being female in patriarchy. It is living proof that Buddhist institutions do not respect and nurture the Buddha-embryo present in women in the same way that they nurture the Buddha-embryo present in men.

One can shed many tears and write many pages concerning the patriarchal and androcentric institutions and record-keeping practices that have tainted and corrupted Buddhism historically. On the other hand, for Buddhism, history is not normative or exemplary, so Buddhists cannot cogently call upon the authority of tradition or the past to maintain Buddhist patriarchy. In fact, in one apocryphal story, the Dalai Lama is reported to have told a woman questioning the Buddhist record, "That's history! Now it's up to you." That story can and also should be reversed. We can say to the leaders of Buddhism, who deserve the respect they have earned, "Now it's up to you! Recognize and empower female *gurus*!" The deliberate cultivation of female *gurus* and teachers is the most critical agenda facing contemporary Buddhists and the single most important requirement for achieving a genuinely post-patriarchal Buddhism. This is equally true for those forms of Buddhism that do not revere the *guru* as formally, for the teacher is always central to the transmission of Buddhism from generation to generation.

Fortunately for Buddhism, it is currently meeting a movement seeking liberation that is its own equal, though not its duplicate. As Buddhism came West, for the great good fortune of both movements, its first decades of relatively widespread acceptance in the West coincided with the growth of feminism as a strong spiritual force in the West. As a result, the initial generation of Western Buddhists includes many, many women who are Buddhists themselves, first and foremost, who do not see their main function as enabling male practitioners but as developing their own Buddha-nature. Were it not for the magic of timing, of the simultaneous arrival of many Asian Buddhist teachers and a generation of Westerners steeped in feminist values, Buddhism would have little possibility of being liberated from its sexism by Western feminism. Tibetan Buddhism has a term for such a mutually appropriate synchronicity—"auspicious coincidence."

Completing *trikaya* theory through cultivating the presence and teaching authority of female *nirmanakayas* would have a more powerful impact than any other act or symbol in ending the shame associated in patriarchal culture with being female and undoing the scapegoating of women for samsaric existence. Seeing a woman on the *guru's* throne, teaching the Dharma, and granting initiations and blessings would be powerfully transformative for both men and women. For men, the experience of devotion to a female *guru,* accompanied by all the longing and yearning that characterizes nontheistic *guru* devotion, would undo the negative habitual patterns, learned in early childhood under patriarchal child-rearing practices, that scapegoat women for the limitations and finitude of life.[28] Here would be a woman undoing *samsara* for the male by her teaching presence. For women, this presence will be affirming, empowering, and encouraging in a way that nothing else can be. At last Buddhist women will have the same kind of role model that Buddhist men have always had! For both genders, it will be definitively, incontrovertibly clear that there is no shame in being female, that it is okay to be a woman.

Completing current forms of Buddhist theory, however, will not be the only blessing that comes with the presence of female teachers. Sometimes Buddhists imagine that Buddhism after patriarchy is merely a matter of equal rights. It is imagined that things will end when women regularly take on the teaching role in Buddhism and that these women will do nothing more than continue to present the same messages that the male teachers have always presented, that only their form and presence, but not their message, will be different. That such women will present only the same messages seems unlikely, however. It seems unlikely that males speaking out of patriarchal conditions have said everything that needs to be said about liberation. It seems unlikely that, when women finally participate in Buddhist speech, they will not add to the sum total of Buddhist wisdom about liberation. A genuinely post-patriarchal Buddhism will include the one thing that Buddhism has always lacked—large numbers of well-trained, thoroughly practiced, articulate women who are not male identified. Certainly the example of Christianity, in which feminist analysis is far more developed than in Buddhism, strongly suggests that the androgynous voice does not merely amplify what had always been said but adds to it significantly. And this androgynous voice will be articulated, whether or not the Buddhist authorities recognize it as the wisdom of the Buddha.

NOTES

1. Gross, "Female God Language."

2. Gross, "Hindu Female Deities" and "Steps toward Feminine Imagery."

3. Griffiths, *Christianity,* 136.

4. In some Tantric imagery, the personification of *prajna,* Manjusri, carries a sword that cuts through dualistic fixation, or, alternately, cuts both elements of a dichotomy. "The sword of *prajna*" is a favorite image for the process of letting go of false dichotomies and dualisms.

5. Beyer, *Cult of Tara,* 55.

6. *Yidam* is the term used for a *sambhogakaya* manifestation that is one's "meditation Deity," the focus of one's self-visualization in so-called Deity yoga.

7. A *mantra* is a short verbal formula, repeated over and over in meditation, that captures verbally the essence of the *yidam* and stabilizes one's meditation on that *yidam.*

8. Templeman, *Origin of Tara Tantra,* 11-12.

9. Wilson, *In Praise of Tara,* 125.

10. Wilson, *In Praise of Tara,* 105-66.

11. Wilson, *In Praise of Tara,* 301.

12. Wilson, *In Praise of Tara,* 190-93.

13. Wilson, *In Praise of Tara,* 305-6.

14. Wilson, *In Praise of Tara,* 191-93.

15. Allione, *Women of Wisdom,* 30; Trungpa, "Sacred Outlook," 234.

16. Allione, *Women of Wisdom,* 31-34, contains discussion of some meanings that can be attributed to some of her implements and aspects of her pose. See also Trungpa, "Sacred Outlook," 238-40. Another description of her and the meaning of her implements, in her role as consort of Cakrasamvara, is found in Dawa-Samdup, *Sri Cakrasamvara-Tantra,* 20-21.

17. A *mandala* is the mythic universe a *yidam* inhabits and that the mediator visualizes. It consists of a circle or a square oriented around the center and protected by boundaries, with gates in the cardinal directions.

18. Trungpa, "Sacred Outlook," 238–40. This article also provides additional praises and an extensive commentary without which these praises would be quite opaque.

19. One of the *samaya* obligations taken on by a practitioner of Vajrayana Buddhism, though not other forms of Buddhism, includes a vow not to denigrate women "who are nature of *prajna* and *sunyata,* showing both."

20. Some first-time readers of Tibetan hagiographical literature might question this claim, because the literature does include frequent "miracles." Such events do not contradict the humanity of the main characters but are based on other Tibetan and Vajrayana beliefs concerning the ability of an "accomplished human" (*siddha*) to control the elements. For further discussion of this motif, see my article "Yeshe Tsogyel."

21. All forms of Buddhism regard human rebirth as extremely auspicious, in part because only in the human realm, not in the realm of the "heaven dwellers" or in any other realm of sentient existence, is enlightenment possible. Tibetan contemplations encourage one to treasure the "precious human birth" and to use it wisely before all-pervasive impermanence takes its toll. Because other

Buddhist contemplative exercises that foster detachment by focusing on the foulness of the human body or on a rotting corpse are better known to Western students of comparative religion, it is important to clarify that one needs the "precious human body" to engage in such contemplations.

22. Hookham, *Buddha Within.*

23. This colloquial translation of the term *tathagatagarbha* is from the oral teachings of Chogyam Trungpa.

24. This statement applies to the realm of meditation instruction and spiritual discipline. In the traditional Tibetan social world and also in the realm of religious institutions, such as monasteries and leadership roles, gender roles were expected and enforced.

25. For an extended discussion of the symbolism of masculine and feminine principles in Vajrayana Buddhism and a feminist interpretation and reconstruction of them, see my book *Buddhism after Patriarachy.*

26. These are the Three Jewels, or the Three Refuges, the most basic elements of Buddhism and the focus of the Refuge ceremony in which a non-Buddhist, by going for refuge to the Three Jewels, becomes a Buddhist.

27. Yeshe Tsogyel is found on the Nyingma lineage tree and is supplicated in lineage chants, the only exception to this generalization of which I am aware.

28. Gross, *Buddhism After Patriarchy,* 234-40, 249-55.

WORKS CITED

Allione, Tsultrim. *Women of Wisdom.* London: Routledge and Kegan Paul, 1984.

Beyer, Stephen. *The Cult of Tara: Magic and Mystery in Tibet.* Berkeley, Calif.: University of California Press, 1973.

Dawa-Samdup, Kazi. *Sri Cakrasamvara-Tantra: A Buddhist Tantra.* New Delhi: Ditya Prakashan, 1987.

Griffiths, Paul J. *Christianity through Non-Christian Eyes.* Maryknoll, N.Y.: Orbis, 1990.

Gross, Rita M. "Hindu Female Deities as a Resource for the Contemporary Rediscovery of the Goddess." *Journal of the American Academy of Religion* 46 (1978): 269-91.

———. "Female God Language in a Jewish Context." Pp. 167–73 in *Womanspirit Rising: A Feminist Reader in Religion,* edited by Carol P. Christ and Judith Plaskow. San Francisco: Harper and Row, 1979.

———. "Steps toward Feminine Imagery of Deity in Jewish Theology." Pp. 234–47 in *On Being a Jewish Feminist: A Reader,* edited by Susannah Heschel. New York: Schocken, 1983.

———. "Yeshe Tsogyel: Enlightened Consort, Great Teacher, Female Role Model." Pp. 11–32 in *Feminine Ground: Essays on Women and Tibet,* edited by Janice D. Willis. Ithaca, N.Y.: Snow Lion, 1989.

———. *Buddhism after Patriarchy: A Feminist History, Analysis, and*

Reconstruction of Buddhism. Albany, N.Y.: State University of New York Press, 1993.

Hookham, S. K. *The Buddha Within.* Albany, N.Y.: State University of New York Press, 1991.

Templeman, David, trans. and ed. *Origin of Tara Tantra by Jaw-nan Taranatha.* Dharamsala, India: Library of Tibetan Works and Archives, 1981.

Trungpa, Chögyam. "Sacred Outlook: The Vajrayogini Shrine and Practice." Pp. 226–41 in *The Silk Route and the Diamond Path: Esoteric Buddhist Art on the Trans-Himalayan Trade Routes,* edited by Deborah E. Klimburg-Salter. Los Angeles: University of California at Los Angeles Art Council, 1982.

Wilson, Martin. *In Praise of Tara: Songs to the Saviouress.* London: Wisdom Publications, 1986.

16

EMILY ERWIN CULPEPPER

Missing Goddesses, Missing Women: Reflections of a Middle-Aged Amazon

I want to begin with a true story. It chronicles my journey to some further realizations about benefits and limitations of contemporary Goddess imagery and its usefulness as a resource for feminist activism. I write in the spirit of conversation, an approach I call "narrative theory."[1] As an activist, a central commitment of my analysis is to use a writing style accessible outside, as well as inside, the academy. This method arises from feminist consciousness-raising. It acknowledges the fundamental importance that dialogue among women reflecting on our experiences has in the creation of theory. This approach is one of many emerging methods of feminist theory that do not privilege predominant patriarchal norms for scholarship.

MEDITATIONS ON MENOPAUSE

A new colleague, whom I know only slightly, called me to ask for resources to help her develop more affirming feelings about menopause. She had just begun to experience hot flashes and a visit with her gynecologist confirmed her sense that her menopause process had begun. To her dismay and, I think, somewhat to her surprise, her reactions were tumultuously ambivalent and mostly negative. For a new acquaintance, she was very frank, approaching me as a possible resource on the recommendation of a mutual friend. She reached out over the telephone in a few minutes snatched from classes, meetings, and appointments in that way that women who are feminists sometimes have of taking the plunge to ask another feminist whom we do not really know very well for support. In this way, women have often turned to each other to share confidences and together to make sense of our lives.

I have long been interested in menstruation and menopause, so I talked easily about some of the various resources from the women's health movement that consider menopause from a woman-centered perspective.[2] I especially recommended starting with Rosetta Reitz's book, *Menopause: A Positive Approach,* as a classic self-help and consciousness raising text by a woman in menopause.

As the baby boom generation grows older, there is beginning to be more attention to menopause, including in some women-centered and feminist writing. My own interest in menopause has become more tangible as I prepare for this process, which I will begin in the next several years. I was happy my colleague felt she could call and admired her courage in speaking so openly about vulnerable feelings of loss, a sense that this change had come "too soon," and her struggle with the realization that she had no deeply positive images for what menopause might mean in her life.

Then she asked specifically for any materials from feminist spirituality that described rituals for envisioning menopause positively. I talked about the general practice of designing one's own rituals, creating ways to meditate on and celebrate (individually or with others) what we need for strength, healing, and social change. As part of this approach, I described contemporary Goddess witchcraft and its use of Goddess symbolism as inner imagery for the self.[3] Yes, she said, this possibility particularly interested her. She wanted not only practical feminist health information, but suggestions, guidelines, catalysts for plumbing and transforming the inner sense of despair she felt.

I began to describe contemporary interest in Triple Goddess imagery (drawn initially from European and American paganism) that has become an important central symbol in contemporary, wiccan-inspired, grassroots feminist spirituality. This symbol system depicts aspects of the Goddess and a woman's life as mirroring each other, each in three stages, with menarche and menopause identified as the ritual transitions between them. Names for the stages may vary somewhat, but typically a woman's life stages are described as girl/woman/elder. These life stages are envisioned as manifesting Goddess aspects of Maiden/Mother/Crone (or sometimes: Virgin/Mother/Crone). Menarche marks the transition from identity as girl/Maiden into an identity as woman/Mother. Then menopause marks the change of identity from woman/Mother to elder/Crone.

For many feminists this imagery has provided a vital symbolic frame of reference creating sustenance through contemporary witchcraft and other forms of feminist spirituality and philosophy during the last two decades. Maiden/Mother/Crone—each aspect of the Triple Goddess has received attention in diverse ways. These mythic identities are understood as dimensions of a woman's deep Self that ritual and reflection can open up within us as sources of insight and energy. The Crone has been of special interest, with multiple symbolic meanings, including: insight from long experience, wisdom, and sage judgment; rage, vengeance, and justice; and knowledge of death and rebirth.[4]

Previously, I have been especially concerned with ways in which Triple Goddess imagery relies too centrally on a reproductive (and usually implicitly heterosexual) model for women's lives.[5] Focusing on the Goddess as Mother produces what I have called "generic erasure" of many women's realities. I have argued that the middle stage of our lives needs to be imagined as a sense of full female adulthood and agency, whether or not we become mothers. It is sufficient to note here that feminist spirituality does emphasize that all Goddess imagery needs to be freely, creatively interpreted. Also, each aspect of the Triple Goddess is imagined to be present in each stage of a woman's life. In other words, there is a complex interplay of these aspects. For example, my girl self (the playful and eagerly exploring Maiden) is also chronologically my earliest/oldest self—that is, the Maiden can also be the Crone. And my current self is always my youngest self. Thus, the triple aspects are understood dynamically and holistically and not in a simple linear fashion.

Getting back to my colleague—yes, she said, this was just the kind of resource she was seeking. She wanted concrete imagery for developing rituals or meditations for self-affirmation at menopause. Would I send her some references when I had time? Certainly, I would be happy to. I planned to copy a few representative selections, maybe some suggestive rituals. But after I hung up, I began to feel uneasy as I contemplated the primary resources. Something in what I sensed that my caller needed (and I needed!) was missing. As I looked over the materials, I began to realize what was starting to feel wrong. Most written sources from feminist spirituality that address menopause have focused on the transition from midlife adulthood to one's Crone stage, becoming a female elder. It is essential to stress that the written sources are not fully indicative of the much more diverse grassroots practices. This is true of any religion or spiritual path but is especially true of feminist spirituality with its emphasis on spontaneous creative invention and variation, its gleeful opposition to uniformity and dogma. Nevertheless, written records do carry weight and have a shaping influence, particularly because the emerging number of books is one way this grassroots movement is spreading. In these written materials, a wrinkled wise old woman (from diverse cultures) is the primary picture envisioned.

In a climate of virulent ageism, we definitely need powerful imagery validating old women and our experiences with aging. As Baba Copper has written, "One of the primary definitions of patriarchy is the absence of old women in power."[6] Though it needs far more attention, there has been some magnificent feminist theory, in the last decade especially, analyzing aging and ageism—including ageism among feminists.[7] Ingrained white Western patriarchal definitions of women's worth focus on our subordinate service as youthful sexual objects or adult mother objects. In this misogynist context, menopause is deeply, culturally charged with negative meanings. Standard medicine and psychology view menopause as something to cure. As Daly,[8] Reitz, and others have observed, menopausal women are seen as deviants. Medical texts speak of ovarian failure and lost femininity. With such intense socialization and constant negative stereotyping, it is no wonder some women experience the "change of life" as a dreadful sentence that feels more like an end than a change.

Such hostile, derogatory images of female aging are a potent part of making menopause a disturbing and painful time for some women. The fear of being an old woman reviled and ridiculed by the dominant society is a major, embedded, destructive image that we need to examine and exorcise. Our task is not simply a matter of recognizing distorted views of female aging. The interstructured oppressions of patriarchy make aging into a difficult and dangerous territory for many women.[9] Clearly, Crone imagery can be an important means for confronting and transforming our fears. Discovering one's Crone self can better enable us to face harsh realities and to envision old age in creative and powerful ways.

A nagging and unsettling realization began to surface, however. Triple Goddess imagery essentially asks women at menopause to leap into an elder role. While potentially vital and powerful, woman elder/Crone imagery is not actually in many ways appropriate or accurate here. I began to find this prospect silly and, in fact, ageist itself. Did I really want to send my colleague material that said menopause meant she now should become a sort of instant tribal elder?[10] "Look me in the eye," Barbara MacDonald has asked in resistance to her experiences with ageism.[11] I took her advice and imagined looking my colleague in the eye as I handed her resources that would essentially depict her life post-menopause as if she were immediately to enter old age. Do not pass go. Do not continue as you are but jump into this potent archetype. Hmmmm. Was I having another feminist "click" experience? Or was my growing reluctance about this material a manifestation of my own internalized ageism? I remembered conversations with feminist theologian Nelle Morton. How angry it made Nelle when after her retirement from teaching (and certainly well past her menopause) well-intentioned women began referring to her as their foremother, as if she had retired from life. Not that Nelle minded being appreciated or having her early work honored, but she smelled the anesthetizing gases of ageism in this "promotion" to archetypal status. Her voice echoed in my mind, conjuring up MacDonald's pointed observation that too many younger feminists seem more comfortable with pictures of dead foremothers on their walls than with the real presence of old women.[12]

These voices encouraged me to take my reservations seriously and to analyze more fully. Attunement to such inner dialogues and rendering the part they play in analysis have become for me important parts of constructing a narrative form of theory. Sharing our thought process on the page, tracing out a line of thought and its inspiration, helps to make feminist theory more accessible, without succumbing to condescending notions of simplification. Of course, reference to inner voices is taboo in conventional patriarchal scholarship. (Always knew she was crazy!) This method I am working with leaves behind the pretense of pure objectivity and shows a thinker's mind at work. Feminist authors are increasingly exploring many diverse methods of rendering visible our engagement with our work, placing it in context.

Examining my responses, I found women from my past, women I *would* call Crones, rising up inside my mind. Such real life Crone imagery is vital and important to me. I am blessed to have grown up in a fairly matrilineal culture (the deep South) in which I had many experiences with strong, witty, independent, and loving old women. Their lives and my connections with them are part of who I am, including my eager response to feminism. (These relationships were virtually all white, one of the damages of the 1950's segregation that permeated my childhood.) In a graduate theology course in the early seventies, we were asked to write the title and chapter headings for our autobiography. My title, "All I Want Is to Be An Outrageous Old Lady," came easily because I had tangible examples in mind.

> *My Great-aunt "Wese"*—an eccentric, independent southern spinster. A woman who made great sense to me, even though her ideas about racial and sexual equality and the importance of being clear about money had become set (as in "set in her ways") so firmly against the *status quo* that they had driven her a bit mad.

Marme—my grandmother, less thought provoking than her intractable sister Louise but still fascinating in the stubbornness she quietly asserted, though that stubbornness was otherwise so at odds with her traditional views on manners.

Aunt Edith—who visited regularly and whom I discovered at about age twelve was an aunt because she was Marme's best friend since childhood. She had her own version of confident independence and a droll, fully-present humor that spilled over the limits of being a "lady."

"Ma" Butt—our landlady for most of my childhood until adolescence. She named herself my "adopted grandmother." A widow, she shared her half of the house with a widowed boarder/friend. "Miz Butt" transcended jokes on her incongruous name (which she firmly insisted upon) with her expansive manner and her solid working-class pride.

Essential to these connections was Helen—my mama, an energetic, cheerful, and loved-filled woman. Her friendships with these Crone women established the context in which I knew them. In these interwoven, intergenerational female relationships, I can clearly see a *living* Triple Goddess. I have no interest in romanticizing the Crones of my childhood or the many others I remember. They were not perfect archetypes but real women, complete with complexities, disappointments, and ambiguities. "Crone" does name for me part of their powerful legacy I carry inside. But they do not stand in my inner imagery for the transformational time at menopause. They stand well beyond that.

Calling up these Crones of my childhood helps me name who and what are missing when there is a primary focus on becoming a Crone at menopause. Triple Goddess imagery does not provide a clear name for the later midlife time of our lives. Full, mature, and thriving female adulthood is what I have in mind. I do have childhood images for what this can be. Certainly, there are my experiences of Mama in her prime. (She told me once about having hot flashes and coping with sudden menstrual flooding at work. I remember my teenage embarrassment. But I also remember how she laughed at her own consternation over this unexpected episode. And she also told me that she was glad that being a social worker meant she was in an all-women's office.) I remember here many of my middle-aged female school teachers and also Mama's "girlfriends," now middle-aged, but friends since her high school days. I remember Essie, who was Mama's age and had worked for my family since I was in grade school. (This was my only childhood relationship to break the color line, which produced and shaped but did not completely define it.) These women were past their menopause, but they were not Crones.

"Middle-aged" is the best name this culture can provide, a term that certainly has derogatory connotations. Middle-aged women—target of jokes, often depicted in dominant U.S. culture as neurotic if white, and stoically strong or invisible if women of color. "Middle-aged" does not exactly strike me as an exciting name to reclaim (compared to "witch," "bitch," "dyke," or "queer"—to mention a few I enjoy reclaiming). In my late forties, I am aware that "middle-aged" is definitely a description I am supposed to resist. To feminists and nonfeminists alike, the term "middle-aged" connotes boring, being on the way out (of fashion, of status, of access to power). A clue to prompt further investigation.

The lengthening average life span in industrialized countries, especially among women, is surely an important feature of the situation. Although women's increasing longevity in this society varies by race and class, women of all groups are living longer. If a woman lives into an increasingly typical old age, at menopause she might well expect to have two, three, or more decades of life ahead of her. These are years for which patriarchal role models and the economic marginalization of women do not well prepare us. Likewise, the increasing participation of more and more women in the paid economy (which brings more attention to those women who have always worked outside the home) means that women at midlife and older are more visible in the public/patriarchally noticed world.

Perhaps we need middle-aged Goddesses—another stage that certainly would upset the Triple Goddess scheme. From this vantage point, we can see even more clearly that the Triple Goddess model for women's lives relies on daughter/mother/grandmother relationships. As I have described in my own life, this intergenerational imagery can be positive and valuable. But it also reveals even more fully that women's reproductive roles are the basis of meaning for the Triple Goddess. Her primary name has always been drawn from the role in the center, the Mother or the Great Mother, despite assertions in feminist spirituality that there is no intent to define women by this role.

The other primary symbolism usually correlated with the Triple Goddess is lunar imagery. The resemblance of the twenty-nine-and-a-half-day lunar month to the average menstrual cycle is one reason for this ancient association. In this adaptation of lunar imagery, the waxing/full/waning phases of the moon are identified with Maiden/

Mother/Crone and girl/woman/elder. Contemporary feminist spirituality has a disturbing tendency to collapse together the meanings of the waning moon with the dark moon and correlate this combination with the Crone.[13] Such a combination merges imagery of waning with imagery of death and distorts them both. This collapse of symbolic meanings emphasizes a sense of Crone as one of extreme old age, near to and including death.

Certainly meditations on mortality, on changing physical abilities, on waxing and waning energies are relevant aspects of addressing our aging. But it is ageist to equate aging with decline and death. Thus, overly focusing on the reproductively based Triple Goddess can become reductionistic (however unintentionally), implying general decline once a woman's reproductive capacity has ended. This process only replicates the dominant culture's negative and fearful stereotypes of menopausal women as decaying has-beens who are coming apart and dangerous.

More complexly explored, we would consider how waxings and wanings might be part of any stage in our lives. For example, for many heterosexually active women, waning reproductive ability has meant waxing freedom in sexual expression when released from concerns over conception. While many white women have described adolescence as a waning of personal freedom, many black women describe a female heritage encouraging them at adolescence to prepare for adult independence, a waxing of womanist identity. For women who have relied (consciously or unconsciously) on status derived from patriarchal standards and rewards for beauty, age brings waning status. Yet for many women, menopause comes at a time in life when they feel quite strong, powerful, and in their prime. Margaret Mead coined the term PMZ (Post-Menopausal Zest) to name this little-discussed experience of many women.[14] Generalizations are always dangerous, of course, as the specific material circumstances of women's lives vary greatly. For many women, limitations from interstructured patriarchal oppressions greatly increase at this time of life. Increasing numbers of women, however, are speaking up to say that menopause and aging open up new energies and opportunities.

A primary motivation for Goddess imagery is to express our vision, our fullest sense of possibilities for women. For middle age and for menopause, we need more mythic, spiritual, psychic resources. One of the few such resources is Christine Downing's book about her experiences, *Journey through Menopause: A Personal Rite of Passage*. Downing cites as a motivation for her book the lack of positive models for menopause and the need for these in our psyches.

> I knew myself to be at the point of transition from early to late adulthood. . . . Yet I knew almost nothing of the distinctively female ways of navigating this passage and felt myself to be confronting a transition for which my culture had somehow conspired to keep me unprepared. I felt alone, uninformed, somewhat afraid—and yet also curious and expectant. I was at the brink of a centrally important life-change and had no knowledge of the myths or rituals that had helped women throughout history live this transition with hope, dignity and depth.[15]

Downing calls for a remythologizing of menopause. "I would wish us to learn to view menopause developmentally rather than pathologically, as a life phase rather than a degenerative or deficiency disease, and to see it not only as a physiological event but as a psychological one, as a soul experience."[16] Downing's work in religion and depth psychology led her to turn to Greek Goddess imagery in hopes of finding some guidance. She considers the familiar Triple Goddess and the importance of the Crone as an image for female old age. She examines ways such imagery can be helpful for confronting patriarchal distortions of the Crone as a frightening, fearful image that can surface with particular vividness at menopause.

But eventually Downing concludes that what she most deeply needs is to construct for herself a rite of passage, to mark and reflect upon the stages of her life and her future at this change of life. Dreams and inner psychic imagery are her means of preparation. Her discoveries lead Downing to realize that for her, menopause is not so much about becoming a Crone as it is a journey, a body-event and soul-event that will be taking her from one stage of life to another. Following a familiar pattern for rites of passage with phases of separation, transition, and return, she decides that a literal journey to enact the inner psychic and physiological ones best suits her as the way to celebrate her menopause.

Though I find features of Downing's analysis problematic, she does not claim that the discoveries she makes are necessarily what other women will find. Rather, she is following the basic feminist method of offering her story, her narrative, about realities that patriarchy has made taboo, unspeakable, missing.

> I have written this book as an account of my journey through menopause, in the hope that it will initiate a new openness among us about this area of our lives.
>
> My experience is somewhat idiosyncratic. It is part of the cost of the imposed silence that I cannot know how much of it is typical or how much of it will be illuminating to others. . . . [17]

Returning from her journey, Downing (somewhat to her surprise) has left behind the Triple Goddess and the Crone. She has come instead to an understanding that for this time in her life, she needs Goddess imagery that affirms centeredness in her place in life, imagery for "maturity" not diminished to the cloying connotations of this word. For Downing, given her frequent preference for immersing in Greek imagery, the Goddess she finds is Hestia, symbolized by the fire of the hearth, holiness in the everyday. Searching her own inner mythology for Goddess imagery to illuminate her life as she moved past menopause did not lead to the Crone. Downing found that, although fears about her Crone self needed to be confronted, in important ways the Crone's fullest power is yet to come. Downing's experiences and reflections illuminate the need for strong, female-identified psychic imagery for mature middle age, for PMZ, joyful and not tamed by embedded ageist fears.

There are only a few other such written explorations. Another ground-breaking book that opens up more women's stories about menopause is an anthology, *Women of the Fourteenth Moon.*[18] This collection offers almost a hundred selections drawn from essays, poetry, and fiction about diverse aspects of menopause. The authors are not as ethnically and racially diverse as we need and have come to expect in feminist work. It is a beginning, though limited in its representation. The title essay offers a new mythic image for post-menopause that does not focus on Crone imagery. As Eleanor Piazza explains:

> The name "Woman of the Fourteenth Moon" came to me as I sought an honoring name for menopausal women. Simply, if there are thirteen full moons in a given year, a woman who has not had a period for a year will begin a new phase in her life upon the fourteenth moon without bleeding.[19]

The women in Piazza's ritual group were from diverse backgrounds. They had not been able, however, to find ceremonies for menopause from their various peoples; only fragments of customs served as resources. She goes on to describe menopause ceremonies they created to celebrate this passage and their new status. Again, the spirit is one of offering their story as a testimony to what is missing and as a catalyst for creativity.

> Ceremonies are experiential and unique to each community that creates them. We are fortunate to have the skeleton, the bones, of our ceremony brought to us by such diverse heritages as this community provides. We are black, white, red, yellow, and brown. Each year we flesh it out differently, and each year we learn from the ceremony itself.[20]

A final resource that develops mythic Goddess imagery about menopause and aging into a more complex and differentiated pattern is Zsuzsanna Budapest's "Rites of Middle Age." In a section from *The Grandmother of Time* entitled "Rites of Passage," she writes:

> This time called middle age is the bulk of our lives.
> Society despises us in this flower of our lives.[21]

Budapest offers a "Crowning Ritual for Middle Age." She describes this ritual as marking a woman's acceptance and the acknowledgment by others of her powers in midlife, which she calls "her role in life as queen." She describes one such ritual by her friend Maggie.

> Being a queen means that in the middle of her life, Maggie will treat herself with respect and use her powers as a mature woman to take care of business. Being a queen means that she will not minimize her own importance, that she will consciously affirm her role to lead.[22]

This ritual focuses on what is missing if we simply leap from midlife to cronehood. It celebrates a strong and growing sense of self, an important affirmation at a time when cultural images of menopause as decline are pressing in upon many women. I must note, however, that designating midlife with the role of "queen" is highly problematic to me, even though *queen* comes from the root *gyn* (female). Because "queen" draws its imagery from historical associations with royal, hierarchical, oppressive social organization, I cannot affirm it.[23]

I do, however, want to affirm Budapest's creative exploration of the need for midlife rituals. A positive feature of her rites for middle age is that she includes not only this midlife ritual for maturity (and what shall we call it instead of queen?) but also three other separate rituals for women: "Rites of Passage for Menopause," "Ritual for Removal of Womb, Breasts, Ovaries," and "Croning Ritual—Entering the Wise Age."[24] Budapest does not collapse these significant life experiences into one rite of passage, as overreliance on the Triple Goddess tends to do.

Although women certainly should and do choose any time they feel inspired to have a croning ritual, it is especially interesting that Budapest's timing for the croning ritual is *not* reproductively based. It is not merged into a menopause ritual. Instead, she bases her croning ritual in viewing life chronologically from an astrological perspective.

> When the great planet Saturn spins back for the second time in your natal chart, you are fifty-six years old. This is the age we recognize as the

> doorway into the age of wisdom. This time in a woman's life is really devalued in modern society. A very unkind treatment is allotted to those of us in this age group. Watch out, because soon most of America will be in this age group, and it will be fashionable to be old—just wait and see![25]

Affirming and celebrating midlife realities, goals, and visions—as well as facing menopause—felt like important parts of what my colleague was struggling with. Diverse images, information, and strategies seem more creative and dynamic than a condensed menopause/Crone ritual. One of the reasons "menopausal woman" (read: "menopausal bitch") is such a hostile epithet in this society is that so many misogynist attitudes about women, our aging, our power, and our bodies are focused into it. Patriarchal society uses this significant life transition as a weapon against us. We must dismantle these damaging stereotypes, uncover the traditions of women who have resisted them, create what is missing.

SOME LIMITS OF GODDESS IMAGERY AS A CATALYST FOR SOCIAL CHANGE

These reflections on menopause rituals and Goddess images have led me further to examine thealogy, especially its role in our efforts for women's liberation. Although obviously not for everyone, feminist spirituality is a catalyst and tool for significant numbers of women who are changing our lives and creating social change. It is this link with creating social change with which I am continually concerned.

We need depth symbolisms. Such imagery is vital to our consciousness of deep inner states of being, emotions, passions, existential philosophies, intellectual analysis, convictions, moral orientations. By being conscious of, elaborating on, and sharing these deep meanings, we can be better equipped for political struggle and our fullest living.

Goddess imagery can function as one form of such liberating depth symbolizing if we remain attuned to how we utilize it. Goddess images—whether drawn from large or small pantheons, whether envisioned as creatrix, ancestor, or inner dimensions of self—are images of divinity. They are mythic. As such, they connote a sense of timelessness, eternity, essence. This timeless quality is both an asset and a limitation. When functioning as a fulcrum, as a place that enables deep centering in the face of oppression, then Goddess imagery can be a means for liberating movement and biophilic sustenance.[26] When naming experiences that may feel limitless, Goddess imagery can be a vital means for adequate expression of enormous realities we need not to deny.

I think here of both positive and negative experiences. Most painfully, I think of conversations with women who are survivors of childhood sexual abuse or other violence. For many such survivors, mythic female images of rage have been powerful for naming the depth of their experiences and for healing and moving beyond the control of the abuse. My own experience as an adult with being physically attacked and fighting back grew into a life-saving experience of the emergence of my Gorgon self.[27] I will never doubt that she exists in a timeless, necessary, and intensely real way.

Goddess imagery can also be one way to name experiences of ecstasy in life. Identifying with the web of life, with the planet and the cosmos are examples of such mystic experience for many of us. Another instance would be moments of intense loving communication with others. Holistic focus on creative tasks can also have such meaning. Such experiences plumb depths and dimensions of ourselves that can call forth mythic imagery to point toward their ultimacy. Often the images and vocabulary of male-dominated cultures are inadequate to name these vital perceptions. Indeed, the images and vocabulary often deny or distort them.

Just here, however, is where we need to be alert to the power of our own symbolisms. This timeless, essential quality can become static, or a place of escape, or even a means of oppression. I believe that the more standardized spiritual/existential imagery becomes—whether as religious creed, secular intellectual dogma, or political absolutism—the more institutionalized and less flexible it becomes. This rigidity is a danger of archetypes.

As Daly has noted, archetypes can become too fixed, limiting us.[28] Thus, we need to assess the limitations of Triple Goddess imagery (and any other such images—especially our favorite ones) in light of women's multiple realities. Otherwise, Goddess imagery or any depth symbolism can become colossal stereotypes, closing off rather than opening up meaning. (Some other suggestive examples of depth symbolisms not usually thought of as spiritual would be: democracy, socialism, free speech, individualism, free market economies, and so on.)

One means of assessing how depth symbolism is functioning is to pay attention to the contexts in which we find it and to reflect on its effects. This reflection is an ongoing dialogue, and we will not all agree on the relevant parts of the context or assessments of function. That disagreement is inherent in the diversity of our existence, however, and such dialogue is part of the multiple conversations with which we construct reality.

To return to the consideration of menopause as my major example here, the full context of a woman's life shapes the meaning of menopause and any symbolisms for this process. One woman's liberating ritual may well be overly romantic or stereotyping to another. When considering the meanings of Triple Goddess imagery in ancient pagan cultures, there is so much context we do not and will never have. Pondering menopause and ancient Goddess images, I have found myself wondering just what the diverse experiences of women in antiquity might have been. When might they have begun menstruation, and when might it typically have ceased? There is no agreement on these matters. For example, due to varying assumptions about living conditions, diet, and typical number of pregnancies, opinions vary widely as to whether or not women in prehistoric times menstruated frequently. What might menopause and the Triple Goddess have meant in worlds so different from our own? What might the Crone have meant in a gatherer/hunter culture? Would many women have lived to old age?

Such questions do not mean that hypotheses are pointless but that we must remember how much we do not know. This partial knowledge is one reason why debates over the relation of ancient Goddess images to the roles of women and men in those cultures persist and will continue to do so. Theories and intuitions about the past can be very inspiring, but we have more secure grounding in the present when we remember these are hypotheses.

Additionally, the tendency to timelessness and essence means that Goddess imagery by its nature will not open up the full range of women's lives, nor should we expect it to do so. Although there are many Goddess images, and feminist wiccans are fond of saying that the Goddess has a thousand faces, these images have a tendency toward an idealized form. Thus, although Goddess images explored by feminists in our society have become increasingly culturally diverse—a real strength—this does not mean they fully depict the range of women's lives and needs. Archetypes highlight extremes. This quality is precisely the realm of both their strength and weakness. Consider the attributes of age, physical shape, behavior, and expression. I have a hard time thinking of a "Goddess of mixed emotions," for example, though I have no trouble thinking of many that change from one intense emotion to another. Or, as another example, where are the Goddesses whose weight does not appear to be dramatically idealized? Many Goddesses are shape changers, but the shapes are primary, intense, and highly distinct.

We also need to recognize that Goddess imagery, because of its timeless, archetypal nature, can promote a tendency to universalize. When a particular Goddess image feels intensely right because it expresses a profound reality for us, we need to remember that this depth perception is still grounded in our own experience. It may certainly connect us with others, but they must say so. Generalizing from our experience to an assumption that we have fully understood other women's experiences erases their realities. Such universalizing misses their true being. Ultimately, it can oppress them. This does not mean we cannot suggest connections. We must be mindful of these risks and our concrete differences, however, in our attempts to bond with each other. These assets and limitations, strengths and weakness of Goddess imagery underscore the importance of grounding such symbolizing in the particular material, historic, and social conditions of our lives. Careful attention to the lives of real women keeps our primary focus on liberation. Such attention helps us notice not only what we need but who is missing. We must notice who is absent, because a primary mechanism of oppression is, like totalitarian regimes everywhere, "to disappear" our realities—by erasure, making invisible, silencing, subordination, assimilation, reversal, denial, distortion, torture, murder.

To make this more concrete, consider the following reflections exploring some such limitations in ideas I have proposed earlier in this essay. I offer them as examples of the need to remain open to contradictions. I believe it encourages more ethical and political honesty to examine ways in which lives of other women may lead to truths different from our own. In these differences, as well as in our similarities, lie the seeds of fruitful conversations and more creative, effective analysis and action. Here is another reason for not making Goddess spirituality into a religion. Religions usually end up promoting the idealized belief that they are adequate explanatory systems with resolutions to life's contradictions.

- Consider my own earlier affirmation of the Triple Goddess as a form that movingly names the female intergenerational relationships in my childhood. Although this means there is, then, some "truth" for me in this way of experiencing the Triple Goddess, it is my truth and I must claim it and offer it as such. It is not an absolutely true, universal myth. It might not, for example, function this way at all for women who have broken and disturbing relationships with women in their families. Although some have said to me that such Triple Goddess imagery is an inspiration for potential healing and wider worlds, others have found this very imagery a hollow mockery. What is most difficult is that sometimes the difference between their experience and my own produces a painful distance we work to bridge. (For example, conversations with women who survived incest and other severe abuse have been especially significant for me here.)

• Consider the increasing cultural diversity of Goddess imagery in feminist spirituality, to which I earlier referred as a positive development. Yet there are dangers here of colonizing the traditions of cultures other than one's own. Native American women have especially addressed the problem of white people uncritically adopting Native American traditions as part of the dominant culture's current faddish attention, romanticizing and demanding access to them. Although our sources of inspiration and appreciation can certainly be diverse, it is important to distinguish between one's own response to an image from another culture and the meanings an image has in its original context. We need to examine what our choices are as we seek inspiration and whether they fall into oppressive patterns we do not intend. To do this, we must be open to hearing from each other.

• Consider my critique of overreliance on reproductively based roles to name women's realities. I have chosen not to be a mother. Goddess as Mother does not function for me as a liberating name for my deep Self. Nor does "mother" function as a generic term for creativity, though I realize that it sometimes does for other women who are not mothers. Additionally, as a lesbian, I am critical of mother-based imagery for its compatibility with heterosexism in this society (despite that fact that there are, of course, lesbian mothers and grandmothers). Yet it is just here I must be careful not to replicate in another form the very universalizing and generic erasure I have criticized. I do not deny my own experiences, and I urge other women to consider the limitations of generic mother-Goddess imagery in this society. I do not want to deny, however, the realities of women who do experience Mother and Grandmother Goddess imagery as liberating. Again, the voices of Native American women are instructive here. Brooke Medicine Eagle, for example, describes tribal cultures with strong women-centered traditions in which "mother" and "grandmother" are titles of honor in ways that do not seem to marginalize nonmothers.[29]

As activists working for social change, we need to be aware of the double-edged nature of spiritual, mythic imagery in our lives. The inherent tendency of mythic imagery toward absolutizing and universalizing warns us that we must temper its use. Goddesses must not eclipse the diversity within each of us and among all of us. Mythic time, although often an underexplored aspect of being in industrialized societies, is only one rhythm of our being. Successful work for social justice includes learning to value the mundane, concrete details of making social change. Attention to the cosmic *and* the concrete will help us live the paradoxes of life more creatively and effectively. When either dimension is missing, we miss parts of ourselves and we miss each other.

SOMETIMES WHAT'S MISSING IS HUMOR!

A final observation on Goddess imagery is that although it can aid in the expression of sublime and profound realities, this very strength can also sometimes give it a tendency to be overly serious. Oppression is cruelly serious, but one of the delights of liberation is that its motive is biophilic joy and a belief that life is worth living. As Emma Goldman is reported to have said in response to pressures from other political activists that she be more serious, "If I can't dance, it's not my revolution."

In this spirit, I invoke the Goddess Hilaria.

> HILARIA, undoubtedly one of the most widely acknowledged and revered of the Found Goddesses, is always good for a laugh. . . . Especially dear to Her are those known for their Wicked Laughs, and She listens lovingly to the cackles that rise like suddenly freed birds from the throats of encircled Crones.[30]

I discovered Hilaria in a wonderfully irreverent book by Morgan Grey and Julia Penelope, *Found Goddesses: Asphalta to Viscera.* I also became acquainted with the likes of Videa (whose high-tech shrines are now found in most homes), Inertia (with her powerful Rites of Procrastination), Paranoia (Goddess-of-the-Ever-Watchful), Pollyanna (She-Who-Overlooks), and Gettuffa (Our-Goddess-of-Self-Defense).

These found Goddesses are an inspiration for new uses of Goddess imagery in the everyday material conditions of our lives. Since Goddess imagery is one means for leverage against the weight of oppression, we should surely elaborate this frame of reference to include more fully Goddesses as a means of levity. Patriarchal society demands that we take it seriously. As "fumerist" (feminist humorist) Kate Clinton has observed, "making light" is certainly one effective means for dealing with patriarchy.[31]

Thus, as I adjust to wearing bifocals while I teach, I wonder if there is a Bifocalia and how she might aid me. Computeria, previously thought by many to be hostile to women, has surely come to my aid in typing this chapter—the first on my computer. Perhaps as I sit in too many meetings in what Diana Beguin has so aptly termed "academentia,"[32] Hilaria will help save my sanity—and help me realize sooner when to leave!

Sometimes I think humor is really the ultimate taboo in political struggle and scholarship. It is a sign we have gone too far. The threat is that we will not be taken seriously (read: "We've committed the sin of not taking them seriously"). So let us conclude with an extended devotional passage from *Found Goddesses* on a Goddess most helpful to me. She is a true Muse, and I often employ her tokens as rewards when I write. As you will see, in good feminist fashion, she will bring us full circle to our initial concern with menopause.

> CHOCOLATA is believed by many to be merely an occasional, or periodic, aspect of Munchies, because She frequently appears only at specific times during lunar cycle or under similar conditions. Her most devoted adherents, however, who are legion, maintain that Chocolata is a major Goddess, deserving ritual observances of her own. . . . These are major thealogical debates unlikely to be settled in the near future, and we won't try to resolve them here. Of more importance, we believe, are indications that some forms of Chocolata worship can be traced back to the Amazons.
>
> What we have been able to find out suggests diverse connections between the rituals of Chocolata and the most ancient roots of our own spirituality. Chocolata is often found in small, edible statues that resemble bunnies or cream-filled eggs (around the time of the Vernal Equinox), or fat, bearded figures with bags slung over their shoulders around Winter Solstice, and in small pointed breast-like pieces commonly called "Kisses.". . . One linguist, who has spent much of her life decoding the ancient language of the Amazons, has discovered that the mysterious name M & Ms, is an esoteric aspect of Chocolata that means "Menstruation and Menopause."[33]

NOTES

1. I have especially focused on this method of intertwining personal narrative with critical analysis when seeking to open up issues in contemporary feminist debates. Sharing the examination of my own thought processes while wrestling with certain issues clearly invites the reader to participate. This approach moves beyond the "objective" and "authoritative" voice of conventional scholarship. It can sometimes more adequately convey the lived ambiguity and nuances of issues. I have particularly explored this narrative form of inquiry in an article examining pornography as a kind of "sacred speech" in patriarchy ("Are Women's Bodies Sacred?") and in an article on feminist spirituality interested in Goddesses but not organized as a Goddess religion ("Spiritual, Political Journey").

2. Boston Women's Health Book Collective, *The New Our Bodies, Our Selves;* Callahan, *Menopause;* Doress, et al., *Ourselves, Growing Older;* Greenwood, *Menopause, Naturally;* Montreal Health Press, *Menopause;* Reitz, *Menopause;* Taylor and Sumrall, *Women of the Fourteenth Moon;* Taylor, "Menopause."

3. Budapest, *Grandmother of Time;* Starhawk, *Spiral Dance;* Stein, *Goddess Celebrates;* Walker, *Crone and Women's Rituals.*

4. Daly, *Gyn/Ecology;* Walker, *Crone.*

5. Culpepper, "Contemporary Goddess Thealogy."

6. Copper, *Over the Hill.*

7. For example, MacDonald and Rich, *Look Me in the Eye.*

8. Daly, *Gyn/Ecology.*

9. Culpepper, "Ageism, Sexism, and Health Care."

10. Native American women have also criticized a tendency of non-Native Americans to appropriate Native American traditions into their spirituality. Facile, romanticized use of Native American imagery of tribal elders does not respect these traditions. Although one may draw inspiration from many sources, we need to guard against a kind of New Age spiritual colonialism that co-opts.

11. MacDonald, *Look Me in the Eye.*

12. MacDonald, *Look Me in the Eye,* 16-17.

13. Culpepper, "Contemporary Goddess Thealogy."

14. Attributing PMZ to Mead has become part of contemporary women's oral network. Though I have been unable to document a source, this attribution to Mead is widespread and I want to honor that oral tradition here.

15. Downing, *Journey through Menopause,* 3.

16. Downing, *Journey through Menopause,* 13.

17. Downing, *Journey through Menopause,* 16.

18. Edited by Taylor and Sumrall.

19. Piazza, "Women of the Fourteenth Moon," 263.

20. Piazza, "Women of the Fourteenth Moon," 266.

21. Budapest, *Grandmother of Time,* 190.

22. Budapest, *Grandmother of Time,* 190.

23. Significantly, the etymology of "hierarchy" reveals that it originated as a description of holy orders and religious rule. The original role of religious authority in legitimating systems of social ranking highlights one of the reasons I do not think making Goddess imagery into a religion is ultimately a liberating

path. As a feminist freethinker, I oppose the creation of theacracies as well as theocracies.

24. Budapest, *Grandmother of Time,* 191-94.

25. Budapest, *Grandmother of Time,* 193.

26. Mary Daly created the word "biophilic": "By biophilic I mean life-loving. This term is not in the dictionary, although the term necrophilic is there, and is commonly used" (Daly, *Gyn/Ecology,* 10 n.).

27. Culpepper, "Ancient Gorgons."

28. See Daly, *Pure Lust.*

29. Medicine Eagle, "Grandmother Lodge."

30. Grey and Penelope, *Found Goddesses,* 63.

31. Clinton, *Making Light.*

32. Daly and Caputi, *Websters' First New Intergalactic Wickedary.*

33. Grey and Penelope, *Found Goddesses,* 25-26.

WORKS CITED

Boston Women's Health Book Collective. *The New Our Bodies, Our Selves.* New York: Simon and Schuster, 1990.

Budapest, Zsuzsanna E. *The Grandmother of Time.* San Francisco: Harper and Row, 1989.

Callahan, Joan C., ed. *Menopause: A Midlife Passage.* Bloomington, Ind.: Indiana University Press, 1993.

Clinton, Kate. *Making Light.* whys crack records, 1982.

Copper, Baba. *Over the Hill: Reflections on Ageism between Women.* Freedom, Calif.: Crossing Press, 1988.

Culpepper, Emily Erwin. "Ancient Gorgons: A Face for Contemporary Women's Rage." *Women of Power: A Magazine of Feminism, Spirituality and Politics* 3 (1986): 22-24, 40.

———. "Contemporary Goddess Thealogy: A Sympathetic Critique." Pp. 51–71 in *Shaping New Vision: Gender and Values in American Culture.* Vol. 2, The Harvard Women's Studies in Religion Series, ed. Clarissa Atkinson, Margaret Miles, and Constance Buchanan. Ann Arbor, Mich.: University of Michigan Research Press, 1987.

———. "Are Women's Bodies Sacred? Listening to the Yes's and No's." Pp. 199–209 in *Sacred Dimensions of Women's Experience,* edited by Elizabeth Dodson Gray. Wellesley, Mass.: Roundtable Press, 1988.

———. "The Spiritual, Political Journey of a Feminist Freethinker." Pp. 146–65 in *After Patriarchy: Feminist Transformations of the World Religions,* edited by Paula Cooey, Bill Eakin, and Jay McDaniel. Maryknoll, N.Y.: Orbis Books, 1991.

———. "Ageism, Sexism and Health Care: Why We Need Old Women in Power." Pp. 191–209 in *Facing Limits: Ethics and Health Care for the Elderly,* edited by Gerald R. Winslow and James W. Walters. Boulder,

Co.: Westview Press, 1993.

Daly, Mary. *Gyn/Ecology: The Metaethics of Radical Feminism.* Boston: Beacon Press, 1978.

———. *Pure Lust: Elemental Feminist Philosophy.* Boston: Beacon Press, 1984.

——— and Jane Caputi. *Webster's First New Intergalactic Wickedary of the English Language.* Boston: Beacon Press, 1987.

Doress, Paula Brown, Diana Laskin Siegal, and The Midlife and Older Women Book Project. *Ourselves, Growing Older: Women Aging with Knowledge and Power.* New York: Simon and Schuster, 1987.

Downing, Christine. *Journey through Menopause: A Personal Rite of Passage.* New York: Crossroad, 1987.

Greenwood, Sadja. *Menopause, Naturally: Preparing for the Second Half of Life.* Volcano, Calif.: Volcano Press, 1989.

Grey, Morgan, and Julia Penelope. *Found Goddesses: Alsphalta to Viscera.* Norwich, Vermont: New Victoria Publishers, 1988.

MacDonald, Barbara, with Cynthia Rich. *Look Me in the Eye: Old Women, Aging and Ageism.* San Francisco: Spinsters Ink, 1983.

Medicine Eagle, Brooke. "Grandmother Lodge." Pp. 261–63 in *Women of the Fourteenth Moon: Writings on Menopause,* edited by Dena Taylor and Amber Coverdale Sumrall. Freedom, Calif.: Crossing Press, 1991.

Montreal Health Press. *Menopause: A Well Woman Book.* Toronto: Second Story Press, 1990.

Piazza, Eleanor J. "Women of the Fourteenth Moon—The Ceremony." Pp. 264–67 in *Women of the Fourteenth Moon: Writings on Menopause,* edited by Dena Taylor and Amber Coverdale Sumrall. Freedom, Calif.: Crossing Press, 1991.

Reitz, Rosetta. *Menopause: A Positive Approach.* New York: Penguin Books, 1977.

Starhawk. *The Spiral Dance: A Rebirth of the Ancient Religion of the Great Goddess.* San Francisco: Harper and Row, 1979.

Stein, Diane, ed. *The Goddess Celebrates: An Anthology of Women's Rituals.* Freedom, Calif.: Crossing Press, 1991.

Taylor, Dena. "Menopause: Last Blood." Pp. 92–106 in *Red Flower: Rethinking Menstruation.* Freedom, Calif.: Crossing Press, 1988.

——— and Amber Coverdale Sumrall, eds. *Women of the Fourteenth Moon: Writings on Menopause.* Freedom, Calif.: Crossing Press, 1991.

Walker, Barbara G. *The Crone: Woman of Age, Wisdom, and Power.* San Francisco: Harper and Row, 1985.

———. *Women's Rituals: A Source Book.* San Francisco: Harper and Row, 1990.

Index of Women and Goddesses

Index of Subjects